ALSO BY FREDERICK CREWS

The Pooh Perplex

Skeptical Engagements

The Critics Bear It Away: American Fiction and the Academy

The Memory Wars: Freud's Legacy in Dispute (with other authors)

Unauthorized Freud: Doubters Confront a Legend (editor)

Postmodern Pooh

Follies of the Wise: Dissenting Essays

FREUD

Sigmund Freud, about 1890

FREUD

The Making of an Illusion

Frederick Crews

METROPOLITAN BOOKS

HENRY HOLT AND COMPANY   NEW YORK

m

Metropolitan Books
Henry Holt and Company
Publishers since 1866
175 Fifth Avenue
New York, New York 10010
www.henryholt.com

Metropolitan Books® and m® are registered trademarks of
Macmillan Publishing Group, LLC.

Library of Congress Cataloging-in-Publication Data

Names: Crews, Frederick C., author.
Title: Freud : the making of an illusion / Frederick Crews.
Description: New York : Metropolitan Books, [2017] | Includes bibliographical
   references and index.
Identifiers: LCCN 2017000826| ISBN 9781627797177 (hardcover : alk. paper) |
   ISBN 9781627797184 (electronic book : alk. paper)
Subjects: LCSH: Freud, Sigmund, 1856–1939. | Psychology—History. |
   Psychoanalysis—History.
Classification: LCC BF109.F74 C74 2017 | DDC 150.19/52092—dc23
LC record available at https://lccn.loc.gov/2017000826

Our books may be purchased in bulk for promotional, educational, or business use. Please
contact your local bookseller or the Macmillan Corporate and Premium Sales Department at
(800) 221-7945, extension 5442, or by e-mail at MacmillanSpecialMarkets@macmillan.com.

First Edition 2017

Designed by Kelly S. Too

Photo research and editing provided by
Liz Seramur of Selected Shots Photo Research, Inc.

Printed in the United States of America

1 3 5 7 9 10 8 6 4 2

For good friends and Freud scholars:

Malcolm Macmillan, who set the highest standard

Han Israëls, who defied the censors

Allen Esterson, who has lived for truth

However far human beings may reach with their knowledge, how-ever objective they may seem to themselves to be: in the end they carry away nothing but their own biography.

—FRIEDRICH NIETZSCHE*

It's not a lie if *you* believe it.

—GEORGE COSTANZA, IN *SEINFELD*

* *Human, All Too Human,* #513 (1878).

CONTENTS

LIST OF ILLUSTRATIONS

Frontispiece: Sigmund Freud, about 1890 (Photo © PVDE / Bridgeman Images)

1. Jacob Freud and his son Sigismund, age eight (Photo © Tallandier / Bridgeman Images)

2. Amalie Freud and her son Sigismund, age sixteen (akg-images / Interfoto)

3. Eduard Silberstein, Freud's best friend in adolescence (© S. Fischer Verlag GmbH)

4. Martha Bernays and Sigmund Freud in 1885, during their engagement (Photo © PVDE / Bridgeman Images)

5. Minna Bernays, Freud's future sister-in-law, age eighteen (Mary Evans Picture Library / SIGMUND FREUD COPYRIGHTS / Everett Collection)

6. Ernst Fleischl von Marxow, Freud's teacher, friend, and fellow user of cocaine (akg-images / Imagno)

7. Freud's colleague Carl Koller, who discovered cocaine anesthesia (Mary Evans Picture Library / SIGMUND FREUD COPYRIGHTS / Everett Collection)

8. André Brouillet's 1887 painting *A Clinical Lesson at the Salpêtrière*, depicting Jean-Martin Charcot's induction of a hysterical fit (Private Collection / De Agostini Picture Library / Bridgeman Images)

A NOTE ON SOURCES

For an understanding of Freud's pre-psychoanalytic development and his character in general, the most revealing documents are his and Martha Bernays's *Brautbriefe*, or engagement letters, exchanged between 1882 and 1886. Upon the death of Anna Freud in 1982, the letters were donated to the Freud Archives in the US Library of Congress, where, at her stipulation, they were hidden from view until 2000. That was not an exceptional measure. The first director of the archives, Kurt Eissler, saw to it that other papers would remain unavailable for many more decades, extending as far forward as the year 2113.

Nevertheless, some *Brautbriefe* have long been familiar, at least in part, to the reading public. Ernst Freud published 97 of them in his 1960 edition of his father's selected letters, and Ernest Jones quoted or cited more than 200 in his authorized biography. That may sound like a lot, but 1,539 engagement letters of Freud's and Martha's have survived; and not surprisingly, those that fail to tally with his legend have until recently remained either unpublished or redacted.

Recently, however, German transcripts of all of the *Brautbriefe* have been made available on the Library of Congress's website. Moreover, the full *Brautbriefe* have begun to be published, in five volumes, by a team of scrupulous German editors. Freud scholarship will be revolutionized when this slow-motion event has concluded. As of this writing, three volumes have appeared, taking the correspondence through September 1884. I have gratefully consulted those texts and the comprehensive notes that accompany them. And, with assistance, I have translated those letters not already published in English.

Because the Library of Congress transcripts contain errors, prudence might dictate that any new study of the early Freud be postponed until all five volumes of the definitive edition have appeared. For me at age eighty-four, however, another prudential consideration takes precedence. I must tell what I know about Freud, hoping that some inevitable mistakes and omissions won't be so grave as to invalidate my inferences.

In quoting published materials that were translated from German, such as James Strachey's *Standard Edition* of Freud's complete psychological writings, I have occasionally preferred a more literal translation, especially where it makes a substantive difference of meaning. Every such change is indicated in the citation. Paragraph breaks have been inserted into a few lengthy passages.

Finally, readers may wonder why, in the chapters that follow, generic physicians are always *he* and generic patients are always *she*. This blunt solution to the always vexing pronoun problem recognizes, but isn't meant to endorse, a historical reality: in Freud's early career nearly all providers of psychotherapy and hypnotism were men, and most of their clients were women.

ABBREVIATED TITLES

CP   Sigmund Freud, *Cocaine Papers*. Ed. Robert Byck. New York: Stonehill, 1974.

FF   *The Complete Letters of Sigmund Freud to Wilhelm Fliess, 1887–1904*. Trans. and ed. Jeffrey Moussaieff Masson. Cambridge, MA: Belknap of Harvard U., 1985.

FMB   Sigmund Freud and Martha Bernays, *Die Brautbriefe*. 5 vols. (projected). Eds. Gerhard Fichtner, Ilse Grubrich-Simitis, and Albrecht Hirschmüller. Frankfurt: S. Fischer, 2011—.

FS   Sigmund Freud, *The Letters of Sigmund Freud to Eduard Silberstein: 1871–1881*. Ed. Walter Boehlich. Trans. Arnold J. Pomerans. Cambridge, MA: Belknap of Harvard U., 1990.

J   Ernest Jones, *The Life and Work of Sigmund Freud*. 3 vols. New York: Basic, 1953–57.

L   *Letters of Sigmund Freud*. Ed. Ernst L. Freud. Trans. Tania and James Stern. [1960.] New York: Dover, 1992.

SE   *The Standard Edition of the Complete Psychological Works of Sigmund Freud*. 24 vols. Trans. James Strachey, with Anna Freud, Alix Strachey, and Alan Tyson. London: Hogarth, 1953–1974.

SK   Sigmund Freud, *Schriften über Kokain*. Ed. Albrecht Hirschmüller. Frankfurt: Fischer Taschenbuch, 1996.

FREUD

Preface

Among historical figures, Sigmund Freud ranks with Shakespeare and Jesus of Nazareth for the amount of attention bestowed upon him by scholars and commentators. Unlike them, he left behind thousands of documents that show what he was doing and thinking from adolescence until his death at age eighty-three. Although many of those records were placed under lengthy restriction by followers who felt both financial and emotional incentives to idealize him, that blackout has at least partly expired by now. More revelations will emerge, but they are unlikely to alter the outlines of Freud's conduct and beliefs as they appear in the most responsible recent studies.

Nor, surely, will much more be learned about Freud's intricate relation to the currents of medical, philosophical, political, and cultural thought that affected him, or about his own effect on later currents.[1] We know that he was the beneficiary of various long-term trends that influenced his own thinking and then accelerated in the twentieth century. They include a backlash against scientific positivism; an Ibsenesque discontent with bourgeois hypocrisy; a current of Nietzschean "dark Romanticism," celebrating the Dionysian element that Christian teaching had equated with sinfulness; the rise of a bohemian avant-garde, devoted to anti-establishment feeling and sexual license; increased urbanization and social mobility, accompanied by rejection of patriarchal authority;

and a waning of theological belief, allowing psychotherapy to inherit some of religion's traditional role in providing guidance and consolation to the unhappy. The disaster of World War I virtually guaranteed that Freud's pessimistic, instinct-centered philosophy would prevail, at least among intellectuals, over sunnier models of the psyche.

If Freud's career and its impact are so well understood, what justification could there be for another lengthy biographical tract? The question appears especially pertinent in view of the fall that Freud's scientific reputation has suffered over the past forty-five years.[2] In 1997, for example, the standard academic work on cognition and emotion referenced 1,314 texts, only one of which was by Freud.[3] And in 1999, a comprehensive citation study in the flagship journal of American psychology reported that "psychoanalytic research has been virtually ignored by mainstream scientific psychology over the past several decades."[4] The situation has not improved in the twenty-first century. As one otherwise sympathetic observer put it in 2010, "the scientific standing of psychoanalysis and of its therapeutic claims has been severely compromised both by a lack of empirical support and [by] its dependence on an outdated biology."[5] It might be merciful, then, just to turn our backs on an increasingly deserted scene.

But Freud, even stripped of his scientific pretensions, is destined to remain among us as the most influential of twentieth-century sages. Without those pretensions, in fact, his cultural sway becomes a more intriguing phenomenon. Although the peers who knew his writings perceived the flaws in his system,[6] intellectuals in later years were spellbound by his self-portrayal as a lone explorer possessing courageous perseverance, deductive brilliance, tragic insight, and healing power. Much can still be learned from that episode of mass infatuation, in which I myself naïvely participated fifty years ago. And the serio-comic history of the psychoanalytic movement itself is instructive as a cautionary demonstration of what can happen when a pseudoscience, lacking any objective means of adjudicating internal differences of judgment, becomes a worldwide enterprise whose outposts inevitably loosen their ties with the founding center and generate new vortices of dogma.[7]

My main concern here, however, is with Freud in person—and, indeed, with only one question about him. How and why did a studious, ambitious, and philosophically reflective young man, trained in rigorous inductivism by distinguished researchers and eager to win their favor, lose perspective on his wild hunches, efface the record of his mistakes, and establish an international cult of personality? The record from his years of obscurity and struggle can show how he was affected by clashing impulses: his sense of duty, his fear of disgrace and of prolonged poverty, his yearning for celebrity, his initial willingness to conform and to ingratiate himself, and his resentment of the institutional authority to which, for a while, he nominally bowed. As we will see, the balance among those factors was tipped by crucial experiences, between 1884 and 1900, whose import for psychoanalysis has been almost entirely overlooked.

It may seem odd that this part of the story has never been told in full detail. But lack of attention hasn't been the problem. Rather, biographical Freud studies have been dominated by partisans of psychoanalysis with a vested interest in preserving the legend of epochal discovery. Nearly all of Freud's apologists, heeding a tacit plea on his part to be exempted from dispassionate evaluation of his claims, have engaged in protective discourse: ascribing special acuteness to the master, always granting him the benefit of the doubt, and, when there appears to be no dodging the evidence of his illogicalities and ethical lapses, blaming them on the autonomous operations of his unconscious mind.

By exaggerating Freud's competence in various respects, this Freudolatry has obscured the central drama of his career. His temperament and self-conception demanded that he achieve fame at any cost. His apologists tell us, as Freud himself did, that the cost was irrational opposition from a prudish world. As we will see, however, the cost was much steeper: it was nothing less than his integrity as both a scientist and a physician.

Although many readers expect a sensible book about Freud to manifest its objectivity by weighing certain hard-won contributions against certain errors or excesses, such predetermined evenhandedness renders him more puzzling than he actually was. We have been told, for example, that he disregarded every element of scientific prudence *and* that he achieved fundamental breakthroughs in psychological knowledge.[8] How, then, did he do it? No one can say; the attempted explanations vaporize into the useless notion of "genius." It is better, I suggest, simply to ask what the biographical evidence tells us at every juncture. If, as a result, we lose a former hero, we may at last gain a consistent picture of the man.

On one point, though, nearly all readers will want to insist upon a concession that won't be made below. Believing that Freud, whatever his failings, initiated our tradition of empathetic psychotherapy, they will judge this book to have unjustly withheld credit for his most benign and enduring achievement. Still worse, they may judge the author to be a disbeliever in psychotherapy itself. I will show, however, not only that Freud had predecessors and rivals in one-on-one mental treatment but also that he failed to match their standard of responsiveness to each patient's unique situation. As for my estimation of psychotherapy, I regard it as potentially helpful to the extent that it dispenses with a reductive style of explanation.

Nevertheless, analysts who believe that their discipline has now "gone beyond Freud" will find no comfort in my chapters. Whatever its recent improvements, psychoanalysis remains what Frank Cioffi sarcastically dubbed a testimonial science.[9] That is, the evidence offered in support of its propositions consists almost entirely of assurances that Freud and others have found them to be true. A vast first-person literature, recounting what individual analysts have purportedly learned from their patients, can be selectively taken to prove one or another tenet. But regarded as a whole, the same literature cancels out to zero, because the anecdotes favoring one proposition are no better grounded than the opposing ones.

Of course, hard-core partisans can be counted upon to dismiss this book as an extended exercise in *Freud bashing*—a notion that gets invoked whenever the psychoanalytic legend of lonely and heroic discovery is challenged. To call someone a Freud basher is at once to shield Freud's theory from skeptical examination and to shift the focus, as Freud himself so often did, from objective issues to the supposedly twisted mind of the critic. Like other aspects of Freudolatry, the charge of Freud bashing deserves to be retired at last. The best way to accomplish that end, however, is just to display the actual record of Freud's doings and to weigh that record by an appeal to consensual standards of judgment.

· ·

PART ONE

SIGMUND THE UNREADY

· ·

A man with unbridled ambition is bound at some time to break away and, to the loss of science and his own development, become a crank.

—Freud, letter to Georg Groddeck*

---

* 6/5/1917; L, p. 317.

· 1 ·

Between Identities

1. PROSPECTS AND BURDENS

When Sigmund—*né* Schlomo Sigismund—Freud enrolled in the University of Vienna in 1873 at age seventeen, he bore with him the high expectations of a family that desperately needed him to become a salary earner. His father, Kallamon Jacob, formerly a wholesale wool merchant in Freiberg, Moravia, had gone bankrupt, and a year's further search for business in Leipzig, Germany, had proved fruitless.

Relocated in Vienna since 1860, Jacob had long since given up actively looking for work. The Freuds were surviving mainly on charity from local and distant relatives, including the two sons from Jacob's first marriage, who had emigrated to England and become modestly successful shopkeepers in Manchester.

If Sigismund had been the only child of Jacob and Amalie Freud, their future would have looked brighter, but the marriage was distressingly prolific in offspring. Although Jacob was already forty, with one or possibly two marriages already behind him, when he married the twenty-year-old Amalie, Sigismund's birth proved to be the first of eight. And five of his siblings were sisters, unlikely to find middle-class employment or to make advantageous matches. Jacob was of no more financial help to his brood than Dickens's Mr. Micawber, to whom his son would later compare him.

Freud's childhood was marked by incidents whose traumatic effects he subsequently judged to have been severe. His Czech nanny in Freiberg, who functioned as a surrogate mother when Amalie went from one pregnancy to the next, had been abruptly fired and jailed for stealing. Years later, Sigismund was haunted by the awful thought that his ill wishes toward his first immediate sibling, Julius—born when Sigismund was just seventeen months old, and dead six months later—had somehow killed the baby. And his relocation from Freiberg to Leipzig and thence to a lower-class Jewish enclave within the Viennese district of Leopoldstadt, where he would grow up in the midst of overcrowding, illness, and penury, was evidently a protracted trial.

One incident in particular stands out as a source of continuing mortification. In 1865 Sigismund's uncle Josef was sentenced to ten years in prison for having counterfeited rubles; a well-founded suspicion persisted that Sigismund's half-brothers in Manchester had been involved in the scam. (The phony bills, after all, had been made in England.) Sigismund was nine when the Viennese newspapers were trumpeting the sting operation that had caught the Jewish forger Josef Freud. The boy and later the man may never have fully recovered from that shame.

The easygoing Jacob was proud of Sigismund and assumed loving charge of his early education, including his acquaintance with Judaism. Jacob looked forward each year to reading aloud the Passover Haggadah, and he twice presented his son with a Hebrew-German "Samuelson Bible"—the same volume both times, rebound for the adult and backsliding Sigmund and inscribed with a traditional cluster of sacred passages.[1] But Jacob had little use for theology. He had embraced the movement known as *Haskalah*, which sought to bring European Jews out of their cultural isolation and, at the same time, to promote scriptural study in a nonliteral, nonmystical, ethical spirit.[2] The editorial content of his son's Bible, which moralized the epic tales of Moses and David, was itself an expression of *Haskalah* humanism.

This undogmatic idea of what it means to be a Jew was amplified by the teenage Sigismund's religious studies, which were required by his college-preparatory school, the Sperl (Leopoldstadter Communal) Gymnasium. In extracurricular sessions with Samuel Hammerschlag, who would remain his friend in later years, he learned to regard the ethical aspect of Jewish thought as consonant with enlightened social values. From Hammerschlag, too, he came to value the heroic strain in another ancient tradition, that of the Greek and Roman classics.

In boyhood, Sigismund had idolized his father and associated him with the noblest Hebrews of the Bible. As his own dream of greatness took hold, however, disillusionment set in. Having grasped that parents can exercise a measure of choice regarding the size of their families, and finding himself required, vexatiously, to look after five young sisters and a final brother, the boy grew impatient with a father who had gone on engendering children while failing to provide for them.

Moreover, Sigismund was shocked when Jacob, seeking to let him know how bad things had formerly been for Jews in Freiberg, confided that he hadn't fought back against gentile bullying. After learning of such "unheroic" conduct, Sigismund compensated by fantasizing himself as Hannibal, the Semitic Carthaginian general whose father had made him swear to "take vengeance on the Romans"—metaphorically, on the established Roman Catholics of Austria.[3] Such daydreaming became chronic as Sigismund, with dawning consciousness of his family's humble state, identified not just with Hannibal but also with the world-shaking Alexander, Caesar, and Napoleon, among others.

Meanwhile, his more practical ambitions were swelled by his irreligious mother, Amalie, who openly favored her firstborn at the expense of his siblings. Relying on the forecast of a fortune teller and on old-wives' superstition, she insisted he was destined for a brilliant career. Sigismund appears to have taken the prophecy in earnest and to have accepted his special privileges in the household as nothing more than his due. But by giving birth to seven more children, and by withdrawing into mourning over baby Julius when Sigismund was not yet two years old, Amalie left him with a permanent sense of abandonment.

In different ways, both of Freud's parents would strike the eventual theorist of the "family romance" as unworthy of his innate nobility and as an impediment to his social ascent. Along with thousands of other beneficiaries of the emperor Franz Josef's lifting of anti-Jewish restrictions, they had both emigrated from Galicia, a region that now includes parts of Poland and Ukraine; Amalie had also passed some of her childhood still farther east, in Odessa. Strong-willed, boisterous, and histrionic, with "little grace and no manners," this emotional "tornado" of a mother remained closer to her eastern roots than her upwardly mobile son would have liked.[4] Jacob was more subdued, but too much so; his resignation to defeat gave Sigismund a constant reminder of how far he could fall if he were to lose his foothold on the ladder of professional success.

Jacob and Amalie Freud, whose personalities were even farther apart than their ages, agreed on one important point: the best hope for a turnaround in the family's circumstances lay with Sigismund's academic achievements. The parents were heartened when he proved to be a precocious reader, a deft student of Greek, Latin, and history, and, after home schooling until age nine, the academic star nearly every year in his class at Leopoldstadt's multiethnic gymnasium. If Sigismund were to continue on the same prize-winning path, he would presumably earn the support of influential university professors. And in the distance lay respectable and remunerative career opportunities in a number of fields, from law and medicine to business, banking, higher education, and civil service.

Freud's parents were not mistaken about his mental agility. Before founding and leading an international movement, he would become a skilled anatomist, the holder of a prestigious postgraduate fellowship, a pediatric neurologist, a family doctor, and a scientific author. None of those achievements and honors, however, would slake his appetite for greatness or earn him more than temporary peace of mind. Already disposed to regard himself as disadvantaged by his humble origins and poverty, he would gradually acquire a sense of isolation, a mistrust of others' motives, and a panicked conviction that only some extraordinary breakthrough or windfall could allow him to realize his dreams.

2. ROOM TO BE TOLERATED

The most important contributor to that feeling of narrowed access to recognition was the psychological weight of anti-Semitism. Freud himself, in his autobiographical remarks, recalled that burden and emphasized the adjustment of attitude he had needed to make in order to press ahead with his career. Interestingly, though, he said nothing about a topic that will concern us much later: the effect of prejudice on the shaping of psychoanalysis.

Freud's eventual doctrine would constitute a turning of the tables on the anti-Semites—a "transvaluation of values" that delegitimized the Christian dichotomy between spirit and sexual passion. But Freud couldn't acknowledge that impetus without exposing the "science" of psychoanalysis as an ideological production. Consequently, anti-Semitism figured in his retrospect only as an obstacle to be negotiated in his path to discovery of universal psychological laws. From Freud's account we could never suspect either that he retained a lifetime grudge against gentiles or that—as we will find—one strain of anti-Semitism affected his own apprehension of fellow Jews.

Looking backward in his *Autobiographical Study* of 1925, Freud maintained that his struggle with prejudice had already been fully engaged in his adolescence. "Anti-Semitic feelings among the other boys," he wrote of his concluding school years, "warned me that I must take up a definite position. . . . And the increasing importance of the effects of the anti-Semitic movement upon our emotional life helped to fix the thoughts and feelings of those early days."[5] But a look at the record will show that until he was about nineteen and beginning medical school, he hadn't expected to be handicapped by his ethnicity.

We cannot doubt that Freud did experience some of the slights described in the *Autobiographical Study*. Even though, by the time of his graduation, Jews made up a full 73 percent of the Sperl Gymnasium's pupils, that majority constituted no insurance against snubbing. The rapid increase in Jewish enrollment, from 68 to 300, during the years of Freud's attendance was well suited to producing hostility from gentile teenagers who perceived "their school" as having fallen into alien hands.[6] Nevertheless, the adolescent Freud didn't regard prejudice as a credible threat to his advancement. A favorable sociopolitical climate encouraged him to believe that his opportunities would be almost limitless if he properly "Germanized" himself. This is not to say that his early fondness for Goethe, Schiller, and Heine was feigned. Rather, he saw

no conflict between retaining his identity as a Jew and becoming culturally German.

That Freud aimed at Germanization from the outset is most clearly
indicated by his early decision to alter his given name. In either 1869
or 1870, no later than age fourteen, he began registering for his school
courses not as Schlomo Sigismund but as Sigmund, and his early letters
also show him experimenting with the new version before definitively
adopting it in his signature.[7] Quite a bit of baggage was then left behind.
"Schlomo," honoring Freud's paternal grandfather, means "Solomon."
"Sigismund" was his parents' tribute to a sixteenth-century Polish mon-
arch who had protected Jews against pogroms. But quite recently the
name had come to stand, like the later "Hymie," for the generic Jew in
anti-Semitic jokes.[8] In contrast, "Sigmund" would have evoked the Norse
hero Siegmund in the *Niebelungenlied*, a work that was then serving
as a rallying point for pan-Germanic sentiment; Wagner's *Die Walküre*
(1870) strongly advanced that connection.

Although Freud wasn't trying to pass for a gentile, as a refashioned
Sigmund he was announcing his eagerness to become as *kulturdeutsch*
as anyone else. And he had an imposing model to follow. His first close
friend—a fellow Jew and on-and-off classmate in the Leopoldstadt
gymnasium—was Heinrich Braun, who would go on to attain promi-
nence in Social Democratic politics and journalism; he even served
briefly in the German parliament. The debonair, charismatic Braun, a
bold rebel, encouraged Freud to supplement his school curriculum with
implicitly subversive books by the progressive British historians W. E. H.
Lecky and Henry Thomas Buckle and by the gentile German skeptics
Ludwig Feuerbach and David Friedrich Strauss.[9]

Braun confided to Freud his plan of acquiring a law degree and then
becoming a radical politician. Smitten by his panache, Freud thereupon
decided he would follow that very course himself. Although he soon
thought better of the idea and opted for a medical career, it was a telling
sign of the times that two young Jews could plausibly imagine themselves becoming socialist leaders, operating freely within the broader society to accomplish reforms that would be applauded by Jews and gentiles
alike.

An even more impressive crossing of ethnic lines was effected by

Braun's eventual brother-in-law, Victor Adler, whom Freud came to know (and envy, and dislike) at the University of Vienna. A physician in private life, Adler believed that his political organizing and parliamentary initiatives extended naturally from his concern for patients who were experiencing class oppression. As the founder of the first Social Democratic party in Austria, Adler would manage to legislate universal manhood suffrage in a land where the nobility's illusions were still being humored. In 1907, thanks to Adler, the workers could vote at last, and they made his party the strongest in Austria. When the whole empire imploded at the end of World War I, it was the dying Adler who "led the orderly and peaceful revolution which removed the last formalities of Habsburg rule."[10]

Neither Adler nor Braun, then, felt significantly limited by anti-Semitism. Nor, apparently, did Freud himself feel persecuted in his schoolboy years, as can be inferred from two fragmentary sets of extant correspondence: a handful of letters to his Freiberg companion Emil Fluss, with whom he had reconnected in a visit to his birthplace at age sixteen, and a more extensive collection, composed mostly in errant self-taught Spanish between the ages of fifteen and twenty-five, that he sent to his closest teenage friend and "private academy" confidant, Eduard Silberstein. Both Fluss and Silberstein were Jews, and Silberstein, one year behind in the gymnasium, had been exposed to the same local atmosphere as Freud. While each set of Freud's letters occasionally mentions Jewish ethnicity, neither of them contains so much as a hint of ill treatment.

We meet in these archly ironizing documents a bookish, ponderously playful, sententious adolescent who exudes optimism about his studies and his plans for a sterling career. His literary and philosophical orientation is already German. He often sounds as if he is parroting judgments that were pronounced in class by his teachers. But there are signs, as well, of youthful cynicism about an older generation's pomposities. Jewish, Christian, and imperial Austro-Hungarian customs alike are treated satirically, with an implication that forward-looking youths in this modern age can no longer be bothered with religious or patriotic nonsense.

According to Freud's *Autobiographical Study*, a wall of anti-Semitism,

more formidable than the occasional taunts of schoolboys, greeted him
as soon as he undertook his higher education at seventeen:

> When, in 1873, I first joined the University, I experienced some appre-
> ciable disappointments. Above all, I found that I was expected to feel
> myself inferior and an alien because I was a Jew. I refused absolutely
> to do the first of these things. I have never been able to see why I
> should feel ashamed of my descent or, as people were beginning
> to say, of my "race." I put up, without much regret, with my non-
> acceptance into the community; for it seemed to me that in spite of
> this exclusion an active fellow-worker could not fail to find a little
> place [*ein Plätzchen*] in the framework of humanity. These first
> impressions at the University, however, had one consequence which was
> afterwards to prove important; for at an early age I was made familiar
> with the fate of being in the opposition and of being put under the
> ban of the "compact majority." The foundations were thus laid for a
> certain independence [*eine gewisse Unabhängigkeit*].[11]

This stirring paragraph bears only an oblique relation to the truth.
To begin with, had Freud really been so alone and despised during his
first years at the University of Vienna? Although Jews composed only
10.1 percent of the Viennese population in 1880, they already made
up 21 percent of the university's students, and most of them who were
enrolled in 1873 appear to have felt at home there. Even the nationalist fraternities had yet to turn against Germanizing secularists such as
Freud. Although he had no taste for drinking and dueling, he told Silberstein that he could have joined such a fraternity in either of his first
two years.[12]

Other letters from Freud suggest that he was delighted to be out of
high school and immersed in a broadening program of reading. As he
wrote to Silberstein after one year of study, he regarded his continuing
youth to be a time of undiluted self-development, without the need to
give a thought to earning money or attending to other people's judgments and demands.[13] "Never before," he reported a year later, "have
I enjoyed that pleasant sensation which may be called academic happiness, and which mostly derives from the realization that one is close to

the source from which science springs at its purest and from which one will be taking a good long drink."[14]

If Freud had been met with ostracism on entering the university, he surely would have wanted to end the ordeal as speedily as possible, but he lingered over an eclectic potpourri of courses. Nor does it appear that he was deprived of an active social life. Although he was by no means gregarious, and although he continued to associate privately only with Jews, he had numerous gentile acquaintances. One of his first acts as a student was to join an influential club, the *Leseverein der deutschen Studenten Wiens* (Reading Society of Viennese German Students), in which Jews and gentiles freely mingled.[15] Significantly, that club's mission was to forward the cause of Germanic culture in Austria, with the ultimate hope of seeing the western half of the empire disembarrassed of its Slavic Hungarian twin and completely integrated into Germany.

The prevailing mood of the *Leseverein* was naively utopian. As a fellow Jewish medical student who knew Freud, Solomon Ehrmann, recollected of the club, "We abandoned the altars upon which our fathers served and offered ourselves—in common with our fellow man of a different confession—to what was allegedly new, because we were told that now a new ideal, the ideal of humanity, the fraternization of mankind, was to be worshiped."[16] Ehrmann's remark suggests that comradeship between Jewish and gentile members, however awkward it may have proved in the execution, was mandated by the club's guiding principles.

Freud would remain a member of the *Leseverein* until its dissolution by a pro-Slavic imperial administration in 1878, when open tension had surfaced between Jewish and gentile members.[17] By then Freud would understand that pan-German nationalism had acquired an explicitly anti-Semitic character and that the *Leseverein* would offer him no shelter. But in the early years Victor Adler, Heinrich Braun, and Freud himself felt sufficiently welcome to take active roles in the club's activities. Indeed, Adler would be one of its leading officers until the end. And when Freud described to Silberstein the issues currently exercising the *Leseverein*, he wrote not as someone who might have been suspected of dual loyalty but as a fully equal participant.

We can see, then, that Freud's *Autobiographical Study* misrepresented his university experience in at least two respects. He hadn't been expected to feel inferior as soon as he arrived, and he hadn't been excluded from casual social contact with gentiles. On the contrary, he had sought it out in the *Leseverein* and had been pleased to blend in with the membership at large, adopting at least some of its values as his own. He hadn't even resigned when anti-Semitism did finally erupt within the club. All in all, his desire for acceptance seems to have been much stronger than we could have inferred from his self-description as an outcast who had nobly embraced his fate.

3. ADJUSTMENTS OF ATTITUDE

Long before he felt anti-Semitism to be closing in on him, Freud allowed it to exert an influence over his own perceptions. He was aware that the identifiably "eastern" Jews were already objects of scorn. As a son of two Galicians himself, he might have been suspected of being less than fully Viennese. The implicit goal of his self-improvement was to distance himself from his origins. Thus he was perturbed whenever he encountered Jews who struck him as "too Jewish" in their appearance and deportment.

As early as 1872, for example, at age sixteen, Freud told Emil Fluss how repulsed he was by an encounter with a family on a train:

> Now, this Jew talked in the same way as I had heard thousands of others talk before, even in Freiberg. His very face seemed familiar—he was typical. So was the boy, with whom he discussed religion. He was cut from the cloth from which fate makes swindlers when the time is ripe: cunning, mendacious, kept by his adoring relatives in the belief that he is a great talent, but unprincipled and without character. . . . I have enough of this riffraff [*Gesindel*]. In the course of the conversation I learned that Madame Jewess and family hailed from Meseritsch: the proper compost-heap for this sort of weed.[18]

This burst of venom was far from unique. In 1875, at age nineteen, Freud wrote to Silberstein about a new acquaintance who "is undoubtedly brilliant, but unfortunately a Polish Jew."[19] In 1878, at twenty-two, he told the same friend that he was appalled by the behavior of a *"grobber Jüd"*—a coarse Jew—at a dinner party.[20] At age twenty-seven, in recounting a funeral to his fiancée, he characterized one speaker as a fanatic who manifested "the ardor of the savage, merci-less Jew."[21] Further, at twenty-nine he told his fiancée that he had been disagreeably struck by the sight of "somewhat wretched Jewish faces" in a social gathering in Berlin.[22] And in the same year he described an acquaintance as "a typical little Jew with sly features."[23] It would seem, then, that the young Freud's chief response to anti-Semitism wasn't to protest against its invidious stereotypes but to hope that they wouldn't be applied to himself.

The success of Freud's strategy—acquiring *kulturdeutsch* manners and holding to an antithesis between better and worse categories of Jewishness—depended entirely on the willingness of gentiles to observe the same distinction. But a stock market crash in May 1873, several months before Freud attended his first university classes, initiated an irreversible hardening of the public mood. When a full decade of hard times followed the collapse, gentile artisans found their opportunities cramped and their wages depressed—so they reasoned, anyway—by Jewish laborers and peddlers. The resultant frustration, along with resent-ment of the corrupt financiers who had brought liberalism into disre-pute, sufficed to revive an ethnic demonizing that the state-established Catholic church had never disowned. Now, for the first time, anti-Semitic agitation struck demagogic politicians as a useful means of swelling party ranks and swinging elections.

A telltale incident from the period of Freud's medical studies can illustrate how he must have been pushed from the cautiously fraterniz-ing mentality of the *Leseverein* to this sense of an unbridgeable chasm between the ethnicities, all the more devastating because he had been taken by surprise. In 1875 the University of Vienna's medical school, where Freud was finally settling down to concentrate on degree require-ments, suffered an ominous convulsion. Most of the school's professors and students believed that, under an open-admission policy, aca-demically unprepared eastern Jews were becoming disproportion-ately represented. In a book-length report on the situation, the famous surgeon-professor Theodor Billroth proposed placing *numerus clausus* limits on the enrollment of Hungarian and Galician Jews.

But he didn't stop there. Although many of Billroth's distinguished colleagues were Jewish, he maligned all of them by implication. Jews, he asserted, constitute a single nation, no less distinct than Persia or France, and members of that nation will never be capable of understanding the Romantic German mind. In a wild emotional flourish, he declared that "pure German and pure Jewish blood" could never commingle.[24] Demonstrations and violent clashes between Jewish and German-nationalist students quickly followed.

Billroth would later repent of his inflammatory words and renounce anti-Semitism altogether. It can easily be imagined, though, that when Freud studied surgery under him for three semesters in 1877 and 1878, their relations must have been tense.[25] From the midseventies on, mutual suspicion affected all cross-ethnic interactions within the medical school and the university-affiliated hospital where Freud would serve his internship.

Jewish-gentile relations in Austria became even more ominous in the 1880s. The Berlin professor Eugen Dühring's malicious tract of 1881, *The Jewish Question as a Racial, Moral, and Cultural Question*, served as a match to the tinder of Viennese anti-Semitic sentiment. In the following year, the German nationalist movement, many of whose most early supporters had been Jewish, produced the splinter Austrian Reform Association, whose platform included repealing the civil rights of Jews. The decade also witnessed the rise of the Christian Social party, whose rabble-rousing leader, Karl Lueger, advocated having Jews stripped of their positions in civil service and the professions. On April 8, 1897, Lueger would be confirmed as the mayor of Vienna, an office he would hold for the following thirteen years. By the nineties, open derision of Jews as a racially unitary group—rootless, avaricious, shifty, hideous, and diseased—became commonplace in the press.[26]

In fact, however, it was not until the Nazi *Anschluss* of 1938, annexing Austria to Germany, that hatred of Jews would become an official position of the state. Until then, as Freud understood, gentile Austrians of the "better class," though bigoted in their opinions, tended to maintain a hypocritical civility toward those Jews whose conduct mirrored their own. The latter felt pressure to conform in all outward respects while they assumed, with good reason, that the smiles of their peers and superiors in the workplace were far from benevolent. They knew that well-earned preferment could be denied without explanation and bestowed instead on a gentile administrator's incompetent cousin or nephew. If a Jew happened to be predisposed to anxious suspicion, this world of trapdoors and false appearances would be sure to elicit it.

Indeed, Eduard Silberstein's usually optimistic and self-satisfied correspondent is scarcely recognizable in the touchy and suspicious Freud of the 1880s. True, the latter personage was burdened with new problems relating to his engagement and his career. But in his twenties Freud seems to have contracted a morbid distrust of other people's motives toward himself. Fearing arbitrary rejection on the grounds of his "race," he would try (not always successfully) to be unusually humble and diplomatic with authorities who held his future in their hands. Then he would despise them all the more for having put him through that demeaning ordeal.*

Freud would never attempt to deny his ancestry, and he never doubted that cultivated Jews were ethically and intellectually superior to gentiles of any stripe. But he also became, and remained, acutely class conscious. Vienna's heightened anti-Semitism stifled any remaining sympathy he might have felt for the masses, both Jewish and gentile, and made him wish for closer association with prosperous, achievement-oriented Jews who stood above reproach.

This selective closing of ranks would be epitomized in his joining B'nai B'rith five months after Karl Lueger's confirmation as mayor of Vienna. At that time B'nai B'rith was a fraternal order of mostly wealthy, service-minded Jews whose local chapter had been formed in 1895 to pursue progressive goals without relying on the wider Austrian polity.[27] Until the psychoanalytic movement came to preoccupy him full-time, Freud would be one of that chapter's most active and devoted members, and he would remain on its rolls until his flight to London

---

* As an embittered Freud would tell Jacob Meitlis in 1938, among gentiles "basically all are anti-Semites" (quoted by Yerushalmi 1991, p. 54).

in 1938. Significantly, he would read early chapters of *The Interpretation of Dreams* not to a university audience but to his lodge brothers, who could be relied upon for encouragement even though his argument was exotic to their ears.

But this tightening of Freud's bond with worldly, philanthropic Jews would be accompanied by a hardening of his antipathy to Jewish religion in all of its outward forms. He even briefly considered declaring himself a Christian simply in order to avoid a rabbinical wedding. His bride, the pious granddaughter of a distinguished Hamburg rabbi, would be admonished that no religious observances could be tolerated in his household. He would arrive late for his father's religious funeral and would skip his mother's altogether. His sons would not be circumcised, and it is said that none of his children, while living at home, ever entered a synagogue. At Christmas they would gather around the traditional German tree and exchange gifts in the manner of the Christians.[28] And at the end of Freud's life, on the eve of the Holocaust, he would publish *Moses and Monotheism*, wherein it would be maintained that the great leader and teacher of the Hebrews—a "Freud figure," as every reader has noticed—was no Jew but an Egyptian prince, murdered by the ignorant idolators whom he had tried to enlighten.[29]

In part, Freud's spurning of Judaism was a straightforward expression of his disbelief in supernatural claims. Yet many other Viennese professionals who shared his atheism were willing to pay token deference to the customs still observed by their elder relations. And Freud, as we recall, had been schooled in Jewish tradition by a father and an instructor who placed no emphasis on theology. The implacability of his anti-Judaism expressed a determination to cut every tie to Leopoldstadt and its culture of meek acquiescence to inferiority. Later, Freud would aim at both explaining and replacing all religions with psychoanalysis; but he might never have arrived at such a grand project if orthodox customs and rituals hadn't proved such an attractant for anti-Semitic mockery.

In spite of his apprehensions, Freud isn't known to have ever been deprived of a career opportunity because of ethnic bias.[30] Rather, anti-Semitism was an important factor in his life because, descending on him just when he was preparing for a life in medicine, it amplified his self-doubts, distorted his attitude toward gentile colleagues, and aroused a permanent rage against Christian smugness. One result would be a peculiarly inward form of revolutionism, symbolically anti-Christian but outwardly respectable and nondenominational. The public reforms of Victor Adler, Heinrich Braun, and Freud's sometime neighbor Theodor Herzl would strike him, by comparison, as relatively shallow and, at the same time, as likely to stir up needless trouble.

Insofar as family ties and traditions constitute a source of emotional strength, it was unfortunate that Freud's drive for success pitted him against his origins. The race hatred that troubled his young manhood was largely to blame for that alienating effect. I have already suggested, however, that his insecurity had earlier sources as well. As we will see, some challenges in the realms of love and work, *Liebe und Arbeit*, would exacerbate nervous tendencies in Freud that must have been present all along. And it was those tendencies and their consequences, in tandem with the soaring ambition he had contracted in more innocent years, that would lead him to make his extraordinary claims about the nature of the mind.

2

Getting By

1. SOME LIMITATIONS

According to the canonical version of Freud's career, a strong vocation for scientific inquiry drew him, beginning from a concern with the physiology of simple sea creatures, through histological study of nerve cells in lower vertebrates, to investigation of the structure of the human brain stem, to brain pathology in human neurological diseases, and finally—after he learned from Jean-Martin Charcot that clinical observation yields richer results than mere anatomy does—to the successful treatment of psychoneuroses. In this way, it is said, he prepared himself to deduce from his patients' utterances the laws of normal and abnormal motivation. And along his path toward psychoanalysis, the brilliant young physician made himself a significant figure within a remarkable number of fields, from evolutionary biology and pediatric neurology to brain pathology and psychopharmacology.

Already in the 1880s, according to the legend, Freud was resolving key problems, decisively advancing the Darwinian paradigm, and barely missing out on the full development of the neuron theory for which Heinrich von Waldeyer-Hartz and Santiago Ramón y Cajal gleaned the credit in 1891. At each station of his journey he allegedly took command of a more difficult and significant field than the last, sometimes arriving at the brink of a fundamental breakthrough but instead, because his restless intellect required new challenges, moving ahead to more complex problems.

Although (the narrative continues) Freud found himself able at last to characterize his principal discovery, the unconscious, in strictly psychological terms, his long apprenticeship in anatomy had served him well, admonishing him that mind events are also brain events and that a science of interpretation is still a science, answerable to rigorous standards of corroboration. Thus the Freudian neuroscientist Mark Solms, believing that "today psychoanalysis stands as one of the last outposts of the great clinical traditions of internal medicine," depicts Freud's pre-psychoanalytic writings as congruent with, and progressively pointed toward, his psychological breakthrough.[1]

These claims are considerably inflated. Nevertheless, they do refer to an actual record of accomplishment. Between 1877 and 1900, Freud published six extensive monographs, forty articles, and an enormous number of reviews. In books such as *On Aphasia* (1891), the collaborative *Clinical Study on the Unilateral Cerebral Paralyses of Children* (1891), and *Infantile Cerebral Paralysis* (1897), he usefully surveyed and evaluated the extant range of theories on neurological topics. Taken together, these miscellaneous books and papers formed the basis for the professional recognition he would be granted by colleagues, including his 1885 appointment as a *Privatdozent* (unpaid lecturer) at the University of Vienna, his receipt of a traveling fellowship in the same year, and the prestigious unpaid post that he held, from 1886 through 1895, in Max Kassowitz's First Public Institute for Sick Children. Further signs of esteem ensued, including his membership on several editorial boards for learned journals, his selection as a contributor on the topic of childhood palsies to a major encyclopedia of medicine, and his *Professor Extraordinarius* title in 1902.

By most objective accounts, however, none of Freud's pre-psychoanalytic writings were pivotal for the modern development of any discipline. Although Gordon Shepherd devotes a chapter to him in his treatise on neuron theory, for example, Shepherd concludes that

Freud's papers deserve to be ranked with a large number of others.[2] And in Joseph D. Robinson's definitive study of how synaptic transmission came to be recognized, Freud's name goes altogether unmentioned.[3] His early record, furthermore, is notably discontinuous, showing little follow-through. He skipped from one self-contained task to another, augmenting the sum of generally accepted knowledge and deftly criticizing premature conclusions reached by others but never crucially testing any of his own hypotheses.

Even Solms, the foremost champion of Freud-as-scientist, feels obliged to admit that his most promising-looking papers regularly stopped short of drawing important conclusions that appeared to be just a step away. For example, Freud exposed the "intersexuality" of the eel, "but without recognising the significance of his findings."[4] And again, he identified some properties of the neuron but was "far too vague and reserved" to take another step.[5]

Freud had to work around handicaps that were unusual in a medical scientist. Numbers and equations left him cold, and he often got details wrong or contradicted himself about them in the course of a paper. "To be tied down to exactitude and precise measurement," Ernest Jones observed, "was not in his nature."[6] As Freud himself would tell his close friend Wilhelm Fliess, "You know that I lack any mathematical talent whatsoever and have no memory for numbers and measurements."[7] Thus he felt compelled to exclude statistics from almost all of his technical as well as his anecdotal writings.

The near absence of charts and tables from Freud's scientific papers might be regarded as a peripheral matter if it weren't symptomatic of a basic weakness of temperament: a lazy reluctance to collect sufficient evidence to ensure that a given finding wasn't an anomaly or an artifact of careless procedures. This flaw could go unnoticed so long as Freud was microscopically analyzing dead tissues, any one of which could stand for countless identical others. For the purpose of establishing laws in most fields, though, large samples are indispensable. As a psychologist, Freud would consistently ignore that requirement. Instead, he would rest comprehensive generalizations on untested insights from a few cases or even from just one, his own.

2. THE MISSING SPARK

Freud's early record, creditable but hardly predictive of greatness, calls for a reassessment of his native qualifications for the role of innovator. Let us start from the beginning of his intellectual development. Extant documents offer little support for the assumption that he had been a scientifically inclined youth whose curiosity about nature took him, in stages, toward an eventual confrontation with the baffling human mind. To be sure, he loved walking in the woods and bringing home rare flowers.[8] But his schoolboy letters show that his orientation in adolescence was overwhelmingly literary, historical, and philosophical. Indeed, one of his early ambitions had been to become either a poet or a novelist.[9]

According to Freud's own testimony, it was a literary experience that first aroused his interest in science at age seventeen. Then he felt inspired by an oral reading of "Nature," a prose-poem attributed— wrongly, as it happens—to Goethe.[10] That text was a paean to the variety and creativity of the living world, whose secrets, it was said, would always remain safe from prying inquirers. Although the poet's rapture before mysterious forces made for an odd introduction to the methodical rigor of Viennese research, it spoke to a kindred feeling in Freud. Decades later he would aver that every organism is suffused with instincts of "life" and "death"—shadowy powers in the vitalistic tradition of early-nineteenth-century *Naturphilosophie*.

Naturphilosophie, championed by Hegel, Fichte, and Schelling, among others, consisted of Romantic speculation about the structure and animating energy of the natural world. It offered a metaphysical program that presumed to unite the individual sciences. In practice, however, its untested premises discouraged experimentation along strictly materialist lines, and thus it was anathema to positivists such as Hermann von Helmholtz and Freud's first mentor, Ernst von Brücke. When Freud chafed against the rigors of empirical norms, it was inevitable that he would fashion his own variant of *Naturphilosophie*.

Like other elements of Freud's legend, the "Nature" story exaggerates his early autonomy and clarity of purpose. It is hard to believe that

his choice of a degree program was determined solely or even principally by a literary work. He already knew that he lacked the temper of
a politician, such as Heinrich Braun or Victor Adler; and the world of
business, to which his father had hoped to attract him by sending him
on a post-graduation visit to his entrepreneurial half-brothers in
Manchester, was tainted by scandals, including the disgrace and imprisonment of his uncle Josef, the forger. Meanwhile, a concentration in
medical science appeared to make sense on mundane grounds, with or
without a special gift or even interest on his part.

That Freud at seventeen wasn't fired with zeal for scientific investigation is clear from his announcement to Eduard Silberstein, *after*
having listened to the reading of "Nature" and having opted for a
medical degree, that he meant to devote his first university year to the
philosophy faculty and to "purely humanistic studies, which have nothing to do with my later field."[11] When he did enroll in a few science
courses, he wrote tepidly that he was "moderately satisfied because
I am spending my time in a way that, while it could be much better, is
by no means among the worst. I am referring to my work in the sciences, albeit not the right sort of work."[12] And when he found that the
analysis of zoological tissues did suit him well enough, he thought of
seeking a joint Ph.D. in philosophy and zoology—a program that would
have necessitated his permanently transferring from the faculty of medicine to that of philosophy.[13]

Philosophy, indeed, was Freud's real intellectual passion in the first
phase of his studies. The hero of his late teens was Ludwig Feuerbach,
"whom I revere and admire above all other philosophers."[14] By 1841
Feuerbach had already developed the thesis Freud would elaborate in
The Future of an Illusion (1927): that the God posited by Jewish
and Christian theology is nothing other than a projection of human
needs and fears. And it was as a Feuerbachian that he was drawn,
by way of a stimulating challenge, to the Catholic philosopher Franz
Brentano, whose courses in the university and whose private conversation he found more attractive than any scientific lectures or laboratory exercises.

Brentano was also a systematic psychologist, and Freud must have
been struck by his insistence that, after stringent reform, psychology

might acquire sufficient rigor to be accepted as an authentic natural science. But Brentano's conception of the mind, which excluded the possibility of unconscious mental phenomena, could hardly have pointed Freud toward psychoanalysis.[15] Nor, when Freud decided to probe the psychical underworld, would he heed Brentano's stern admonitions about empirical accountability.

In the legend of Freud's orderly march toward founding a new discipline, his scientific and medical instructors in the university come off badly on the whole. "Being a rebel," wrote his friend and last physician Max Schur,

> Freud was contemptuous of the "Old Guard" at the medical school of the University of Vienna . . . who had been awarded honorary titles either because they were chairmen of departments, or were noted for some special achievement, or had merely arrived at a certain seniority and "knew the right people."[16]

These, presumably, were the dinosaurs who would later prove themselves too set in their ways to perceive the merits of psychoanalysis. The Freudian community continues to think of them as advocates for a narrow positivism that couldn't have satisfied a budding revolutionary.

In reality, Freud had attended the most advanced medical school in the world—a mecca for visiting physicians from the rest of Europe and North America—and he had been awestruck by its great tradition.* Its luminaries—Rokitansky in pathology, Brücke in physiology, Meynert in psychiatry, Hyrtl in anatomy, Arlt and Jaeger in ophthalmology, Schrötter, Gruber, and Politzer in otolaryngology, Billroth in surgery, Hebra in dermatology, Nothnagel and Bamberger in internal medicine, Chrobak in obstetrics and gynecology—were celebrated in Vienna because they ranked among the best in the world at their specialties. And their brightest students would become sterling innovators in the next generation.

---

* Ernest Jones related that Freud "as a young student at the University of Vienna . . . used to stroll around the great arcaded court inspecting the busts of former famous professors. . . . He then had the phantasy . . . of seeing his own bust there in the future" (J, 2:14).

At a time when medicine was still emerging from the arid dicta of Hippocrates and Galen, whereby all diseases were ascribed to disproportionate humors or "animal spirits," Vienna set the model for specificity in diagnoses and etiologies (causes of disorders). True, the university suffered from aging infrastructure, overcrowding, and unhygienic conditions that encouraged the spread of infection. But its morale was sustained by enthusiasm for new instruments, new techniques, and new correlations between organic deficits and symptoms of disease. Observation of the human organism (both alive and in autopsies) was to be exact; the results of such observation were to be the deciding factor in the choice between rival hypotheses; and explanations of biological phenomena could appeal only to commonly acknowledged laws of chemistry and physics, not to undetectable imagined energies.

The idea that Freud's instructors in science and medicine were wanting in general curiosity is far from the mark. Hermann Nothnagel, for example, pursued classical studies in his free time; Theodor Billroth was an accomplished musician and a close friend to Brahms; and the physiologist Ernst Fleischl von Marxow read widely, taught himself Sanskrit, and translated Dante for his own satisfaction. Ernst Brücke, the son and grandson of painters, was himself a painter and the author of three academic books on art, and several of the papers that he wrote during the period when Freud worked under him addressed broadly humanistic problems.

Nor did Freud's elders draw an arbitrary line between their scientific and cultural interests. Brücke's chief assistant, Sigmund Exner, aspired to determine how it was possible, physiologically, for human beings to exercise intelligence, morality, and free will. And Freud's other key mentor at the university, Theodor Meynert, the son of a painter and a drama critic, indulged in speculative explanation of higher functions by reference to hypothetical structures within the brain. Although most of those efforts came up short, they erred on the side not of pedantry but of rash adventure.

The question, then, is not whether Vienna's medical professors were worthy of Freud; it is why he dreaded taking most of their courses and then found those courses difficult to pass. The main reason is that he was ill prepared both by educational background and by disposition. His gymnasium education had been geared toward *Bildung*, or the formation of a cultivated gentleman, with heavy doses of Greek, Latin, history, and literary classics. And he soon found that a philosophical interest in Darwinism was no substitute for scientific aptitude. "I was compelled," he confessed much later, "during my first years at the University, to make the discovery that the peculiarities and limitations of my gifts denied me all success in many of the departments of science into which my youthful eagerness had plunged me."[17]

A normal progression to the M.D. degree in the University of Vienna entailed five years of coursework, promptly followed by the *rigorosa*, or three comprehensive qualifying examinations. Freud's path was more meandering. He took six years to meet his course requirements, after which time, despite his family's need for him to become financially independent, he put off the *rigorosa* for another two years. Only in 1881 did he muster the courage to sit for those tests, which he did pass but without distinction.

3. THE DOCTOR IN SPITE OF HIMSELF

Although Freud had been exposed to the best medical education that the world of the 1870s had to offer, the actual life of a physician was repugnant to him. Nor did he ever discover in himself the least talent for that role. Ernest Jones, who knew him intimately, noted in him an active "aversion to the practice of medicine,"[18] and Freud himself would always be candid about his disinclination for tending to illness. "Neither at that time," he wrote, "nor indeed in my later life, did I feel any particular predilection for the career of a doctor."[19] Never, he recalled, had he felt a craving to be of service to suffering humanity.[20] Malfunctioning bodies revolted and depressed him, and he wished to see as little of them as possible. His sister Anna would one day reveal that the sight of blood had been intolerable to him.[21] As late as 1927 he would own that he had "never really been a doctor in the proper sense."[22]

By his twenties, Freud was willing to contemplate any program he could master without having to vivisect animals or deal with really sick people. That requirement was met by the microscopic analysis of already prepared zoological specimens, an activity conducted in the recently modernized Institute for Comparative Anatomy, headed by a brilliant forty-one-year-old professor, Carl Claus. A quick and diligent learner of procedures set forth by others, Freud distinguished himself sufficiently to be sent, on two occasions in 1876, to Claus's Zoological Experimental Station in Trieste, where his mentor gave him the task of trying to confirm an earlier researcher's hypothesis about the recogniz-ability of testes in eels.

The result was Freud's first scientific paper, a competent though inconclusive production that was remarkable chiefly for its author's age, twenty-one, and for its unusual tone, which the psychoanalyst and historian Siegfried Bernfeld, the earliest inquirer into Freud's period of apprenticeship, would characterize as "always self-assured—at places, even cocky."[23] The inappropriateness of that tone to an assigned project already suggests a strain between Freud's ambition and his limitations. Bernfeld detected hints that the novice researcher—"tempted to rebel-lion and competition," and living in "an irritating atmosphere full of frustration, doubts, and comparisons"[24]—resented the relatively young Claus's sway over him and was determined to project more independence than he actually possessed.

Freud's deeper yearning, apparently, was for a mentor whom he could emulate without suffering feelings of envy and aggressive rivalry. Just such a figure was Ernst Brücke, the most honored of active profes-sors in the faculty of medicine and a preeminent physiologist from the 1840s until his death in 1892. Freud was expected to enroll in at least one course of Brücke's and to take a turn in the laboratory of his Physio-logical Institute. As soon as he met the great man in 1876, however, Freud had no more fervent desire than to remain by his side and win his approval.

Freud would stay affiliated with the dingy institute, which lacked both running water and a gas supply, for six briefly interrupted years, first as a research student and then as an unpaid "demonstrator," or teaching assistant, entrusted with preparing specimens and slides for classes taught by Brücke and his second and third in command, Sigmund Exner and Ernst Fleischl von Marxow. The chief goal of Freud's striv-

ing between 1876 and 1882 was to put himself in line for inheriting
one of those two assistantships, should it become vacant.

Fleischl and Exner were well-off professors who didn't need to rely
on their meager income from the institute. Freud's situation was more
stressful. He was aspiring to a position that would pay him very little
and be his only source of funds. And his microscope studies, though
meritorious, were mostly assignment driven, as opposed to the path-
finding work of both Exner and Fleischl. Thus there seemed to be little
chance that he would ever be appointed a professor of physiology.
And succession to Brücke's directorship was even farther out of reach.
Exner, the first in line for that position, did obtain it, and he kept it
until 1917, when the psychoanalyst Freud was sixty-one years old.

But the young man we have been coming to know was not so much
seeking one career as he was shrinking from another, that of a doctor.
His six years with Brücke can be understood as a long postponement
of commitment, during which time he craved not only recognition but
also respite from the nagging hostility—exacerbated by consciousness
of anti-Semitism—that he felt toward contemporaries who were more
privileged or honored than himself. Brücke's objectivity and his posing
of sharply defined, manageable tasks, along with the Jewish Fleischl's
cordiality and solicitude, created a supportive environment for Freud,
who found, after the shock of discovering that he could barely pass his
science courses, that his field work in Trieste had equipped him well
to meet Brücke's technical demands. Subsisting on gifts and loans, he
might have been content to stay within the Physiological Institute for
many more years.

Freud's receipt of the medical degree in 1881 prompted no alteration of his plan—or lack of one. On June 16, 1882, however, his life
took a fateful turn. That was the day when he and Martha Bernays,
a fellow Viennese, became secretly engaged. Both were poor; both wanted
to raise a family; and neither of them could countenance the idea of
subjecting that family to destitution. They wouldn't be able to marry
at all, then, without a prospect of steady and substantial income from
Sigmund's work. It remained for Brücke to draw Freud aside and point
out the obvious corollary. He must leave the institute, resolve to become
a private physician, and enter Vienna's General Hospital as a rotating

resident, trying out specialties until he found one that he could bear to practice. One month later he undertook that very ordeal.

3. MAKING THE ROUNDS

Like many another candidate, Freud had acquired his M.D. without ever having treated a patient. Now, from 1882 to 1885, he would see hundreds of them, chiefly in the hospital's departments of surgery, internal medicine, psychiatry, neurology, and dermatology, but also more briefly in ophthalmology and naso-laryngology. The senior physicians in charge of those branches, including Billroth, Nothnagel, Meynert, and Franz Scholz, were all eminent practitioners of anatomy-based research. All but the neurologist Scholz, who had outlived his engagement with his field, were imparting advanced techniques to eager residents and visitors.

Yet Freud was only going through the motions of becoming a skilled physician. During his two months in the hospital's surgery department, when Billroth was apparently on vacation, he learned for sure that he wasn't born to wield a scalpel. Under Nothnagel in general medicine, he was reminded of his repugnance for diseased people. His stints in dermatology and naso-laryngology left him uninspired, and he couldn't handle the instruments employed in the latter specialty without betraying his lifelong clumsiness. And under Meynert and Scholz, the two physicians who dealt with what we would now call mental patients, he sustained his morale only by reverting to the one investigative activity he had mastered, the solitary microscopic analysis of tissue specimens.

Apart from its laboratory, where both Freud and Meynert preferred to spend their time, the hospital's psychiatry unit was little more than a holding pen for the disturbed, most of whom would be transferred, after an average stay of eleven days, to the Psychiatric Asylum of Lower Austria, just outside Vienna.[25] Only a few patients, those exhibiting syndromes of particular relevance to Meynert's current pathological research, were retained, and some others were discharged outright. With the help of young staff physicians such as Freud, Meynert would reach a cursory diagnosis, just sufficient to indicate whether the patient should be retained or transferred. It was only after a patient's death that he or she might draw the chief's full attention. Postmortem analysis of retrieved brains could allow him to correlate lesions with disorders and thus to isolate the segments responsible for functions that had gone awry.

In Meynert's department between May and September 1883, Freud performed clerical duties and participated in the fast-turnover processing of cases. Albrecht Hirschmüller, studying case summaries that Freud prepared for Meynert's disposition, found them to be perfunctory and full of careless errors. And he notes that Freud's extant letters from the period convey an eerie indifference to victims of mental illness.[26] Hirschmüller perceives no inner engagement on Freud's part with mental factors—not even when the case at hand was a fascinating instance of folie à deux, a much-studied syndrome at the time.[27]

Freud completed his hospital residency by spending fourteen months, from January 1884 through February 1885, attached to Scholz's department of "nervous diseases"—a blanket term that encompassed some illnesses of undetermined etiology. He despised Scholz and earned his enmity by complaining about the administrator's parsimonious and unsanitary management of the unit. For that and perhaps other reasons, Scholz found Freud antipathetic, eventually demanding that he be transferred out of the department. But so far as we know, the two men didn't quarrel over principles of treatment. Freud wasn't yet inclined to challenge the prevailing "therapeutic nihilism," the view that medical conditions are either incurable or self-limiting and that intervention is usually deleterious.

4. AN ACCIDENTAL NEUROLOGIST

Given his loathing of Scholz and apparent lack of concern for patients on the neurology ward, it may seem anomalous that Freud passed more than a year on that ward and that he decided to specialize in the same field himself. But the reason for his choice can be found in an opportunity that had come to his notice shortly after he left Meynert's psychiatric service. In September 1883 Nathan Weiss, a friend of Freud's and an assistant to Scholz, hanged himself in despondency over the unraveling of his recent marriage. At the time of his death, Weiss was already a neurology *Dozent* in the University of Vienna—the very position to which Freud would be advanced in September 1885.*

When Weiss died, Freud went to his sagacious older friend and benefactor Josef Breuer for career counseling. Breuer himself, as we will later see, had compiled a distinguished record in physiology but had opted to earn his living as a family doctor. He advised Freud to build his credentials in neurology while continuing to get trained in general medicine. Then he would be able to accept local patients who presented virtually any complaint, and meanwhile he would be earning a reputation in one specialty—the one, we may note, that Breuer knew to be lucrative, thanks to the number of chronically agitated and fabulously wealthy ladies at the apex of Viennese Jewish society. Later, in another private conversation, Hermann Nothnagel seconded the wisdom of Freud's laying the groundwork for becoming a private neurological specialist while applying to take Weiss's vacant place in the university's medical faculty.[28]

Freud was determined and adaptable. He quickly familiarized himself with the extant neurological literature in German, English, and French. Yet his speedy acceptance as a neurological expert in his own right requires explanation. By the time of his appointment to the university docentship, he had published, apart from book reviews, just one article that could be classified as neurological in topic, a single-case study of a brain hemorrhage.[29] How had he convinced the senior professors and hospital department heads that he was a neurologist at all?

A partial answer is that neurology, a relatively new field, was struggling through an identity crisis that revolved around syphilis, at that time the most intently investigated and controversial of diseases. The fact that its full course entailed both paralysis and insanity helped to confound attempts to draw a clean line between neurology and psychiatry. In addition, neurologists were divided over how to address states of nervous debilitation, some of whose symptoms appeared to be

---

* Freud's actual period of service began after his return from Paris in April 1886; he didn't begin offering courses until October of that year.

shared with epilepsy. In the 1880s, then, it wasn't easy to say who was and wasn't a bona fide neurologist.

Authorities such as Brücke, Exner, Fleischl, and Meynert, moreover, were following Freud's career with sympathetic interest. They believed him capable of performing well in an untried discipline that wasn't far removed from their own. Although static, descriptive neuroanatomy—his real specialty—wasn't neurology, it was a necessary foundation for advances in the discrimination and treatment of nervous diseases. But it wasn't Freud's as yet meager work in neurology proper that impressed his elders; rather, it was his steady earnestness, his total record of publication on scientific topics, and his exposure to neurological and quasi-neurological case work, first under Meynert, then under Hermann von Zeissl in the General Hospital's syphilis ward, and finally during his long period under the nominal supervision of Scholz.

Freud himself, however, understood that he was ill-equipped to become a first-rate neurologist. The sticking point was his distaste for neurophysiology, the study of the living nervous system whose dissected elements he could expertly examine under glass. As Siegfried Bernfeld flatly stated, in Freud "the ability for physiological work was missing."[30] And without an intimate knowledge of physiology, abnormalities couldn't be illuminated in an original way.

Already in 1878, as an undergraduate, Freud had spent six months in association with Vienna's Institute of General and Experimental Pathology, where, under the eminent Salomon Stricker, he had endeavored to carry out an assigned project having to do with the operation of saccular (versus tubular) glands. No one was better qualified for introducing Freud to active physiological work; in Jones's words, Stricker was "credited with having transformed pathology from an anatomical to an experimental physiological discipline."[31] According to Stricker's report, delivered publicly and aloud, Freud's effort was a complete failure. Stricker himself, in fact, had been obliged to carry the project to completion.[32] And now in 1884, knowing that a good neurological researcher was also expected to be a physiologist, Freud returned to Stricker's institute for a second and more urgent try. For several months, as Bernfeld relates, he "accomplished nothing."[33]

Decades later, Freud would still feel touchy about his second

failure with Stricker. The work he had been assigned in Brücke's Physiology Institute, he complained, having been "too closely restricted to
histology" (tissue analysis), had left him unprepared.[34] But this was a
weak alibi for the fact that all nonhistological inquiry was outside his
ken. During his six years in Brücke's laboratory, neither Brücke nor
Exner nor Fleischl had been overcommitted to the microscope. It was
Freud, wishing to continue the successes he had enjoyed under Claus,
who had been unwilling or unable to expand his scientific horizon
beyond inert tissues.

In Meynert's laboratory, which was freely available to him from
May 1883 into the summer of 1885, Freud kept on pursuing the investigation of such specimens. In his application for the *Dozentur*, or
university lectureship, he made it clear that he expected to remain
committed to neuroanatomy. And soon thereafter, when he went off to
study under the clinically oriented Jean-Martin Charcot, he anticipated
spending his research time peering into a microscope once again. Even
after becoming a convert to Charcot's psychological agenda, he would
go right on composing papers about the anatomy of the brain. He did
so because he was good at it—and, for the time being, at little else.

In view of his late start in a field that was alien to his disposition,
Freud compiled a worthy record in neurology as it was then understood. But we shouldn't be surprised that he kept searching for other
routes to fame, or that in 1885 he would leap from pathological anatomy
to a total enthusiasm for Charcot's work with hypnotism and hysteria.
Then at last he would feel that a scientific line of thought was fully
engaging the subjective and holistic concerns that truly excited him.

3

Forsaking All Others

1. BLISS DEFERRED

Before getting to know Martha Bernays in April 1882, Freud had taken a dim view of young women, evidently regarding them as potential obstacles in his path of self-betterment. At age seventeen he had observed to Emil Fluss, "How wise are our elders to burden the fair sex with but little knowledge of natural science!! (I see we are all agreed that women are born for something better than to acquire wisdom.)"[1] The best policy, he had believed, was to avoid female company altogether. Rebuking Eduard Silberstein for his flirtations, he had warned of women's ready susceptibility to seduction, thanks to their lack of any "inherent ethical standard" and to their educationally programmed "ineptitude for life's serious tasks."[2] An upright man, he declared, ought to abstain from offering flattery to creatures "who are unstable, incapable of grasping their own unimportance, and whom nature has . . . inclined to be vain."[3]

The young Freud stood in no danger of becoming a seducer himself. Although his letters to both Silberstein and Fluss at age sixteen were much concerned with puppy love for Fluss's thirteen-year-old sister, Gisela, what those passages chiefly display is his fear of social contact with the opposite sex. Gisela was never informed of the tepid infatuation. When Freud got over it—or perhaps in order to get over it—he sent Silberstein a mock "epithalamium" (nuptial ode) whose grotesque verses bristle with sexist contempt for the ordinary creature, now recast as the grotesque river monster Ichthyosaura, who had been glorified in his fantasy.[4]

As numerous commentators have observed, Freud's adolescent musings about the Fluss family had less to do with any winsome traits on Gisela's part than with a daydream of replacing his own uncouth mother with Gisela's well-read, equable, and modernizing one. Freud himself told Silberstein that he had "transferred my esteem for the mother to friendship for the daughter."[5] That was perhaps the earliest example of an extant proto-psychoanalytic reflection. Yet it was also a portent of future difficulty with perceiving and accepting women apart from their preassigned roles in his psychodrama.

All it took for Freud to fall in love with his future wife—so he would profess, and so his biographers have duly repeated—was one brief view of her at the dining table of his parents' apartment as she was peeling an apple and chatting with his sisters. Martha, however, was not stunningly beautiful, and Freud himself would consider her less attractive than her sister Minna, four years younger, who was also mingling with the Freud girls in that period. Although Martha would prove, in her extensive premarital correspondence with Sigmund, to possess admirable traits of temper, character, and intellect, he could hardly have divined them from her apple peeling.

Stories of love at first sight are charming, and doubly so when we perceive that one or both of the involved parties had nothing of a material nature to gain from their union. Martha's father had died suddenly in 1879, and a desperate shortage of funds on both sides would cause their engagement to extend through more than four years of deprivation and worry, especially on Sigmund's side. But Martha Bernays owned a treasure that Freud may have found attractive: the prestige of the Bernays name itself.

A "decisive factor" in his choice of a wife, Freud would write to his daughter Mathilde in 1908, had been his "finding a respected name."[6] It is impossible to believe that he had known nothing about Martha's family before catching sight of her from a doorway. Her sister Minna appears to have already gotten engaged, two months earlier, to his best friend at the time, Ignaz Schönberg. Moreover, Sigmund was cordially acquainted with Martha's brother, Eli. He must have been aware that one of their grandfathers had been the chief rabbi of Hamburg and a relation and associate of Heinrich Heine's, and, further, that two of their uncles (one deceased) were eminent scholars.

Even before getting to know Martha, then, Freud may have decided that it was time for him to marry someone above his parents' social station. But not far above, for he believed that his poverty, ethnicity, awkwardness, ugliness (as he imagined), and lack of good prospects barred him from using marriage to leapfrog over class barriers. The much-reduced Bernayses, struggling to pay their bills, were quite good enough for a man with Freud's considerable liabilities and untested talent. It also helped that Freud, self-conscious about his stature at 5'7", was several inches taller than his fiancée-to-be.

As for the family he aspired to join, it was Emmeline Bernays, not her pragmatic, forthright, and fun-loving daughter, who cared about social distinctions and correct appearances. Against her wishes, her husband, Berman, had moved the family to Vienna when Martha was eight. Even without a cushion of wealth, the widow now hoped that her two girls could marry back into the comfortable circumstances they had once enjoyed in Wandsbek, a small town outside Hamburg. Finding herself at the head of an Orthodox household, Emmeline also expected her daughters to choose husbands who respected Jewish faith and ritual. She had already tried to arrange such a marriage for Martha—who, however, had bravely held out in the hope of making a love match.

If Freud, the son of a bankrupt idler and the nephew of a felon, believed he could win the hand of a Bernays, it must have been because he calculated that Emmeline's claim to social superiority was not so foolproof as she liked to think. Her late husband had himself served a jail term for fraud and had tried without much success to make a fresh start in Vienna. After his death, the family had been kept solvent only by gifts from Martha's uncle Michael and by the modest salary of her brother, who had assumed his dead father's job as secretary to an economist. Eli himself would soon demonstrate the near parity of the two families by marrying the eldest of Freud's sisters, Anna, in October 1883.

And the sharp-tongued, independent-minded Minna, once her own fiancé succumbed to tuberculosis in 1886, would have to accept the demeaning role of "lady's companion."

When a favorably impressed Martha, after some secret walks and talks, consented in June 1882 to marry Sigmund, the pair confronted an obstacle. It was unthinkable that Emmeline would rejoice at the idea of handing her elder daughter to an impecunious, atheistical laboratory assistant from a barely respectable family. Although the couple, after six furtive months of keeping "Mama" in the dark, finally revealed their intention to her, they did so only after Eli Bernays had announced his own engagement to Freud's sister Anna.

Sigmund already disliked the pious, imperious Emmeline Bernays. Their relationship was further poisoned when, a year after the secret betrothal, Emmeline compelled her two engaged daughters to move back with her to Wandsbek, an expensive two-day train ride from Vienna. Sigmund's antipathy now turned to fury. Yet he fully shared the bourgeois outlook that underlay Emmeline's reservations about him; marriage without money was unthinkable. Thus he had to endure an extended agony of frustration, visiting Wandsbek only four times in an engagement that would stretch across nearly four and a half years.

2. A CASE OF NERVES

When Sigmund and Martha were apart, they corresponded at a rate that would put any epistolary novelist to shame. Those missives, wrote Ernest Jones, leaving Martha's participation out of account, make us party to

> a tremendous and complicated passion, one in which the whole gamut of emotion was evoked in turn, from the heights of bliss to the depths of despair with every grade of happiness and misery being felt with unsparing intensity. It may be said with all circumspection that, quite apart from the special interest attaching to Freud's personality, the set of letters would be a not unworthy contribution to the great love literature of the world. The style is at times reminiscent of Goethe, but the delicacy of feeling, the exquisite tenderness,

the precision of phrasing, the range of vocabulary, the wealth of allusion, and, above all, the distinction, the profundity and nobility of thought they display, are Freud's own.[7]

What a major event it would have been, then, if all of those letters, briefly placed at Jones's disposal by Anna Freud, had been published in unexpurgated form for any reader, not just for a few trusted Freudians, to absorb and assess! Until recently, however, the public had seen only a modest selection of Freud's engagement letters, primly redacted by his heirs with the aim of forming "a portrait of the man"[8]—a portrait, that is, of a steadily affectionate fiancé, sometimes ill-humored but gradually led by the strength of his love toward greater self-command.

The full archive allows some less complimentary inferences to be drawn—inferences that Jones himself, to his credit and to Anna Freud's unease, felt obliged to concede. As he remarked in dismay, confidentially, to Siegfried Bernfeld, "Martha comes out of the letters excellently but Freud was very neurotic!"[9] Jones could see that the state of being engaged had elicited an infantilism in Freud that must have been present all along; and some of his strangest behavior, which Jones noted but passed over lightly, had occurred toward the end of the long delay.

Freud's *Brautbriefe* kept hinting at a delicacy in his own constitution that was strikingly at variance with the tireless vigor he sometimes exhibited in the out-of-doors. The letters contain frequent reports of physical and psychological complaints for which he sought Martha's sympathy. The physical ones ranged from insomnia, indigestion, severe headaches, and nasal mucus to sciatica, "rheumatic" pains, and constriction of the throat. Graver afflictions, including typhoid fever and a mild case of smallpox, were stoically endured, but the net impression conveyed by the extant letters is that most of Freud's symptoms were tightly intertwined with his anxieties. Although it is impossible to estimate the contribution of hypochondria to his woes, we can be sure that his frequent accounts of pain, faintness, fatigue, and indisposition conveyed an extra message to his intended: her mate might prove to be more a patient than a lover.

As for his psychological health, Freud dwelled on feelings of loneliness and depression from which he had presumably been rescued by Martha herself. The rescue, however, needed to be continually renewed. "Frozen on an island in the icy sea," he wrote her from Paris in January 1886, "that is your beloved now. Except that every other day, I know not how, the warm mail comes floating along from Wandsbek, and the ice melts as it comes through."[10] In the preceding month he had warned, "My health, my mood, and my inclination to work are all dependent on my hope to see you again; and if it does not happen, who knows how soon I will have another *break down*.' "[11] Sometime before December 1885, then, Freud had presumably experienced at least one nervous collapse.[*]

"Many wounds that went deeper than you knew have been closed," Freud told Martha in 1884.[12] But it seems more likely that those wounds were being aggravated by the stress of his new situation. "At times," he disclosed sixteen months after his betrothal, "I have something like attacks of despondency and faintheartedness which you, my dear and good one, must not share."[13] Three months later he reported, "I have days on end—they always come one after the other, it is like a recurring sickness—when my mood slackens for no apparent reason, and I tend to get exasperated with amazing ease."[14] In August 1884 he confessed that he had "experienced during the past fourteen months only three or four joyful days, when I had some small success. . . . And that is too little for a human being who is still young and yet has never been young."[15]

What was the matter? In Freud's own view, darkened by a prevailing theory of racial degeneration that took the inbred Jews as its prime exhibit, his heredity was far from optimal. As he told Martha, he regarded his extended family as marked by "a considerable 'neuropathological taint' "—exemplified, notably, by his first cousins in Breslau. Two of the four had gone insane, and a third was hydrocephalic and feeble-minded. But Freud was able to add, with less than complete

---

[*] Perhaps Freud was referring to an ominous tailspin that had lasted for several weeks in 1875, featuring insomnia, mood swings, and a feeling that, as he told Silberstein, his "limbs had been glued together and were now coming apart again" (2/21/75; FS, p. 89).

reassurance, that in his nuclear family the only disorders were his own "neurasthenia," or "nerve weakness," and that of his sister Rosa.[16]

The reigning view assigned the symptoms of neurasthenia—chiefly depressive lassitude, general anxiety and tremors, hypersensitivity, headaches, insomnia, and digestive problems—to overwork. Significantly, however, Freud would contravene that judgment and maintain that the syndrome was a direct outcome of onanism. To his early biographers, it was all but self-evident that he had been masturbating his way through his long engagement and making himself sick with guilt over it. The bachelor's secretiveness about his habit, Jones privately wrote to Bernfeld in 1952, "was certainly neurotic." He added, however, that the theme would not be suitable for inclusion in a biography—not, that is, in the kind of biography he was intending to write.[17]

Masturbation per se can hardly account for the feelings of anxiety and emptiness to which Freud often fell victim. A depressive tendency was fundamental to his makeup. Yet he did believe the alarmist medical lore of his day regarding the evils of "self-abuse"; and the one consequence of the habit that he would later emphasize above all others was that a man who is given to masturbating before marriage will suffer from "diminished potency" as a husband.[18] Although he would prove capable of intercourse, we will see that he experienced dysfunction and that it troubled him deeply. In retrospect, it would appear that neither masturbation nor his cloying endearments in the *Brautbriefe*—"little princess," "my treasure," "fair mistress," "angelic girl," "my sweet little woman"—reassured him that his forthcoming marital obligation was going to be a joy.

3. FASHIONING THE PERFECT WIFE

Freud was already experiencing a problem that he would one day ascribe to all men: an inability, held over from early childhood, to reconcile female sexuality with maternal purity and devotion. His bride was supposed to arrive intact, submissive, and sexually ignorant, but also to reciprocate a lust that he hoped would outlast the honeymoon. Yet she was also expected to coddle him as her indulged son. That role, in Freud's estimation, was a woman's highest calling. As he would put

it in 1933, "Even a marriage is not made secure until the wife has succeeded in making her husband her child as well and in acting as a
mother to him."[19]

In the same juvenile vein, Freud morosely reminded his fiancée that
their ideal happiness couldn't last for long, because "dangerous rivals
soon appear: household and nursery."[20] He feared that Martha's everyday wifely tasks, with or without children underfoot, were going to
rob him of her full attention. But worse, the thought that she would
be apportioning her affection between him and their actual offspring
was as distressing to him as had been the arrival of the seven younger
siblings who siphoned maternal love away from Amalie Freud's *goldener Sigi*.

Because Freud was concerned to protect his fiancée from sexual
knowledge, it has been assumed that she must have exemplified the
aversion to eroticism that he would later ascribe to virgins in general.
The *Brautbriefe*, however, show us a very different Martha—a coquettish
one who allowed herself to be kissed by another man *after* pledging
herself to Freud, and who took pleasure from inflaming her beloved's
desire. In one letter, for example, she recounted a dream in which the
two of them held hands, gazed into each other's eyes, and then "did
something more, but I'm not saying what."[21] Note, too, that this ama-
tory teasing came less than two weeks after the start of the secret
engagement.

When he wasn't complaining about his present ailments and future
neglect, the unhappy fiancé was instructing his beloved in how to
become a properly deferential mate. He made it clear that she would
have to change some of her ways, and the sooner the better. It was precisely Martha's most admirable qualities—unselfconscious candor
and spontaneity, a trusting nature, freedom from class prejudice, loyalty
to her family and its values—that struck him as in need of revision.
Thus he rebuked her for having pulled up a stocking in public; forbade her to go ice skating if another man were along; demanded that
she sever relations with a good friend who had gotten pregnant before
marriage; and vowed to crush every vestige of her Orthodox faith and
to turn her into a fellow infidel.

The area in which Martha most urgently needed reeducation, Freud believed, was that of excessive regard for her own family. He had coveted its name in 1882, but the very illustriousness of Martha's connections prompted a worry that she and other Bernayses might look down on him as a parvenu. As a son of two Galicians whose culture had scarcely extended beyond the Hebrew Bible and the Talmud, he was quick to suspect a well-connected North German of harboring a prejudice that he himself privately shared. He would try relentlessly, then, to extirpate everything "Bernays" about his fiancée and bride. "From now on," he admonished her in a falsely jovial decree, "you are only a guest in your family, like a gem that I have pawned and that I am going to redeem [*auslösen*] as soon as I am rich."[22]

Likewise, despite the syrupy passages in his *Brautbriefe*, Sigmund wanted Martha to remember that she herself was nothing very special. Just nine weeks into the engagement, for example, she was informed that her looks were hardly out of the ordinary.[23] (In stressing her sober virtues instead, Sigmund was evidently trying to discourage her from flirting with other men.) And at times he teased her patronizingly about her want of worldly experience and her inability to collaborate in his work. After she had tried to help him with a translation project, he wrote, "I am nothing short of delighted by my little woman's unskillfulness."[24]

Sigmund's excuse for rehearsing Martha's limitations was that he occasionally performed the same exercise on himself. As he wrote on November 10, 1883, "Since I am violent and passionate with all sorts of devils pent up that cannot emerge, they rumble about inside or else are released against you, you dear one."[25] The vices he acknowledged were a bad temper, a penchant for hatred— "I can't hold out against silent savagery"—and "a tyrannical streak" that made "little girls [namely, Martha] afraid" and rendered him all but unable to "subordinate [him]self" to any other person.[26] In owning up to such traits, however, Freud wasn't resolving to curb them in his marriage. "You see what a despot *I* am," he warned just one month into the engagement.[27] Martha was to understand that the despotism would persist.

The couple's engagement included no period of romantic comradeship before Martha's new master began laying down the rules. She was told from the outset that she would be expected to serve his needs, manage his domestic existence, and honor his decisions in all other matters. The dollhouse diminutives with which he addressed her only reinforced the message that his darling girl was to live only for him, exercising no individual will. As for "feminine" means of gaining advantage, he declared that they wouldn't be tolerated. "I will let you rule [the household] as much as you wish," he decreed, "and you will reward me with your intimate love and by rising above all those weaknesses that make for a contemptuous judgment of women."[28]

Although Freud was echoing the separate-spheres ideology of his era, he did so in awareness of more liberal views that were beginning to attract serious notice. Indeed, in 1880 he himself had translated into German, as an assignment for a fee, a volume of John Stuart Mill's works that contained the century's most stirring plea for gender equality, *The Subjection of Women*.[29] There he encountered a passionate argument against the oppressive attitudes and customs that had spared European males from having to vie academically, professionally, and politically with fifty percent of their contemporaries.

To Freud's way of thinking, Mill's position was nonsense. "For example," he reported to Martha in bafflement, the author "finds an analogy for the oppression of women in that of the Negro. Any girl, even without a vote and legal rights, whose hand is kissed by a man willing to risk everything for her love could have put him right about this."[30] And he added,

> It is also a quite unworkable idea to send women into the struggle for existence in just the same way as men. Should I think of my delicate, dear girl as a competitor? The encounter could only end by my telling her, as I did seventeen months ago, that I love her, and that I will make every effort to get her out of the competition and into the unimpeded, quiet activity of my house. . . .
>
> No, here I stand with the elders. . . . The position of woman cannot

be other than what it is: to be an adored sweetheart in youth and a beloved wife in maturity.[31]

Freud didn't ask his fiancée whether she agreed with those sentiments. Her expression of a contrary opinion would not have counted—except, of course, as a sign that she was not yet reconciled to her destined role. As Ernest Jones observed with unusual bravery, Freud was insisting on nothing less than "complete identification with himself, his opinions, his feelings and his intentions. She was not really his unless he could perceive his 'stamp' on her."[32] And again, the relationship "must be quite perfect; the slightest blur was not to be tolerated. At times it seemed as if his goal was fusion rather than union."[33]

This zeal to remake another personality doesn't look promising for a career in psychotherapy, a field that relies on empathy with the traits of others. As is well known, Freud would remain puzzled by women but would cover his ignorance with dogma about a biological inferiority that causes all of them to remain childish, envious, and devious. That hurtful doctrine would be rooted not in clinical findings but in prejudices and fears the theorist had manifested long before aspiring to expertise about the mind.

4. TANTRUMS

We have only just begun to see how much trouble Freud would have in taking a steady view of others. Despite his bouts of nervous lassitude, for example, he showed himself to be a very whirlwind of destructive energy in one respect. From the first weeks of his engagement he was intermittently gripped by a ferocious jealousy and sense of betrayal.

The first object of his hatred was his future mother-in-law, whose understandable wariness toward him he misperceived as implacable hostility. He was outraged that that she retained a measure of authority over her daughters, and so he demanded of *both* sisters that they refrain from taking her part against him. If Martha meant to persist in placing her mother's wishes ahead of his own, then "you are my enemy; if we don't get over this obstacle we will founder. You have only an either-or. If you can't be fond enough of me to renounce your family for my sake, then you must lose me, wreck my life, and not get much out of the family yourself."[34]

Two other "enemies" were the violinist and composer Max Mayer, a distant cousin of Martha's, and Fritz Wahle, an artist companion of Sigmund's. Martha now looked upon both of those ex-suitors as well-intentioned friends, but Freud felt threatened by them; and Wahle, he knew, was still in love with Martha. Sigmund commanded his fiancée to cease addressing Mayer by his first name and to have nothing further to do with Wahle. When thinking of the latter, he wrote, "I lose all control of myself, and had I the power to destroy the whole world, ourselves included, to let it start all over again . . . I would do so without hesitation."[35] Three years later his anguish over the thought of Wahle was still acute.

And then there was Martha's sociable and adventuresome brother Eli, who bore Freud only the kindest feelings. The two had been on good terms before the engagement, and Freud was indebted to him on several counts. Eli had restored the Bernays family to a semblance of financial viability; he had chivalrously backed Martha's refusal to enter into a marriage of convenience; and in 1883 he would once again manifest his superiority to crass materialism by marrying Freud's own penniless sister Anna. Just two weeks after getting engaged, however, Freud announced to Martha that Eli would thenceforth become his "most dangerous rival."[36]

Before long, Freud declared that Eli had become "unbearable" to him.[37] He went out of his way to pick quarrels with the mystified friend—maintaining, for example, that Eli had behaved rudely toward his youngest sibling, Alexander.[38] For two years he refused to speak to the despised one, nor would he attend his own sister's wedding to him. And in the closing months of the engagement, his rage against Eli reached and sustained a truly paranoid intensity.*

----

* Some of the epistolary evidence from this period may have been destroyed. Freud's engagement letters seem to have continued until shortly before his wedding day, September 13, 1886. Jones read such letters, based some inferences on them, and briefly quoted from three of them, dated May 13, June 5, and July 6 of that year. Yet Ernst Freud declared in 1960 that "letters written by Freud to Martha during the final four months of

In order to meet his summer expenses in 1886, Freud had undergone the humiliation of borrowing a hundred German marks from Martha, who could ill afford to part with them. He knew, however, that she owned some other funds—as did her sister Minna—that had been consigned to Eli for investment. In the third week of May 1886, Freud became obsessed with getting his hands on Martha's share of that money, which he needed chiefly to buy furniture for their apartment; and he began asking her, and then hounding her, to demand Eli's surrender of it.

In Freud's defense on the financial issue, it must be said that Eli's record of moneymaking schemes was less than sterling; he possessed both the heart and the history of a gambler. Whether he was more cautious with his sisters' funds isn't known.* When inquiries about restitution were made, he professed, plausibly enough, that the sums in question were illiquid; they couldn't be turned into ready cash without a costly loss of principal. But Eli's hesitation convinced Freud that he had embezzled Martha's and Minna's nest eggs, and he directed Martha to require immediate restoration of the stolen amount in full.

Between May 20 and June 17, 1886, Freud made at least nine demands that Martha get her money back from Eli. By the latter date she had temporized for so long that Freud began to lose control. On June 18 he told her to convey a threat to Eli: her fiancé was prepared to inform "the robber's" superiors at work about the embezzlement and to have his income garnished. Martha, however, had no intention of treating Eli so harshly. Instead, she tried to placate Sigmund by scraping together another fifty marks and sending it to him—an expedient that only heightened his mortification at being financially dependent on a woman and a Bernays. Now he began to rave that the "highly genteel" Wandsbek household, with its classy Hamburg credentials, loathed him as a Polish boor.[39]

---

their engagement have unfortunately not been preserved" (L, p. 7n). What had the missing letters revealed? Jones wrote, tantalizingly, that "for more reasons than one [it was] not feasible" to reproduce long passages from them (J, 1:120).

* Élisabeth Roudinesco asserts, without attribution, that Eli was being blackmailed by a former mistress with whom he had fathered a child (Roudinesco 2016, p. 37).

Freud was goaded again when Eli, given to understand that the problem was furniture, proposed to guarantee payment on the items that Sigmund and Martha might otherwise be unable to buy on terms. On June 20 Sigmund instructed Martha to reject the offer on the grounds that a merely verbal assurance by such a "scoundrel" was worthless. But because the now exasperated Martha didn't reply at once, Freud took matters into his own hands and wrote directly to Eli—who, no doubt alarmed by Freud's apocalyptic frame of mind, immediately sent off the entire owed sum. Freud wasn't grateful; in a *Brautbrief* of June 22 he crowed vindictively over his defeat of the "coward" who had just accommodated him.

Freud was scarcely appeased when Martha then received a surprise dowry from another relation, enabling the long-postponed wedding to be scheduled at last. By virtue of its Bernays source, the gift only reminded him of his own poverty and dependency. Thousands of gulden, suddenly added to his bank account, would constitute a mortification if he hadn't earned them himself.

With Eli's repayment now in hand, and with a new scheme of borrowing furniture instead of purchasing it on credit, Freud believed he could safely marry at last. But Martha's unwillingness to renounce her brother when commanded to do so had sent him into a frenzy that didn't soon abate. Announcing a determination to have nothing further to do with the double brother-in-law who had efficiently complied with his ultimatum, Freud turned his wrath on his "future obedient wife,"[40] who didn't yet realize that her "primary duty" was to be "loving and not defiant."[41]

Freud's conduct in the Eli matter lends weight to Emmeline Bernays's comparison of him, in a reproving letter, to a "spoiled *child*" who thinks he can get his way by throwing fits.[42] In letter after letter he berated Martha for disloyalty, bluntly voicing a doubt as to whether she was worth marrying at all:

- I must only obtain a promise from you *never to lend him money again or to invest it with him* or you and I are really through.[43]
- If I accept [what you said in your latest letter], there is only one

conclusion to be drawn: that you have chosen between me and Eli, and that we need not be concerned about our coming together.[44]

- Just a few days ago I would have laughed if someone had told me that you and I would not marry because we could not agree and do not trust each other's love. And yet here we are. And I see no way out, for I cannot give in.[45]
- The consideration that a thoughtful girl has for everyone else does not apply to her fiancé.[46]
- You were everything to me, but as Eli's sister you are of no use to me.[47]

Elsewhere Freud did acknowledge that he had been difficult, but the responsibility, he was convinced, lay entirely with Martha: "If I have become unbearable recently, just ask yourself what made me so."[48] To his inflamed imagination the Bernays family, including his fiancée, was a unified phalanx opposing his blameless intentions. And, fantasizing about how despised he was in Wandsbek, he mused grimly, "one who is happy to be a noble martyr finds such opportunities quite often."[49]

Most ominously for the future student of universal human nature, Freud believed that Martha, in defying his wishes, had shown herself to be at the mercy of irrational impulses from which he himself was immune. "And if she behaves thus despite her love," he pronounced, turning her into a third-person object of clinical scrutiny, "what flaws must there be in her personality?"[50] In his jealous fury he sincerely believed he was treating her objectively, "without bitterness."[51] "My judgment," he informed her, "turns out to be the right one every time."[52]

As Freud's emotional tempest finally began to subside, he was ready to make peace with Martha, but only on terms of unconditional surrender. With her savings now transferred to his possession, he let her know that a fraction of the new family's funds, if she conducted herself appropriately, would be allocated to her future comfort. Don't worry, he reassured her: "my little bird will always find a cage and a lump of sugar."[53]

On September 13, 1886, Sigmund and Martha were finally able to wed in a Viennese civil ceremony, followed a day later by a religious one in Hamburg. By then, however, Martha must have realized that her husband would require continual humoring and was never going to be her friend. Driven frantic and rendered ill by his rages, she had begged him only for "a little respect"; but she would never receive it.[54] The untold story of their marriage, sentimentalized by Jones, would be Freud's complete extinction of a personality that had once been playful, ardent, and ready for shared adventure.

PART TWO

THE FIRST TEMPTATION

When I've thought sufficiently long about you and
about cocaine, I think about money and again about
money.

—Freud to Martha Bernays, 6/12/84*

* FMB, 3:401.

4

White Magic

1 A BRUSH WITH FAME

A fateful turn in Freud's career occurred in 1884, halfway through his engagement. He was preoccupied at the time with trying to secure enough money to warrant settling down with Martha Bernays. The substantial sum, he believed, wouldn't be forthcoming unless he could capitalize on an innovation in science or medicine. But what could it be? Freud was still a newcomer to neurology; the laboratory studies that he could execute deftly were only conventional science, destined at best to modify somebody else's theory; and circumstances were nudging him toward a life of dutiful routine.

Above all, Freud lacked basic confidence in his abilities. If he had possessed an aptitude for discovery, he mused in his self-pitying letters, fame and wealth would have been his for the plucking. Instead, he sensed within himself a troubling imbalance between his ambition and his gifts. "Now for a long time," he wrote, "I have known that I am no genius. . . . I am not even very talented; my whole capacity for work probably stems from my traits of character and from the absence of outstanding intellectual weaknesses."[1]

It would be a fine thing, Freud believed, if the goals of becoming wealthy and of making a scientific name pointed to a single course of action. Because money came first, however, there was never much likelihood that he would take on a research project for the sheer sake of its intellectual appeal. As he protested to Martha after she had rallied him, in one letter, to follow his scientific inclination wherever it led, "this isn't going to happen; . . . I intend to exploit science instead of allowing myself to be exploited by it."[2] His goal, as he put it elsewhere, was to attract recognition not only from his peers but also from "the well-paying public."[3] Scientific advances are rarely if ever generated from such a motive.

There was, however, one possible egress from Freud's dilemma. His mentors had taught him that gains in anatomy and physiology are made possible not only by the development of higher-resolution microscopes but also by improved techniques for staining specimens to be viewed under glass, so that the structure of nerves, muscles, and veins can stand out more clearly. Even though such a refinement would be only an instrumentality, not a substantive discovery, the world of medical science would be indebted to the inventor of a superior stain.

Here was one potentially important achievement that did lie within Freud's reach, and for which years of labor had adequately prepared him. Already in 1877, serving as Brücke's laboratory assistant, he had attempted to improve the then accepted method of staining; and in 1879 he had published a brief notice announcing just such an achievement. His claim, which appeared to be warranted by good results within the Physiology Institute, was that his mixture of nitric acid, water, and glycerine facilitated the preparation of nerves for sharper viewing "in a guaranteed and effortless way"[4]—a phrase, we may note, conveying a distinct hint of salesmanship. For whatever reason, though, Freud's formula does not appear to have caught on outside the confines of the institute.[5]

In the fall of 1883, now employing Meynert's facilities instead of Brücke's, Freud returned to the task of fashioning a better stain. The idea this time was to utilize a solution of gold chloride in a formula whose application could isolate myelin (nerve sheathing) more clearly than ever before. By February 1884 Freud was reasonably certain that he had succeeded. In step-by-step instructions, he dictated precise quantities of ingredients and spelled out how they were to be handled. And now he made sure that his innovation would get noticed. He submitted a full accounting to the *Archiv für Anatomie und Physiologie* and two shorter, identical papers to the *Centralblatt für die Medicinischen Wissenschaften* and the English journal *Brain*.[6]

Freud's *Brautbriefe* in the months preceding publication of the gold chloride papers show mood swings between elation and worry. His technique worked well enough to produce some impressive slides that were greeted with hurrahs when shown to Josef Breuer and to Freud's former colleagues at the Physiological Institute.[7] If the beauty of those results were matched by dependability and uniformity from one laboratory to another and from year to year, Freud's distinction would be assured. Several letters to Martha, however, indicate an awareness of continuing inconsistent results, and no letters indicate that the difficulty was overcome.[8]

Scientific discretion called for a delay while the cause of unreliability was being tracked down. Freud did spend months trying to improve his formula. Stymied, however, he opted to submit the papers for publication as they stood, irrationally hoping that no one would notice the problem he had failed to solve.

Although Freud's proposal was a near miss, both its originality and its value have been overstated by most commentators. His was not the first attempt to develop a myelin stain based on gold chloride; it was the third, after those of Joseph von Gerlach in 1872 and Paul Flechsig in 1876. And all three techniques were consigned to oblivion by the most successful of Carl Weigert's several stains, introduced in the same year as Freud's, 1884. An 1888 review of the field witheringly characterized Freud's alternative as useless.[9] In 1897, annotating the bibliography he submitted in his bid for a professorship, he was constrained to admit that his long-abandoned innovation had proved "no more reliable than other methods of gold staining"—which is to say that it had failed.[10]

It is all the more striking, then, that Freud's 1884 papers violated scientific convention by resorting to crass propaganda. "Failures of unknown cause," the longer article boasted, "which in other gold-toning procedures give histologists cause for complaint, can be ruled out in the present method. . . . One can count with certainty on obtaining long series of sections of identically colored preparations." And in

Brain Freud was even more emphatic: "This method will never fail (as all [other] methods of staining by gold chloride will do)."[11]

Freud's bravado in these sentences was as ominous as it was precipitous. Here we already observe a penchant for indulging in boosterism when the intrinsic worth of his science was as yet untested. We may recall in this connection Siegfried Bernfeld's comment that the tone of his very first scientific paper was "always self-assured—at places, even cocky." A tendency to braggadocio, it seems, was there from the beginning.

2. THE CURE-ALL

Freud's *Brautbrief* of April 21, 1884, reveals that he was already preparing to invest his hopes elsewhere:

> My mind is also occupied now with a project and a hope that I want to tell you about. . . . It is a therapeutic test. I have been reading about cocaine, the effective ingredient of coca leaves, which some Indian tribes chew in order to make themselves strong against hardship and overexertion. A German has tested this remedy on soldiers and actually reported that it produces wondrous strength and capacity for work. Now I want to get some of this substance for myself and, for obvious reasons, try it out on cases of heart disease, then on nervous exhaustion, particularly in the miserable condition after morphine withdrawal.[12]

So began, on a note of restrained hope, a three-year odyssey that would render the then twenty-seven-year-old Freud conspicuous for his singularly enthusiastic, broad-spectrum advocacy of an alkaloid (crystallized plant extract) whose practical uses and terrible risks would be debated around the world.*

---

* The threat to Freud's legend posed by his cocaine involvement has been managed, on the whole, either by hurrying past it—see, e.g., Gay 1989; Makari 2008; Phillips 2014; Roudinesco 2016—or by ascribing exaggerated value to his papers on the topic. In 1974 Robert Byck, collaborating with a vigilant Anna Freud, translated and collected Freud's cocaine essays and some related documents in a useful volume, but deferred editorially to Anna's filial piety. "All of Freud's papers on cocaine," Byck declared with more gallantry than candor, "can be said to be thorough in their review, accurate in their physi-

The German physician mentioned in Freud's letter was Theodor Aschenbrandt, a surgeon to the Bavarian artillery who had acquired some cocaine prepared by the Darmstadt pharmaceutical company Merck—the only European firm to have succeeded in deriving a relatively stable, uniform, chemically potent version of the drug. Aschenbrandt's paper related how, during autumn maneuvers in 1883, six exhausted and/or unhealthy soldiers, after drinking a cocaine solution, had proved themselves capable of extraordinary exertions without suffering ill effects.

By the time he wrote to Martha, Freud had been further emboldened by a number of articles in back issues of a Detroit magazine called the *Therapeutic Gazette*. The most influential of those items was an 1880 submission from Dr. W. H. Bentley, who reported that, over a number of years, he had alleviated various ailments, from dyspepsia to tuberculosis, with "erythoxolon coca"—more properly *Erythroxylon coca*, or cocaine.[13] And one claim in particular, for a reason that will become clear, couldn't have failed to electrify Freud. Bentley asserted that, using cocaine supplied by the American firm Parke, Davis & Co., he had repeatedly curbed both morphine and alcohol dependency without putting new addictions in their place.

Bentley's counsel to his medical colleagues was at once straightforward and harebrained. Repeatedly during a given session when the patient felt a craving for morphine or whiskey, he or she was to be offered a mouthful of cocaine solution. When the original craving no longer recurred—in other words, when the cocaine high had obliterated the desire for anything else—the physician would know that he had arrived at the right prescription: the sum of the amounts of medicinal fluid that had been imbibed. Afterward, rather than linger by a bedside, Bentley would ship the addict from one half to three pounds of the saturated fluid and wait to hear by mail how the cure had turned out.

Apparently, Freud found nothing worrisome in such a procedure. He was reassured, no doubt, by the fact that no fewer than sixteen articles in

---

ological and psychological experimentation, and almost prescient in their consideration of points which have become major issues in modern psychopharmacology" (CP, p. xxvi). More recently, Albrecht Hirschmüller has provided a textually reliable German edition (SK)—one whose commentary, however, keeps straining to shield Freud from criticism.

the *Therapeutic Gazette* had declared cocaine to be both safe and efficacious. Freud either didn't notice or didn't care that the *Gazette*, far from being a legitimate medical journal, was in fact a house organ of Detroit's own Parke, Davis pharmaceutical firm. Indeed, the listed editor was none other than the company's owner, George S. Davis. But the testimonials that Freud savored fell into alignment with his own positive thoughts about cocaine, and that was evidence enough for him.

Freud did perceive that the professional American literature on cocaine treatments, even in the *Therapeutic Gazette*, had all but ceased four years before his own introduction to the topic. After 1880, as he remarked in the first of his four cocaine papers,

> information regarding successful cures became rarer: whether because the treatment became established as a recognized cure, or because it was abandoned, I do not know. Judging by the advertisements of drug dealers in the most recent issues of American papers, I should rather conclude that the former was the case.[14]

For the breakthrough-seeking Freud, then, the American medical community's puzzling new reticence was less telling than the continued efforts of the pharmaceutical industry to market its product.

As Freud informed his fiancée, it was already common knowledge that Andean natives had traditionally fortified themselves for heroic feats of labor by chewing coca leaves. The alkaloid cocaine, however, was unknown to the Incas and their descendants. It is much faster acting and more powerful than the leaves from which it is extracted, and some of its effects are markedly different. Moreover, drinking a solution could cause the active chemicals to accumulate in organs more rapidly than would the chewing—or, more precisely, the wadding into a cheek—of leaves whose juice gradually seeped out.

When judging Freud's pronouncements about cocaine, however, it will be important to keep at bay anachronistic judgments deriving from the modern cocaine plague. In the closing decades of the nineteenth century there were no statutes banning or even regulating the sale or consumption of cocaine in Austria or anywhere else, and its most concentrated forms, crack and freebase, were as yet unknown. In the United States, low-grade cocaine was being added to soda pop, cigars, and cigarettes, consumed as a general tonic, and prescribed to ease hay fever, sinusitis, and even teething. Meanwhile, one cocaine-laced wine, Vin Mariani, in circulation since the 1860s, was still being consumed internationally in the first years of the new century. Its devotees included President McKinley, Czar Alexander II of Russia, and Queen Victoria, and it was endorsed in advertisements by Pope Leo XIII, who was said to carry it everywhere in a hip flask.[15]

Vin Mariani, concocted by the French chemist Angelo Mariani, was made by steeping wine in coca leaves, whose taste was so bitter that care had to be taken to keep the concentration low. In fact, Mariani's policy was to choose the least bitter leaves in his stock, and those were the ones containing the least cocaine. The drink did induce a high, thanks to the fact—unknown to anyone before 1990—that alcohol and cocaine together produce a third potent intoxicant, cocaethylene. But no amount of Vin Mariani or other coke-laced products would have been likely to result in cocaine addiction. As a result, the broad public was slow to perceive a social problem with cocaine. And many doctors remained complacent about the drug because they, too, were aficionados of Vin Mariani.

Freud's own underestimation of the drug's risks, however, derived not from ignorance of its power but from his own thrilling introduction to it. Cocaine itself, in the purest form then known, began at once to warp his judgment. Though close to penniless, he had purchased an expensive gram of the alkaloid from Merck. On April 30, 1884—*Walpurgisnacht*, or the folkloric night of supposed witchcraft and trafficking with the Devil—he tasted cocaine powder and imbibed his first .05 gram solution of it, marveling at its mood-elevating capacity. And from that night forward he would regard the drug as the most precious and restorative substance on earth.

On *Walpurgisnacht* in Goethe's *Faust*, Mephistopheles offers the hero a magical elixir that grants him both sexual and intellectual mastery. *Faust* was already Freud's favorite work of serious literature, and it would remain so. The figure of Dr. Faust, risking his soul for freedom from the ethical constraints that render the experience of other mortals so impoverished, would become central to his later self-conception as the founder of an anti-Christian science that could penetrate forbidden realms.

Scarcely a month after disclosing his new interest, Freud was already sure that the "magical remedy" (*Zaubermittel*) would prove to be his ticket to worldly success.[16] He had continued to take the drug himself and to feel emboldened by it. Meanwhile, he had begun sending small amounts of it, along with commendations of its benefits, to his fiancée, to his sisters, and to trusted colleagues, who would presumably be encouraged to prescribe it to their patients for the alleviation of various complaints.[17]

Freud's enthusiasm was boundless. A letter to Martha of May 9, 1884, excitedly recounted how, freelancing from his hospital work, he had employed cocaine to banish the pain of a sufferer from mucus obstruction. He was also finding signs of "brilliant success" with depression and indigestion. "If all goes well," he announced, "I will write an essay on it, and I expect it will win its place in therapeutics, by the side of morphium and in place of it." If so, "we need have no concern about being able to stay in Vienna and to possess one another soon."[18]

3. INSTANT AUTHORITY

Freud's pursuit of celebrity through the promotion of cocaine was conducted in the hours he could spare from his hospital duties and from his resumed search for still other medical novelties to which he might attach his name. Given his apparent ignorance of cocaine prior to April 1884, the speed with which he acquired an air of expertise is surprising. According to another *Brautbrief*, he completed his comprehensive-seeming essay "On Coca" a mere two months after mentioning that he had just been introduced to cocaine by reading Aschenbrandt and Bentley.[19] By July 1 the paper had appeared in the *Centralblatt für die Gesamte Therapie*.[20] Twenty-five pages long, and laden with seventy-eight footnotes citing the literature in several languages, it recounted Freud's own sanguine observations while touching with a knowledgeable air on every aspect of the drug's history, uses, and apparently minor limitations.

The earliest modern commentators on this article, Siegfried Bernfeld and Ernest Jones, were eager to put maximum distance between psychoanalysis and the racy topic of cocaine. As a result, they manifested considerable distaste for "On Coca." Beginning in the 1970s, however, Freudians promoted the essay to the status of an early masterpiece. Eberhard Haas praised Freud's "careful study of the literature"; Albrecht Hirschmüller found his summary of that literature to be nothing less than "brilliant"; and Robert Byck called the work "as up-to-date today as when first published."[21]

In order to effect this rehabilitation, however, the celebrants have had to discount a good deal of evidence. Hirschmüller himself, for example, points out that Freud's reading occupied less than two weeks of his spare time; that he ignored large bodies of work from France and South America, including a long monograph and a groundbreaking dissertation; and that he discussed accessible travel literature without having bothered to read it. Indeed, although Hirschmüller extols the sheer number of works summarized in "On Coca," he concedes that Freud's expert-looking references were mostly lifted, without investigation, from an 1883 *Index-Catalogue of the Library of the Surgeon-General's Office of the United States Army*.

Freud's hyperactive state when assembling his fortnight's-worth of skimming resulted in an extraordinary number of inaccuracies. He transcribed the Surgeon-General's bibliography erroneously, misstating names, dates, titles, and places of publication. His reference form was inconsistent, resulting in no fewer than five ways of specifying one periodical, the shady *Therapeutic Gazette*. Even his chemical formula for cocaine was imprecise; and when he "corrected" it in his second paper, he got it wrong again. Such carelessness amounted to a revealing departure from the standards maintained in his previously published articles. Surely cocaine itself was impinging on Freud's willingness and ability to edit his hasty work.

At various points "On Coca" hinted that its author possessed a long and judicious familiarity with cocaine and its effects. "Time and again" (*zu wiederholten Malen*), wrote Freud, as if looking back on many years of pharmaceutical experience, he had relieved his colleagues' stomach problems with cocaine.[22] Copious experience with patients could also be inferred from his endorsement of cocaine regimens to intervene against depression, heart problems, and "all diseases which involve degeneration of the tissues."* And in relating how the drug had affected him personally, Freud remarked, "I have observed the same physical signs of the effect of cocaine in others, mostly people of my own age."[23] How many people of any age, with or without digestive problems, could he have studied in two months while going about his hospital duties? To say that those subjects were "mostly" his coevals implied an improbable number of subjects and an exaggerated span of study.

In his enthusiasm, Freud was especially drawn to reports by the earliest European coca researcher, Paolo Mantegazza, a boisterous Italian neurologist, anthropologist, and sexual reformer. "I have carried out experiments and studied, in myself and others, the effect of coca on the healthy human body," Freud wrote; "my findings agree fundamentally with Mantegazza's description of the effect of coca leaves."[24] And a few pages later he offered this reassurance: "Mantegazza's exhaustive medical case histories impress me as being thoroughly credible."[25] Those were irresponsible statements. Freud's "experiments" and "findings" were nonexistent. Indeed, it had been scarcely two weeks since he had begun reading the standard literature.

More basically, Freud was confounding "the effect of coca leaves"— the leaves that Mantegazza had been excitedly gnawing in Peru in 1858, three years before cocaine had been chemically isolated—with cocaine itself. The very title of Freud's paper—not "On Cocaine," as it is sometimes cited, but "On Coca"—fostered that same confusion, which was never rectified in the body of the text. The misrepresentation was as gross as if he had judged the physiology of wine consumption by citing that of grapes, or as if he had confused hashish with hemp.

Freud does appear to have had firsthand familiarity with Mantegazza's *Sulle virtù igieniche e medicinali della coca e sugli alimenti*

---

* CP, p. 67; SK, p. 73. In Freud's day syphilitics were treated with mercury, whose devastating effects on the nervous system were poorly understood. In commending one physician's report that cocaine increased patients' tolerance for mercury, Freud proposed that, with cocaine as an adjuvant, more of the heavy metal could be ingested in a given dose (CP, p. 69; SK, pp. 76–77).

nervosi in generale (1859). If so, his faith in the sobriety of Mantegazza's assessments wasn't shaken by passages like this one, recalling a coca high that was, to put it mildly, untypical of the traditional Peruvian experience:

> I sneered at the poor mortals condemned to live in this valley of tears while I, carried on the wings of two leaves of coca, went flying through the spaces of 77,438 worlds, each more splendid than the one before.
>
> An hour later I was sufficiently calm to write these words in a steady hand: "God is unjust because he made man incapable of *sustaining the effect of coca* all life long. I would rather have a life span of ten years with coca than one of 1000000 . . . (and here I had inserted a line of zeros) centuries without coca."[26]

We cannot tell how much of Mantegazza's dizzy report was owing to his concentrated dose of coca leaves and how much to his irrepressible joie de vivre, which shines through all of his writings on ethnography and sexual hygiene. What we can be sure of is that Freud, in offering a blanket endorsement of Mantegazza on coca, was manifesting his own surrender to the charms of cocaine.

As a physician, though, Freud was most exhilarated by the many cures of morphinism that had been narrated in back numbers of the *Therapeutic Gazette*.* "On Coca" conveyed an impression that such cures were commonplace in America. Coca, Freud wrote (meaning cocaine), appears to have "a directly antagonistic effect on morphine."[27] Moreover, it probably doesn't get stored within the organism, and therefore "there is no danger of general damage to the body as is the case with the chronic use of morphine."[28] Hospitalization of the patient, then, is quite unnecessary; the whole regimen can be brought to a successful end, with only trivial complications, in a matter of days.[29] And Freud

---

* Thanks chiefly to overmedication, morphine dependency was the most common addiction in the late nineteenth century. As with other opiates, increased craving could lead to cardiac arrest, coma, and death. Although some addicts succeeded in regulating their intake, the resultant struggle produced a continual misery.

recounted that he had personally "had occasion to observe" just such a happy outcome.[30]

Freud didn't utterly suppress the darker side of the cocaine record. He passed along reports of toxicity and therapeutic failure—only, however, so as to deem them largely unmerited.[31] In most instances, he suggested, weak or impure preparations must have been to blame. Uniformly good outcomes would presumably be obtained with the higher-grade product being manufactured at last by Merck (misspelled throughout as "Merk")—a product dependably possessing "the full or at least the essential effects of coca leaves."[32] Thus the corrective for any disappointing results from cocaine treatment would be cocaine itself, now stronger than before and stripped of impurities. And any temporarily experienced toxicity, Freud assured his readers, would be likely to diminish with repeated use.[33]

Although the cocaine literature struck Freud as untrustworthy wherever it raised doubts, he entertained no such reservations about its highlights. Facts and rumors alike were uncritically passed along, just so long as they were positive. Coca (meaning cocaine) is more potent than alcohol, Freud wrote, but "far less harmful," since even repeated doses "produce no compulsive desire to use coca further."[34] Indeed, he affirmed that a more typical response, which he had corroborated in his trials on himself, is aversion to repeated use.[35] And in its South American homeland, he insisted in a misleading non sequitur, coca (now meaning only the leaf) had yielded numerous benefits to health, nutrition, equanimity, and social cohesion. According to Freud's judgment, then, there were no reasons to refrain from adding cocaine to Europe's therapeutic armamentarium and expanding the number of its applications as soon as possible.

4. SELF-TREATMENT

"The psychical effect of *cocaïnum muriaticum* in doses of 0.05–0.10g," Freud wrote in "On Coca,"

> consists of exhilaration and lasting euphoria, which does not differ in any way from the normal euphoria of a healthy person. . . . One

senses an increase of self-control and feels more vigorous and more capable of work; on the other hand, if one works, one misses that heightening of the mental powers which alcohol, tea, or coffee induces. One is simply normal, and soon finds it difficult to believe that one is under the influence of any drug at all.[36]

In this passage the "one" (German *man*) who gets energized by cocaine, thus attaining "the normal euphoria of a healthy person," is clearly the statement's author, who indirectly reveals that when lacking cocaine he feels himself to be less than in control and productive.

In a 1953 essay that Anna Freud attempted to suppress, Siegfried Bernfeld acknowledged the early Freud's need for cocaine.* The drug, wrote Bernfeld, "was an almost perfect remedy against his neurasthenic spells. . . . Cocaine simply jacked up [his] mood and capacities from their depressed state to a more normal level."[37] And Ernest Jones, no doubt in consultation with Bernfeld, made essentially the same point in his biography. "Cocaine heightens vigor," he wrote,

> only when this has been previously lowered; a really normal person does not need the fillip. Freud was not in the latter fortunate position. For many years he suffered from periodic depressions and fatigue or apathy, neurotic symptoms which later took the form of anxiety attacks before being dispelled by his own analysis.[38]

These statements by Bernfeld, Jones, and Freud himself bear an implication of cardinal importance for our study. If Freud needed cocaine in order to reach a "normal" state, one in which he felt capable of putting forward his ideas, it follows that his writings were typically influenced by cocaine. Those writings, moreover, included the texts containing his first articulation of psychoanalytic theory. For, as we will see, and as the postwar psychoanalytic directorate tried to keep us

---

* After the editor of the *International Journal of Psycho-Analysis* sent Bernfeld's typescript to Anna Freud, she implored Bernfeld not to publish it, and she asked Ernest Jones to intercede with the journal. The paper was then rejected, but published elsewhere. See Steiner 2000, 2013.

from realizing, Freud's so-called cocaine episode evidently reached almost to the turn of the twentieth century.

According to Jones's biography, in the mideighties Freud took cocaine only "on occasion" and in very modest doses of one hundredth of a gram.[39] The *Brautbriefe* show us, however, that he resorted to the drug quite frequently in order to cope with low moods, stomach upsets, headaches, lethargy, exhaustion, neuralgia, and sciatica. "In my last severe depression," he revealed to Martha on June 2, 1884, "I took coca [*sic*] again, and with a small amount was lifted to the heights in a wonderful fashion. I am just now busy collecting literature for the song of praise to the magical substance."[40] And on May 17, 1885, he wrote that on the previous day he had taken cocaine to treat his third migraine headache of the week. That was his standard nostrum for migraines. Just one complaint, then, had apparently accounted for three cocaine doses in a seven-day period.

As for the amount that Freud typically ingested at a sitting, a letter to his fiancée in October 1884, referring to his testing on animals of a closely related alkaloid, shows that Jones's figure was low by at least a factor of ten. "Today we killed the first rabbit with it," wrote Freud, "with a dose of 0.1g, the same as my own usual cocaine dose."[41] That amount is also implied by a June 1885 letter in which he told Martha how to apportion the half gram, roughly, of cocaine that he was enclosing in a vial. He instructed her to divide it into either eight small doses or five large ones—that is, between .0625g and .1g each. The top level, we see, matched Freud's own "usual" amount.[42] But if he thought that his delicate sweetheart, whom he repeatedly charged with insufficient robustness, could safely absorb .1g of cocaine at a time, it seems likely that he felt himself able to handle somewhat more.

We learn from his letters that Freud fortified himself with cocaine whenever he anticipated a threat of public embarrassment. Just before taking the oral examination for his promotion to the *Privat-dozent* lectureship, for example, he "acquired a considerable quantity of cocaine, after which I immediately became a different man."[43] Nervous fatigue, too, called for cocaine therapy. "I won't be tired," Freud told his fiancée while preparing for a long train ride to visit her, "because I'll be traveling under coca, in order to keep down my terrible impatience."[44]

One begins to wonder not how often he took the drug but whether there were more than a few days when he failed to find an excuse for doing so.

That Freud felt no compunction about closely following one cocaine dose with another may be illustrated by the following story, narrated in stages to his fiancée. In May 1885, still feeling weak from a mild bout of smallpox, he decided to travel by train to the nearby Semmering range for some strenuous hiking. Martha wouldn't need to be concerned about his debilitation, he assured her: "The magical remedy cocaine will keep me free from all fatigue."[45] He brought along a whole gram of the drug, or ten times his usual dose.

Although we don't know how much of Freud's supply remained after two exhilarated days of ascent and descent in sunshine, rain, and hail, the amount of his provision is telling. It seems likely that he paused for cocaine whenever he felt his level of energy waning. If that was his customary practice, it would seem that he was spared from really drastic dependency in this period only by his relatively safe means of ingesting dilute solutions of the drug. But we no longer need to wonder how the "neurasthenic" young doctor managed to hike as tirelessly as had Aschenbrandt's soldiers.

Most significantly for the future theorist of sexual neurosogenesis, cocaine impressed Freud as an aphrodisiac. Early in "On Coca" he reported that, according to Mantegazza, a Peruvian Indian would increase his coca chewing "when he takes a woman."[46] And near the end of the essay he became more explicit:

> The natives of South America, who represented their goddess of love with coca leaves in her hand, did not doubt the stimulative effect of coca on the genitalia. Mantegazza confirms that the *coqueros* sustain a high degree of potency right into old age; he even reports cases of the restoration of potency and the disappearance of functional weaknesses following the use of coca. . . .
>
> Among the persons to whom I have given coca [*sic*], three reported violent sexual excitement which they unhesitatingly attributed to the coca. A young writer, who was enabled by treatment with coca to resume his work after feeling out of sorts for rather a long

time, gave up using the drug because of the undesirable secondary
effects which it had on him.[47]

Supposedly, Freud distributed "coca" with no thought of improving
the recipients' sex lives. He implies that Austrian men, unlike the savage
Incas, prefer to remain erotically subdued. We are meant to believe,
then, that the unexpected arousal in three cases was offensive to those
who felt it and that a fourth victim of "excitement" was so distressed
that he never took the drug again. And needless to say, "On Coca"
remains mum regarding the role of cocaine in its author's own sexual
economy.

As we see from the *Brautbriefe*, however, no cocaine effect was
more important to Freud than the enhancement of desire. For the semi-
cloistered Freud as for the aging but still yearning Faust, the promise
of sexual power over a young virgin was a lure with which the ascetic
pursuit of knowledge couldn't compete. Granted, Freud didn't expect to
exercise that power until his wedding night. Such was his insecurity,
though, that he employed cocaine just to overcome a reluctance to
think about having a helpless Martha at his mercy.

Certain *Brautbriefe* illustrate this effect with startling clarity. Before
setting out on the hiking trip already mentioned, for instance, Freud
allowed himself a revealing fantasy about future jaunts with his wife
over the same terrain: "You'll be fed [*gefüttert*] with cocaine," he wrote,
"and will have to give me a kiss at every resting place."[48] Here cocaine, in
a letter probably written under its spell, was envisioned as an instrument
of sway over the passive beloved, whose deliciously anticipated resistance would melt under the drug's power.

Again, writing to a reputedly wan Martha scarcely a month after he
first imbibed the drug, the usually prim but now randy fiancé expressed
himself as follows: "Woe to you, little princess, when I come. I will kiss
you quite red and feed you quite plump. And if you are naughty you
will see who is the stronger, a gentle little girl who doesn't eat or a big
wild man who has cocaine in his body."[49] Once again Freud's tone
was bantering, and his manifest topic this time was merely the restoration of Martha's health; yet he was also announcing that he planned to
be libidinally supercharged by cocaine. And here, too, he conceived of

his chemically eroticized self not as the affectionate companion of a dear person but as a powerful mate who would have his way, luxuriating in the crushing of maidenly reluctance.

Ernest Jones understood that for Freud the sexual meaning of cocaine was primary. The shaky fiancé had allowed an aphrodisiac to take control of his brain, and Jones regretted it. "Depression," he wrote,

> like any other neurotic manifestation, lowers the sense of energy and virility; cocaine restores it. . . . To achieve virility and enjoy the bliss of union with the beloved, [Freud] had forsaken the straight and narrow path of sober "scientific" work on brain anatomy and seized a surreptitious short cut: one that was to bring him suffering instead of success.[50]

The "suffering" cited by Jones referred to the trouble Freud would soon bring down on himself by becoming the cheerleader for a dangerous drug. Freud's comeuppance, Jones wanted us to believe, was ultimately salutary, because afterward, sobered, he could resume the objective frame of mind that led to psychoanalysis. But Freud never did return to that condition; he would spin his theory out of guesswork arising partly from reflections on his own libidinal plight. And he would do so, as Jones well knew, at a time when cocaine was driving his thought process more tyrannically than ever before.

Prior to his introduction to cocaine, Freud had shown little interest in nervous psychopathology. A change of outlook was required before his science of the repressed could be envisioned even as a distant project. Where did that change begin if not here in 1884, with the capacity of cocaine to heighten the user's self-absorption, sex drive, erotic fantasy, and sense of contact with deeper realms of experience? There is evidence in the *Brautbriefe* to show that in the two final years of his engagement, Freud's still operative prudery, moralism, and deference to authority were beginning to meet opposing temperamental currents. And along with that development, we will see, came a dawning sense that cocaine could both banish his nervousness and liberate him from the tyranny of conformism.[51]

5

A Friend in Need

1. "YOU NEEDN'T BE AT ALL JEALOUS"

Of all the relationships in Sigmund Freud's life, the one that has been least understood, in both its nature and its importance, was his bond with Ernst Fleischl von Marxow.* Intellectually, as we will see later, Fleischl led him onto highly significant terrain. Emotionally, he aroused powerful currents of affection and rivalry that would be stirred again in the 1890s by Freud's dearest and most influential friend of all, Wilhelm Fliess. But Fleischl also played a central role in Freud's romance with cocaine. The uncensored *Brautbriefe* allow us at last to weigh the effect of cocaine on Freud's dealings with Fleischl. To do so is to reopen the belittled, hushed-up question of whether the drug was, in fact, a crucial determinant of Freud's path to psychoanalysis.

We have already mentioned Fleischl as having been one of the two assistants in Ernst Brücke's Physiological Institute. But he was also a distinguished scientist and academic. In the 1870s, when he was still very young, Fleischl had done pioneering studies in the electrophysiology of nerves and muscles, and he had advanced his discipline even

---

* Some commentators represent the name as "Ernst von Fleischl-Marxow," but "Ernst Fleischl von Marxow" appears on the title page of his posthumous *Gesammelte Abhandlungen* (1893), edited by his younger brother Otto. Both versions of the name can be found in Freud's writings.

more fundamentally by inventing superior devices for making fine measurements of electrical stimuli. Later, turning his attention to the brain, he was the first researcher to show that stimulation of vision and hearing produces electrical activity in the cerebral cortex. And in the 1880s, adding ophthalmology to his mastered disciplines, he developed a number of widely adopted instruments and made key discoveries about relations between the optic nerve and the retina. Freud had taken four courses from him in the University of Vienna's medical school in 1875–77. By 1880, at age thirty-four, Fleischl was already a full professor.

Few acquaintances left a stronger impression on Freud. Until he entered Brücke's institute in 1876, Freud had met no physician or scientist whom he could unreservedly admire. In Brücke's laboratory, he recalled in a late revision of his *Autobiographical Study*, he found men "whom I could respect and take as my models: the great Brücke himself and his assistants Sigmund Exner and Ernst Fleischl von Marxow."[1] Exner's vaingloriousness, however, grated on Freud, while the stern, sixty-year-old Brücke was intimidating. Fleischl, at thirty, was more accessible in every way: unpretentious, helpful, articulate, broadly inquisitive, and contagiously passionate about his scientific work.

When Freud moved from being Fleischl's classroom student to being his subordinate in the Physiological Institute, he found in him a friend, protector, and collaborator. The daily proximity ended with Freud's departure for the General Hospital in 1882, but his relationship with Fleischl only deepened. Freud and Fleischl were both philosophically inclined Jews who had been trained in scientific positivism but who also cultivated broadly humanistic interests. Both of them were lengthily engaged. Both felt the pressure of high parental expectations, and both (though for very different reasons) had to struggle against despair.

Freud owed a great deal to Fleischl, who supported him as an examiner for both his medical degree and his elevation to *Privatdozent*. Fleischl lobbied for him with the power brokers Theodor Meynert and Hermann Nothnagel. When Freud, in a dark mood, thought of resigning from the General Hospital and thus losing all hope of a docentship, it was Fleischl who talked him out of it. Fleischl took him to electrical exhibitions in Vienna, explaining the latest developments and giving a novice the benefit of his thorough grounding in physics. And when Freud wrote his brief account of his gold chloride procedure for the London journal *Brain*, the actual submission was made by Fleischl.

The assistance was also financial. Among Vienna's "Coterie"—the affluent Jewish professionals who cared passionately about the arts and sciences—it was felt that no promising career ought to be thwarted by want of means.[2] Generosity flowed freely toward bright, diligent, needy aspirants like the young Freud. Thus "loans," most of them forgiven, from Fleischl, Josef Paneth, and Josef Breuer kept Freud afloat for several years as he sought to establish a career.

When Freud expressed frustration about his inability to afford a trip to Wandsbek to visit his fiancée, Fleischl was ready to provide the funds. He also shepherded patients and private students to Freud, and gave him expensive equipment for conducting his own electrical studies. It was Fleischl, in 1885, who got Freud a summer job in a suburban Viennese clinic. And money from Fleischl supplemented Freud's traveling fellowship when he passed the fall and winter of 1885–86 in Paris.

Most important for Freud, however, was the magnetism of Fleischl's personality. Darkly handsome, socially adept, effortlessly brilliant in the lecture hall, he evoked in Freud a mixture of affection, awe, and self-doubting competitiveness. "He is a thoroughly outstanding man," Sigmund wrote to Martha shortly after getting engaged,

> in whom nature and education have done their best. Rich, skilled in all physical exercises, with the stamp of genius in his energetic features, handsome, sensitive, gifted with all talents and capable of forming an original judgment about most things, he was always my ideal, and I wasn't satisfied until we became friends and I could take a pure delight in his ability and worth.[3]

Freud's admiration, however, was also mixed with two other feelings: jealousy and pity. The first effect stemmed from professional rivalry. From 1876 until 1882, as we have seen, Freud had yearned to replace either Fleischl or Exner on Brücke's staff; and of the two it was

Fleischl whose tenure appeared likely to be foreshortened by illness and addiction. As things developed, Fleischl had stayed on while Freud was persuaded to resign. The misery Freud experienced after leaving Brücke's institute spurred a lingering resentment of Fleischl for having clung to the position Freud had coveted. In later analyzing a dream ("Non Vixit") involving his already deceased friend in the context of the Physiological Institute, Freud acknowledged that he had harbored a death wish against him—and indeed, that he still did, long after Fleischl's actual demise.[4]

As for pity, Fleischl deserved it all too amply. When he was working as an assistant to the great pathologist Carl von Rokitansky in 1871, a horrific accident changed his life forever. Performing an autopsy at age twenty-four, he contracted a potentially fatal infection of his right thumb. The subsequent partial amputation of that thumb was already a significant handicap that precluded further dealings with cadavers. But the ensuing neuromas—tumors on damaged nerve endings—grew more agonizing with every attempt to treat them. Injected morphine was the only feasible means at Fleischl's disposal to blunt his pain sufficiently for him to keep working without a cognitive deficit. He became a drug addict; and, seeing no way out, he told Freud that he expected to kill himself.

Fleischl's tragic plight drew Freud closer to him, but Fleischl himself, absorbed in both his suffering and his research, remained somewhat aloof. On October 25, 1883, Freud confided to his fiancée:

> You're partly right about Fleischl, Marty. Our relationship isn't at all one of real friendship; he hasn't become a friend in the way that Breuer is. There is always a gap surounding him, an aura of unapproachability, and when we've been together he has always been too occupied with himself to come near me. But I admire and love him with an intellectual passion, if you will allow such a phrase. His disappearance will touch me in the way that an ancient Greek would have been moved by the destruction of a holy and famous temple. I love him not so much as a human being, but as a precious work of the Creation. And you needn't be at all jealous.[5]

In telling Martha not to worry, Freud was betraying an awareness that his own affection was now awkwardly divided. And a further, if fainter, implication was that the awkwardness could be resolved only by the "disappearance" of his suicidal friend, prematurely eulogized here.

"Freud's sexual constitution," admitted Ernest Jones, "was not exclusively masculine."[6] Viewed in the retrospect of a lifetime, early signs of that fact can be noted. Sigismund's first infatuation, we recall, had been with his dashing schoolmate Heinrich Braun. When Braun, reappearing at the University of Vienna, then spurned Freud and chose Victor Adler as his best friend, Freud was wounded and embittered. Meanwhile, Eduard Silberstein, whom he had warned against traffic with females, had been his inseparable companion and confidant for many years. And now, in the early 1880s, another masculine attachment—this one insufficiently reciprocated—was serving a comparable function for him.

In this light, one paragraph from a letter to Martha of June 27, 1882, seems particularly meaningful:

Then I looked around his room, thought about my superior friend, and it occurred to me how much he could do with a girl like Martha, what a setting he could provide for this gem, how Martha . . . would admire the Alps, the waterways of Venice, the splendor of St. Peter's in Rome; how much pleasure she would get from sharing the recognition and influence of the beloved one, how the nine years that this man has over me would mean as many unparalleled happy years of her life compared to the nine miserable years spent in hiding and near helplessness that I must anticipate. I was compelled to picture for myself, with torment, how easily he, who spends two months of each year in Munich and frequents the most select society there, could meet Martha at her uncle's house. I became curious as to how Martha would suit him. Then I suddenly broke off the daydream; it was clear to me that I could not relinquish the loved one, even if to be with me weren't the right place for her. . . . Can't I for once have something better than I deserve? Martha remains mine.[7]

Here, near the outset of his involvement with two desired persons, Freud mentally steps aside and couples them. Only gradually and fitfully will he gain confidence that he himself can secure and retain Martha's love. Meanwhile, his submission to Fleischl, unconvincingly revoked at the end of the passage, suggests something beyond cerebral passion.

Freud's craving for deeper intimacy with Fleischl was also a desire for greater equality with him, so that he would no longer feel threatened by his former teacher's superior attributes and attainments. "Now I have an advantage over him," Sigmund had written soon after Martha accepted his proposal, when Fleischl's own hopes of marrying had already been dashed.[8] By the spring of 1884 Fleischl's enslavement to morphine had rendered him still more vulnerable in Freud's eyes. Now, however, Freud saw an opening for ingratiating himself with his "ideal" in a way that could cancel the distance between them and, in the bargain, lift Fleischl out of addiction and earn great renown for himself.

2. DOCTOR AND PATIENT

When Freud told his fiancée on April 21, 1884, that he had ordered a supply of cocaine after reading of its capacity to bolster endurance, he added that he intended to "try it out on cases of heart disease, then on nervous exhaustion, particularly in the miserable condition accompanying morphine withdrawal (as, for example, Fleischl)."[9] Freud's eagerness to wean Fleischl from morphine was not that of a researcher who has already found and tested a medical novelty. Indeed, his skimming of the cocaine literature, as reflected in "On Coca," wouldn't even be undertaken until June 5, 1884—a full month, therefore, after he had begun treating Fleischl.[10] The only procedural advice he could find consisted of the promotional tales that even the trashy *Therapeutic Gazette* had long since ceased to offer.

Like all of his medical colleagues in the 1880s, however, Freud was aware that morphine withdrawal, even in expert hands and under ideal conditions, is arduous and risky. As he wrote to Martha on May 9, 1884,

> You should know that a man who is used to taking large doses of morphine and then suddenly stops taking it suffers the greatest misery for 6–8 days: vomiting, diarrhea, chills and sweats that lead from one fainting spell to the next, intolerable psychic depression, and above all a continuous craving for morphine. And since the patients' wills are weak anyway, they cannot resist the cravings, and they interrupt the withdrawal treatment again and again. For this reason, treatments are carried out only in asylums.[11]

Freud must have realized that the usual challenges and dangers would be immeasurably greater with an untested remedy. Yet he never seems to have contemplated a hospital stay for Fleischl. Nor did he address the obvious prudential questions that were raised by his scheme. What precautions, such as the conducting of animal studies and the compiling of long-term case histories, ought a physician to observe before setting out on a controversial regimen of detoxification? Which methods, if any, of administering the drug would be both safe and effective? And how much follow-up would be required before one could say for sure that cocaine and morphine are truly antagonists?

What, moreover, was the envisioned action of cocaine in Fleischl's course of withdrawal? As Freud acknowledged in "On Coca," cocaine is not a soporific but a stimulant to the entire nervous system.[12] It does relieve pain and produce a transitory euphoria, but for that very reason it can trick the subject into believing that his need for the other drug is being removed rather than temporarily suppressed. What means would Freud, as the observer of Fleischl's progress, employ to distinguish between release from addiction and mere intoxication?

Without thinking the matter through, Freud imagined that Fleischl would somehow get free of both morphine and the rationed cocaine that would be exhausted in the brief course of therapy. But he couldn't say how, afterward, Fleischl was supposed to manage the ongoing pain from his neuromas. Freud's plan, such as it was, would leave the "cured" Fleischl no less excruciated than he had been before his initial recourse to morphine for pain relief. And now Fleischl would have at hand his syringe, his new taste for cocaine, and, between hits, a state of abstinence-induced restlessness and anxiety for which the medicine of choice would probably be more cocaine.

Just two weeks after first mentioning that he had taken note of cocaine, Freud approached Fleischl with the idea of a cure that could begin at once. His letter to Martha describing the visit makes no mention of the treatment protocol. Instead, it focuses on his intention of helping the stricken friend through the period of withdrawal. "Then I was with Fleischl," he wrote on May 7, apparently referring to the same day,

> and there I again experienced so much of the misery that grieves me. I proposed cocaine to him and he has clutched at the idea with the haste of a drowning man. I will often go to him, help him to organize his books, show slides, etc. It is an incomparable misery.[13]

Freud must have handed over his first therapeutic concoction, if not the entire batch, on the day he secured Fleischl's consent. The result—wholly positive, so far as Freud was concerned—was announced to Martha on May 9:

> Triumph, rejoice with me. Something good has come of the cocaine, after all. Something very good. Imagine—it is, as I suspected, a remedy for morphine withdrawal and the horrible conditions it causes, and to my delight, the first patient in whom I observe it is none other than Fleischl. He has taken no morphine for three days, but has substituted cocaine and is in excellent spirits. He now hopes that he will be able to finish the entire period of morphine abstinence this way, and then we will both be happy people.
>
> ... And now Dr. Fleischl is in the best state of well-being, insofar as his pains permit it. He is completely without the usual complaints and craving for morphine, and his only indications of the morphine withdrawal are chills and a mild case of diarrhea. He is beside himself with astonishment and gratefulness. And I am so happy.
>
> ... If it ends well, I will write my article about it, and I suspect

that then this remedy will win its place in therapy, alongside and above morphine.[14]

This exultant letter didn't entirely lack signs of uneasiness on Freud's part. By then Fleischl had completed only a fraction of the challenge Freud set for him:

There is one thing I am still afraid of: what will happen when the eight days that the condition [of withdrawal symptoms] usually lasts have passed? Will the craving for morphine come back when he stops taking cocaine, or will it remain absent, as if he had completed the usual period of abstinence? I hope for the latter, but I am very seriously worried.[15]

Clearly, then, protracted vigilance was called for, along with the postponing of any public announcement of success.

"On Coca" was completed on or about June 28, six weeks after the intended termination of the cocaine cure. From that essay we are meant to infer that Fleischl's good fortune persisted through the entire treatment period and beyond:

I had an opportunity to observe a man's sudden withdrawal from morphine through the use of cocaine. During an earlier cure he had suffered the most severe withdrawal symptoms. This time, so long as the effects of cocaine lasted, his condition was tolerable and notably free of depression and nausea. The only permanent symptoms recalling his abstinence [from morphine] were chills and diarrhea. [During his cure] the patient stayed out of bed and was completely functional. In the early days he took three decagrams of Cocaïnum muriaticum daily; after ten days he could dispense with it altogether.[16]

Here we may note in passing that Freud seems curiously reluctant to take credit for the reported wonder, which, instead of having been produced by himself only weeks earlier, was merely "observed" by him on a temporally unfixed occasion. He isn't just protecting Fleischl's anonymity but also dissociating himself from the case should it later prove a liability. Nevertheless, the success that he now reports is spectacular. And the cure's implied distance in time from the hour of writing about it—for how else could Freud know which symptoms were "permanent" (*permanenten*)?—is its most confidence-inspiring feature.

Freud's slipperiness in this passage—the thematic centerpiece of "On Coca," making the most impressive claim for the drug's therapeutic power—bespeaks a muffled awareness that a pronouncement of cure after a mere six weeks is inappropriate. His obscuring of the timetable, however, pales in significance when we consult further *Brautbriefe* from May and June 1884 and try to reconcile his published claim with what he there disclosed to his fiancée. If "On Coca" is to be credited, Fleischl spent ten days off morphine while ingesting .3g of dissolved cocaine daily, and thereafter he happily dispensed with both morphine and cocaine, experiencing only chills and diarrhea as the "permanent" side effects of the cure. But the letters tell a very different story.

3. COMPLICATIONS

Late on Monday, May 12, 1884, when the projected regimen was about half over, and three days after Freud had invited Martha to "rejoice with me," he sat down to give her a distressing update:

> Fleischl is in such a sad state that I cannot enjoy the cocaine success at all. He continues to take it, and it continues to protect him against the miserable state of morphine use. But he has had such frightful pains in the nights from Friday to Saturday and from Saturday to Sunday that he lay there as if unconscious until 11 a.m. Then in the afternoon, under the influence of cocaine, he was quite well. Early Monday I wanted to visit him, but he didn't answer my knocking. Two hours later, the same result. Finally Obersteiner, Exner, and I pulled ourselves together, got the key from the servant, and went in. There he lay, quite apathetic and not answering our questions. Only after some coca did he come to himself and tell us that he had had terrible pains. These attacks afflict the soul; in that state he can only

become maniacal or kill himself. I don't know whether he took morphine during these attacks. He denies it, but one shouldn't believe a morphinist, even if it's an Ernst Fleischl.[17]

Here we learn, in contradiction of "On Coca," that Freud's cure had devastated his patient; that the regularly administered portions of cocaine were supplemented on at least two occasions (May 11 and 12) by emergency doses that were needed to arouse Fleischl from a near coma; that Freud had no way of knowing whether or not Fleischl was already back on morphine; and that, as a consequence, the findings of the planned experiment were already contaminated and could have no validity. But we also learn something more troubling than all of these facts in combination. Although Freud realizes that Fleischl can now "only become maniacal or kill himself," he still refers, incomprehensibly, to his own "cocaine success."

We might reasonably expect that Freud would show remorse for the peril into which his ill-considered initiative has plunged his friend. To assume so, however, would be to underestimate the eerie coldness and self-preoccupation that many observers, including some of his most loyal disciples, would remark in him on later occasions. The following cheerful lines just precede the May 12 account of Fleischl's torment:

About cocaine—it flourishes. I have gained some experience with its effect on stomach aches, not enough for publication and for convincing others, but enough for me. I cured Albert H. of a hangover with it, and myself of the pressure and discomfort that follows dinner; I have seen the sensitivity of a patient's stomach to pressure disappear after a small dose; I expect a great deal from it. I have not yet had cases of real vomiting or cardiac insufficiency and am, of course, watching for them impatiently. I am very active. I have told Bettelheim about it and have induced him to try it; I have brought the eternally good Breuer to buy four grams to try on his people. . . . Darling, how is your stomach? As soon as I know more about [cocaine's] effects, I will decide whether I should send it to you. I believe it is a magical substance.[18]

The callous heartiness of this passage fits nicely with the next report, on May 14, about Fleischl's condition and Freud's own latest
career-enhancing feat:

> So yesterday I gave my lecture. Despite a lack of preparation, I spoke
> quite well and without any hesitation, which I ascribe to the cocaine
> I had taken beforehand. I told about my discoveries in brain anat-
> omy, all very difficult things that the audience certainly didn't under-
> stand, but all that matters is that they get the impression that I
> understand it. . . . It was good company: Billroth, Nothnagel, Breuer,
> Fleischl, and all the others. . . . Fleischl says that he hasn't taken
> morphine for six days and is relatively well, but he looks so awful,
> talks so wearily, and doesn't sleep. He slept badly before, too. On the
> whole, cocaine has been a triumph with him, but he is doing poorly
> for the other reasons.[19]

In passages like this one, we observe the adjustment of attitude that
will characterize all the rest of Freud's dealings with Fleischl. He
sympathizes with his friend and is grieved by his suffering—for which,
however, he accepts no responsibility. Having wagered his medical
acumen entirely on cocaine, he seems incapable of asking himself
whether his provision of the drug might have contributed to Fleischl's
pitiable state. If cocaine has been good for Freud, it must also have
been good for Fleischl.

Freud did notice that the agony of the morphine-deprived Fleischl,
when he wasn't high on cocaine, had become intolerable. His surgeon,
the eminent Theodor Billroth, had previously gotten nowhere by repeatedly carving away at the ever smaller stump of Fleischl's thumb.
Now, however, Billroth thought he might have better success with a
new procedure, applying electricity to the exposed nerves. Just how
such a measure was supposed to control pain is unclear. From Freud's
vantage, however, the intervention couldn't come soon enough. "I have
also asked [Breuer] to ask Billroth," Freud wrote on May 12, "to perform
the new operation he has in mind as soon as possible, because otherwise he, Fleischl, will go to pieces in one of these attacks."[20]

Billroth was to be assisted in the treatment by Dr. Carl Bettelheim, an army surgeon. Bettelheim, as it happens, had listened credulously to Freud's recruiting for cocaine, and he had been persuaded to sample the drug himself. In addition, on Freud's advice he had begun dispensing it to his patients. These developments bore on the question of how Fleischl's pain was to be blunted during and after the surgery. Billroth intended to employ morphine—thus, we see, effectively terminating the experiment of morphine withdrawal. Inspired by Freud, however, Bettelheim wanted cocaine to be used as well, presumably by injection. And indeed, it would appear from a *Brautbrief* of May 24 that cocaine was chosen as Fleischl's primary painkiller, with morphine held in readiness to be supplied as necessary.

It was a chastened Dr. Bettelheim who, on May 20, informed Freud how the previous day's electrocution of neuromas had gone. As Freud told Martha,

> Bettelheim was just with me and told me that Fleischl fared very badly after yesterday's operation, and further that he has not seen any good in cocaine. He does not have decisive cases, however, and he did not give enough [cocaine]. Of course I must continue the observations myself.[21]

So Fleischl was now worse off than ever, and the explanation was apparent to Freud: an insufficient quantity of cocaine had been administered during an otherwise promising operation. The fickle Bettelheim, in Freud's opinion, had no right to pass a globally negative judgment on cocaine when he had been too stingy with it to produce the excellent results that Freud had led him to expect.

Fleischl's unbearable pain in the wake of his surgery had immediately discredited Bettelheim's cocaine-favoring viewpoint and had handed the initiative back to the traditionalist Billroth, who had mercifully reached, again and again, for his hypodermic needle and morphine supply. Freud's next letter, on May 23, expressed his disappointment over that shortsighted measure:

> Fleischl's condition is as follows: he was operated upon on Monday, was urged by Billroth to take considerable amounts of morphine,

had the most horrible pains after the operation, and was given he does not know how many injections. Until then he had managed excellently with the cocaine. So the cocaine has stood the test very well. He will wean himself from the morphine again as soon as the wound has healed.[22]

As Freud did recognize, Fleischl's detoxification program had now been returned to square one. But Fleischl had never entirely gone off morphine in the first place. Rather, he had tried and failed to cure an addiction by dosing himself with the most addictive drug yet produced by the human race. The net effect of Freud's counsel, then, had been to turn Fleischl into a double addict.

4. THE PERSISTENCE OF BELIEF

In the months following Fleischl's introduction to cocaine, Freud had many opportunities to observe his friend's continued and gradually debilitating ingestion of that drug. On July 12, 1884, he told Martha that, in order to dispel a miserable mood of his own, he had *asked Fleischl* for "a little coca, which he regularly takes."[23] And on October 5 of the same year he reported that Fleischl had ordered so much cocaine from Merck that the company had expressed curiosity about the nature of his interest. Freud could now be certain that he had been wrong to dismiss the possibility of cocaine dependency. Obviously, he owed the world a retraction not just of that point but of the cure that he had characterized as well established.

But such a disavowal would never come. In early 1885 Freud republished "On Coca" as a freestanding pamphlet, with minor corrections and an "Addenda" section containing three numbered items.[24] Two of them bore directly on his experience with Fleischl:

2. On the Effect of Coca in Cases of Morphine Addiction

The usefulness of cocaine in cases of morphine collapse has recently been confirmed by Richter (Pankow), who also favors the view, expressed in the above text, that there is an antagonistic relationship between the effect of cocaine and that of morphine.

3. On the Internal Application of Cocaine

Since at present various authors seem to harbor unjustified fears about bad effects from the internal application of cocaine, it is not superfluous to emphasize that even subcutaneous injections, such as I have used with success against long-standing sciatica, are entirely harmless. The toxic dose for humans is very high, and there seems to be no lethal dose.[25]

Freud was digging in his heels. Thanks to his boasts in the original version of "On Coca," other physicians had begun applying cocaine to morphine detoxification, and he had started marshaling positive reports while ignoring the cautions of skeptics. The latter included Fleischl's own doctor, Joseph Breuer, whose wisdom Freud usually heeded in this period. Seeing what was happening to Fleischl in the wake of Freud's cocaine treatment, Breuer had disapproved of Freud's writing "On Coca" and had nothing good to say about the drug.[26] By defying Breuer's well-considered judgment, the drug-influenced Freud was taking the first step toward his eventual scorn for his ex-mentor as a timid vacillator.

As for Freud's own claim of an "antagonistic relationship between the effect of cocaine and that of morphine," he had actually seen no sign of it since the first three days of Fleischl's treatment. If he had been attentive to evidence lying before his eyes, he would have been troubled by Fleischl's apparent devolution into a chronic user of both drugs. What he wanted, however, was not greater accuracy or responsibility but victory, and for that purpose he couldn't resist citing an author who had simply trusted what he had read in "On Coca."*

We see from Freud's Addendum 3 that by January 1885 the climate of opinion surrounding cocaine was already beginning to darken. "Various authors," Freud indicated, were regarding the drug with alarm.

---

* Dr. Richter, the author cited in Freud's Addendum 2, had asserted not only that cocaine "completely cancels the effect of morphine" but also "the other way around" (Hadlich 1885, p. 21). That is, he held the view that *morphine* is an excellent means of yielding symptom-free withdrawal from *cocaine* addiction. Freud cited Richter without mentioning that statement.

But he summarily deemed the critics' fears "unjustified" (*unberechtigt*). Virtually no amount of cocaine, he assured his physician readers, would harm their patients, much less kill them, and subcutaneous injections, unmentioned in the original essay, were now commended as "entirely harmless."

From February 1885 onward, Freud's references to Fleischl in the *Brautbriefe* show a clear recognition that his friend's twin addiction was now irreversible. It is hard, then, to imagine what further evidence he might have required before concluding that injected cocaine poses grave risks to health. Yet on the third day of March 1885, and once again on the fifth, he delivered a wholly upbeat lecture, "On the General Effect of Cocaine," recapitulating "On Coca" and the physiological experiments we will examine later.* And on both occasions he reiterated, with small variations, his prior claims about the Fleischl case.

Freud's lecture was given before the Physiological Club and the Psychiatric Society, both of whose members knew Fleischl personally and were long familiar with his morphine dependency. No one could have doubted the identity of the subject described. Nor could Freud have ruled out in advance the contingency that Fleischl himself might be in the audience, listening to his own case being mischaracterized. Freud must have thought that he was telling the truth. If so, however, he was deluded to a degree that can be accounted for only by the distortion of his own judgment by cocaine.[†]

The operative heart of Freud's lecture, however, was its counsel to fellow physicians. "On the basis of the experience I have gathered with cocaine effects," he asserted,

---

* Freud not only gave his lecture twice; he published it twice as well, in April and again in August 1885 (Freud 1885c, 1885d).

† One sign of Freud's indifference to facts appears in his contradictory handling of details regarding Fleischl's treatment and progress. In "On Coca" Fleischl was said to have been given .3g of cocaine per day "during the first days of the cure"; but in this lecture it is .4g, apparently sustained over twenty days. (That period, of course, extended well beyond the June 19 date of Fleischl's surgery, when he absorbed large amounts of both morphine and cocaine.) It may not be worthwhile to look for self-interested calculations behind these changes. Freud probably relied on his faulty memory, not even bothering to reread his own published words.

I would have no hesitation in recommending, in similar withdrawal cures [to Fleischl's], that cocaine be given in subcutaneous injections of 0.03–0.05 grams per dose, and that nothing is to be feared from the accumulation of doses. On several occasions, I have even seen cocaine quickly eliminate the manifestations of intolerance that appeared after a rather large dose of morphine, as if it had a specific ability to counteract morphine.[27]

Thus Freud was urging his colleagues to load their syringes with cocaine and get down to the task of rescuing morphinists, as he had done (or perhaps only observed) "on several occasions." Was there more than one such occasion? Freud referred to his "experiences," plural, and Ernest Jones, for one, was inclined to believe him.[28] But no further cases emerge in the *Brautbriefe*. Apart from the Fleischl affair, then, Freud's contribution to the deadly cocaine epidemic that was then beginning may have been made not through further treatments but through wantonly broadcast advice.*

---

* Albrecht Hirschmüller, hoping to show that Freud's counsel was plausible enough in its day, points out that cocaine continued to be used in morphine withdrawal throughout the 1880s (SK, p. 33). That fact, however, doesn't exonerate Freud; it attests to the scope of his dangerous influence.

6

The Wrong Discoverer

1. A MEDICAL MILESTONE

The reverberant influence of Freud's 1884 essay "On Coca" cannot be explained without reference to events outside the text itself. Its author, after all, was only a twenty-eight-year-old intern who possessed no prior experience with stimulants, much less a record of pertinent research. Pharmacology had been the weakest link in his lackluster qualifying examinations for the M.D. degree.[1] As his omnibus article manifested, furthermore, he was hardly writing as a pioneer in the subdiscipline of cocaine studies. A quarter-century had already elapsed since curious Europeans had begun informing themselves about the scientific properties of coca and its salts, and across the ocean Parke, Davis had been vigorously marketing its "coca elixir" since 1875. Why, then, would readers pay attention to the views of a newcomer like Freud?

"On Coca" aroused little interest in the first three months of its existence, and by then Freud was losing confidence that cocaine would prove to be the handiest means of jump-starting his career. His essay alone, in any case, couldn't have led immediately to a rash of cocaine use. Throughout Europe the substance itself was scarce, prohibitively expensive, and generally disprized as useless. In Merck's business of manufacturing such pharmaceutical alkaloids as morphine and quinine, cocaine was an afterthought. Merck kept it available in minuscule quantities merely on the chance that some positive function might be found for it, and its steep price bespoke a near absence of competition for European sales. So tiny was the demand, indeed, that Freud's own modest purchases, along with Fleischl's, came to Merck's notice and constituted the firm's alert to a possibly heightened level of interest.

There the boomlet might have ended were it not for another development that Freud inspired without expressly intending to do so. It was a colleague of his, the young physician Carl (sometimes Karl) Koller, who provoked a well-merited sensation over cocaine in the fall of 1884, thus triggering a chain of events whose consequences are still being felt today on a worldwide scale.

Koller's breakthrough—the proof that a cocaine solution can numb the cornea and conjunctiva and thus allow pain-free eye surgery on a conscious patient—was a major event in the history of medicine, inaugurating the era of local anesthesia. And one minor effect of that electrifying news was the rescue of "On Coca" from obscurity. Koller generously acknowledged that his awareness of cocaine had come about through Freud, who had brought cocaine to his notice both conversationally and by a hint, dropped into the concluding paragraph of "On Coca," that the drug might prove useful as an anesthetic. For the three ensuing years, therefore, most readers assumed that Freud must be Europe's preeminent authority on the drug.

Koller had been one of Freud's acquaintances since at least 1880, when they were university medical students together. He was a gifted researcher/physician who excelled in both capacities. At the remarkable ages of twenty-two and twenty-four he published two groundbreaking papers accounting for the formerly puzzling emergence of the mesoderm (middle germ layer) in the chicken embryo. That work, achieved through analytic reasoning as opposed to observation, was widely praised, reprinted, and acknowledged in standard textbooks. But two years later, when Freud introduced the twenty-six-year-old Koller to cocaine in the spring or summer of 1884, Koller was still a lowly assistant in the ophthalmology department of Vienna's General Hospital.

Neither Koller nor Freud was the first investigator to conceive of cocaine as a possible anesthetic. The chemist who first isolated and analyzed the cocaine molecule in 1861, Albert Niemann, had immediately noted its numbing effect. In 1865 the French physician Charles Fauvel had some success employing a tincture of cocaine as an anesthetic for operations on the throat. In 1868 the Peruvian surgeon Thomas Moreno y Maíz had noted the anesthetic effect of cocaine on laboratory frogs and had called for further research.[2] "The local action of this substance is very marked," wrote Moreno. "Could one use it as a local anesthetic?"[3] And in 1880 two Frenchmen, S. Coupard and F. Bordereau, remarked that locally applied cocaine abolished the corneal reflex in animals.[4] But because of the impurity, irregularity, and frequent chemical inactivity of the available drug supplies, those investigators were unable to replicate their positive results. It was the improved quality of cocaine itself that allowed Koller to do better in 1884.

After hearing his department chief, Carl Ferdinand von Arlt, lament the absence of an ocular anesthetic, Koller had spent years trying to develop one. He pursued the goal through animal studies, sequentially but fruitlessly experimenting with chloral, bromide, morphine, and subfreezing temperature. He had all but forgotten those efforts when serendipity struck in 1884. "Upon one occasion," he wrote,

> another colleague of mine, Dr. Engel, partook of some [cocaine] with me from the point of his penknife and remarked, "How that numbs the tongue." I said, "Yes, that has been noticed by everyone that has eaten it." And in the moment it flashed upon me that I was carrying in my pocket the local anesthetic for which I had searched some years earlier. I went straight to the laboratory, asked the assistant for a guinea pig for the experiment, made a solution of cocaine from the powder which I carried in my pocketbook, and instilled this into the eye of the animal.[5]

This account was corroborated in 1919 by the assistant on the scene, Josef Gaertner. With Gaertner's help, the already convinced Koller had quickly anesthetized the eyes of a frog (not a literal guinea pig), a rabbit, and a dog, with breathtaking results. Immediately afterward,

> We trickled the solution under the upraised lids of each other's eyes.
> Then we put a mirror before us, took a pin in hand, and tried to
> touch the cornea with its head. Almost simultaneously we could joy-
> ously assure ourselves, "I can't feel a thing." . . . With that the discov-
> ery of local anesthesia was completed.[6]

Only one necessary step remained: a successful cocaine-aided cata-
ract surgery, which was performed by Koller on August 11, 1884. A
report of that achievement—written but not delivered by Koller, who
had no funds for traveling and no permission to leave the General
Hospital—was presented to an international convention in Heidelberg
on September 15. Then ensued a worldwide acknowledgment of the
breakthrough, a plethora of experiments confirming and extending
Koller's inference, and the rapid introduction of cocaine anesthesia not
just into ophthalmology but wherever mucous membranes required
surgery—in gynecology, proctology, urology, and otolaryngology.

Very soon, moreover, the daring American surgeon William Halsted
was able to report that a subcutaneous injection of cocaine could dis-
arm nerves for many other types of operations, including dental surgery.
By proving that cocaine numbed the descending branches of a nerve as
well as the nerve itself, Halsted inaugurated "regional" anesthesia, whose
culmination was James Leonard Corning's development of a total spinal
block in 1885.[7] It wasn't until the early twentieth century that cocaine
was finally supplanted by safer alkaloids such as lidocaine and procaine
(Novocain). Meanwhile, cocaine production swelled, competition forced
the price to drop, and, inconspicuously at first, recreational use began to
overtake medical applications, with far-reaching social effects that neither Freud nor Koller nor anyone else had anticipated.

2. A SUPPORTING ROLE

Apart from passing along, in "On Coca," the familiar speculation that
cocaine might serve as an anesthetic, Freud had played no active role

in the development of cocaine anesthesia. The opening paragraph of his second cocaine paper, published on January 31, 1885, took justified credit for Koller's awareness of cocaine while also acknowledging that Koller and only Koller had thought of adapting the drug to eye surgery:

> To bring the coca plant and its alkaloid, cocaine, to the attention of physicians, I published in the July issue of Dr. Heitler's *Journal of Therapy* a study on this subject based on a review of reports contained in the literature and on my own experiments with this long-neglected drug. I can report the unexpectedly rapid and complete success of that effort. While Dr. L. Königstein, at my suggestion, undertook to test the action of cocaine in alleviating pain and restricting secretions in pathological eye conditions, my colleague in this hospital Dr. Carl Koller, *independently of my personal suggestion*, happened upon the felicitous idea of inducing complete anesthesia and analgesia of the cornea and conjunctiva by means of cocaine, whose power to numb mucous membranes had been long known.[8]

As we see, in granting Koller's priority Freud mentioned another figure in this story, his and Koller's mutual friend Leopold Königstein. He was an older ophthalmologist who, at Freud's suggestion later that summer and fall, conducted cocaine experiments of his own. Before leaving Vienna for Wandsbek in September, Freud had urged him to test the drug's power to assuage eye afflictions such as trachoma and iritis. That inquiry into analgesic—not anesthetic—applications failed because Königstein, or perhaps an erring pharmacist, employed a solution that stung the eyes instead of soothing them.

Königstein possessed the knowledge and skill to have beaten Koller to the discovery of cocaine anesthesia. He might well have done so if he hadn't been initially directed by Freud to explore nonsurgical relief of ocular pain. By mid-September 1884, when Königstein finally did use cocaine for effective anesthesia, Koller's victory announcement was already a fortnight old. Königstein, however, couldn't face the obvious fact that he had lost out, and he told his good friend Freud that he didn't intend to be eclipsed by Koller. After all, he reasoned, he had

happened upon some significant cocaine effects that Koller had overlooked.

Freud knew that Königstein couldn't prevail in a priority dispute,
but he also felt invested in his ongoing work. Königstein, he wrote to
Martha, had "really discovered something."[9] Consequently, he didn't
simply advise Königstein to back off. Instead, mediating between the
disputants, Freud got them to agree that each would read a paper on the
same occasion, a meeting of the Vienna Society of Physicians on October
17, 1884.

To Freud's dismay, however, Königstein's paper breached scientific
etiquette by making no mention of Koller's pioneering achievement.
Whereupon Freud skillfully interceded once again, writing to Koller, "I
am aghast at the fact that in K's published paper there is no mention of
your name; and I don't know how to explain it in view of my knowledge of him in other respects; but I hope you will postpone taking any
steps until I have talked to him, and that you will, after that, create a
situation in which he can retract."[10]

So successful was Freud's intervention that Koller and Königstein
managed to resume their formerly collegial relationship. Indeed, when
Freud's father, after being examined by Koller, underwent successful
glaucoma surgery in April 1885, the cocaine anesthetic was administered by Koller, the knife was wielded by Königstein, and the whole
procedure was attended by Freud. There they were in alliance, cocaine's
three European medical champions, thanks to a timely exercise of tact
that would find no parallel in Freud's vindictive later years. And the very
alacrity with which Koller and Königstein welcomed his role as arbitra-
tor speaks well of his reputation, at the time, for professional objectivity.

Freud was delighted when Koller, in his public announcement of
September 1884, acknowledged his influence; at the time he expected
nothing more. Here was one boost to his medical standing, to be followed, he was sure, by still greater ones as the cocaine revolution
spread through Western medicine in novel manifestations. As the
months went by, however, Freud grew restless and annoyed. In October
he complained to Martha, "Coca has really brought me much honor,
but we haven't gotten much out of it, or not enough."[11] In the same

month, he told his sister-in-law Minna that "the lion's share [of credit] has gone to others."[12] Listening to Koller and Königstein read their papers on October 17, Freud estimated that Koller had given him a mere five percent of the credit; and Königstein's welcome praise couldn't banish the thought that he, Freud, had erred in not undertaking the work himself. He could have done a better job than Königstein, he boasted to Martha, and he would have succeeded if only he hadn't been "misled by people's incredulity on all sides."[13] By December 1884 Freud was still a minor celebrity, as Koller's announcement continued to cause "a giant stir throughout the world,"[14] but the very scope of Koller's renown left him feeling uninvolved and forlorn. "It's been so long since I've published," he lamented.[15]

Some hints in the medical literature had led Freud to anticipate that the next frontier would be subcutaneous injections of cocaine, with which Königstein, at his urging, had begun experimenting in October. (Ernst Fleischl's evident self-medication by that means hadn't set off alarms with Freud.) When he attempted to treat neuralgia with injected cocaine, however, he obtained no result. It appears that he was just dowsing with his hypodermic needle, hoping that the miracle drug had more wonders to reveal. And his ideas for further cocaine applications—among them the alleviation of seasickness, sciatica, and diabetes—weren't working out, either.

Bit by bit, Freud came to understand that Koller's achievement was the kind of world-historical advance that had occupied his own daydreams. Meanwhile, as Koller's fame spread and physicians everywhere rushed to expand upon his work, Freud's general sponsorship of cocaine no longer served a purpose. Fatal mishaps with cocaine overdoses, furthermore, were teaching physicians to be wary of miracle-cure propaganda such as Freud's. His March 1885 lectures in that spirit stirred vocal opposition among his auditors. Taken aback, he told Martha that thenceforth he would curtail his public association with the drug.[16] That resolution wouldn't hold, but it accurately reflected Freud's belief, at the time, that Koller's well-deserved fame had eclipsed his own and had obviated any need on his part to keep drawing attention to cocaine.

3. FRIENDS FOR NOW

During the eventful month of September 1884, Freud had been in Wandsbek consorting with Martha Bernays. In his first subsequent letter to her, he broke the news of Koller's sensational revelation, though without bothering to identify him by name.[17] Soon enough, however, Koller became a familiar presence in the correspondence, always in positive contexts. Koller's and Freud's reputations were still intertwined, and Freud was feeling mellow toward the man "who has brought such fame to cocaine and who recently has become an ever closer friend of mine."[18]

The letter mentioning this bond also contained a gripping story about events that had thrown the entire General Hospital into turmoil. In Theodor Billroth's clinic, Koller had responded to an assistant's anti-Semitic insult by punching him in the face. Challenged to his first and only duel, Koller then amazed everyone by decisively winning the swordfight. As a greatly relieved Freud wrote to his fiancée, "It turned out well, little woman. Our friend is quite unharmed, and his opponent got two proper gashes. We [Jews] are all heartily happy, a proud day for us. We are going to give Koller a present as a lasting reminder of his victory."[19]

Koller's anesthesia announcement had brought him closer to Freud than in their undergraduate days, and now the duel on January 6, 1885, appeared to guarantee their solidarity. As Freud wrote to him with questionable tact twelve months later, "It is now about a year since I first knew that you were somebody worthwhile. For the great discoveries are always made by great discoverers."[20] Koller, he told Martha, was a veritable Maccabee, a hero of Jewish liberation.[21] He had done what Freud had only fantasized doing: to risk everything for the honor of his people and, however provisionally, to score an actual victory.

In the wake of the duel, Freud sent the hero this letter:

Dear Friend:
I have missed spending the evening with you. After the vehement excitement of the last days I felt the need to unburden my heart to

two of the dearest people, Breuer and his wife. You may guess what
we were talking about, and what Breuer's comment was. It would
give me great pleasure if you would accept my offer to use the
intimate term *du* as an external sign of my sincere friendship,
sympathy, and willingness to help. I hope that the shadows which
seem to threaten your life at present will soon vanish and that you
will always be what you have been in these last weeks and days,
a benefactor to mankind and the pride of your friends.

Your Sigm. Freud[22]

The "shadows" mentioned here refer to gentile retribution that, as
anyone could now predict, would forever doom Koller's chances for
advancement either in the General Hospital or in the university that directed it. Indeed, only a few months later the shunned researcher would
begin a dreary odyssey through various cities of Germany, Holland, and
France before finally settling all but anonymously in New York.

Freud empathized with Koller's plight, which was what his own
might have been if he hadn't kept his aggressive impulses in check.
Koller, he wrote to Martha, possessed "a considerable claim on my
sad thoughts."[23] The man who had brought him favorable notice and
had upheld his ethnic honor was being hounded out of Vienna while
Freud himself continued to maneuver within the corrupt system for a
promotion and a fellowship to Paris. As a probationer who worried
about being disadvantaged by nepotism and racist bias, he wouldn't
be lodging complaints about injustice to a fellow Jew. He could, however, offer discreet support to Koller, whom he characterized to Martha
as his "secret patient."[24]

Freud's subsequent letters to the itinerant Koller show solicitude
not only about his search for refuge and employment but also about
his physical and mental state. Writing to Koller from Paris on New
Year's Day 1886, Freud recollected that he had initially "given up" on
his dejected friend when they parted company in Vienna, since Koller had
made "such a pitiful impression" on him at the time.[25] Eventually, however, Koller recouped his strength and resolve, and then Freud concluded, dubiously, "I really think you are cyclic"—or, as we would
now say, bipolar.[26]

When Freud was planning to visit Martha on his way to Paris in the fall of 1885, he hoped Koller would board the train en route and accompany him for some hours.[27] Since no *Brautbriefe* would have been written when Sigmund and Martha were together, we may never learn whether that reunion took place. Freud's proposal, however, shows that Koller, more than a year after their parting, still meant a good deal to him.

Soon, however, the correspondence between Freud and Koller began to dwindle, and after 1887 they would never meet again. Koller's daughter, Hortense Koller Becker, refers to "a sharp exchange of letters" in 1895 "over a ridiculous, imagined slight to a female relative of Freud to whom my parents had offered help and hospitality."[28] That flare-up, which had a precedent in Freud's accusation that Eli Bernays had grievously insulted his brother Alexander, occurred in a period of maximum hostility toward bewildered former friends, notably the gentle Breuer. But Koller, if not Freud, was willing to discount the brief unpleasantness. Finally revisiting Vienna in 1926, he tried to pay a call on Freud, but found him unavailable.

4. THE NARRATIVE EVOLVES

Freud's unwavering defense of Koller's priority against Leopold König-stein's improper challenge, along with his fraternal relations with Koller into the 1890s, manifested an understanding that, where cocaine anesthesia was concerned, he and Koller had never been rival investigators. As he wrote as late as 1899 in *The Interpretation of Dreams*,

> Once, I recalled, I really *had* written something in the nature of a *monograph on a plant*, namely a dissertation on the *coca-plant*, which had drawn Karl Koller's attention to the anaesthetic properties of cocaine. I had myself indicated this application of the alkaloid in my published paper, but I had not been thorough enough to pursue the matter further.[29]

Fifteen years after the event, then, Freud was still willing to state that his inertia in 1884 had left him out of the running for the prize attained by Koller. This final acknowledgment extended his record of commendable behavior toward both Koller and Königstein.

Were it not for Freud's susceptibility to jealousy and self-aggrandizement, there would be nothing further to say about his role in the story of local anesthesia. But that story, or rather its partisan recasting, continued into the 1930s and beyond, taking on some remarkable embellishments.[30] The later Freud didn't just envy the simplicity and reliability of Koller's innovation; he also realized that psychoanalysis would look more convincing if its founder had previously shown himself to be a discoverer in Koller's mold. Over the years, in private communications that were then recounted to other analysts, Freud rearranged history to imply that he had personally shown Koller the crucial numbing property of cocaine; that he had very nearly preempted Koller; and even that he had actually discovered cocaine anesthesia on his own and had been cheated of credit by the unscrupulous rival.

The one statement of Freud's about cocaine that is remembered in the psychoanalytic community is the following reminiscence, appearing in his *Autobiographical Study* of 1925:

I may here go back a little and explain how it was the fault of my *fiancée* that I was not already famous at that youthful age. A side interest, though it was a deep one, had led me in 1884 to obtain from Merck some of what was then the little-known alkaloid cocaine and to study its physiological action. While I was in the middle of this work, an opportunity arose for making a journey to visit my *fiancée*, from whom I had been parted for two years. I hastily wound up my investigation of cocaine and contented myself in my monograph on the subject with prophesying that further uses for it would soon be found. I suggested, however, to my friend Königstein, the ophthalmologist, that he should investigate the question of how far the anaesthetizing properties of cocaine were applicable in diseases of the eye. When I returned from my holiday I found that not he, but another of my friends, Carl Koller (now in New York), whom I had also spoken to about cocaine, had made the decisive experiments upon animals' eyes and had demonstrated them at the Ophthalmological

Congress at Heidelberg. Koller is therefore rightly regarded as the discoverer of local anaesthesia by cocaine, which has become so important in minor surgery; but I bore my *fiancée* no grudge for the
interruption.[31]

Freud's narrative manifestly conceded full merit to Koller for having applied cocaine to local anesthesia. Koller's daughter, however,
reading in the light of later developments, perceived that there was

> something in the tone of this paragraph which can be accounted for,
> not by [Freud's] feelings at the time of the discovery, when he still
> expected to reach other even greater results with cocaine, but only by
> his feelings a few years later, when these hopes were gone and only
> its value in surgery shone on undiminished.[32]

Putting a cheerful face on the embittering fact that Koller alone had
won lasting honor from cocaine, Freud was hinting that he himself
would have been the discoverer were it not for two factors: his delega-
tion of the inquiry to Königstein and his untimely trip to Wandsbek.

Many commentators have scrutinized this passage, most of them
psychoanalysts trying to determine to what degree Freud blamed
Martha Bernays for his failure to catch the brass ring. As has frequently
been noted, the paragraph bears a teasing, equivocal aspect. Does
Freud hold Königstein responsible for having failed to execute the suggestion (never actually made) that he probe the *anesthetic* potential of
cocaine? Is Freud here confessing to an amiable weakness in having
allowed himself to be amorously distracted? Is he simply bantering
coyly about long-past events that were rendered trivial—so he may be
suggesting—by the great scientific insights that have long since rock-
eted him beyond Koller's modest orbit? Or is he still seething with
"denied" resentment toward the ostensibly absolved Martha?

The paragraph contains even more uncertainties. By calling his involvement with cocaine both peripheral ("*abseitig*") and deep ("*tief-
gehend*"), for example, Freud was skating near to oxymoron. Both
adjectives were needed, however, to establish his alibi for failure. Only
a deep interest could place him on Koller's level of mastery, yet that

same interest had to be peripheral to other concerns, or surely he wouldn't have been deterred by so insignificant a factor as a rendez-vous with his fiancée.

Several distortions of fact in Freud's statement suggest that more is at stake here than meets the eye. Sigmund and Martha hadn't been apart for two years, but only one; his visit to Wandsbek wasn't arranged at the last moment but had been planned for months; and it assuredly didn't interrupt research that had been on the verge of scooping Koller.[33] By leaving the impression that he had been busy studying cocaine's "physiological action" when he was suddenly called away to Wandsbek; by depicting himself as having hastily inserted his June pre-diction about anesthesia in "On Coca" while packing for that trip in September, as if his research into anesthetic uses of cocaine had then been interrupted; and by falsely claiming that he had directed König-stein's attention to specifically anesthetizing effects, Freud was mis-stating not just the timeline but both the nature and the persistency of his cocaine involvement in the summer of 1884—all with the aim of retroactively lending a Koller-like purposefulness to a period in which his cocaine interests had actually been diffuse and dilettantish.*

In order to see how supererogatory it was of Freud to imply, belat-edly, that he had nearly preempted Koller, we need only reflect that the latter clinched his priority through performing an eye operation. In the General Hospital, Freud had rejected the offer of a surgical apprentice-ship because, as he told Martha at the time, he simply wouldn't be up to it (*weil ich da nichts kann*).[34] Nor was he conversant with ocular diseases. Not until March 1885, six months after Koller's announce-ment of success, did Freud serve a brief internship in the hospital's oph-thalmology department, learning such basics as how to manipulate an ophthalmoscope, test for visual field, and prescribe for glasses.[35] And thereafter he was still unable to recognize his father's patent symptoms

---

* In the first edition of the *Autobiographical Study*, Freud had written that he didn't blame Martha for *mein damaliges Versäumnis*—that is, for his own *omission* or *negli-gence* at the time. The phrase preferred by Strachey and Jones—*die damalige Störung*, "the *interruption* at the time"—dated from 1935, when Strachey was preparing a sec-ond English edition of Freud's memoir (SE, 20:15n). Eleven years after having accused himself of inattentiveness, Freud had altered his text to imply that in 1884 a siren had lured him away from his important work.

of glaucoma—which, he wrongly assured the worried sufferer, were of no particular importance.[36]

As we know, moreover, Freud was disgusted by palpable diseases and was made queasy by the sight of blood. He wanted little to do with cutting of any kind—least of all, we can be sure, with the slicing of eyes. Siegfried Bernfeld, remarking on Freud's ocular squeamishness, quaintly ascribed it to castration anxiety.[37] The interpretation was gratuitous, but Bernfeld understood that a temperamental aversion had played a role in Freud's failure to seize the initiative that fell to Koller in 1884.

5. TRADING PLACES

Among the unflattering tendencies that Freud's first biographer, Fritz Wittels, had noted in his sometime master was an obsession with his failure of 1884 regarding anesthesia.[38] An infuriated Freud demanded a retraction; supposedly, he had long since forgotten about the insignificant Koller affair.[39] But Wittels, who had been a member of Freud's inner circle from 1907 to 1910, had often heard him speak unguardedly about the matter, and everything else that he wrote in 1924 about Freud's character—also sternly denied—rings true.

Another disciple, Hanns Sachs, recalled a lecture of unknown date in which Freud reminisced about the events of 1884. Here, approximately, were Freud's words as Sachs transcribed them:

> "Among my friends, when I was a young interne at the General Hospital, was one who seemed obsessed with the idea of finding a new ophthalmological therapy. Whatever medical problem was discussed, his thoughts and questions went in the same direction: Could this be used for the eye?—so that he became occasionally a bit tiresome by his monomania. Well, one day I was standing in the courtyard with a group of colleagues of whom this man was one, when another interne passed us showing the signs of intense pain. [Here Freud told what the localization of the pain was, but I have forgotten this detail.] I said to him: 'I think I can help you,' and we all went to my room where I applied a few drops of a medicine which made the pain dis-

appear instantly. I explained to my friends that this drug was the extract of a South American plant, the coca, which seemed to have powerful qualities for relieving pain and about which I was preparing a publication. The man with the permanent interest in the eye, whose name was Koller, did not say anything, but a few months later I learned that he had begun to revolutionize eye-surgery by the use of cocaine, making operations easy which till then had been impossible."[40]

This secondhand narrative probably has some basis in fact. In May 1884, gathering material for his first paper on cocaine, Freud was issuing the drug to any of his acquaintances who complained of digestive symptoms and was then recording the outcomes, which tended to be positive.[41] And when he himself told a version of the Sachs story in 1934, he specified that his colleague's disorder had been intestinal. Perhaps, then, Carl Koller did witness such a demonstration. What stirs doubt, however, is Freud's intimation, as reported by Sachs, that this was the germinal moment for Koller's discovery.

Sachs's account, which wasn't meant to be critical, evidences envious malice on the part of the psychoanalytic Freud. As the story celebrates Freud, so it belittles the "obsessed" and "tiresome" Koller, who is now such a reduced personage that his name barely requires mention. This lesser being, it is hinted, acquired fame by capitalizing on an insight freely proffered by the unpossessive Freud, himself too normal to fall into "monomania." As for the odd detail that Koller "did not say anything" at the time, its sinister implication is that the Iago-like Koller may already have been scheming to steal, "months later," credit that properly belonged to Freud.

By 1910, in fact, Freud had convinced himself that he was the true discoverer of cocaine anesthesia. In that year he angrily insisted on the point with his patient Albert Hirst.[42] Later, Kurt Eissler "wrote to Jones about a similar-sounding [to Hirst's] version of the cocaine episode that he had heard from Freud's disciple Paul Federn."[43] Who besides Freud himself could have told Federn about his secret priority over Koller?

Long before the flurry of interest in Hirst's recollection, psychoanalytic insiders had picked up signals from Freud that Koller's behavior toward him in 1884 had been dastardly. There was room for only one hero in the story of cocaine anesthesia, and that hero was going to be Freud. The man who had once felt guiltily indebted to his "dear friend" Koller, as he had repeatedly addressed him in letters after 1884, and who had looked up to him as a noble Jewish knight, now saw him only as a nuisance. And whenever the older Freud had no more use for someone who had been important to him, a barrage of auxiliary attacks on the offender's character and/or mental health was sure to follow.

The year 1934 witnessed a number of fiftieth-anniversary tributes to the unjustly obscure Koller from within his profession. Among them was a warm speech by the Viennese ophthalmologist Josef Meller, which was published first in the *Wiener Klinische Wochenschrift*, where it came to Freud's attention, and then as a booklet.[44] On November 8, 1934, Freud wrote to Meller acknowledging the article's mention of his own role in 1884 but protesting the unseemly lavishing of attention on Koller. Meller, he chided, was quite mistaken in his positive account of Koller's character:

> K. Koller, somewhat younger than I, was—and probably still is—a pathological personality, a self-tormenting quarreler, who was generally disliked because of his disputatiousness and his continual acts of aggression. . . . Koller's morbid nature had an organic foundation, of which he was well aware. He did not deny the indications of hereditary syphilis in his family, and he was very unhappy about that. In his continual neurotic complaints he had chosen me as his confidant.[45]

Freud then went on to recount a version of the story that would later be remembered, with variations, by Hanns Sachs, whereby the wise young cocaine expert had taken a suffering colleague up to his room with others, including Koller, and had produced an instant cure of stomach pain. In the Meller variant, Freud went even farther, "recollecting" that on that occasion he had allowed Koller to taste cocaine and had mentioned to him its numbing property.[46] Now the story was that the sneaky Koller had been literally fed the great secret by Freud but had still failed to digest it until months later.

Freud's venomous letter to Meller was known to at least two of the inner-circle psychoanalysts who fashioned his modern image in the postwar years. Siegfried Bernfeld and Ernest Jones both understood that, regardless of the unbelievable elements in Freud's recasting of the anesthesia story, a death sentence on Koller's reputation had been passed along to them. Bernfeld's 1953 essay on Freud's cocaine adventure established the correct line: Koller had tried to undermine Freud's contribution from the outset and had grown increasingly strident on the point in later years, maliciously altering the timeline of events to make it look as if he had never been influenced by "On Coca."*

In 1953 Jones made the same accusation, adding that Koller "did not reciprocate Freud's chivalrous behavior" in the matter of Koller's priority dispute with Königstein.[47] The skillful Jones capped his assault on Koller (who had died in 1944) with invidious armchair psychoanalysis. Already in 1884, according to Jones, Koller was showing "some disturbance in his personality. . . . In hospital days Freud had treated him privately for a neurotic affection; 'negative transferences,' as they are called, often endure."[48]

By the 1970s the received view in Freudian circles was that the rascal Koller had snatched from Freud an honor that the latter had been too high-minded, and too bent on more important issues, to bother claiming for himself. The only remaining question was why Freud, a genius, had neglected to beat the plodding Koller to the finish line. "Why did Freud not make use of the intervening time between finishing his paper in June and his departure in September?" asked Eissler. "Why did he procrastinate and then, shortly before leaving, entrust the whole experiment to his friend [Königstein]?"[49]

Freud's champion found the answer in the stars:

> Curiously enough, there is a high degree of probability that, if Freud had made that epochal discovery, it might have given his subsequent development an entirely different direction. World fame—acquired too early and by an accidental and, so to speak, unmerited success—might conceivably have become his undoing, as it probably was for Koller.[50]

---

* Bernfeld produced no citations to warrant his charge; the four publications by Koller that were listed in his bibliography do not substantiate it in any way. Although Koller in his old age did get confused about dates, he always declared unequivocally that he was indebted to Freud for having introduced him to cocaine.

This was unabashed teleology. Supremely gifted though Freud was, according to Eissler, it was his destiny to miss an early triumph so that he could be spared for greater things. Such, at its most extreme, is the hagiography that, usually in milder form, has largely obscured the prosaic motives, errors of judgment, and limited scientific capabilities of the man who simply didn't bother to ascertain whether cocaine might serve as an effectual aid to surgery.

7

Expert Judgments

1. CONSULTING PHYSICIANS

As Carl Koller's fame spread in the fall of 1884, Freud felt increasingly annoyed at having been left behind. But that was about to change, albeit in a minor key. Back in May, almost certainly at Fleischl's instigation, the Merck company had processed an order from the Physiological Institute for ten grams of cocaine.[1] Now Merck, according to a *Brautbrief* of October 5, had "noticed [Fleischl's] large consumption" of cocaine and inquired about it; and Fleischl, in replying, had mentioned Freud and "On Coca."

On Fleischl's advice, Freud sent Merck an introductory letter and a copy of the essay. "I hope that because of this," he wrote to Martha, "my name will remain linked to coca in the factory's catalogs."[2] In default of having discovered something new about the drug, Freud now looked forward to being cited as an endorser within a pharmaceutical company's sales brochure.

The man who had written to Fleischl was probably Emanuel Merck, the aged owner of his company. He must have assumed that a large drug order emanating from the esteemed Physiological Institute was connected to a research project—not, certainly, to a private cocaine habit. Fleischl's reply has not survived, but we can infer from subsequent events that he didn't disabuse his correspondent of the illusion that he was a scientific investigator into drug properties. It was in that connection that he recommended direct contact with his knowledgeable colleague Dr. Freud.

In order to win Merck's trust, the distinguished Fleischl needed only to refrain from disclosing his cocaine dependency. As for Freud, we can be sure he told Merck what he never tired of announcing in this period: that he had overseen Europe's first weaning of an addict from morphine via cocaine. Of course he wouldn't reveal that the addict in question had been Fleischl, or that the patient was now unable to abstain from either substance. In Merck's eyes Freud and Fleischl were a team of objective researchers looking into the therapeutic properties of a drug that Merck had undervalued until the announcement of Koller's breakthrough. If the team arrived at spectacular findings of its own, Merck wanted to be the first to hear about them.

Clearly, Fleischl and Freud hadn't set out to pose as a research team. But the Darmstadt firm had boxed them in. If Fleischl weren't to be outed as an addict, he had to disguise himself as a cocaine investigator; and Freud had to protect Fleischl from being exposed to Merck as his anonymous patient.

Merck found the story believable and promptly issued a "circular" touting various applications of cocaine. It referred favorably to Freud's study of the drug and named Fleischl as one of his expert informants.[3] Thus both Freud and Fleischl, a renowned university professor and an aspiring neurologist, were allowing their names to be conscripted for a sales campaign. More seriously, because Merck's circular was widely printed in medical journals, the two physicians were helping to deceive others about the safety of a drug that was already causing Fleischl preliminary symptoms of dependency.

Cocaine and Its Salts was written and signed by Emanuel Merck himself. It appeared in both German and English, depending on the venue of distribution.[4] The brief document did touch on Carl Koller's advance in ophthalmological surgery, which had been announced at Heidelberg just a month earlier. For the most part, however, Merck drew his examples directly from "On Coca" and from Freud's and Fleischl's personal claims about morphine withdrawal:

During the past few months, Prof. Dr. E. v. Fleischl, in Vienna, and
Dr. Sigm. Freud, Physician in the General Hospital in Vienna, have
diligently occupied themselves with this preparation. The former, particularly, has determined that cocaine, by hypodermic injection, has
proved itself to be an invaluable adjuvant to morphine withdrawal,
even sudden withdrawal. This fact alone should give the remedy an
enduring place among the treasures of the physician.[5]

Of particular significance here is the association of Fleischl's name
with cocaine *injections*. It appears that Fleischl had switched from oral
to subcutaneous absorption no later than May 19, 1884, the day of his
Billroth surgery. Now he was an enthusiast of the more radical method.
And Freud, even though he could plainly see that no "abstinence" from
morphine was being illustrated by Fleischl's serial injection of *two*
addictive drugs, had revised "On Coca" to bring it into conformity
with Fleischl's preference for the hypodermic needle. Emanuel Merck, in
all innocence, would now propagate the noxious advice to the medical
world:

In cases of gradual or long-continued withdrawal, decreasing doses
of morphia and increasing doses of cocaine are given. In cases of
absolute and sudden abstinence, doses of 0.1 g are injected as often
as the morphium hunger is felt. Confinement in institutions becomes
quite unnecessary with this method. Dr. Freud, who, with others, saw
such a case pass into positive convalescence after ten days' cocaine
treatment (0.1 g subcutaneously three times a day), is of the opinion
that a direct antagonism exists between morphine and cocaine.[6]

It might be thought that Freud and Fleischl, realizing from the
publication of Merck's circular that their ruse had compromised their
medical probity, would have resolved to cease billing themselves as
experts on morphine withdrawal by means of injected cocaine. On the
contrary, they seem to have become more committed to the masquer-
ade. Their behavior in that regard was so out of character as to require
a special explanation: their common personal use of the drug, which

notoriously weakens inhibitions that rest on social or professional convention.

In November 1884, shortly after the publication of Merck's pamphlet, a brief notice titled "Cocaine" appeared in the Philadelphia journal *Medical News*.[7] Its authorship, listed only as "From Our Special Correspondent. Vienna," was in doubt until the psychoanalyst and Freud scholar Alexander Grinstein showed that Freud had previously published in the same journal and had used exactly the same designation.[8] Further evidence for Freud's responsibility can be found in the familiar content of the notice itself. Under the cover of anonymity, Freud was apprising American doctors of new findings about cocaine, including these:

> Some experience has been collected in Vienna about the interesting drug. Prof. Fleische [*sic*] and his colleagues here have seen the excellent effect of cocaine during the period of "abstentiae morphiae." Persons used to large amounts of morphia for many years, could bear the privation of this alkaloid without suffering the well-known tortures which are usually connected with it. Even in cases in which the morphia was not withdrawn gradually, but stopped at once, cocaine showed the best effects.[9]

"Fleische" here is probably an American printer's typo for "Fleischl." If so, however, Freud's little article contained a big lie. The historical Fleischl was indeed a medical professor, but he wasn't performing morphine withdrawals and he didn't have a number of academic collaborators who were helping him to do so.

Just why Freud chose to leave himself out of that account, both as author and as cocaine researcher, is open to interpretation. His reluctance, however, was not without precedent. Already in "On Coca" he had characterized the Fleischl case as one that he had merely observed, not engineered. There, it appears, he was hedging his bet on the long-term outcome of Fleischl's cure. Taking cognizance of the practical-joke aspect of the *Medical News* article, Han Israëls plausibly suggests that it may have been concocted jointly by Freud and Fleischl.[10] Even if it wasn't, they must have taken satisfaction from Freud's deceiving the Americans into crediting the existence of a chimerical research program.

Once again, a grave breach of medical ethics was being perpetrated. A single case with a dubious result was being misrepresented and inflated into numerous successful ones, thus lending false corroboration to a treatment regimen that many American doctors would have shunned if they had been correctly informed. We needn't wonder that, in this instance, Freud declined to sign his name to statements that could have been held against him if subsequent treatments went awry or if the team of "Prof. Fleische and his colleagues" were exposed as fictitious.

Freud and Fleischl had one more deception to perpetrate. In the *St. Louis Medical and Surgical Journal* of December 1884, there appeared a signed article by Freud titled "Coca." Although it was mostly a condensation of "On Coca," this text was added:

> Prof. Fleischl, of Vienna, confirms the fact that muriate of cocaine is invaluable, subcutaneously injected in *morphinism* (0.05–0.15 grm. dissolved in water); a gradual withdrawal of morphine requires a gradual increase of cocaine, but a sudden abstinence from morphine requires a subcutaneous injection of 0.1 grm. of cocaine. *Inebriate asylums can be entirely dispensed with*; in 10 days a radical cure can be effected by an injection of 0.1 gram of cocaine 3 times a day. It is evident that there is a direct antagonism between morphine and cocaine.[11]

In the world outside Freud and Fleischl's imagination, the positive findings and the recommended dosage ranges that Freud was stipulating here could have been arrived at only through extensive trial and error. The impression was given, then, that Fleischl had accumulated an extensive practice from which he had gleaned and analyzed copious notes on the procedures essayed, the immediate results, and followup, leading to the general observation that cocaine unfailingly blocks a morphine craving. That impression was reinforced by the emphatic conclusion that hospitalization was never needed. This was Freud's most pernicious statement about cocaine and, at the same time, his boldest lie about the evidential basis for his confidence. He could hardly have falsified the record so grossly without the approval of the cocaine-besotted Fleischl, with whom he remained on excellent terms after the publication of this imposture.

2. RESEARCH FOR SALE

Although Freud always held physiological theory and experimentation in high regard, he didn't feel comfortable, in his own laboratory work, venturing beyond the anatomical analysis of tissue structures. In the fall of 1884, however, for the only time in his life, he did plan and execute physiological experiments—namely, tests of effects on the human organism wrought by cocaine and by one of its near cousins. To be sure, here too he was undertaking nothing that seriously challenged his ingenuity. Nor was he testing an original hypothesis. But at least he was proceeding beyond the casual subjective reporting in "On Coca," published earlier that year. Now his results, purportedly belonging to impersonal, value-neutral research, would be gleaned from instrument pointers moving across a numbered background.

It was, once again, the Merck company that prodded Freud into taking action. The Mercks, father and sons, had on hand only a small quantity of cocaine, but they were better positioned than any competitors to launch into expanded production if the market demanded it. And now that further medical applications for the drug were being discovered, the company began exploring possible uses for other derivatives of coca.

The most promising of those chemicals was ecgonine, an alkaloid that is naturally found in the coca leaf but is also generated by the metabolizing of cocaine itself. Merck's managers could isolate ecgonine, but they knew nothing about its effects when ingested. Rather than try to interfere with the important cocaine research they imagined Fleischl to be conducting in Brücke's Physiological Institute, they turned for expert assistance to his apparent associate Freud.

Understandably, Freud was unsure of his qualifications for the assignment. Because ecgonine, unlike cocaine, had never been administered to animals in order to assess its toxicity, he knew he would have to undertake animal experiments; but whether through squeamishness or inexperience or both, he seems to have dreaded that task. Fleischl, on the other hand, would presumably have known just how to proceed, and Freud accepted the Merck commission only after securing Fleischl's agreement to join in the effort.

Merck's offer arrived at a moment when Freud was more than usually amenable to other people's initiatives. On October 7, 1884, he had written to Martha Bernays in high excitement about his latest brainstorm, which was soon revealed to be the curing of diabetes with cocaine injections. One might think that the necessary research toward that end would have occupied him for an extended period. Just four days later, however, he complained that "my big undertaking has failed me except for a little trifle."[12] But then he immediately went on to disclose Merck's proposal. He had accepted it with alacrity and had already secured Fleischl's promise of assistance. It seems that he was compensating for his latest disappointment by acquiescing to the next suggestion that came his way.

On October 18 Freud told Martha that a 100-gram shipment of ecgonine was on its way from Merck. He believed that this was the company's entire supply of the chemical—a fact he found reassuring, because his monopoly of ecgonine, he remarked, would prevent anyone else from eclipsing his priority. If there was something interesting to be learned about ecgonine, he now reflected, he might yet feel himself to be a real researcher after all.

As for the work itself, though, Freud wasn't ready to give it his wholehearted attention. In that same letter, he informed Martha that he expected six projects to occupy him during the next half year: "ecgonine, if it serves any purpose"; brain anatomy; the writing up of a completed medical treatment; another paper about an ongoing case; research on electricity; and experiments with an unspecified new instrument that Fleischl had been developing. Still another task, the conducting of an extracurricular medical course for profit, would also soon compete with the ecgonine study.

The first order of business with ecgonine was to determine how hazardous it was. To that end Freud and Fleischl acquired frogs, a rabbit, and a dog, each of which was apparently to be administered increasing doses of the drug and then observed for effects on its nervous system, up to and including death. Yet curiously, Freud couldn't wait even one day for those results to begin accruing. On the evening of October 20, just hours before the animal experiments were to begin, he himself ate a "tiny grain" of ecgonine to see what it would do to him.[13] If the drug had been highly poisonous, that rash deed could have immediately ended his life. Instead, no effect was noticed beyond a feeling of repugnance toward ecgonine itself.

Freud and Fleischl did begin injecting their laboratory animals with ecgonine on October 21, and on the 26th they managed to kill a rabbit with .1g of the drug. On the next day, however, Freud complained to Martha that Fleischl was proving to be an unpunctual and unreliable collaborator. Although Fleischl promised to do better, his combination of illness, drug dependency, rival projects, and apparent lack of interest in ecgonine soon caused him to drop out. By then, Freud had accumulated one dead rabbit and a number of frogs exhibiting cramps, agitation, paralysis, and other signs of toxicity.[14] But he hadn't learned enough, or hadn't sufficiently calmed his nerves, to proceed alone with the animal studies, which went no further.

Freud reverted to trying the effect of ecgonine on himself. On November 2 he took a dose to ascertain whether it would suppress his hunger and lift a cross mood, as cocaine would have done; neither improvement ensued. Freud's half-serious approach to that research is indicated by a droll aside in a *Brautbrief* of that same day: "One shouldn't be writing a letter to his little darling during an experiment with a new poison, right?" As he mentioned a day later, he experienced an extraordinarily vivid dream that same night. Given the role of such dreams in the formation of psychoanalytic theory, this is an arresting fact.

Freud's curiosity about ecgonine took a brief uptick at that point. But by November 6 he was telling Martha, "Your guess was right; ecgonine is rubbish, and unfortunately it's depriving me of many great, undetermined discoveries." Although he vowed to continue his investigation, the sole reason for persisting, he said, was his obligation to Merck. And it was in that halfhearted spirit that he began measuring the effect of ecgonine on human muscle power and reaction time.

3. UNINTELLIGENT DESIGN

Freud's report to Merck regarding ecgonine has not survived, but we can infer what it was like from an article that he wrote soon afterward. Because the instruments he had assembled for testing ecgonine were still in his possession, he decided that he might as well apply the ecgonine tests to cocaine, too. The results of his cocaine experiments formed the basis of his next paper on the drug, "Contribution to Knowledge of the Effect of Cocaine," published in January 1885.[15] The paper is of considerable interest, not for its findings but for the light it casts on Freud's ability to devise and execute meaningful research.

Both Siegfried Bernfeld and Ernest Jones deemed Freud's "Contribution" to be a sloppy piece of work. Bernfeld called the experiments "poorly and haphazardly designed, and reported without sufficient precision,"[16] and Jones lamented that "the facts are recorded in a somewhat irregular and uncontrolled fashion that would make them hard to correlate with anyone else's observations."[17] Later Freudians, however, have sometimes claimed that the "Contribution" recorded a great discovery and that it deserves recognition as a founding document of psychophysiology. But in this instance Bernfeld and Jones were entirely right.

The impetus behind Freud's "Contribution" obviously came from Merck's ecgonine assignment. But the sense of a more purposeful motive was fostered by the autobiographical remarks found in the paper itself, which mentioned neither Merck nor ecgonine. Freud portrayed himself as a cocaine specialist who was marching ahead with his own research agenda. The success of "On Coca" in inspiring Koller's and Königstein's discoveries, he wrote, had now led him to supplement his investigation of cocaine's subjective and therapeutic effects with a physiological inquiry. "As a means of designating the action of coca [sic] by changes in measurable quantities . . . , I decided to test both the motor power of certain muscle groups and psychical reaction time."[18]

For the conduct of his experiments, Freud supplied himself with three crude devices. Two of them were dynamometers: springmetal clasps that, when squeezed, move a pointer along a scale indicating how much maximum strength has been exerted. He possessed a one-handed model and a heavier and more accurate two-handed one, but after using the latter for four days, he had to abandon it because of blisters.[19] The lighter instrument, contracted with his other (right) hand, was then put into use.

In order to measure reaction time, Freud employed a neuroamoebimeter, a vibrating metal strip that emits a sound. As his paper explained, the subject was supposed to stop the vibration as soon as he heard the tone; an automatic pen then recorded how many vibrations, at 1/100th-second intervals, had occurred. Freud's general plan, then, was to check how the ingestion of cocaine would affect both strength and reaction time as recorded by the dynamometers and the neuroamoebimeter, respectively.

The work that Freud produced with those tools was unrigorous in the extreme. The problems began with his set of chosen subjects—namely, himself. Obviously, if one wants to learn how the strength and reaction time of humans are affected by a drug, one must sample a varied population, averaging out idiosyncratic findings. But Freud decided to play every role: experimenter, experimental subject, data collector, evaluator of results, and reporter to the scientific community.

When it came time to draw up his paper in the last week of 1884, Freud must have realized that he had better say something about his failure to test anyone else. This is what he wrote:

> I repeatedly carried out on myself, or had carried out [on me], these
> two series of experiments. I realize that such self-researches have the
> shortcoming, for the person who conducts them, of claiming two kinds
> of believability in the same matter. But I had to proceed in this way for
> external reasons [*aus äußeren Gründen*] and because none of the indi-
> viduals at my disposal showed such a regular reaction to cocaine
> [as my own]. The results of the investigation were, however, also con-
> firmed through my testing of other persons, mostly colleagues.[20]

Here is a peculiar array of statements. Freud seems to be saying, first, that some impediment kept him from finding volunteers to experiment on; second, that he could, after all, have enlisted some people to whom he had previously given cocaine; but third, that there was insufficient uniformity in their subjective reactions to the drug; fourth, that he therefore had no alternative to becoming the sole subject himself; but fifth, that it all turned out for the best, because a new set of subjects, "mostly colleagues," fully confirmed his inferences. The aspiring physiologist thus declared, in the space of a few lines, that he both did and didn't try his experiments on other parties, who both were and weren't capable of matching his own reactions.

Within Freud's hairball of contradictions we can discern a premise that reveals his basic misconstrual of experimental science. Supposedly investigating specieswide characteristics that couldn't be known in advance, he had nevertheless decided that his results must show a certain regularity based on a shared affinity for cocaine. But since some of his acquaintances hadn't responded well to the drug, he had found himself compelled to eliminate the very possibility of variation by studying nobody's reactions but his own. Thus, he implied, he had made himself the sole subject as a methodological precaution. And though, in now writing his report, he understood that some readers might strain at a plea for "two kinds of believability"—the attribution of general validity to a one-subject study and the designation of that subject as the evaluator of the garnered data—he himself professed to see nothing amiss in the arrangement.

Freud's paper propounded several judgments: that cocaine, after being swallowed, does enhance both strength and reaction time, the former more distinctly than the latter; that the effects are greatest when the subject begins from a more or less depressed state; that the explanation of efficacy therefore probably lies not with the direct action of the drug on nerves or muscles but on its capacity to dispel a low mood; that, independently of other factors, and with or without cocaine, the same individual will show markedly different ranges of strength from one day to another; and that regular-looking fluctuations of strength can be correlated with the time of day, from lowest power in the early morning to a peak sustained from forenoon through the rest of daylight, followed by a slow and steady decrease in the evening. Freud noted that this pattern appears to match the well-known daily temperature curve in *Homo sapiens*.

None of these conclusions is implausible, and the point about a diurnal waxing and waning of muscle power has been seized upon by some Freudians as a major breakthrough. Had Freud so thought of it, however, we must wonder why, as one who was never shy about claiming priority, he didn't boast about his achievement. Instead, he consistently neglected to list the "Contribution" among his writings, and he seems to have regarded it as a hindrance to his reputation. As he confided in a letter of 1936, the paper "should never have been published."[21]

From a methodological standpoint, indeed, the "Contribution" may rank among the most careless research studies ever to see print. Consider, in addition to the flaws already remarked:

- Freud made no effort to control his cocaine dosages, varying from .1g to "a little more cocaine" to "a small indeterminate amount of cocaine."
- The intervals between his trials varied from five minutes to almost three hours.
- He never stated how many trials he had conducted.
- He switched types of dynamometers in the course of the experiment but made no allowance for their different properties, and he overlooked the difference in strength between his two hands.
- He failed to weigh the effect of autosuggestion on his application of more pressure after he had taken cocaine.
- In testing both time-of-day effects and cocaine effects, he neglected to isolate them from one another. The diurnal variations in strength, he limply observed, "do not have much to do with the action of cocaine per se."[22]
- His "Remarks" column in his tables sometimes recorded his mood, sometimes his state of energy or fatigue, sometimes his activity just prior to trying his strength, and sometimes nothing at all.

As is often the case in shoddy research, some of Freud's conclusions may have been serendipitously correct. But they weren't warranted by the presented data, and therefore they lacked any utility for subsequent investigators. The most charitable assumption we could make is that cocaine beclouded the writing as well as the conduct of Freud's study.

4. A TESTIMONIAL

In March 1885, as we know, Freud twice lectured to colleagues about cocaine, reiterating his false claim of having liberated Fleischl from morphine dependency. The second lecture went over better than the first, and Freud reported to Martha that two members of that audience, representing a distinguished journal and a newspaper, had approached him about further publication on the topic.[23] Such appeals were all that was needed to alter his plans. Lacking a strong commitment to any of his several projects, he was ready to oblige anyone who could promise him exposure and/or payment; and cocaine was the only theme producing such offers.

A postcard to Martha dated April 11, 1885, brought news of another such opportunity. "Money," Freud wrote,

> is coming into view somewhere on the business horizon again. For an American company that is bringing cocaine into the market, I'm supposed to attest to their product; or rather, to test whether it's as good as Merck's and to publicize the result. For that I'll receive 50–70 florins, of course quite independently of the investigation's outcome. It really isn't work at all but a pleasure, and for the first time I'll get paid for my authority.

The firm in question was none other than Parke, Davis & Co., whose compendium of improbable reports, the Detroit *Therapeutic Gazette*, had thrilled and confused Freud a year earlier. Now the company wanted to put him to work as an expert testifier to the quality of its brand.

Albrecht Hirschmüller has reconstructed the circumstances that lay behind this offer.[24] Parke, Davis had been selling a "fluid extract" of cocaine whose high price and undependable quality rendered it, even inside the United States, uncompetitive with Merck's better-controlled product. But Parke had recently conceived the idea of radically altering the means of manufacture. Instead of shipping whole leaves over thousands of miles, with inevitable deterioration in transit, Parke decided to have raw cocaine extracted on the site of collection in Bolivia and then refined at headquarters back home. Several dramatic misadventures attended that effort, but it began to prove its value sometime in 1885, and in the following year Merck adopted the same policy.

It would be useful to learn whether Parke, Davis's cocaine had already gained in quality by the time Freud was asked to endorse it. What we do know is that two Parke brochures, issued later in 1885, aggressively promoted a variety of related items, including not only cocaine per se and an apparatus for subcutaneously injecting it but also a cocaine wine, cocaine cigarettes and cigars, and a derivative suitable for inhalation. These were the recreational products whose virtue, if only with respect to their cocaine content, would be certified in advance by Dr. Freud.

Why Freud? As Hirschmüller relates, an American spokesman would have been suspected of nativist chauvinism in favoring Parke, Davis over Merck. A European, therefore, was required—one who had already noted positive uses of cocaine and had conducted sober-looking studies of its effects. Freud alone apeared to meet those specifications. The one apparent risk in choosing him, then, was that the young physician in far-off Vienna might interpret his task too seriously and reach a finding that Merck's brand of cocaine was really the better of the two.

A published excerpt from Freud's report allows us to infer that he led Parke, Davis to expect findings in at least five areas. The two easiest trials would rate the brands' relative taste and euphoric potential. Third, as Freud had already set out to do with ecgonine, he would test each substance's potency by gauging its ability to produce spasms and paralysis in laboratory animals. Fourth, as with cocaine in his "Contribution," he would compare effects on human strength. And finally, with an implicit nod to Carl Koller, he would determine whether the drugs were equally suited to anesthetizing an eye. If it was ever intended in earnest, that was a substantial agenda.

On April 25, 1885, Freud told his fiancée that he had just received some "good" cocaine. We can infer, then, that the trials for taste and euphoria were performed at once and that he found Parke's drug congenial. He added that he had also placed an order for rabbits to be used in his experiments. We can only guess how long it took for the animals to arrive. But on April 27, having spent just two days with the new cocaine, Freud relayed to Martha the news that Parke's cocaine was fully the equal of Merck's in all respects—one of which, presumably, was its toxicity to small animals.

Freud supplied no information about his means of reaching that omnibus judgment; the whole narrative occupied a single sentence. It is impossible to believe that he had already received the animals, subjected them to the same procedures that he hadn't been able to conduct alone in the case of ecgonine, run and analyzed the dynamometer tests, and satisfied himself that Parke's substance anesthetized the eye in just the way that Merck's did. What he did say was that the outcome pleased him, because now he could be "all the more certain to receive the 70 florins."

Freud's approval of the American cocaine was put to use in a way that proved both controversial and mysterious. The *Wiener Medizinische Presse* of August 9, 1885, contained an article titled "On the Different Cocaine Preparations and Their Effect." The article featured an insert that was explicitly credited to Freud; it was reproduced from his positive report to Parke. Ostensibly, however, the article itself had been written by someone else.

That article, published in a respectable medical weekly, makes a shocking impression even today. It is transparently a piece of advertising for Parke, Davis and a correspondingly mean assault on Merck. In this purportedly objective paper, the word "Parke" appears thirteen times. Parke's drug is alleged to be purer, more soluble, more stable, more pleasant in odor and color, and less expensive than Merck's or than that of another rival, the Dresden firm Gehe & Co. Clearly, Merck is the real target. Merck cocaine, the author declares, is so unreliable that production has had to be suspended, and thus the product is not even to be found for sale.

Actually, the potency of American cocaine had been so low and variable in 1884 that one manufacturer, Squibb, did suspend production, with a public apology, until the raw cocaine supply improved in

1885. Parke, Davis, in contrast, had upgraded its product without interrupting its sales effort. As for Merck, its cocaine was already good enough in 1884 to vouchsafe Koller's discovery and its many ensuing spinoffs, and it had found no reason to cease manufacture or make excuses.[25] The *Wiener Medizinische Presse* article appeared particularly malicious in falsely alleging that Merck cocaine could no longer be acquired at all.

Understandably, Emanuel Merck didn't hesitate to protest this assault on his company in the guise of an independent report. In an open letter published in a subsequent number of the same journal, he debunked all of the article's misstatements about Merck cocaine and deplored the editors' prostitution of their pages to an obviously commercial appeal.[26] But the author of the offending article, a certain "Gutt." whose apparently abbreviated name appeared at the end, offered no rebuttal. His job of Merck bashing had been done.

Who was "Gutt."? That word could have designated, among others, either the Viennese editor Herman Guttmacher, as Robert Byck assumed in 1974, or—Albrecht Hirschmüller's preference—Hans Gutt, a local physician and author. But both attributions are fragile. Herman Guttmacher edited a competing magazine, the *Wiener Klinische Wochenschrift*. Why would he favor his rival publication with an article, and why would his name be abbreviated there? As for Hans Gutt, no period was called for at the end of his name. Furthermore, neither Gutt nor Guttmacher, so far as is known, took any interest in cocaine, much less in recommending one of its brands over another. Only one person in Vienna had a stake in such differential judgment—the same Dr. Freud whose high opinion of Parke, Davis's product is reproduced in the article's insert, leaving a perhaps calculated impression that "Gutt." was someone other than himself.*

There are weighty reasons for concluding that "Gutt." was indeed Freud. The author appears thoroughly familiar with "On Coca," whose structure he recapitulates, whose judgments he entirely seconds, and

---

* The word "Gutt.," if coined by Freud, may have hinted at a *Gutachter*, or the provider of an expert opinion. Freud's report to Parke, Davis was precisely a *Gutachten*, and that is the term he used in describing his assignment to Martha Bernays.

whose final sentence about future anesthetic applications he quotes and deems prophetic. He also cites Freud's "mathematically" exact findings, published elsewhere, about cocaine's enhancement of muscular strength. Who besides Freud could have found exactitude in his scatterbrained "Contribution"?

In addition, "Gutt." handsomely ranks Freud, "the rediscoverer of the coca plant," with Drs. Königstein and Koller as having produced "brilliant results" with cocaine. (No examples of Freud's corroborated scientific or therapeutic achievements with cocaine were supplied, because none existed.) The author even states, only half truthfully, that Koller's and Königstein's researches were undertaken at Freud's urging (*auf Veranlassung Dr. Freuds*). Even apart from the attributed insert, Freud gets mentioned seven times to the far more famous Koller's two. Thus "Gutt.'s" article is a broadside not only for Parke, Davis's cocaine but for the authoritative Dr. Freud as well.

Both Byck and Hirschmüller acknowledged that Freud's authorship of the entire venal article had once been accepted by scholars—an assumption that looks more credible than ever now that we can read in a derestricted *Brautbrief* that Freud had agreed to "publicize" his Parke-friendly judgments. The article reads like a literal-minded fulfillment of that charge. So far as Byck and Hirschmüller were concerned, though, the case was closed; one of them put forward his "Gutt," the other his "Guttmacher," with dialogue-stopping adamancy. Apparently it was inconceivable to those authors that the ever ethical Freud had stooped to trickery and self-promotion in this instance. But we have seen, earlier in this chapter, that he had already perpetrated several comparable deceptions in the preceding year.

Whatever the truth about "Gutt." may be, "On the Different Cocaine Preparations and Their Effect" conveyed its denigration of Freud's former benefactor, the Merck company, in a way that maximized the illusion of objectivity while protecting Freud from exposure as a shill for Parke. The experimental results obtained by the quoted "Dr. Freud" were rendered in dry, neutral-sounding language, while the untraceable and unpunishable "Gutt.," a fervent admirer of that same Dr. Freud, nakedly assailed Merck's reputation.

All three of Freud's opportunities for physiological research—his ecgonine study, his tests of cocaine's effect on strength and reaction time, and his evaluation of Parke cocaine—exhibit the same pattern. Tasks of modest significance, bearing no relation to his scientific and medical training, were accepted in the absence of a fruitful project of his own. He was ill prepared to execute the relatively straightforward work, and he performed it sketchily, without feeling motivated to correct for his biases.

Quite the reverse, in fact. Some of Freud's stipulations, such as the exclusion of subjects who didn't already share his positive reaction to cocaine, were meant to ensure agreeable findings. His concern was not with pursuing an inquiry to its logical end but with simulating that effect while cutting as many corners as he could. And there is evidence to suggest, most deplorably, that he sold faked test results for the use of advertising copy and published, under an assumed name, a high estimation of his own knowledge and research. If so, we are dealing with a very different man from the one depicted in the standard biographies.

8

The Survivor

1. CASH AND SYMPATHY

When the bare facts of Freud's relations with Ernst Fleischl are set forth, it is tempting to regard Freud as a sociopath. Before Freud offered him cocaine, Fleischl, though continually suffering, was a brilliant scientist, polymath, and man of the world. Afterward, he gradually became what Freud called "a broken man" and "a mass of eccentricities,"[1] subject to insomnia, hallucinations, inability to eat, personality changes, and horrific wasting as he lapsed into invalidism and died in 1891. Freud bore a large measure of responsibility for that transformation, yet he refused to own up to it during Fleischl's lifetime. On the contrary, he represented his prescription of cocaine against Fleischl's morphine habit as having proved a signal success.

But the Freud of the 1880s was no sociopath. Rather, he was an insecure and ambitious young man who, having been steered into a profession for which he lacked aptitude or strong interest, was desperate to achieve distinction by any means that lay at hand. He probably felt that an admission of blame in the Fleischl case would have permanently disgraced him, leaving him with no medical livelihood, no academic prospects, and therefore no chance of settling down with Martha Bernays. He was far from unmoved by Fleischl's plight. With the sole, if huge, exception of his failure to address Fleischl's double addiction, he behaved with compassion toward his stricken friend.

In the year following Fleischl's introduction to cocaine, however, Freud's solicitude for him sat awkwardly with another, more self-interested, feeling: a desire to put some of the well-off Fleischl's money to his own urgent use. Fleischl had access to more funds than he would ever need, while Freud, scarcely able to afford the train fare to visit his fiancée, had little hope of putting aside enough to justify setting a wedding date. He had already been periodically "borrowing" from Fleischl. When he learned, in June 1885, that he had won a traveling fellowship to study with Jean-Martin Charcot, his financial anxiety became more acute. He wouldn't be able to stay in Paris for the full period if his meager fellowship weren't privately supplemented.

Freud can sound callous and conniving when telling Martha of his efforts to extract money (*pumpen*) from Fleischl. But we can also see that he felt sheepish about asking for handouts in the period of his friend's steep decline. He was borrowing from a doomed man—one whose ability to remain ambulatory, or even alive, he estimated in months.[2] And he knew that approaching the debilitated Fleischl for money would be a delicate matter. Fleischl was often attended by colleagues and others whose presence would forestall any such initiative. Furthermore, on a given day he might prove either too sedated or too hyper to be reachable. But there were times when the trial had to be made, and Freud kept looking for the right opportunity.

On March 4, 1885, he disclosed to Martha that new loans from Fleischl were on his mind: "I am contemplating a bit taking poor Fleischl, who has a lot of money now, at his word for a few months." The *Brautbriefe* show that this plan was successfully implemented, though not without setbacks. Seeing that Fleischl was rarely alone, Freud apparently put one request into a hand-delivered note, to which he got an encouraging reply. "I received the enclosed letter from Fleischl," he wrote Martha on March 12, "and then I went to him, and he slipped me the money secretly; there are always lots of people around."

But just three weeks later, Freud was angling for another loan, this time in vain:

I was with Fleischl today but couldn't get anything from him (*konnte aber nichts von ihm kriegen*), because Prince Liechtenstein, Chrobak, and Obersteiner were there, and then a French professor and his wife came also, and at last I left. The poor man—he hadn't slept for eighty-six hours, and he faints six times a day. He hasn't left his room for eleven weeks.[3]

Most interesting of all, however, is a letter of March 10, 1885, written less than a week after Freud told Martha of his intention to step up his borrowing. The relevant paragraph was reproduced in part by Ernst Freud in the selected *Letters*. According to that volume's translation:

I wrote to Fleischl yesterday, but did not insist on an answer because writing is so difficult for him. On Friday or Saturday, when I have come to the end of my money, I will go and see him. I wonder if he will lend me anything. . . . [4]

Although little about the Fleischl connection can be inferred from Ernst Freud's sampler of correspondence, here we do perceive a willingness to let the public know that in 1885 Freud had been hoping for at least one loan. But the concluding ellipsis arouses curiosity. Repairing to the *Brautbriefe*, we find the sentence that was omitted: "If [he does lend me the money], he may no longer be here when we need to think about paying it back" (*Wenn, so dürfte er nicht mehr da sein, zur Zeit, da wir an's Zahlen denken dürfen*).

In suppressing Freud's remark, his editor son was hewing to a tacit rule of Freudian discourse. Freud's comment about not needing to return money to a dead man was the kind of datum that couldn't be allowed to fall into the hands of anyone outside the trustworthy inner circle. The censored speculation had already been seen, of course, not only by Ernst Freud but also by his sister Anna and by Ernest Jones, Siegfried Bernfeld, and Kurt Eissler, none of whom ever publicly remarked on it.

Already in the 1950s, however, Jones had established a model for steering clear of the whole topic of unreimbursed loans. "Freud borrowed sums from [Fleischl] on several occasions," Jones wrote, "and when he left for Paris Fleischl told him to be sure to write if he was in need. He died before he could be repaid."[5] Actually, as Jones well knew, Fleischl died in October 1891, five and a half years past Freud's return from Paris and well after he had established a residence with Martha and acquired a prosperous clientele. But on the chance that the debt was never repaid, Jones thought it wise to imply an early exit of the creditor.

How shocking is it, really, that Freud made prudential calculations about Fleischl's disappearance? Who, in his situation, could have prevented such thoughts from crossing his mind? If there is a scandal here, it resides not in Freud's blunt observation to Martha but in the cravenness of his followers and heirs, who seem to have feared that the psychoanalytic edifice might topple if the leader were ever to appear self-serving.

If Freudians weren't so spooked by Freud's responsibility for Fleischl's woes, they could find much to admire in his ongoing concern for his friend. The *Brautbriefe* show, for example, that in the summer of 1885, when Freud was looking forward to several months of personal research on polyneuritis, he was nevertheless willing, if requested, to drop everything and spend the entire period tending to Fleischl at the latter's summer home in St. Gilgen, near Salzburg.[6] Freud would have been paid by the Fleischl family, and that was a factor in his deliberations. "I would get some money out if it," he reflected, "but the main motive would be that without losing anything [i.e., income], I can do some good for such a beloved and unfortunate friend."[7]

On the other side of the ledger, though, was Freud's awareness that he was temperamentally unsuited to nursing a patient whose convulsions, anxiety attacks, and other erratic behavior required around-the-clock attention. The job, he wrote, would be "frightfully difficult."[8] Yet he was ready to make the sacrifice—"to repay," he wrote, "some of the great deal that I have learned" from Fleischl. After much hesitation, however, Fleischl rendered the problem moot by choosing one of his brothers to be his summer caretaker.

The Fleischl affair presents severe challenges to Freud's legend, but the limitations that it demonstrates include neither avarice nor ingratitude nor indifference to the misery of a friend. Instead, the negative revelations are Freud's medical impetuousness and incompetence, his inability to think clearly when his reputation was imperiled, and his penchant for making false public statements about his accomplishments.

2. CODEPENDENT

No one, not even Fleischl's physician Josef Breuer, was better situated than Freud to study his drug use. At that time, we know, Breuer strongly disapproved of cocaine, and Fleischl may have been reticent with him about his new habit. But Freud was a fellow cocainist. The intimacy he had long sought with Fleischl was secured through their shared affection for the drug, producing what Freud proudly characterized to Martha as "a friendly confidentiality."[9]

Thanks to his many visits with Fleischl, some of them lasting from early evening until morning, and to his nearly nonstop *Brautbriefe*, Freud has left us a rich record of Fleischl's states during those fourteen months. The ruination wasn't linear, nor did mind and body fail at the same rate. Freud repeatedly alludes to an undiminished brilliance and even to fresh scientific projects on Fleischl's part (though nothing is heard of the latter after November 1884). Nevertheless, just how inspired the newly loquacious, excitable Fleischl was in actuality may be doubted— for his auditor, too, appears at times to have been in an altered condition.

One result was that when Freud heard Fleischl's wild monologues, which bounded without intermission from one recondite topic to another, he felt transported. As he told Martha on May 21, 1885, "I literally intoxicate myself with his company." That was shortly before Fleischl's worst crisis, in June; but even afterward Freud still relished "the magical attraction [*zauberischen Reiz*] of an intimate association with Fleischl, the mental stimulation."[10]

The letters in which Freud related the excitement he felt in Fleischl's company are of great significance for a grasp of the metamorphosis that was occurring in 1884–85, when Freud's bourgeois ambitions, centered upon Martha Bernays, clashed with the spirit of rebellious adventure that would eventuate in psychoanalysis. "Every time," he wrote on May 21, 1885, "I ask myself if I will ever in my life experience anything so shattering and exciting as these nights with Fleischl." Returning from another all-nighter on May 26, he wrote of "the intellectual elation, the clarification and stimulation of so many opinions." And he added, portentously, "This fairyland [*Feenreich*] of intellect and unhappiness does a great deal, of course, to alienate me [*mich . . . entfremden*] from my surroundings; I am less comfortable in the hospital than scarcely ever before."[11] In the Brücke school of science there was no room for a fairyland of any description. But Freud, we remember, saw cocaine as a magical substance; and now his friend, whose fearless mind encircled the globe and made Vienna and its sober professors appear hopelessly drab, was showing him the same magic that Mephistopheles dangles before Faust.

Freud had other motives for wanting to believe that Fleischl's intellect was still intact. He loved the man and shrank from the evidence that the old Fleischl was slipping away from him. And so long as he could keep admiring Fleischl's brilliance, he could postpone a full reckoning with the disastrous result of his own intervention. But there could be no mistaking the significance of Fleischl's direct avowals of anxiety and despair. Already by October 15, 1884, Martha was informed that his "psychical state" had worsened, and on November 8 he was said to be "miserable."

A no less obvious sign of Fleischl's dependency on both a stimulant, cocaine, and a soporific, morphine, was his shuttling between insomnia and somnolence. As early as May 25, 1884, three weeks after Fleischl had started using cocaine, Freud described him as sleeping all day and staying awake all night. On other occasions, when Freud would attend him until morning, bursts of random fluency would alternate with hours of unconsciousness.[12] No doctor, least of all one who fancied himself cocaine's ambassador to Europe, could have failed to link those phenomena with drug intoxication.

In his *Brautbriefe* of this period, however, Freud almost never mentions cocaine and Fleischl's ill health in the same connection. The reason cannot lie in any reluctance on Freud's part to tell Martha about cocaine. He was sending packets of it to her for the improvement of her health and mood while he continued to chronicle its wondrous effects on himself. On July 12, 1884, angered by having been refused permission for a hospital leave to visit Martha, he calmed himself with some cocaine that was borrowed from Fleischl.[13] On May 17, 1885, he relayed the news that a serving of cocaine had banished a migraine—though it had also left him unable to stop working or, later, to fall asleep. And on May 21, after spending another harrowing night with his erratic friend, he wrote that he was neither exhausted nor despondent, thanks to the bit of cocaine he had taken in the morning.

Freud vividly recounted Fleischl's bodily decay, his suffering, and his descent into petty vanity.[14] Yet between May 1884 and May 1885, the *Brautbriefe* indicate a total reluctance to ascribe those changes to the drug. So far, indeed, was Freud from facing the truth that on May 21, 1885, he boasted to Martha, "You can see how much I have changed the world with cocaine from the fact that Fleischl has already spent 1800 marks on cocaine. A good part of our fortune, isn't it?" And on May 30, just days before Fleischl's total collapse, Freud reported having *loaned* him half a gram of cocaine; he promised to send the same amount along to Martha when the loan was repaid.

The apogee of Freud's willful blindness, however, may have been reached several months earlier, on January 7, 1885. At that time he had embarked on a private medical trial in which he attempted to treat sufferers from sciatica and facial neuralgia by injecting them with cocaine. If those projects bear fruit, he fantasized, "money is just going to fly in to me." We are left in the dark regarding the number of his neuralgia patients and the particulars of their treatment. On January 6, though, Sigmund had told Martha that, while the work was going well, the cases were too few. A day later he was still hopeful; and now, significantly, the name of Fleischl was invoked:

> My object has a special name: it is called neuralgia, face-ache. [I wonder] whether I will succeed in curing it. . . . I am very excited about it, because if it succeeds, the attention necessary for our life [together] will be assured for some time. We will have all we wish for, and perhaps even Fleischl can be helped.

Perhaps even Fleischl can be helped. Some scholars believe that this plan was actually executed and that Fleischl's precipitous decline in 1885 was a direct consequence of subcutaneous cocaine administered by Freud.[15] But that is unfair; Fleischl had already switched, on his own, from oral to hypodermic cocaine ingestion. The real shocker is that in January 1885, having had every opportunity to note the depredations of a severe cocaine habit, Freud was so illogical that he contemplated assisting an already injecting cocainist by means of cocaine injections.

It is evident, in any case, that Fleischl became sicker and wilder in the first half of 1885, though still without explicit recognition by Freud of what the problem was. On March 10, 1885, Freud estimated that his friend wouldn't be alive much longer, and on March 16 he reported that Fleischl had been sleepless for the past fifty-two hours and was "slowly collapsing." How low would Fleischl have to sink before Freud acknowledged the role of cocaine in his plight?

When Freud finally did mention both morphine and cocaine, in a letter of May 21, after Fleischl had treated him to a night of disordered antics, it was in a therapeutic, not a diagnostic, context. Fleischl's dazzling conversation, wrote Freud, was "interrupted by states of the most complete exhaustion [but] sustained by morphine and cocaine." Thus Freud, far from blaming the two drugs for Fleischl's rambling, gave them credit for combating his fatigue.

A letter of June 5, 1885, reported new horrors but once again failed to address their cause:

> At 9:30 p.m. I went to Fleischl and found him in such a state—Brücke and Schenk were there—that I quickly got Breuer. Then of course I spent the night there, the most frightful night I have ever experienced, and I have been duly cast down by it.

By June 8, 1885, Fleischl was entering the worst of his known cocaine crises, featuring not just insomnia, anxiety, and uncontrolled volubility but also convulsions and hallucinations of insects crawling all over his skin. At that point, finally, Freud conceded that the source of distress was cocaine. Not cocaine per se, however, but excessive amounts of it: "He took frightful doses that have greatly harmed him." Freud distinguished between such rashness and Martha's own prudence with the cocaine he had recently mailed to her: "I am glad you liked the cocaine so much; you won't get habituated to it like him."

Ernst Freud deleted this entire passage from his published version of the letter without signaling the omission with an ellipsis.[16] Thus readers were deprived of an important insight. Already by 1885 Freud had come to believe that addicts have no one to blame but themselves. As he primly observed to Martha, "How terrible to be a nervous person! I could not forgive anyone for it; it is the beginning of psychic devaluation; all the gifts of body and mind are made worthless by that state. Well, we are not and do not want to become like that."[17]

In mid-June an important turning point was reached. Mortified by Fleischl's worsening helplessness, Breuer now directed his patient to give up cocaine altogether, and he enlisted a small team of physician friends to conduct an around-the-clock vigil while Fleischl endured the torments of withdrawal. A letter of Freud's on June 14 shows him taking a turn at Fleischl's bedside:

> Then I spent the night with Fleischl. I think I have not yet told you that by continuing to use very great quantities of cocaine, he has finally contracted a kind of delirium tremens just like an alcohol delirium. But that has been overcome now; he takes no more cocaine, but is very miserable and has a series of attacks of cramps every night. It was like that tonight, too. He spent the rest of it tolerably well, but I fell asleep then, until I woke up at 6:30 in the morning and went out to Döbling to teach.

We wonder at this point whether Fleischl was able to complete the cocaine withdrawal, and we are also curious to know how Freud acted as he witnessed his friend struggling to be rid of the very substance that he himself had thrust upon him. A letter of June 26 bears on both matters:

> Since his pains have become intolerable, Fleischl has been suffering at night from attacks of fainting with convulsions, during which he should not be left alone. On top of that he is sleepless or sleeps very irregularly; on the whole, he is immoderate in everything, from work, eating and not eating, to the taking of medicines, the division of the day, etc. A host of eccentricities that have always been peculiar to him are developing themselves ever more uninhibitedly now.

Since I gave him cocaine, he has been able to suppress the spells of unconsciousness and to better control himself, but he took it in such enormous quantities (1800 marks for cocaine in three months, about a gram a day), that in the end he suffered from chronic poisoning, could not sleep at all, and finally, over a number of consecutive nights, had delirium tremens, just as alcoholics get.

The worst outbreak was during the evening when I came there by chance, got Breuer, and then spent the night with him. Since then, Breuer has maintained a certain power over him, and has extracted his promise to forgo cocaine; and since then his behavior really is more human. He is only weaker, sleeps badly and irregularly, and has his attacks every night. During the nights when he did not sleep, Breuer and Exner sat up with him in turn.

In contrast to the quick and easy morphine withdrawal that Freud thought he had effectuated eleven months earlier, Fleischl was now undergoing a traditional, closely supervised regimen of detoxification. But Freud remained as confused as ever. In the passage just quoted, he congratulates himself for having *helped* Fleischl by means of cocaine, supposedly enabling him "to better control himself" in managing symptoms that are laid entirely at the door of morphine.

3. THE AFTERMATH

Several further impressions of Fleischl can be gleaned from *Brautbriefe* written after the tension-filled events of June 1885. Two encounters are especially memorable. On July 31 the St. Gilgen–bound Fleischl took poignant leave of Freud, who told Martha about it on the next day:

Yesterday I said goodbye to Fleischl. I had to go before long because I had a migraine; he wanted to keep me longer. . . . We agreed to write to each other, to St. Gilgen and then to Vienna, and the repeated "Please write if you need something" cannot be misunderstood. I think, will I ever see him again? He and Schönberg and another friend, Koller (of the cocaine), have many claims on my sad thoughts.[18]

Fleischl would be away for only a month. But Freud himself would be departing for Wandsbek and Paris at the end of August, just before Fleischl's scheduled return, and Freud wouldn't be back in Vienna until the following spring. Fleischl might well have died by then. In fact, however, he held on for six more excruciating years.

When Freud returned from Paris in early April 1886, he sought out Fleischl in the Physiological Institute. The reunion was at once warm and appalling. During the eight months of separation Fleischl had wasted badly:

In the room I see two backs. The broad one belongs to Exner; the other is narrow, and the thin legs around which the trousers flap, the head with the wild hair—that is Fleischl. Great reunion. Fleischl looks miserable, more like a corpse. He has some reason for going downstairs, probably to inject himself, and I promise to follow him shortly.[19]

During Freud's stay in Paris, Fleischl had neglected to respond to a plea for yet another loan. Now he placed the blame on his sufferings at the time. "I have to tell you," Freud wrote his betrothed,

that Fleischl has apologized repeatedly about the money he didn't send. He says that of course he simply forgot about it, as he does everything now, and he is putting himself at my disposal immediately. Of course I have refused. He looks miserable, is said to hallucinate constantly, and it will probably be impossible to let him remain in society much longer.[20]

Almost all of the remaining references to Fleischl in the *Brautbriefe* concern Freud's visits to his apartment in May 1886. They closely resembled the encounters of the previous spring and summer, when Freud would typically pass a whole night tending to his friend with alternating horror at his agony and wonderment at his still lively intellect. "I go to Fleischl quite often," wrote Freud on May 5, "and I still find him mentally very strong." "Despite all the cracks," he declared three days later, "mentally he is still a giant." But Fleischl was also sleepless and prey to such severe anxiety attacks that Freud had to comfort him until as late as 7 a.m.

After May 30, 1886, Fleischl disappears from the extant *Braut-briefe*, which themselves declined in frequency as Sigmund and Martha's September wedding approached. The last pertinent entry I have seen reads as follows:

> Yesterday during the night I was with Fleischl. Of course I helped to bring him through one of his anxiety attacks. For the rest, though, he was very nice, and he told me heaps of stories about [the Swiss author] Gottfried Keller, with whom he is great friends.[21]

Thus the documented portion of the friendship ends in much the same way as it began, with, on Freud's side, a mixture of sorrow over Fleischl's state and deference to his worldly knowledge and connections. Even today, reading these lines, we ourselves must marvel along with Freud at the mental vitality, all but disembodied, that persisted in Fleischl after so much attrition.

From this date until Fleischl's death in 1891, information about his health and state of mind is sparse. No credence can be given to Freud's self-serving remark about Fleischl to Josef Meller in 1934: "After a surprisingly easy morphia withdrawal he became a cocainist instead of a morphinist, developed bad psychic disturbances, and we were all happy when later on he returned to the earlier and milder poison."[22] We can be sure, though, that Fleischl's trajectory was downward. The large circle of people, male and female, who had once reciprocated his cordial interest in them must also have dwindled. Josef Breuer, in a letter written shortly after Fleischl's death, referred to "this wretched crumbling of such a brilliant character." And the same letter, glancing back to relatively happier times, mentioned "the frightful distance between the previous and the present Ernst."[23]

Breuer's letter introduced another tantalizing complication. "Apart from his pains," he mused, "the only times when Ernst wasn't deeply unhappy were when, befuddled and half daffy from chloral, he fell into a complete loss of judgment about everything and himself."[24] The reference here was to the sedative chloral hydrate, which was then being widely prescribed without much regard for its dangers. Both Breuer and Freud administered it liberally to patients complaining of nervousness or insomnia. Fleischl may have developed such a tolerance for morphine that he switched from morphine to chloral without losing his dependency on cocaine, which is more addictive than either of those drugs.

Fleischl's long ordeal did leave Freud feeling sheepish about having steered his friend toward cocaine, and he was finally able to say so almost directly in *The Interpretation of Dreams*: "I had been the first to recommend the use of cocaine, in 1885, and this recommendation had brought serious reproaches down on me. The misuse of that drug had hastened the death of a dear friend of mine."* Even here, we observe, Freud dodges responsibility for having actively thrust the cocaine cure upon Fleischl. The reader infers that Fleischl had acted on his own, straying into misuse of the drug instead of employing it wisely as recommended by Freud.

Many years later, Freud would disclose to Marie Bonaparte that only once in his life had he kissed a woman's hand—that of Fleischl's mother as she stood beside his deathbed.[25] We can surmise that behind his formal gesture of condolence lay considerable anguish and remorse. It is safe to say, nonetheless, that Fleischl's importance to Freud in subsequent years didn't come down to a straightforward matter of guilt and atonement.

Consider the following eloquent fact. When pictures were taken of Freud's consulting room in 1938, the cluttered office was seen to contain a photograph positioned above the famous couch: a portrait of the handsome Fleischl in his prime. It is unimaginable that the combative, perennially self-justifying Freud would have kept that image staring out at him for decades if its principal meaning to him were accusatory. With the healing of time, he must have settled into thinking of Fleischl with unalloyed affection and gratitude.

---

* SE, 4:111. Freud's dating of "On Coca" here was a year late. It has been suggested that he may have been thinking of the time when he began advocating subcutaneous injection of cocaine—a more intimate link to the outcome of the Fleischl case.

9

Exit, Pursued

1. THE FIRST ALARM

In July 1885 Freud caught a hint of trouble that, two years later, would bring his cocaine advocacy to a humbling end, causing him to regret it for the rest of his life. In that month he learned of an article, just published in a journal for neurologists, disputing his counsel that cocaine injections be utilized for morphine withdrawal.[1] The author, Albrecht Erlenmeyer, wasn't just a physician holding a contrary opinion. He was the director of an institution near Koblenz dedicated to treating nervous disorders and to breaking addictions, with particular emphasis on morphine, and he was already known as the leading expert on the topic.

Unlike Freud, who had observed one case whose catastrophic outcome he continued to hide, Erlenmeyer could draw on more than a decade's-worth of pertinent experience. Through trial and error he had arrived at what he considered to be the safest and most humane approach to morphine withdrawal. It was a six- to twelve-day tapering of morphine administration under supervised conditions that minimized the agonies of deprivation while also guarding against backsliding. The book that he published on the topic in 1887, *Morphine Addiction and Its Treatment*, became a standard text, running through several editions and translations. It was recently reprinted in abridged form as a medical classic.[2]

Erlenmeyer's 1885 article did not address the problem of cocaine addiction. Instead, it confined itself to the inefficacy of using cocaine to combat morphinism. Freud, the author lamented, had taken at face value the suspect American stories of that cure. Although the articles that Freud cited had largely stopped after 1880, he had ascribed the near silence to a likely professional consensus in favor of the treatment. It was far more likely, Erlenmeyer observed, that the testimonials vanished because the regimen itself had been found to be worthless.[3] He was puzzled that Dr. Freud could remark on the American hiatus with incurious complacency and then plunge heedlessly ahead.

Erlenmeyer next addressed himself to the anonymous Fleischl case as Freud had recounted it in "On Coca." Nothing in Freud's report struck his critic as supporting the claim that cocaine acts as an antagonist to morphine. Insofar as Freud's description was credible, it raised more questions than it answered. Among other anomalies, the patient's ongoing diarrhea and chills didn't tally with the assertion that he had been restored to a "normally functioning" (*leistungsfähig*) state.

Erlenmeyer also focused on a second cocaine regimen discussed in "On Coca." Freud had cited another doctor's reported case of a woman who was receiving occasional morphine shots to treat her migraine headaches. The treatment had worked, yet a few hours after each injection the patient would experience typical symptoms of morphine abstinence. Trying cocaine instead, she and her physician found it to be ineffective against migraine, but the cocaine did seem to ease the morphine withdrawal. From these facts Freud had inferred that the case showed cocaine to be adapted to weaning patients from morphine *addiction*—a state whose relevance to that case was nil, since the patient had felt no strong craving for morphine and had simply used it as an occasional headache remedy.[4]

Both in that example and in the Fleischl case, Erlenmeyer showed, cocaine had acted just like morphine itself. That is, it had temporarily quieted the ill effects of sudden morphine deprivation. As Erlenmeyer drily observed, this is what happens every time a morphinist shoots up with morphine. If it is nonsense, he wrote, to say on that basis that morphine is an antagonist to morphine, then it is equal nonsense to award the same role to cocaine. Freud had established nothing more than an incidental resemblance between two drugs.

Erlenmeyer's own approach to research was more methodical. As the head of a clinic seeking improved therapies, he himself had tried out Freud's suggestion, injecting cocaine beneath his patients' skin. Indeed, he had done so 236 times, all scrupulously recorded with regard to the number of injections employed for each given amount of cocaine, from .005g to .06g. On 232 of those occasions the patient had been a morphine addict. Erlenmeyer thus possessed extensive relevant data whose margin of error was minuscule and whose cumulative meaning was opposite to what Freud had claimed.

The physiological effects of substantial cocaine injections, Erlenmeyer found, were unpleasant: a racing pulse, constricted arteries, sweating, and a rise in blood pressure and temperature, with additional anxiety and dizziness occurring at the highest drug concentrations.[5] Euphoria was also noted, but it tended to last for only ten to fifteen minutes. Above all, the anticipated withdrawal from morphine simply didn't occur. Cocaine "has no effect on the restlessness and sleeplessness, nor in the least does it influence the lack of appetite and the diarrhea."[6]

Here, then, was a formidable challenge to Freud, posed by a major authority on drug withdrawal. It rested on a wide evidential base drawn from controlled and documented experience, and it had been published in a respected journal that was required reading for Freud's fellow neurologists. For the first time in his career, Freud's scientific and medical judgment was being harshly challenged in print. If Erlenmeyer's critique couldn't be refuted, Freud was now obliged by medical ethics to recant his wild advice to fellow doctors. How did he in fact respond?

On July 9, 1885, writing to his fiancée just a month after Fleischl's worst crisis, Freud had this to say about the new turn of events:

> Dr. Erlenmeyer, the editor of a neurological journal, has published in
> it a long article with a single purpose: to ridicule me for my recom-
> mendation to use cocaine for morphine addiction. It is badly done,

however—only distortions, stupid objections, and, lastly, badly organized observations to refute the argument. Of course I will not reply. It has the advantage, though, that people are learning it was I who recommended cocaine for morphinism. They could never have gathered that from the works that confirm my position—works in which my name isn't mentioned. So one can always be grateful to one's enemies.

Ernest Jones, who must have perceived something here that didn't comport with his depiction of the imperturbable Freud, took care to disguise this letter's defensive petulance. Pretending to reproduce the entirety of "Freud's comment," Jones omitted the sentences showing that Erlenmeyer had wounded Freud's pride.[7] And since he offered no hint regarding the content of Erlenmeyer's critique, readers were left to assume that the article had been insubstantial and that the unruffled, forbearing Freud had found it amusing and even flattering.

2. THE TROUBLE MOUNTS

With the encouragement of both Carl Koller's discovery and Freud's promotional essays, some physicians had begun to regard cocaine as a panacea. As Steven B. Karch observes, the drug was touted as "the cure for almost every conceivable disorder, from prostate enlargement to nymphomania, asthma, sea sickness, hemorrhoids, and hay fever."[8] The choice of nymphomania was especially ironic; even the sexually wary Freud had remarked on cocaine's ability to heighten desire and reduce inhibition, and he had jocularly warned Martha to watch out for the consequences in his own case. It was probably the eroticizing property of cocaine that principally drove the public's shift of interest from strictly medical applications to thrill seeking.

Recreational cocaine's potential for harm would remain underappreciated until the turn of the century. By then, however, artists, intellectuals, and other members of the lay public, having been introduced to the drug by the cocaine snuff that companies like Parke, Davis were then marketing as treatments for asthma and hay fever, would have discovered that pure snorted cocaine could hit the nerve centers sooner and harder than a swallowed solution. But already in 1885, the year of Erlenmeyer's paper and of Fleischl's psychotic collapse, complaints of grave harm were being voiced.

At first, reports of addiction came less frequently than reports of mishaps in supervised medical procedures. It was hard to become addicted without frequent subcutaneous shots, which could be self-administered by physicians, dentists, and pharmacists but by few others. In contrast, hundreds of patients were getting either a small number of injections in a brief regimen of attempted morphine withdrawal, or they were receiving one-time topical anesthesia applied before surgery to eyes, throats, noses, ears, gums, genitals, or rectums. It was this latter type of application that first drew the world's notice to the most serious cocaine risks. An excessive single dose that was absorbed by mucous membranes, it was found, entered the bloodstream directly and could trigger a blackout, convulsions, or a fatal heart attack or stroke.

By the end of 1885 it was already clear that Erlenmeyer's charge against cocaine—that it didn't serve its intended purpose in morphine withdrawal—was the least of its liabilities. In addition to the surgical blunders, a few reported cases of addiction among health workers had sufficed to raise a general alarm about dependency. Cocaine, it was now being correctly inferred, was far more addictive than morphine and far more devastating in its effects. Many morphinists, including Fleischl prior to acquiring his cocaine habit, could integrate their morphine craving into fairly productive daily routines; but cocaine craving, once acquired, appeared to be all-consuming and all-destroying.

The example of cocaine addiction from the 1880s that is now most famous involved the boldest of American surgeons. This was William Halsted, who, inspired by Koller, proved the merit of using cocaine for nerve-block anesthesia.[9] Unfortunately, his trials with injection into various body sites addicted many of his assistants and himself. By 1886 he was shooting an awesome two grams per day, and soon his personality had altered almost as drastically as Fleischl's. Two attempted withdrawal cures in a mental hospital, rashly employing subcutaneous morphine to blunt abstinence symptoms, only succeeded in rendering Halsted, like Fleischl, a double addict.

Although Halsted's drug involvement was kept private during his lifetime, other cases of spectacular addiction among doctors did come to light in 1885 and soon thereafter. The tide of informed opinion was beginning to turn. In November 1885 an editorial in the *New York Medical Record* stated that the cocaine user, having acquired an insatiable craving, "becomes nervous, tremulous, sleepless, without appetite, and he is at last reduced to a condition of pitiable neurasthenia."[10] And in 1887 the same journal declared that "no medical technique with such a short history has claimed so many victims as cocaine."[11]

It didn't escape the notice of critics that, on both sides of the Atlantic, cocaine addiction among doctors was occurring most frequently as a result of self-administered treatment for morphinism. Understandably, then, resentment was sometimes aimed directly at Freud, identified as the chief proponent of that false remedy. A typical 1885 warning was that of Louis Lewin, the already eminent German pharmacologist whose later book *Phantastica* (1924) would become, worldwide, the most frequently consulted text on psychoactive drugs and plants. Criticizing Freud by name, Lewin denied that a morphinist could be motivated to replace his drug of choice with cocaine; he added that a likelier result would be enslavement to both drugs at once.[12]

Freud must already have been feeling uneasy, then, when Erlenmeyer returned to the attack on cocaine in a more adamant and sweeping, if succinct, essay in May 1886. In his 1885 article Erlenmeyer had presented evidence that cocaine doesn't work as a means of breaking the morphine habit. By the next year his own experience had taught him that this argument, though true, had missed the most urgent point that needed to be made. Cocaine, he now knew, was the most dangerous drug on earth.

This second essay quickly became famous and has remained so, because it featured the two most quoted sentences ever written about cocaine. Thanks to its ravages, wrote Erlenmeyer, cocaine addiction had become in short order "the third scourge of mankind," following addiction to alcohol and morphine.[13] And, enlisting a folk saying, he declared that the idea of curing morphinism through cocaine was a matter of "casting out the Devil with Beelzebub."[14]

During the previous ten weeks alone, Erlenmeyer recounted, his attention had been called to thirteen examples of cocaine addiction, drawn from his own practice and from cases to which he had been summoned as a consultant. The fateful cause was always subcutaneous injections that had been applied for the purpose of morphine withdrawal. The ineffectiveness of those shots for their intended purpose had led some doctors to administer higher and more frequent doses of cocaine, with catastrophic results. In such cases, wrote Erlenmeyer, the patient

> would like to free himself from cocaine voluntarily, but this is no longer possible. The absence of cocaine from the organism makes itself felt through a variety of unpleasant, bothersome feelings that leave him temporarily incompetent. He needs cocaine in order to work, he longs for cocaine—he is addicted to cocaine.[15]

Now that Erlenmeyer had become directly familiar with cocaine dependency, he could draw a clinically useful distinction between the symptoms of addiction and those of unmet craving during withdrawal. The cocaine addict who still has ready access to the drug, he wrote, is recognizable by weight loss, insomnia, a corpselike aspect, and various other disturbances. But during attempted abstinence he will also suffer cardiac and respiratory irregularities, fainting, and severe depression. If he does get cured through a slow, isolated regimen of weaning, he will remain profoundly demoralized. And even the most carefully supervised cure will be forestalled by immediate relapse when the drug is once again accessible.

Erlenmeyer couldn't have known that he was describing, among others, Ernst Fleischl, both in his addicted state and in the horrors of his attempted withdrawal in the summer of 1885. But Freud knew it, and he must have wondered how long it would be before Fleischl's publicly exposed condition would eventuate in his own total disgrace.

3. GIVING NO QUARTER

Fourteen months separated the publication dates of Erlenmeyer's 1886 article and Freud's final presentation on cocaine. The latter was one of eighteen pieces that were solicited in 1887 by the *Wiener Medizinische Wochenschrift*, whose editors wanted to bring physicians up to date on the latest developments in local anesthesia by means of cocaine.[16] Freud, now feeling cornered, ignored the assigned topic and used the occasion to parry charges against cocaine; he alone discussed morphine withdrawal and cocaine addiction.

In almost all discussions of Erlenmeyer's second essay, his sentence about "the third scourge of mankind" is said to have blamed Freud in person as the bringer of a universal plague. According to the received story, Erlenmeyer threw down the gauntlet to Freud, leaving the latter with no recourse but to defend himself in print. Hence Freud's last public statement on cocaine is regarded as a justified rebuttal to the most damning accusation that would ever be launched against the future psychoanalyst. But Freud wasn't mentioned in this second article; nor did Erlenmeyer allude to him in any way.

Freud's 1887 article was titled "Remarks on Cocaine Addiction and Fear of Cocaine, with Reference to a Lecture by W. A. Hammond."[17] The first half of that title sounded a war cry. Readers who knew Erlenmeyer's 1886 essay "On Cocaine Addiction: Preliminary Communication" were left in no perplexity about Freud's hostile allusion to it. In German, Erlenmeyer's title had been "*Über Cocainsucht: Vorläufige Mitteilung.*" Freud's contained the phrase *über Cocaïnsucht und Cocaïnfurcht.* "Fear of cocaine," Erlenmeyer's fear, was awarded equal syntactic weight with "addiction to cocaine," as if the two were of comparable importance.

No previous title of a work by Freud had contained a literary flourish of any kind, much less a satirical barb. Even when drawing on his own experience, he had represented himself as a neutral vehicle of knowledge. Now, though, readers were being introduced to his mordant side. Here was a preview of Freud the patronizing attacker, a man who would appropriate all objectivity to himself while blaming disagreement on his opponents' defective state of mind.

Prior to July 1887 Freud had reiterated and expanded his claims for cocaine without making the slightest concession to dissenters, whom he invariably brushed aside as misinformed. His "Remarks" now began in the same uncompromising, self-vaunting spirit:

> Karl Koller's brilliant application of the anesthetizing property of cocaine to the healing of the ill and to the advancement of the art of medicine obscured for a while the fact that the new medication has also laid claim to a notable role in the treatment of internal and nervous disorders. Later, however, *one* of these uses of cocaine, which I may attribute to my work "On Coca," . . . came to the general attention of physicians. I refer to the usefulness of cocaine for combating morphine craving and the alarming withdrawal symptoms that crop up during the abstinence cure. I had drawn attention to this property of cocaine as noted in American reports (in the *Detroit Therapeutic Gazette*), and at the same time I reported the surprisingly favorable course of the Continent's first morphine withdrawal by means of cocaine.[18]

Freud's feet, we gather from this opening, were still planted where he had set them in 1884. He was as proud as ever to have found his inspiration in the pages of the *Therapeutic Gazette*. And despite the two-plus years that had now elapsed since he witnessed Fleischl's delirium tremens under cocaine, he declared once again that his treatment of May 1884 had been a triumph.

Not everyone, Freud knew, had as yet lost faith in cocaine treatments. Without asking himself whether his fellow holdouts ought to admit that they too had erred, Freud saw an opportunity to summon them to his aid as critics of Erlenmeyer's judgment. Perhaps he could make Erlenmeyer, rather than himself, look like the reckless party:

> There now ensued a very energetic contrary argument by Erlenmeyer (in his *Centralblatt*, 1885), who, on the basis of a large number of imposing tests, denied cocaine any utility in morphine cures and represented it as a dangerous substance, owing to its effect on vascular innervation. Nevertheless, Erlenmeyer's findings rested on a clumsy

experimental error, which was immediately exposed by Obersteiner, Smidt and Rank, et al. Instead of administering the drug according to my recommended dose (several decigrams) *per os* [by mouth], Erlenmeyer had given minimal amounts in subcutaneous injections and thus had gotten a transient toxic effect from doses that were ineffective over the long term. The authors who refuted him had, for their part, fully confirmed my original statements.[19]

This is the most impudent paragraph Freud had published to date on any topic. To be sure, it displays a debater's subtle cunning: Freud chooses to rebut just the first of Erlenmeyer's two pertinent articles, the one in which only transient toxicity was addressed. By complaining that Erlenmeyer has administered *too little* cocaine, he obscures the fact that Erlenmeyer's second and more important article dealt with the risk of overdoses. This tactic allows Freud, some paragraphs later, to warn, hypocritically, against more permanent harm, as if he had ascertained that problem on his own.

What causes astonishment, however, is Freud's avowal that he has never advised doctors to administer cocaine by any means other than orally. Hadn't he advocated "entirely harmless" cocaine injections in his February 1885 supplement to "On Coca," and hadn't he, shortly thereafter, told two audiences and two sets of readers that "nothing is to be feared from the accumulation of [injected] doses"? Freud would seek to obscure his record on many later occasions, but for sheer misrepresentation of his own published statements, and for gambling on his readers' inability to remember what he had written, the anti-Erlenmeyer passage has no peer. He was disavowing no fewer than five emphatic assertions, oral and published, that he had made within a single recent year.

Confronted with Freud's 1887 reversal of what he had said in 1885, and noting that the 1885 article was excluded from all of his subsequent résumés, Freud boosters have opted to believe that he "repressed" any memory of having written the earlier paper. Siegfried Bernfeld labeled the omission a parapraxis, or Freudian slip.[20] So powerful and enduring was this defense mechanism, according to Bernfeld, that it compelled Freud, again without his conscious awareness, to discard or burn all offprints of the two articles. And Ernest Jones seconded "the alert Bernfeld" in all respects, from the "unconsciously determined" turnabout on the wisdom of injections to the "unconscious repression" that caused copies of the 1885 paper to be absent from Freud's library and bibliography.*

But Freud didn't forget that he had championed subcutaneous injection of cocaine. He deliberately asserted the opposite, that he had *objected* to the practice in one or more publications that had been shockingly ignored by Erlenmeyer. The reason he didn't cite those publications was that they didn't exist, and the reason he didn't cite his 1885 lecture/article was that it did exist and was incriminating.

Freud's 1887 apologia invoked "Obersteiner, Smidt and Rank, et al." to back up his chastisement of Erlenmeyer for having stupidly employed cocaine in subcutaneous doses that were at once insufficient and toxic. But Freud was enlisting authors who had simply adopted his own claims in "On Coca." Nor had any of them criticized Erlenmeyer; indeed, Smidt and Rank had praised him.[21] By 1886, moreover, Obersteiner, as Freud knew from close personal acquaintance, had become much warier of therapeutic cocaine.[22] Thus Freud's marshaling of "anti-Erlenmeyer" authorities was an exercise in cynical deception.

4. BLAMING THE PATIENT

Freud's job of damage control in his "Remarks" required that he take some cognizance of Fleischl-like horror stories—which were now too numerous and convergent to be written off—while nevertheless ducking responsibility for his advocacy of the misguided protocol that had produced them. As we have seen, one part of his strategy was simply to deny that he had ever recommended cocaine injections. Another part was more nuanced. Freud would repeat Erlenmeyer's observation about the increasing incidence of double addiction from subcutaneous treatments, but, omitting any mention of the article in which Erlenmeyer

---

* J, 1:96. Even the usually careful Hirschmüller endorses this strained judgment, citing Bernfeld's "impressive study" without contemplating alternative hypotheses (SK, p. 24).

had deplored that phenomenon, he would present it as his own independent finding.

In doing so, Freud once again strove to absolve cocaine of bearing a special degree of risk:

> The value of cocaine for morphinists got lost, however, for other reasons [than any problem with cocaine itself]. The sick people themselves began to get hold of the drug and to subject it to the same abuse to which they were accustomed with morphine. Cocaine was supposed to serve them as a substitute for morphine, but it must have proven a quite insufficient substitute, for most morphinists quickly arrived at an enormous dosage of 1g pro die in subcutaneous injection. It turned out that cocaine used in that way is a much more dangerous enemy of health than morphine. Instead of a slow wasting, we get rapid physical and moral deterioration, hallucinatory states of agitation as in alcohol delirium, a chronic persecution mania, which according to our experiences is characterized by the hallucination of small animals in the skin, and cocaine craving instead of morphine craving—these were the sad results of trying to cast out the Devil with Beelzebub.*

Here Freud is largely paraphrasing Erlenmeyer's second paper and even appropriating its "Beelzebub" phrase, as if he had just thought of it himself. In all of the traits that he specifies here, however, he is also accurately describing Fleischl. The detail that stands out in this regard is the sample addict's intake of one gram of cocaine per day—the very figure that Freud, in June 1885, had mentioned to his fiancée as Fleischl's own average consumption in recent months. What would Freud's readers have concluded about him, we may wonder, if they had learned that his model for the cocaine-crazed degenerate was the very man about whom, three paragraphs earlier in this essay, he boasted "the

---

* CP, p. 172; SK, p. 125. In this passage the phrase "according to our experiences" (*nach unseren Ehrfahrungen*) includes a plural pronoun but is clearly meant to refer to Freud's own clinical encounters with patients who have come to him after hooking themselves on cocaine. But so far as we know at present, Freud had no such record to draw upon, apart from watching Fleischl's unraveling without doing anything about it.

surprisingly favorable course of the Continent's first morphine withdrawal by means of cocaine"?

Erlenmeyer, Freud wrote, blamed cocaine itself for bad results,
whereas it was chiefly out-of-control morphinists—people like Fleischl,
he could have said—who were giving cocaine an undeserved bad name:

> I cannot refrain from making an obvious observation that will strip
> away the horror of the so-called third scourge of the human race, as
> Erlenmeyer so pathetically calls cocaine. *All reports of cocaine addic-
> tion and of resulting deterioration refer to morphine addicts*, people
> who were already ruined by one demon and who, because of weak-
> ened willpower and a need for stimulation, would abuse, and actu-
> ally have abused, any stimulant offered to them. *In our experience
> [bei uns] cocaine has claimed no other, no victim of its own.**

What is "pathetic," we must wonder, about trying to alert readers to
a grave and growing menace to public health? Later in his essay, Freud
writes of "the so-called cocaine addiction" (*die sogenannte Cocainsucht*),
as if there were actually no such thing.[23] Moreover, he misrepresents
Erlenmeyer as having called cocaine, rather than cocaine addiction, "the
third scourge of mankind." Thus he depicts his adversary as a temper-
ance prude—and, of course, the home-team historians have loyally
followed suit.[24]

Freud's strategy was now to grant the existence of cocaine dependency but to restrict the phenomenon to morphinists. But there were
already a few known nonmorphinist cocaine addicts when Freud wrote
his essay. Even if none had yet been identified, furthermore, it would
still have been illogical and irresponsible on his part, when medical
cocaine was still fairly new and recreational use was in its infancy, to
assert the impossibility of such cases.

---

* CP, p. 173; SK, p. 126; emphasis as found. Taking Freud's cue, both Bernfeld and
Jones laid all blame for Fleischl's condition on Fleischl himself. Cocaine, Bernfeld
declared, "was an unreliable helper and Fleischl a weakling . . ." (Bernfeld 1953, p. 610).
The modern Freudians Jürgen vom Scheidt (1973) and Eberhard Haas (1983) have taken
the same line. In Haas's "lovely study" (Hirschmüller, SK, p. 31), the pain throbbing from
the stump of Fleischl's thumb is reconfigured as a psychosomatic "self-castration."

The desire to stand up for his favorite drug prompted Freud to insert into his "Remarks" still another cocaine testimonial, the last one he would ever write:

> I have manifold experience with the long-continued use of cocaine by persons who weren't morphinists, and I have taken the drug myself for months without perceiving or experiencing any particular condition similar to morphinism or any yearning for continued use of cocaine. On the contrary, there occurred, more frequently than I would have liked, an aversion to the drug, which gave cause for curtailing its use.[25]

As he had done before, here Freud asserted that cocaine is so disagreeable as to be self-limiting in its employment—a claim that is belied by his own fond encomiums to the "magical substance" in the *Brautbriefe*.

Freud had taken cocaine—orally, we presume—for years, not months as he maintained; and his discernment, particularly regarding cocaine itself, appears to have been weakened by the habit. In that sense he showed signs of psychological addiction to the drug. But he was not physically addicted. He ingested cocaine for specific ends—to cure a headache, to combat stage fright and a sense of inferiority, to feel more sexual—and then he apparently didn't take it for days at a time. Moreover, his occasional drinking of dilute cocaine, further weakened by metabolic breakdown, would not have turned him or anyone else into an addict. Thus his autobiographical example was beside the point.

The last five paragraphs of Freud's "Remarks" synopsized a talk by Dr. W. A. Hammond, "a well-known foreign authority." Hammond had been a young, reform-minded Surgeon-General of the United States during the Civil War (though he was court-martialed and dismissed). Afterward a professor of nervous and mental diseases, he believed cocaine was no more addictive than coffee or tea. Freud gladly cited that opinion without pointing out that it had been strenuously disputed by Hammond's colleagues in the New York Neurological Society.[26]

Freud's 1887 essay was written at a time when medical sentiment regarding cocaine was in transition from optimistic to monitory—that is, from Freud's previously stated judgments to Erlenmeyer's most recent ones. Such an awakening didn't call for a middling, difference-splitting response by physicians; the recent reports of harm required urgent concern and a fresh assessment of the drug's limitations. Freud's article, aiming at advantage rather than truth, mimed such a reconsideration while largely discouraging it.

In later years Freud found his article embarrassing, and he did what he could to bury it. Freudian disciples have accepted that tacit repudiation with relief; like Freud himself, they have been only too willing to write off a "mistake" along with the rest of the unfortunate "cocaine episode." I have dwelled on this concluding pronouncement on cocaine, however, in order to show that while it does contain errors of fact and judgment, there is nothing inadvertent, much less "unconscious," about it. It is actively evasive, malicious, and dishonest.

. . . .

PART THREE

BLIND SUBMISSION

. . . .

It is difficult for most people to suppose that a scientist who has had great experience in certain regions of neuropathology, and has given proof of much acumen, should have no qualification for being quoted as an authority on other problems; and respect for greatness, particularly for intellectual greatness, is certainly among the best characteristics of human nature. But it should yield to respect for the facts.

—Freud, Review of August Forel's *Hypnotism*, 1889*

---

* SE, 1:92–93.

· 10 ·

A French Connection

1. AT THE CROSSROADS

Among the turning points in Freud's life, none was more decisive for the founding of psychoanalysis than his receipt of a modest traveling fellowship from the Ministry of Education in June 1885. The grant would take him to Paris and its Salpêtrière hospital, where, from October 1885 through February 1886, he would submit himself to the reasoning and the personality of Jean-Martin Charcot, then the most famous neurologist in the world. "It was assuredly the experience with Charcot in Paris," wrote Ernest Jones, "that aroused Freud's interest in hysteria, then in psychopathology in general, and so paved the way for . . . [his] developing psychoanalysis."[1]

That was Freud's own opinion, too.[2] Indeed, though Charcot's reputation plummeted immediately after his death in 1893 and never fully recovered thereafter, Freud would always maintain that the Charcotian approach to hysteria had provided his own psychological system with a firm scientific underpinning. In the eyes of his followers, he was Charcot's rightful heir. And thus, with a considerable skewing of the Frenchman's actual position in nineteenth-century medicine, Charcot became saddled with the role—as the historian

Toby Gelfand puts it sardonically—of John the Baptist to Freud's Christ.*

Anticipating that a better-connected *Sekundararzt* (Assistant Physician) would get the travel grant, Freud had planned to resign his internship in the General Hospital in August 1885, spend the next month in Wandsbek with Martha Bernays, and then begin his private medical practice in Vienna with no higher goal in mind than to become wealthy enough to marry. The fellowship erased that agenda and sent his hopes soaring once again. As he wrote to Martha on June 20 with comic hyperbole but genuine delight,

> Oh, how wonderful it will be! I am coming with money and staying
> a long time and bringing something beautiful for you, and then I will
> go on to Paris and become a great scholar, and then come back to
> Vienna with a big, big halo, and then we'll get married soon after, and
> I will cure all the incurable nervous cases.[3]

It is unsettling to read such giddy prose. We already know how cornered Freud would be feeling two years thence, when he would have to wriggle out of his denounced cocaine advocacy through falsehoods and rhetorical ploys. That trap was already being set for him in July 1885 by Fleischl's horrendous collapse and Erlenmeyer's first polemic, with Freud himself named as the chief offender. As one scholar, contemplating the escape to Paris, observes, "It was a good time for him to get out of town."[4]

If so, however, Freud remained oblivious to his peril. The gathering storm, one portent of which he had already encountered in a restive lecture audience, left him unrepentant. In Paris and again in Berlin shortly thereafter, he would go on administering cocaine to others as a panacea.[5] And on occasion, straight into the spring of 1886, he would express unmixed gratification at being recognized as a drug authority.[6]

Freud had good reason to feel that his prospects were brightening

---

* Gelfand 1989, p. 293. Asti Hustvedt, for example, holds that Charcot deserves honor because "the brilliant founder of psychoanalysis" believed so (Hustvedt 2011, p. 7). According to Hustvedt, Charcot "did nothing less than pave the way for psychoanalysis" (p. 62). See also Robinson 1993, pp. 24–35; Micale 2008, p. 251; Makari 2008, p. 18.

in the summer of 1885. After extensive lobbying among the university's medical faculty, he knew that his application to be promoted to *Privat-dozent*, or unpaid lecturer, in Neuropathology was going to be approved. Here, then, was a second coup. "I have attracted broad attention because of the travel stipend and the simultaneous lectureship," Freud told Martha on July 1; "among my colleagues—the Jewish ones, that is—I am of course a kind of national hero." Fresh in Freud's mind was another "national hero," Carl Koller, who had won a duel with a bigot and been ostracized because of it. Freud, in contrast, saw a clear path ahead. His new academic title, his fellowship award, and his forthcoming association with the celebrated Charcot ought to provide just the edge of distinction he would need, upon his return, to attract a better class of patients and secure his and Martha's livelihood.

Freud's two victories were won in part by a display of obeisance to standards that he had already begun to resent. The regnant positivism of Germanic medical schools, including his own, left no room for subjective considerations. Reacting against the vague Romantic *Naturphilosophie* of an earlier generation, the Germans were dogmatically bent on reducing mind events to brain events, as if motives and emotional vicissitudes were of no account. Hence the emphasis on postmortem brain analysis—a fine means of sorting diseases but also a means of keeping disturbances of feeling at a distance. When German psychiatrists did take an interest in patients' minds, they concerned themselves almost exclusively with psychoses, which, though beyond a hope of cure, might prove correlatable with telltale changes in brain tissue.

Freud had known which parts of his record to emphasize in his two campaigns for advancement. When submitting his credentials for *Privatdozent* in January, he had omitted all of his cocaine papers except the relatively diffuse survey "On Coca." Highlighted instead were his histological publications, including studies of human brain anatomy that he had recently undertaken with the faculty position expressly in view.[7] And he had promised that, if appointed, he would lecture only about diseases of the nervous system, with particular attention to brain pathology. That was just what the medical professors, most notably Brücke, Nothnagel, and Meynert, needed to hear. But did it represent the actual state of Freud's interests in 1885?

The same question can be asked about the self-portrayal in his fellowship application. Extreme tact, if not duplicity, was called for in that instance. By the mideighties Jean-Martin Charcot had become a highly controversial figure in Viennese circles—one who, according to the majority judgment, had compiled a brilliant record of discovery but had then taken a fateful misstep. He had turned his attention from demonstrable ravages of the brain and nervous system to an illness of contested authenticity, hysteria. And, to the horror of positivists, he had made room for *ideas* as a factor in its causation.

Worst of all from the German standpoint, Charcot had chosen to study hysteria by means of hypnotism. That practice was still tainted by its association with the long-discredited pseudoscience of Mesmerism (or "animal magnetism"), the therapeutic fad that had swept across Europe before the French Revolution. Franz Anton Mesmer and his fellow "magnetizers" had employed rituals and hypnotic commands to "rebalance" their patients' internal stores of magnetic fluid in harmony with fancied polarities in the universe at large. More scandalously still, they had triggered and sometimes exploited orgasms in susceptible women. Temporarily squelched by devastating reports from two scientific commissions, the practice had flared up again in the early nineteenth century.[8] And the brash Charcot was now adapting latter-day Mesmerism to purposes of psychological experimentation.

Freud knew, then, that he wouldn't be sent to Paris in order to study hysteria and hypnotism under Charcot. Selecting his words carefully, he stressed his background in neuroanatomy and asked only for an opportunity to exploit "the wealth of material on nerve diseases provided by the Salpêtrière clinic."[9] Charcot was then counting hysteria among those diseases, but it went unmentioned in Freud's application. The fellowship committee was sure that the young aspirant, whose microscope studies had manifested an aversion to ungrounded guesswork, would be using the Salpêtrière's facilities only for postmortem researches into damaged brains.

There is every reason to believe, however, that Freud chose Paris because of Charcot's unorthodox concerns. Hypnotism already intrigued him. As early as 1880 he had expressed interest in, and may have attended, a much-discussed demonstration by a show-business magnetizer, the itinerant performer Carl Hansen, who made a specialty of hypnotizing and then humiliating troublemakers (or were they confederates?) who had denounced him as a fraud.[10] Josef Breuer, Freud's most trusted adviser, had been smitten by Hansen's demonstration and, as we will see, had employed hypnotism himself in a case that was extensively discussed with his protégé. It mattered, too, that one local adept of hypnotism, who in more carefree days had amused the intellectual elite by "putting to sleep" both people and animals, was none other than Freud's beloved Fleischl.

Moreover, hypnotism had other defenders in Vienna. Moriz Benedikt, a maverick neurologist and electrotherapist and an old friend of Charcot's, was an early champion of hypnotherapy for nervous conditions. In July 1885 he told Freud what to expect from working with the French master.[11] And still another practitioner was Heinrich Obersteiner, in whose Vienna clinic Freud briefly served not long before leaving for Wandsbek and Paris.[12] On June 23, 1885, Freud wrote to Martha that Obersteiner had been showing him "some very successful hypnotic experiments with a female attendant," and he added, "In Paris, you know, there is a great focus on hysteria, hypnotism, and the like."

Freud did expect to be conducting brain tissue analysis at the Salpêtrière; his fellowship application hadn't misrepresented his plans. His mood, however, was another matter. Fleischl and cocaine together had left him impatient with conventional ideas; he dreaded sinking into the tedious routine of a family doctor; and he was already attracted to the larger-than-life image of Charcot, the ruler of a medical empire and, reputedly, the most dominant personality in Europe.

2. "THE NAPOLEON OF THE *NÉVROSES*"

The son of a carriage maker, Charcot rose to wealth, international prestige, and power in medical, social, political, and artistic circles, until he became the most prominent self-made man of the early Third Republic. Medical discovery was his ticket to fame. He contributed fundamentally to the understanding of gout, arthritis, rheumatism, epilepsy, cerebral hemorrhage, muscular atrophies, aphasia, and other afflictions, while also advancing knowledge of the brain, spinal cord, and peripheral nerves. Early in his endeavors, moreover, he threw light on pulmonary and kidney diseases; he is also counted as a founder of geriatric medicine.

In recognition of such achievements, Charcot was appointed, in 1872, the sole Professor of Pathological Anatomy in the Paris Faculty of Medicine. In 1882 he received the world's first chair in diseases of the nervous system. And the culminating honor, election to France's national Academy of Sciences, was awarded in 1883, two years before Freud's visit. Nine volumes of Charcot's *Complete Works* (meant to reach fifteen, but halted after his death) were supplemented by another four volumes of clinical reports, case histories, and reflections.[13]

In every phase of his career, Charcot's aim was to shrink the number of disorders that had to be classified as *névroses*. It would be wrong (though it is often done) to translate that term as "neuroses," as if in contrast with the more disabling psychoses. Following the example of his hero, the psychiatric reformer Philippe Pinel, Charcot reserved *névroses* to designate those neurological disorders (of whatever severity) whose pathology hadn't yet been established, such as dystonia and Parkinson's disease.[14] He had in mind this sense, for example, when he characterized the *névroses* as "an incoherent group."[15] A given malady would cease to be a *névrose* when Charcot or someone else secured a definitive connection between its observable symptoms and the lesions that were causing them.[16]

Charcot's feats of disease analysis were achieved through what he called the "anatomo-clinical" approach, as contrasted with the German "anatomo-pathological" one. They were not diametrical opposites, since both methods made use of autopsy analysis. But whereas such microscopic study was all-important to the anatomo-pathologists, Charcot—following the precedent of the great René Laennec—also drew up symptomatic models based on extensive observation of living patients. With his meticulous compilations of symptoms, he could then reason in detail about the correlation between subsequently discovered lesions and the progressive features of each infirmity. In this manner, for instance, he was able to show that Parkinson's disease and multiple sclerosis are separate entities.

Charcot was aware that many patients suffer from more than one disorder and that therefore no individual can be safely assumed to personify a given syndrome. His aim was to cross-check his case histories until a single model of the disease in its purest form emerged. That model would then constitute the clinical side of the anatomo-clinical enterprise. The method wasn't foolproof, but its triumphs were many. They captivated the lay public as well as other physicians and aroused the pride of a chauvinistic government, which lionized Charcot alongside his friend Louis Pasteur.

Charcot's accomplishments were enabled and largely guided by the nature of the site where they occurred, the largest medical facility in the world. The Salpêtrière complex, consisting of some forty-five buildings in eastern Paris, had already undergone a number of transformations since its origin as a saltpeter (gunpowder) warehouse, safely remote from the urban center, in 1634. More a hospice than a hospital, it had once sheltered as many as 5,000 female apprentices, retirees, prisoners, cripples, and lunatics. In 1849 it had come under government authority and had been reconceived as a home exclusively for poor, aged, infirm, and mentally disabled women. When, in 1852, Charcot first accepted an internship there, the chief function of the dreary town-within-a-city was to keep those women off the streets of Paris. By the early 1860s its insane population included about 1,500 women, while some 3,000 others were housed in separate units. The latter group languished with various chronic illnesses while also cooking, cleaning, and gardening for what one observer poetically characterized as the Versailles of pain.[17]

Any other physician, after a few token years, would have wanted to be promoted out of that isolated, statically custodial facility. Instead, with steely aplomb, Charcot—the "senior physician" of the hospital from 1862 until 1893—turned "this vast emporium of human suffering," as he called it, into "a seat of theoretical and clinical instruction of uncontested utility."[18] At his death, the Salpêtrière's level of care was still less than exemplary, but it had long been the world's informal headquarters for neuropathology.

Charcot's forte was a unique combination of diligence, self-discipline, close observation, intellectual clarity, rational method, executive decisiveness, and sheer force of will, enabling him to control the research of some twenty physicians—among them the subsequently renowned Joseph Babinski, Pierre Marie, Georges Gilles de la Tourette, Alfred Binet, Paul Richer, Charles Richet, D.-M. Bourneville, Albert Pitres, and Fulgence Raymond. While Charcot lived, those talented doctors functioned as his eyes and ears in the wards of his hospital. They routinely submitted their draft papers to him for review before publication in one of the several journals that he founded and controlled. Members of the "School of the Salpêtrière" were expected to second his ideas; and if they did so, no obstacles lay in their path to academic and administrative advancement.

When Charcot's followers dubbed him "the Napoleon of the *névroses*," they weren't reaching for a strained analogy. Not only did he look like a stoutish Bonaparte; he cultivated the association, especially in his hand-in-coat photographic portraits, one of whose prints he would inscribe to Freud. And within the Salpêtrière he held absolute sway. When he put a question to his audiences or readers, he would have the answer ready and would deliver it with an air of finality.[19] Though he nominally welcomed dialogue, he was known to forestall disagreement with an unnerving stare.[20]

Under Charcot's direction the Salpêtrière, while remaining shabby and overcrowded, became an extraordinarily modern educational center, employing concerted multimedia effects to shape both medical and lay opinion. Charcot and his staff filled their publications with an unrelenting stream of papers embodying his outlook. They lavishly utilized the new medium of photography, electrically projecting slides to illustrate lecture themes and circulating other images that appeared more convincing than any argument.

At its chief's urging, the hospital added—along with its outpatient clinic—laboratories, consulting rooms, a photography center, a museum, and an auditorium where visitors from around the world could attend his lectures, which were two hours in length but never less than engrossing. And through it all, Charcot exercised the skills of a master diplomat, securing cordial relations with foreign doctors, state officials, journalists, and anyone else who might prove useful to him.

So cogent, pointed, and aptly illustrated were the more formal of Charcot's lectures—the ones he gave on Friday afternoons—that they could be published by assistants with little editing while he himself, wasting no time, forged ahead with his theoretical studies. Even his more spontaneous Tuesday morning talks—the famous *leçons du mardi*, initiated in 1882—were lucid enough to be readily transposed to print.

Such, then, was the sway of the great figure who had decided in the later 1870s to add one more jewel to his crown by doing for hysteria what he had already done for rheumatoid arthritis and multiple sclerosis: not to cure the disorder but to establish its typical signs and course and then to match that knowledge with whatever could be gleaned from autopsies. If he were to succeed, as he fully expected to do, hysteria might not be any more manageable than before, but it would have earned a place alongside the respectable, certifiably organic illnesses of humankind.

3. HYSTERIA SCIENTIZED

No ailment stands in greater need of critical understanding than hysteria. As early as the seventeenth century, the English physician Thomas Sydenham noted the only unifying feature in the hysterical grab bag. Hysteria, he said, was protean, taking on the aspect of more stable diseases. Indeed, it had a way of mimicking only those maladies of which the patient was previously aware. That meant, however, that its symptoms, taken all together, amounted to a suspect *embarras de richesses*. As the skeptical psychiatrist Charles Lasègue wryly observed, hysteria had been made into "the wastepaper basket of medicine."[21]

In theory, a hysteric could show any number of the following manifestations: hyperesthesia (excessive sensitivity), anesthesia (loss of sensation), or hemianesthesia (loss of sensation on one side of the body); contractures; catalepsy (the fixity of a muscle in a given position and state); locomotor impairment; lethargic apathy and its opposite, emotional storms; local paralyses; intense pain; palpitations; tics and tremors; constant coughing; hiccups; sobbing; severe headaches; sensations of choking or suffocating; stiffness; stigmatic hemorrhages and blistering; nosebleed; fainting; functional blindness in one or both eyes; abulia (weakness of will); inability to speak in one's native language, or at all; anorexia; nausea and vomiting; false pregnancy; diarrhea; constipation; prolonged sleep; excessive secretions of various kinds; and amnesic "absence" from normal self-awareness, including fugue states and the bizarre phenomenon of multiple personality.

A debate continues as to whether it ever made sense to posit a single medical phenomenon underlying such variability. Everyone grants by now that hysteria, if it exists at all, is not a disease on the neurological model of multiple sclerosis, much less on the germ- or virus-based model of tuberculosis or AIDS. The issue is whether it nevertheless qualifies as an authentic disorder—not just a mode of perverse behavior but a malfunction of the brain, producing certain kinds of consciously unwished-for symptoms.

In Charcot's time and for the two preceding centuries, the majority opinion among physicians was that hysteria is "the female malady" par excellence.[22] Theory on the topic was suffused with misogyny.* On some accounts, a hysterical penchant was native to female physiology and temperament. And most doctors also believed that resistance to women's "natural" role within the family made them sick. It is no accident, then, that feminist movements have regularly been characterized by their opponents as "hysterical," or that the grossly somaticizing forms of the disorder, already rare by the turn of the century, went into eclipse with the arrival of "the New Woman" after World War I.

We will see that Charcot was not above misogynistic prejudice. As a man of the Enlightenment, however, he thought of himself as having put all popular superstition behind him. The idea that hysteria is a gynecological condition was still being used to justify grotesque surgical interventions that he publicly deplored.[23] Yet the same commitment to skepticism left him reluctant to declare that the disorder was simply

---

* As Martha Noel Evans has pointed out, "The association of activity, mastery, and rationality with maleness transforms the investigation of hysteria into a mythic struggle with the mysteries of its female object. . . . Epistemological mastery of hysteria parallels and often fuses with a mythology of male control over female unruliness" (Evans 1991, p. 3).

bogus. As a militant secularist, he took satisfaction from finding medical explanations, in both epilepsy and hysteria, for the church's stock-in-trade miracles: raptures, possession, stigmata, faith healing, and exorcism.

Charcot's interest in hysteria was expressed as early as 1858, when neurology barely existed and when French psychiatry was still almost exclusively concentrated on *aliénés*, or the outright insane.[24] He noticed that France's public hospitals contained a great many *demi-fous*— "neurotics" in our more recent parlance. To label most of them as hysterical, predisposed by weak heredity to fall ill, was to claim a huge terrain for one of the new disciplines, either psychiatry or neurology. The ambitious Charcot must have calculated that neurology would be the winner if he got there first. Nor could he have failed to notice that another Paris hospital, the Charité, had already begun focusing on hysteria in the early 1870s.[25] That was when he himself began planning to include the disorder among the illnesses systematically investigated at the Salpêtrière.[26]

In 1872 the closing of one dilapidated wing of his hospital resulted in the transfer into Charcot's direct care of about 150 sane epileptics and "hysterics" who had previously been obliged to mingle with the *aliénés*. Thenceforth they would be housed only with one another—a more merciful arrangement for them but also, as it turned out, a potential source of diagnostic confusion. Another key development was the opening of an outpatient clinic in 1881, affording the director access to information about thousands of additional cases.

By 1878 Charcot was fully committed to solving the riddle of hysteria. The exalted academic chair that he received in 1882 carried an expectation that he would unify his research interests and gather fresh material—which, as it happened, lay right before him in Salpêtrière inmates whom he designated as hysterics. Their relative longevity, a nuisance to the "anatomo-" half of his program, afforded an exceptional opportunity for protracted observation in what he called his "museum of living pathology."[27]

It was a delicate task for Charcot to uphold the reality of hysterical manifestations, resembling as they did epileptic discharges on one side and conscious dissimulation on the other. But he expected victims of incurable nervous diseases such as epilepsy to show a number of telltale signs that could distinguish them from the hysterics: a progressive worsening of their handicap, a deterioration in general health, an imperviousness of their symptoms to suggestion or to the relaxing effect of anesthetics, and a sense of frustration or despair in the face of their affliction, contrasting sharply with the *belle indifférence* of many hysterics.[28] There was also the problem that hysteria could be easily feigned. Charcot was confident, furthermore, that through other tests— some as simple as a sudden pinprick on a putatively unfeeling limb— he could reliably discriminate between true hysterical symptoms and pretended ones.

Charcot's goal was to bring order to the hodgepodge of hysterical symptoms. He demoted some of them to peripheral status and claimed to have found a strong sequential pattern in those that remained, which he deemed to be invariably indicative of hysteria. His signature concept was *la grande attaque hystérique*, more often called simply *la grande hystérie*, or major hysteria, which supposedly defined the progress of a quintessential fit of "hysteroepilepsy."* First, according to Charcot, there would be an "epileptoid" phase, with grimaces and spasmodic gestures; then *grands mouvements*, or acrobatic contortions such as a "clownish" arching of the back; third, *attitudes passionelles*, or the acting out of private hallucinatory scenes; and finally, a "terminal delirium," or melancholic lament over disagreeable recollections.

In practice, Charcot found that one or more phases might be absent from a given attack. But that variability didn't reduce his faith in the correctness of his model, which made allowance for any number of *formes frustes*, or partial manifestations. Although he rounded out the picture with the notions of *petite hystérie* and *hystérie ordinaire*, their miscellaneous symptoms didn't interest him. Those minor patterns lacked the regularity that he sought as a lawgiver, and they appeared to be less subject to controlled manipulation than were the features of major hysteria.[29] Late in a stellar career, then, Charcot gambled his hard-earned reputation on the genuineness of one entity, *grande hystérie*.

---

* Charcot came to regret that term for its seeming implication that hysteria is a subset of epilepsy; he found himself having to insist that the two maladies were unrelated (Charcot 1894, p. 253).

The most influential of Charcot's notions was that of *psychologi-cally traumatic* hysteria, especially as it applied to males. In 1884—not long, then, before Freud's arrival in the fall of 1885—the Salpêtrière admitted several men who had seemingly recovered from physical shocks but had then developed paralysis of a limb. At an earlier point in his career, Charcot would have assumed that the men's "hysterical" impairments could be explained as the delayed effects of brain lesions, incurred during the physical shocks they had undergone. That was exactly what authorities in Britain and Germany were saying in 1884 about a post-accident condition they called "railway spine."

But by this time Charcot, who eventually published sixty-one case records of male hysteria and who kept files on many more, had been thwarted in his quest for a link between hysteria and brain damage. For a while, he had fallen back on the conceptual expedient of "func-tional" or "dynamic" lesions, possibly of a chemical nature, that could affect nerves and muscles without leaving the kind of evidence that an autopsy might disclose. But that postulate, while satisfying a theoreti-cal demand, was a blind alley, since it didn't lend itself either to cor-roboration or to disproof through available means of testing. The only recourse left for Charcot, if he wasn't to capitulate to the railway-spine school of thought, was to posit a *mental* mechanism of symptom causation that began its operation moments after the trauma but was completed later.

Charcot had already shown, astutely, that hysterical paralyses typi-cally affect a whole limb, as if they were acting out a thought ("I can't move my arm") rather than including only the nerves and muscles descending from a given point of injury. He then set about to show that many of his male patients' handicaps, even when they had been pre-ceded by a physical impact, were indeed mental in nature and had resulted from *ideas* relating to their injuries. Hysterical paralyses, as he put it, depend on the imagination but are not imaginary.[30]

It was in order to establish and display this truth that Charcot felt compelled to make use of hypnotism. Unlike his disapproving col-leagues in other European centers of research, he felt confident that hypnotism, thanks to the efforts of James Braid, Rudolf Heidenhain, and Johann Czermak, among others, had finally shed its disreputable origins and proved its merit as science. Impressive papers on the technique by his own assistant Charles Richet had tipped the balance for him. And as a student of medical history, he knew that Mesmerists, whatever their analytic failings, had described phased attacks that closely resembled *grande hystérie*.[31] The phases had originally referred not to unprompted hysterical fits but to effects of the magnetizing routine; but since Charcot, along with many other observers, believed that only hysterics could be hypnotized, a carryover to his conception of hysteria was unavoidable.

Charcot's method of demonstration was to hypnotize patients who were *not* already saddled with a paralysis or catalepsy; to command that, upon awakening, they would feel themselves unable to move a certain limb; and then to note that the resultant temporary symptom was indistinguishable from the long-term incapacity of patients who had acquired their disability a while after having received a physical or mental blow. Thus the imposed *suggestion* that temporarily impairs a hypnotic subject appeared to have an exact counterpart in the *auto-suggestion* that can impair a trauma victim after the trauma and its immediate sequelae are over. Furthermore, Charcot observed that not only the motor aspects of hysteria but also its dissociative features—patently counterfactual beliefs, trancelike states, amnesia, identity distortion—could be closely matched in deep hypnosis.

Before long, Charcot was referring to *grand hypnotisme* as a disorder in its own right, albeit one that needed to be activated through the subject's collaboration with an operator. Though only sporadic and situational, the *névrose* of *grand hypnotisme* was said to be no less uniform in its essential features than was *grande hystérie*. Indeed, the two entities, as Charcot envisioned them, substantially overlapped. Both of them included catalepsy and hallucinations, and hysterical "somnambulism" was matched by hypnotic "lethargy."

In Charcot's judgment, autosuggestion could "create a coherent group of associated ideas that install themselves in the mind as a sort of parasite, remaining isolated from the rest while being able to translate themselves overtly into corresponding motor phenomena."[32] On the whole, the "parasitic" ideas that he deduced from hysterical symptoms were straightforward, along the lines of "My leg has been injured; I'm afraid I can't walk." Occasionally the instances he cited lent themselves to more complex interpretation. One patient had lost the use of his right arm and leg, and later his power of speech, after having mistakenly shot a friend's dog on a fox hunt. We can grasp how congenial such an example would be to the later theorist of masochism, the punitive superego, and the somatization of guilt.

The implications Charcot drew from his "living experiments" with hypnotism were far-reaching. He hypothesized that a sudden trauma produces an emergency brain alteration, or *condition seconde*, involving a heightened suggestibility that is akin to that of a hypnotized person. In such a state, the trauma victim not only fears the loss of a physical capability but acts it out mentally, inadvertently rehearsing the paralysis or contraction or hemianesthesia to come. Noticing, moreover, that the actual debility could be delayed for days or even weeks, Charcot interpreted the gap as evidence that the process of symptom formation was still "incubating," or undergoing "mental elaboration."

He also observed that a symptom could grip an individual who hadn't been injured at all but had merely been spooked by a close call or had undergone an emotional setback. Such disproportionality between the event and its apparent consequence obliged the theorist to keep widening the scope that he allowed to strictly mental considerations. Eventually, in spite of his belief in hereditary degeneration as the root cause of all *névroses*, and in spite of his attempted reduction of psychology to "the rational physiology of the cerebral cortex,"[33] he conceded that "hysteria is, in an absolute manner, a psychical malady."[34] And that concession, however grudging, would serve as Freud's invitation to theorize about the mental causation of symptoms without misgivings or compromise.

There is much more to be said about Charcot's assumptions and procedures; and much more *was* said, as we will see, by doubting contemporaries, not all of whom were averse to the practice of hypnotism. On the contrary, it was precisely a just assessment of the uses and limitations of hypnotism that allowed Charcot's brightest critics to perceive what was amiss with his reasoning. The best psychological minds of the 1880s would readily perceive where Charcot had gone wrong. Would Freud be one of them?

11

The Travesty

1. ZONES OF CONFUSION

The story repeatedly told by Freud and by subsequent adherents to his movement was that Charcot, by applying the same rigorous rationality that he had marshaled to unlock other *névroses*, had brought hysteria impressively within the purview of experimental science. The story, however, is false. Charcot didn't conquer hysteria; it conquered him. Not only did the Napoleon of the *névroses* fail to explain the generation of hysterical symptoms; the symptoms that he studied were shaped by his means of investigating them. His seemingly novel method constituted not a scientific advance but a disastrous reversion to Mesmerism. And in his zeal to make his patients' behavior conform to his demands, he violated medical standards and created an institutional travesty.

This was the judgment passed unanimously, if belatedly, by Charcot's contemporaries and successors within the Salpêtrière itself. When he died unexpectedly in 1893, they and others already knew that his conception of hysteria had been arbitrary and self-confirming. No sooner had he departed than most of his lieutenants, who had chafed under the necessity of humoring his illusions, rushed to declare that they had always been doubters. With astonishing rapidity, the phenomenon of *grande hystérie* then vanished as completely as Prospero's cloud-capped towers. By 1906 Pierre Janet, the only Salpêtrière veteran who continued to express gratitude for earlier guidance, felt obliged to state that "nobody nowadays any longer describes the attack of hysteria as Charcot did."[1] And upon acceding to Charcot's academic chair in 1911, Jules-Joseph Dejerine, who had bided his time for decades under one-man rule, declared, "It seems now certain . . . that the crises delineated by [*grande hystérie*] are nothing other than coaching and imitation."[2]

Unanswered doubts had long been accumulating. How could Charcot maintain *both* that hypnotically gleaned knowledge is uncontaminated *and* that he could make a hypnotized subject believe anything he pleased? And why was the Charcotian brand of hysteria rarely found outside the Salpêtrière, and then only in venues managed by graduates of his teaching? Such keen, though temporarily cowed, scientists as Babinski and Binet, who both would later denounce the Salpêtrière's hysteria operation as a sham, must surely have wondered where and when their patients had acquired the sequenced grand-hysterical symptoms that Charcot regarded as definitive of the disorder.

Because Charcot regarded all hysteria in the light of degeneration theory, his reports about patients typically dwelled on their ancestry, their moral lapses, and their medical vicissitudes prior to arrival at his hospital. Nowhere, however, was he able to lay out a prior history of phased major attacks in his specific sense of the term. Patients would usually be placed under his care for one or two complaints that might or might not deserve to be considered hysterical, such as a paralyzed arm or a susceptibility to convulsions; but soon, at least in the cases that would then be featured in the house literature, the full expected pattern would develop. Even without either party's conscious intention to deceive, frequent subjection to hypnotism at the hands of biased personnel was eliciting the desired symptoms and suppressing others.

Consider, for example, the bricklayer's apprentice known as "Pin . . ." (Pinaud), who took up residence at the Salpêtrière in March 1885, seven months before Freud's arrival. In the aftermath of a fall that had rendered him briefly unconscious in 1884, Pinaud had gradually lost the use of his left arm, which was completely paralyzed by the time Charcot first saw him. That was his only presenting symptom upon admission.

Just four days later, though, Pinaud was found to be harboring no fewer than four *hysterogenic zones*—anatomical loci where hyperexcitability appeared to be concentrated and where an investigator's pressure could immediately trigger an aura followed by an attack. Even more gratifyingly, after the staff's "insisting a little further" with pressure on the newly discovered zones, Pinaud manifested what Charcot called an "absolutely classical" attack, the first of many in which he exemplified every feature of major hysteria.[3]

Likewise, the patient called "Augustine" (Louise Augustine Gleizes) entered the Salpêtrière in 1875 suffering from "paralysis of sensation in the right arm and attacks of severe hysteria, preceded by pains in the lower right abdomen."[4] We aren't told what was meant by severe hysteria in her case. What we do know is that she acquired a persistent leg paralysis during hypnotic experimentation in the hospital—a likely sign that, once again, the investigative method was generating symptoms. Augustine's attacks rapidly assumed a uniquely Charcotian form and greatly accelerated in frequency.

Perhaps the best proof that Salpêtrière hysteria was *une hystérie de culture*, as Charcot's adversaries called it, lies in the fact that patients who exited the hospital soon overcame their susceptibility to *grande hystérie*.[5] A widely discussed case was that of Charcot's most frequently exhibited hysteric, Blanche (born Marie) Wittmann. Transferred to a different hospital, the Hôtel-Dieu, Wittmann came under the care of another practitioner of hypnotism, Jules Janet (Pierre's brother). After several months of treatment, Wittmann no longer appeared hysterical at all—until, that is, she reentered the Salpêtrière and began serving again in Charcot's public demonstrations. In the interim, a calmer personality had emerged—one that Wittmann, according to Janet, claimed to have deliberately held in abeyance as she was miming grand-hysterical attacks.[6]

It is clear that *something* was seriously the matter with Charcot's patients; otherwise they wouldn't have been remanded to a hospital of last resort. But their "hysteria" appears to have been learned behavior, acquiring regularity in the Salpêtrière itself. As I have mentioned, in 1872 Charcot inherited a ward full of diagnostically sane patients, some of whom were classified as hysterics and the others as epileptics.

Much later, in 1925, his disillusioned former disciple Pierre Marie gave one possible account of what had happened next. The young hysterics, he wrote, had closely observed their fellow patients, "and because of their tendencies to mimic, . . . they duplicated in their hysterical fits every phase of a genuine epileptic seizure."[7] If Marie was correct, this was how "hysteroepilepsy"—later stripped of the second, but more revealing, half of its name—had entered the world.

But were Charcot's "hysterics" suffering from hysteria in the first place? Or were they, for the most part, epileptics of a relatively mild variety that hadn't yet been acknowledged by the medicine of Charcot's day? Lacking the encephalogram and therefore having to rely on gross behavioral symptoms, most physicians at that time reserved the diagnosis of epilepsy for fits entailing a full *grand mal* loss of consciousness. In London, however, John Hughlings Jackson was already identifying intermediate forms of epileptoid damage that caused violent mood changes, memory gaps, and delusions but not convulsions.[8]

Modern observers have argued that many of the Salpêtrière's "hysterics" were in fact experiencing either syphilis or conditions identified many decades later: temporal lobe epilepsy and frontal lobe epilepsy, whose manifestations coincide with most of the peculiarities that Charcot regarded as hysterical.[9] We now know that temporal lobe epileptics can "learn" to undergo electrical brain discharges (focal seizures) in response to cues.* Alternatively, some of Charcot's patients may have been exhibiting "PENS"—psychogenic non-epileptic seizures—which, even today, are impossible to distinguish from true epilepsy without the aid of video EEG.† On either interpretation, the patients' pathological manifestations were being cultivated and ingrained in a setting where they were supposed to have been treated.

As for the male victims of collisions, combat, and falls whom

---

* As Arthur F. Hurst observed long ago when studying victims of "shell shock," a neurologically damaged patient may be exceptionally prone to acquiring new symptomatology under the suggestive interrogation of physicians (Hurst 1920, pp. 6–7, 30–31).

† See Bodde et al. 2009. Augustine's medical history in the Salpêtrière appears significant in this light. The patient, who had suffered convulsions from childhood onward, may have been an out-and-out epileptic. But the fact that her seizures completely ceased toward the end of her stay in the Salpêtrière appears to be more consistent with PENS.

Charcot invoked to expand the scope of hysteria, the passage of days or weeks before the appearance of their "excessive" debilities struck him as impossible without the added contribution of fears and fantasies. We know today, however, that concussive brain injury and its resultant hemorrhaging, clotting, oxygen starvation, and hypoglycemia can gradually produce the symptoms that Charcot branded as hysterical.[10]

Freud believed that Charcot's positing of male hysteria was his boldest, most liberating move; and some Freudians are still making the same argument today. But the existence of male hysteria had already been urged by Paul Briquet in 1859. And Charcot, in the very act of making room for it, displayed prejudices that demeaned women while straining his conception of the disorder's traits. For as soon as a few male cases had come to his notice, hysteria was found to have branched into a less annoying, more stoical form.

Charcot's male hysterics were described as robust, no-nonsense laborers who, despite having undergone grave physical trauma, maintained some *sangfroid* even in their token *attitudes passionelles*. Depressed and taciturn victims of compromised immunity and misfortune in the workplace, they were making trouble only for themselves. In Charcot's characterization, the very uniformity of male hysteria—"remarkable in the permanence and tenacity of the symptoms"[11]—came across as a tribute to the stronger sex.

The women patients in the Salpêtrière, though they had been exploited and abused for decades, struck Charcot as histrionic and deceitful without, in many cases, having been rendered that way by anything but irritants to their already fragile feminine temperaments. "One finds himself sometimes admiring," he wrote, "the amazing craft, sagacity, and perseverance that [hysterical] women will put in play for the purposes of deception."[12] Their wiles are most ingenious, according to an exasperated Charcot, "when a physician is to be the victim."[13] And even when they weren't dissembling, women were said to be capricious in their symptom display. The hysteria of a certain female patient, he told his colleagues, was "by nature essentially unstable and mobile, as is the sex it prefers to afflict."[14]

In Charcot's estimation, the most common hysterogenic zone was the ovaries—"the fundamental zone," he called it.[15] The Salpêtrière's female hysterics would go into convulsions or catalepsy when their lower abdomens were pounded by a fist or squeezed by the hospital's most notorious device, the mechanical "ovarian compressor." Contact with other suspected hysterogenic zones, though less frequent, was also productive; but the matrix of trouble remained below.

The Salpêtrière's male patients would appear to have constituted a living refutation of any theory that associated hysterical pathology with female organs. Because he had uncovered hypersensitive spots in the "hysterical" female body, however, Charcot anticipated similar results for at least some of his men. "With several male patients," as Mark Micale relates, "he found that hysterical fits could be induced with the application of pressure to the groin. Seven of his hysterical males, or eleven percent, also displayed these supersensitive points along the spermatic cord, on the skin of the scrotum, or in the testes."[16]

In an encyclopedic presentation of hysteria as it was understood at the Salpêtrière, Charcot's assistant Paul Richer maintained that every resident hysteric possessed a hyperesthetic ovarian zone.[17] All of the examples he provided, however, were female; and the female model influenced what was being discovered in the men. Thus, when Pinaud obligingly produced four hysterogenic zones, one of them was found to reside just above a testicle, but the other three were quasi-female in location. One appeared "beneath the left breast," and two were found "in each of the iliac areas"[18]—the very sites where Charcot would have palpated ovaries if Pinaud had been a woman.*

How could Charcot and his assistants have come to believe in such absurdities as quasi-ovarian zones in men? The answer is that their principal tool of inquiry, hypnotism, was perfectly suited to conveying the operator's thoughts to the subject. Such communication, of course, is the essence of recreational and therapeutic hypnotism, in which

---

* Evidently appealing to feminist sentiment in our own time, Mark Micale hails Charcot for having demasculinized the hysterical male body. "In the ultimate equation of the two sexes," he writes, Charcot "even attributed hysterical pain in the female organ believed to most differentiate men from women—the ovaries—directly to men," thus forging one of the great neurologist's "signal departures in the history of medicine" (Micale 2008, p. 160). To put it mildly, however, such departures were less than useful to later generations of doctors.

direct commands are issued; but when research subjects are interro-
gated under hypnosis, they are typically alert for *unintentionally "tele-
graphed"* signals of the operators' expectations, and they are usually
eager to comply. Thus, any hypothesis that was being entertained at the
Salpêtrière would be sure to meet with corroboration when it was hypnotically tested on a patient.

2. SALPÊTRIÈRE FOLLIES

As a consequence of that fallacious practice, the research hospital that
had done so much to promote sound practices in medical science fell
victim to a number of popular misconceptions. Chief among them was
a mechanistic fad known as Burq's metalloscopy and metallotherapy.[19]
Victor Jean-Marie Burq, resuming Mesmer's path, had announced to a
skeptical world that he could perform three related wonders. He could
diagnose a syndrome by observing the patient's reaction to certain
metals; he could restore sensation to the limbs of benumbed patients
by pressing metals or magnets against their skin; and by the same means
he could shift a patient's anesthesia from her left side to her right, or vice
versa.[20] Supposedly, no psychological interaction was required to produce the dramatic effects.

   In 1877–78 Charcot had headed a commission whose charge was
to evaluate the plausibility of Burq's unorthodox science.[21] The submitted report was uncritically positive. Rather than ask himself how
Burq might be self-deceived, Charcot had duplicated his experiments—
including, unfortunately, the inadvertent presentation of cues that were
registered and obeyed by the subjects. In hemianesthetic hysterics, Charcot wrote, "the nervous fluid, if one will pardon the expression, does not
transport itself to one side until after it has in part abandoned the
other."[22] The lord of the Salpêtrière had drawn closer to the crank
practice of Mesmerism, with its own theory of redistributable "nervous
fluid," than is commonly realized.

   Burq's procedures, once speciously validated, were adapted for use
in the Salpêtrière's exploration of hysteria.[23] Throughout the 1880s,
Charcot encouraged research by Babinski, Binet, and Charles Féré into
metallic, magnetic, and electrical transfer of sensations and neuropathic

conditions. And significantly, he didn't object when, in 1887, Binet and Féré chose *Animal Magnetism* as the title for their Charcotian manual on hypnotism.[24]

Binet and Féré's work purported to show how, through the action of "aesthesiogens" such as magnets, a symptom could be moved not merely from one side of a subject to the other but from one subject to another.[25] The trend reached Swiftian absurdity in the work of Charcot's rash disciple Jules Bernard Luys, who maintained that a patient's morbid thoughts and whole deranged personality could be absorbed into an iron crown, which, when placed on a second subject's head, would download its noxious contents into his mind.[26] Yet even this silliness was outdone by Babinski, who succeeded, by his own reckoning, in transferring hysteria from a woman to a pig—a counterpart of Jesus' miracle, recounted in Matthew 8:28–34, of sending demons into a herd of swine.[27]

The Salpêtrière even experimented with producing its own stigmata. The staff subscribed to "dermagraphism," or the alleged capacity of hysterics' skin to function as a magic slate that would retain words and images inscribed with a stylus. The medical artists would mark chests, backs, and limbs with such rude notations as "Satan," "demoniac," or "dementia praecox," and would sometimes sign and date their work. In at least one instance, a Salpêtrière patient was instructed to bleed, somewhat later, from the raised letters, and allegedly did so.[28]

Most unexpectedly in view of Charcot's sober early feats, he allowed the Salpêtrière to become a site of experiments in hypnotic clairvoyance and telepathy.[29] Mesmer's followers had ascribed paranormal gifts to certain subjects under somnambulism, and Blanche Wittmann was regarded as just such a seer. Charcot believed that Wittmann, when hypnotized, could communicate telepathically and perform seemingly impossible card tricks. Although he stopped short of claiming that she was in contact with a spirit world, the line separating Salpêtrière medicine from spiritualism had grown perilously thin.

Thanks to a droll little book by the Belgian polymath Joseph Delboeuf, we know that madcap trials were being conducted in Charcot's hospital during Freud's time there. Delboeuf was the most widely accomplished intellectual in Europe—a holder of doctorates in both physics and mathematics, the author (at age twenty-nine) of a brilliant critique of Euclidean geometry, an expert in optics, a professor of Greek and Latin philology, and a philosopher of science. In *A Visit to the Salpêtrière* (1886) he narrated what he had witnessed in the last week of 1885. Kibitzing and even role playing in tests of the inmates' powers, Delboeuf had understood at once that the Charcotians were deluding themselves. It was characteristic of his ceaseless curiosity that, after debunking Salpêtrière-style hypnotism, he became a hypno-therapist himself, and a successful one.[30]

The first thing Delboeuf noticed about Charcot's staff members was that they were treating their experimental subjects as robots or cadavers. They chatted about them in their presence and poked them to demonstrate hysterical reflexes. Charles Féré, Delboeuf drily remarked, "played [Blanche Wittmann] like a piano."[31] And in the presence of their experimental subjects, the Salpêtrière investigators discussed just what effects they anticipated seeing, as if such information couldn't pos-sibly influence the behavior that followed. Who, Delboeuf wondered, was manipulating whom? In a mischievous paradox, he characterized one of Charcot's subjects as "a mannequin of unequalled intelligence."[32] It was the Charcotians who saw only a doll before them; Delboeuf saw a woman who was tailoring her behavior to the requirements that she watchfully assessed.

Was there, Delboeuf asked, a "sleep"-inducing spot on the crown of a hysteric's head?[33] Only in the Salpêtrière! Again, the visitor couldn't be convinced that magnets, rather than obvious cues, were inducing Blanche Wittmann to exchange her right-side "catalepsy" with her left-side "lethargy."[34] The testers had remained unsuspicious even when Blanche obligingly crossed her opposite arms and legs as the magnet approached and segued between cartoon expressions of gai-ety and sadness.

Delboeuf felt no need to pass explicit judgment on that charade, or on another scene—a so-called *mariage à trois*—that illustrated the Salpêtrière penchant for banal theatrics. The experimenters

> persuaded a sleeping girl that she had two husbands, one on her left side and the other on her right, and that she owed a scrupulous faith-

fulness to each of them. Monsieur Féré and I were the two husbands. Each of us could caress *his half*; she received our caresses with marked pleasure. But woe betide either of us who tried to transgress on the other's side. When I attempted it, I received a well-delivered slap; M. Féré got a slightly more timid one.[35]

Such were the puerile antics of a research group that had once led the world in neurological discovery.

The tactful Delboeuf understood that his methodological criticisms wouldn't be welcome at the Salpêtrière. If the Charcotians had been sincere about determining the efficacy of magnets, he perceived, they needed only to emulate the French royal commission of 1784 in testing whether feigned magnetism, coupled with suggestion, would produce different outcomes than were found by employing real magnets. If not, the hypothesis of inadvertent suggestion would be proven; but that was the very outcome Charcot's assistants wished to forestall.*

3. A ONE-MAN SHOW

The lore of hysteria contains no more striking souvenir than André Brouillet's huge painting *A Clinical Lesson at the Salpêtrière*, first hung in 1887. With photographic realism it depicts Charcot lecturing in a consultation room to a group of distinguished physicians as a staffer (it is Babinski) props up the voluptuous Blanche Wittmann, whom Charcot has hypnotically sent into a faint that presages a major attack. To its Parisian viewers the painting was a source of national pride, with its focus on an authoritative Charcot calmly drawing a lesson from a "living experiment." To the physicians who had been recognizably depicted as onlookers, the work was a flattering who's-who of France's neurological avant-garde. (A few eminent laymen were included, too.) And to Sigmund Freud, who would hang a lithograph of Brouillet's

---

* Delboeuf's influence can be detected in one of the most effective critiques of Salpêtrière science, Armand Hückel's 1888 booklet *The Role of Suggestion in Certain Phenomena of Hysteria and Hypnotism*. Hückel recounted the design and results of numerous ingenious experiments proving that the Charcotians were failing to guard against the effects of unintended suggestion.

work on a wall of his consulting room, the scene evoked his own inheritance from the great teacher who had grappled with the demons of the unconscious.

Today, however, what we are likely to see in this image is not an experiment but a well-rehearsed act. Brouillet's rendition of Charcot's audience—twenty-seven men in dark suits, intently absorbed in a feat to which they are lending perfect trust—tells us that in the Salpêtrière, Charcot's judgments were the only ones that counted. And another significant clue to orthodoxy can be discerned here. On a wall to one side of the lecturing master hangs a large charcoal drawing by Paul Richer, depicting a female patient contorted into one of the *grands mouvements* occurring in the second phase of a Charcotian attack. This was the *arc-de-cercle*, a rigid posture of "clownism" in which the head and feet, pressed against the floor, support a grotesquely arched back. Tellingly, the image is situated where Charcot's hypnotized patient would have faced it prior to "going under." The Salpêtrière's rooms contained many similar illustrations, which served as reminders, if any were needed, of just how *grande hystérie* was supposed to look.

Charcot's detractors were well aware that the event depicted in Brouillet's painting was made possible by a tacit conspiracy. They knew, in the first place, that staff members in the wards were competing to present their leader with subjects who exemplified, in the right order, all four phases of the major-hysterical attack. As for the patients, the dependable performers among them were slipped coins for their cooperation and, in some instances, promoted to adjunct staff roles that enabled them to serve as models of the good hysteric and to tyrannize over their former equals. If they aspired to such privileges and to the glory of being depicted in a lavish annual book, the *Iconographie Photographique de la Salpêtrière*—sold around the world to fascinated readers—they were well advised to cultivate and perfect the necessary antics.[36]

From a memoir by the famous dancer known as Jane Avril (Jeanne Beaudon), who spent eighteen months as a patient in the Salpêtrière, we learn that its women hysterics conspired to deceive their doctors on ward visits by faking "extravagant contortions" so as to "capture attention and gain stardom."[37] Even as they were serving as what the

Swiss neurologist Paul Dubois called Charcot's "marionettes" and "circus horses," those women led him on and laughed behind his back.[38] If his staff members perceived the game—and surely some of them did—they couldn't summon the courage to disabuse their self-infatuated supervisor.

Aloof from firsthand inspection of the wards, Charcot relied on visual documentation of hysterical traits, first through sketches made by his subordinate Paul Richer and then through allegedly candid photographs. His trust in the objectivity of such evidence, he claimed, was absolute. But again, as one can tell from leafing through the *Iconographie*, both the recorders and the patients knew what was expected of them.[39] In many instances it is all too apparent that the pictures were posed. Indeed, the state of photographic technology at the time ensured that expressions were being held steady for the camera.

Especially suspect were the tableaux corresponding to well-known literary scenes and to representations of Charcot's hobbyhorse: the correspondence between individual stages of *grande hystérie* and forms of religious mania, including demonic possession, beatific vision, ecstasy, and a reliving of the Crucifixion. The images of resident actresses in such kitschy attitudes reinforced Charcot's conviction that those stages were valid "for all countries, all times, all races."[40] But what they actually exemplified was hierarchical Salpêtrière teamwork, whereby patients, nurses, interns, photographers, illustrators, and assistant physicians all catered to *le maître*'s predilections.

Every week, Charcot would hold an informal Tuesday demonstration for colleagues and students, observing outpatients (not regulars such as Wittmann) and reasoning aloud about as yet undetermined diagnoses. It was these *leçons du mardi*, in which Charcot risked erring in public or arriving at no conclusion at all, that elicited the most wonderment from his admirers. But the Tuesday sessions were not so spontaneous as they appeared. The eight or ten sample patients of the day were typically selected by Charcot himself in prior conferral with his lieutenants.[41] The impression that the master's powers of observation and analysis were being exercised on total strangers was just that, an impression—a stage effect owing to hidden collaboration.

Charcot's Friday lectures, in contrast, were production numbers.

He had decided, audaciously, to invite the nonmedical public to attend those gatherings in the hospital's 400-seat auditorium, where his presentation would be enhanced by a dramatic deployment of slides, footlights, limelights, and darkening shutters.[42] All of fashionable Paris, along with the literary elite (Zola, de Maupassant, Daudet, and Mirbeau, among others), gathered to watch patients be hypnotized and then convulsed by a mere gesture or touch. Even the great Sarah Bernhardt attended such events in order to refine her simulating of hysteria on the stage.

Typically, Bernhardt and the other onlookers would be treated to a complete major-hysterical fit, performed under deep hypnosis by one of Charcot's reliable resident swooners. Afterward, a second command would restore the "sleeper" to her prior state of consciousness, presumably with no recollection of the contortions and ravings just concluded. Having served a didactic purpose, the patient would then be escorted back to her teeming ward, while the gathered visitors, convinced that they had witnessed a disease in action, would marvel at Charcot's command of the mind's secret levers.

When Charcot lectured on symptomatic tremors, he would introduce three or four female patients to whose hats his assistants had attached rods topped by feathers, producing a ludicrous maximum of agitation. Intimate facts about the sufferers' low backgrounds, peculiarities, and misdeeds would then be recounted as they stood shamefacedly before a gawking audience.[43] This was thoughtless cruelty. As Delboeuf remarked indignantly in 1889, hysterics can benefit from therapy, but not if they have been maintained in a disabled state for purposes of "public demonstration and courses."[44]

4. PATIENTS OR VICTIMS?

Charcot's fame brought him affluent private clients, including millionaires, Russian dukes, the Queen of Spain, and the emperor of Brazil. He was willing to make mansion or palace calls anywhere in Europe. Needless to say, the grandees weren't informed of his view that hysteria is brought about by hereditary degeneration. His treatment consisted of detaching them from their complicit family members, prescribing various conventional measures, and trading on his reputation as a miracle worker whose sheer presence and encouragement could banish illness. By those placebogenic means, which implied a cannier understanding of "hysteria" than the one he officially supported, he often obtained gratifying, if probably transitory, outcomes.

His hospital patients, however, received his attention only insofar as they served as models of hysteria à la Charcot. The Salpêtrière did contain a hall filled with therapy contraptions, however ineffective, and its hysterics were periodically ushered from their wards en masse and strapped onto the quaint devices. But Charcot wasn't merely indifferent to their progress. Because he was exclusively concerned with research and display, he was positively vexed when, for whatever reason, symptoms went away.

One patient's paralyzed hand, for example, was scheduled for electrical therapy when Charcot ordered the treatment deferred because, in his own words, "any attempt of this kind would, perhaps, bring about the return of motion and heal it, and he [Charcot] intended for his audience to witness whatever might come about."[45] Or again, when Pinaud's paralyzed arm began to regain its mobility "prematurely," Charcot regretted the fading of "this monoplegia so perfectly suited to study."[46] Hence he lied to the patient, convincing him that no cure had occurred. "Unfortunately," wrote Charcot, the new paralysis that he thereby created "didn't last for more than twenty-four hours"; after another attack, it was gone forever.[47] *Le patron*, as he was often called, made no attempt to disguise his annoyance at that outcome.

Charcot was so indifferent to his hospital patients' welfare that when some of them became asymptomatic and were then hired as "ward girls" to perform menial chores, he continued to have them hypnotized and prodded to suffer cataleptic attacks that could be studied by his physicians. Unsurprisingly, some of the new workers relapsed and were then restored to their earlier status as inmates. One of them was the much-exposed Augustine, whose symptoms had inexplicably abated in 1879. No longer a patient, she was hired as a ward girl. The doctors, however, were displeased that she no longer suffered from catalepsy, contractures, and hallucinations, and they began inducing them again through hypnosis. Before long, she was once again producing symptoms on her own—but with clear signs of exacerbated mental derangement as well.[48]

Callousness toward the sick wasn't limited to those selected for display. Charcot suborned some female patients to spy on others and report back about faked symptoms. "I had there the best possible police," he wrote of two such spies, "that of women over women, for you are aware that if women enter into any plot among themselves they very seldom succeed."[49]

Again, any patient, at any unannounced moment, could be pricked with a pin to test for dissimulation of anesthesia or subjected to a demeaning experiment such as the "dermagraphism" described above. More ambitiously, the *Iconographie* crew undertook to freeze catalepsy on film by administering shocks while patients were arrayed before the camera. One famous image shows six stupefied women, their arms held out in statuesque recoil, a moment after they were startled by the crashing sound of a gong that was struck in an adjacent room. The response, if genuine, was epileptoid, but Charcot regarded it as a proof of hysteria.[50]

Charcot and his staff were also much concerned with observing and measuring secretions that might yield knowledge of hysteria's dark interior operations. That project was largely focused on the various fluids, especially vaginal ones, exuding from patients in states of pathological somnolence or rigidity. Peremptory stripping, genital prying, and the collecting of samples for analysis were therefore a routine occurrence within the wards.[51] And the *Iconographie* didn't hesitate to report on what was observed, such as the "voluminous breasts, hairy armpits, and pubic region" of the much-photographed Augustine.[52]

Searching for hysteria's hieroglyphs below the waist, the Salpêtrière's inquirers attached correspondingly less importance to what was being expressed through vocal cords. Thus, when patients railed against the early sexual abuse and emotional torment that must have contributed to their illness, Charcot paid no attention to their complaints. "You can see how hysterics scream," he told one Tuesday seminar. "One might say that it is much ado about nothing."[53]

Among all of the Salpêtrière's means of maintaining dominance and compelling desired behavior, the most pervasive was the administration of drugs. Patients were doped with ether, chloroform, ethyl valerate, morphine, and/or amyl nitrite to start or stop attacks and to test whether alleged paralyses and contractures would persist under an enforced relaxation of muscles. Augustine received every one of those drugs, and both she and Blanche Wittmann developed a desperate craving for ether.[54] Charcot's assistant D.-M. Bourneville, having discovered that Augustine indulged in erotic reverie when subjected to ether, was especially fond of inducing that state in her and then insisting that she write out her fantasies. Augustine was reluctant to do so, but her craving for the drug overcame her inhibition.

Drugs were employed in the wards on a daily basis as a means of repaying obedience or, alternatively, of securing orderly behavior. Patients who balked at continuing to perform illustratively in lectures could expect to be rendered submissive through forced drugging. A narcotized patient, dependent on the authorities for her next fix, was unlikely to withhold compliance, much less to incite her wardmates to rebellion.

When things went smoothly in Charcot's Salpêtrière, it functioned less as a hospital than as a center of propaganda and a site for dehumanizing experiments. But when the subjects balked, they found themselves treated like felons in a dictator's prison. The nominally therapeutic showers, baths, and "faradizations" then became means of reprisal, submitting the uncooperative to prolonged chilling or ramped-up electricity. The ovarian compressor also doubled, when necessary, as an instrument of discipline. And the Salpêtrière had its own version of "the hole"—namely, the insane ward, into one of whose cells a straitjacketed Augustine was carried, and then handcuffed to the wall, after an attempted escape. Until she fled for good in 1880 by recruiting an accomplice and disguising herself as a male visitor, Augustine was approaching the condition of the debased *aliénées* whom Pinel had once encountered in the same hospital.

And then there was "Célina," whose fits had usually been arrested through ovarian compression:

When the attacks persisted, however, and in an effort to calm her blatant sexuality, her doctor cauterized her cervix. This operation,

which was all the more painful to the patient because she also suffered from vaginismus . . . , was repeated four times. . . . They then
treated her with ether, to which she became addicted.[55]

The burning of her cervix and the disabling of her mind with ether, like
the fastening of Augustine to a wall, must have served as a lesson to her
watchful sisters: be hysterical in the correct manner!

Charcot's Salpêtrière had indeed become a vast laboratory, not for
the elucidation of hysteria but for the inadvertent demonstration of
everything that can go wrong when egotism, ambition, hierarchical
authority, and unchecked power are "scientifically" brought to bear on
a helpless population of unfortunates. A week's visit had been more
than enough for Delboeuf to grasp the foolishness and sadism of the
enterprise. His stay overlapped with that of Freud, who would be on
hand for over four months. Now we will see how Freud—reputedly the
most thoughtful and observant of psychologists—responded to the
same body of evidence.

12

Attachment Therapy

1. INITIATION

On October 13, 1885, Freud arrived in Paris and took up residence in a hotel in the Latin Quarter, expecting to remain in the city for three months. As things turned out, he stayed, with a Christmas-season absence in Wandsbek, until February 28, 1886—and even then he didn't go straight home, instead passing two more weeks among pediatric neurologists in Berlin. Still another visit to his fiancée intervened before he returned to Vienna on April 4.

Earlier in Vienna, Freud had felt relatively comfortable in his university, in its hospital, and in a tight-knit, mutually solicitous Jewish community, including his own needy but always affectionate and supportive family. In Paris, however, he was going to be an unknown outsider armed only with a letter of introduction from Moriz Benedikt—a "fairly crazy person," as he confided in a *Brautbrief* of July 1, 1885, who "is extremely unpopular with us at home." And Freud would be bidding for recognition in a language that he had begun to study only shortly before arriving—a language in which, as he wrote to his future sister-in-law Minna Bernays after more than six weeks in Paris, he couldn't say "*du pain*" clearly enough to make himself understood.[1] "My heart is German provincial," the same letter confessed, "and it hasn't accompanied me here."[2]

In Paris, Freud's usual headaches and indigestion were exacerbated by a heightened sense of anonymity, helplessness, and "laziness," his term for a depressive paralysis of will. Typical was his report to Martha of October 31:

Again today I am not yet completely well. Not a continuous nausea; but after lunch a miserable feeling of dizziness, an overheated head, sleepiness, and irritability. At the same time, I am always so hungry that I struggle not to eat twice or three times as much, and, as I mentioned, it is quite different from my Viennese condition, which involved a weariness that lasted all day and no specific stomach symptoms.

Freud's own explanation of such sharpened torment was that it resulted from the thwarting of his drive for professional success—a frustration that Paris, vibrant but withholding, seemed to amplify. His health in general, he felt, and hence his ability to settle down, stood at risk if the pressure to achieve were to continue much longer. The cure that he pondered was, once again, to renounce all scientific aspirations and to resign himself to mediocrity. Thus the keynote of his initial phase in Paris was surrender to intimidation, a feeling of having been overwhelmed in advance of any effort.

That feeling had two main focuses, Charcot and the city itself. Both of them loomed in Freud's imagination as all-powerful without needing to make room for his drab foreign self. Understandably, then, he was in no rush to present his meager credentials at the Salpêtrière. Instead, he spent most of his first week taking long walks, frequenting museums and theaters, and moping over his isolation—"not a word of German, no familiar faces, no jokes, no signs of affection all day long."[3] His anonymity in the bustling streets must have struck him as a fore-taste of the cold reception awaiting him at the mammoth asylum.

It was natural, then, for the lonely stranger to console himself with a good deal of cocaine, which never seems to have been in short supply. Before he left Paris at the end of February 1886, the drug would play an important role in steadying his nerves for social interaction. In the early stage of his visit, it must have appealed to him as his only reliable comfort. References to his use of cocaine crop up frequently in the Paris *Brautbriefe*, and many of his reported thoughts, deeds, and mood swings bespeak its influence.

It was in Paris, for example, that Freud underwent his first known hallucinatory experiences. In *The Psychopathology of Everyday Life* (1901), attempting to distance himself from "spiritualism," he would make the following remarkable disclosure:

> During the days when I was living alone in a foreign city—I was a young man at the time—I quite often heard my name suddenly called by an unmistakable and beloved voice; I then noted down the exact moment of the hallucination and made anxious enquiries of those at home about what had happened at that time. Nothing had happened.[4]

"Quite often," we see, Freud was undergoing auditory hallucinations in Paris; and instead of immediately recognizing their unreality, he had had to make "anxious enquiries" by mail to be sure that Martha hadn't spoken to him from 600 miles away. Hallucinations are a common result of cocaine intoxication.

Not even cocaine, however, could prevent Freud from deciding that the French were a cold, arrogant, and dishonest folk. Yet little by little, Paris melted the hostility of its unhappy critic. In its sheer antiquity, monumentality, and variety, the city he couldn't expect to impress was itself the most impressive thing he had seen. The medieval and Roman ruins at the Musée de Cluny and the Assyrian and Egyptian remains at the Louvre helped to imprint on him an archaeological conception of the past. Attending migraine-inducing plays at the cramped and stuffy Comédie Française and the Porte St. Martin in the hope of improving his French, reading Victor Hugo's *Notre-Dame de Paris*, and repeatedly visiting the great cathedral itself and the Louvre, he soon began to feel less like a bewildered alien and more like an intellectual tourist whose horizons were being broadened.

Paris was also opening Freud's eyes to a side of life that he still found rather alarming: uninhibited behavior. In the mid-1880s, unabashed candor about the body and its needs was the best-known trait of the city whose international icon wasn't yet the Eiffel Tower but the Folies

Bergère. It is easy to picture how Freud's agitation must have been heightened by the daily parade of saucy faces and swaying hips that he witnessed during his strolls. And sex for hire was both legal and ubiquitous in Paris. Freud apparently told Marie Bonaparte, late in life, that he hadn't entered his marriage as a virgin.* Perhaps, then, at twenty-nine he did learn a thing or two about copulation, thus beginning to catch up with other European men of his generation.

2. OVERAWED

Freud mustered enough courage to enter the Salpêtrière on October 19, 1885. But out of nervousness, no doubt, he had left Benedikt's letter of introduction back in his hotel. Charcot was on duty, but Freud thought it advisable to delay presenting himself until the following day. When he did so, his fear of a curt reception was allayed at once. Benedikt's letter, he perceived, was all Charcot needed to accept him as a legitimate visitor who ought to be accorded the usual privileges.

Freud's first description of Charcot to his fiancée was an evocative vignette:

> At ten o'clock M. Charcot arrived, a big man of fifty-eight, wearing a top hat, with dark, strangely soft eyes (or rather, one is; the other is expressionless and has an inward cast), long wisps of hair stuck behind his ears, clean shaven, very expressive features with full protruding lips—in short, like a worldly priest from whom one expects a ready wit and an appreciation of good living.†

---

* For many years, a typescript transcribing or summarizing Bonaparte's diary was held by the New York psychoanalyst Frank Hartman, who showed parts of it to Peter Swales on November 20, 1980. According to Swales's recollection, Hartman concurred that the diary refers to Freud's confession about the loss of his virginity.

† 10/21/85; L, p. 175. In the 1960 translation of Freud's *Letters*, he appears to have perceived the diminutive Charcot as "tall"—an oddity that has been counted as evidence of oedipal awe. But the word in question was only *großer*, meaning simply "big." Charcot had by then become stout, and Freud was probably referencing his waistline rather than his height.

Freud's medical apprenticeship in Austria had taught him to assume that any learned mentor will project an air of stern authority. Imagine his surprise, then, at finding Charcot to be relaxed, urbane, droll, and forthcoming in the presence of subordinates and others. "Altogether," he wrote after their first meeting, "the atmosphere is very unconstrained and democratic. Charcot lets fall in passing such an abundance of the shrewdest remarks, asks many questions, and is always so polite as to correct my miserable French."[5] That this show of openness was itself a display of power—that of a ruler who can afford to be cordial because no one would dare to contradict him—did not occur to Freud, nor would it do so later.

In the *Brautbriefe* a month later, we find Freud wholly possessed both by Charcot's self-presentation and by his science. Now he is ready to defend the Frenchman against all doubters. Interestingly, however, this new loyalty has only reinforced his own defeatism. Charcot's dazzling accomplishments have shown him the futility of lesser efforts:

> Charcot, who is one of the greatest of physicians, a brilliant and prudent man, is simply ripping away all of my opinions and purposes. After many of his lectures I go away as I do from Notre Dame, with new feelings about perfection. But he assails me; when I go away from him I no longer have any desire to work at my own silly things; I've been lazy for three days now without making self-accusations about it. . . . I can't say whether the seed will ever bear fruit, but I know for certain that no other man has had a comparable effect on me. . . . When I get home I feel quite resigned and say to myself: the great problems are for men between fifty and seventy; for us young people there is life itself.[6]

Why was Freud so demoralized? The reason he gave Martha was incoherent. If no one besides men between the ages of fifty and seventy could solve major problems—already an absurd supposition—that must have been because those achievers had devoted themselves to a field of inquiry when they were no older than Freud and had kept at it for decades. The apparent lesson would be to buckle down now in the hope of becoming Charcot's peer, or at least his worthy colleague, with the passage of time.

But Freud, we remember, wanted fame and wealth in the short run. He seemed to feel, bizarrely, that what he craved was already the property of another. Instead of emulating Charcot's dedication, he was inclined to step aside and become an armchair Charcotian—or, rather, a Charcot acolyte, staying as close to the great man as possible, hanging on his every word, and hoping to attract his notice.

Now that Freud was fully aware of Charcot's psychological interests, he felt especially lukewarm toward the neuroanatomical project—microscopically studying diseased brain tissue from dead children—that Charcot's assistants, under the master's obliging direction, had set up for him in the hospital's laboratory for pathology. Indeed, he would abandon the work altogether after a couple of desultory months. Explaining his decision to Martha on December 3, he provided no fewer than seven reasons for having quit, from a stomach catarrh and insufficient space to "the very healthful effects of calmness" and "the impossibility of lunching near the Salpêtrière." The inconveniences were real enough, but Freud's capitulation, so unlike Charcot's early perseverance in far more trying circumstances, marked the chasm between their temperaments.

Freud's one obsessive desire was to draw Charcot's favorable attention to himself. Nothing was worse than the thought that he was doomed to remain insignificant in the master's eyes. "My well-being is really quite poor overall," he wrote on November 12, 1885,

> and I am so terribly afraid of doing anything, and unhappy about all the little hindrances. I think now I am beyond the worst of it, but the whole month has been a loss, and I must make good use of the next two if I want to finish a project. The French are still very arrogant and inaccessible, and I am not so pleased with Charcot anymore, either. He never speaks a word to me or any other foreigner, and one feels so cramped and isolated.

Appalled by such mewling, the levelheaded Martha reminded her betrothed that he was privileged to have been given this free time for self-development in a foreign capital. Rebuked, on November 17 he made an attempt to be philosophical. "Charcot is an extraordinary person," he grudgingly reflected, "whether he is speaking to me or not."

Two days later Freud was in better spirits, and he managed to tell Charcot of a clinical project he had in mind—a joint venture with Pierre Marie, who had been Charcot's *chef de clinique*, or master assistant, at the time he was delegated to accommodate the visitor. In fact, as we learn from an earlier letter, it was Marie who had proposed the idea to Freud.[7] Although we don't know the specifics, Marie's intention was to offer Freud an opportunity to relate his anatomical studies to observation among the Salpêtrière's hysterics.[8] Charcot immediately authorized the step. Here, then, it might be supposed, was the moment when Freud began his transition from neurology to clinical psychology.

Freud, however, dreaded the forthcoming task. "In my disheartened and sullen state," he wrote on November 12, "I've considered that this new work will hold me here longer and put me into even greater unrest and agitation." And a week later he reported, "It looks as though Marie wants to withdraw, so I don't know what I will be able to accomplish."[9] For whatever reason, one of Charcot's most influential lieutenants had changed his mind about working with the newcomer.

Having arrived in Paris with credentials as a neurological histologist, Freud had been provided with means for inquiry in that direction, but had backed away. Having then professed allegiance to Charcot's conception of hysteria, he had been given a second opening; but it had only heightened his anxiety, and the offer was soon withdrawn. This novice, it seemed, was going nowhere in his career and didn't have to be further indulged. That would scarcely have mattered to Charcot, who was accommodating toward all visiting physicians while never allowing himself to be distracted from his own busy schedule.

For Freud, however, a day of reckoning had come. On Saturday, November 28, he wrote to Martha:

Last week's sirocco, or else my turning away from ambition, my renunciation of a publication from here, and my decision to win you by giving up everything having to do with my career, probably explains the fact that since Monday I have stayed home in the afternoons—reading Notre-Dame de Paris by V. Hugo or leafing through the archive—without feeling guilty about it. I have long known that my life could not be completely consumed by neurology, but only here—why here, in the chaos of Paris, I do not know—did it become clear to me that it could be given up entirely for the sake of a dear girl. And yet I am not entirely uneasy about all of this; this time will evoke a fond memory for me someday when we are sitting together.

Here Freud is reporting after almost a week of having sequestered himself in his hotel room each afternoon instead of returning to the Salpêtrière. His morose behavior has been childish, and so is his logic as he now retreats from painful thoughts about failure to cozy thoughts about marriage. He has, of course, long since won the hand of his "dear girl," but now he fancies that she can be secured only by his renouncing all career aims. Martha has presented him with no such ultimatum; on the contrary, she likely would have little use for a milquetoast husband who thought he had to choose between her love and meaningful work. Freud's sickly denials—"without feeling guilty about it," "not entirely uneasy"—indicate a losing battle against self-condemnation.

His reference to "the archive" points to still another symptomatic action. Having intended to lay out five francs for a memoir by Charcot, he has instead, unaccountably, allowed himself to spend a staggering eighty francs for an entire set of the Salpêtrière team's papers since 1880, with an ongoing subscription for still more articles as they become available.[10] Martha has professed herself horrified by this extravagance, and on December 1 Freud sheepishly agrees with her:

I myself am startled by the outlay. . . . I wouldn't have bought [the archive] if I'd had something else to fill up my time here. However, I have withdrawn from both the histological and the experimental work—or I will have to withdraw—and for that reason I wanted to compensate myself with the literature.

Freud was baffled by his own "psychologically interesting blunder."[11] Was he under the influence of cocaine when he spent sixteen
times more money more than he intended? Or, as he implied, had he
been depressed and at sea about his failure to get engaged in any
project?[12] The two possibilities aren't mutually exclusive.

For the moment, in any event, Freud has settled into being a reader
rather than a doer. "I sit at home in the afternoons," he reports, "reading and resting my excited brain."[13] And Hugo's text makes for less
nervous reading than Charcot's. "Recently," Freud writes, "I caught
myself enjoying old Victor Hugo's Notre Dame de Paris more than
neurology."[14] As for career prospects, "My inclination to take care of
myself so that I am not unfit for action, and to give up all of my ambitious projects, has not diminished in the least."[15]

What does Freud intend by "not unfit for action"? He may be
referring to the undemanding life of a private physician who is no
longer striving for fame as a discoverer. It would be easy, he may be
thinking, to reach into his medicine bag for standard nostrums instead
of vexing himself with theories. Secondarily, he may have in mind his
capacity to perform as a normal husband, without being disabled by
excess stimulation of his nervous system.

That second meaning would help to explain why he poses a choice
for himself between neurology and Martha. Typical in this regard is a
letter of April 29, 1886, in which Freud, after complaining that low
moods and bodily weaknesses often persist after one of his frequent
headaches has abated, tells his fiancée, "I'm afraid you're getting a man
who isn't worth much—or [perhaps] you won't take him at all." Surely
he is worrying here about more than his limitations as a breadwinner.

When Freud wrote that he was renouncing "ambitious projects,"
he didn't mean all projects whatsoever. Throughout his time in Paris,
he would revise previously suspended papers and contemplate new
ones. Such busyness helped him to feel usefully occupied when he knew
he was getting nowhere at the Salpêtrière. With a friend from Vienna,
for example, the accomplished Russian neurologist Li Verij Dark-
schewitsch, who was then a fellow visitor at the hospital, he planned
and completed a paper on brain anatomy, published in 1886. The paper

expressed judgments that both men had reached independently before coming to Paris.

Again, as soon as Freud had given up on his laboratory study, he began to write a textbook—never to be completed—on nerve pathology.[16] In view of his limited experience, the project appears to have been grandiose. Later comments to Martha about the book indicate that its drafting was just a means of coping with a gathering sense of futility.

That sense reached a culminating point in early December, when Freud resolved to cut his fellowship visit short and leave Paris as soon as possible. He was sure he would miss the great city, which he adored now that it was no longer coupled in his mind with his sinking fortunes at the Salpêtrière; and he would miss Charcot, who was still a god in his eyes. But with regard to professional training and achievement, he felt like a beaten man. His fiancée's rallying letters could restore him to optimism only momentarily. It was at this point, on December 14, 1885, that he mused despondently to Martha, "who knows how soon I will have another *break down*."

Freud's plan had been to quit Paris before Christmas, visit Martha over the holidays, and return to Vienna with nothing tangible to show for his Parisian experience. But an old acquaintance with whom he had been reunited in Paris, Giacomo Ricchetti—a Serbian-born Jewish physician, twenty-four years his elder—urged him to return to Paris in January and resume his relations with Charcot; and Ricchetti's counsel prevailed. The reason for this alteration of intent, however, wasn't that Freud could now envision himself becoming, after all, a keen scientific investigator of hysteria. Rather, he had found an effective means of ingratiating himself with Charcot after all, and Ricchetti helped him to see that by staying through February he might consolidate his advantage and be able to count on Charcot's future support.

3. TRANSLATED TO SOMEBODY

"Today I had a silly idea," the otherwise despairing Freud had written to his fiancée on December 9, 1885:

The third volume of Charcot's Leçons has not been translated; how would it be if I asked him for permission to do it? If only the permission has not already been granted to the translator of the first two volumes! That will probably be the case, and it would be best if I abandoned the idea. I will just make an inquiry to see whether truly nothing can be done.

The substantial book in question, which would appear in French in 1887, a year *after* Freud's German translation of it, was not Charcot's *Leçons du mardi* but the third and last volume of his *Leçons sur les maladies du système nerveux.*[17]

The role of translator wasn't a new one for Freud; we recall that in 1880 he had rendered a number of texts by John Stuart Mill into German. This time, he was more concerned about being adequately remunerated. Subsequent letters show him quarreling with the publisher over payments and calculating whether they might suffice to advance the date of his wedding. Clearly, however, there were overriding motives in this instance: enhancing his reputation through linkage with a great name, gaining Charcot's confidence, and keeping the hero present in his mind beyond the approaching time of their separation.

Freud's qualifications for turning French into German were hardly self-evident. Only five months had elapsed since his first submersion in the language. When witnessing Sarah Bernhardt and others on the stage in October and November 1885, he had gleaned only an approximate idea of what they were declaiming. But Freud was a quick learner when he needed to be, and in Paris he had been reading French prose by Victor Hugo and by Charcot himself. Besides, Charcot had lectured and written in a relatively unadorned style about matters that weren't obscure to a fellow neurologist.

Given Freud's stymied and depressed condition in December 1885, the morale-building import of his "silly idea" would be hard to overstate. The prospect was far too important to be broached in casual conversation with Charcot, especially in Freud's halting and mispronounced French. A diplomatic effort was called for. At once Freud drafted a letter and enlisted his friends the Ricchettis to improve it.

Two days later he could report, "Mme. Ricchetti corrected it, and M. Ricchetti, who puts great faith in compliments, sprinkled in some phrases that were flattering to Charcot."[18]

The letter opened in this baroque manner:

> Fascinated for two months now by your speech, immensely interested by the subject you so masterfully treat, it has occurred to me to offer myself to you for the translation into German of the third volume of your *Leçons*, if in any event you want a translator and if you consent to avail yourself of my work.[19]

Charcot, who formally concurred three days later, must have felt lucky to be acquiring an interpreter possessing such previously unsuspected grace of written Gallic expression.

By the time, nearly forty years later, that Freud came to write his *Autobiographical Study*, the circumstances attending this letter had acquired a different cast for him. For the first part of his Parisian stay, he claimed in those pages, he had gone unnoticed at the Salpêtrière and hadn't been allowed to participate in staff activities. But "one day in my hearing," he wrote,

> Charcot expressed his regret that since the war he had heard nothing from the German translator of his lectures; he went on to say that he would be glad if someone would undertake to translate the new volume of his lectures into German. I wrote to him and offered to do so. . . . Charcot accepted the offer, I was admitted to the circle of his personal acquaintances, and from that time forward I took a full part in all that went on at the Clinic.[20]

A lovely story, but it is untrue in both spirit and detail. In the first place, Freud, just as soon as he introduced himself to Charcot, had been given laboratory space for the anatomical project he had meant to conduct. Charcot in person had written to an academic colleague to obtain diseased brain samples for that undertaking. So, too, Freud had been granted total access to Charcot's wards, had followed him about, and had mingled freely with the staff. Later, as we know, Charcot had authorized him to conduct another investigation in the sole company of his recent second-in-command, Pierre Marie—an unusual privilege for a young visitor. Freud's contention that he had been neglected until he became Charcot's translator served to cloak the fact that he had already failed twice at generously proffered research projects and was expecting to leave Paris prematurely in a crestfallen and disturbed state.

At the end of 1885 and in the first months of 1886, the fixed routine of translating was ideally suited to the restoration of Freud's equipoise. He was hard at work by December 13, the day after hearing back positively from Charcot.[21] His rendition of the first lecture (out of twenty-six), he wrote to Martha on the following day, would soon be completed and ready for the author's perusal.

On December 16, just a week after having been struck by the possibility of enhancing both Charcot's fortunes and his own, Freud had found a publishing house, Toeplitz & Deuticke, whose owner was willing to launch the book simultaneously in Leipzig and Vienna. By January 10, 1886, he had already mailed off a segment of prose to Franz Deuticke in Vienna. In May, two of the lectures appeared as an article in the *Wiener Medizinische Wochenschrift*. And not long after July 18, 1886, the date that Freud appended to his preface, the book itself would be published.

A marvelous alteration of his status awaited Freud in the new year. It didn't become apparent right away, because Charcot was sidelined with an illness for two weeks, leaving Freud, now relocated in a noisy *pension*, to confess, "I need only Charcot's restoration to be contented here."[22] When Charcot returned on January 13, Freud, eager for any sign of approval, believed that he detected a new warmth of manner:

> Today Charcot was here again with all of his magic, but looking pale, and he has aged quite a bit in the last few weeks. When he saw me, he approached me, shook my hand, and said a few words, I think *ça ne reviendra plus*. I had said, *bien heureux de vous revoir en bonne santé!* Despite my feeling of independence, I was quite proud of this attentiveness, since he is not only a man to whom I must subordinate myself, but also one to whom I am glad to be subordinate.[23]

We may wonder how much actual attentiveness was shown by Charcot in this perfunctory encounter. But he did begin treating Freud as someone who could be of use to his international reputation. Their relationship would bear fruit again in 1892 with the first of two translated volumes of the *Leçons du mardi*.[24] And the logistics of translation, review, and revision would provide a basis for the two men to stay in epistolary contact—though with increasing edginess on Charcot's side, we will find, as he began to perceive that Freud possessed a strategic agenda of his own and was not going to be swayed from it by old loyalties.

The improved regard in which Freud had basked after Charcot's return to work became a major theme of the remaining letters from Paris. To have been denominated Charcot's translator involved the right to consult with him privately, not just at the hospital but also in his noble old townhouse at 217 Boulevard Saint-Germain, in the most fashionable neighborhood of Paris. To Freud that house was scarcely less awe-inspiring than Notre Dame, and to be granted entry into its inmost shrine, Charcot's study, was a fairy-tale experience.

Freud began to feel himself the preferred courtier of a king:

Now I am the only foreigner at Charcot's. Today, when a number of small separate offprints (English) arrived, he handed me one of them, and soon afterwards I had an opportunity to make a certain impression on him. He was talking about a patient, and while the others were laughing, I interjected, "*Vous parlez de ce cas dans vos leçons,*" and quoted a few of his words. That seems to have pleased him, for an hour later he said to his assistant, "*Vous allez prendre cette observation avec M. Freud.*" Then he turned to me and asked whether I would like to "*prendre une observation*" with M. Babinski. Of course I had no objection. It is a case that he [Charcot] seems to find interesting. It doesn't seem so to me, but I will probably have to write a paper about it jointly with the assistant. But the point of the story is that he paid attention to me at all, and that the assistant was as if transformed.[25]

This passage, frankly narrating an attempt to gain an advantage through flattery, illustrates once again the sway of Freud's emotional needs over his scientific decisions. Because Charcot's word is law for him, he will "probably have to" become the coauthor of a paper whose topic he finds uninteresting. As he clearly states, "the point of the story" is a sign of recognition from Charcot—one that has also raised his standing in the eyes of an assistant.

The assistant in question was hardly a nonentity. Although Joseph Babinski was a year younger than Freud, his 1885 medical thesis on multiple sclerosis was just then drawing wide admiration, and he was known at the time as Charcot's favorite student. Soon after Freud's arrival he had succeeded Pierre Marie as head intern, a position he held into 1887. Babinski would develop into one of the most formidable clinical neurologists of his long lifetime, with more than 200 papers and many discoveries to his name. He would also become, for a while at least, the most influential supporter of Salpêtrière doctrine regarding hysteria.

Freud's letter of January 27 continues:

I took on the case at 11 a.m., when Charcot was away. I tackled the case and realized to my astonishment that I could actually communicate with a Frenchman. The conclusion of the observation was postponed until 4 p.m., and the assistant invited me (!!) to lunch with him and the other hospital doctors in the Salle des Internes—as their guest, of course. And all this as a result of one nod from the master!

. . . Thus the whole day was spent in the Salpêtrière. . . . Then the assistant, who probably wasn't eager to compete with me in the investigation, went away, and as I am no beginner like him, in a quarter of an hour I found out everything, and I communicated it to him.

The prospect of collaborating with a physician of Babinski's caliber could have figured for Freud as a rare opportunity. What comes through instead in this letter is an unseemly gloating. The rival had to be not simply bested but deleted from consideration.

As Freud wrote on the following day, "The conquest of Charcot is making rapid progress."[26] His greatest pleasure during these weeks appears to have consisted of feeling himself to be not merely a bona fide member of the royal entourage but uniquely singled out for praise.

Thus a seemingly trivial event on February 9 provided him with an exquisite thrill. A pretentious Viennese hydrotherapist who wished to meet Charcot had called on Freud at his pension, and they had gone to the Salpêtrière together. The man, wrote Freud,

> regards himself as a great neuropathologist. He made all kinds of condescending remarks which I took in my stride, sure of a forthcoming revenge. He had a letter of introduction to Charcot containing an extravagant flattery: that he had arrived to meet the greatest of living physicians. From this he expected I don't know what kind of reception. I was sure, though, that it would be quite cool. Indeed, as he handed over the letter, Charcot said only "*À votre service, Monsieur!*" Then he added, "*Vous connaissez M. Freud?*" He was taken aback by that, while I lowered my head, silently pleased.[27]

The insecurity and spitefulness that would characterize many of Freud's better-known episodes are already conspicuous here. More interesting, however, is the way those traits were skewing his perceptions. It doesn't take much acquaintance with French to know that "*Vous connaissez M. Freud?*" was a scarcely less automatic gesture than "*À votre service.*" Indeed, it was as formalistic as "*Charmé de vous voir,*" whose hollowness Freud had at last comprehended. But the mere fact that Charcot had spoken his name struck Freud as a devastating rebuke to the interloper.

4. ALMOST FAMILY

The Ricchetti couple, whose company Freud had enjoyed since mid-November, had left Paris on January 26, but not before Giacomo had accidentally won Freud an invitation to a prized Tuesday soirée in Charcot's Saint-Germain mansion. Charcot had meant to invite only Ricchetti, but the latter was standing next to Freud at the time. Ever correct in decorum when dealing with physicians, Charcot turned to Freud and extended the same offer to him.

Given Freud's problem with spoken French, the Tuesday parties— he attended three of them in addition to three private editorial meetings in Charcot's study—were an ordeal for him. Each invitation to an evening event, however, was seized upon with pride, and the cards themselves were mailed to Wandsbek as precious souvenirs. The last of the three evenings would doubtless be boring, Sigmund wrote on February 1, because the novelty of his presence would have worn off and no one would take an interest in him; but he would nevertheless go "gladly because I can proudly declare in Vienna that I was invited to Charcot's house six times."

The *Brautbriefe* show Freud dipping into his dwindling funds to purchase formal evening attire, begging Martha to send appropriate neckties, and calming his nerves with cocaine before each Tuesday crossing of the splendid threshold. Without that chemical boost, he imagined, he wouldn't be brave enough to converse with the invited notables. It was easier, of course, for him to chat with already known staff members from the Salpêtrière who had been deemed worthy of attending, such as Babinski, Marie, and Gilles de la Tourette. Freud welcomed signs of cordiality from them while continuing to imagine, on slender grounds, that his own status was special. And for that purpose, too, cocaine was surely helpful.

More than one commentator has proposed that Freud, in setting Charcot on a pedestal and claiming a special relationship with him, was figuring himself as Charcot's rightful son. Such an interior drama, in the imagination of a child who has outgrown an idealization of his biological father, would form the theme of a 1908 essay by Freud called "Family Romances."[28] As he expounded the pattern there, a boy who daydreams that he belongs to a high-status surrogate family "is turning away from the father whom he knows to-day to the father in whom he believed in the earlier years of his childhood."[29] Only neurotics, Freud alleged, fail to put this normal fantasy behind them as they pass through adolescence into adulthood.

For the psychoanalytic Freud, the family romance would figure as a derivative of the Oedipus complex. No textual evidence suggests, however, that Freud imagined himself a rival for the embraces of Mme. Charcot. He was impressed by her wealth but unmoved by her "round" and "not very distinguished-looking" person.[30] But if we strip the family romance to its barest essence—namely, the longing to be incorporated into a grander household—there can be little doubt that Freud was engrossed in it by early 1886.

Freud and many other guests in Charcot's mansion shared a hope of career advancement through the master's favor. The surest avenue to it, however, would be enlistment in Charcot's literal family; and that is where Freud's thoughts now turned, however idly. The Charcots had two children, a son of nineteen and a daughter of twenty. Both of them figured in Freud's virtual reality—one as a despised rival for Charcot's affection, the other as a more legitimate princess than the one addressed as such in the *Brautbriefe*.

Freud's references to Charcot's son in his letters to Wandsbek were coldly dismissive, as if the young man, ten years his junior, possessed no imaginable merit beyond his surname. As for his first name, Jean-Baptiste, Freud couldn't bring himself to remember it correctly. But the petite, vivacious Jeanne Charcot, whom he would call "highly gifted" in his obituary essay on her father, drew his intense interest.[31] "Now just suppose I weren't already in love and were a proper adventurer," he teased in a *Brautbrief*;

> it would be a strong temptation to get drawn in, for nothing is more dangerous than when a young girl bears the features of a man one admires. Then people would laugh at me and toss me out, and [but?] I'd be the richer for the experience of a beautiful adventure. It is better as it is—.[32]

Here Martha Bernays—shabby-genteel, provincial, still loyal to her religion, and orphaned by a father who had served jail time for fraud—was being told that her fiancé entertained thoughts of wooing the cultivated daughter of a sumptuously rich mother and the man he most admired in the world. The subtext for Martha could hardly have been plainer: *For your sake I am sacrificing romance, affluence, and professional advantage.* No wonder Freud sounded repentant after hearing back from the feisty maid of Wandsbek.

It was Charcot himself, however, not his daughter, to whom Freud really felt attached. The Frenchman was less his teacher than his patron saint—the protector who had blessed him and whose name, in an act of profoundest homage, he would bestow on his firstborn son, Jean Martin Freud. When quoting Shakespeare, collecting antiquities, studying demonology, or visiting the sites of gruesome episodes in the history of Christianity, Freud wouldn't just be following Charcot's example; he would be appropriating portions of his identity.

On February 25, 1886, taking his final leave of Charcot, Freud arrived with a purchased photographic portrait of his idol, suitable for signing and framing. He needn't have bothered; Charcot had plenty of them to give away. The one he politely signed, with a boilerplate inscription, would be mounted on a miniature easel and placed on the desk of Freud's consulting room.[33] And to complete the furnishing of that first office, Sigmund would instruct Martha on April 7, 1886, to embroider a tablet bearing this trite motto:

IL FAUT AVOIR LA FOI

J. M. Charcot

Whatever Charcot had meant by "faith," for Freud it probably signified trust in his own success, predestined or at least assisted by association with his master.

5. EVERYTHING IN ORDER

Although Freud's stay in Paris had been made meaningful by his contact with Charcot, he was aware that he had failed to prove himself superior to other apprentices. His sense of unworthiness was especially sharp on the evening of February 2, 1886, as he braced himself for one of those intimidating soirées at Charcot's mansion. The cocaine that he had just ingested to instill social courage, he wrote to his fiancée, was making him "talkative" (*geschwätzig*) about the factors in his life that were militating against easy victories. In a passage already quoted in part:

> [I suffer from] poverty, long struggle for success, little favor among men, excessive sensitivity, nervousness, and worries. . . . I think that people notice something alien in me and that the real reason for this

is that in my youth I was never young, and now that I am entering
maturity I cannot mature properly. There was a time when, full of
ambition and eagerness for knowledge, I vexed myself day after day
because nature hadn't, as she sometimes does in one of her good
moods, stamped my face with the mark of genius. Since then I have
long known that I am no genius, and I no longer understand how I
could ever have wanted to be one. I am not even very gifted.[34]

In the midst of this maudlin confession, however, and without mentioning any field of research interest to which he felt attached, Freud
turned the despairing assessment on its head and envisioned a great
triumph after all. Through solid traits of character and a lack of outstanding intellectual weaknesses, he wrote, and "under favorable conditions," he might yet "achieve more than [the eminent physician]
Nothnagel, to whom I consider myself far superior, and possibly reach
the level of Charcot."[35]

But not even cocaine, the evident muse of this passage, could make
Freud believe himself capable of achieving greatness through hard
work alone. Instead, the drug coaxed forth his old fantasy of world
conquest. The people who disprized him and held him back were in
for a shock if they thought he was going to keep on groveling and suppressing his anger:

> Do you know what Breuer told me one evening? . . . He said he had
> discovered that hidden under the cover of my shyness there lay an
> extremely daring and fearless man. I had always thought so, but I
> never dared tell anyone. I have often felt as though I had inherited all
> the defiance and all the passions with which our forebears defended
> their temple and that I could gladly throw away my life for one great
> moment.[36]

The Freud who makes a debut here is the one who will later show
martial zeal as the leader of a militant soldiery. In 1886, however,
heroic martyrdom was as much glory as he could imagine. And even
so, his actual conduct in Paris, where he had sulked in his hotel when
not insinuating himself into Charcot's good graces, had been far from

valiant. The fantasist of mighty deeds had "never dared tell anyone" how "daring and fearless" he was.

If Freud, at the end of his Paris stay, felt at least intermittently energized, it wasn't because he had discovered his vocation as a therapist or theorist; it was because he now sensed himself to be a vehicle of Charcot's own transcendent force. That incorporation of the dominant male had already been hinted in a *Brautbrief* of December 12, 1885. There Sigmund told Martha that the courage he had recently shown in approaching Charcot with an idea of his own had been supplied to him by Charcot himself.[37] By freely submitting to one man, he wrote, he had overcome the need to subject himself to anyone else.[38] As Sigmund told Martha two months later, "I have been left with a valued, exalted memory of Charcot, almost, in its way, like [the feeling I had] after the ten days with you. It's as if I have experienced something beautiful that can nevermore be taken from me. In dealing with colleagues I feel ever more self-confident, adroit, and expert."[39]

Freud's expertise, however, was that of a conformist who, notably unlike Delboeuf, had completely overlooked the fallaciousness of Charcot's procedures. At the Salpêtrière, he had peripherally served an enterprise in which four kinds of factors were conjoining to produce examinable symptoms: the preexisting medical conditions of the inmates, the culture of the wards, the expectations of the indoctrinated medical team for reinforcement of Charcot's theory, and the carrot-and-stick extension of those expectations into incentives for compliance. A whole sociology of meretricious "knowledge production" in coercive circumstances could have been inferred from a clear-minded analysis of that spectacle. But Freud's record of critical reflection in Paris is a cipher.

Both before and during his stay in Paris, Freud had been exposed to much trenchant criticism of Charcot's operation. As early as 1878 an unsigned editorial in *The Lancet*—a preeminent journal to which Freud himself would contribute before receiving his travel grant—had disparaged Charcot's quixotic advocacy of metallotherapy, adding:

> The question appears to us to be beset with pitfalls of fallacious
> inference far more grave and numerous than Professor CHARCOT

is disposed to admit; and we think that the profession will do well to suspend its judgment until some more independent evidence is forthcoming than that furnished by the well-trained patients of the Salpêtrière.[40]

Those well-trained patients were already an international scandal by the time of Freud's arrival in Paris. But the ongoing denigration of Charcot appears to have left no impression on him. His concern was not with passing judgment on methods and conclusions or with attending to patients' stories but with forestalling a collapse of his own self-esteem. To that end, he had sought a transfusion of confidence from Charcot in person; and that process could succeed only if he believed in his idol's infallibility.

This yen for borrowed power, though, was unpropitious for a future career in psychology. Closely regarding Charcot over a period of months, Freud had never noticed the egomaniac, the impresario, the fortune hunter, the manipulator, the torturer, or the insecure tyrant whose cordiality was premised on an understanding that he must never be contradicted. A young man who felt compelled to overlook such obvious traits would be questionably equipped, later, to penetrate the far less accessible realm of "the unconscious."

Some writers who have been appalled by Charcot's coldness cannot bring themselves to believe that Freud revered him. In *Augustine (Big Hysteria)*—"one of the most important plays," it has been said, "in the new feminist theatre of hysteria"—Anna Furse depicts an alarmed, offended young Freud in rebellion against his overbearing and unfeeling host.[41] This invented Freud, already equipped with proto-psychoanalytic curiosity and acumen, proffers sympathy to the abused Augustine. He is on his way to becoming hysteria's Pinel, humane and pathbreaking.

All's fair when dramatic conflict must be generated for theatrical ends. In this instance, however, the most strained liberty taken isn't "Dr. Freud's" anachronistic presence at the Salpêtrière circa 1880, when Augustine tricked her jailers and fled; it is his disapproval of Charcot's callousness. The Frenchman's power over his hysterics actually thrilled Freud and aroused his envy. Thus, when he succeeded at last in ingratiating himself with *le maître*, "I have only to say one word to Charcot," he gloated in a letter of February 1886, "and I can do whatever I like with the patients."[42]

As an outsider, Freud probably took little advantage of that license. That he savored it, however, indicates his solidarity with Charcot in regarding the Salpêtrière's inmates as less than fully human subjects. Not once, so far as we can tell, did he consider whether their welfare was being served by the daily humiliations to which they were subjected. Nor, then, necessarily, did he question whether Charcot's recourse to hypnotism—that overpowering of one mind by another—was the best means of probing for the wellspring of hysteria. The practice, insofar as Freud could master it, would become his own chosen means of inquiry, with results that, like Charcot's, would be dictated not by psychological insight but by the suggestive imparting of presuppositions. He was digging himself a deep hermeneutic pit—one from which, as we will see, he would never be able to emerge.

13

In Dubious Battle

1. BEARDING THE ELDERS

By the time he left Paris at the end of February 1886, Freud had to have known that a fierce debate over hypnotism and contaminated knowledge was in process between Charcot and his eventual nemesis, Hippolyte Bernheim of the University of Nancy, 175 miles east of the capital. In 1882 Bernheim, a neurologist, had been converted to hypnotic cures by observing the feats of a country doctor, Ambroise-Auguste Liébeault, who had been offering pro bono treatments to the local peasantry. Bernheim himself soon became famous for removing symptoms through hypnotic suggestion.* But for that very reason he understood, as Charcot did not, that hypnotism couldn't serve as a reliable tool of inquiry. His guiding rule, a kind of Uncertainty Principle of psychology, was this: One cannot uncover a subject's mental state or history by a method whose application changes that subject. The rule is especially pertinent to hypnotism, which aims directly at rendering the subject obedient to the operator's suggestions.

The key term *suggestion*, it must be recognized, bears two conflict-

---

* See, e.g., Bernheim 1965, pp. 215–407. It is well established that hypnotism can affect not only psychological dispositions but also the gastrointestinal, cardiovascular, and respiratory systems and even the skin. See, e.g., Paul 1963; Orne and Dinges 1989; Frank and Frank 1991.

ing senses, covering both a deliberate and an unintended alteration of a subject's beliefs and behaviors. Charcot knew that he was experimentally "suggesting" such changes (a paralysis, a contraction, a hallucination), but he never grasped that he was accidentally "suggesting" (telegraphing) his wish that the subject fall into line with Salpêtrière expectations. It was his neglect of the latter meaning that caused him to mistake a conscious mental act—compliance with his tacitly understood desire—for evidence of a preexisting susceptibility to *la grande attaque hystérique*.

The keenly reflective Bernheim understood that hypnotism is only a special case of a general phenomenon whereby a powerful party can impose beliefs on a weaker one. And thus he also saw that a failure to take suggestibility into account would inevitably lead researchers to overlook their own influence on their findings. When later psychologists implemented experimental controls and took subliminal influence as an object of study in its own right, they were acting in Bernheim's spirit. So, too, every modern student of false-memory formation owes a debt to Bernheim, who warned that persistent pressure could induce a cowed subject to "remember" scenes that had never occurred.

Bernheim's position was stated in two books whose publication closely surrounded Freud's stay in Paris: the concise 1884 *De la suggestion dans l'état hypnotique et dans l'état de veille* (waking state) and the ampler and more celebrated 1886 *De la suggestion et de ses applications à la thérapeutique*.[1] Charcot didn't deign to reply, but as the threat loomed ever larger, he trained his biggest guns on Bernheim: Georges Gilles de la Tourette, Joseph Babinski, Alfred Binet, and Charles Féré. They stayed on the offensive from 1884 through 1889, reiterating Salpêtrière orthodoxy in journals and books and ridiculing inadvertent suggestion as an empty concept. But by the end of the decade, Bernheim was the clear victor. Even in 1885, all parties knew that the Salpêtrière dispensation would survive only if its proponents could refute the charge that suggestion had corrupted every one of their findings.

Even Freud would finally have to address Bernheim's challenge—not, however, because he registered its full import but because he could no longer ignore the trend of informed opinion. But in the late winter of 1886, he couldn't afford to ponder Bernheim's argument at all. And so, when he now ventured forth to uphold Charcot's wisdom, he made sure to leave the war between Paris and Nancy completely out of account.

Freud had planned to spend three weeks in Berlin before proceeding to Wandsbek and then Vienna. As things worked out, he had to tuck a brief Wandsbek visit (March 26–29) into a Berlin stay that lasted from March 1 until April 3. His *Brautbriefe* of March 1886—a month he spent among pediatric neurologists, preparing for his role as the head of a planned neurological department in Max Kassowitz's Public Institute for Children's Diseases—betray a new combativeness that was centered on the defense of Charcot against all naysayers.*

The well-established German physicians, Freud wrote, were impervious to Charcot's appeal. "It is strange how everyone here believes there is a great deal of humbug at Charcot's clinic," said a letter of March 6, "and that the things he is studying are merely curiosities." Rather than ask himself whether the critics might have a point, Freud judged them to be behind the times. As he remarked on March 5, "There is no doubt that the people who oppose Charcot are very backward. The comparison showed me the man's true greatness." Undeterred, he lobbied with some Germans on behalf of his "dear old master" (*meinem lieben alten Herrn*),[2] and he felt he was making converts among an open-minded younger generation.[3]

Although Freud was apprehensive about returning to Vienna as a militant Charcotian, he was full of energy and resolve. "I have completely forgotten my shyness," he wrote on March 18. And on March 25: "Little nostalgia for Vienna, but no fear of it, either." Finally, on April 2, his last full day in Berlin, he stated with ominous pugnacity, "I am fully prepared, . . . and 'Proud in my breast, assured of victory'—and will very much remember that the age of the nebbish is at an end." Indeed it was. The nebbish of pre-Parisian days, now cured of bashfulness by Charcot, cocaine, and Paris itself, had been sup-

---

* The Kassowitz position—part-time, unpaid, but prestigious—had been tentatively offered to Freud while he was away in Paris. He would hold it from 1886 to 1895, collecting valuable case material for publications in neurology. Curiously, however, he would make no use of that evidence in his psychological theorizing and would even deny that he possessed any firsthand acquaintance with child patients. See, e.g., SE, 7:193n; 9:214; 20:39.

planted by an implacable zealot who felt a mission to plant the cult of his dear master in Vienna.

But first, Freud had some explaining to do. He had been paid, albeit meagerly, to achieve two goals in Paris: to learn how neurological research was being handled there and to conduct his own postmortem study of children's diseased brains. From his Viennese colleagues' point of view, he had reneged on both promises and was arriving home empty-handed. Thus his reentry called for careful diplomacy and repair.

The written fellowship report that Freud submitted to the medical faculty on April 22, 1886, however, displayed no such tact.[4] There he stated, as he hadn't in his original application, that his main goal in visiting the Salpêtrière had been to weigh the frequently heard complaint that the latter-day Charcot and his fellow workers were uncritical and inclined to "dramatize" their hasty findings about hysteria.[5] That was what Freud's superiors, with good reason, still believed, and they must have been curious to learn about the tests of validity that their fellowship holder had applied to Charcot's claims. But no such tests had been brought to bear, and Freud skirted the issue. Instead, he wrote of "the great man's" sincerity, charm, and openness of manner, as if such traits guaranteed correct scientific results. "The attraction of such a personality," Freud declared, "soon led me to restrict my visits to *one* hospital and to seek instruction from *one* man."[6]

Freud went on in his report to expound Charcot's favorite syndrome of *grande hystérie*. He even included the "hysterogenic points" as Charcot had purportedly found them in the accident victim Pinaud.[7] By virtue of Charcot's efforts, according to Freud, "hysteria was lifted out of the chaos of the neuroses, was differentiated from other conditions with a similar appearance, and was provided with a symptomatology which, though sufficiently multifarious, nevertheless makes it impossible any longer to doubt the rule of law and order."[8]

More than a few eyebrows must have been raised by such categorical certainty, proffered without a hint of the evidence that had supposedly rendered skepticism "impossible." Freud did mention that his recently visited colleagues at Berlin's famous Charité hospital had as yet failed to notice the Charcotian "stigmata" of hysteria in their outpatients.[9] Among the many observers who remarked on the scarcity of *grande hystérie* beyond the Salpêtrière, he may have been the only one who didn't grasp that the integrity of the disorder was cast into doubt by that circumstance.

Most dogmatically, Freud endorsed Charcot's strangest conception, the *névrose* called "*grand hypnotisme*." It made no manifest sense to classify hypnotism, which is a two-party consensual practice, as a disorder, but Charcot had been driven to that extreme by his belief—definitively refuted by Bernheim and Delboeuf—that only hysterics can be hypnotized. For Charcot, *grand hypnotisme* differed only slightly from *grande hystérie* yet was somehow a syndrome of its own. The redundancy of the two *névroses* didn't trouble Freud, who counted *grand hypnotisme* among Charcot's most wonderful discoveries. "I found to my astonishment," he wrote, "that here were occurrences plain before one's eyes, which it was quite impossible to doubt, but which were nevertheless strange enough not to be believed unless they were experienced at first hand."[10] Every stage magician hopes that his audience will consist of precisely such eyewitnesses as Freud.

The student-turned-teacher had only just begun his campaign to reeducate the Viennese. On two occasions in May 1886, he delivered (probably identical) lectures on hypnotism to learned bodies, Vienna's Physiological Club and its Society for Psychiatry and Neurology.[11] And then he presumed to address the most distinguished forum of all: the Society of Physicians, whose ornate marble lecture hall, whose demand that every lecture offer a novel thesis and fresh evidence, and whose tradition of unsparing criticism from the floor had intimidated more seasoned presenters than himself. But this was the defiant new Freud, who couldn't be deterred from a set purpose.

The event, first scheduled for June 4 but then postponed until October 15, proved to be a humiliation and a watershed in Freud's life. His text hasn't survived; it probably suffered the fate of other documents that he periodically destroyed. Siegfried Bernfeld and then Henri Ellenberger, however, collating the Society of Physicians' minutes with extensive newspaper accounts, were able to reconstruct not only the substance of Freud's lecture but also the comments it provoked.[12] And Ellenberger, bypassing Freud's own later, misleading, comments about the event, set forth facts that undermined one of the pillars of the Freud

legend: the idea that he had been ridiculed and then shunned by trog-
lodytes who were too convention bound to accept his "innovations."

Freud's lecture, titled "On Male Hysteria," focused on a single
case that had preoccupied the Salpêtrière's researchers during the last
months of his visit. The patient was, once again, the bricklayer's apprentice Pinaud.[13] Three days after a fall that had knocked him unconscious, Freud related, Pinaud had developed left-side anesthesia and an
impairment of hearing and taste—followed, weeks later, by nervous fits
and finally by the attack of complete *grande hystérie* that Charcot had
found so gratifying. Moreover, Pinaud had exhibited "hysterogenic
zones" in his chest and in one testicle. Nevertheless, at last notice he
had appeared to be gradually returning to normal.

Freud apparently neglected to mention that this patient's specifically
Charcotian symptoms had materialized only at the Salpêtrière and after
contact with the staff. Instead, citing an alcoholic father and a nervous
sister, he ascribed the entire "hysteria" to hereditary degeneration. In
his view, then, the case vindicated not only male hysteria but also the
ultimate predisposing cause of *grande hystérie*, exactly as pronounced
by Charcot.

No doubt Freud later regretted the emphasis of his lecture on hysterogenic zones and degeneration, two doctrines that would soon be
going out of style. If his lecture had been published, it would have constituted evidence that Freud in this period was parroting Charcot's
judgments instead of thinking for himself. But there is another inconvenience here—one that would never be faced by Freud or by his
modern adherents. All of the symptoms experienced by Pinaud before
his Salpêtrière initiation, and some of his subsequent symptoms as
well, were consistent with progressive effects of brain trauma.

The patient's distortions of hearing and taste, his one-sided anesthe-
sias, and his "generalized fits" without loss of consciousness strongly
suggest partial epileptic seizures. The timeline of the case poses no
obstacle to that diagnosis. Years can intervene between brain trauma
and the onset of afflictions like those mentioned here; nevertheless, healing within the brain can yield the early improvement noted by Freud.

Nothing about the case of Pinaud, then, requires the invoking
of a psychogenic wild card such as hysteria. We can say with high

probability that the patient had suffered injury to the right side of his brain, where his left-sided motor functions were being imperfectly controlled, and that the sequelae of his injury manifested themselves progressively over a period of weeks and then began to subside. Although the correlation between specific brain regions and symptoms like Pinaud's wasn't yet established in 1886, the prudent diagnostic course—the course Charcot himself would have followed in the 1870s—would have been to leave conceptual space for the existence of nerve damage while waiting for finer instruments of detection to arrive. But because Charcot was no longer exercising such caution, Freud, too, perceived no need for it.

In choosing to defend the existence of male hysteria, Freud committed another blunder. Few theorists anywhere, including those in his lecture hall, still believed that hysteria, if it existed at all, was unique to womankind. Charcot, who was always decorous in acknowledging predecessors, traced the theory of male hysteria to the seventeenth century, and he freely granted that his more immediate source for the idea had been Paul Briquet's 1859 *Treatise on Hysteria*.[14] But the Germans, according to K. Codell Carter's definitive review of the evidence, "seem to have regarded male hysteria as even more common than did Charcot."[15] And one member of Freud's audience, Moriz Benedikt—Charcot's good friend and annual visitor, and the author of Freud's letter of introduction to him—had been an outspoken advocate of male hysteria since 1868.[16] Benedikt must have been taken aback to hear that Charcot's agreement with his position was now being characterized as a novelty.

As Ellenberger learned, Benedikt was not alone in regarding Freud's thesis as supererogatory. From the floor, the neurologist Moritz Rosenthal protested that male hysteria, about which he had published an article sixteen years earlier, was an uncontroversial reality and therefore not worth discussing. Maximilien Leidesdorf, in whose sanatorium Freud had briefly served in 1885, added that it was impossible, when impacts were followed by somatic impairments, to exclude the factor of organic damage to the brain. But the severest rebuke was offered by the chairman of the meeting, Heinrich von Bamberger, who had been on the committee that had chosen Freud over other fellowship candidates. Bamberger commented, "In spite of my great admiration for Charcot and my high interest for the subject, I was unable to find anything new in the report of Dr. Freud because all that has been said has already long been known."[17] This was the official verdict: Freud had proffered no original research and had wasted his betters' time.

2. A SECOND TRY

Among the oral responses to Freud's October 15 talk, the most constructive and consequential seems to have been that of his laboratory mentor from 1883, Theodor Meynert. Like others in the hall, Meynert respected Charcot's early work but had no patience with theories that relied on hypnotism to produce their evidence. So far as he was concerned, *grande hystérie*, whether male or female, was phony science. And in Meynert's view, the unavailability of Pinaud for close reexamination in Vienna meant that Freud's sole, and secondhand, example possessed no utility for discriminating between Charcot's psychologically traumatic hysteria and so-called railway spine, which could be fully explained by reference to organic damage.

Quite often, Meynert remarked from the floor, he had encountered cases in which epileptoid physical and mental symptoms resembling Charcot's hysteria had been straightforwardly produced by accidents. As Frank J. Sulloway relates, "Meynert suggested that it would be interesting to see if any such cases exhibited the exact symptoms described by Freud, and he offered to put at Freud's disposal any appropriate material in his clinic, so that a more exact demonstration could be arranged."[18] This was a discreet way of letting Freud see that he had neglected to show why hysteria had to be invoked to account for Pinaud's afflictions. Meynert was now inviting Freud to examine cases of *nonhysterical* accident victims and to ascertain whether their troubles differed at all from those of the patients Charcot had classified as traumatic hysterics. If no consistent distinction could be noted by Freud or others, Charcot's category would have to be judged superfluous.

As we know from the subsequently published text of his second address to the Society of Physicians in the following month, however, Freud came away from the question period with a different understanding.[19] He thought he had been challenged only to produce "some cases in which the somatic indications of hysteria—the 'hysterical stigmata' by which Charcot characterizes this neurosis—could be observed in a clearly marked form."[20] It ought to have been obvious that such instances, in the absence of detailed comparison with purely organic cases, could have no bearing on the objection that Meynert had raised on October 15. But that objection had passed over Freud's head. He felt that if the Viennese physicians could only be made to see what he had been shown at the Salpêtrière, they, too, would bow to Charcot's authority.

Freud therefore set about the quixotic task of returning to the society with a male Charcotian hysteric in tow. No such patient was under his care. Eventually, however, he succeeded in borrowing a suitable-seeming candidate from a young laryngogolist. The debilitated man, no doubt hoping to learn of new treatment options, agreed to stand before a meeting of the society on November 26, 1886, when Freud would describe his symptoms and illustrate them by prodding various regions of his body.

Freud's sample patient, a twenty-nine-year-old engraver whom he called August P., was suffering from many handicaps, the worst of which were repeated attacks of convulsions and a pronounced insensitivity on the left side of his body. It is doubtful, prima facie, that ideas had produced those effects. And indeed, August P. had undergone a major physical shock. "In his eighth year," Freud disclosed, "he had the misfortune of being run over in the street; . . . and he fell sick of an illness which lasted for several months, during which he suffered frequently from fits . . . [that] continued for some two years."[21]

The epileptoid aspect of the case, though unremarked as such by Freud, is salient here in both childhood and adulthood. To quote Freud:

His present illness dates back for some three years. . . . His brother threatened to stab him and ran at him with a knife. This threw the patient into indescribable fear; he felt a ringing in his head as though it was going to burst; he hurried home without being able to tell how he got there, and fell to the ground unconscious in front of his door.

It was reported afterwards that he had the most violent spasms. . . .
During the next six weeks he suffered from violent left-sided headaches and intra-cranial pressure. The feeling in the left half of his
body seemed to him altered.[22]

In the three-year period between those events and Freud's lecture,
August P. had endured between six and nine further attacks of convulsions.[23] That history was strongly suggestive of a brain defect as posited by Meynert. Ever loyal to Charcot, however, Freud concluded that
those seizures must have been ideogenic. And he averred that August P.,
like Pinaud, displayed telltale hysterogenic zones, one of which extended
from "the left spermatic cord" to that abdominal area "which in women
is so often the site of 'ovaralgia.' "[24]

Freud ventured to end this second talk by expressing a "hope of
being able to restore the patient in a short time to normal sensitivity."[25]
Even if he had had more to offer his nervous clientele at this time than
placebo treatments, however, such healing of a man in August P.'s condition would have been little short of miraculous. And Freud's boast
rang doubly hollow: August P., to whom he had only recently been
introduced, wasn't his patient in the first place.

3. LOOKING BACK IN ANGER

The Freud of autumn 1886 was not impressing anyone with his medical astuteness, his grasp of logic, or his independence of mind. Nevertheless, he was still capable of addressing his senior colleagues in a
respectful and open manner. If his two addresses to the Society of Physicians regarding male hysteria mark a pivotal point in his career, it
isn't because they caused irreparable damage to his reputation. Rather,
it is because the rebuke he suffered for his gullibility toward Charcot
inflamed his incipient sense of isolation and persecution, rendering him
less willing than he had previously been to seek common ground with
colleagues. And that estrangement, as yet only a tense feeling rather
than an actual break, would be magnified in recollection until it figured as heroic resistance to orthodoxy.

Here is what Freud wrote in his 1925 *Autobiographical Study* regarding his 1886 presentations on male hysteria:

> The duty devolved upon me of giving a report before the "Gesell-schaft der Aerzte" [Society of Physicians] upon what I had seen and learnt with Charcot. But I met with a bad reception. Persons of authority, such as the chairman (Bamberger, the physician), declared that what I said was incredible. Meynert challenged me to find some cases in Vienna similar to those which I had described and to present them before the Society. I tried to do so; but the senior physicians in whose departments I found any such cases refused to allow me to observe them or to work at them. One of them, an old surgeon, actu-ally broke out with the exclamation: "But, my dear sir, how can you talk such nonsense? *Hysteron* [*sic*] means the uterus. So how can a man be hysterical?" ... At length, outside the hospital, I came upon a case of classical hysterical hemi-anaesthesia in a man, and demon-strated it before the "Gesellschaft der Aerzte." This time I was applauded, but no further interest was taken in me. The impression that the high authorities had rejected my innovations [*Neuigkeiten*] remained unshaken; and, with my hysteria in men and my production of hysterical paralyses by suggestion, I found myself forced into the opposition. As I was soon afterwards excluded from the laboratory of cerebral anatomy and for terms on end had nowhere to deliver my lectures, I withdrew from academic life and ceased to attend the learned societies. It is a whole generation since I have visited the "Gesellschaft der Aerzte."[26]

This passage contains a number of deceptive implications and out-right untruths:

- Freud hinted that his second audience had applauded tepidly, with-out discussion, because the prestigious doctors had already decided that he was to be treated as a nobody. But they had complied with his request for another hearing, and the reason no discussion ensued is that *all* of the many presentations at that session were limited to ten minutes.[27]

- There is no evidence to show that Freud was barred from Meynert's Laboratory of Cerebral Anatomy or from any other venue in the wake of his lectures on hysteria.
- Neither before, during, nor after his two lectures did Freud ever produce "hysterical paralyses by suggestion," nor did either of his lectures contain what he called "innovations."
- Freud was by no means "forced into the opposition" in 1886. Instead of withdrawing from academic life, he was just then undertaking his obligations as a *Privatdozent*. He would continue to give courses and single lectures after being granted the rank of *Professor Extraordinarius* in 1902.[28] In 1924, a few months before writing that he had withdrawn from academic life in 1886, he told Oskar Pfister, correctly, that he had kept on lecturing at the University of Vienna (although sporadically) until 1918.[29]
- Freud remained active in several medical societies at least until 1904.[30] As for his claimed exclusion from the Society of Physicians, he nominated himself for membership in 1887.[31] The fact that he was then elected proves that the objections to his lecture on male hysteria hadn't been meant personally. He was still a member at the very time, in the mid-1920s, that he was depicting himself as a pariah.

Whether deliberately or through memory distortion, everything that Freud asserted in 1925 about his setback in 1886 was false. Yet there is also a strain of continuity across those thirty-nine years. In his first months back from Paris, Freud was in a paranoid frame of mind. Colleagues who refused the Salpêtrière revelation were his enemies, whom he expected to mock and reject him. When they didn't do so, he still felt hated by them. By 1925 he had invented a complete story that was true to his feelings if not to the facts.

Already by 1888, Freud had selected a foe for life: Theodor Meynert. Because Meynert had openly disapproved of his surrender to Charcot and hypnotism, Freud believed that his former mentor was out to destroy his career. Yet Meynert, *after* the unpleasantness at the Society of Physicians lecture, had offered him not only his own lecture course in brain anatomy but also an assistantship in his laboratory, a boon that, if Freud had accepted the offer, could have placed him in an advantageous position for eventually inheriting the great psychiatrist's professorship.

Over the next several years, Freud repeatedly taunted Meynert in print for his aversion to hypnotherapy and his supposed failure to have properly understood Charcot. The feud would be carried into Freud's 1891 book *On Aphasia*, which was in part a critique of Meynert's conception of the brain. When Meynert died in the following year, Freud paid an obligatory condolence call on his widow and was presented with the choice of some books from the late psychiatrist's library. "Last week," he wrote to a friend, "brought me a rare human pleasure: the opportunity to select from Meynert's library what suited me—somehow like a savage drinking mead from his enemy's skull."[32]

Freud would get vicious again in *The Interpretation of Dreams*, where he first passed along the gossip that Meynert had been a chloroform sniffer in his youth and then "recalled" a purported incident from Meynert's final days:

> I had carried on an embittered controversy with him in writing, on the subject of male hysteria, the existence of which he denied. When I visited him during his fatal illness and asked after his condition, he spoke at some length about his state and ended with these words: "You know, I was always one of the clearest cases of male hysteria." He was thus admitting, to my satisfaction and astonishment, what he had for so long obstinately contested.[33]

This "recollection" rings false. In the first place, the two men's mutual antipathy by 1892, along with Freud's distaste for direct confrontations, renders it at least questionable that he would have called on Meynert while the latter was dying. Second, Meynert's part in the quarrel, after he was goaded by Freud in 1888, had consisted of just one expression of disappointment that a former student of physiology was now a Mesmeric aficionado. And most tellingly, Meynert had never denied the existence of male hysteria, much less participated in an "embittered controversy" over it. Indeed, he had acknowledged purported cases of male hysteria in his clinic. Thus it is preposterous to suppose that he belatedly admitted, to his victorious detractor, that he belonged to a previously denied class of neurotics.*

In broad respects, the record is clear: it was Freud who set out to antagonize Meynert and who substituted invective for a reasoned defense of Charcot and hypnotherapy. His hostility and spitefulness were still active more than thirty years later. In launching a permanent vendetta against his former teacher and benefactor while blindly adhering to the Salpêtrière gospel, Freud was showing himself to be a man in the grip of strange passions. These were not healthy signs for a career, just then beginning, that would purportedly be devoted to objective investigation of the mind.

3. THE DOUBLE AGENT

Not long after undertaking his private practice, Freud realized that he could no longer ignore Bernheim's ascent to preeminence. Characteristically, his first impulse upon finally reading the latter's *De la suggestion* in late 1887 was to consider translating the book into German.[34] His offer was accepted; and when, in July 1889, he paid his own visit to Bernheim in Nancy, *Die Suggestion und ihre Heilwirkung* (healing effect) was already in print.[35]

In 1887 virtually all concerned parties knew that the world of psychology wasn't big enough to hold both Bernheim and Charcot. Yet when Freud wrote a long encyclopedia entry on hysteria in the spring of 1888, his sole reference to Bernheim gave no hint of conflict. "The direct psychical treatment of hysterical symptoms will be considered the best some day," he wrote, "when the understanding of suggestion has penetrated more deeply into medical circles (Bernheim-Nancy)."[36]

In early 1888, then, Freud must still have believed that Bernheim's

---

* Freud's later supporters have noticed something fishy about the deathbed story, but they dare not say it was false, for then they would be calling Freud a liar or a hallucinator. "Regardless of whether it was true, factually or symbolically," writes one commentator, "the episode captures in miniature a fascinating dynamic: the masculine personification of positivistic science exerting himself to officially suppress the reality of hysteria that lurks just beneath the surface of his own sex" (Micale 2008, p. 241). The same writer subsequently remarks, "Meynert railed against the idea of male hysteria, until his own private deathbed confession" (p. 271).

therapeutic emphasis nicely dovetailed with the objective research find-ings of the Salpêtrière. Those findings included the purported discovery, hailed by Freud, that hysterical contractures can be removed through "bringing about a *transfert* by means of a magnet."[37] Apparently, he hadn't understood that the debunking of *transfert* was the crowning indictment in Bernheim's case against the Salpêtrière. Indeed, in 1888 Freud perceived no incompatibility between commending Bernheim and reiterating Charcot's gospel regarding male and female hystero-genic zones, magnetic "aesthesiogens," and even the uses of the gro-tesque ovarian compressor, all of which notions were anathema to the Nancy perspective.[38]

Thus Freud contracted to translate *De la suggestion* and made sub-stantial progress in doing so before paying much heed to its argument. Belatedly, however, he did realize that Charcot would not take kindly to a blanket endorsement of his archrival. Indeed, Freud may have been alerted to the Bernheim problem by Charcot himself.[39] But it then occurred to him that he was well situated to perform an unusual service for his touchy mentor in Paris. As he wrote to Wilhelm Fliess on August 29, 1888,

> With regard to the *Suggestion* book, you know the story. I undertook the work very reluctantly, and only to have a hand in a matter that surely will deeply influence the practice of nerve specialists in the next years. I do not share Bernheim's views, which seem to me one-sided, and I have tried to defend Charcot's point of view in the preface.[40]

In short, Freud had now decided to undermine Bernheim's claims prophylactically in the opening pages of Bernheim's own book, before any anti-Charcotian reflections could enter the reader's mind. And that plan, once conceived, was so appealing to Freud that he couldn't wait for the book's publication in early 1889. In a two-part article of September 1888, he excerpted his preface in order to notify the world that Bernheim's stand on hypnotic suggestion was mistaken.

The only paragraphs of the preface that Freud withheld in his article were the first two, in which Bernheim's work would be unreservedly commended. Those paragraphs were necessary to the preface because without them *Die Suggestion und ihre Heilwirkung* would have looked like sheer sabotage; but the same paragraphs had to be omitted from Freud's article so that Bernheim could be diminished in comparison with Charcot.

In both documents, the preface and the spin-off article, Freud summarized the Nancy/Paris dispute, which hinged on the nature of hypnosis. For the Charcotians, he wrote, hypnosis was a unique state of the nervous system, producing the phenomenon of *grand hypnotisme*; but for Bernheim "all hypnotic manifestations would be psychical phenomena, effects of suggestions."[41] Thus:

If the supporters of the suggestion theory are right, all the observations made at the Salpêtriére are worthless; indeed, they become errors in observation. The hypnosis of hysterical patients would have no characteristics of its own; but every physician would be free to produce any symptomatology that he liked in the patients he hypnotized. We should not learn from the study of major hypnotism what alterations in excitability succeed one another in the nervous system of hysterical patients in response to certain kinds of intervention; we should merely learn what intentions Charcot suggested (in a manner of which he himself was unconscious) to the subjects of his experiments—a thing entirely irrelevant to our understanding alike of hypnosis and of hysteria.[42]

Indeed, Freud added, the hysteria diagnosis itself was imperiled by Bernheim's thesis:

If suggestion by the physician has falsified the phenomena of hysterical hypnosis, it is quite possible that it may also have interfered with the observation of the rest of hysterical symptomatology: it may have laid down laws governing hysterical attacks, paralyses, contractures, etc., which are only connected with the neurosis through suggestion and which consequently lose their validity as soon as another physician in another place makes an examination of hysterical patients.[43]

Here, for once, Freud had grasped exactly what stood at issue and how essential it would be to determine where the truth lies. And here is where a genuine scientist, seeing an opportunity to resolve a major medical controversy, would have wanted to weigh the experiments of Bernheim, Delboeuf, and others and perhaps embark on further tests that might explode or validate *transfert* and *grand hypnotisme*.

Freud, however, lacked both the institutional means and the emotional detachment that would have been requisite to such an undertaking. Instead, as he would later do whenever psychoanalytic tenets were in trouble, he shifted into an ad hominem register, asking what kind of people would be comforted by the suggestion argument. His answer was *people who can't face the truth*: "I am convinced that this view will be most welcome to those who feel an inclination—and it is still the predominant one in Germany to-day—to overlook the fact that hysterical phenomena are governed by laws."[44]

There followed, in Freud's article and preface, some bluffing that will sound familiar to attentive students of his psychoanalytic works: "There is no difficulty in proving piece by piece the objectivity of the symptoms of hysteria." "*Transfert* in particular . . . is indubitably a genuine process." "We may accept the statement that in essentials [hysteria] is of a real, objective nature and not falsified by suggestion on the part of the observer." And if any further proof of *grand hypnotisme* were needed, Freud offered assurance that the Salpêtrière itself would speedily provide it.[45] That remark alone sufficed to show that he was oblivious to the risk of confirmation bias.

Having decided that he had better associate himself with Bernheim as soon as possible, but then having closed ranks with Charcot against him, Freud now experienced a further slippage of belief. As the 1880s drew to a close, medical opinion was settling the dispute conclusively in Bernheim's favor.[46] Influential works by Albert Moll, August Forel, and Albert von Schrenck-Notzing, along with those of Delboeuf, apparently tipped the balance.[47] And so Freud perceived that his categorical defense of Charcot was no longer sustainable.

Meanwhile, Charcot's reputation was crumbling for other reasons as well. His idea that diseases are clustered in "neuropathic families," each of which battens on a given "degenerate" line of people, was rendered obsolete by the spectacular achievements of Louis Pasteur and Robert Koch in identifying specific microorganisms as pathogens. Freud now had to live down such backward declarations as this, from his 1888 encyclopedia entry on hysteria:

> The aetiology of the *status hystericus* is to be looked for entirely in heredity: hysterics are always hereditarily disposed to disturbances of nervous activity, and epileptics, psychical patients, tabetics, etc., are found among their relatives. Direct hereditary transmission of hysteria, too, is observed, and is the basis, for instance, of the appearance of hysteria in boys (from their mother). Compared with the factor of heredity all other factors take a second place and play the part of incidental causes, the importance of which is as a rule overrated in practice.*

Now Freud found himself in a box. If he were to publish an article disavowing Charcot's exploded doctrine, he would have to explain why he had previously believed it. The only reason had been hero worship. Moreover, readers would want to know about the objectively documented cases of Freud's own that warranted his change of opinion; but his therapeutic record, as we will find, was a blank. Above all, if he were simply to join the camp of Charcot detractors, he would be forfeiting the advantage he most cherished for his career: the impression that he had been anointed by the greatest of all neurologists.

Freud appears to have realized, however, that he could uncouple himself from Charcot through the same means he had applied to Bernheim: translating one of the authority's books while disputing some of its tenets through subversive annotation. It may have been Freud himself who urged Charcot to contract, in 1891, for a German edition of the Tuesday lectures of 1887–88, which were about to be revised for French publication.[48] In any event, he knew that his previous rendering of the *Leçons sur les maladies du système nerveux* would make him the natural choice to translate the new *Leçons du mardi*. If Freud's

---

* SE, 1:50. Note that both Charcot and Freud, for all their insistence on male hysteria, believed that the disorder could be inherited only from the maternal side.

plan succeeded, Charcot would come off looking sufficiently meritorious on the whole, but readers would discover from the notes that his translator deserved to be counted among those critics who were thinking for themselves.

We can trace Freud's waffling about hypnotic theory just by following the twists in his editorial policy. He had challenged some of Bernheim's judgments in the preface and notes to his 1889 translation of *De la suggestion*; but when, in 1892, he rendered into German another of Bernheim's works, *Hypnotisme, suggestion, psychothérapie*, he allowed the text to speak for itself.[49] And nearly all of his criticisms of *De la suggestion* would be deleted from his translation of the second edition in 1896. But a converse development can be observed in his treatment of Charcot, whose fortunes were heading in the opposite direction from Bernheim's. As a self-appointed envoy from the Salpêtrière in 1886, Freud had allowed Charcot's formal lectures to appear in German accompanied by a glowing preface and, with the author's consent, just a few friendly notes and an altered title. But the poisonous notes he added to Charcot's *Leçons du mardi* in 1892–94 showed that he no longer regarded the beleaguered master's word as sacrosanct.

The German edition of Charcot's Tuesday lessons, *Poliklinische Vorträge*, was published in five installments between 1892 and 1894.[50] In accordance with his intention of giving with one hand and taking away with the other, Freud employed his preface to heap fulsome praise on "the great discoverer" and "sage" at whose feet he had sat "spellbound" in 1885–86, when "the magic of a great personality bound his hearer irrevocably to the interests and problems of neuropathology."[51] That titan's work, Freud hinted, was now being advanced, albeit with certain discriminating corrections of perspective, by the translator himself—a man who knew Charcot intimately and enjoyed his favor. As for the critical footnotes that would follow, Freud unctuously admonished, "I hope these remarks will not be understood as though I were trying in any way to set my views above those of my honoured teacher."[52] But that was just what he had in mind.

As we will see, by 1892 Freud was preparing to announce that he and Josef Breuer, not Charcot or anyone else, had unlocked the best-guarded secrets of hysteria, and that they would soon publish their findings in a collaborative book. For the moment, he would use his footnotes to Charcot's *Leçons* to herald the coming revelation. "Abnormalities of sexual life," he announced, not hereditary predisposition, constituted the key determinants of several psychoneuroses, including hysteria.[53] And still more confrontationally, he asserted that Charcot's whole conception of "neuropathic families" of diseases was mistaken.[54]

Charcot, for example, had included syphilis in the "arthritic" family, isolating it from two other syndromes that were then widely, and correctly, regarded as late stages of the same disease: tabes dorsalis (or locomotor ataxia) and general paralysis of the insane. Freud not only sided with the critics; he declared that his own experience as a physician proved Charcot wrong.[55] According to Freud, he had learned from his practice that Charcot's "provoking factors" for tabes actually bring about another disorder, "neurasthenia cerebrospinalis."* To Charcot's astonishment, the formerly accommodating Viennese psychotherapist, who couldn't have treated more than a handful of syphilis cases and had never speculated about their etiology, was now portraying himself as the superior expert in the classification of disorders.

In the longest (and penultimate) of his extant letters to Freud, on June 30, 1892, Charcot vented his indignation. "A stable mind," he wrote, could not have been so irrational as to associate tabes dorsalis with syphilis. And now the once diplomatic lord of the Salpêtrière bared his fangs. The proof of the arthritic grouping of diseases, he sneered, could be found in Freud's own lineage, *les familles juives*.[56] Jews, Charcot meant, were a degenerate race, and their inbreeding over the centuries had left them vulnerable to precisely those afflictions he had declared to be a natural set.

Charcot's final note to Freud, written two months before his death, perfunctorily conveyed what Toby Gelfand calls "a certain coolness."[57] He wished to hear nothing further from or about a man who had exploited his trust in order to upstage him and take the part of his enemies. But what about Freud himself? In the increasingly bigoted

---

* Allegedly a derangement of the spinal cord, neurasthenia cerebrospinalis would soon be exposed as nonexistent. See Savill 1908, pp. 128–131.

atmosphere of 1892, was he going to accept the imputation that he belonged to a putrefying "race"?

4. BACKTRACKING

That question had been on Freud's mind at least since medical school and steadily during his fellowship period at the Salpêtrière, when Charcot was already expounding an innate Jewish affinity for contracting diseases. However dismayed Freud may have been by such a blow to his self-esteem, he had meekly borne the humiliation at the time. In a *Brautbrief* of February 10, 1886, which we mentioned earlier, he had surveyed the medical record of his relatives and himself and deemed it all too illustrative of Charcot's point.

The first book of Charcot's that Freud translated, on nervous diseases, had said little about ethnic traits. The *Leçons*, however, dwelled pointedly on Jewish family trees and even on exemplars of "the wandering Jew" that the author had encountered as outpatients. There was, Charcot wrote, a uniquely Jewish "neuropathy of nomadism," compelling its victims to relocate from one country to another.

That view was developed in a book titled *The Wandering Jew at the Salpêtrière*, published while Freud was halfway through annotating the *Leçons*. Charcot wasn't the author, but the work had been composed under his supervision. In it, Henry Meige, one of Charcot's assistants, opined that the "Israelites," among whom "enormous intellectual strengths" were found side by side with "mental aberrancies," suffered disproportionately from a nervous malady: geographical restlessness.[58] As Freud probably knew, his own father, in his early days as a wool trader in Moravia, had been registered with the authorities as a Galician "wandering Jew."[59] And Sigmund was well aware that prejudicial laws, not "neurosis," had kept Jacob on the move.

Now Freud might have been tempted to launch a thoroughgoing critique of Charcot's pseudo-objectivity, whereby the effects of social oppression were "scientifically" construed as innate pathology in the persecuted group. In no extant documents, however, did he contemplate such a step. If the idea occurred to him, he must have found it incompatible with his ambitions. A Jewish physician who complained

about anti-Semitic theory would be branding himself as a troublemak-
ing outsider. Freud, in contrast, was looking forward to being known
as a universalist, precisely in the mode of Charcot. And he still wanted
Charcot's prestige to serve as his membership card in the nondenominational fraternity of science.

More particularly, he wanted to join the company of those psychologists who had been drawing conclusions about the structure of
the mind from hypnotic (or otherwise inhibition-loosening) methods,
just as Charcot had done. Bernheim and Delboeuf had shown that
such an enterprise could never be secure against self-deception, and
Freud had belatedly, and grudgingly, conceded that their position was
a respectable one. But if he were to join Charcot's own former staff
members in acknowledging, as they all did in the 1890s, that Salpêtrière
research on hysteria had been a farce, he would be tying his own
hands.

These considerations explain why Freud's obituary essay on Charcot, published in September 1893, proved to be a tissue of obfusca-
tions. The essay, nominally a tribute to the lost master, was a thinly
disguised promotion for Freud's and Breuer's just-emerging position on
hysteria, which was going to complete and correct Charcot's work. Of
course the final acrimony between Freud and Charcot went unmentioned. For us today, nonetheless, echoes of the quarrel can be heard.
Freud wrote, for example, that Charcot "was very sensitive about the
accusation that the French were a far more neurotic nation than any
other and that hysteria was a kind of national bad habit."[60] He couldn't
have raised that point without recalling that the Jews, in Charcot's
opinion, were the "nation" that was disproportionately prone to nervous disorders.

In Freud's idealization, Charcot had uplifted the whole disprized
class of hysterics, who had been considered malingerers until the great
humanitarian demonstrated "the genuineness and objectivity of hysterical phenomena."[61] More specifically, Charcot had made the following "surprising discoveries": the four stages of *grande hystérie*; its status
as the master pattern; the "localization and frequent occurrence of the
so-called 'hysterogenic zones' and their relationship to the attacks";
the frequent occurrence of male hysteria; and a broadening of the

number of symptoms that could now be recognized as hysterical.*
Freud even praised Charcot for having found that hysteria "was a form
of degeneracy, a member of the 'famille névropathique'"—though two
pages later the same idea was said to "require sifting and emending."[62]

Freud reserved his highest praise for Charcot's experimental method,
which "assured him for all time, too, the fame of having been the first
to explain hysteria":

> While he was engaged in the study of hysterical paralyses arising after
> traumas, he had the idea of artificially reproducing those paralyses,
> which he had earlier differentiated with care from organic ones. For
> this purpose he made use of hysterical patients whom he put into a
> state of somnambulism by hypnotizing them. He succeeded in prov-
> ing, by an unbroken chain of argument, that these paralyses were the
> result of ideas which had dominated the patient's brain at moments
> of a special disposition. In this way, the mechanism of a hysterical
> phenomenon was explained for the first time.[63]

But now the moment had come for Freud to make a show of independence by playing off Bernheim against Charcot:

> The restriction of the study of hypnosis to hysterical patients, the
> differentiation between major and minor hypnotism, the hypothesis
> of three stages of "major hypnosis" and their characterization by
> somatic phenomena—all this sank in the estimation of Charcot's con-
> temporaries when Liébeault's pupil, Bernheim, set about construct-
> ing the theory of hypnotism on a more comprehensive psychological
> foundation and making suggestion the central point of hypnosis.[64]

Freud's strategy, then—designed both to prop up Charcot's reputation and to indicate a need for his own improvements—was to maintain that Bernheim's critique had destroyed grand hypnotisme but had
left grande hystérie unscathed. Needless to say, that was illogical; if

---

* SE, 3:21. As we have seen, Charcot had actually tried to simplify hysteria by relegat-
ing to insignificance all of its symptoms that didn't occur within grande hystérie.

inadvertent suggestion had contaminated one part of Salpêtrière research, the rest had been disqualified, too. Freud was sacrificing cogency to the more pressing cause of safeguarding his own "research" into hysteria.*

An obituary needn't meet the criteria expected of a scientific paper. In all of Freud's theoretical statements we have examined thus far, however, whether they be about hypnotism, hysteria, or cocaine, we perceive the same self-advancing character. The aim isn't to solve a problem but to put Freud himself in the most favorable light, either as a seasoned inquirer, a recognized associate of a leading figure, an astute critic of that figure, or a discoverer who will soon reveal an important truth. In his drive to become famous for *something*, Freud saw himself falling behind the most creative and rigorous thinkers in his field. His only recourse was to attach himself sycophantically to great reputations and then to undermine them, leaving himself positioned as our sole guide to a wiser course.

---

* Freud would continue to invest uncritical faith in phenomena that Charcot had elicited through flawed experimentation. Hysterogenic zones, for example, would figure in his portion of the 1895 *Studies on Hysteria* (see, e.g., SE, 2:148–151); he would inform Fliess that he possessed such a spasm-inducing spot on his own torso (3/13/85; FF, p. 120); and in December 1896 he would still be detecting Charcot's "clownism," or *grands mouvements*, in his own patients (12/17/96; FF, p. 218).

1. Jacob Freud and his son Sigismund, age eight

2. *Amalie Freud and her son Sigismund, age sixteen*

3. *Eduard Silberstein, Freud's best friend in adolescence*

4. *Martha Bernays and Sigmund Freud in 1885, during their engagement*

5. Minna Bernays, Freud's future sister-in-law, age eighteen

6. *Ernst Fleischl von Marxow,*
Freud's teacher, friend, and
fellow user of cocaine

7. *Freud's colleague*
Carl Koller, who discovered
cocaine anesthesia

8. *André Brouillet's 1887 painting* A Clinical Lesson *at the Salpêtrière, depicting Jean-Martin Charcot's induction of a hysterical fit*

9. *Joseph Delboeuf, Charcot's most incisive critic*

PART FOUR

PLAYING DOCTOR

My colleagues are of the opinion that I make a diagnosis of hysteria far too carelessly where graver things are in question.

—Freud, *The Psychopathology of Everyday Life**

---

* SE, 6:166.

14

Medicine Man

1. SETTLING IN

On April 25, 1886, Freud inaugurated his private practice, characterizing himself in a small newspaper advertisement as a Docent in Neurology who had just "returned from spending six months in Paris."[1] In
that inconspicuous fashion he assumed a role that, sustained over more
than half a century, would bring him worldwide attention as an alleged
healer, scientist, and wise commentator on human nature and fate. We
mustn't suppose, though, that any portents of that outcome could have
been detected at the outset. Freud saw nothing uplifting or even promising in the medical vocation; he doubted his capacity to meet its minimum requirements; and his overriding concern with income militated
against reflection about the sources of his patients' maladies.

In the spring and summer of 1886, Freud was in an especially poor
state for launching a career. Soon after repatriating on April 4, he had
begun to feel anxious and frustrated. The fervor for Charcot that had
recently energized him in Berlin wasn't going to be helpful in positivist
Vienna. His *Brautbriefe* from the next three months show a higher
incidence of physical and psychological complaints—chiefly migraine
headaches, crippling depression, and outbursts of fierce anger—than in
any comparable period during his four-and-a-half-year engagement.

"What bothers me most," he wrote on April 29, "is the continuing tired mood and general weakness once the headache has passed."

Missing from the extant letters is Freud's earlier fantasizing about thrills in the marriage bed. In his current mood—"I am . . . not enjoying anything, have not looked cheerful for weeks, and am, in short, so unhappy"—he wouldn't have been susceptible to Martha's charms.[2] If he was nevertheless determined to avoid any further postponement of the wedding day, now scheduled for September 13, it was partly because he felt himself to be aging prematurely and becoming less adaptable to a woman's needs and peculiarities. "How long are people young," he asked his fiancée, "how long are they healthy, how long can they maintain the flexibility that allows them to adjust to changes in the other person's condition?"[3] Freud had recently turned thirty when he wrote that lament.

In a letter of June 5 he concisely expressed his sense of what was bringing him down: "Money and nothing but money, my sweet" (*Geld u. nichts als Geld, mein Liebchen*). And he added: "You can easily believe how this has changed me." Indeed, before learning in July that Martha would be getting an unexpected dowry, Freud worried constantly about whether he could earn enough to support a household in Vienna. If not, he and his bride might have to emigrate to his least favorite country, the mob-ruled United States. (Be sure to take a napkin with you in that case, advised Breuer, because you are probably going to become a waiter.)[4]

Freud's money trouble had been partly of his own making. In Paris he had squandered some of his meager resources. His benefactors Paneth and Breuer had evidently become distrustful and had declined to send him another sou;[5] and even Martha suspected that her beloved was acquiring the habits of a *boulevardier*. Back in Vienna, interestingly, Freud at first sensed an ongoing reserve in both Breuer and Paneth, as if they had lost some of their former confidence in his self-discipline.[6]

Once reestablished in Vienna, Freud was drawing on the just-released second half of his fellowship stipend to pay for lodging, employ a maid, purchase medical equipment, support his birth family, and underwrite recuperative trips taken by his mother and a sister. Meanwhile, he felt ethically bound to refuse emergency help offered by the visibly shrunken Ernst Fleischl. That was commendable, but it left Freud unsure whether he would be asking Martha to become the wife of a pauper.

But it was not in Freud's nature to economize. In April, preparing to open his practice, he had already secured elegant, strategically located quarters at Rathausstrasse 7, paying a rent beyond his means. In August, contemplating his September wedding, he took on an even grander and more expensive suite at Maria Theresienstrasse 8. This would be the Freud residence and the site of his medical practice until the family moved to the now famous Berggasse 19 apartment, with its seventeen rooms, in 1891.

Among other vexations, Freud learned at the end of June that he would be called up for reserve military service from August 9 through September 10.[7] That stint turned out to be a pleasant vacation from his worries; as he wrote to Minna Bernays, he was marching "with the help of cocaine."[8] The prospect of military duty, however, meant that any income stream from chronic patients would be interrupted and perhaps foreclosed. The logical conclusion, drawn by Sigmund's prospective mother-in-law, was that he ought to delay getting married until at least the end of the year. But she sensed, correctly, that he wasn't going to budge. Your "ill-humor and despondency," she scolded him, "border on the pathological."[9]

When he wasn't laid low by headaches and black moods, Freud went about soliciting favors he would need for three purposes: attracting patients to his practice, securing permission to give his fall university course on some topic he had already mastered, and gaining access to patient records and other research material that could lend substance to his lectures in that course. In addition, then, to opening his practice, giving talks to physicians' gatherings, completing his Charcot translation, working in Theodor Meynert's laboratory, and beginning his part-time duties at the Kassowitz Institute before their official start, Freud paid diplomatic calls on Moriz Benedikt, who controlled the policlinic's records at the General Hospital; on Hermann Nothnagel, who, if well disposed, could send many patients his way; and on Meynert himself, who would have to step graciously aside if Freud's university course were to deal with his own specialty, brain anatomy.

Some of this lobbying was successful beyond Freud's expectations, and some of it was disappointing. All of it, however, was distasteful to him. He no longer felt like the deferential underling who had humbled himself before members of fellowship and appointment committees. It was still necessary for a while longer to court sponsorship, but once it was acquired, Freud felt unclean. "I am becoming fashionable," he wrote on April 15, "and I do not like it at all."

Both Breuer and Charcot—the first in personal discussion, the second in demonstrations at the Salpêtrière—had piqued Freud's interest in one "neurological" disorder, hysteria. In his financial straits, however, he was in no position to turn away any patients who could be enticed across the threshold of his consulting room. Thus, for example, he willingly kicked back twenty percent of one early fee to a tour leader who demanded payment for steering a wealthy Russian patient his way.[10] The Russian's ailment didn't matter; his affluence did.

In the first years of his doctoring, Freud's preoccupation with the rank and financial status of his patients was incessant. Only "very minor people" (sehr kleine Leute), he complained on June 1, 1886, were willing to seek his ministrations. Again on June 13 he fretted, "I have no new work from the better social classes." Instead, he wrote, he was reduced to dealing with some Romanian Jews—people, he complained, who paid badly and were unpleasant in the bargain. In July he was elated to learn that a Portuguese count had been sent his way for treatment, but this proved to be too much of a good thing. As he would find, it was impossible to remonstrate with such a cavalier eminence over unpaid bills.[11]

Breuer had impressed upon the novice an obligation to accept outright charity cases. Only through such altruism could a physician demonstrate a trustworthy degree of community mindedness. But for Freud, this added vexation was almost too much to bear. To make matters worse, he felt obliged to take on a certain number of freeloading patients who could have afforded to pay. It was customary to waive fees for clients who were themselves doctors or who had been referred by friends—one of whom proved to be Freud's Paris companion Giacomo Ricchetti.[12]

Freud was astonished by the naïve trust that patients invested in his imagined healing power. "Yesterday," he reported on May 17, 1886, "a very dear, busy colleague also came by my clinic, and today his wife was here in tears, looking for reassurance. I had to laugh! As if I were master of life and death!" We can be sure, however, that Freud kept his laughter to himself. He was beginning to share Charcot's long-held belief that it is no part of a doctor's role to dash the misplaced hopes of his social equals or superiors.

It was only with Martha Bernays that Freud allowed his self-doubts to show. "Another question," he wrote, "is whether I will be satisfied with this as an occupation, and I can tell you that it is a sad way of earning one's bread, and one must have a great deal of humor and energy in order to avoid being irritated and ashamed by one's ignorance, embarrassment, and helplessness."[13] "Most of it I do not understand," he confessed, referring to medical lore in general; "whenever I succeed at something, I am very happy."[14] But success came rarely. "I have yet to help any patient," he wrote on May 4. And by June 8, seven weeks into his private career, he could congratulate himself for only one excellently progressing case—a case, as will be seen, that he had misunderstood.

3. THE CONVENTIONAL WISDOM

With exceptions that are not to his credit, Freud initially shunned medical experimentation; he wished to provide his clients with whatever mode of therapy they would have been offered by his competitors. In the 1880s the most popular of such nostrums was still electrotherapy, or the administering of "galvanic" (DC) or "faradic" (AC) shocks that were thought to alleviate any number of complaints, from neurasthenia and hypochondria to neuralgia, paralyses, spinal degeneration, and psychoses. This therapeutics, dating back to the late eighteenth century, was largely ineffectual, but it was still being endorsed by leading physicians, and Freud didn't hesitate to practice it.

In doing so, he was following the career advice of the eminent internist Hermann Nothnagel. When Freud had suddenly decided to become a neurologist in 1884, Nothnagel had admonished him that if he wanted referrals, he would need to specialize in electrotherapy. Freud had already attempted, unsuccessfully, to conduct experiments with an electrical device,[15] and he had lectured to visiting Americans about "electricity and electrodiagnosis."[16] Within the General Hospital, furthermore, he had begun to try electrotherapy, as the following passage from a *Brautbrief* of March 23, 1885, reveals: "Today I made an attempt to electrify my crazy [*meschuggenen*] patient, and the fellow passed out altogether and fell flat on the floor. That is quite unpleasant. I wasn't frightened, but the psychical impression that it made on him was very bad."

By April 29, 1886, when his practice wasn't yet a week old, Freud had managed to borrow a patented generator and to direct its current into a female patient, without discernible benefit. Undeterred, he kept on prescribing and carrying out electrotherapy after he had replaced the borrowed machine with a purchased one of his own. And because the electrified clientele assumed, erroneously, that Freud knew how to effect cures, most of them returned day after day for more of the same.

When we think of nineteenth-century electrotherapy, we probably imagine a low current flowing through electrodes attached to the subject's forearms. But Freud was drawing his instruction from Wilhelm Heinrich Erb's 1882 *Handbuch der Elektrotherapie*, which specified different techniques for different disorders; and Freud related that he had followed those instructions to the letter.* Erb insisted that the electricity be sent right where it was needed. To combat urinary incontinence in females, for example, he prescribed sending a "tolerably strong current for one or two minutes" through a wire inserted into the urethra, producing a "somewhat painful sensation"; and for erectile dysfunction, the penis and occasionally the testicles would be subjected to the same "tolerably strong" current.[17]

As we can tell from the *Brautbriefe*, what Freud liked about electrotherapy was its extended course of treatment. In 1886, he regretted only that he couldn't use the lucrative procedure more frequently. "One

---

* Erb was a distinguished neurologist and a professor at the University of Leipzig. Before writing his best-selling handbook, he had made major contributions to the understanding of syphilis and several muscle-wasting diseases. In touting electrotherapy for a spectrum of disorders, however, he appears to have allowed his judgment to be corrupted by the profits he was reaping from sales of his machine.

of my patients," Martha was told on May 26, "seems to have finished after only seven sessions. That will happen fairly often, and one must be content, but it demonstrates the uncertainty of all calculations." Three days later he reported a happier result: He had just been paid for another patient's eighteen sessions, presumably electrotherapeutic.[18] As he had written of one patient when he was moonlighting from the hospital in 1885, "I hope she gets herself electrified a lot, so that your summer stay can turn out richer."[19]

In his *Autobiographical Study* of 1925, Freud claimed that he had been "soon driven to see" that Erb's electrotherapy was a worthless placebo, and so he had promptly "put [his] electrical apparatus aside."[20] But when was that? Ernest Jones asserted that Freud forsook his generator after just twenty months of application—that is, through the end of 1887. It is certain, however, that he was still practicing electrification uncritically in February 1888.* And the late Peter Gay, in the only sentence he devoted to the topic in his biography, proposed that Freud was still electrifying patients "in the early 1890s."[21]

In a lecture of May 1892 to the Vienna Medical Club, Freud brought electrotherapy into the argument. Why should we expect one hypnotic session to resolve a case of neuralgia, he asked, when it may take many sessions of electrotherapy to yield that result?[22] Here is Freud, then, having privately treated nervous illnesses for six years, endorsing electrical treatments whose inutility he had supposedly perceived almost at once in 1886. If he was telling the truth when he asserted in 1925 that he had lost faith in Erb's curative claims near the outset of his career, he had knowingly allowed patients to be deceived while his own wallet grew fatter. But the burden of evidence suggests that he retained an indolent trust in electrotherapy until his patients' dissatisfaction, aroused by public controversy, became a problem for him.

We might suppose that the inquisitive Freud, once he began drawing generally "nervous" patients into his practice, would have been eager to establish close rapport with them and to draw out their traumatic

---

* In that month, having diagnosed "cerebral neurasthenia" in a patient, Freud reported to Fliess that, before becoming pregnant and relapsing, she had made "steady improvement with galvanization and *demi-bain* [hydrotherapy] treatment" (2/4/88; FF, p. 18).

histories. But in the early years, this does not appear to have been the case. Freud's usual therapy for "nerves" was conventional: to refer the patient to a rest cure in a sanatorium or spa.

The standard authority on such therapy, the American physician Silas Weir Mitchell, had targeted his regimen to nervous women, whose troubles, he believed, stemmed from inappropriate striving to compete with men—a problem about which Freud harbored similar feelings. Since 1873, the Weir Mitchell system had featured, as Elaine Showalter says,

> seclusion, massage, immobility, and "excessive feeding." For six weeks the patient was isolated from her friends and family, confined to bed, and forbidden to sit up, sew, read, write, or do any intellectual work. She was expected to gain as much as fifty pounds on a rich diet that began with milk and built up to several substantial daily meals.*

Freud went along with the Weir Mitchell program and its emulators, sending patients to facilities that paid him a modest fee for each day's residence of his patient.[23] Once out of his supervision, however, such patients might never return, and this he found disagreeable. As he candidly recalled in his *Autobiographical Study*, "prescribing a visit to a hydropathic establishment after a single consultation was an inadequate source of income."[24] Therefore, he wrote, he had immediately abandoned referring patients for baths and massage.

But once again, Freud's recollection was mistaken. As Ernest Jones conceded, he "was still using those . . . methods in the early nineties."[25] Nor, while the Weir Mitchell regimen remained in vogue, did he ever voice a doubt regarding its effectiveness. In October 1887, for example, we find him reporting to his in-laws that "a few days ago I put Frau Z. on a fattening cure"[26]—a sign of adherence to Weir Mitchell's philosophy, whereby the addition of body fat was thought to

---

* Showalter 1993, p. 297. The classic description of Weir Mitchell confinement is Charlotte Perkins Gilman's famous autobiographical story, "The Yellow Wallpaper," written in 1889 and published in 1892. Gilman, who had been driven temporarily insane by isolation and sensory deprivation, sent her story to Weir Mitchell himself in the hope that he would finally curtail his destructive advice. He did so, but without notifying or crediting Gilman.

restore a childbearing capacity that had been weakened by unwholesome female intellectuality.[27]

In January of the same year, Freud had published a glowing review of Weir Mitchell's translated book *Fat and Blood, and How to Make Them*, averring that the author's "procedure, by a combination of rest in bed, isolation, feeding-up, massage and electricity in a strictly regulated manner, overcomes severe and long-established states of nervous exhaustion."[28] He reiterated the point in his 1888 article "Hysteria":

> In recent years the so-called "rest-cure" of Weir Mitchell . . . has gained a high reputation as a method of treating hysteria in institutions, and deservedly so. . . . This treatment is of extraordinary value for hysteria, as a happy combination of "*traitement moral*," with an improvement in the patient's general nutritional state. . . . The best plan is, after four to eight weeks of rest in bed, to apply *hydrotherapy* and *gymnastics* and to encourage plenty of movement.[29]

By the time of *Studies on Hysteria* in 1895, almost a full decade after his practice had begun, he was blending Weir Mitchell principles with newer practices that we will discuss later. As he put it, "I have adopted the habit of combining cathartic psychotherapy with a rest-cure which can, if need be, be extended into a complete treatment of feeding-up on Weir Mitchell lines."[30]

Another popular way of treating hysteria was more sinister. From the 1870s until the century's end, women who were diagnosed as hysterical were often placed in the care of gynecologists who subjected them to harsh procedures—hysterectomy, ovariectomy, clitoridectomy, and urethral cauterization—that would presumably extirpate the source of trouble.[31] Charcot and Breuer condemned such cruelty, and Freud was unsure of its efficacy.[32] In 1888 he declared, with waffling circumspection, that the importance to hysteria of "abnormalities in the sexual sphere"—that is, genital defects—was "as a rule over-estimated."[33]

But that may not have been the end of the matter. The physician who, after Breuer, seems to have given the young Freud the most referrals was the noted gynecologist Rudolf Chrobak, whom Freud would later call "perhaps the most eminent of all our Vienna physicians"; Chrobak happens to have been one of the chief proponents and busiest performers of surgical cures for hysteria.[34] As a historian notes, Chrobak was "extraordinarily active in the castration of nervous women, having performed in a few years 146 operations."[35] Significantly, the practice of medical referral tends to be reciprocal. If Chrobak helped to jump-start Freud's marginal career by referring patients to him, it is all but certain that Freud directed some female "hysterics" into Chrobak's care.

In this connection, two *Brautbriefe* from 1886, when read in tandem, are of more than passing interest. On May 13, 1886, near the outset of his practice, Freud alluded to "the delicate aspects" of a case involving a nervous American doctor and his "beautiful and interesting" wife, about whom Freud was planning to consult Chrobak.[36] Ten days later he reported that the same woman "was operated on yesterday." It is hard to avoid the inference that the novice physician swallowed his misgivings and steered at least one unfortunate woman into a barbaric treatment.

The same result could come about simply by leaving medical dogma unchallenged. In 1894 one of both Breuer's and Freud's unsuccessfuly treated patients, "Nina R.," was being railroaded toward "castration" at the hands of the fanatical German gynecologist Alfred Hegar. The supposedly timid Breuer protested vigorously, citing the physical and psychological harm caused by such butchery and calling the "epidemic" of female castration "a gynecological scandal."[37] Freud, however, though he disapproved of Hegar's views,[38] appears to have said nothing. Nina R. was indeed remanded to Hegar's clinic, where she was at least temporarily spared by the discovery that she was suffering from tuberculosis. If she did remain unmutilated, it was not because her primary physician, who would later depict himself as a man of exceptional moral courage, had intervened to protect her.

4. CLINICAL TRIALS

If a physician needs money so badly that he is reluctant to turn away any patient who can afford his fees, the potential destruction he can wreak is considerable. When a well-known local actor, Hugo Thimig, approached Freud in May 1886 complaining of dysfunction and/or pain in a wrist, Freud hesitated to refer him to a qualified orthopedic surgeon. Why not have a go at repairing the damage himself? His extensive knowledge of anatomy, however, was not matched by surgical experience or deftness. Of his various internships, not a single one of which had stimulated his intellect or suited his disposition, the most antipathetic had been in surgery. Even Jones felt obliged to concede Freud's "lack of surgical skill."[39]

The squeamish, irritable Freud applied his scalpel to Hugo Thimig's wrist in the dubiously aseptic environment of his consulting room in Rathausstrasse 7. On May 15, 1886, he told Martha of a devastating letter from Thimig expressing consternation (*Bestürzung*) that the operation hadn't succeeded. Humbled and disconcerted, Freud returned the fee that the wounded Thimig had gallantly proffered.

The Thimig case tells us something important about Freud: his malpractice in the Fleischl affair was not a fluke. Motivated in both instances by an ungrounded hope for a good result, he overrode normal precautions and placed a patient's health in needless jeopardy. And though both fiascos made him feel ashamed, neither of them taught him to become more circumspect. He would have a long career of acting on impulsive, sometimes fatal misjudgments.

Like other physicians of his day, Freud continually relied on pain-deadening drugs to treat both ordinary anxiety and a number of otherwise intractable conditions. And, as Jones acknowledged, his favored means of delivering those drugs was by injection. Starting in 1884, Jones laconically remarked, Freud had "employed [the hypodermic needle] a good deal in the next ten years for various purposes."[40]

What distinguished Freud from most of his fellow doctors in the later 1880s was his panacea of choice: cocaine. Neither Fleischl's scarecrow aspect nor the warnings that were now appearing in the medical press deterred him from continuing to self-medicate with the drug and try its effects on patients reporting various ills. Indeed, he was already acting as an informal cocaine doctor in Paris and Berlin before returning to Vienna to open his practice.

On February 23, 1886, shortly before leaving Paris, Freud had been summoned to visit a bedridden young cousin of Martha's, Jules Bernays, who was suffering from fever, an extreme inflammation of the throat, nocturnal delirium, and an inability to swallow. For Freud, who disliked Jules and who groused at having to treat him gratis, these grave symptoms pointed merely to a case of "throat croup" (*Halscroup*), for which he couldn't recall the standard treatment.[41] Deciding anyway, however, to make himself "master of the situation," he reached for his cocaine supply and painted the drug directly on Jules's throat. The correctness of his diagnosis and prescription, he believed, was demonstrated by Jules's immediate ability to swallow some wine and milk.

Freud paid three further calls on Jules Bernays in close succession, applying more cocaine and inducing sleep with morphine. (The Fleischl case had not dissuaded him from employing those drugs in combination.) Ascertaining that the patient retained an ability to eat and drink, he assured him that the illness had been banished for good (*dass alles vorüber sei*).[42] But Jules remained sick, and another doctor concluded that he was suffering from diphtheria—a conclusion that Freud angrily disputed in a letter from Berlin on March 6. The case, he told Martha, was an inflammation of the throat, period. And the thought that the whole Bernays clan now disagreed with him was infuriating. "Am I mentioned in the horror story about Jules's diphtheria?" he asked on March 9. "You have not said anything about it. I am still afraid of hearing that I provided the wrong treatment 'in the family.' As you know, I did not treat him at all, and he did not even have diphtheria."

Freud, however, *had* treated Jules, ineffectually, and his diagnosis had evidently been mistaken. But he didn't want to hear anything more about the matter. In Berlin, less than two weeks after hotly defending his handling of the case, he was daubing cocaine on the throat of an aristocratic acquaintance, Sally Levisohn—whose only symptom was a cough—and fretting that the pharmacist might not have prepared a sufficiently strong concentration of the drug.[43]

When Freud opened his practice the following month, he looked forward to administering cocaine for a spectrum of illnesses. On the very first day, he told Martha that he had been able to "provide some relief" for a man with stomach pains.[44] And two days later he said that another patient had looked him up because he recalled having been previously helped by cocaine.

In early May 1886, two weeks after declaring himself ready for consultation, Freud accepted a sciatica patient for treatment. Despite his previous lack of success with injecting cocaine directly into an affected site, he convinced himself that it was going to work this time. Over an eleven-day period, the new patient appeared in Freud's consulting room on every working day, presumably for another injection on each visit. Not surprisingly, the man became distinctly euphoric. And so did Freud, who wrote that

> the sciatica patient, to Breuer's amazement, is on his way to recovery, and is actually scheduled to be released on May 15. As Breuer tells it, the man can hardly compose himself for "rapture," and he is already telling me about a lingering pain his wife has in her arm, and about all kinds of other people who have rheumatism. Since I restored him with an injection I had created, I am naturally more than a little proud, and I only hope that nothing happens and I can discharge my first healed patient.[45]

As predicted, Freud declared the man cured on May 15—by which time, for all we know, he may have created not just a giddy enthusiast for cocaine therapy but an addict as well. Of one thing we can be sure: cocaine does not cure sciatica. But Freud, once again, felt no desire to follow up the case. Having entered his ledger as the very first success of his private practice, it held no further interest for him. And having spared himself any unpleasant surprises regarding side effects, addiction, or relapse, he was well disposed to keep providing cocaine— swallowed, painted, or injected—for any of the numerous disorders to which it appeared to respond.

The most fundamental defect in Freud's ministrations, however, wasn't his choice of questionable remedies; it was his inaptitude for reaching correct diagnoses. His unchecked inclination was to find that the patient suffered from whatever ailment was preoccupying Freud at that moment. From 1887 into the nineties, the choice was usually hysteria. And when a given patient was subsequently shown to be harboring an organic disease, Freud still maintained that hysteria was part of the clinical picture.

Consider two cases of uncertain date that were narrated in *The Psychopathology of Everyday Life* (1901). In the first instance, Freud had taken on "a young man who had not been able to walk properly after an emotional experience":

> At the time I made a diagnosis of hysteria and I subsequently took the patient on for psychical treatment. It then turned out that though my diagnosis had not, it is true, been incorrect, it had not been correct either. A whole number of the patient's symptoms had been hysterical, and they rapidly disappeared in the course of treatment. But behind these a remnant now became visible which was inaccessible to my therapy; this remnant could only be accounted for by multiple sclerosis. It was easy for those who saw the patient after me to recognize the organic affection. I could hardly have behaved otherwise or formed a different judgement, yet the impression left was that a grave error had been made; the promise of a cure which I had given him could naturally not be kept.[46]

This is a characteristic "confessional" passage by Freud, half retracting an admission in the act of making it. The idea of a diagnosis that was neither correct nor incorrect is far from clear. And Freud's claim of having rapidly dispelled "a whole number" of hysterical symptoms is suspect, not only because he never possessed an efficient means of making symptoms vanish but also because his diagnosis was implausible. It had initially rested on the man's difficulty in walking, which was later fully explained by his multiple sclerosis. Freud misled this patient while fooling himself as well; and he chose to remain deceived even after having been proved wrong.

The same chapter of the *Psychopathology* contains another such account, at once sheepish, defensive, and confused. A fourteen-year-old girl, Freud wrote, had come to him with "an unmistakable hysteria, which did in fact clear up quickly and radically under my care":*

> After this improvement the child was taken away from me by her parents. She still complained of abdominal pains which had played the chief part in the clinical picture of her hysteria. Two months later she died of sarcoma of the abdominal glands. The hysteria, to which she was at the same time predisposed, used the tumour as a provoking cause, and I, with my attention held by the noisy but harmless manifestations of the hysteria, had perhaps overlooked the first signs of the insidious and incurable disease.[47]

This girl's "hysteria" was "noisy," we can gather, because she was screaming in pain. Not even her prompt death from cancer could induce Freud to reconsider his diagnosis or his assertion that his care, so far as it went, had been a great success. Would any other doctor, not excepting Charles Bovary, boast of having snappily "cleared up" the very symptoms that had made a quick and deadly reappearance?[48]

Because the girl with stomach cancer would have died in any event, Freud was blameless in her death (though surely not in her suffering). With his arsenal of potent drugs, however, he was tempted to overmedicate other patients and then fail to perceive that drug toxicity was causing symptoms of its own. Even if the initial diagnosis may have been right, the new iatrogenic condition would disastrously progress without alarming Freud. That, of course, is just what happened with Fleischl, but his case was not unique.

Consider the patient known as "Mathilde S." (Schleicher), the daughter of a well-known Viennese painter, whom Freud treated intermittently over a two-and-a-half-year period beginning in early 1889.[49] Mathilde struck Freud as an inhibited, self-reproachful, delusional melancholic and insomniac featuring "zirkuläre Verstimmung," corresponding roughly to what would later be called manic depression or bipolar disorder.[50] At the time, Freud was treating nervous cases with

---

* According to Freud's letters to Fliess, the girl was actually thirteen. See 6/12 and 6/18/00; FF, pp. 418, 419.

hypnotism, under which the lulled patient would be commanded to quit her symptoms; and he tried it again in this instance. We know from his reminiscences, however, that he had trouble hypnotizing anyone; in all likelihood, therefore, Mathilde's hypnotic induction was facilitated by one or more soporific drugs.

Freud regarded Mathilde's treatment as successful, and so did she at first; but then she developed so many new symptoms of a transparently manic character—including an obscene display of longing for sex with Freud himself—that in October 1889 she was sent into a Viennese psychiatric clinic where Freud was serving as a consulting physician. Albrecht Hirschmüller continues the story:

> While the patient was hospitalized, use was made of the entire range of medications available at the time: morphine, chloral hydrate, valerian, bromide, digitalin, opium, scopolamine, and sulfonal, a sedative that had recently been discovered. Unwanted and extremely severe side-effects resulting from the chloral hydrate endangered the patient's life. But she recovered and left the clinic in May 1890, still suffering from melancholia.
>
> Freud resumed treatment, prescribing alternating high doses of chloral hydrate and sulfonal, but apparently did not hypnotize her further. In the autumn she displayed a heightened pattern of vomiting, abdominal pains, and retention of urine, which was red in color. At the end of September the patient died. Shortly afterwards, a warning was issued against [sulfonal], and Mathilde's clinical symptoms were recognized as the expression of the presence of a severe hepatic porphyria resulting from the medication. In a report that was succinct and clear, Freud assumed responsibility for the fatal consequences of his treatment.[51]

In brief, then, Mathilde Schleicher died as a result of an overdose of a relatively new drug whose deadly properties were unknown to Freud or anyone else. But there is more to the story. Freud had either prescribed or failed to countermand a ghoulish smorgasbord of morphine, chloral hydrate, valerian, bromide, digitalin, opium, scopolamine, and sulfonal: extremely severe, indeed life-threatening, side effects of the chloral hydrate, at least, were noted before her discharge. Yet when Freud resumed her care, he put her back on "alternating high doses of chloral hydrate and sulfonal." And he apparently kept her on the fatal regimen straight through the period of her terminal vomiting, cramps, and red urine. Just weeks after Mathilde's death on September 24, 1890, a medical article revealed that sulfonal can cause porphyria and destroy a patient's liver.[52]

Freud's brief and impersonal report on Schleicher's treatment and its outcome stated that the sulfonal, previously administered on a trial basis (*probeweise*), had rendered her "very anesthetized" or "stupefied" (*sehr betäubt*).[53] Freud had apparently welcomed that result, which he sought to duplicate in the next phase of therapy—even though Mathilde's deterioration had already shown that the sulfonal had been at best ineffective and possibly noxious. Not knowing how to remove her symptoms, he aimed to mask them through recourse to the same drugs that had almost killed her; and this time he terminated the case altogether through medical manslaughter.

5. A SKELETON IN THE CLOSET

While Freud owned up to his treatment of Schleicher, there were many incidents in his career that he wished to keep in darkness. None is more tantalizing than the suicide of Pauline Silberstein, the first wife of his best friend in adolescence. Pauline had come to Vienna from Romania in 1891 to be treated by Freud for a nervous condition. According to one account, she had rented some space in his own apartment/office building, the rebuilt "*Sündhaus*" on Vienna's Maria Theresienstrasse.* On May 14, 1891, Pauline died instantly upon plunging over a balustrade on an upper story of the building.

In Freudian circles, the favored version of this rarely discussed tragedy is that Pauline, suffering from major depression, climbed the stairs and leaped before Freud could meet her for their very first therapeutic

---

* The "house of repentance" was so named because, as the former Ringtheater, it had been the site of Vienna's most horrendous fire, killing some 600 audience members in 1881.

hour. Kurt Eissler, for one, insisted that Sigmund and Pauline were totally unacquainted when she jumped.[54] And that is the inference we are meant to draw from Walter Boehlich's Eissler-influenced introduction to the Freud/Silberstein letters.[55] But there are reasons to believe otherwise.

Fondly recollecting his late friend in a letter of 1928, Freud stated to Eduard's Romanian B'nai B'rith chapter that he "once had occasion to attend to [Silberstein's] first wife."[56] He would hardly have said that about a patient who killed herself before the first appointment. And no less persuasive is a recollection by Eduard's granddaughter, who resisted Eissler's strenuous insistence that Freud and Pauline hadn't met.[57] According to this descendant, she had been told by her mother and by three of the mother's cousins that the miserable bride "was treated unsuccessfully by [Eduard's] friend Sigmund Freud, and threw herself from a window [sic] in Freud's apartment building."[58] Within the Silberstein family tradition, it is clear, Pauline's death was linked to Freud's dealings with her.

We cannot declare with any assurance that Frau Silberstein jumped *after* consulting with Freud on that grim day. He isn't mentioned in any of the journalistic or police reports, and there are contradictions among the newspaper accounts and also between them and the official police report.[59] The latter declared that Pauline fell in front not of Freud's apartment but of her own quarters in the same building. Would she have taken the trouble to move in there, precisely for the sake of proximity to Freud, but then have done away with herself before her first therapeutic session? That is unlikely, and doubly so in view of the contrary reminiscences by her family members and by Freud himself.

Pauline Silberstein's violent end must have been extremely disturbing to Freud. Imagine his agony in having to break the news to Eduard. He must have realized, as well, that the Viennese public's awareness of his relation (however innocent) to the calamity could have finished off his already tainted reputation as a medical practitioner.

The pattern-obsessed Freud who would later theorize about doubles and revenants would not have been capable of insulating Pauline Silberstein from the rest of his history. He had both a sister and a niece named Pauline, and he remembered (or thought he remembered) that niece as having played a part in one of the most portentous incidents of his early childhood—an episode of cruelty toward a girl.[60] He would later express delight when Wilhelm Fliess, whose sister Pauline had died young, gave a daughter that same name.[61] But this other Pauline vanished without leaving a trace in Freud's heavily autobiographical publications; nor does her misfortune figure in any letters I have seen. The silence is deafening.

Just as a thought experiment, however, let us postulate that Frau Silberstein, having become depressed within her new marriage, did keep her appointment with Freud before leaping to her death. We might wonder, then, what he could have told her about her husband, inducing horror and despair. When Freud was seventeen, he had warned Eduard against female company. And at nineteen, when he and his friend were parted by circumstance, he had written, "I really believe that we shall never be rid of each other; . . . we have come so far that the one loves the very person of the other."

Did Freud still feel that Eduard Silberstein belonged to him and that Pauline had usurped his place? If so, and in view of his overbearing way with patients in general, it would have been in character for him to allow jealousy and malice to override his obligation to the fragile Pauline. But possibility, of course, is not the same thing as evidence. Unless a smoking-gun document comes to light, we will never learn why the bride of Freud's bosom friend hurled herself over the balcony.

15

Tending to Goldfish

1. A BETTER CLASS OF NEUROTICS

When we encountered Freud in the anxious opening months of his practice, he was applying placebo regimens, along with cocaine shots and various potent soporifics, to whatever afflictions came under his care. Such stopgap work, drawing on means whose inefficacy and/or dangers would soon be widely known, was never going to provide him with the steady livelihood that he craved. But he did possess a key advantage—one that he had broadcast in his otherwise imprudent lectures of 1886. This was his connection to Charcot, who was widely, if controversially, regarded as the leading expert on the mysterious syndrome of hysteria. As Freud wrote to his new friend Wilhelm Fliess on February 4, 1888, "My practice, which, as you know, is not very considerable, has recently increased somewhat by virtue of Charcot's name."[1]

It was fortunate for Freud that he had chosen to characterize himself as a neurologist. In the turf war between the relatively new fields of psychiatry and neurology, an informal borderline was being drawn between the psychiatrists' *psychoses* and the neurologists' *neuroses* (not to be confused with Charcot's *névroses*).[2] The demarcation fell between sanity and insanity. Whereas the psychoses were regarded as untreatable brain diseases, a neurotic, retaining an unimpaired or only mildly compromised sense of reality, ought to have been tractable to therapy—perhaps even to a cure. Thus a neurologist, in good conscience, could welcome patients harboring not only hysteria but also *neurasthenia, depression* and its manic counterpart, *phobias, obsessions,* and *compulsions.**

If Freud hadn't been Jewish, such cases would have been unavailable to him in Vienna. At a time when professors of psychiatry, almost all of them gentiles, still regarded hysteria as dissimulation or as a sign of hereditary rot, it fell to "nerve doctors," predominantly Jews, to treat the condition and its sufferers with respect.[3] As Roy Porter observed, doctors to the wealthy, by putting their emphasis on "nervous collapse, nervous debility, gastric weakness, dyspepsia, atonicity, spinal inflammation, migraine, and so forth, . . . could forestall suspicions that their respectable patients were either half mad or malingering sociopaths."[4] Any neurologist could play that tactful game, but only a Jewish one could be counted upon not to believe that sheer Jewishness was the source of a patient's tiresome behavior.

Encouragingly for Freud, a few Viennese physicians who knew of his Paris sojourn began paying him to consult on their own hysteria cases. His protector and counselor Josef Breuer, whom he regaled with stories of Charcot's amazing feats, was sufficiently impressed to redirect some hysteria cases to him, as did the gynecologist Rudolf Chrobak. Both of them mollified wary patients by acting as informal supervisors of his early ministrations. And other referrals probably came, in a spirit of medical-school solidarity, from such colleagues as Moriz Benedikt, Hermann Nothnagel, and Richard von Krafft-Ebing.[5]

Still another supplier of patients—few in number but crucial for Freud's prestige—was Charcot himself. Needless to say, Blanche Wittmann and other Salpêtrière inmates weren't sent to Vienna in order to be relieved of their instructive symptoms. But Charcot, as we have seen, had a placebogenic practice among the European elite. At least two of Freud's future patients (Anna von Lieben and Elise Gomperz) had already been treated by Charcot in Paris; and it was natural for Charcot

---

* Inconsistently, Freud tended to count paranoia as a neurosis; nor was it helpful that he sometimes called the neuroses "neuro-psychoses."

to tell such clients that they could entrust themselves to a bright young neurologist in their home city who was translating some of his works.

It was Breuer, however, who made the difference between success and failure for the initially struggling Freud. Breuer was the most sought-after private internist in Vienna, serving as the physician to virtually every family in the Jewish *haute bourgeoisie*. Indeed, he was treated as an equal within "the Coterie"—that tight circle of intermarried millionaires and their families, clustered around the *Ringstrasse*, who were sponsoring and mingling with the stars of Viennese high culture. The Coterie also welcomed such distinguished thinkers as Theodor Meynert, Sigmund Exner, Ernst Fleischl, and the philosopher Franz Brentano, who actually married into the Gomperz clan.

Although the young Freud was known to all of those figures, he didn't aspire to join their company in the glittering salons hosted by Josephine von Wertheimstein and by her sister Sophie von Todesco. What he hoped to gain through Breuer's mediation was a medical specialization as a "nerve doctor" to the very rich. And it was just within the Coterie that the most fascinating cases of "hysteria" and other neuroses could be found—cases demanding long-term attention that Breuer, after a major misadventure to which we will return in later chapters, had neither the time nor the inclination to undertake. Freud, we will see, didn't share Breuer's reservations about wasting his patients' time and money. For the kind of involvement, lasting months and years without arriving at a point of resolution, that some affluent clients demanded, he was more than willing to be of service.

It was ironic, however, that Freud meant to trade on the impression that his tutor Charcot had mastered hysteria. In the first place, as we have noted, many of the "hysterics" in the Salpêtrière were probably misdiagnosed epileptics. Second, Charcot had never attempted to cure or even mollify them, but only to establish—falsely, as it happened— the objective reality and the triggering mechanism of their disorder. Third, his principal tool of demonstration, the hypnotic provoking of well-rehearsed symptoms, was useless. And fourth, Charcotian hysteria, whose ultimate cause was thought to be "hereditary degeneration," scarcely resembled the mind-set of the pampered socialites who would now be sent to Freud.

The paralyses, contractures, and obscene screaming of French wash-erwomen, prostitutes, and derelicts bespoke not only their real afflic-tions but also their subordination within the Salpêtrière and the larger world. Freud, however, would encounter articulate ladies and gentlemen who expected to be humored for their persistent eccentricities and aver-sions. To be sure, they also tended to arrive in his office with preexist-ing diseases; but his predilection for interpreting miscellaneous organic symptoms as psychogenic would confuse matters further, widening the already huge chasm between Parisian and Viennese "hysteria."

If Freud had been motivated by intellectual curiosity, the stark divergence between the two hysterias would have been enlightening for him. He had in hand all the evidence that would have been needed to challenge the integrity of a syndrome that was shifting its character according to both social circumstances and the preconceptions of physicians.[6] Such sophisticated relativism, already forwarded by the independent-minded Joseph Delboeuf, would become widespread in the 1890s, resulting in the all but total demise of the hysteria diagnosis in the early twentieth century.

Freud, however, would contribute less than nothing to that awak-ening. As we saw, he had blinded himself to the imitation, bribery, and deceit that were responsible for the chimera of *grande hystérie*. Now he was bent on using his French credentials as an attractant for business. To that end he would promote the misapprehension, which he surely didn't believe, that the Salpêtrière had admirably prepared him to treat the local gentry's psychological complaints.

2. A WEALTH OF OPPORTUNITY

One often reads that Freud, in spite of his theoretical missteps, deserves credit as the first psychologist to have taken his patients' mental anguish seriously, listened closely to their stories, and offered them his sympathetic understanding. As Hannah Decker pointed out long ago, however, empathy-based care was commonplace in the years preced-ing the emergence of psychoanalysis.[7] Some of Freud's early patients were handed along to him by colleagues (Breuer, for example) who had already shown plenty of solicitude. Freud's habit, moreover, would always be to overlay his patients' complaints with a ready-made framework of explanation; therefore he was impatient, not sympathetic, with their efforts at self-understanding.

In this respect Freud differed markedly from his contemporary Paul Dubois, headquartered in Berne. Dubois taught his patients how to alter their manner of coping with the immediate difficulties they faced. His "persuasion therapy," which would become a serious rival to psychoanalysis in the early twentieth century, was ancestral to every branch of cognitive treatment that flourishes today. The fact that it was swept away in the Freudian tide must be counted as a setback in the history of mental care.

In any event, a Hippocratic sense that each human being deserves respectful treatment was never part of Freud's perspective. Most people struck him as contemptible. "I have found little that is 'good' about human beings on the whole," he would write to Oskar Pfister. "In my experience, most of them are trash."[8] And he was unforgiving toward what he called the "moral cowardice" of hysterics.[9] If he admired certain patients for their intelligence or good conversation, he looked down on others and hoped he could avoid their company altogether. As he wrote in Studies on Hysteria, "I cannot imagine bringing myself to delve into the psychical mechanism of a hysteria in anyone who struck me as low-minded and repellent."[10] That attitude would only become more adamant when he at last acquired a surplus of applicants for therapy and could tell many of them to take their complaints elsewhere.

As Freud had surely noticed at the Salpêtrière and in Vienna's General Hospital, it was the wretched of the earth whose mental problems tended to be most severe. But Freud, unlike some conscience-stricken followers who would be drummed out of his movement, had no sympathy for the lower orders. Indeed, he actively despised them. As he would tell his patient and disciple Marie Bonaparte, recalling an early visit to a penniless old woman, "as I had to clear my throat, I spat on the stairs instead of spitting into my handkerchief like a well-brought-up man. But it was out of contempt for the poor house, for the poor people who were my only patients at that time."[11]

How fortunate, then, that poverty itself, for which Freud held the downtrodden entirely responsible, appeared to be a contraindication

for healing through psychotherapy. As he would explain, for analysts'
eyes only, in 1913,

> experience shows without a doubt that when once a poor man has
> produced a neurosis it is only with difficulty that he lets it be taken
> from him. It renders him too good a service in the struggle for exis-
> tence; the secondary gain from illness which it brings him is much too
> important. He now claims by right of his neurosis the pity which the
> world has refused to his material distress, and he can now absolve
> himself from the obligation of combating his poverty by working.[12]

Freud would preface this sardonic paragraph with a recollection
that he had attempted to treat non-fee cases but had quit the experiment when he realized that without substantial bills to pay, patients
weren't motivated either to accept his authority or to make timely
progress toward termination (never an actual concern).[13] He had
thus been obliged to conclude that saddling neurotics with financial
hardship was therapeutically efficacious; and so he resigned himself to the necessity of making psychoanalysis burdensome on the
wallet.

Thinking back to his early practice, Freud told Bonaparte that he
had "treated only poor people at the time, no princess!"[14] (Bonaparte,
Napoleon's great-grandniece, was a princess of both Greece and
Denmark.) That was largely true of the years 1886–87. Thereafter,
however, Freud was able to attract the wealthy clientele that he desired.
It has been estimated that three-quarters of *all* his patients, from 1886
to 1939, were rich—as opposed, for example, to one-quarter of Alfred
Adler's.[15]

Clients who were essential to the swelling of Freud's own treasure
as he was developing psychoanalysis included these:

- Elise Gomperz, the daughter of a railroad owner. She married a
  famous scholar who was himself the son of a banker. Her family was
  among the most culturally eminent in Vienna.
- Anna von Lieben ("Cäcilie M."), born a baroness, fabulously rich,
  the daughter of a banker, and related by marriage to other great

families in Vienna. She became the wife of another banker who was
subsequently president of the Austrian stock exchange.

- Fanny Moser ("Frau Emmy von N."), descended from aristocrats
  in both Switzerland and Germany. Married to the owner of a watch
  factory, a railroad, and a magnificent castle on the Rhine, she was
  thought to be the wealthiest woman in Central Europe and one of
  the wealthiest in the world.
- Ilona Weiss ("Elisabeth von R."), raised on a great estate outside
  Budapest. She was the daughter of a rich businessman and investor.
- Marie von Ferstel, descended from generations of bankers, and a
  baroness by marriage to an eminent diplomat. Like the other named
  women, she lived in high society and was constantly attended by
  servants.

All of those patients began their treatment by Freud in the nineteenth century, and all but Marie von Ferstel began seeing him fairly
early in his practice. In subsequent years he would treat such well-off
individuals as Albert Hirst, whose father had assumed the management
of a paper factory; Ida Bauer ("Dora"), daughter of a textile magnate;
Anna von Vest, whose father prospered as a notary to still wealthier
men; Ernst Lanzer ("the Rat Man"), whose mother had been adopted
into one of Vienna's premier industrialist families; Baron Viktor von
Dirsztay, son of a wealthy banker, industrialist, and railroad owner;
Sergei Pankeev ("the Wolf Man"), son of a major landowner in Ukraine
and grandson of one of the richest men in Russia; Margarethe Csonka
(the "female homosexual"), daughter of a Rothschild partner who was
also the Austro-Hungarian empire's chief importer of petroleum; Elfriede
Hirschfeld, who married into a Russian fortune; and Carl Liebmann, an
heir to New York's Rheingold Beer millions. Some of those people dissipated their wealth or lost it through war and revolution, but all of
them were flush when they engaged the services of Freud.

One tacit goal of psychoanalytic historiography has been to keep at
bay the realization that Freud, once having been granted access to the
best society, saw a path not just to a decent living but to substantial
wealth. Thus Ernest Jones, in one of his more desperate fibs, declared
roundly that Freud, whose "attitude toward money seems always to

have been unusually normal and objective," "never strove for money as such."[16] Money, bluffed Jones, held "no emotional significance" for the modest drudge who happened upon the unconscious in the course of his selfless research.[17] But then Jones let it slip that the unworldly one was a tax evader who had hidden his fortune in at least one foreign bank account.[18]

Freud's "poorhouse neurosis," as Peter Drucker aptly called it, was impervious to any abatement through prosperity, and he privately acknowledged the compulsive character of his need.[19] Money, he confessed in a 1909 letter to Carl Jung, was "the complex over which, for reasons that go back to my childhood, I have the least control."[20] As he memorably confided to Fliess, in a sentence that was judged insufficiently scientific for inclusion in the original edition of their correspondence, "Money is laughing gas for me."[21]

Money per se, however, was less important to Freud than the social status it might confer. He didn't hesitate to spend lavishly to that end. Even before his practice was altogether secure, he moved from one chic district of Vienna to another and then to a third, where, in a sprawling apartment, he would employ a cook, a housemaid, a charwoman, a governess, and a nanny—before Minna Bernays, herself a considerable ongoing expense, assumed that last role. Midday meals would be sumptuous affairs. Touristical travel and summer vacations at mountain resorts would be regular items in the budget. And even when income was scarce, Freud would ride to his house calls in a luxurious carriage drawn by two fine horses.[22]

Meanwhile, he had begun to cultivate what he later called his second addiction, following tobacco: the collecting of "very beautiful things"—chiefly statuettes from distant and/or ancient cultures.[23] Their essential function, he wrote, was "to keep me in a good mood."[24] The dreamy contemplation of such objects became, after smoking, his favorite activity, connecting him to the fantasizing about myth and history that he had indulged since childhood.

Because he couldn't forgo his luxuries even when patients were in short supply, Freud necessarily regarded Vienna's affluent neurotics less as sufferers who might require his medical attention than as potential enablers of his way of life. His anxiety that they might not appear in sufficient numbers tended to peak every fall, when, after summer vacation, patients from the previous spring might or might not resume their interrupted treatment. Thus on August 27, 1899, Freud told Fliess that in three weeks "the worries begin again whether some negroes will turn up at the right time to still the lion's appetite."[25] The allusion was to a favorite cartoon, in which a yawning lion complains, "Twelve o'clock and no negro."[26]

Fliess didn't need to be told what Freud meant by "negro"; the term belonged to their private code. So, apparently, did a still more expressive metaphor to which the psychotherapist had recourse three weeks later. "A patient with whom I have been negotiating," he wrote, "a 'goldfish,' has just announced herself—I do not know whether to decline or accept."[27] *Goldfish*, unlike *negroes*, was self-explanatory. Not surprisingly, Freud quashed whatever scruples he was harboring in this instance. A week later he wrote, "The goldfish . . . has been caught."[28] This was the Baroness Marie von Ferstel, who, before deciding around 1905 that Freud was nothing but a "charlatan,"[29] would swell his funds more handsomely than any other patient.

To haul in such a trophy catch would be of little avail, however, if the goldfish were to decide precipitously that the cure had promptly occurred. This is not to say that Freud didn't want to make hysteria vanish; to do so would have brought him instant fame and worldwide demand for his services. In fact, however, neither he nor anyone else had found a key to uprooting the neurotic disorder that might or might not spontaneously disappear in a given case, but was more likely to segue arbitrarily from one troublesome symptom to another.

As that realization gradually sank in, Freud settled for helping his patients through an endless string of emergencies. And, as he could hardly fail to notice, such troubleshooting proved to be a rewarding business plan. Hence the import of a statement he made to Fliess on August 1, 1890, explaining why he wouldn't be able to join his friend in Berlin for a valued reunion. Among the reasons given for canceling, this one came first: "my most important client [*Hauptklientin*] is just now going through a kind of nervous crisis and might get well in my absence."[30]

That sentence—it would of course meet the cold steel of Anna

Freud's scissors—may look at first like one of Freud's mordant jokes. But the paragraph in which it appears leaves no doubt that he was in earnest. This patient was his *Hauptklientin* because she was the principal source of his income at the time. If left alone, she might overcome her "crisis" all by herself, and that would never do. Freud needed to make himself the sole instrument of whatever solace she might be granted, thus extending his receipt of fees into the indefinite future.

3. THE STRUGGLE FOR MASTERY

Before Freud could gain such power, he had to make an impression of all-around competence. The task was rendered more difficult by his outsider status. His well-heeled clients had been bred to tyrannize over inexperienced providers such as himself, and they already subscribed to their own medical theories, derived partly from reading and conversation and partly from the specialists who had previously attended them.

Typical in this regard was "Nina R," whom we have previously encountered. Before being seen by Breuer and then Freud, she had contested Richard von Krafft-Ebing's view of her nervous condition. There was little hope, then, for Freud. His formal write-up of her case noted that the patient's "considerable intelligence" had allowed her to dispute his every therapeutic move. "In the end," wrote Freud, "she remained her own doctor and gave us [himself and Breuer] the right to console her, to be pleasant with her, and to listen to her complaints, under the condition that we respected her ceremonial which she had built up around herself and did not disturb her cherished habitudes."[31]

The grandees could summon Freud at any hour of the day or night, even during his vacations, and have him do their bidding.[32] If some of them wanted only to amuse themselves, make trouble, and squander their husbands' money, he would have to play whatever part they assigned him. And in their web of intermarried families they possessed a gossip network that could instantly blackball him if he were to give offense—for example, if he curtly told a patient that her self-diagnosis was mistaken.

In these conditions, the young Freud had little freedom to assay new therapies without begging permission from clients who regarded him as a probationer and a deputy. It appeared to him, then, that his role was destined to remain reactive and palliative. "The carriage is expensive," he lamented to Fliess in 1888, "and visiting and talking people into or out of things—which is what my occupation consists in—robs me of the best time for work."[33]

Toward the end of 1887, however, twenty months into his private career, Freud found himself contemplating a potential instrument for neutralizing the kind of class inequality that was burdening him. Until then, restrained by fealty to Charcot, he had refused to read Hippolyte Bernheim's momentous *De la suggestion et de ses applications à la thérapeutique*, detailing feats of hypnotherapy wrought by himself and his Nancy predecessor in that vein, Liébeault. But those well-documented successes with removing individual physical symptoms had inspired other physicians, many of them eminent, to make pilgrimages to Nancy and observe both Liébeault and Bernheim in action.* The pilgrims themselves had then become hypnotherapists and were now reporting excellent results of their own.† Although Charcot had scoffed at the vulgar idea of actually *helping* patients through hypnotism, the practice had become so popular that Freud felt compelled to join in.

In a chapter that he contributed to a popular book in 1890, Freud would marvel that hypnotism "endows the physician with an authority such as was probably never possessed by the priest or the miracle man."[34] The subject, he wrote, "becomes obedient and credulous—in the case of deep hypnosis, to an almost unlimited extent."[35] And he would tell a lecture audience in 1892 that hypnotic suggestion obliges one brain

---

* The visitors included, from Germany, Albert Moll and Albert von Schrenck-Notzing; from Switzerland, August Forel; from Belgium, Joseph Delboeuf; from Sweden, Otto Wetterstrand; from Holland, A. W. van Renterghem; from Britain, A. T. Myers, Frederic W. H. Myers, John Milne Bramwell, Humphry Rolleston, Edmund Gurney, and Charles Lloyd Tuckey; and from the United States, Morton Prince, Hamilton Osgood, and J. M. Baldwin.

† In 1889, for example, Forel mentioned that in only one year, 1887, Wetterstrand in Stockholm had hypnotically cured 718 ailments, with only nineteen failures; that van Renterghem in Amsterdam, over a mere three months, had cured 162 out of 178; that Fontan and Ségard in Marseille had cured 100 with very few disappointments; and that he himself had helped 171 out of 295 (Forel 1889, pp. 10–11).

to absorb the ideas of another without interposing criticism.[36] That looked like an ideal means of having his way with otherwise haughty clients. As he recollected in 1925, "there was something positively seductive in working with hypnotism. For the first time there was a sense of having overcome one's helplessness; and it was highly flattering to enjoy the reputation of being a miracle-worker."[37]

Here, however, we run into a major anomaly. According to Freud's own testimony, he was helpless to send his clients into deep trances. Indeed, he found it hard to generate any stage of hypnosis at all. As he would confess in 1895,

> I soon dropped the practice of making tests to show the degree of hypnosis reached, since in quite a number of cases this roused the patients' resistance and shook their confidence in me.... Furthermore, I soon began to tire of issuing assurances and commands such as "You are going to sleep! ... sleep!" and of hearing the patient ... remonstrate with me: "But, doctor, I'm *not* asleep." ... I feel sure that many other physicians who practise psychotherapy can get out of such difficulties with more skill than I can.[38]

This obstacle to effective treatment was owing in part to inherent handicaps in Freud's situation. All of the experts agreed that hypnotism was easily accomplished when subjects observed one another "going under," as they did in both Charcot's and Bernheim's institutions. But as Freud himself pointed out in an 1891 paper titled "Hypnosis," "patients of a higher social class" wouldn't stand for being hypnotized in the company of others.[39] Nor, he could have added, would they readily defer to the authority of a novice physician—"shy and very young," as one patient's daughter recalled—who had recently emerged from the wrong side of Leopoldstadt.[40]

Most of the blame for Freud's vexations is traceable to his own touchiness and lack of confidence. If he was poorly adapted to doctoring in general, he was even less suited to practicing hypnotism. In "Hypnosis" he wrote that even when the procedure works, "both physician and patient grow tired far sooner" than with other medical endeavors. There was too stark a contrast, he wrote, "between the

deliberately rosy colouring of the suggestions and the cheerless truth"—
the truth, that is, that no serious progress was being made.[41]

As August Forel opined in 1889, a good hypnotist will face many
setbacks but will find a way to make accommodations and win the
trust of resisting subjects; but a practitioner who displays anxiety, mistrust, depression, or fear of mockery won't be able to prevail.[42] The
hypersensitive Freud suffered from all of those liabilities. Even when
he had succeeded in hypnotizing one young patient, for example, he
was so exasperated by her failure to improve that he shouted at her
while she was "under."[43] One cannot imagine a deft hypnotist venting
his irritation in such a manner.

Was Freud lying, then, when he referred to having put some patients
into hypnosis? No, there is reliable evidence to indicate that he sometimes induced either that state or a plausible facsimile of it. But if
Freud's hypnotic skills were so poor, how could he have hypnotized
(or thought he was hypnotizing) certain patients, mined them for
insights into "the unconscious," and secured their long-term fidelity
to his practice?

This question admits of several possible answers. Some patients
came to Freud after having been hypnotized by a number of other therapists. Being naturally "dissociative" types, they would have been hyp-
notizable by Freud or virtually anyone else, including themselves. Some
other patients must have been dissimulating in order to gratify him or
to keep in play a dialogue they found intriguing or diverting. Freud
knew that fakery was possible, but he didn't care; the therapy business
would proceed in any event. Finally, some of his patients seem to have
accepted tacit invitations to doze off—and he didn't mind that outcome, either. On May 28, 1888, for example, he wrote to Fliess, "I
have at this moment a lady in hypnosis lying in front of me and therefore can go on writing in peace. . . . The time for the hypnosis is up. I
greet you cordially."[44]

Even Freud's few model informants, however—his equivalents for
the dozen divas of the Salpêtrière—might have proved recalcitrant
were it not for another weapon in his therapeutic arsenal: drugs. Jones,
we recall, discovered (but declined to illustrate) that Freud wielded the
hypodermic needle freely in his private practice. We saw that with one

frequently hypnotized patient, Mathilde Schleicher, he countenanced the administration of no fewer than eight calmants, any one of which could have loosened her inhibitions.

Alone among Freud scholars, Peter Swales has drawn the likely connection between that drug effect and Freud's ability to extract confessions (whether true or false) from some patients in spite of his awkwardness with hypnotic technique.[45] In 1891, as Swales points out, Albert von Schrenck-Notzing mentioned "how the administration of narcotics is sometimes necessary for the purpose of diminishing resistance to hypnosis."[46] We know that Freud employed drugs to manage his patients' behavioral outbursts; but wouldn't he also have wanted to blunt their reluctance to let go of daylight consciousness and spill their secrets?

Another aspect of the drug issue invites speculation. Writing around 1914, P. D. Ouspensky noted that narcotics were being regularly used not only for "weakening the resistance to hypnotic action" but also for "strengthening the capacity to hypnotize."[47] Ouspensky's disclosure opens a window on the possibility that Freud used drugs—including his favorite, cocaine—on himself as hypnotist as well as on his subjects, thus facilitating "free-floating attention" and a quasi-paranormal conversation between one "unconscious" and another. If so, it would be little wonder that he experienced chronic trouble telling the difference between his patients' memories and their fantasies, or between their "free associations" and his own.

4. TIES THAT BIND

With or without the added factor of psychoactive drugs, Freud's early reliance on hypnotism raises troubling questions about the extent to which his patients—those who didn't walk away—may have sacrificed their emotional and intellectual independence to him. Forgetting the checkered history of Mesmerism, we tend to think of a hypnotized person's vulnerability as a temporary matter, ending with the command to "wake up" or with the execution of a harmless posthypnotic task. But Freud's contemporaries, even those who dismissed stories of Svengali-like zombification, were alert to potential abuses.

August Forel, for instance, likened the gifted hypnotist to Napoleon (one of Freud's principal heroes) and warned against the "magnetic" leader's power to turn others, especially women, into servants
of his will.[48] And the Charcotians pro tempore Binet and Féré, though
disdainful of alarmism about robotic murderers, remarked that someone who is hypnotized for several days in a row by the same person
tends to stay obsessed over the entire period. Those authors, too,
warned against "elective somnambulism," or the subject's lingering
infatuation with the operator.[49]

Freud himself couldn't disagree. He candidly noted that "if circumstances demand a persistent use of hypnotism, the patient falls into a
habit of hypnosis and dependence on the physician[,] which cannot be
among the purposes of the therapeutic procedure."[50] There was a real
danger, he wrote, of the patient's "becoming too much accustomed to
the physician personally, of losing her independence in relation to him,
and even of perhaps becoming sexually dependent on him."[51]

In practice, however, Freud ignored that risk and continued trying
to hypnotize patients at least until 1896. Indeed, he subjected some of
them to several hypnotic sessions per day, often for hours at a time.[52]
And he did so at first not for a specific therapeutic or investigative purpose but as a routine soporific that might be applied over a number
of years. Naturally, then, his repeated hypnotic efforts, whether or
not they produced authentic hypnosis, tended to result in attachment
to his own person. He was cultivating the abjection that he publicly
condemned.

When we think of Freud collecting evidence for his protopsycho-
analytic formulations, we tend to picture him as the taciturn, note-
taking listener who sits apart from his supine patient, avoiding both
physical and ocular contact and offering only an occasional gentle hint
that the patient might want to free associate to an especially promising
utterance that she has just made. As we will later see, that was an idealization, for public consumption, of more coercive behavior on his
part. In the first years of his practice, however, he wasn't even pretending to be austere and enigmatic. Instead, he was acting quite literally as
a hands-on therapist, courting sensual responses to his own person.

Hypnotism itself, for one thing, entailed a close face-to-face encounter in a darkened room after "any tight clothing [had been] taken off."[53] In some instances Freud would lower the patient's eyelids with his fingers.[54] For mood softening, he often attached electrodes to various portions of the patient's body and applied a gentle current.[55] And because "the subject-matter of the suggestions which are to be imparted ... is not always suitable for conveyance to other people closely connected with the patient," no spouse or friend could be on hand to witness these preliminaries or their sequel.[56]

In addition, one of Freud's usual resources was massage. For "soothing and lulling" prior to hypnotic induction, he recommended "stroking the patient's face and body with both hands continuously for from five to ten minutes."[57] More focused manipulation of symptomatic regions would then ensue. As Freud advised, "Stroking and pressing on the ailing part of the body during hypnosis gives excellent support in general to the spoken suggestion."[58] And since he remained a firm believer in Charcot's hysterogenic zones, chief among which was the lower-abdominal "ovarian" segment, one begins to grasp why some of his female patients fled in haste while some others, whose husbands had forsaken their erotic company for that of mistresses, were happy to keep returning.*

These ministrations usually, but not always, occurred in Freud's consulting room. As I have mentioned, however, he was continually on call to rush over to a wealthy lady's residence and assist her through an emergency. Writing in 1932, Sándor Ferenczi recalled that Freud, before becoming contemptuous of all hysterics as a pack of deceivers, "occupied himself passionately and devotedly with helping neurotic patients (lying on the floor for hours when necessary next to a person in a hysterical crisis)."[59] Difficult as it is to envision the propriety-conscious Freud performing such horizontal labor, we will see that Ferenczi's recollection of what Freud related to him tallies with other reports from the same era.

---

* On the supposition that they knew what was ailing female hysterics who lacked a competent sexual partner, many Victorian physicians directly masturbated them under the pretext of "massage" (Starr and Aron 2011). The fastidious Freud probably avoided that practice, but not by much. When, in one session, he asked "Emmy von N." why she was so restless, "she informed me that she had been afraid that her period was going to start again and would again interfere with the massage" (SE, 2:67).

Thus it is evident that Freud, whether or not he thought of himself in that light, was encouraging unfulfilled women to put him into the role of a surrogate lover. On a lesser scale he was reverting to the therapeutics of Mesmer, who, a century earlier, had provoked orgastic convulsions by touching women all over and pressing their knees between his own for hour after hour.[60] And, again like Mesmer, he was conditioning his hysterics to produce further episodes of writhing, raving, and release. The man who would later write of "secondary gain from illness" was making himself into his patients' principal source of such gain.

This way of putting the matter, however, slights Freud's own emotional involvement in his clinical role. As Delboeuf understood, long-term hypnotic influence is a two-way process; the hypnotist is assigned a part in the subject's emotional drama.[61] In Freud's later terminology, this was countertransference—a phenomenon he was reluctant to confront in the early years because, both personally and professionally, he feared engulfment in chaotic sexual feeling. By drily intellectualizing about hysteria's impersonal laws, he was evading a circumstance—the vulnerability of the therapist himself to sexual temptation—that would be driven home to him two decades later when his disciples Ferenczi and Jung, among others, would jeopardize the cause of psychoanalysis through scandalous affairs with patients.

The fact that Freud could only rarely induce a true hypnotic state should be borne in mind when we find him claiming, on early occasions, that he had removed symptoms from patients under hypnosis. But because of the erotic suggestiveness of his *attempts* to hypnotize, he did occasionally succeed in bringing a woman into the credulous dependency against which the critics of hypnotism had always warned. Then the stage was set for "clinical proof" of whatever ideas he might hold, however temporarily, about the cause and cure of the neuroses.

16

Lessons Taken and Applied

1. CONSCIOUS OF THE UNCONSCIOUS

Beginning around 1889, Freud approached his therapeutic tasks with the assumption that all sufferers from hysteria have willfully forgotten, or *repressed*, disturbing experiences that still *unconsciously* prey on their minds. The feasibility of that idea, he wrote in his *Autobiographical Study*, had been demonstrated to him when, in the company of a patient, he had visited Hippolyte Bernheim in July of that year. "I was a spectator of Bernheim's astonishing experiments upon his hospital patients," he recollected, "and I received the profoundest impression of the possibility that there could be powerful mental processes which nevertheless remained hidden from the consciousness of men."[1]

Hidden psychodynamic processes, Freud believed, were theoretically required to explain Bernheim's success in inducing *posthypnotic amnesia*. In that routine, a subject typically receives a command under hypnosis; forgets, upon awakening, that she has received it; nevertheless robotically carries out the ordered task; but then forgets that she has done so. Here, in Freud's view, were several proofs of repression, showing that the mind can be divided against itself.

This, however, was not at all what Bernheim himself, influenced by Delboeuf, was coming to believe in 1889. By then both men had noticed that posthypnotic amnesia occurs not uniformly but only if the subject is explicitly ordered to forget. If she is ordered to remember, she does so. In either case, then, she is exhibiting what Delboeuf called *complaisance*, a conscious willingness to play the hypnotic game according to the operator's rules. Indeed, Bernheim was now so convinced that there was nothing more to the practice—that, in Delboeuf's famous dictum, "there is no such thing as hypnotism"—that he would soon be turning to direct waking suggestion for his feats of healing, and with the same good effects as before.*

Because Freud himself was a struggling hypnotherapist who had read the literature, taken instruction, and already tried to convey posthypnotic commands to his patients, it seems unbelievable that he waited until 1889 to find a convincing example of induced amnesia. Part of what he wished to get across in the *Autobiographical Study*, however, was that the great Bernheim had staged an experiment solely for him as a respected peer. Readers were meant to gather, additionally, that Freud had been one of the first, not one of the last, visitors to be impressed by Bernheim's skill and that the others had failed to notice the connection between hypnotism and the unconscious mind.

In spite of his tactical nod to Bernheim, Freud usually depicted himself as a lonely pioneer in the exploration of the unconscious. Its mysteries were supposedly inaccessible to less courageous researchers than himself—and that included just about everyone. In order to accept that representation, however, we must erase most of what is known about the psychological discourse of his time.

Ever since Charcot, in 1882, dared to introduce trance states into sanctioned French medicine, a countercurrent to positivism had taken hold in Europe, welcoming alleged paranormal phenomena and reviving certain aspects of *Naturphilosophie*—the "science" of vitalistic energy flows connecting the depths of the psyche to the cosmos at large. Subliminal mental operations were once again regarded in some quarters as legitimate objects of inquiry. Charcot's mentor in hypnotism, Charles

---

* Delboeuf 1891. Delboeuf's article bearing that sentence as its title shows that what he doubted was the existence of *hypnosis* (not hypnotism) as a physiological state occurring nowhere else. See also LeBlanc 2000, pp. 89–91; Borch-Jacobsen 2009, p. 132.

Richet, posited the existence of what he called an "unconscious ego"—a portion of the mind that, as two scholars remark, "was constantly on the watch, formed inferences, and performed acts, all unknown to the conscious ego."[2] By the time Freud was forming his own ideas about a second mind, consciousness was being represented as froth on the surface of a turbulent sea. It was merely, as Théodule Ribot put it in 1881, "the narrow gate through which a very small part of [cerebration] appears to us."*

Freud was one among a number of theorists who believed that the psychoneuroses are caused by troubling thoughts or memories. The Leipzig neurologist Paul J. Möbius called hysteria a "disease of the imagination,"[3] and his emphasis on the mind as pathogenic agent was shared by a still more eminent Leipzig colleague, Adolf Strümpell. In a celebrated lecture and in many professional conferences, Strümpell urged that somatic symptoms will often prove to have resulted not from physical illness but from "primary psychological processes."[4] He and Möbius, both of whom were warily monitored by Freud, would disappear from public memory once the legend of Freud's originality had taken hold.

Freud was also a latecomer to the idea that mental disturbances can have sexual causes. As early as the 1860s, for example, his combative senior colleague Moriz Benedikt had theorized that hysteria is caused by recollected misadventures and maladaptations, especially sexual ones, that continue to affect the sufferer's mind beneath the threshold of consciousness. The term "libido" was Benedikt's long before it was Freud's. And in the early 1890s Benedikt's therapeutic measures included probing insistently for memories of sexual "pathogenic secrets."[5]

More generally, the quarter century after 1880 was the golden age of sexology, whose major figures—Richard von Krafft-Ebing, Albert Moll, Iwan Bloch, Albert von Schrenck-Notzing, and Havelock Ellis— exerted a decisive and multifarious influence on Freud. There is no sexual topic in his writings, from homosexuality, bisexuality, sadomasochism,

---

* Ribot 1881, pp. 26–27. As Rosemarie Sand (2014) has extensively documented, the idea that consciousness encompasses only a small part of mentation, and that a motive for action must overcome contrary motives before the act can be initiated, goes back at least as far as Leibniz in the seventeenth century.

and fetishism through infantile masturbation, the pregenital "component instincts," the psychosexual stages, and even the evolutionary origin of sexual disgust, that wasn't anticipated and largely shaped by his readings.[6] Many of those debts were acknowledged at the time, but all of them were eventually suppressed in favor of the specious appeal to clinical experience. To a still underappreciated degree, the contents of the psychoanalytic unconscious would be the contents of the sexological tomes on Freud's bookshelf.

The year of his visit to Nancy, 1889, witnessed more psychodynamic ferment than ever before. At that moment, in Henri Ellenberger's words,

> Dessoir in Germany and Héricourt in France tried to make an inventory of the knowledge acquired on the unconscious mind. Moriz Benedikt published case histories illustrating his observations on the secret life of daydreams and suppressed emotions (especially of the sexual kind) and their role in the pathogenesis of hysteria and neuroses. . . . Physicians not only described and classified varieties of sexual deviations, but also studied the masked effects of sexual disturbances on emotional and physical life.[7]

Mental activity in the absence of consciousness, moreover, was the common theme of two international conferences in Paris, on hypnotism and on "physiological psychology," that Freud was then expecting to attend. (Although he traveled there in the company of Bernheim and Liébeault, he may have skipped most of the sessions.)[8] A typical offering was Max Dessoir's paper titled "The Double Ego" (Le double moi).[9] All of us, Dessoir maintained, possess the makings of a second personality. "Our conscious psychical life," he urged, "rests on a substratum of hallucinatory nature, where long-forgotten images reside"; and "the theory of lower consciousness opens a new path for the psychical treatment of nervous and mental illnesses."[10] The other participants— including such luminaries as Delboeuf, Babinski, Bernheim, Forel, Hippolyte Taine, Émile Durkheim, William James, and John Hughlings Jackson—quarreled on a number of points, but nobody in either conference doubted the utility of psychotherapy for patients who had lost touch with their deeper selves.

One of the presenters in the hypnotism conference was Pierre Janet, who at age thirty had already become the cynosure of the psychology profession by virtue of his acclaimed 493-page book *L'autonomisme psychologique*. And he was already sounding quite "Freudian" (to modern ears) before Freud had written a word about retrieving memories from the repressed unconscious. Consider just one of the cases recounted in his book, that of a nineteen-year-old in Le Havre, "Marie."[11] She had suffered from convulsions and delirium during her menstrual periods, from occasional hallucinations at other times, from functional blindness in one eye, and from anesthesia on one side of her face. By unearthing the patient's memories of shocking events, so Janet claimed, he had located a traumatic experience corresponding to each symptom; and by then hypnotically modifying the bad recollections, he had caused each symptom to dissolve.

Almost simultaneously with Janet's *L'autonomisme*, Delboeuf published a book, *Le magnétisme animal*, describing his own experiences at Nancy. In that work, which Freud surely read, Delboeuf claimed to have cured a hysterical woman by hypnotically "effacing" a traumatic memory. His observations of the case, Delboeuf wrote,

> tend to make me believe that many nervous states or mental illnesses have as their origin a natural suggestion that has acted at this special moment. . . . [In the light of my described case], one could explain how a hypnotist contributes to the cure. He puts the subject back into the state in which the trouble manifested itself and verbally combats that same trouble, now reborn.[12]

Thus the memory would be "reborn," according to Delboeuf's scenario, in order to be hypnotically expunged once and for all.

Such evocation and erasure of unconscious material would soon became Freud's goal with his "hysterics" of the early nineties. He would be trying to convince each hypnotized patient that even if she tried, she would no longer be able to envision the dreaded scenes that lay behind her symptoms. In making that effort, however, Freud wouldn't be innovating but attempting to catch up to the latest therapeutic fashion. And, as with hypnotism per se, he would never be able to match his contemporaries' success.

2. TEACHER AND PUPIL

Although Freud was by no means a pioneer, then, in theorizing about sexuality and the unconscious, by 1890 he was working with several ideas that defied the conventional wisdom of the hour. These were a belief in *long-delayed* symptom formation along sexual lines, a faith that such connections could be uncovered merely by attending to a patient's behaviors and unguarded turns of phrase, and a therapeutics of concerted emotional release. As we will see, and as Freud acknowledged, the last of those novelties originated with Josef Breuer. But the source of the first two convictions long remained unknown and was therefore assigned, unhelpfully, to the black box of "clinical evidence."

Unbeknownst to most Freudians, however, this hole in the record was filled in 1986 by an admirable feat of independent scholarship, Peter J. Swales's long essay "Freud, His Teacher, and the Birth of Psychoanalysis." Swales's immediate purpose was to identify and characterize one of Freud's anonymous early patients—the very patient, in fact, who had accompanied him to consult with Bernheim in Nancy. But what the historian discovered in the process was nothing less than the source of fundamental convictions to which Freud would cling for the next fifty years.

Several passages in Freud's contributions to *Studies on Hysteria*, the book that he and Breuer would jointly issue in 1895, hint that someone whose case history he didn't feel at liberty to set forth—he called her "Frau Cäcilie M."—had actually been his most informative patient and the main influence on the book itself. Although he knew her better than any of the four women whose stories he would tell in greater detail, "personal considerations" required that she be kept in the background. Freud would say enough, however, to indicate that she had understood her own hysteria in novel terms that he found compelling. And in private he was more emphatic. If you knew her, he wrote to Wilhelm Fliess in 1897, "you would not doubt for a moment that only this woman could have been my teacher (*meine Lehrmeisterin*)."[13]

Swales found that this was Anna von Lieben, the immensely rich baroness who joined another baroness, Fanny Moser ("Frau Emmy von N."), as the most important of Freud's early patients. She was the *Hauptklientin* whom he couldn't allow to "get well in [his] absence." Her husband's fee payments were the principal basis of Freud's economy in a period, 1887 to 1893, when he was risking insolvency in order to make himself thoroughly presentable as a "society doctor."* Even so, in this instance the benefit to his wallet was secondary to decisive intellectual stimulation.

Born the Baroness Anna von Todesco, the daughter of a banker and, from 1871, the wife of another banker, Anna was related, through intermarriages, to three other great Jewish families in the Coterie: the houses of Gomperz, Auspitz, and Wertheimstein. She had divided much of her time between a grand rural villa and the Viennese palace into which her parents had moved when she was about fifteen. Then Anna's mother had hosted glittering soirées attended by such luminaries as Brahms, Liszt, and Johann Strauss. After 1888, the extended Lieben family relinquished the palace but occupied a whole urban apartment building.

The Coterie was a hub of eccentricity and nervous illness, including psychoses that required institutionalization. For originality, oddness, and imperiousness of behavior, however, no one could match Anna von Lieben. A melancholy, introspective poet, a portrait painter, and a musician, she was also gifted at chess, which she enjoyed playing against two opponents at once. Upon her command, shopkeepers would reopen after closing time so she could ransack their shelves in one glorious burst of spending. She was as nocturnal as a raccoon. A chess professional was stationed outside her bedroom in readiness for

---

* Just when Anna von Lieben's treatment by Freud began is a matter of dispute. Christfried Tögel (1994, pp. 129–132) argues for 1886, but his circumstantial evidence appears to be weak.

impromptu games that could last until dawn. In the eyes of the young Hugo von Hofmannsthal, she was "half crazy."[14]

Lieben had long been obese. Outside her hearing, Freud expressed himself rudely about her weight. She was *der Koloß*, "the colossus" or "the hulk."[15] When she was staying at the sumptuous Villa Todesco in Hinterbrühl, south of Vienna, she required that lamb cutlets be delivered from the city each morning in time for her favorite breakfast. Now and then, though, she would consign herself to a slimming spa or try a diet consisting entirely of champagne and caviar. But because ambulation was difficult for her, she passed most of her waking hours reclining on a divan—the serendipitous inspiration, it has been surmised, for her young physician's couch therapy.

In her adolescence Anna had contracted an unspecified "female illness," to which she soon began adding other debilities. One of them, according to Freud, may have been organic in nature: a facial neuralgia. But when the pain subsided under apparent hypnosis, he began to suspect a psychogenic cause.[16] Other woes, ranging from trivial to grave, struck him as pointing less ambiguously to psychological distress. Anna was easily upset by small annoyances; she had long felt misunderstood by family members who considered her a malingerer; she was given to Weltschmerz; and she would fall into states of weakness and confusion, requiring a sympathetic doctor to rally her back to normal awareness. With one major exception that we will discuss, this seems to have been all that was wrong with Lieben when Freud took over her case, which he would nevertheless characterize as "my most severe and instructive" one.[17]

Lieben obtained some relief through the sifting of her memories. That she, not Freud, took the lead in that process is indicated not only by his tribute to her pedagogical role but also by the fact that, through many years of valetudinarianism, she had believed in both traumatic memory and the conversion of ideas into symptoms. She was a connoisseur of grievances, big and small, and had amassed such a store of them in her journals that it was easy for her to coordinate symptoms with memories. Thus she put her therapist on the path of "reading back" from the coded language of a symptom to the nature of the supposed experience lying behind it.

But that was just one of the lessons Anna von Lieben would teach her trusting doctor. Here are the others:

- **Pathogenic moral shocks.** Charcot regarded his lower-class patients at the Salpêtrière as simpletons who could experience fear but not moral reflection or even shame. Lieben and her kind, however, were brought up to cultivate refined feeling, purity of thought, and correct behavior. Lieben believed, and so Freud came to accept, that the nervous systems of proper ladies could be disrupted by just about anything—including their own unruly desires—that offended their high ideals. Anna's model of neurosogenesis through disgust and self-reproach had a measure of verisimilitude in her rarefied milieu. Freud, however, would claim it to be the rule for the human mind in general.

- **Metaphors as pathogens.** A theory of symbolization was already implicit in the idea of somatic conversion, but Lieben possessed a more radical notion that she had apparently been pursuing for years. The mind's hysteria-generating faculty, she believed, could forge a symptom from a figure of speech that had once come to mind at a stressful moment. Psychoneurotic symptoms, then, were charades, and by guessing which metaphor was being mimed, the patient or her doctor could coax remembrance of the traumatic event back into consciousness.

  Studies on Hysteria contains a number of quaint examples from Anna/"Cäcilie's" case and others. Why did Cäcilie feel a pain in her heel? Not because she was vastly overweight or because she may have had plantar fasciitis, but because she had once feared that she might not "find herself on a right footing" with certain strangers.[18] Why did she experience a neuralgic pain in her cheek? Because an insult from her husband had felt "like a slap in the face."[19] Such glib exercises, accepted by Freud without hesitation, would endear him to science-envying littérateurs; but he was flouting all that he had learned in medical school about attribution of causes and aligning himself with the most fanciful diagnosticians of the Middle Ages.

- **Dream interpretation.** Anna's favorite uncle, Theodor Gomperz, was an authority on dreams and their significance in tribal societies.

Whether or not he influenced her, it is certain that she kept a record of her dreams and their supposed messages. One journal entry was headed "*Traumesdeutung*," or dream meaning, closely anticipating the title of Freud's magnum opus. Although Freud was already interested in dreams, Lieben's affinity for symbolic translation probably colored her own view of them, and therefore Freud's.

- **Sex.** From adolescence onward, Anna keenly felt the absence of fulfillment in love. During the entirety of her work with Freud, she kept a therapeutic journal that was later destroyed by a son-in-law on the grounds that "it was full of private and indecent things, even perhaps outright obscenities."[20] Her married sex life, such as it was (she had five children), had ended, and her husband had openly taken a mistress. Momentously for Freud's development, Lieben ascribed her nervous state to sexual frustration. She believed, moreover, that certain behaviors could be understood as surreptitious expressions of desire. One of her poems, for example, suggests that women smoke as a substitute for being kissed. Here Freud, as a reader, was being tutored in the implacability and deviousness of the sex instinct.

- **Layered memories.** A letter from Breuer to Forel in 1907 disclosed that Lieben, under prodding from Freud, had kept retrieving ever earlier memories until she was drawing material from her putatively forgotten childhood. This had been exciting to Breuer and Freud alike, and it led Freud to one of his most doctrinaire ideas: that a trauma in adolescence or thereafter always reactivates a much earlier one that wasn't understood as threatening at the time.

- **Free association.** Citing a 1921 statement by A. A. Brill, Swales maintains that Freud learned his free association technique, whereby the client is encouraged to say whatever comes into her mind, in sessions with the voluble Lieben after their joint visit to Nancy in 1889. There are grounds for believing that Brill's information was conveyed to him by Freud. To be sure, Freud's distant recollections were error prone; and free association isn't mentioned in the *Studies*, published two years after Lieben's treatment ended. Nevertheless, we can surmise that Anna, with her own habit of seeking causal links through symbolic clues, influenced Freud in this respect as well.

We can see why Freud was so grateful to Anna von Lieben. At the same time, it is dumbfounding that root principles of his science may have been derived from a database consisting of one patient's musings about her history. Delboeuf had warned that therapeutic schools get born when physicians judge their first patient to be representative and then read the same traits into all of the others.[21] Not even Delboeuf, however, could have envisioned that a doctor would adopt a patient's own hunches wholesale without exercising critical judgment and would then pretend that he had been gradually drawn toward the same conclusions by impartial study of many other cases.

3. DRAMA SCHOOL

From the scattered passages about "Frau Cäcilie M." in *Studies on Hysteria* it is hard to discern what Freud had hoped to accomplish, therapeutically, with Anna von Lieben. Indirect evidence, however, tells us that at some early point in the treatment, he began attempting the memory extirpation that had been commended by both Delboeuf and Janet. In July 1889, writing to his sister-in-law Minna Bernays during his stay in Nancy, he remarked that she could grasp his way of treating Lieben if she were to read Edward Bellamy's novel of 1880, *Dr. Heidenhoff's Process*. In Bellamy's plot, a woman suffering from melancholia and hysteria is cured by an electrical machine that erases her traumatic memories as she concentrates on them. Freud possessed no such machine, but his hypnotherapy, though clumsy enough to warrant his seeking remedial instruction from Bernheim, was apparently directed to the same end.[22]

Freud's idea of ultimate *symptom* removal, however, corresponded neither to Bellamy's science-fiction notion nor to the serious proposals of Janet and Delboeuf. For those two authors, a traumatic memory was the sole irritant behind a given hysterical symptom. To efface the memory, then, would be equivalent to dissolving a kidney stone or an embolism; nothing further would remain to be done. But for Freud, the toxic element in hysteria was the panic-driven *emotion* that the traumatized patient had never allowed herself to feel. It constituted a repressed "quantity of affect" that would have to be coaxed forth in therapy and reattached to the now consciously remembered experience.

Years earlier, in 1880–82, just such a regimen had been practiced with a young Viennese woman, Bertha Pappenheim, by Freud's older friend and confidant Josef Breuer. Working more as partners than as physician and obedient patient—indeed, it was Pappenheim who took the initiative—the two parties had developed a routine whereby Pappenheim *lived through* past incidents, some of which may have been pathogenic; and her suffering had appeared to dwindle during that phase of her treatment.

Breuer and Freud had been discussing Pappenheim's therapy off and on since at least October 1882, shortly after Breuer disengaged himself from active involvement in her case.[23] Their dialogue had evidently become more intense after Freud's return from Paris in the spring of 1886. On Charcot's authority he had accepted a traumatic account of hysteria formation that must have looked at least somewhat compatible with the Pappenheim case as he understood it from Breuer. No doubt Breuer and Freud, who each exchanged letters with Charcot at the time, were reassessing Pappenheim's hysteria from a Charcotian point of view.

Once Freud's general practice began narrowing to the psychoneuroses, Breuer's experience with Pappenheim became still more interesting to him. The proof can be found in his 1888 essay "Hysteria," where, while admitting that conventional treatments were yielding hit-or-miss results, he briefly and enigmatically endorsed another approach. Hypnotic suggestion, he wrote,

> is even more effective if we adopt a method first practiced by Josef Breuer in Vienna and lead the patient under hypnosis back to the psychical prehistory of the ailment and compel him to acknowledge the psychical occasion on which the disorder in question originated. This method of treatment is new, but it produces successful cures which cannot otherwise be achieved.[24]

That statement curiously failed to mention what was distinctive in "the Breuer method," as Freud would later call it. Readers of the 1895 *Studies on Hysteria* would learn, however, that Breuer had aimed at *catharsis*, or the purgative discharge of obstructed affect, a consummation occurring because a restored memory had been reunited with feelings that the hysteric-in-the-making had been too frightened or ashamed to express at the time. For both the early Breuer and the early Freud, catharsis figured as a therapeutically provoked means of *abreaction*, the healthful release of affect that normally allows even a trying experience to be "worn away" without pathological consequences.

Breuer's conception hadn't arisen from his practice but from a scholarly book that, although largely neglected when it was first published in 1857, caused a sensation when its second edition appeared in 1880.[25] Oddly enough, the author was the uncle of the future Martha Freud, the classicist Jacob Bernays. It was a treatise on Aristotle's own theory of catharsis, whereby the viewers of a stage tragedy were said to be purged of pity and terror by empathizing with the dramatic representation of those emotions. Bernays's volume was all the rage in the Coterie, to which both Breuer and the intellectually avid Pappenheim belonged.

Bernays's interpretation of a few cryptic lines in Aristotle's *Poetics* was debatable.[26] Even more so was his attempt to transfer the theory from a theatrical to a therapeutic context. And more problematic still was the idea that "catharsis" really accounted for any perceived progress within the convoluted Pappenheim case, to which we will soon be returning in detail. It is certain, nevertheless, that Breuer and Pappenheim *thought* they were following the Aristotle-cum-Bernays prescription. Freudian theory about the necessary release of pent-up feelings in psychotherapy can be traced, then, not to clinical victories by himself or others but to a brief cultural fad in 1880.

Whatever their origin, it must be understood that Freud's premises, from the end of the 1880s into the early twentieth century, inclined him to regard a patient's emotional agitation as a sign that repressed traumatic memories were being reluctantly dragged closer to the surface of consciousness. Thus he was pleased whenever he could discompose a patient; and if her symptoms then became more numerous and severe, so much the better. This was the opposite of the psychotherapeutic ethos as it was generally regarded at the time. But Freud was adamant, for he conceived of the clinical encounter as an attempt not to assuage the client's present state but to flush out her demons and subdue them.

It makes sense, then, that Anna von Lieben's symptoms worsened in the fall of 1888, a year or so after Freud had begun treating her through attempted hypnotism. Then she developed what he called "a really surprising wealth of hysterical attacks," including "hallucinations, pains, spasms[,] and long declaratory speeches."[27] The last of those manifestations may have been modeled on *attitudes passionelles*, the fourth and most ludicrous phase of Salpêtrière-style *grande hystérie*, about which Anna could have heard either from Freud or from Charcot in person—for she had already voyaged to Paris for at least one consultation with the lionized Frenchman.

Lieben's case also began to acquire an eerie similarity to Pappenheim's a decade earlier. The women were personally acquainted; Breuer was the family physician to both; and Freud, as we will see, was then urging Breuer to turn Pappenheim's alleged "cathartic cure" into a showpiece of therapeutic efficacy. In these circumstances, Lieben had all the inspiration she needed to reprise the symptoms of Breuer's early patient. And she did, matching not only Pappenheim's dissociated monologues but also her hallucinations and aphasia in her native language.

Freud and Lieben were caught up in an iatrogenic tango whose dips and bends grew more extreme. He couldn't afford to reflect that he might be part of her problem instead of its solution. He even failed to register the significance of a crucial fact that he would innocently pass along to readers of the *Studies*. Once he had begun soliciting Anna's traumatic memories, they were "accompanied by the acutest suffering and by the return of all the symptoms she had ever had"; but when questioned by a different therapist, "she would tell him her story quite calmly."[28] Freud himself, then, was nudging Anna to act out, and the supposedly repressed and terrifying recollections that he elicited lost their affective charge when he wasn't on hand to cue them.

3. THE CABINET OF DR. FREUD

The circumstances and outcome of the Lieben case do not inspire confidence either in the cogency of Anna's brainstorms or in the utility of Sigmund's healing efforts. With regard to the former, Lieben was a spoiled, willful, histrionic tyrant whose self-absorption and self-pity were underwritten by her wealth. She was more in need of something constructive to do than she was of therapy, which only provided a stage for her long-running theatrics. Freud would allow readers of the *Studies* to infer that his five years of symptom banishing had left her in an improved state. He would never mention in print what he knew: at some point after his lengthy treatment of her was broken off, she had become a total nervous invalid and had remained in that state until her fatal heart attack in 1900.

In addition, Lieben's daily existence had featured a practice that would lead even a psychoanalyst to wonder whether she was really giving Freud unmediated access to the unconscious. She was a drug addict. From an early age she had used morphine, on which she was now dependent. Almost certainly, then, some of her "hysteria" symptoms— the unrehearsed ones—were signs of morphine craving and deprivation. Morphine must have been a major determinant of her sudden enthusiasms and retreats, her somnolence by day and insomnia at night, her nonstop talking and associational games, her lapses into semi-consciousness, her absorption in fantasy, her extraordinary dreams and nightmares, and her drifting back to the real or imagined childhood scenes whose counterparts would be featured in Freud's psychodynamic theory. And morphine, rather than transference, was what chiefly governed her compulsive reliance on Freud, who supplied her essential daily fix.*

From comments made by Lieben's heirs, Swales learned that in the period of her treatment by Freud, her morphine supply was maintained on the premises of her Vienna apartment in a locked cabinet. A trusted nurse/housekeeper, taking orders from Freud, regulated her access to it. But when a scheming governess won Anna's favor and vied for possession of the valued key, Freud took the governess's part against the loyal but outflanked nurse. Thus he ensured that the shift in household command wouldn't curtail his ability to exercise a measure of control over Anna's behavior.

Freud would relate in *Studies on Hysteria* that he had been summoned to "Cäcilie's" quarters once or twice a day to deal with her spasms and ranting. "As a rule," he wrote, "I was sent for at the climax of the attack, induced a state of hypnosis, called up the reproduction of the traumatic experience and hastened the end of the attack by artificial

---

* If Lieben could "sleep" hypnotically only with the aid of morphine, the abatement of her neuralgic pain under hypnotism was hardly a sign, as Freud surmised, that it was psychosomatic.

means."[29] That last phrase was a euphemism for morphine injections, which, we can be sure, never failed to do their job of returning the addict to tranquility.

As Swales remarks, Freud's reluctance, in 1895, to spell out his "artificial means" is understandable given the freshness of his own and some readers' memories of his catastrophic cocaine boosterism and the agonized death of Fleischl in 1891. As a scientific matter, however, his refusal to bring morphine into the discussion of Lieben's case was dishonest. Even if he failed to notice that her addiction was the common denominator of her strange conduct—and what physician, during five years of personally administering the narcotic, could be so blind?—he owed his readers the knowledge that hysteria wasn't the only possible explanation for that behavior.

It could be argued in Freud's behalf that concern for Anna was the reason for his silence about her morphine use. Sincere devotion to confidentiality, however, would have required that he refrain altogether from depicting the mental state of his conspicuous Viennese neighbor. The person Freud protected was himself. In his 1888 "Hysteria" article he had warned that a hysterical nervous system "reacts in a positively perverse manner to narcotics such as morphine and chloral hydrate."[30] If he had been frank about Lieben's addiction, readers would have been able to perceive that he had used morphine to keep her in thrall. And then they would have realized that the typical behavior of a drug addict is hardly a suitable foundation for deducing the universal traits of a psychoneurosis.

The best judges of Freud's conduct toward Anna von Lieben were her family members, including her children, who witnessed his comings and goings. They heard her screams and caught glimpses of her tumbling about on the carpet with her therapist, who would then render her compliant through incantations and injections. The children feared and loathed him as der Zauberer, the magician.[31] Among the five of them, however, the older ones may have realized that morphine rationing, not sorcery, was the key to the sinister power held over their mother by her incessant visitor.

On November 27, 1893, Freud wrote to Fliess that he now had "a quite unusual lack of patients," for he had "lost" (verloren) the one we now know to have been Anna.[32] "Lost" implied that the case had been snatched away from him. It may be that Leopold von Lieben, knowing that Freud was keeping his wife on morphine while her condition worsened, and probably believing, with good reason, that Freud was exacerbating her fits, had decreed that no further bills from the therapist would be honored. But Anna herself had grown exasperated with Freud several months earlier. On April 17 he had written to Minna Bernays that his patient "has just now been in a state in which she can't stand me, because it's a matter of suspecting that I don't treat her out of friendship, but only for money."[33] Those were the terms on which Freud and his "teacher" parted company.

Overlapping with his treatment of Lieben, Freud had as a patient her in-law Elise Gomperz, handed off to him by Charcot. Elise, indeed, was one of Freud's very earliest patients, and the first one who belonged to the exclusive Coterie. She, too, retaining a typical array of contemporary upper-class hysterical symptoms, got gradually worse instead of better; but because she became fixated on Freud's own person, he was able to keep her in treatment for seven years and then to renew the relationship, briefly, a year later.[34] Her case, as a fiasco that displayed no innovations of technique or theory, was excluded from *Studies on Hysteria*.

Freud had already disappointed the Gomperz clan by unsuccessfully treating Franziska von Wertheimstein—the unstable niece of Elise's husband, the eminent scholar Theodor Gomperz—in the first half of 1888. In the spring or summer of that year she suffered a complete nervous collapse, after which Freud had been obliged to remand her to the care of Richard von Krafft-Ebing. The latter had placed her in a rest home, where she remained for the entire following year.[35]

Gomperz (who was also Anna von Lieben's uncle) put the blame for Elise's abjection squarely on Freud. When, in January 1893, she was sequestered from Freud in a spa, Theodor wrote to her:

> I am very pleased to learn that . . . you are starting to feel better, and regret only that you also consult Freud from a distance. . . . Only and always ear-confession and hypnosis—from that we have seen no wonders; I could only ever see increasing deterioration. All reasonable people—Breuer and Freud here excepted—warn incessantly about the continuation of these now more than fruitless experiments.[36]

And in April 1893 Gomperz admonished his wife again, directly charging that Freud was the cause of her exacerbated nervous state.[37]

Given the ties between the Gomperz and Lieben families, it was inevitable that neither Charcot nor Breuer could prevent the Coterie from unanimously turning on Freud. To say that he was then regarded as an ineffectual therapist would be an understatement. He seems, rather, to have been so despised that his bad repute became a legend to be relayed through the generations. As late as 1982 Elise and Theodor's granddaughter told a researcher, "In this house one doesn't speak of Freud—not at all." And in 1984 Anna's granddaughter, in another interview, exploded (in English), "He had been no good at all!"[38]

That Freud was widely regarded with suspicion in this period is also reflected in a reminiscence by Arthur Koestler's mother, born Adele Jeiteles, who was sent to the young neurologist around 1890 because an occasional tic was causing her head to bob. Freud appears to have immediately decided that the tic was hysterical, in which case it could be traced to a sexual shock. In a 1953 interview with Kurt Eissler, Adele described her precipitous exit from physicianly dealings that struck her as perverse.* In the words of Michael Scammell,

> Adele was not impressed. "Freud massaged my neck and asked me silly questions," she complained to Koestler some fifty years later. "I told you he was a disgusting fellow." She told Kurt Eissler . . . that she had visited Freud only reluctantly ("you were held to be half-crazy if you went to Dr. Freud") and had disliked him on sight, mainly because of his black side-whiskers. She said that while massaging her neck Freud had asked her if she had a sweetheart. Shocked, she refused to answer and hurried away as fast as she could. Freud's interest in sex was "scandalous and outlandish," and though her girl-friends couldn't wait to hear about her visit, Adele claimed that no one in her circle took him seriously.[39]

---

* Eissler intended to keep that interview, along with others by Arthur Koestler and his wife, out of public view for nearly seven decades, but Koestler's biographer Michael Scammell, ignoring a threat of legal reprisal, found a copy among Koestler's papers and quoted it (Scammell 2009).

17

Traumas on Demand

1. LED IN CIRCLES

When Freud persuaded Breuer, in June 1892, to join him in announcing a breakthrough in the understanding and treatment of hysteria, he still anticipated a measure of success with Anna von Lieben. Although she had never been a tractable hypnotic subject without the aid of morphine, and although she was apparently worse off than when Freud had begun treating her four or five years before, the doctor and patient together must have imagined that they had proved how neurotic symptoms arise and how they can be dispelled. Freud seems to have hoped, then, that he was on the verge of achieving a "causal" mode of therapy—one that could uproot the disorder itself, and not just its latest manifestations, by freeing the original traumatic memory and its severed affect from their entrapment in the unconscious. Perhaps the first such victory was going to be achieved with Lieben herself. But it didn't happen.

The case on which Freud would lay the most theoretical weight, that of "Emmy von N." (Fanny Moser), was in fact his most humbling failure. His relations with Moser spanned just two inconclusive May–June periods, one year apart.* Those relations were suspicious on both

---

* Were those years 1889 and 1890, or 1890 and 1891? Scholars have disputed the point. See, e.g., Andersson 1979, Swales 1986, Ellenberger 1993, and Tögel 1994.

sides and sometimes openly antagonistic. Moser's cooperation with Freud's proposals was never more than halfhearted. And the arrangement came to an end, in this instance, not through a husband's exasperation but through the volatile patient's own decision to take her troubles elsewhere.

But why, then, would Freud allot a long segment to "Emmy von N." in the *Studies*? Part of the reason may have been Moser's geographical remoteness. She had only been visiting, not inhabiting, Vienna when Freud treated her. Residing at a safe distance in a grand chateau that lay well outside Zürich, she was unlikely to learn that her case had been discussed in print. Freud was thus at unusual liberty to be candid about her peculiar behavior. More positively, Moser was one of the very few patients he had been able to hypnotize at will—or so he believed. As a result, her case was the only one he could produce in which memory retrieval under hypnosis actually seemed to have occurred.

Even on its manifest surface, however, the story of Emmy von N. would fall short of illustrating either the existence of repressed memory or the alleged correlation between recovered memory and meaningful therapeutic gain. What the case did show, from its very first day, was a cluster of symptoms that would have led any trained observer to hypothesize the presence of an organic disorder. In Freud's words:

> Her speech was from time to time subject to spastic interruptions amounting to a stammer. She kept her fingers, which exhibited a ceaseless agitation . . . , tightly clasped together. There were frequent convulsive *tic*-like movements of her face and the muscles of her neck, during which some of them, especially the right sterno-cleido-mastoid, stood out prominently. Furthermore, she frequently interrupted her remarks by producing a curious "clacking" sound from her mouth which defies imitation.[1]

Ola Andersson, however, appears to have come across good evidence that Freud's stated timetable—May–June 1889 and May–June 1890—was correct. In either case, Moser's treatment overlapped with Lieben's.

Moreover, Freud added, every two or three minutes the patient would contort her face in an expression of horror, reach out her hand, and exclaim, "Keep still!—Don't say anything!—Don't touch me!"[2]

These behaviors call to mind Tourette syndrome, which had been identified in 1885, the year Freud arrived at the Salpêtrière; and there, we remember, he was acquainted with Georges Gilles de la Tourette himself. Indeed, on February 9, 1886, Tourette had taken Freud to his apartment after a soirée at the Charcot mansion and had handed him an offprint that was probably his paper describing the newly isolated disorder.* In his case history, however, the neurologist Freud didn't mention the possibility of a neurological disease. As with Anna von Lieben's neuralgia, he was interested only in assigning as many symptoms to hysteria as possible. Hence he offered his patient no help whatsoever in understanding and coming to terms with her medical condition.

I have mentioned that the Baroness Fanny Moser was probably the wealthiest woman in central Europe.[3] Born Fanny Louise von Sulzer-Wart in 1848, the thirteenth of fourteen children, she was the daughter and granddaughter of very prosperous businessmen. Her great wealth, however, was acquired when, at age twenty-three, she married the sixty-five-year-old widower and tycoon Heinrich Moser, who would live for only four more years, bequeathing his immense fortune entirely to her.

But then began the most trying episode of Fanny's life and a source of never-ending misery. The disinherited children of Heinrich Moser's first marriage spread a rumor that Fanny had poisoned her husband after he altered his will in her favor. Lawsuits followed, and the corpse was exhumed. Although it showed no trace of poison, the murder tale had acquired a life of its own. Thenceforth Fanny was shunned not only by her in-laws but by other aristocrats, whose friendship she desperately courted through lavish but fruitless displays of hospitality.

Fanny appears to have been a devoted and well-appreciated wife during her four years of marriage; hence her receipt of the whole estate. But as Henri Ellenberger noted, Fanny was isolated and tormented by

---

* See 2/10/86; L, p. 208, and Pappenheim 1980, p. 270. Although Tourette's paper (Gilles 1885) didn't mention the fact, Tourette syndrome typically shows periods of remission. Here, possibly, was a further opportunity for Freud to draw false correlations between his therapeutic efforts and Moser's less troubled phases.

an inability to win respect within the only circle that mattered to her.[4] When Freud met her, the widow had spent some fifteen years frantically trying to recapture her childhood sense of security and acceptance within the highest society.

Freud perceived at least part of that psychosocial basis for "hysteria." He would acknowledge in the *Studies* that his patient's fears of people had their origin in "the persecution to which she had been subjected after her husband's death."[5] The question, however, was how she could now be assisted in coping with it.

Freud seems to have had no idea of what would and wouldn't prove therapeutic for his nervous client. After he instructed Moser to stop being afraid of mice, for example, he reminded her of "the story of Bishop Hatto."[6] According to legend, God punished the wicked bishop by having him eaten alive by a vast swarm of rats. Was Freud surprised when Fanny manifested "extreme horror" at his recitation? What did he suppose he was accomplishing? At the time, he had already been treating neurotics for several years, yet he appears to have told his patient the gruesome, upsetting fable simply because it had popped into his mind.

Freud had spent four months working with Moser and had compared notes with at least three of her other physicians (Breuer, Forel, and Wetterstrand) by the time he characterized her in *Studies on Hysteria* as "a true lady," distinguished by "refinement of manners," "humility of mind," and "an unblemished character."[7] Indeed, her moral purity served as his chief exhibit for denying that hysteria was a sign of degeneracy. And when he then altered his diagnosis and declared her to be a typical victim of a syndrome he had recently purported to isolate, anxiety neurosis, it was because a "sexually abstinent woman" would necessarily be prone to that ailment.[8] Fanny, however, was far from abstinent. Ola Andersson and Ellenberger, looking into her activities, found that "she nearly always seems to have had lovers and erotic relationships, sometimes with doctors whom she consulted at the spas, or who lived in her house as her personal doctors."[9]

We can gather that Fanny made an exception for the straight-backed Dr. Freud. Not only did she not seduce him; she seems to have gone out of her way to preserve his ignorance. Although Freud massaged "her whole body" twice a day, with emphasis on the abdominal area where she reported gastric pains and "ovarian neuralgia," and though he also hypnotized her twice daily, probing for intimate revelations, only superficial ones were granted.[10] Moser's sex life was a poorly kept secret in her household and the environs of her chateau, but it remained a dark continent to the Henry Stanley of the unconscious.

Moser's dalliances with her medical attendants point to something important about her case, belatedly registered by Freud but never sufficiently taken into theoretical account. Perhaps realizing that she had an incurable disease and not just "hysteria," Fanny was merely going through the motions of behaving like a good patient. Indeed, she may have been deliberately subverting the role. Medicine, like everything else in her life of frustration, appears to have bored her and struck her as useless; but at least she could strip her caregivers of their pretension to objectivity and healing power. Whether or not their clothes literally came off, she always teased forth and then insulted their professional pride.

"I noticed to my astonishment," Freud wrote, "that none of the daily visitors to [Fanny's] house recognized that she was ill or were aware that I was her doctor."[11] "During the times of her worst states," furthermore,

> she was and remained capable of playing her part in the management of a large industrial business, of keeping a constant eye on the education of her children, of carrying on her correspondence with prominent people in the intellectual world . . . well enough for the fact of her illness to remain concealed.[12]

Freud and Moser, then, like Freud and Lieben, had jointly conjured an array of symptoms and tantrums that seemed to be reserved just for him.

Marks of Fanny's guile are plain to see in the daily summaries of therapy sessions that Freud would reproduce in *Studies on Hysteria*. Unlike Anna von Lieben and most of his other early clients, she took to hypnotism with suspect alacrity, seeming to fall into "complete somnambulism (with amnesia)" on only his second try with her.[13] In the midst of one such slumber, "she expressed a desire for me to wake her up from hypnosis, and I did so."[14] Patently, then, she hadn't been "asleep" at all. And the oblivious Freud added, "I have come across many other proofs that she kept a critical eye upon my work in her hypnotic consciousness."[15]

According to Freud's Lieben-inspired theory of repression, the memories that have generated symptoms are sealed away and require a therapist's prompting in order to emerge. But Fanny not only agreed at once that her anxiety stemmed from early traumas, she soon began to parade them in facile abundance:

> This series of traumatic precipitating causes which she produced in answer to my question why she was so liable to fright was clearly ready to hand in her memory. She could not have collected these episodes from different periods of her childhood so quickly during the short interval which elapsed between my question and her answer. . . .
>
> . . . She said that in general she thought of these experiences very often and had done so in the last few days.[16]

Those "last few days" were in fact the first days of Moser's treatment. She had been mulling over Freud's communicated expectations and had decided to cooperate by reinterpreting her entire life within the framework of his theory. It must have seemed to her like a risk-free experiment and a means of involving her new doctor in her tangle of idiosyncrasies. Her effortless recall of pertinent memories, unimpeded by repression, constituted an *embarras de richesses*—but it didn't embarrass Freud, who was delighted to get so much confirmation that he was on the right track.*

As Fanny's therapy settled into routine, she found her twice-daily massage sessions especially suitable for telling Freud what he wanted to know. "Nor is her conversation during the massage so aimless as would appear," he observed in his notes:

> On the contrary, it contains a fairly complete reproduction of the memories and new impressions which have affected her since our last

---

* Freud's notes from his first three weeks of treating Moser in 1889 make it clear that he was then striving to "wipe out" scenes that Fanny spontaneously generated in production-line style. As Malcolm Macmillan has shown, some of Freud's language in describing his technique closely paralleled Delboeuf's in *Le magnétisme animal* (Macmillan 1979, p. 307).

talk, and it often leads on, in a quite unexpected way, to pathogenic
reminiscences of which she unburdens herself without being asked to.
It is as though she had adopted my procedure and was making use of
our conversation, apparently unconstrained and guided by chance,
as a supplement to her hypnosis.[17]

"This," wrote James Strachey in an editorial comment, "is perhaps
the earliest appearance of what later became the method of free association."[18] If so, the fatal defect of that method was already on view.
The patient was being coached to produce just the "traumatic" material
required by Freud's theory. Only later did it dawn on him that "what
I was allowed to hear was no doubt an *editio in usum delphini* [a
bowdlerized edition] of her life-story."[19] Yet he persisted in imagining
that Fanny's "edited" disclosures held import for both the causation
and the correction of her symptoms.

After a psychological relapse, a patched-up quarrel with Freud,
and a stay in a sanatorium, Moser returned to his care for a second
eight weeks of therapy, a year after the first. He judged it at the time
to be wonderfully effective. In *Studies on Hysteria*, five years later,
he was still taking credit for the fine outcome. The reported improvement, however, soon evaporated—thanks entirely, Freud believed, to
Fanny's malice toward her therapist: "By an act of will as it were, she
undid the effects of my treatment and promptly relapsed into the
states from which I had freed her."[20] It seems that when Moser got
better, it was Freud's doing and a sign that his theory was correct; but
when she worsened again, it was her doing and an attempt to rob him
of his victory.

Reluctantly, Freud granted that "there had been little change in her
fundamental character."[21] In fact, as he knew, Moser soon found herself institutionalized once again, this time with his approval as a consulting physician. He had run out of ideas for treating her himself. We
cannot say that he had made his patient's condition worse; it seems
doubtful that he exerted much long-range influence on her at all. That
he offered his dealings with her as a model for other physicians,
however, is remarkable; it suggests how far his desire for fame was out-
reaching his capabilities at the time of *Studies on Hysteria*.

As Freud observed in a footnote added to his 1924 edition, his debacle with "Frau Emmy" had been only one of many run-arounds on her part. According to a colleague (it was Forel) whom he encountered a few years after having been added to her list of vanquished physicians,

> She had gone through the same performance with him—and with many other doctors—as she had with me. Her condition had become very bad; she had rewarded his hypnotic treatment of her by making a remarkable recovery, but had then suddenly quarrelled with him, left him, and once more set her illness going to its full extent. It was a genuine instance of the "compulsion to repeat."[22]

"The same performance"; "rewarded"; "once more set her illness going to its full extent"; "the 'compulsion to repeat'": these locutions, written almost thirty years after *Studies on Hysteria* was first published, betray the aging Freud's chagrined awareness that Moser had led him a merry chase.

In 1895, however, he was still claiming to have erased one of her symptoms after another through hypnotic commands and reactivation of traumatic memories. The idea that such recall (with or without hypnosis) is the best weapon against hysteria would become a key rationale for psychoanalysis as a theory of repression and therapeutic derepression. Yet Freud's only warrant for that idea was his transitory success at local symptom removal—a success that Fanny may have staged, for her own diversion, in order to keep him running in rings.

On July 19, 1889, Freud, who was on his way to Nancy with Anna von Lieben, signed the guest book that Fanny Moser kept at the chateau outside Zürich that she had bought two years before. At some later moment, however, she attached a small piece of paper next to Freud's name. That was her accustomed way of reminding herself, "Never invite this person again." *

---

* Ellenberger 1993, p. 282. The story of Freud's incompetence in this case extends beyond his direct traffic with Fanny Moser. Her elder daughter (also named Fanny), then nearing the end of adolescence, was rebellious, and Freud was asked to evaluate her psychological condition. He found the girl to possess "abnormal development," a "path-

2. PRESSING FOR ANSWERS

Looking back in his 1925 *Autobiographical Study* and other late reflections, Freud depicted himself as having moved systematically through several methodological phases in his treatment of neurotics. In each period, readers were told, he had achieved good results and gathered useful knowledge, but he had also encountered obstacles that needed to be overcome. Behind the notion of orderly advance lay a picture of a steady inductivist, testing various techniques and refining or rejecting them according to their demonstrated degree of efficacy.

Presumably, then, we ought to be able to find moments of demarcation at which Freud dropped one method in favor of the next one. And, accordingly, we should also find that his success rate, if mapped on a graph, would rise dramatically whenever he adopted a new procedure. But nothing of the kind is to be seen in the actual record. Because Freud drove many patients away and, with the others, never achieved more than temporary symptom abatement followed by relapses or new outbreaks, he had no means of determining whether one means of treatment worked better than another. And any claim that he abandoned a given technique at some definite early moment will inevitably be contradicted by a later sign that he was still using it or recommending it to colleagues.

If Freud had actually found one of his methods to be outstandingly effective, he surely would have said so in a contemporaneous paper, owning up to the comparatively poor results he had gotten before the

---

ological disposition," and "unbridled ambitions which were out of all proportion to the poverty of her gifts" (SE, 2:77, 83). And he anticipated a descent into paranoia because of the girl's "neuropathic heredity" on both sides of her family (ibid., p. 83).

In *Studies on Hysteria* Freud neglected to relate what had happened next. As a result of his drastically negative evaluation, the younger Fanny was confined in a mental clinic. Once set free, however, she won her mother's permission to pursue a vocation for science. After earning a baccalaureate at Lausanne, she studied at three other universities, earned a Ph.D. with a dissertation on "The Comparative Development of the Lungs of Vertebrates," and became a working zoologist and the author of a distinguished tract on jellyfish (Ellenberger 1993, p. 283). Later she wrote a two-volume book on a favorite topic of Freud's, parapsychology, and even corresponded with him about that shared interest, somehow without his realizing at first that "Fanny Moser-Hoppe" was the same person he had once considered slow-witted and destined for lunacy.

change and offering data to validate the sharp improvement thereafter. But that was never his way. At every stage he represented himself as a successful therapist whose ideas had been confirmed by his patients' gains. Only much later, in surveying his career from the high ground of his eminence, would he lay claim to landmark moments when, with the aid of a new technique or hypothesis, frustration had given way to success.

One such fable was sketched in a letter of 1918 to Fanny Moser-Hoppe, the daughter of "Emmy von N." There, excusing himself for having botched her mother's therapy, Freud ventured, "It is precisely because of this case and its outcome that I recognized that treatment by hypnosis is a method that possesses neither sense nor value and that I needed to create psychoanalytic therapy."[23] By "psychoanalytic therapy" he meant the free-association technique, whereby the therapist allows the patient's unguided thoughts to lead the two parties, cooperatively, to repressed memories or other causally significant material.

But it had taken Freud about four years, *after* "Emmy" set him loose, to complete the methodological shift that was here compressed into an ideal moment. Such telescoping can occur in anyone's distant recollections. More surprising, though, is Freud's claim to have suddenly abandoned a tool that he had gone right on employing after the fiasco of the elder Fanny's treatment.

A more public story, and one that has a place of honor in birth-of-psychoanalysis lore, was told in the *Autobiographical Study*. One day, he wrote, he had hypnotized "one of my most acquiescent patients, with whom hypnotism had enabled me to bring about the most marvellous results."[24] On awakening, this woman had disconcerted him by throwing her arms around his neck, thereby revealing to him "the nature of the mysterious element that was at work behind hypnotism."[25] The engine of the hypnotic effect was thus revealed to be raw libido, a factor that threatened to undo the rational work of psychotherapy. "In order to exclude it, or at all events to isolate it," Freud had decided, "it was necessary to abandon hypnotism."[26]

This is a characteristic narrative in several respects: its unsubstantiated boast of "marvellous" healing, its pretension to an innocence of mind that gave way to a reluctant awareness of sexuality, and its implication that Freud had discovered something wholly unsuspected until then. In reality, the association between therapeutically induced trances and erotic vulnerability had been a staple of polemic and debate since the controversy over Mesmerism in the 1780s. And in Freud's own era, the campaign against licentious hypnotism had been led by someone about whom he fumed every day, Theodor Meynert.* It would have been unlike Freud to admit that he had come to agree with the man he had hated more fiercely than any other at the time. Instead, he maintained that a single incident, detached from any context of discourse, had obliged him to forgo a tool he had been wielding to good effect with the patient in question and presumably with many others.

Although Freud did begin trying nonhypnotic forms of interrogation on other patients (and for other reasons) around 1892, the idea that one hug put an end to his practice of hypnotherapy is false. Remarkably in view of his want of skill, he continued attempting to hypnotize some patients until 1896, the year that he himself later declared to have been his last as a hypnotherapst.† And he kept on privately commending hypnotism to colleagues until at least 1919.[27] None of this conduct reflects the aversion that he supposedly contracted "one day," circa 1892.

In several twentieth-century writings Freud would raise further objections to hypnotherapy. The hypnotized patient, he wrote, can "suggest to himself whatever he pleases" without profit to his treatment.[28] If a good result does somehow occur, it will surely come undone, because "all the processes that have led to the formation of the symptoms" have remained unaffected.[29] And too much depends on a positive rapport between the hypnotist and patient.[30] Under hypnosis, moreover, the patient loses contact with present reality.[31] Finally, the state of hypnosis can become addictive, "as though it were a narcotic."[32]

Behind the scenes, Freud and his movement would never be free

---

* As Sulloway recounts, "Meynert believed that much of the basis of the hypnotic trance was sexual. By inhibiting the subject's higher cortical activity (and thus his conscious control over his own body), hypnosis encouraged . . . the involuntary release of sexual impulses in the *sub*cortex" (Sulloway 1992, p. 44; emphasis as found).

† See SE, 7:260, where, in a lecture of 1904, Freud said that he hadn't used hypnotherapy "for some eight years." That statement fits well with a letter to Jung of 10/7/06 in which Freud mentioned that he had given up hypnotism a decade earlier (Freud/Jung 1974, p. 6).

from a worry that psychoanalysis was no better than hypnotherapy and possibly worse, because it took longer, it was costlier, and, while turning many of its patients into missionaries for its worldview and its business, it failed to address symptoms in a targeted manner. The reservations Freud did express about hypnotherapy—that its effects were only temporary, that it fostered retreat into a dreamworld, and that it created an unhealthy dependency—would be brought against psychoanalysis itself for a century and more. And indeed, when we hear of modern analyses lasting for decades, long after the presenting complaint has been forgotten by both parties, we must wonder how prudent it was of Freud to charge that hypnotism can be addictive.

It isn't true, of course, that psychoanalysis began when Freud abandoned hypnotism. Although free association became, and remains, the methodological core of psychoanalysis, we mustn't forget that there was an intervening phase, Freud's recourse to "concentration" and soon thereafter, to concentration under "pressure." As he later explained,

> When, therefore, my first attempt [at hypnotism] did not lead either to somnambulism or to a degree of hypnosis involving marked physical changes, I ostensibly dropped hypnosis, and only asked for "concentration"; and I ordered the patient to lie down and deliberately shut his eyes. . . . It is possible that in this way I obtained with only a slight effort the deepest degree of hypnosis that could be reached in the particular case.[33]

Freud was unsure whether the new concentration technique was yielding genuine memories. But then (so he claimed) he brought up a germane memory of his own. On his visit to Nancy in July 1889 with Anna von Lieben in tow, he had seen Bernheim lay his hand on an awakened subject's forehead and thereby induce her to recall the whole blanked-out episode of her hypnotic trance. "This astonishing and instructive experiment," Freud remarked,

> served as my model. I decided to start from the assumption that my patients knew everything that was of any pathogenic significance and

that it was only a question of obliging them to communicate it. Thus when I reached a point at which, after asking a patient some question such as: "How long have you had this symptom?" or "What was its origin?," I was met with the answer: "I really don't know." . . . I placed my hand on the patient's forehead or took her head between my hands and said: "You will think of it under the pressure of my hand. At the moment at which I relax my pressure you will see something in front of you or something will come into your head. Catch hold of it. It will be what we are looking for.—Well, what have you seen or what has occurred to you?"[34]

But here was a chronological anomaly. If Bernheim's 1889 demonstration of forced recall under forehead pressure was "astonishing and instructive" to Freud, and if he wasn't getting satisfactory results from hypnotism, why did he wait until 1892 to begin implementing Bernheim's lesson?

Malcolm Macmillan has supplied one likely explanation. It was in 1892 that Alfred Binet, in a book titled *Les altérations de la personnalité*, reprinted a passage in which Bernheim recounted having placed his hand on a woman's forehead and successfully demanded that she recall what he had done to her under hypnosis.[35] The passage would have been especially striking to Freud because Bernheim had taken liberties with the propriety-conscious woman, lifting her skirt and pinching her thigh. Her reluctant, mortified recall of those boundary violations required an overcoming of sexual shame—a feat that would have reverberated with Freud's new emphasis, in 1892, on the repression and derepression of erotically charged memories.

Although there was only the most tenuous relation between Bernheim's "recovered memories" and Freud's, the application of "pressure" was heartening for the latter. The technique, he would write, "yielded me the precise results that I needed"; and he added, "It has always pointed the way which the analysis should take and has enabled me to carry through every such analysis to an end without the use of somnambulism."[36] Hence Freud developed what he called "a literally unqualified reliance on my technique."[37] To his convenience in reaching conclusions but to the detriment of his science, he would never again encounter a sign that he was on the wrong interpretive track.

Thenceforth, if a patient responded to the demand for a traumatic memory by saying "I really don't know," her noncompliance was already accounted for in Freud's theory. It exemplified *resistance*—a psychical counterforce emanating from the long-buried experience that the patient was claiming not to remember. And by creating discomfort and annoyance by means of continuing to reapply pressure until he obtained a satisfying result, Freud could glean further pseudo-evidence that he was grappling with demonic forces in the unconscious.

By 1892 that belief, which he owed partly to Anna von Lieben and partly to theorists such as Dessoir and Janet, had become a dogma for him. Dropping any pretense of investigative neutrality, he began implementing his pressure technique in a prosecutorial manner. With Freud's hand on her brow, each patient was given to understand that if she were serious about getting well, it would not be a permissible option to withhold details of her sexual history.

Faced with that ultimatum, a patient could only break off her treatment or serve up plausible-looking reminiscences accompanied by suitable signs of distress. Freud, whose aim was to unearth repressed traumas that would accord with his theory, encouraged his patients to feel horrified by abuses that they may or may not have actually endured. In this manner he helped to perpetuate "hysteria," which could exist as a malady only so long as physicians were soliciting and rewarding the display of its stigmata.

3. A LEG TO STAND ON

If Freud was telling the truth about his near-perfect success with the pressure technique, there ought to have been no dearth of complete case histories exemplifying such healing. But only two of his published cases, each occupying a segment in the 1895 *Studies on Hysteria*, even mention the application of forehead pressure. They are the tales of "Miss Lucy R." and the much fuller narrative regarding "Elisabeth von R.," paraded as Freud's "first full-length analysis of a hysteria."[38]

"Lucy" had asked Freud to address just one symptom: olfactory hallucinations, especially featuring the smell of burned pudding. Because they *were* hallucinations, Freud asserted categorically that they had to be hysterical in nature.[39] Yet he already knew that Lucy had lost her general sense of smell and that she suffered from chronic suppurative rhinitis. In the midst of the nine-week treatment, moreover, another doctor found that Lucy had also contracted caries of the ethmoid bone.[40] Freud couldn't have known that that disease can cause a brain infection, or that a variety of temporal lobe epilepsy can result in olfactory hallucinations.[41] Nevertheless, the discovery of Lucy's caries ought to have put an end to his claim that she was a hysteric. Instead, he employed his recently adopted pressure technique to obtain smell-related memories, from which he fashioned a hypothesis that the source of Lucy's hysteria was (as usual) unreciprocated love—in this instance, for her employer.

There is every reason to doubt that a person suffering from two organic conditions, both involving her nose, could have had her sense of smell restored just by promptly and cheerfully agreeing with a supposition put to her by Freud. In the case history, however, soon after Lucy's last "traumatic memory" has bubbled up, she appears to Freud "as though transfigured."[42] And in a chance meeting with him four months later, she assures him that her recovery has endured. Did such a meeting really occur, and did Lucy really look upon Freud as an awesome healer?*

"Elisabeth," we now know, was Ilona Weiss, a wealthy twenty-four-year-old whose family had moved from Budapest to Vienna in her childhood. In the fall of 1892 Freud had been summoned, probably by Breuer, to look into her severe problems with ambulation.† Ilona bore herself strangely, had great pain in walking, and needed to rest soon after rising to her feet, even when she had merely been standing still.

In that period, Freud still felt some responsibility to check for a

---

* Mikkel Borch-Jacobsen, citing numerous parallels, declares that Lucy R. was none other than Freud's sister-in-law Minna Bernays (Freud 2015, pp. 384–385n). If so, the case history contains much further duplicity, beginning with the very pretense that "Lucy" was a patient instead of an occasional guest in Freud's home. See, however, Skues 2017.

† Christfried Tögel (1994, p. 136) maintains that the dates Freud gave for Weiss's treatment were a year later than the actual ones. Until better evidence than Tögel's is produced, however, it seems best to follow what is said in *Studies on Hysteria*.

possible organic basis of a patient's disability, and in this instance he found it: "muscular rheumatism," marked by "numerous hard fibres in the muscular substance."[43] But Breuer had led him to expect hysteria in Weiss, and he found that as well. The decisive clue was that she *didn't complain enough* about her agonies! Surely, wrote Freud, this was the *belle indifférence* of the hysteric as classically described by Charcot.* In addition to her suspiciously "cheerful air," furthermore, Ilona seemed to get erotic enjoyment from being pinched in an area of her right thigh that Freud, again following Charcot, unhesitatingly identified as a hysterogenic zone.[44] Ergo, Weiss was a hysteric. Yet this "intelligent and mentally normal" patient wasn't exhibiting a single symptom of the disorder as it was then customarily described.[45]

Was Ilona really indifferent to her pains, as Freud claimed on one page of the *Studies*? Or, as he conceded two pages later, did she "attach sufficient importance" to them, but without allowing them to get her down?[46] The latter attitude is usually praised as stoicism. For Freud, however, the uncomplaining woman's attention "must be dwelling on something else, of which the pains were only an accessory phenomenon— probably on thoughts and feelings, therefore, which were connected with them."[47] That was all the pretext he needed to circumvent "rheu- matic infiltration" and get straight to work on Ilona's memories and metaphors.

Although Weiss refused to theatricalize her pain, she didn't hesitate to reveal, with indignation, that her general situation in life was unsat- isfactory. Her married sister had died; her mother had undergone a serious eye operation; she herself, hobbled and homebound, had been cast into the role of a nursemaid for her father before he too died; and she had lost an opportunity to marry a desirable man. Formerly, she had longed for musical training and engagement with the world; now she bitterly resented the assumption, held by everyone who remained around her, that her highest goal ought to be marriage.[48] Protofeminist sentiments welled up in her.

---

* Ibid., p. 135. Here and there in his text, however, Freud contradicts himself by refer- ring to Ilona's experiencing more pain than her "rheumatism" alone warranted. But how could he have known that, since she was taciturn on the subject?

Those feelings themselves struck Freud as indicators of hysterical pathology. For, as we have seen, he regarded female aspiration as ipso facto abnormal. Now, hinting at a problem of gender identity, he wrote that Weiss was "greatly discontented with being a girl."[49] "The independence of her nature," he determined, "went beyond the feminine ideal."[50] Yet it is evident that his patient was a healthy-minded woman who, having suffered misfortune, prejudice, and a physical disability, was responding with understandable bitterness.

In order to exercise and demonstrate his theory, however, Freud needed to show that the patient's symptoms, one by one, had been exacerbated by a special hysterical mechanism. His challenge was to convince himself and others that rheumatism itself, in Ilona's case, had somehow suspended its rules of operation so as to make way for the rules of hysteria. The latter, as he apprehended them, dictated that each hysterical symptom must result from an emotional shock and that some symptoms will also reenact their corresponding traumas by miming them.

In order to explain Ilona's difficulties with her legs, then, Freud needed to elicit some memories to which he could attach symbolic connections. If a likely-looking thematic link occurred either to Ilona or to Freud himself, that would be sufficient proof that hysterical "conversion" had amplified a preexisting pain. And sure enough, even before Freud applied pressure to her forehead, her case began to yield up its secrets to him.

The large hysterogenic zone on her right thigh, for example, was explained by the fact that her ailing father used to rest his leg there when it was being bandaged. Freud refrained from elaborating, but sex was on his mind, and we can picture him bearing down on Ilona for the particulars of that daily scene. Her left leg, too, had stories to relate in code. Freud soon satisfied himself that "every fresh psychical determinant of painful sensations had become attached to some fresh spot in the painful area of her legs."[51] Thus those limbs contained a virtual diary of traumata written in nerve and muscle; and with the patient's cooperation Freud could read it off like a translator.

As for symbolization, Freud stopped short of proposing that Weiss, like Anna von Lieben with her neuralgia and heel pain, may have *acquired* her symptoms by acting out certain metaphors. But he did edge close to that claim by purporting to find diagnostic clues in conventional expressions:

> The patient ended her description of a whole series of episodes by complaining that they had made the fact of her "standing alone" painful to her. In another series of episodes, . . . she was never tired of repeating that what was painful about them had been . . . the feeling that she could not "take a single step forward." . . . I could not help thinking that the patient had done nothing more nor less than look for a *symbolic* expression of her painful thoughts and that she had found it in the intensification of her sufferings.[52]

In order for Freud to draw connections like these, it wasn't even necessary for Weiss to speak. All he needed was the information that she had been either walking, standing, or lying down at times of emotional strain. Remarkably, he regarded all three activities as exercising her legs. Thus almost any negative experience on Ilona's part could be counted as having been leg related and therefore potentially hysterogenic. Freud found it noteworthy, for instance, that she had been "*standing* by a door when her father was brought home with his heart attack."[53] What other position could she have taken by the door?

As for the therapeutic effect of Freud's interpretations, he wanted his readers to believe that he had wrought a fairly steady improvement in Weiss, interrupted only by occasional "spontaneous fluctuations"—each of which, however, he could prove to have been "provoked by association with some contemporary event."[54] Thus both the decreases and the increases in her pain level could now be regarded as psychically determined, leaving her organic illness completely out of the picture. But if her agony kept "fluctuating" during his treatment, neither her better nor her worse days were significantly correlated with his psychotherapeutic measures. Freud was producing no real effect on Ilona, and finally he admitted as much: "her pains had manifestly not been removed; they recurred from time to time, and with all their old severity."[55]

At the time he wrote up Weiss's story, Freud already believed that her lack of frequent orgasms would have sufficed to produce a neurosis. But since he was discussing her case in a book cowritten by Breuer—who, as we will see, was more moderate about the role of sexual problems in hysteria—he chose not to bring that point into focus. Instead, he kept his account of Weiss's pathology on the novelistic plane of "love." Her romantic ambitions, rejected by her supposedly prim conscious mind, had been thwarted, and that was why she had fallen ill.

In order to wrench her unhappiness into hysteria, Freud needed to seize upon an incident that could do service as a pathogenic moment, preceded by adequate mental health and followed by a neurotic heightening of pain. It was at this point in the treatment that Freud, despairing of his ability to induce a hypnotic state, began to apply "pressure." The effect was dramatic. "It was surprising," Freud reported, "with what promptitude the different scenes relating to a given theme emerged in a strictly chronological order. It was as though she were reading a lengthy book of pictures, whose pages were being turned over before her eyes."[56]

Freud ought to have been suspicious of such friction-free cooperation. Like Fanny Moser's immediate avalanche of memories, it was hardly compatible with a theory of intrapsychic conflict and resistance. And, again like Moser, Weiss seemed to be giving him *everything but* the ultimate psychogenic scene that he required. Yet by renewing his pressure, by warning that "she would never be free of her pains so long as she concealed anything," and by insisting that she *did* remember the origin of her disability, Freud finally prevailed to his satisfaction. Ilona came up with a serviceable incident from two years before.

Day and night, she had nursed her ailing father for the last eighteen months of his life, even sleeping in an adjacent bed so that she could attend to his every need. Thus her opportunities to intermingle with eligible bachelors had been drastically curtailed. Even so, according to Freud, she thought that one attractive young friend of the family regarded her fondly. Once, seeking a few hours of respite and hoping to encounter this potential suitor, she attended a party where his presence was expected. Indeed, he was there; the two young persons felt a new degree of closeness; Ilona stayed out later than she had intended;

and the potential beau had accompanied her to the door. But when she then checked on her father, she found that his pulmonary edema had taken a turn for the worse. Ilona reproached herself for selfish neglect and never abandoned her father again. As a result, no courtship and love match ensued.[57] In Freud's summation, "the erotic idea was repressed from association and the affect attaching to that idea was used to intensify or revive a physical pain which was present simultaneously or before."[58]

"While she was nursing her father," Freud wrote,

> she for the first time developed a hysterical symptom—a pain in a particular area of her right thigh. It was possible by means of analysis to find an adequate elucidation of the mechanism of the symptom. It happened at a moment when the circle of ideas embracing her duties to her sick father came into conflict with the content of the erotic desire she was feeling at the time. Under the pressure of lively self-reproaches she decided in favour of the former, and in doing so brought about her hysterical pain.[59]

Four pages later, however, and without seeming to notice that he was contradicting himself, Freud made a stupefying admission. Weiss's pain level, he wrote, hadn't increased at all at the time of the alleged "conversion." Indeed, he was unable to infer the occurrence of any pain that could be labeled hysterical during the following *two years*. "On the evidence of the analysis," he wrote,

> I assumed that a first conversion took place while the patient was nursing her father. . . . But it appeared from the patient's account that while she was nursing her father and during the time that followed . . . *she had no pains whatever and no locomotor weakness.* . . . The patient had behaved differently in reality from what she seemed to indicate in the analysis.[60]

Here Freud appeared to be on the brink of conceding that "the analysis" was erroneous. If "the pains—the products of conversion— did not occur while the patient was experiencing the impressions of the first period, but only after the event, ... while she was reproducing those impressions in her thoughts,"[61] it is clear that Freud's reconstruction of "her thoughts" during "the first period" rested only on speculation, which would now have to be disavowed. But no: Freud preferred his intellectual handiwork to the facts of the case. Accordingly, he charged Ilona herself with having left one impression by her behavior and a contrary one "in the analysis"—even though, in fact, she had strenuously disagreed with the latter. And he suddenly discovered a handy new psychological law: "Conversion can result equally from fresh affects and from recollected ones."[62]

Freud thus reserved the right to conjoin widely spaced, seemingly unrelated events and to assert that one of them had been caused by the other. Further, a physical sensation (Weiss's pain at the bedside) could be considered to have been relegated to the subject's unconscious, in storage for later perception, without her ever having noticed it at the time. Thus Freud now allowed for experiences themselves not to be registered as such, in which case the lack of any sign of their presence was no longer an obstacle to establishing causal relations involving them.

4. WALTZING ILONA

Freud would seem to have completed his explanation of Weiss's hysteria, albeit arbitrarily, with his story of a conversion that left no traces until it was "remembered" two years later. But because his treatment was still going nowhere, he felt compelled to supplement one tale of thwarted love with a second one. His grand surprise, both for his readers and for Ilona herself, was the news that she had long been in love with her brother-in-law; that she had entertained a morally repugnant fantasy, even before he was widowed, of marrying him; but that several impediments to the union were insuperable. Weiss had then "repressed her erotic idea from consciousness and transformed the amount of its affect into physical sensations of pain."[63]

This romance theme—a woman's making herself sick with unrequited, possibly guilty love—would prove to be a favorite of Freud's. It attested to his belief that all heterosexual females from the better classes, even when they profess an unladylike longing for independence, really want to subordinate themselves forever to some fine gentleman. (And, on the instinctual plane, they would thereby forestall a buildup of toxic "excitations.") The fact that Ilona admired her upright, responsible brother-in-law, then, must have meant that she was in love with him.

Any lingering doubt was dispelled when, one day during a house call, Ilona and Freud heard the brother-in-law arrive at her dwelling and inquire after her:

> My patient thereupon got up and asked that we might break off for the day. . . . Up to that point she had been free from pain, but after the interruption her facial expression and gait betrayed the sudden emergence of severe pains. My suspicion was strengthened by this and I determined to precipitate the decisive explanation.[64]

Here Freud outdid himself in thickheadedness. Weiss had been sitting down, immobile and pain free. Intending, with the social correctness of her class, to greet a visitor without keeping him waiting, she abruptly stood up—an action Freud knew to be always painful for her. But instead of bringing this elementary consideration to mind, he regarded the incident as proof of his hysterogenic hypothesis.

If Weiss had been in love with her brother-in-law, that fact would have been steadily known to her conscious mind. But she denied it, and she objected to Freud's presumption in trying to inform her of her own feelings. As we have seen, however, a patient's disagreement could only strengthen Freud's conviction that he was right. He actually welcomed Ilona's "resistance to the attempt to bring about an association between the separate psychical group and the rest of the content of her consciousness,"[65] because his theory of repression demanded that the patient feel threatened by a confrontation with the hidden truth.

Freud was eager to wrap up Weiss's case in time for his summer vacation of 1893.[66] But had anything been accomplished? He wanted to think so:

> Her condition was once more improved and there had been no more talk of her pains since we had been investigating their causes. We

both had a feeling that we had come to a finish, though I told myself that the abreaction of the love she had so long kept down had not been carried out very fully. I regarded her as cured and pointed out to her that the solution of her difficulties would proceed on its own account now that the path had been opened to it. This she did not dispute.[67]

"This she did not dispute." The reader is meant to conclude that Ilona had come around to Freud's view of her case. All Freud has done, however, is tell us what she *didn't* say. And in view of events that soon followed, we can guess that if she "didn't dispute" his summary, it was because she had learned that there was nothing to be gained from opposing him.

Just a few weeks after the final session, Freud received "a despairing letter from [Weiss's] mother," to whom, breaking professional confidentiality, he had disclosed his brother-in-law hypothesis:

At her first attempt, she told me, to discuss her daughter's affairs of the heart with her, the girl had rebelled violently and had since then suffered from severe pains once more. She was indignant with me for having betrayed her secret. She was entirely inaccessible, and the treatment had been a complete failure. What was to be done now? she asked. Elisabeth would have nothing more to do with me.[68]

This, then, was the upshot of Freud's "first full-length analysis of a hysteria": zero therapeutic gain, permanent alienation of the patient, and a worsening of her bad relations with her mother. Two months later, though, Freud allegedly heard from a colleague who said that Ilona was now much improved. And in the spring of 1894, he wrote, he was delighted to spot his ex-patient dancing athletically at a ball—no less liberated from hysteria than the "transfigured" Miss Lucy R. Thus, after all, Freud was vindicated in "a kind of conviction that everything would come out right and that the trouble I had taken had not been in vain."[69]

It would be good to know who else saw Ilona whirling about the ballroom floor. Freud was not known to frequent such events. The spring of 1894, furthermore, was almost a year after the end of Weiss's treatment. We have no idea of any ministrations, physical or psychological, that she may have received in the interim. But here again we encounter Freud's lifelong habit, once he had parted company with a patient, of regarding any subsequent betterment, no matter how remote in time, as his own doing.

Years later, Ilona Weiss entered into a satisfactory marriage—which, however, didn't mellow her discontent or mitigate her leg pains, from which she continued to suffer until her death in 1944. According to her family, no remission had ever occurred. Her daughter related that the desperate Ilona had consulted many specialists, who variously diagnosed her illness as rheumatism, sciatica, and neuritis.[70] She hadn't forgotten Freud, though. Speaking to her daughter long after her treatment of 1892–93, she said that Freud had been "just a young, bearded nerve specialist they sent me to." Freud had attempted "to persuade me that I was in love with my brother-in-law, but that wasn't really so."[71]

Weiss's daughter recalled those words when meeting with Anna Freud in January 1953, and Peter Gay read Anna's memorandum about the conversation before it was deposited in the Freud Archives and immediately embargoed for fifty years by Kurt Eissler.[72] Although Gay quoted the daughter's words about the bearded neurologist and his mistaken hypothesis, he said nothing about the other important revelation in the document: that Ilona retained her disability for life.

Instead, Gay offered a loyalist account of the outcome. Neglecting to mention Freud's pressure technique, he alleged that mere "uncensored talking" had yielded "brilliant results" for both Weiss and Freud. Talk "proved the key to her cure"—a cure validated by Freud's sight of his ex-patient briskly dancing.[73] The "Elisabeth von R." case, Gay added, "demonstrates how systematically [Freud] was now cultivating his gift for close observation."[74] As for Ilona's slighting remarks about Freud, Gay suggested that she may have unconsciously repressed Freud's correct interpretation of her case.[75] It was Gay, however, who "repressed" the inconvenient evidence that Ilona had never been cured.

· ·

PART FIVE

HIS TURN TO SHINE

· ·

Freud is a man given to absolute and exclusive formulations: this is a psychical need which, in my opinion,
leads to excessive generalization.

—Josef Breuer to August Forel, 11/21/1907*

---

* Quoted by Cranefield 1958, p. 320.

18

Now or Never

1. THE JANET MENACE

Because the cases of Anna von Lieben, Fanny Moser, and Ilona Weiss would all be showcased in *Studies on Hysteria* (1895) as instructive examples of Freud's therapy, we must assume that they stood among the most imposing of his early ministrations. As we have seen, however, each of the three treatments was aborted after the patient, having experienced either no benefit or a worsening of symptoms, became exasperated with her single-minded doctor. Of special note is Lieben's conclusion, after five years of intimate exchanges, that Freud had been out to enrich himself all along.

Physicianly concern, we might think, would have motivated a stymied Freud to reconsider his assumptions and goals. To admit that he had been making no headway, however, would have been too discouraging for a man who dreamed of fame and who saw it eluding him at an accelerating pace. He had failed at hypnotherapy. Unlike him, moreover, the leading psychological theorists were active in university and/or hospital communities that offered hundreds of patients and continual dialogue with peers. Thus they could compile many case histories whose positive outcomes and efficient day-to-day progress had been attested by neutral observers. Meanwhile Freud, working in private, was having trouble retaining, much less helping, any clients at all. The conclusion he evidently drew from this sad plight was that there would never be a better time than the present to put himself forward as an authoritative discoverer and healer.

One rival in particular appears to have sent Freud into emergency mode. This was Pierre Janet, whose precocious *L'automatisme psychologique*, as I have mentioned, was the toast of the psychological world in 1889. Freud's hope of rising in that world rested in large measure on his ability to portray himself as the rightful and chosen successor to Charcot, whose posthumous loss of credit he would never fully acknowledge. Already by 1890, however, it was clear that Charcot stood in awe of Janet, not of the distant Freud; and in 1892 he ceased to respect Freud at all.

Freud and Janet had both attended the Salpêtrière in 1885, and each of them soon thereafter capitalized on his association with Charcot. But while Charcot became disillusioned with Freud in 1892, *L'automatisme psychologique* had dazzled him so thoroughly that he had created a laboratory of pathological psychology within the Salpêtrière in 1890 and offered its directorship to the young author. Indeed, Charcot's own increased hospitality to psychological explanation in the last few years of his life was entirely owing to Janet, to whom he deferred as the reigning expert on hysteria.

That was the main, but by no means the only, aspect of Janet's career that must have aroused Freud's envy. Unlike Freud, who had to sacrifice, scheme, and endure bitter humiliation in order to overcome the handicaps of his origin, Janet was born into privilege and opportunity. His education was the best that France could offer. As the son of a well-off attorney, he was able to attend a Parisian school that had educated many outstanding achievers in science, literature, politics, and war. Then he had won admission to the elite École Normale Supérieure, whose pupils were expected to become lycée "professors" immediately upon graduation. One of his classmates was the future sociologist Émile Durkheim; and in the year ahead of him stood the philosopher-to-be Henri Bergson, with whom he would remain intellectually affiliated.

Janet's early interests were primarily philosophical, but he was no metaphysician. As a confirmed positivist in the mode of Auguste Comte, he believed that philosophy must be grounded in verifiable facts about human consciousness. And because he realized that introspection can't develop such facts, he chose to invest his faith in observation and experiment. He concluded at an early age that if one wishes to understand the normal mind, pathological states are the most promising objects of study. Mental aberrations, he realized, expose variables that are obscured by the integrated functioning of the ego (*le moi*).

Inspired by Charcot's turn toward hysteria in the late 1870s and by his dramatic rehabilitation of hypnotism in 1882—the year of Janet's own graduation from high school—the younger man had embraced both topics. He set a course that would take him from freelance clinical study to a Ph.D. in philosophy at the Sorbonne, to the directorship of Charcot's laboratory in the Salpêtrière, to a medical degree in 1893, to still another career in private and hospital psychotherapy, and finally, from 1902 until his death in 1947, to a distinguished professorship of experimental and comparative psychology in the Collège de France.

In his early, Charcot-inspired years, Janet was not immune to the fallacies that accompanied Salpêtrière-style experimentation, with its assigning of paranormal gifts and multiple personalities to subjects who were merely responding to the expectations of their manipulators.[*] Even before he corrected those errors, however, his accounts of his therapeutic experience left an image of a humane, decisive, and resourceful physician who had established empathy with patients who were needier in every way than Freud's. A substantial database of cases, his own and others', lent weight to the bold notions he was drawing from them. And he radiated confidence. Lacking either a financial or a psychological need to put himself forward as a leader, he sought consensus, distributing credit to others and prudently allowing for unresolved issues and for exceptions to his rules.

---

[*] Some of Janet's early ideas, later abandoned, caused him to be resurrected in the 1980s as the guiding spirit of a movement that would have appalled him: the conjuring of previously unsuspected "memories" of ostensible childhood sexual abuse by means of therapeutic hypnotism, drugs, and persistent innuendo, along with the hounding of "perpetrators" for whose crimes no independent evidence was either sought or found.

In academic psychology, as opposed to psychotherapy, a more generous appreciation of Janet took hold in the 1970s and continues to gain strength. See, e.g., Hilgard 1977; Perry and Laurence 1984; Gauld 1992; Kihlstrom 2001.

Janet's conception of the mind hinged on a distinction between mere sensations, which are physiologically registered but not necessarily perceived, and full perceptions, which, ideally, are actively cognized and integrated into the individual's sense of selfhood. Healthy persons, he wrote, can process and reconcile a relatively large number of perceptions at once, allowing for a constant adaptation to reality. But a mixture of hereditary weakness and unfortunate experience leaves some people without much integrative capacity.

According to Janet, those people may become either hysterical, suffering from behavioral dysfunctions, or "psychasthenic," suffering from obsessions, phobias, or an inability to make decisions or feel pleasure. In either case, Janet held that a portion of their mental life would have become chronically "disaggregated" from their selfhood, sapping their energy, distracting them, rendering them very suggestible, and generating symptoms. Owing to a "shrinkage of the field of consciousness," their "fixed ideas" would be immune to alteration unless those ideas could somehow be brought forward and addressed in therapy.

The nature of that therapy understandably worried Freud. Janet was using hypnosis with the intent of gaining access to unconscious memories and thoughts that were purportedly issuing in ideational and bodily symptoms; and he was claiming to effect cures through awakening and manipulating the rejected material. That was just what Freud, doubtless influenced by Janet himself among others, was *unsuccessfully* attempting to do with his own patients. Although his emphasis on exclusively sexual etiologies deviated from Janet's model, he was going to have trouble convincing knowledgeable readers that he had arrived at his therapeutic rationale through trial and error of his own.

The immediate occasion for Freud's alarm in 1892 appears to have been three widely noticed lectures on hysterical anesthesia, amnesia, and deliberate suggestion that Janet delivered at the Salpêtrière on March 11 and 17 and April 1. The texts were soon published in the *Archives de Neurologie*, a journal whose editors were then awaiting a long-promised article from Freud himself. In the first lecture Janet expounded what he called the "crude, very common physiology" that appears to govern hysterical symptom choice. The ideas of our organs that we unconsciously form, he said, can isolate and disable a whole arm, foot, or eye in defiance of nerve structure. Thus, Janet concluded, hysterical anesthesia must be recognized as an altogether psychological disorder—"an illness of the personality," as he put it in his final sentence.[1]

Janet's idea about unconscious mental control of whole physical units went only modestly farther than Charcot's earlier remarks on the same theme. Nevertheless, it constituted a lightbulb insight for Freud. In the July 1893 paper that he finally submitted to the *Archives de Neurologie*, "Some Points for a Comparative Study of Organic and Hysterical Motor Paralyses," he wrote that hysteria "takes the organs in the ordinary, popular sense of the names they bear."[2] And if that is so, the starting point of the symptom-forming process isn't likely to be an organic insult to the brain as first envisioned by Charcot; instead, it is probably "an alteration of the *conception*, the *idea*, of the arm, for instance."[3]

For both Freud and Janet, then, the agent of hysterical pathogenesis was a psyche that could unconsciously impose its quaint notions on the soma, overriding actual physiology in blocking sensation to an entire hand or limb. The mind, it seemed, could oblige whole body parts, conceived in commonsense terms, to act out its morbid charades. Here was an available justification, though hardly a complete one, of Freud's symbol-reading approach to etiology, diagnosis, and cure. But Freud was simply echoing Janet. Not only were his French terms *moi conscient* and *association subconsciente* taken from his young competitor; his whole discussion of hysteria formation implied Janet's system of *agrégation* and *désagrégation* of perceptions and ideas.

The importance of that borrowing can be gauged by the strenuousness of the efforts made by Freud and others to cover it up. To be sure, his 1893 paper, written for a journal whose readers were keenly aware of Janet's lecture texts, *had* to acknowledge those texts. "I can only associate myself fully with the views advanced by M. Janet in recent numbers of the *Archives de Neurologie*," he wrote;[4] and again, "I follow M. Janet in saying that what is in question in hysterical paralysis, just as in anaesthesia, etc., is the everyday, popular conception of the organs and of the body in general."* In his 1925 *Autobiographical Study*, however, Freud would state that his thesis of 1893 had already been conceived when, in 1886, he had approached Charcot with an idea for a paper:

> I discussed with the great man a plan for a comparative study of hysterical and organic paralyses. I wished to establish the thesis that in hysteria[,] paralyses and anaesthesias of the various parts of the body are demarcated according to the popular idea of their limits and not according to anatomical facts. He agreed with this view, but it was easy to see that in reality he took no special interest in penetrating more deeply into the psychology of the neuroses.[5]

The Freud of 1925 gained three advantages from that representation. First, he belatedly made his shy and deferential twenty-nine-year-old self look keen, assertive, and more inquisitive than the narrow Charcot. Second, he could now backdate his psychosomatic outlook to 1886, thus establishing precedence over any number of competitors—of whom Janet was the foremost—who had come along later in the eighties. And third, he could bask in Charcot's alleged acknowledgment that his idea, whatever it was, had been correct. In actuality, Charcot had disagreed with it. In a letter of February 25, 1886, Freud had told his fiancée that "even if [Charcot] could not accept it, he did not want to contradict me."

Brautbriefe of March 15 and 18 and April 7, 1886, and letters to Wilhelm Fliess of December 28, 1887, of February 4, May 28, and August 29, 1888, and of May 30, July 10, and July 24, 1893, attest to Freud's vexing inability to finish the project. After seven years of frustration, and thanks only to Janet, he was at last able to refine Charcotian doctrine in one respect: the form taken by a paralysis could be determined by a symbolizing mind. But then, in a footnote to his trans-

---

* SE, 1:170. Freud could have found Janet's thesis briefly stated in *L'automatisme psychologique* (Janet 1889, p. 280), but he evidently overlooked it there. Macmillan (1997, p. 95) notes that paralyses were the only category of major hysterical symptoms *not* covered in Janet's three lectures. Thus Janet's "leftovers" may have determined the scope of Freud's paper.

lation of Charcot's Tuesday lessons, Freud made so bold as to assert that the master had *asked him*, presumably as a peer investigator, to undertake the study: "When I was leaving the Salpêtrière, Charcot suggested to me that I make a comparative study of organic and hysterical paralyses."* Janet's crucial role in the story was omitted in 1925, leaving Charcot and Freud as scientific colleagues on the same plane of expertise.

Whenever the later Freud rearranged his history in a self-flattering spirit, the psychoanalytic establishment considered it de rigueur to go along with the revised tale. Thus Ernest Jones declared baldly that the "Comparative Study" was already complete by August 1888. "For some strange reason," however, its publication was delayed for five more years.[6] Since Freud had offered no explanation, only referring evasively to "accidental and personal reasons" for postponement, Jones thought it best to delve no further.

James Strachey, as the editor of Freud's 1893 paper for the *Standard Edition*, saw that he couldn't be so insouciant as Jones. Dates of composition, if not prominent influences, would have to be faced. Strachey did what he could to avoid contradicting either Freud or Jones. It seems, he wrote, that "the paper was already written at this early date"—namely, April 1886.[7] But then Strachey sheepishly mentioned the very late addition of Part IV, where the relevant discussion occurs, and admitted that none of the article's psychodynamic elements could have been intended at the outset.

Still, wrote Strachey, "it seems not impossible that when [Freud] had finished the first draft of this paper he already began to have some faint notion of an explanation of the facts contained in it which involved these new ideas, and he may for that reason have held back its publication while he went into the question more deeply."[8] In this manner, Freud's having taken seven years to finish one derivative article became a sign of creative ferment tempered by judiciousness.

The deeper indebtedness to Janet that Jones, Strachey, and Freud himself wished to obscure is evident from some arresting resemblances

---

* Charcot 1892–94, p. 268n. In reality, Freud had chosen a broader topic, which he must have found unmanageable. See SE, 1:12.

of terminology. Janet, coining the term, wrote of "subconscious" (*sub-conscient*) ideas that continue to produce effects beneath the dominant ego's awareness.* Freud would locate the corresponding ideas in "the unconscious," a reified agency within the psyche. In choosing that term, he was avoiding Janet—but not by much. Again, Janet called his method of treatment "psychological analysis" (*analyse psychologique*). In 1894, writing in French, Freud employed that very term.[9] But soon thereafter he would claim to have invented a revolutionary method that bore a shortened version of the same name.

Freud's first published use of the term "psychoanalysis" would occur in a French journal article of 1896.[10] The word he would choose was *psychoanalyse*, written with an "o" that sounded not just unnecessary but barbaric to French ears. And the spelling was especially strange in view of its context. Freud wasn't yet giving a name to his own procedure but merely saying that it constituted "*une nouvelle méthode de psychoanalyse*," where *psychoanalyse* referred to the generic category of analyzing the mind. Why, then, the bad French? The answer, it would seem, is that Freud was already looking ahead to a Germanizing of Janet's *analyse psychologique*. Later in the same year, with its signature "o" now permanently installed, *die Psychoanalyse* would emerge as a novelty whose only ancestor was alleged to be Breuer, not Janet.[11] Offended by such pilferage and by later insults from Freud, the usually pacific Janet would finally accuse his nemesis of plagiarism.[12]

2. INNOVATION BY PROXY

One way that Freud coped with the Janet menace, we have seen, was to associate himself with an idea avowedly borrowed from his rival but then, elsewhere, to backdate that notion and treat it as his own. That behavior fell within Freud's regular modus operandi: first to trade on an authority's prestige and later to thrust him aside or, if possible,

---

* Although Janet first employed the term "subconscious" in 1888, the concept was already implicit in his theory by 1886 (LeBlanc 2000, pp. 24–25). See also Hirschmüller 1989a, p. 150, listing terms borrowed by Breuer and Freud from Janet and other French sources.

altogether off the stage of history. Such efforts would be futile, however, if he remained a therapeutic nobody, lacking any record of healing and therefore having no basis for advancing his own propositions about the causation and cure of nervous illness.

Feeling thus thwarted in the early nineties, Freud bethought himself once again of Breuer's "cathartic method" and its one arresting application, the 1880–82 case of Bertha Pappenheim. Already in 1888, we noted, he had asserted that Breuer's regimen was producing "cures," plural. What if, now, he could convince his friend that in recent cases he, Freud, had been removing symptoms by the same method and that the two of them were thus in possession of a master key to hysteria? If so, they could publish a book together, vindicating Breuer's anticipation of Janet and others while positioning Freud as the Breuer of a new generation. It might also be possible, Freud realized, to cut into Janet's popularity by disputing his portrayal of hysterics as typically weak and passive. Freud's and Breuer's overbearing Viennese ladies, after all, were quite different.

Freud had now arrived at the most critical moment in his professional life. Given his washout with the Coterie, whose members were forming a consensus that he was untrustworthy and repugnant, his prospects for acquiring further wealthy "hysterics" were dismal. A collaborative book with the well-regarded Breuer, however, could transport him overnight from obscurity to fame, convincing not just the public but even some fellow practitioners that he must have been obtaining excellent results with "the Breuer method." Everything now depended on Breuer, whom we have known thus far only as Freud's usually supportive benefactor and counselor.

Thanks to the long ascendancy of psychoanalysis in the twentieth century and to Freud's self-mythologizing in particular, Breuer is remembered chiefly as the family doctor who dabbled in psychotherapy just long enough to inspire a more resolute investigator than himself. On the other hand, historians who attempt to rehabilitate him at Freud's expense usually stress his psychological insight and empathy. Thus they make him, not the overzealous Freud, into the true originator of whatever was valuable in psychoanalysis. As we will see, however, Breuer's achievement and significance cannot be thus confined. When

regarded through any lens but that of Freudolatry, he appears to have
outshone his restless protégé in all respects that bore on scientific
achievement.

Both Breuer and Freud received a broadly liberal education in
Vienna and strayed from Jewish faith without seeking to deny their
ethnic identity. Both pursued cultural themes in the University of
Vienna's Faculty of Philosophy before settling into medical studies.
Both were influenced by Ernst Brücke; it is assumed that they first met
in Brücke's laboratory, circa 1877.[13] Each of them served an apprenticeship in Vienna's General Hospital and became a lecturer (*Dozent*)
in the university. And they both turned to the practice of general medicine only after finding other goals to be out of reach—a professorship
in physiology for Breuer, a career in anatomical studies for Freud.

Unlike Freud, however, Breuer became an honored contributor to
knowledge of the human organism. In 1868, at age twenty-six, he and
his adviser Ewald Hering conducted elegant experiments showing that
human respiration is controlled by the vagus nerve. The Hering-Breuer
reflex, a monumental discovery, is also said to have been "the first satisfactory experimental demonstration of biological feedback in the
modern sense."[14] And in 1873–75, by testing both animal and human
subjects, Breuer established the function of the semicircular canals in the
labyrinth of the ear, thus solving the puzzle of how balance is maintained
when a head is rotated or accelerated.

By his early thirties, then, and without a laboratory of his own,
Breuer had achieved eminence as a neurophysiologist. He continued to
do basic research after becoming a doctor on constant call. Although
he had resigned his *Dozentur* in 1885, he maintained close personal
and intellectual relations with his academic friends, whose respect and
affection for him were unceasing. His studies continued until at least
1923, when, at age eighty-one, he proposed an experiment to adjudi-
cate the claims of two rival theories.

The Breuer whom we get to know from texts garnered by Albrecht
Hirschmüller bears little relation to the figure depicted by the later
Freud. Especially striking are the excerpts from letters to the theist
Franz Brentano in which he defended and reinterpreted natural
selection, denied that religion deserves a foothold in science, and advo-

cated "vitalism"—by which he meant not the existence of a life force but an acknowledgment of purposiveness in all creatures, whose behavior therefore couldn't be understood entirely in terms of physical and chemical laws.[15] And it is just here, in Breuer's neo-Darwinian vision of life forms as self-regulating organisms possessing "interests," that we find the most profound basis for his dissent from the mechanical reductionism toward which Freud, as we will learn, was trending in the 1890s.

Freud may have been lobbying for Breuer's collaboration as early as 1888. We know, however, that he intensified the campaign after Janet's Salpêtrière lectures on hysteria in the spring of 1892. In 1925 he would report that the Janet factor had proved decisive for Breuer. "At first he objected vehemently," Freud wrote, "but in the end he gave way, especially since, in the meantime, Janet's works had anticipated some of his results, such as the tracing back of hysterical symptoms to events in the patient's life, and their removal by means of hypnotic reproduction *in statu nascendi*."* Breuer must have become convinced, then, that only a joint manifesto, to be followed by refurbishing of the Pappenheim case and by further corroborative case material from Freud, could give him his historical due. On January 1 and 15, 1893, the shared essay, "On the Psychical Mechanism of Hysterical Phenomena: Preliminary Communication," was published in two installments in the *Neurologisches Centralblatt*.

In spite of Breuer's reputation for integrity, the "Preliminary Communication" opened with a deliberately misleading boast: "A chance observation has led us, over a number of years, to investigate a great variety of different forms and symptoms of hysteria, with a view to discovering their precipitating cause."[16] The two physicians, readers were to believe, constituted a long-established team that had been systematically inquiring into many types of hysteria. (Shades of the "cocaine researchers" Doctors Fleischl and Freud.) Their work, moreover, had proved to be magnificent. Although their many patients

---

* SE, 20:21. *In statu nascendi* means "in the nascent state" or "just emerging." Freud's point was that Janet could extirpate a symptom as he was bringing the recollection of its traumatic cause to consciousness.

hadn't at first recalled their precipitating traumas, they had been obliged to do so under hypnosis; and whenever that feat was performed with a properly "cathartic" release of affect, "*each individual hysterical symptom immediately and permanently disappeared.*"[17] Thus, claimed Breuer and Freud, they had isolated the originating mechanism of hysteria "in the clearest and most convincing fashion."[18]

All of this was false. The Pappenheim case, more than a decade before, had permanently sated Breuer's appetite for "catharsis." Again, he and Freud had conducted no methodical research on hysteria, either jointly or apart. Nor had there been anything clear or convincing about Freud's stumbling attempts to correlate symptoms with repressed memories. Nor, for the most part, had he been inducing hypnosis at all. That fact alone, if he had been honest enough to reveal it in the "Preliminary Communication," would have vacated the assertion that his patients had retrieved their traumatic memories only when hypnotized.

At least Breuer and Freud weren't maintaining that they had found a cure for hysteria. More modestly, they held that cathartic memory retrieval could eliminate symptoms one by one after the acute phase of a hysterical attack had spontaneously passed. But then, what advantage did their method possess over the demonstrably successful treatments of Liébeault, Bernheim, Forel, Wetterstrand, and many others? And if those therapists were removing symptoms without recourse to the Breuer/Freud outlook or technique, how could it be said that the Viennese pair had proved their exclusive "psychical mechanism of hysteria"?

The goal of the "Preliminary Communication" was to establish not only the correctness and efficacy of the "cathartic" point of view but also its independence of, and temporal priority to, the work of other recent theorists, especially Janet. Thus, when mentioning Janet by name, the coauthors noted only a curious *analogy* between one of his cases and their own.[19] For well-informed readers, however, Breuer and Freud's debt to Janet must have been glaringly apparent. The "Preliminary Communication" and the ensuing book were studded with Janetian terms and notions, including dissociation, *misère psychologique*, *double conscience*, the role of autohypnotic distraction and fright in hysteria formation, and even a hint of split-personality theory. So congenial would the introductory essay appear to Janet himself, indeed, that he would welcome it as "the most important work that has come to confirm our earlier studies."[20]

While warily steering around their contemporaries, Breuer and Freud did embrace a parent figure, Charcot, in order to supply a precedent for their contention that hypnotism can elicit pristine knowledge of the mental apparatus. Within a few pages they endorsed Charcot's hysterogenic zones of the body, his mental *condition seconde*, his dictum that "hypnosis is an artificial hysteria," and his four-phase *grande attaque*.[21] They even declared that their theory "takes its start from the third of these phases, that of the '*attitudes passionelles*' "—the hokiest feature of Salpêtrière dramaturgy.[22]

What was unfortunate about this retrogressive stance wasn't simply the association with a tarnished idol. The reason Charcot had crashed was that, for all his former rigor as a neurologist, his hysteria research had failed to allow for the effect of unintended and unremarked suggestion in directing a patient's behavior. Breuer and Freud, however, raised the topic of suggestion only long enough to show that they were misconstruing it. With regard to the banishing of symptoms through memory retrieval, they wrote,

> It is plausible to suppose that it is a question here of unconscious suggestion: the patient expects to be relieved of his sufferings by this procedure, and it is this expectation, and not the verbal utterance, which is the operative factor. This, however, is not so. The first case of this kind that came under observation dates back to the year 1881, that is to say to the "pre-suggestion" era.[23]

In other words, Breuer and Freud couldn't possibly have been influencing their patients, for their method was devised before Liébeault and Bernheim had propagated "suggestive" hypnotherapy.

If the two authors believed what they were saying here, they remained ignorant, in 1893, of the elementary difference between the two pertinent meanings of *suggestion*: Bernheim's deliberate demand for obedience or amelioration and an inadvertently signaled expectation that imparts a belief. This confusion or obfuscation ensured that when Freud and Breuer came to describe their case examples in *Studies on Hysteria*, they would be insufficiently concerned that they might have mistaken wishful thinking, compliance, and dissimulation for healing.

Such unawareness, if that is what it was, is harder to explain in Freud's case than in Breuer's. Breuer had made his physiological discoveries without engaging in dialogue with patients, and as a doctor he had reverted to addressing "nerves" with standard prescriptions. Freud, in contrast, was daily immersed in psychotherapeutic interactions; he had translated and edited both of the famous antagonists over suggestion; he had publicly favored first Charcot, then Bernheim, on that very issue; and in his Charcot obituary, coming up later in 1893, he would concede that Bernheim's critique of suggestion had struck a blow against Salpêtrière science. Yet when his own turn came to generalize from his interrogation of patients, he and Breuer waved off the whole topic as an irrelevancy.

It is ironic that while Breuer and Freud were thus committing themselves to the reckless epistemology of the Salpêtrière, their rival Janet was disembarrassing himself of it. Having learned that "Léonie," the only one of his patients who displayed Charcot's four-phase *grande hystérie*, had a long history of being "magnetized" and studied, Janet became vigilant against inadvertent suggestion.[24] Thenceforth, he swore, he would deal only with subjects who hadn't been treated by other investigators; and in each instance he would ask himself not how the patient fit a textbook pattern but how her totality of background factors, personality traits, and observed behaviors made the case unique. Now Janet, having righted his course, was headed toward the more consistent empiricism that would characterize the rest of a great career. Breuer and Freud, however, were sailing into a storm of their own making.

3. SPARRING PARTNERS

On June 28, 1892, Freud informed Fliess, who by then had become his dearest friend, that "Breuer has declared his willingness to publish jointly our detailed theory of abreaction, and our other joint jokes on hysteria."[25] Jokes? Freud's belittling term *Witze* lacked the gravity that the original editors of the Freud/Fliess letters considered appropriate to a foundational announcement. They silently changed the word to "communications" (*Mitteilungen*). In their English-language edition of the letters a further improvement was made; now Freud and Breuer had produced neither jokes nor communications but "work,"[26] suggesting a program of research on a common problem. And James Strachey, joining the conspiracy in the *Standard Edition*, took the prize for mistranslation upward; now "jokes" was metamorphosed into "findings."[27] The guardians of Freud's shrine were taking pains to prevent us from knowing that he had snickered at the collaboration before it had begun.

In spite of their shared obeisance to Charcot and their claim of theoretical solidarity with each other, the shapers of the "Preliminary Communication" were in disagreement on several key points that one or the other had proposed for inclusion. In 1892 the less tractable party was Breuer, who had wanted to help Freud achieve fame but not at the expense of his own convictions. Breuer was willing to countenance, but not embrace, some of the ideas that mattered to Freud, while others had to be muffled or omitted. We can imagine Freud's mounting frustration and anger in the months preceding the January 1893 debut as he chafed against Breuer's ultimatums.

By June 28 Freud may already have sensed that a price in autonomy would have to be paid for coauthorship with Breuer. So eager was he for that prize, however, and so absorbed had he been in drawing up what he thought would be his own portion of the joint manifesto, that he hadn't yet comprehended the veto power wielded by a man who had nothing to lose by backing out of the project. But the true state of affairs began dawning on him soon enough.

On July 12 Freud complained to Fliess, "My hysteria has, in Breuer's hands, become transformed, broadened, restricted, and in the process has partially evaporated."[28] He remained sanguine nonetheless, because he assumed that his prose would be exempt from Breuer's editing: "We are writing the thing jointly, each on his own working on several sections which he will sign, but still in complete agreement."[29] Five months later, however, the sense of accord had vanished, as had Freud's right to produce signed sections within the "Preliminary Communication." Announcing to Fliess the immediately forthcoming publication, he remarked with cryptic bitterness, "It has cost enough in battles with my esteemed partner [*Herr Compagnon*]."[30] Little esteem remained on either side.

The very title of the "Preliminary Communication," referring to a single "psychical mechanism" for hysterical phenomena, obscured a tug-of-war that would continue straight through *Studies on Hysteria*. Freud was already inclined to view all hysteria as resulting from a lively conflict of motives: the subject protects herself from a frightening experience or morally unacceptable idea by *actively repressing it* within her unconscious and converting the undischarged affect into somatic symptoms. But Breuer preferred to believe that the disorder takes hold automatically during a mental absence, or in what he chose to call a *hypnoid state*.

In the "Preliminary Communication," where Breuer held editorial control and where it was imperative that the coauthors appear to be in concert, Breuer's view overshadowed Freud's. The word "repressed," corresponding to Freud's notion of clashing forces within the mind, was allowed to appear only once.* Maddeningly for Freud, Breuer's Janet-inspired "hypnoid states" were categorically declared to be "the basis and *sine qua non* of hysteria."[31]

The tension that had surfaced between Freud and Breuer in the second half of 1892 continued to wax until the publication of *Studies on Hysteria* in May 1895. According to the plan, the intervening period would be occupied with Breuer's writing up the Pappenheim case and with Freud's gathering further examples of effective "catharsis" from his practice. The *Studies* would then consist of the "Preliminary Communication" as an introductory chapter; a second chapter subdivided into the two authors' individually identified case histories; a "Theoretical" chapter by Breuer; and a concluding chapter by Freud, "The Psychotherapy of Hysteria." That plan was carried out, but its execution only dramatized the chasm separating Breuer's views from Freud's.

When Breuer agreed to cooperate with Freud, the latter had already

---

* SE, 2:10. This was Freud's earliest reference to repression in its psychoanalytic meaning. By the time of *Studies on Hysteria*, he was using *repression* and *defense* interchangeably. Still later, *defense* would refer to the totality of thought-transforming mechanisms, of which repression was only one.

been deserted by Fanny Moser, and he hadn't yet undertaken the equally futile treatment of Ilona Weiss. But he still had Anna von Lieben and Elise Gomperz in his care, and he must have impressed Breuer with stories of Lieben's retrieval of traumatic memories. By 1895, however, Breuer knew that Freud had failed with Lieben and Gomperz as well; and meanwhile, no good cases had come along. How, then, was the wondrous cathartic method going to be illustrated by Freud in *Studies on Hysteria*?

That question didn't trouble Freud, who was only nominally committed to "catharsis." It had already done its job of recruiting Breuer, outflanking Janet, and creating the appearance of a unified Breuer/ Freud school of thought. The fact that he hadn't cured any "hysterics" didn't matter, either, for any number of alibis lay at hand, such as the tenacity of the deep-seated disorder and the diagnostic uncertainty of any given case. In 1895 Freud's pride was invested, rather, in three things: his recently adopted pressure technique, his belief that every neurosis has a sexual origin, and his imagined ability to trace symptoms to their traumatic sources.

These would be the themes of his "Psychotherapy" chapter, undercutting Breuer at every point. And those themes could be exemplified well enough, he figured, in the cases of Fanny Moser ("Emmy von N."), Anna von Lieben ("Cäcilie M."), and Ilona Weiss ("Elisabeth von R."), along with two completely uncorroborated cases, one having lasted only an hour in the out-of-doors ("Katharina") and the other unknown to anyone but Freud ("Miss Lucy R.").*

With ample freedom and space to go their separate ways in signed chapters, Freud and Breuer argued for their clashing models of hysteria formation. Breuer adhered to the hypnoid pattern because it struck him as compatible with all known cases of hysteria, including those that rebuffed any hope of recovering traumatic memories. A theory of hysteria generation, he believed, couldn't be deemed adequate if it failed to cover "purely motor convulsive attacks which are independent of any psychical factor."[32] In addition, "high hypnotizability," as

---

* As I have mentioned, the Lieben case, which Freud rightly judged to have influenced him the most, didn't receive a segment of its own.

it is called today, struck Breuer as the strongest predisposing factor for the autosuggestion that might convert thoughts into symptoms. If so, it seemed fitting to him that a dreamy, distracted mind, as opposed to a mind riven by conflict, would be best suited for succumbing to hysteria.

Freud begged to disagree. He could acknowledge, in theory, the existence of "hypnoid hysteria," but he avowed that he had never encountered a case of it. "Defense [repression] hysteria," he proposed, is likely to be the universal type. If so, "the actual traumatic moment . . . is the one at which the incompatibility [between the ego and an idea] forces itself upon the ego and at which the latter decides on the repudiation of the incompatible idea."[33]

But what, Breuer wondered, could this possibly mean? If the ego *decides* to repudiate an idea, then the idea is being pondered and acted upon by a portion of the mind. Who, then, is being spared from thinking about it? In Breuer's measured words, "We cannot . . . understand how an idea can be deliberately repressed from consciousness."[34]

Again, Breuer wanted to be told "how an idea can be sufficiently intense to provoke a lively motor act . . . and at the same time not intense enough to become conscious."[35] And suppose we agree, nevertheless, that the idea can be banished into the unconscious by a single act of repression. Could such a modest event be held responsible for an enduring fissure in the mind? In Breuer's view, the disproportion between the momentary incident and its supposed long-term result could be rectified only by assuming that the patient was suffering from chronic autohypnosis after an initial hypnoid state.[36]

Breuer also noticed disapprovingly that Freud had ascribed homuncular traits—interests, motives, and strategies—to separate portions of the mind. "The pathogenic psychical material," Freud had written, "appears to be the property of an intelligence which is not necessarily inferior to that of the normal ego."[37] Did the mind, then, contain two warring intellects? "We shall be safe from the danger of allowing ourselves to be tricked by our own figures of speech," the incredulous Breuer warned, "if we always remember that after all it is in the same brain, and most probably in the same cerebral cortex, that conscious and unconscious ideas alike have their origin."[38]

Breuer, for his part, was characteristically self-questioning and tentative when explaining his preference for the hypnoid model. He was all the more offended, then, by Freud's insistence on "a single causal nexus" for hysteria.[39] It is imprudent, he wrote, "to give ideogenesis such a central position in hysteria as is sometimes done nowadays" (not mentioning any names).[40] And he added, with injured pride in the face of Freud's scorn, that eclecticism "seems to me nothing to be ashamed of."[41]

Freud's deepest resentment of Breuer had to do with a dispute that smoldered in *Studies on Hysteria*: the etiological role of sexuality. As we will see in Chapter 22, Freud had come to believe that all neuroses, not hysteria alone, are founded in sexual disturbances of one kind or another. Breuer strenuously resisted that proposition, not because he found it shocking but because it struck him as taking Freud's predilection for exclusive causes to a new level of intransigence.

Deeper than all of their differences over theory was a fundamental incompatibility of temperament. Breuer, the renowned experimentalist, understood how essential it is to maintain a cool, skeptical attitude toward one's own ideas.* Freud, however, joined Fliess in continually exaggerating his certainty. Twelve cases to which he alluded in passing had provided him, he wrote in his final chapter, with "*confirmation*" of the psychical mechanism of hysteria. The resistance encountered in therapy was "*no doubt*" the same psychical force that had generated the patient's symptom. Again, the intrusion of irrelevant matter into a patient's associations "*never occurs.*" When we search for a trauma with the pressure technique, "*we shall find it infallibly.*" The procedure "*never fails*"; it has "*invariably achieved its aim*"; and in one instance Freud's confidence in it was "*brilliantly justified.*"[42]

It is no surprise, then, that the doubt-free Freud considered Breuer's great failing to be indecisiveness. Breuer, he scoffed to Fliess in 1896, "unfailingly knows three candidates for the position of *one* truth."[43] What a peculiar demerit issued by one scientist to another! The

---

* "I envy you very much," Breuer wrote to Fliess in 1895; "on my highest holidays I should like to be as sure in my views as you are on any day of the week" (quoted by Hirschmüller 1989a, p. 319).

methodical weighing of rival "candidates for truth" is precisely what had enabled Breuer to become an outstanding physiologist. But Freud, now a believer in privileged intuition, could no longer grasp even the desirability, much less the method, of systematically winnowing hypotheses. If Breuer still disagreed with him, it could only be because the man was temperamentally unsuited to taking risks.

In Freud's view as *Studies on Hysteria* neared publication, Breuer was a contemptible figure. Like Charcot's final rage against the former disciple who had double-crossed him, however, that altered judgment would never be disclosed to the public. Psychoanalysis would require a noble genealogy: first Charcot's outstanding experiments with hypnotic subjects, then Breuer's "discovery of the cathartic method" in one marvelously successful treatment. Freud had persuaded Breuer, over the latter's strong reluctance, to turn Bertha Pappenheim into the immortal "Anna O.," whose recovery of repressed memories had freed her from hysteria. We will now see whether Breuer or Freud—or, for that matter, Pappenheim herself—believed that any such cure had occurred.

19

The Founding Deception

1. ANNA O.

As the celebrated case of "Anna O.," Breuer's treatment of Bertha Pappenheim in 1880–82 would be showcased in Freud's twentieth-century apologetics as the very "foundation of psychoanalytic therapy."[1] Indeed, he would cite that triumph of healing more often than any of his own alleged successes. "The sense of neurotic symptoms," he wrote, "was first discovered by Josef Breuer from his study and successful cure . . . of a case of hysteria which has since become famous."[2] And again: "Breuer did in fact restore his hysterical patient—that is, free her from her symptoms; he found a technique for bringing to her consciousness the unconscious processes which contained the sense of the symptoms, and the symptoms disappeared."[3]

Because Anna O. figures so prominently in official psychoanalytic history, the absence of any effect of the case on Freud's early methods is felt to constitute a puzzle. Why had he begun by addressing "hysteria" with electrotherapy, spa waters, and the Weir Mitchell rigmarole, and then with Bernheimian suggestion, before applying the efficacious Breuer formula, which he would even claim to have commended to Charcot as far back as 1885–86?*

---

* SE, 20:19. It is hard to believe the Charcot story, which was probably another instance

Freudian doctrine itself, however, stands ready to turn the disappointment to advantage. Ilse Grubrich-Simitis, for example, proposes that Freud must have *repressed* his awareness of Breuer's innovation: "the fact that he had thrust aside the memory of it for years suggests that he had resistances of his own to Breuer's findings."[4] We are supposed to believe that Freud, in the very act of listening to Breuer's narrative, felt so threatened that his ego forbade him to recall it—except momentarily when telling Charcot how important it was. Thus his neglect of "catharsis" in his early practice becomes evidence for the power of those mental forces that an older, steelier Freud would uncover in his own mind and then in all other minds as well.

Rather than tie ourselves in such knots, we would do well to examine the Pappenheim case itself, both as Breuer presented it in *Studies on Hysteria* and as we can piece it together from contemporaneous documents. As it happens, there is evidence to show not only how Pappenheim became "hysterical," how she was really treated, and whether the regimen was successful, but also how both Breuer and Freud regarded the case in ensuing years. The story is complex, and patience will be called for. No diligent reader, though, will remain in doubt as to why Freud was reluctant to aim from the start at producing outcomes comparable to this one.

Bertha Pappenheim, three years younger than Freud, was one of four children of a wealthy Jewish couple who had married in 1848. Her upbringing was both privileged and confining. As an Orthodox female, she was steeped in ritual and required to prepare herself, from an early age, for the role of subservient wife. Although she learned English, French, and Italian as well as Yiddish and Hebrew, her activities as a closely supervised young lady were restricted to "riding, going for walks, tea parties, visits to the theatre and concerts, [and] handiwork."[5]

That dollhouse life was grating to the articulate, imaginative, intel-

---

of Freud's habitual backdating. Every staff member at the Salpêtrière knew that Charcot, then annoyed by his upstart adversary Bernheim, disdained hypnotherapy. The apprentice Freud, aiming to ingratiate himself as a good Charcotian, would surely have thought twice before advising the master on that topic. And if he had dared to do so, he would have proudly told his fiancée about it; but apparently he didn't.

lectually keen, and strong-willed Bertha. Nor did it shield her from emotional vicissitudes. On the contrary, her semi-imprisonment within the nuclear family magnified the effect produced on her by a history of strife and tragedy. One older sister, Flora, had died at age two. Her other sister, Henriette, succumbed to tuberculosis at seventeen, when Bertha was just eight. Bertha and her brother, Wilhelm, never got along. Thus she lacked sibling companionship or support in the crucial years of adolescence.

Meanwhile, the arranged marriage of Bertha's parents was evidently cold, leaving bitterness on both sides. Because her doting father preferred her company to his wife's, Bertha depended on no one but him for approval of her talents. But he, too, was taken away from her. His grave illness—pleurisy and a pleural abscess—from the summer of 1880 until his death in April 1881 marked a period of constant anxiety, insomnia, and redoubled family tension for Bertha, who served as his nocturnal nurse until she was forbidden to do so.

Bertha Pappenheim's illness as Breuer reviewed it fell into four phases, each of which presented her physician with new challenges:

Phase One: July 1880 to December 10 of that year. When Breuer first examined the twenty-one-year-old Pappenheim at the end of November 1880, the only symptom known to her family, apart from weakness and loss of weight, was an intense cough, for which he could find no organic cause. He inferred that it was a sign of hysteria—a diagnosis reinforced by his observation in Bertha of lethargy alternating with hyperexcitement. Later, under hypnosis, she would state that she had already been suffering other symptoms unknown to anyone in her household. Tending her father, Siegmund, in July, before her cough resulted in her banishment from his sickroom, she had allegedly experienced a terrifying hallucination of a black snake that was about to bite him, and then a paralysis of her right arm. The hallucination had kept recurring, and the paralysis had taken hold whenever Bertha lapsed into a state of somnambulistic "absence"—the condition that Breuer would later call "hypnoid."

Phase Two: Pappenheim took to her bed on December 11, 1880, and didn't leave it until the following April 1. In rapid succession, as Breuer recounted, there developed

left-sided occipital headache; convergent squint . . . ; complaints that
the walls of the room seemed to be falling over; . . . disturbances of
vision . . . ; paresis of the muscles of the front of the neck; contracture and anaesthesia of the right upper and . . . right lower extremity
[and later] in the left lower extremity and finally in the left arm.[6]

To Breuer, those afflictions appeared to be classic signs of hysteria.
And they were accompanied in Pappenheim's case by psychological
manifestations to which he devoted close and sympathetic scrutiny.
Bertha, he noted, was exhibiting "two entirely distinct states of consciousness" in rapid alternation:

> In one of these states she recognized her surroundings; she was mel-
> ancholy and anxious, but relatively normal. In the other state she
> hallucinated and was "naughty"—that is to say, she was abusive, used
> to throw the cushions at people, . . . tore buttons off her bedclothes and
> linen. . . . She would complain of having "lost" some time and would
> remark upon the gap in her train of conscious thoughts. . . .
>   . . . At moments when her mind was quite clear she would com-
> plain of the profound darkness in her head, of not being able to think,
> of becoming blind and deaf, of having two selves, a real one and an
> evil one.[7]

Shortly before leaving her bed at last, Pappenheim had become
severely aphasic, and finally she fell altogether dumb. It was at this low
point, however, that Breuer, following a hunch, tried an intervention
whose result would impress him profoundly. Suspecting that Bertha's
silence was a reaction against some verbal offense she had absorbed,
he asked her about it—and, immediately abrogating her handicap,
she *told* him that he was right.[8] Although she continued to experience
difficulties with language, ceasing to speak her native German and
switching mostly to English, she had convinced her doctor that simply
by inquiring into the reason for a "hysterical" symptom, he might free
her from its grip. (But how genuine was a disability that could be suspended for the purpose of answering a question?)

Phase Three began with the death of Siegmund Pappenheim on

April 5, 1881, and it extended to December of that year. After a brief period of emotional numbness, Bertha suffered new distortions of speech and vision, and now she would eat only if fed by Breuer. When he brought in a consultant—we now know that it was Krafft-Ebing— she seemed not to recognize his presence. But when that colleague, testing her for dissimulation, blew smoke in her face, Pappenheim underwent the most violent of her fits; and when Breuer next saw her a few days later, she was continually racked by hallucinations and was in the blackest of all her moods.

During her first three phases, Bertha would turn somnolent every afternoon and then, after sunset, pass into a deeper autohypnotic state prior to a night of clear-headed, often exhilarated insomnia. Having noticed that she was muttering fragments of stories during her afternoon "absences," Breuer decided to encourage that means of venting her emotions. And so she became a Scheherazade, exercising a measure of control by telling a daily tale—or, if she had missed a day, two tales. They were "sad and . . . very charming, in the style of Hans Andersen's *Picture-book without Pictures*."[9] Although those narratives gave way to grim hallucinations after her father's death, the process of unburdening through storytelling continued to soothe her.

"In spite of her euphoria at night," Breuer remarked, "her psychical condition deteriorated rapidly. Strong suicidal impulses appeared which made it seem inadvisable for her to continue living on the third floor."[10] On June 7, 1881, he had her transported, against her will, to "a country house in the vicinity of Vienna."[11] (It was an adjunct to the Fries and Breslauer Sanatorium at Inzersdorf.) Once again the patient was furious with her doctor. Either for that reason or some other, she stepped up her hallucinating, her vandalism, and her halfhearted suicide attempts. But then she calmed down, aided by nightly doses of chloral hydrate to induce sleep.

Soon Breuer and Pappenheim, on days when he was able to see her, fell into a routine that took most of the unpredictability out of her mood changes. "I used to visit her in the evening," he recalled, "when I knew I should find her in her hypnosis, and I then relieved her of the whole stock of imaginative products which she had accumulated since my last visit."[12] Afterward, Bertha would feel happy for twenty-four hours, but then she would get increasingly desperate for what she herself named "chimney sweeping" or "the talking cure." If Breuer waited too long between sessions, she would refuse to speak "until she had satisfied herself of my identity by carefully feeling my hands."[13] As for the bad nights after days when no relief had been obtained, only the ever-present chloral could prevent her anxiety from becoming unbearable.

Bertha's physical symptoms began to resolve during her stay at the "country house," thanks in part to her growing regard for the resident physician there, "Dr. B." (Hermann Breslauer).* She grew more reliably cheerful, too. In the fall of 1881 she was allowed to return to Vienna, where her mother had recently changed domiciles. There Breuer resumed his daily service, and things seemed to be going well. But in December "there was a marked deterioration of her psychical condition."[14]

Phase Four began around Christmas 1881, when an eerie pattern emerged. While Pappenheim's less driven self "lived, like the rest of us, in the winter of 1881–2," her autohypnotic self seemed to have turned its mental calendar back to the preceding winter, with amnesia for all that had happened since then. As the flabbergasted Breuer verified by reference to her mother's private diary, this shadow Bertha was reliving, in exact order, the events of the same date in the preceding year.[15] Now he didn't wait for her to fall into trances; instead, he actively hypnotized her twice daily. In the morning session, he would be puzzled by unexplained behavior; but he learned to anticipate that in the second session, when the contemporary Bertha was presumably communing with the ghost of Bertha past, the pertinent memory would surface.

From time to time throughout the eighteen-month relationship between doctor and patient, Pappenheim would "talk away" a symptom, such as an inability to drink a glass of water, by recalling a traumatic moment when that same activity had been associated with

---

* Breslauer was the physician who would disclose the link between sulfonal and porphyria, shortly after Freud's patient Mathilde Schleicher died from an overdose of the drug; see pp. 253–255 above.

disgust or fear. Now, however, she had hit upon a novel means of getting well. She declared that every instance of the symptom's occurrence must be remembered, and in exact reverse order until the original trauma's turn came up.[16]

The Sisyphean character of that enterprise can be illustrated by Bertha's requirement for being relieved of just one class of symptom, her temporary deafness. She and Breuer recognized seven subtypes of that condition, from "not hearing when someone came in" to "not understanding when several people were talking."[17] Every occurrence of each subtype had to be relived in its correct turn, from the most recent instance to the first one, for a total, by Breuer's count, of 303 events.

Pappenheim saved the best for last: a grand finale that, while stretching the one-year rule, enacted a more climactic symmetry by evoking her black-snake hallucination at her father's bedside. Now, preparing for the termination date on June 7 that she herself had fixed—mock-commemorating Breuer's sending her away—she rearranged her room to match her father's chamber on that awful night. At the appointed time, she reproduced the Ur-hallucination for Breuer—whereupon, so he recounted in his *Studies* chapter, she was immediately freed from all of her remaining disturbances.[18] "After this," he wrote, "she left Vienna and travelled for a while; but it was a considerable time before she regained her mental balance entirely. Since then she has enjoyed complete health."[19]

2. ANNA 2.0

Breuer's chapter on Anna O. in *Studies on Hysteria* was in most respects an imposing performance. Following his patient's zigzag advances and reversals, he made her vivid in her complexity and volatility; he explained the stresses that had evidently predisposed her to illness; he showed how difficult it had been for him to arrive at an unambiguous diagnosis; and he didn't shrink from admitting that some of his interventions had proved counterproductive.

This isn't to say, however, that "Case 1" of the *Studies* was a convincing illustration of the theory that Freud and Breuer had put forward in their introductory chapter of 1893, reproduced verbatim in 1895.

Even Breuer was reluctant to award himself credit for Bertha's alleged healing. Breuer judged that Pappenheim's illness had been fueled by anger, frustration, and mourning—emotional states that would naturally subside in new circumstances. When she took a turn for the better, therefore, he didn't feel entitled to credit either his theory or his method. "As regards the symptoms disappearing after being 'talked away,'" he confessed, "I cannot use this as evidence; it may very well be explained by suggestion."[20]

To be sure, Breuer then added that the suggestion hypothesis appeared unlikely, because he had always found this patient "entirely truthful and trustworthy."[21] That, however, was a non sequitur. The most truthful and trustworthy patient in the world might prove highly suggestible, and a liar would surely be less so.

Only one phase of the Anna O. case, the last one, appeared to include memory retrieval in the Breuer/Freud sense. Yet Bertha Pappenheim also experienced gains (as well as setbacks) during the other phases. Note, for example, that she improved when experiencing mellow, "uncathartic" care at Inzersdorf. Again, no memories were being reviewed when Bertha, clearly pleased with herself, coined the terms "talk therapy" and "chimney sweeping." At that time she was just inventing fairy tales and reciting them to a captive audience of one. In Phase Four she did focus on recollection, and her improvement was marked. But even then, some of her symptoms were vanishing without any perceptible correlation with developments in her treatment.

One feature of the Anna O. case as Breuer narrated it did seem to bear provocative implications, but he abstained from theoretical reflection about it. To some extent Bertha's symptoms, however they originated, were *addressed to him*. In the periods of active treatment, her feelings about him seemed to determine whether she would improve or go into another tailspin. Thus her earliest gains occurred as soon as she had won his admiration with her imaginative storytelling. And whenever she resented his absence, she retrogressed.

Pappenheim's compulsive activities, such as having to recite two stories if a day had been missed, allowing herself to be fed only by Breuer, and "checking his identity" when he had been away too long, showed not only that his presence had become essential to her equa-

nimity but also that she meant to rebuke him for any insufficient cooperation with her whims. And when, on two occasions, she drastically
decompensated, it was in response to major betrayals: his subjecting
her to Krafft-Ebing's crude smoke test and his confining her to the
"country house" on a suicide watch. Even her prediction of self-cure on
a certain date contained a built-in reproach. *On June 7 of last year,* she
said to Breuer in effect, *you violated my trust, treated me like a lunatic,
and abducted me, but on this June 7 I will show you that I can get well
just when I choose.*

Bertha had made herself sick when being neglected, insulted, and
undervalued. Now, however, she found that a tender-minded physician
could be induced to play her game instead of his own. Her symptoms,
whatever their source, became the stakes of that game, to be paid out
in improved health only when Breuer allowed himself to be governed
by her. But that was a recipe not for cure but for dragging out the
coyness ad infinitum.

When Breuer's patient then suddenly altered the rules, putting him
through the tedium of her daily "anniversary" ritual, his skepticism
ought to have been aroused. If Pappenheim could really schedule the
completion of her healing in this meticulous manner, the symptoms she
would sacrifice on a given day couldn't have been authentic. Was this
performance designed, then, merely in order to humiliate him? Alternatively, an emotionally wasted Bertha may have been deluding both
her doctor and herself into a belief that her troubles would soon be
over. On either reading, Breuer in this culminating phase seems to
have been bewitched by maneuvers that he countenanced not because
he expected them to be curative but simply because he had ceded
control to Pappenheim.

Some skeptical observers have concluded that Bertha's hysteria was
altogether faked.[22] The subtlest proponent of this position is Borch-
Jacobsen, who emphasizes that Breuer had been summoned by the
Pappenheims only to deal with a persistent cough. The physician, in
Borch-Jacobsen's words, "didn't so much uncover his patient's 'hyste-
ria' as unleash it, by showing her that he was ready to play the game
called Hysteria. The first symptom of Bertha Pappenheim's hysteria was
Breuer's diagnosis of it."[23]

This statement may look hyperbolical in view of the various symptoms Bertha was alleged to have suffered before Breuer took her case. As Borch-Jacobsen points out, however, it is noteworthy that no one in her household, including Bertha herself in her waking life, had noticed anything but the cough. It was only much later, under hypnosis, that she reported the other symptoms.

Oddly enough, the first believer in the dissimulation thesis was Pappenheim herself. Breuer wrote that while she was suffering "a temporary depression" after she terminated her own case in the summer of 1882, she "brought up a number of childish fears and self-reproaches, and among them the idea that she had not been ill at all and that the whole business had been simulated."[24] But Breuer, recalling Bertha's painful contortions, episodes of dread and panic, and frequent inability to eat or sleep, refused to accept that confession. When a case of split personality gets resolved, he had read in the clinical literature, the ex-patient finds it hard to believe that she had been powerless to call off her symptoms.[25] Bertha, he thought, was just being typical in that regard.

In holding to his belief in the reality of Pappenheim's symptoms, Breuer may have been merely shielding himself from ridicule for having been duped. His analysis of her morally upright character, however, rings true—and doubly so, as we will see, in the light of her subsequent career. A total dissimulator doesn't engage in self-reproaches for having cheated. Nor does she inform her physician about the strange detachment she experienced during her sham agonies. Bertha had not only felt alienated from her own suffering; she *told Breuer* that "a clear-sighted and calm observer [had] sat . . . in a corner of her brain and looked on at all the mad business."[26] Her open expression of curiosity about that phenomenon is still another indication that she hadn't manufactured her entire "hysteria" for the sake of misleading her physician. But what, then, was the matter with her?

3. THE DOCTOR'S DILEMMA

It isn't Bertha but Breuer himself who has more recently come under suspicion of untruthfulness. The catalyst was Henri Ellenberger, employing a dramatic feat of research.[27] He cleverly deduced that Pappenheim, *after* her self-termination in June 1882, must have been admitted to a swanky psychiatric facility, the Bellevue Sanatorium in Kreuzlingen, Switzerland. Voyaging there, Ellenberger found a slightly garbled transcript of a Pappenheim case history that Breuer had prepared for the director, Robert Binswanger, along with a later report by Binswanger's assistant physician, a Dr. Laupus. Ellenberger's explosive article, reevaluating the Anna O. case in the light of that evidence, appeared in 1972. And in that same year, inspired by Ellenberger, Albrecht Hirschmüller began visiting Bellevue and turning up further documents—all of them bearing on Pappenheim's delicate health—written by Breuer, Bertha herself, her mother, and a cousin.

The unearthed records have prompted more questions than can be tackled here, but there is no doubt as to which issue is primary. If the Breuer/Freud position of 1893 was that "each individual hysterical symptom" of their cathartically treated patients had "immediately and permanently disappeared" after hypnotic memory retrieval; and if, as Breuer wrote for the *Studies*, all of Anna O.'s symptoms were "permanently removed by being given utterance in hypnosis,"[28] why did the supposedly cured Pappenheim need to enter a sanatorium five weeks after the termination of her case?

In most respects Breuer's retrieved 1882 report corroborated the narrative of his published case history. A tantalizing exception, however, was that the treatment's fourth phase wasn't covered at all in 1882. But this gap in the record has been partly compensated by the discovery of two letters from Breuer to Binswanger, written shortly before Pappenheim's admission to Bellevue, and by a further brief report by Breuer that was meant to prepare the staff for what could be expected from the new guest.[29]

Breuer's language in 1882 and 1895 is so overlapping that we can be sure he was consulting his Bellevue report as he composed his Anna O. segment for *Studies on Hysteria*. Some differences between the two texts, such as Breuer's greater candor in 1882 regarding Bertha's immersion in fantasy, her childish "naughtiness," and her passionate love for her father, can be set down to considerations of tact and genre. Nevertheless, in this instance certain omissions, distortions, and theoretical flourishes in the 1895 text appear to have been motivated by an effort on Breuer's part to wrench the Pappenheim case into alignment with the Breuer/Freud credo of 1893.

In the original write-up, for example, we see more clearly that Breuer didn't regard his therapy as having made contact with the essence of hysteria. He asserted that the course of Fräulein Pappenheim's illness, so far as its worst physical symptoms were concerned, had "passed its peak" (*seine Acme . . . überschritten*) in the winter of 1880–81, and that its psychical manifestations had also "reached their summit" (*ihren Höhepunkt . . . erreicht*) in June 1881.[30] Those developments, Breuer evidently believed, had nothing to do with his interventions.

Again, the necessity of emotional catharsis, a centerpiece of the Breuer/Freud theory, went unacknowledged in 1882. The noun *catharsis* wasn't employed, and the adjective *cathartic* appeared only once. Pappenheim's recollection of her "whims" and "caprices" had apparently been bland in tone, and even her reliving of traumatic scenes had been calmer than we might have expected. Malcolm Macmillan has shown how Breuer, for the *Studies* version, added such intensifying language as "with every sign of disgust," "shaking with fear and horror," and "after giving further energetic expression to the anger she had held back."[31] Breuer was apparently gratifying his collaborator by pumping gratuitous affect into his prose.

It is now certain not only that Bertha was a patient at Bellevue from July 12 through October 29, 1882, but also that she returned to the suburban Fries and Breslauer Sanatorium, to whose adjacent "villa" Breuer had exiled her in June 1881, for at least three subsequent stays: July 30, 1883, to January 17, 1884 (with one eight-day furlough in Vienna); March 4 to July 2, 1885; and June 30 to July 18, 1887. Altogether, that comes to more than thirteen months of post-treatment institutionalization over a five-year span.[32] On each occasion the admitting diagnosis was "hysteria"—although, as we will see, that term may well have been a euphemism for a less fashionable problem.

Extant letters from Breuer and others reveal that he saw Pappenheim after 1882, continued to worry about her case, and surely knew about her various relapses. Someone else who knew about them, both before and after her marriage to Sigmund Freud, was Martha Bernays.

She had long been on cordial terms with the Pappenheims. Indeed, when her own father died in 1879, Siegmund Pappenheim had been appointed Martha's legal guardian. And Bertha was her good friend, whose doings she followed both through direct social encounters and through reports from mutual acquaintances.

A necessary result of this closeness was that Freud, from 1882 until Bertha's move to Frankfurt in 1888, had both reasons and resources for following her vicissitudes. On August 5, 1883, for example, he relayed to his fiancée what he had just been told by Breuer:

> Bertha is again in the sanatorium in Gross-Enzersdorf, I believe. Breuer talks about her constantly, says he wishes she were dead so the poor woman could be free of her suffering. He says she will never be well again, that she is completely shattered.*

And on May 31, 1887, writing to her mother, Martha Freud confided that Bertha, in Ernest Jones's words, "still suffered from her hallucinatory states as evening drew on."[33]

The disparity between such revelations and Breuer's cautious fudging in *Studies on Hysteria* has caused a number of scholars to infer that the real imposture in this affair wasn't Bertha's hypochondria but Breuer and Freud's trumpeting her recovery. Ellenberger initiated this trend by pronouncing that "the famous 'prototype of a cathartic cure' was neither a cure nor a catharsis," and Hirschmüller followed suit.[34] Breuer's treatment of Pappenheim, conceded the late John Forrester, "was in large part a medical disaster."[35] Disbelievers in psychoanalytic claims have voiced the same conclusion with more gusto. "Everything," writes Borch-Jacobsen, "—the whole enterprise of modern psychotherapy—starts from this marvelous tale of Breuer's, almost too good to be true. And it isn't true."[36]

But there are serious obstacles to our agreeing that the gemstone of *Studies on Hysteria* was only a pasteboard fake. As Breuer insisted to

---

* FMB, 2:103. "Gross-Enzersdorf" was Freud's mistake for "Inzersdorf," the site of the Fries and Breslauer Sanatorium. Jones would repeat Freud's error in his biography, thus inadvertently adding an obstacle to later research.

Binswanger, who initially regarded Pappenheim as a dissimulator, her worst physical symptoms couldn't have been playacted. Breuer cited "a contracture of the right arm lasting for 1 1/2 years (and of the right leg lasting 9 months) with persistent chills and severe oedema of the extremities (anaesthesia), which would relax neither when she was asleep nor under intoxication with 5.00 chloral."[37] He could have added that seizures are hard to counterfeit.

Another problem is Breuer's reputation for probity, maintained over a long career. We can grant that, under pressure from Freud and from his own desire to make a good showing, he suppressed some damaging information and equivocated regarding the usefulness of his method. But did he knowingly cheat his readers by portraying a fiasco as a success, thereby inducing fellow therapists to adopt a method that he knew to be inert? Surely Breuer wasn't lying when, in his 1907 letter to Forel, he wrote that with Anna O.,

> my merit lay essentially in my having recognized what an uncommonly instructive and scientifically important case chance had brought me for investigation, in my having persevered in observing it attentively and accurately, and in my not having allowed any preconceived opinions to interfere with the simple observation of the important data.[38]

Hence the attractiveness, at least initially, of a closely reasoned book published in 2006, Richard A. Skues's *Sigmund Freud and the History of Anna O.: Reopening a Closed Case*. On the whole, writes Skues, Breuer's chapter in the *Studies* "cannot be deemed to be seriously misleading."[39] He reminds us, first of all, that Breuer regarded some of Pappenheim's symptoms as belonging to an organic disease that may have both preceded and outlasted her hysteria, and that two other persistent afflictions, a severe facial neuralgia and a dental condition for which she may have undergone a bungled surgery, had nothing to do with hysteria. More controversially, Skues says that Breuer wouldn't have counted disordered thoughts or a distracted mind as hysterical. After those exclusions, Pappenheim's only signs of true hysteria, by Skues's reckoning and presumably by Breuer's, were the physical ones that had vanished by July 1882. As for her several later periods of institutional care, Skues holds that she was merely recuperating from residual effects of both her disorder and its treatment.

Even Skues, however, is baffled by some obscurities and evasions in Breuer's narrative; and it is far from certain that Breuer regarded somatic disturbances as the only genuinely hysterical ones. In his brief report written just before Pappenheim's admission to Bellevue, he characterized her as "convalescing from very severe neurosis and *psychosis of a hysterical nature*."[40] Breuer's sentence reflected his belief, shared by Dr. Laupus among many others, that hysteria does include distorted emotion. "In the unmotivated fluctuation of her moods," wrote Laupus at the end of Bertha's Bellevue stay, "the patient displayed genuine signs of hysteria."[41]

Nowhere, either in 1882 or later, did Breuer assert that Pappenheim's aphasia, hallucinations, and "absences" *weren't* hysterical. If he had thought so, he wouldn't have bothered to claim that those disturbances of mind had disappeared for good during the Phase Four memory cure. It is therefore of interest that all three symptoms actually persisted beyond 1882, though with decreased frequency and intensity. Only by arbitrarily declaring them out of bounds can Skues maintain that by July 1882 "Bertha Pappenheim had effectively recovered from the hysterical symptoms for which she received treatment from Breuer."[42]

During some thousand hours with Pappenheim,[43] Breuer had humored her whims and tried not to be bored by her made-up tales, petty complaints, and banal day-by-day reminiscences. The nonstop talk had become a trial for him, and that must have been one reason why he had tried, unsuccessfully, to send his loquacious patient off to Switzerland in the fall of 1881. As he wrote to Forel in 1907, the Anna O. marathon had taught him "that it was impossible for a 'general practitioner' [the words are in English] to treat a case of that kind without bringing his activities and mode of life completely to an end. I vowed at the time that I would *not* go through such an ordeal again."[44]

Pappenheim was still a burden when they did part company at last. In the brief report that he prepared for the Bellevue team, Breuer warned that she "becomes very insecure and capricious, at times—as she says—'quite crazy.' "[45] And in his letter to Binswanger of mid-June 1882, he wrote that she was then "suffering from slight hysterical insanity, . . . and exhibiting perfectly odd behaviour on visits."[46] *Slight hysterical insanity*. That was what remained, according to Breuer himself, after eighteen months of therapeutic efforts by himself and others.

4. CONVALESCING FROM THE TREATMENT

By depicting Bertha's travails but filing them under a disorder that is no longer taken seriously by physicians, Breuer accidentally exposed the Anna O. case to an abundance of rival explanations. Some observers, as I have mentioned, see Pappenheim as having practiced sheer dissimulation from the start. Others have concluded that she suffered from schizophrenia, from temporal lobe epilepsy, from tuberculous meningitis, from major depression, or from one or another ego disorder known only to psychoanalysis.[47] But the proponents of each "paleodiagnosis" have had an easy time poking holes in one another's hypotheses.

One aspect of the Pappenheim case, however, appears to be less vulnerable than the others to anomalies and gaps in knowledge. I refer to Bertha's reaction to the drugs chloral hydrate and morphine. At some junctures in her history, we know how much medicine was administered, and at what intervals, and over what total period. We also have candid private reports from both Breuer and the Bellevue sanatorium's Dr. Laupus regarding her dependency and the attempts that were made to curtail it. And when all this information is correlated with her symptoms and with familiar effects of those drugs, some conclusions can be drawn that at least partly avoid the trap of arbitrary "diagnosis at a distance."[48]

The health record of Bertha Pappenheim exhibits a number of peculiarities that, taken together, are hard to reconcile either with the dissimulation hypothesis or with the various organic-disease hypotheses. From the outset of Breuer's contact with her, she alternated between states of near normality, manic euphoria, and a lassitudinous despair that was accompanied by paralyses and hallucinations. Her very sanity appeared to hang in the balance, with a precarious alternation between what she herself called craziness and a lucid, self-analytical rationality and adherence to the *politesse* of her class. (Witness, for example, her courteous, objective letter to Binswanger thanking him for his attentions at Bellevue.)[49] But Bertha's fluctuations were curiously diurnal. She was sleepy and "clouded" in the afternoons but hyperexcitable at night, as if in thrall to opposed surges of chemicals in her brain.

These states appear virtually identical to those of Anna von Lieben a decade later. As Peter Swales observed in 1986, the sameness may have owed something both to Freud's influence on the second Anna and to her personal acquaintance with the first.[50] But it also reflected the aspect of both cases that Freud and Breuer calculatedly put under the rug: morphine addiction.

Breuer's omission of that factor from his published case history cannot be explained by a wish to shield Pappenheim from shame. His report took few pains to conceal her identity, and he didn't hesitate to refer, though only in passing, to her other drug involvement. He wrote that at Inzersdorf Bertha "took chloral at night" to combat agitation and that he himself had prescribed it for her "on a few earlier occasions."[51] Only in reading his 1882 report and Dr. Laupus's summary of the Bellevue stay, however, do we learn that the chloral doses had become alarmingly high. Chloral dependency was a major obstacle to cure in Bertha's case. Or rather, along with morphine dependency, it was the very source of the symptoms that lay beyond her control.

Studies on Hysteria contains not a single hint that Breuer had been keeping Bertha on morphine, first to combat intense neuralgic pain that she had been suffering and then for prevention of seizures—which themselves may well have been effects of overmedication. Not only did he withhold this aspect of the case; he sought to mislead his readers about it. Referring to Bertha's time at Inzersdorf in the summer of 1881, he reported that he "had been able to avoid the use of narcotics" in coping with her symptoms.[52] By saying nothing further, he falsely implied that morphine was never a problem for his patient.

In actuality, under Breuer's care Pappenheim had become a double addict. Her most serious debility, as of the summer of 1882 and for five years thereafter, wasn't hysteria but the horror of attempted and failed withdrawal. And her physicians knew about it and drew up their plans accordingly before her admission to Bellevue. "The first task," wrote Dr. Laupus in looking back on her months there, "was to wean her from the morphine addiction."[53]

That task was left tragically incomplete for a number of years. As Pappenheim herself wrote with stoical understatement in her November 1882 letter to Binswanger, "You will realize that to live with a syringe always at the ready is not a situation to be envied."[54] And her condition soon became drastically worse. The evidence is found in Freud's letter of August 5, 1883, relaying Breuer's opinion that only death could now end the "completely shattered" Bertha's agony.

Clearly, Pappenheim was then in a more precarious state than at any time during her treatment by Breuer. On October 31 of that same year, Freud told his fiancée the news from Breuer that her friend Bertha, then recuperating once again at Inzersdorf, "is getting rid of her pains and her morphine poisoning (*ihre Schmerzen u. ihre Morphiumvergiftung los wird*)." Thus it is a certainty that both Freud and Breuer were perfectly aware of the addiction. Can anyone imagine that they had forgotten it when they connived to turn Pappenheim into Exhibit A of the cathartic cure? Even Jones, while cloaking the whole topic of addiction, allowed the truth to be briefly glimpsed: "She improved, however, and gave up morphia."[55]

The fact that Pappenheim did finally succeed in getting clean explains the broadest oddity of her case. As we will see, the haunted, periodically out-of-control Bertha of 1880–82, the "shattered" Bertha of 1883, and the Bertha of 1887 who seemed generally better but "still suffered from her hallucinatory states as evening drew on" became a different person: efficient, purposeful, emotionally steady, constructively creative, and fearlessly devoted to social justice. Yet this Bertha had to have been latent in the "hysteric" who so exasperated Breuer. The mystery dissolves when we realize that her conduct in 1880–82 resulted from chronic intoxication.

It cannot be a coincidence that every one of Pappenheim's symptoms has been listed as a known effect of one or both of her drugs. Large daily doses of chloral hydrate could have been responsible for her dyplopia (double vision), strabismus (crossed eyes), mood swings, aggressive acts, distractedness, and memory loss.[56] Her seizures, paralyses, insomnia, headaches, visual illusions and hallucinations, agitation, anxiety, speech impediments, and even her inability to swallow water are all familiar signs of attempted withdrawal from the same drug. As for morphine intoxication, it can produce euphoria followed by agitation, apathy, malaise, impaired social functioning, drowsiness, and deficits of memory and attention. And failed attempts at withdrawal from morphine could explain Bertha's muscle aches, nausea, insomnia, and depression.

What, then, is left unaccounted for? Only some perverse-looking conduct: Bertha's impish torment of her forbearing doctor. But here we may recall Ernst Fleischl's and Freud's own descent, under the influence of cocaine, to defrauding American medical journals and the Merck Company. Pappenheim's tactics didn't approach that level of deceit, but her judgment was clouded and her fear of abandonment was stark. She clung to sanity by inventing rituals that would ensure continued care from Breuer and a simulacrum of control over her predicament.

The drug effects I have listed were well understood in Breuer's day, when chloral hydrate and morphine were the most frequently employed and most heavily abused of all medications. It is astonishing, if true, that in 1880–82 Breuer didn't consider that he might be dealing with drug poisoning and addiction rather than with "hysteria." But it is unthinkable that he could have remained in ignorance when, for years *after* his treatment of Pappenheim, she continued to exhibit some of the same clinical traits (distractedness, hallucinations, language distortion, aversion to food) while manifestly struggling with the rigors of withdrawal.

Could Pappenheim have been self-administering chloral and morphine in the summer and fall of 1880, before Breuer's treatment began? Serving then as her father's night nurse, she must have had access to his drugs; and morphine and chloral would have been the medications of choice for his pain and insomnia, respectively. Her own insomnia, her fear of losing him, her anger at him for an insult that she disclosed to Breuer, her antagonism toward her mother and brother, and the neuralgia that she had first experienced in the preceding spring all provided motives for recourse to the drugs. When Breuer first saw her, she may have already been intoxicated and on a course toward addiction.

This scenario fits with a curious but well-documented fact. The dosages that proved necessary for effectiveness with Bertha in 1880–82 were much higher than should have been required. Breuer quickly increased her chloral for insomnia to 5 grams per night, a potentially lethal quantity for a normal person. And at Bellevue her daily morphine had to be expanded from 80 to 100 milligrams for the same reason. "Certainly," observes one authority, "it is a dose for someone who is severely dependent on this drug, and . . . no one attains this level of tolerance in a short period of time."[57]

We know of one instance, furthermore, when Bertha's symptomatic behavior resulted *directly* from attempted drug withdrawal. As Breuer wrote to Binswanger,

> 10 days ago the patient was given no chloral for 4 successive nights, and immediately suffered intense agitation. This was followed by a strong hint of delir[ium] c[um] tremore, though this was mixed with states of agitation deriving from other origins to such an extent that it was not very easy to isolate it. In any event, she hallucinated small animals, heard voices, was somewhat inclined to be violent, . . . and so on.[58]

This is a classic picture of withdrawal pangs—much the same ones that Breuer would observe in Fleischl three years later.

There remains the seemingly discordant fact that Pappenheim's state fluctuated in response to her positive and negative feelings toward Breuer and also toward Breslauer and Binswanger at the two sanatoriums. If she was an occasional self-medicator, however, it isn't hard to imagine that at desperate moments she would have consumed extra morphine and/or chloral, whereas at other times she would have adhered to the tapering regimen and have become less symptomatic. After a shaky start at Inzersdorf, for example, her progress there, beginning in the summer of 1881, must have reflected a well-designed program of withdrawal; that successful experience was what made Inzersdorf the obvious choice for her post-Breuer detoxifications.

But why, we must ask, instead of just listening to Pappenheim's interminable ramblings, hadn't Breuer bent every effort to rescuing her from addiction? Not surprisingly, he divined that this same question must be on Binswanger's mind, and he addressed it with notable defensiveness:

> She is receiving daily 0.08–0.1 morphine by injection. My case history will justify me in this matter. I am not engaged in breaking her of this addiction since, despite her good will, when I am with her I am powerless to cope with her agitated state.[59]

Here we see that by June 1882 morphine had become almost as mandatory for Breuer as it was for his patient. After eighteen months under his supervision, she was uncontrollable by any means other than stupefaction by drugs. And he felt remorseful about his failure with her. Writing of her chloral addiction, acquired through a year's-worth of huge doses every night, he remarked, "A considerable degree of responsibility apparently rests with me."[60] Yet, while he hoped that Bertha would "apply her strong will to weaning herself," he shamefacedly added that "here and now, I am preventing her from doing this."[61]

Now we can better understand why, according to Freud in 1925, Breuer had "objected vehemently" to the latter's relentless pleas that the Pappenheim case be resurrected and made the centerpiece of the successful new therapy.[62] The only remaining cause for wonder is that Breuer finally gave in and allowed "Anna O." to be paraded before the world as the beneficiary of a powerful new technique for relieving hysterics of their suffering.

With the inclusion of the respectable-looking Anna O. report in a book cowritten by himself, Freud achieved just the foothold he needed in order to be taken seriously as an expert on hysteria. Unfortunately, however, the case, even after being radically censored and prettified, still appeared to contradict what was, at the time, his most adamantly held idea about the etiology of that disorder: that every hysteria results from the repressed memory of a sexual trauma.

It was not in Freud's nature, however, to be silenced by such an inconvenience. In his view, the Anna O. case now belonged to him.

Although there was little he could do to "Freudianize" the main story without Breuer's agreement, he could at least take revenge on both Breuer and Pappenheim for having denied the sexual dimension that he imputed to their relationship. Tentatively at first, but then more radically once Breuer was no longer on hand to contradict him, Freud would recast the terminating incident until it answered to his need.

20

Adjusting the Record

1. CONSTRUCTION JOB

Although Breuer had complied in part with Freud's desire to make the case of Anna O. sound "cathartic," he had stopped short of aligning it with Freud's doctrine that every neurosis has a sexual basis. Indeed, he had pointedly affirmed, on the opening page of his study, that "the element of sexuality was astonishingly undeveloped" in his patient—a judgment to which he would adhere for the rest of his life.[1] As he told August Forel in 1907, "The case of Anna O. . . . proves that a fairly severe case of hysteria can develop, flourish, and be resolved without having a sexual basis."[2]

So long as that impression went unchallenged, Breuer's case history would boomerang against Freud's etiology of hysteria. The more exclusively and adamantly Freud insisted on sexual causation, the more starkly he was haunted by the recalcitrant example. He found himself caught in a trap. On the one hand, he needed to keep reiterating that Anna O. had been cathartically liberated from hysteria.[3] On the other hand, how could the cure have occurred if Breuer had possessed no inkling of the repressed sexual trauma that had to have underlain Anna's neurosis?

When Freud brooded over an annoyance year after year, however, he usually found a way of neutralizing it that was gratifying to himself and a welcome relief to his followers, even if they first had to stifle some doubts. In the matter of Anna O.'s asexuality, he gradually arrived at two means of removing the impediment. The first was to characterize Breuer as a man whose training and disposition had made it hard for him to recognize sexuality even, or especially, when it displayed itself directly to him. In Freud's estimation, therefore, Breuer's failure to *consciously* perceive a sexual origin for Anna O.'s troubles, far from telling us something about the patient, rendered him a candidate for psychoanalytic assessment in his own right. And second, Freud retold the Anna O. story so as to endow it with a sensational eroticized denouement. In doing so, he demonstrated how much damage he was willing to inflict on other people's reputations—in this instance, both Breuer's and that of the possibly identifiable Bertha Pappenheim—in order to satisfy his thirst for victory.

The tactful and supportive Breuer, unlike Freud, took no satisfaction from prying into his patients' sexual behavior. He never doubted, however, that sexuality was a weighty contributor to neurotic ailments, and he said so plainly in *Studies on Hysteria*: "It is perhaps worth insisting again and again that the sexual factor is by far the most important and the most productive of pathological results."[4] And again: "The sexual instinct is undoubtedly the most powerful source of persisting increases of excitation (and consequently of neuroses)."[5] Indeed, Breuer etched in italics his conviction that "*the great majority of severe neuroses in women have their origin in the marriage bed.*"* Now we can see why Breuer had deemed Pappenheim's sexuality to be "astonishingly undeveloped." He had found it all but incredible that her hallucinations, over an eighteen-month period, had shown no erotic content at all.

Nevertheless, Freud would spread the word among the psychoanalytic faithful that Breuer's inability to accept the full sexual truth about Anna O. was explained by his spinelessness. That then became a mantra to be endlessly recited by one commentator after another.

---

* SE, 2:246. That is just what Freud remembered having been told by Breuer in conversation—though Freud would pretend, in his 1914 *History of the Psycho-Analytic Movement*, that Breuer had voiced that judgment in an unguarded moment and that, hypocritically, he elsewhere maintained the opposite (SE, 14:13).

Ernest Jones established the model in his biography, pointing to "a weakness in [Breuer's] personality that made it hard for him ever to take a definite stand on any question." Breuer, Jones added, was burdened with "a pettifogging kind of censoriousness which would induce him to mar any appreciation or praise by searching out a small point open to criticism—an attitude very alien to Freud's open-hearted and generous spirit."[6] And James Strachey likewise wrote, in introducing *Studies on Hysteria*, that Breuer was "a man full of doubts and reservations, always insecure in his conclusions . . . [and] half-afraid of his own remarkable discoveries."[7]

One such discovery, Strachey meant his readers to infer, was the sexual ingredient in Pappenheim's hysteria. Superficially regarded, the case history appeared to be devoid of any such indication. But Freud, thanks to his symbological code, had rectified that deficiency. "Anyone who reads the history of Breuer's case now," Freud wrote in 1914, "will at once perceive the symbolism in it—the snakes, the stiffening, the paralysis of the arm—and, on taking into account the situation at the bedside of the young woman's sick father, will easily guess the real interpretation of her symptoms."*

Bertha Pappenheim, in other words, while anxiously attending her dying father, was emotionally disturbed, according to Freud's judgment, not by the prospect of a tragic loss but by an unconscious desire to commit incest with the invalid. That lurid proposal, however, was just Freud's hors d'oeuvre for a feast of speculation. Although he merely hinted at it in 1914, by then he had already scripted a new drama surrounding the case, one that represented Bertha as having been temporarily crazed by passion for Breuer himself—who, in turn, had supposedly recoiled in a prudish panic.

According to Freud's reinterpretation, the real key to the Anna O. case had been transference, or a patient's sexual rapport with her

---

* SE, 14:11–12. Freud had evidently worked out this analysis of Anna O.'s mental state in conversations with his disciple Max Eitingon, who elaborated the thesis in an unpublished paper dated October 1909. (See Skues 2006, pp. 57–59.) Clearly, however, the initiative came from Freud. As he wrote to Jung a month later, "So far I have had two of the case histories from the *Studies* brought up to the level of our present knowledge" (11/21/09, FJ, pp. 266–267).

therapist as a surrogate parent. The case was self-explanatory: Bertha, who must have been in love with Breuer, had acquired that fixation only after the death of Siegmund Pappenheim. Yet the most anomalous feature of the Anna O. case now looked more puzzling than ever. If, by 1914, "analysis of the transference" had supplanted derepression of memories as the sine qua non of psychoanalytic cure, and if Breuer hadn't analyzed Bertha's transference but had merely fled from it, how could she have been cured?

As we have seen, Freud was aware that Pappenheim had been unwell for years after leaving Breuer's care. He also knew what her illness was: not hysteria but morphine addiction, induced by Breuer himself. Freud saw no need to trouble the world with that information, but now it occurred to him that the bad outcome of the case might be turned to a good purpose. So far as anyone would be told, Breuer had removed Anna O.'s hysteria; but because he had lacked both Freud's psychoanalytic knowledge and his fortitude, he had failed to deal with the transference that had been created by the successful treatment itself.

As Freud sketched the new version of events in 1914,

Breuer was able to make use of a very intense suggestive rapport with the patient, which may serve us as a complete prototype of what we call "transference" today. Now I have strong reasons for suspecting that after all her symptoms had been relieved Breuer must have discovered from further indications the sexual motivation of this transference, but that the universal nature of this unexpected phenomenon escaped him, with the result that, as though confronted by an "untoward event," he broke off all further investigation. He never said this to me in so many words, but he told me enough at different times to justify this reconstruction of what happened. When I later began more and more resolutely to put forward the significance of sexuality in the aetiology of neuroses, he was the first to show the reaction of distaste and repudiation which was later to become so familiar to me, but which at that time I had not yet learnt to recognize as my inevitable fate.[8]

At this juncture in 1914, with Breuer all too available to rebut any specific allegations, Freud was being deliberately vague in a published work. Had there been an actual "untoward event," or had Breuer merely reacted "as though" (*wie von*) one had occurred? But in 1925, when Breuer lay near death, Freud was somewhat more explicit:

> [Breuer] might have crushed me or at least disconcerted me by pointing to his own first patient, in whose case sexual factors had ostensibly played no part whatever. But he never did so, and I could not understand why this was, until I came to interpret the case correctly and to reconstruct, from some remarks which he had made, the conclusion of his treatment of it. After the work of catharsis had seemed to be completed, the girl had suddenly developed a condition of "transference love"; he had not connected this with her illness, and had therefore retired in dismay.[9]

Here and elsewhere in published comments, Freud was careful to stipulate that his version of events was only hypothetical, a "reconstruction" assembled from hints dropped by Breuer. At the same time, however, he asserted without qualification that he had pieced together the truth "correctly." But if Breuer never backed down, even privately, from his judgment that sexuality had played no part in the Anna O. case, it is hard to imagine what contrary "remarks" he had made to Freud.

Moreover, it made no psychoanalytic sense for Freud to claim that the patient's transference of her oedipal love onto Breuer had begun *at the end* of her eighteen-month therapy. That was a tactical maneuver on Freud's part, erecting a needed wall between his contradictory uses of the same case: as a model catharsis and as a failure to cope with the erotic factor. The supposed eradication of Anna O.'s hysteria remained anomalous, especially in view of the overlooked sexual symbolism Freud had purported to find in her symptoms. But by 1925 he wasn't mentioning the symbols anymore; the whole topic of sexuality was now relocated to the concluding phase of treatment.

Meanwhile, Freud had been leaking the plot elements of his reconstruction not just to the original members of his Vienna circle but also to Jung, the Swedish psychiatrist Poul Bjerre, and Princess Marie Bonaparte, among others.[10] In the rivalrous psychoanalytic community, all such personally disclosed revelations were treasured and proudly transmitted, often with an admixture of further confabulation. Because the tales remained unpublished, Breuer couldn't squelch them; but among the analysts, Freud's campaign to demean him and to eroticize his patient's ailment advanced without opposition.

In 1932, fifty years after a weary Breuer had consigned Bertha Pappenheim to Drs. Binswanger and Laupus, Freud would spell out his latest version of that transition. But he still didn't commit it to print. Instead, he sent a letter to the novelist and biographer Stefan Zweig, protesting that Zweig, an avid Freudian, had been mistaken in reporting to the public that Anna O., under Breuer's hypnosis, had confessed to having experienced inappropriate feelings by her father's sickbed. "What really happened with Breuer's patient," Freud confided,

> I was able to guess later on, long after the break in our relations, when I suddenly remembered something Breuer had once told me in another context before we had begun to collaborate and which he never repeated. On the evening of the day when all her symptoms had been disposed of, he was summoned to the patient again, found her confused and writhing in abdominal cramps. Asked what was wrong with her, she replied: "Now Dr. Br.'s child is coming!"
>
> At this moment he held in his hand the key that would have opened the "doors to the Mothers," but he let it drop.* With all his great intellectual gifts there was nothing Faustian in his nature. Seized by conventional horror he took flight and abandoned the patient to a colleague. For months afterwards she struggled to regain her health in a sanatorium.[11]

If we read this passage while holding open Freud's *Autobiographical Study*, some disturbing inconsistencies come to light. In 1925 Freud wrote that he had discerned a hidden pattern in "some remarks" by

---

* In *Faust, Part II*, Mephistopheles gives Faust a key to a lower realm of "the Mothers"—unnamed deities who control the mysteries of creation.

Breuer; but in 1932 there was an indelibly vivid story, recounted by Breuer himself, featuring a hysterical pregnancy, a direct quotation from a hallucinating Bertha Pappenheim, and an ignominious retreat by the discomposed therapist.

Freud had allegedly heard that narrative before his collaboration with Breuer had begun—that is, prior to the summer of 1892—yet he had been unable to recall it until "long after the break in our relations." Poor Freud! Throughout the first half of the 1890s, he and Breuer had quarreled repeatedly over the issue of sexuality in the Anna O. case, but somehow he hadn't been able to recall Breuer's self-damning confession that he had witnessed the false labor agonies, had fled in a panic, and had abandoned a shattered Bertha to institutionalization.

The 1932 version is incredible on its face, without our needing to check it against subsequently published facts. Not surprisingly, though, it is also refuted by those facts. Breuer had remanded Pappenheim to Robert Binswanger's facility not all at once but after months of negotiations. His reports to Binswanger, far from alerting him to a false pregnancy, admonished that he would find Bertha strangely asexual— important evidence that his later characterization of her sexual innocence was sincere. And her "struggle to regain her health," as Freud had correctly reported to his fiancée, had been all about morphine addiction and the ravages of attempted withdrawal.

In his letter to Zweig, then, Freud was either lying or venting a delusion of his own. One possibility doesn't altogether exclude the other. Although by 1932 Freud may have believed the scenario he had concocted in order to stem the threat to psychoanalysis posed by the Anna O. case, his letter went on to tell an apparent falsehood about more recent occurrences:

> I was so convinced of this reconstruction of mine that I published it somewhere. Breuer's youngest daughter (born shortly after the above-mentioned treatment, not without significance for the deeper connections!), read my account and asked her father about it (shortly before his death). He confirmed my version, and she informed me about it later.[12]

As we remember, Freud was something of a specialist in gleaning precious admissions from people who couldn't be reached for checking. The present instance ranks with the dying Theodor Meynert's self-humbling mea culpa, imparted to his most despised antagonist, to the effect that he had been a secret "male hysteric" all along. Note, furthermore, that in the passage at hand, just one paragraph below Freud's statement that Breuer had told him about the false pregnancy, he calls the same event a "reconstruction." If the first statement were true, nothing would have remained to be reconstructed.

Freud and Dora Breuer probably did communicate after her father's death, and they may have discussed salacious rumors that had swirled around Breuer and his nubile patient at a time when other doctors were raising an eyebrow over their protracted relationship. But Dora couldn't have read about that incident in any published document. The tale of the false pregnancy hadn't been published by Freud or anyone else.* And it wouldn't be tried out on the public until twenty-eight years later, when Ernest Jones set forth the legend that other Freudians would thenceforth believe and pass along.

As Han Israëls has shown, Freud had no need to "reconstruct" the reason for Breuer's termination of Pappenheim's treatment.[13] In a letter to Martha Bernays of October 31, 1883—quite soon, then, after the parting—Freud revealed that Breuer "gave up her care because it was threatening his happy marriage." The letter continued:

> His poor wife could not stand the fact that he was so exclusively devoting himself to a woman about whom he obviously spoke with great interest. Surely, she was only jealous of the demands made on her husband by another woman. Her jealousy did not show itself in a hateful, tormenting fashion, but in a silently recognized one. She fell ill, lost her spirits, until he noticed it and discovered the reason why. This naturally was enough for him to completely withdraw his medical attention from B.P.[14]

---

* In another 1932 letter, this one to the English botanist Arthur Tansley, Freud named the *Autobiographical Study* as the source of Dora Breuer's curiosity (Forrester and Cameron 1999, p. 930). Anna O.'s supposed hallucination, however, isn't mentioned in that text (SE, 20:26).

And Martha replied on November 2 that she tremblingly empathized with Frau Breuer's jealousy.[15]

Freud, then, knew all along that there was a sexual dimension to the Anna O. case, but not the one he would later allege. It consisted of Mathilde Breuer's resentment of the time and attention her husband had been devoting to an attractive young woman. Josef, absorbed in the case, had been slow to notice his wife's distress; but as soon as he did so, he resolved to step away.

These facts shed light on Breuer's initial reluctance to collaborate with Freud and on Freud's later machinations as well. Breuer knew not only that the Pappenheim case had been a medical fiasco but also that he could never disclose the reason why he had withdrawn from it. And Freud was aware that Breuer couldn't contest anything he might choose to say about the matter. As Israëls points out, Freud must have promised Breuer that "the Mathilde factor," along with Pappenheim's morphine addiction, would remain their secret; and much later that secret functioned as blackmail, allowing Freud to lie with impunity about Breuer's supposed sexual cowardice.

2. CLOSING RANKS

Freud's lurid addenda to the case of Anna O. posed a dilemma for the postwar psychoanalytic elite. Devotion to the late founder and to his cause required them to endorse a story that lacked verisimilitude. Jones and Strachey, we now know, fretted over the problem before deciding on a common stance.[16] As Strachey privately acknowledged, the milder version of how Freud arrived at his belief—a mere "reconstruction"— was more plausible than the definite one. But it didn't *sound* better, and therefore both men, coordinating their maneuvers as usual, decided to suppress any mention of reconstruction even as a possibility. Jones fibbed that a letter Freud had written to Martha Bernays on October 31, 1883, provided "confirmation" of the bogus events.* And

---

* J, 1:225. Freud's letter had merely stated that Frau Breuer's extreme jealousy of her husband's professional attentions to Bertha had caused him to terminate the treatment (FMB, 2:384–385).

Strachey, in a *Standard Edition* footnote to Breuer's Anna O. chapter, contented himself with falsely stating that "the whole story is told by Ernest Jones in his life of Freud."[17]

The tale as Jones presented it involved both transference and countertransference, the latter being Breuer's alleged crush on his attractive young patient. Mathilde Breuer's wifely jealousy, wrote Jones, shocked her husband into announcing to the much improved Anna O. that her treatment was now over:

> But that evening he was fetched back to find her in a greatly excited state, apparently as ill as ever. The patient, who according to him had appeared to be an asexual being . . . , was now in the throes of an hysterical childbirth . . . , the logical termination of a phantom pregnancy that had been invisibly developing in response to Breuer's ministrations. Though profoundly shocked, he managed to calm her down by hypnotizing her, and then fled the house in a cold sweat. The next day he and his wife left for Venice to spend a second honeymoon, which resulted in the conception of a daughter; the girl born in these curious circumstances was nearly sixty years later to commit suicide in New York.[18]

This is the canonical telling of how Breuer and Pappenheim parted company, and it is a fabrication. To summarize:

- Although Breuer was fascinated at first by Pappenheim's talents and peculiarities, and may well have felt an initial sexual attraction as well, her obsessive, demanding ways and her impositions on his time and energy had gradually turned her into a burden that he wanted to lay on others—notably Breslauer at Inzersdorf and Binswanger at Kreuzlingen. Meanwhile, he expressed his frustration by stunning his patient with morphine; for otherwise, as he sheepishly explained to Binswanger, he would have been "powerless to cope with her agitated state."[19] Breuer and Pappenheim's relationship was tangled but not discernibly erotic.
- Bertha chose the date for ending her own treatment; she wrapped up the case, or tried to, in one of her commemorative reenactments; and

then she allowed herself to be enrolled at Bellevue in the hope of becoming drug free. Breuer, displaying none of the sexual embarrassment or alarm that Jones's story would lead us to expect, continued to take a benevolent, if more distant, interest in her health.

- The "phantom pregnancy" was indeed a phantom—a product of Freud's scheming to take down his former friend and benefactor.
- Josef and Mathilde Breuer didn't hastily depart for Venice. Indeed, they didn't go there at all. Breuer continued to meet his medical obligations and then the couple repaired to Gmunden, near Vienna, for their customary summer vacation.
- Dora Breuer was born three months before the date on which she was supposed to have been conceived in Venice. And instead of killing herself in New York, she took poison in Vienna when she was about to be seized by the Gestapo. Thus it was obscene on Jones's part to hint that her suicide had been somehow foredoomed by the imagined "curious circumstances" of her birth.

Among commentators who have felt obliged to concede the insubstantiality of Jones's drama, he has been criticized for embellishing the details supplied to him by Freud. Jones, however, rarely felt entitled to deviate from what Freud would have wanted him to say. Apart from his misinformation regarding the death of Dora Breuer, everything in his account probably originated with Freud. Note, for example, that the significantly mistimed conception of baby Dora was already hinted in Freud's letter to Stefan Zweig.

A surviving draft of the relevant segment from Jones's biography, when viewed in conjunction with the published text, shows him struggling to reconcile the oral fable with *Brautbriefe* from 1883 to which he had just been given access.[20] He could see that there was no factual basis for the kiss-and-make-up connubial scene in Venice, eventuating in the birth of a daughter. But he also realized that Freud's slander of Breuer was indispensable to the founding myth of psychoanalysis, and so he dutifully folded it into his text. When Breuer's surviving relatives subsequently proved to Jones that the tale was both impossible and outrageous, they asked him to exclude it from the second edition of his biography; he did not.[21]

If Jones were to have disavowed the main fiction, he would also have had to retract a second one that he had passed along as factual:

> Some ten years later . . . Breuer called [Freud] into consultation over an hysterical patient. Before seeing her he described her symptoms, whereupon Freud pointed out that they were typical products of a phantasy of pregnancy. The recurrence of the old situation was too much for Breuer. Without saying a word he took up his hat and stick and hurriedly left the house.[22]

This second pregnancy yarn may have been nothing more than a corrupted version of the first one.*

Henri Ellenberger challenged the false-pregnancy myth in 1970 and demolished it in 1972.[23] Those were significant developments. Before Ellenberger, Freudians had little objective reason to doubt Freud's word on the issue; afterward, they had every objective reason to do so. But with few exceptions, the only analysts who have acknowledged the gravity of the debacle are those who believe that psychoanalysis can afford to divorce itself from Freud. They are a rare breed. As one of them, Marian Tolpin, courageously observed, "The story about Breuer and his patient is an example of a defensive myth first used by Freud to affirm himself and used subsequently by generation after generation of analysts to affirm the insecurely established group-self of psychoanalysis."[24]

Tolpin was not exaggerating the willingness of her colleagues to enclose themselves within an alternative universe. One analyst, though he cited both of the key texts by Ellenberger, asserted in 1994 that Anna's delusion "was revealed by Freud. . . . Clearly, it is one of the items that Breuer chose to suppress."[25] In 1999 another analyst reaffirmed "the erotic psycho-drama . . . within Breuer's treatment" and credited it with having provided Freud with material for "the Oedipus complex, identification, transference, countertransference,

---

* Skues 2006, pp. 109–110. After the publication of his first biographical volume, Jones was made aware of still another zany rumor propagated by Freud: that Mathilde Breuer had tried to kill herself after Pappenheim's treatment had ended (Borch-Jacobsen 1996, pp. 46–47, 93–103). Jones knew that this latest canard lacked any documentary basis, and so he made no mention of it in his second edition.

repetition compulsion and acting out."[26] A third analyst, crediting
Freud's avowal to Zweig, proposed in 1987 that Pappenheim wouldn't
have undergone a phantom pregnancy unless she and Breuer had been
lovers; ergo, that is what they were.[27] And the leading drum beater
for psychoanalysis "in our time," Peter Gay, though entirely familiar
with skeptical scholarship on the topic, nevertheless declared in 1988
that Freud, in his letter to Zweig, had "revealed" the true sequence of
events.[28]

It was left to Kurt Eissler, of all people, to express indignation at
Freud's viciousness toward Breuer. In spreading false rumors about the
Pappenheim case, Freud had been "ungrateful, indiscreet, and slander-
ous. . . . Freud struck a shattering blow against his benefactor's reputation, almost reducing him to a laughingstock, in connection with an
episode that had never taken place."[29]

True. But how could Eissler have been surprised by such behavior?
The tattling about Breuer and Bertha was not, as he claimed, "an episode in Freud's life without a parallel."[30] Rather, the psychoanalytic
Freud's standard practice was to smear his former associates as soon
as they posed an obstacle to his goals.

3. SOCIAL ACTIVISM EXPLAINED

When Jones announced the identity of Anna O. in 1953, the case described in *Studies on Hysteria* had been over for seventy-one years.
Bertha Pappenheim herself, however, had been dead for only seventeen
years, and she was by no means an obscure figure. In fact, the German
government was about to issue a commemorative stamp in her honor.
By connecting her to the intimate transactions between doctor and
patient in 1880–82 and to the sham denouement of the case, and by
revealing that Breuer and Freud had called her "quite unhinged" in the
next phase of her illness, Jones was inviting "wild analysis" of a woman
who had become celebrated for achievements to which he only glanc-
ingly referred.[31] And that was a pity, because the career of Bertha Pappenheim embodied important lessons that Jones and other psychoanalysts
could have profited from heeding.

The gravity of Bertha's morphine dependency had apparently

shocked her mother, Recha—who would be gratuitously characterized by Jones as "somewhat of a dragon"—into ceasing to disapprove of her aspiration to independence, literary creativity, and work that could make a helpful difference to others.[32] When mother and daughter moved to Frankfurt in 1888, Bertha at twenty-nine immersed herself in feminist tracts, including Jewish ones, that struck her as illuminating her own history of denied opportunity and enforced conformity. Frustration and anger had caused her to act out in childish ways; but now that she was uncontrolled by any man, she saw that she could live a life of freely chosen obedience to principle.[33]

In 1899 Pappenheim would translate Mary Wollstonecraft's *Vindication of the Rights of Woman*. Earlier, and even more significantly for her development, she seized upon the recently discovered fact that she was descended on her mother's side from the famous Glückel von Hameln, a devout widow who had become a successful businesswoman in seventeenth-century Germany, running her own factory and exporting its goods. Glückel had written memoirs for the edification of her many children. Those texts, which Bertha translated from Yiddish into German and republished in 1910, not only described Glückel's vicissitudes in a time of violent anti-Semitism; they also told of her family's charitable works in behalf of destitute refugees from pogroms. Bertha had been groomed for an arranged marriage like her mother's, but she had rebelled against her Orthodox parents' religion. Now she refashioned herself as a modern incarnation of the pious, fearless, and compassionate Glückel.

In addition to writing poems, dramas, and stories for children and adults, Pappenheim began to do welfare work in Frankfurt and to advocate a humane, socially responsible, observant Judaism that stood as a rebuke to the complacent and misogynistic rabbis of her day. She discovered within herself, and cultivated, a rare capacity for blending charm and wit with self-discipline, moral zeal, rhetorical eloquence, and administrative skill. In 1895 she became the director of Frankfurt's Jewish Orphanage for Girls, a position she held for twelve years. Meanwhile, she founded sewing schools, a girls' club featuring a library and a lecture series, and then the national Association of Jewish Women, serving as its first president. By 1900 she was a prominent figure throughout the German-speaking world.

In that year she published a pamphlet, *On the Condition of the Jewish Population in Galicia*, calling attention to the plight of Polish ghetto dwellers, about whom she had learned from refugees in her care. In 1903, traveling to that region, she saw at first hand that poor Jewish girls were being entrapped in an international sex ring whose masterminds were wealthy Turkish Jews. Without hesitation on grounds of respectability, she took up the victims' cause, not only denouncing "white slavery" but personally gathering firsthand information on the phenomenon in Poland, Russia, Greece, Turkey, Egypt, and Jerusalem. She braved danger and shame to rescue prostitutes and orphans, bringing them back with her to a town outside Frankfurt where she had established a home for them. And she didn't merely see to those survivors' nutritional, medical, and educational needs; she served as their affectionate if occasionally admonitory substitute mother.

Pappenheim kept her home for ex-prostitutes and abandoned children in operation throughout the Great War and the devastating inflation, political turmoil, and revived anti-Semitism that followed it. Meanwhile, she continued to travel and to agitate against coerced prostitution, leading an international commission on "white slavery" and later reporting about the phenomenon to the League of Nations. Her work with poor immigrants also took her to England and the United States, where she was received with honor. When Hitler came to power in 1933, she was forced to reduce her activities to the local level. But she never backed down, not even when summoned for interrogation by the Gestapo.

After a long struggle with cancer, Bertha Pappenheim died in 1936, never having lost her humility, her cordiality, her sense of humor, her ethical passion, or her knack of bringing out the best in other people. To educate, she once wrote, is "to act with love, a love which is so strong that it hates what is wrong and not lovable."[34] In a selection of her prayers that was published soon after her death, the following lines appear: "I give thanks also for the hour in which I found words for what moves me, so that I could move others by them. To feel strength is to live—to live is to wish to serve."[35] Among the many who had been uplifted by her devotion to justice were Albert Einstein and her close friend Martin Buber.

Not so Sigmund Freud. For one thing, Pappenheim appeared to have resigned from the very class that Freud had courted and aspired to join. Whereas Bertha had voyaged to Galicia in order to champion the downtrodden, Freud had been eager to efface his own Galician ancestry. And he wished to put as much distance as possible between himself and the urban slum dwellers whom Bertha, unaccountably to him, found worthy of solicitude.

Above all, Pappenheim's apparent celibacy meant to Freud that she had been disabled for her proper biological role. As he declared in his *Introductory Lectures* of 1916–17, "in a certain respect [Anna O.] remained cut off from life; she remained healthy and efficient but avoided the normal course of a woman's life."[36] The implication was that this whole sublimated business of social activism could have been avoided if Breuer had been brave enough to face Bertha's sexuality and encourage its expression within a properly feminine role.

This view was restated more amply in Freud's 1932 letter to Arthur Tansley. Breuer's treatment, he explained, had resulted in a "cure with a defect."[37] The cure had consisted of hastening the end of Anna's excessive mourning for her father. The defect—Breuer's failure to manage her transference love—had driven her crazy: "after Breuer's flight, she once again fell back into psychosis."[38] Although, according to Freud, the patient eventually regained her sanity, she had been permanently stunted. "Today she is over seventy," he told Tansley, "has never married, and, as Breuer said, which I remember well, has not had any sexual relations. On condition of the renunciation of the entire sexual function she was able to remain healthy."[39]

In the mid-1880s Freud had been aware that Pappenheim, a witty and lively friend of his wife's who had visited in his home, was psychologically normal except for her evening hallucinations, which were surely the product not of a diseased mind but of morphine poisoning. Perhaps he had lost that awareness by the time of writing to Tansley. In any event, no one has been able to explain how he could have been sure that Pappenheim, who had been seen in Vienna only rarely and briefly since 1888, was still a virgin at age seventy-three. Breuer's opinion, bizarrely cited in the Tansley letter, was no more up to date than Freud's, and in 1932 Breuer had been dead for seven years. Freud knew nothing more of Pappenheim's life in Frankfurt and elsewhere than did any other reader of her writings—if he perused them at all.

In his own seventy-seventh year, Freud was still reliving the old battle over sexuality and neurosis, and he remained on the lookout for examples of psychoanalytic mechanisms in action. Predictably, then, the only thing that concerned him about Bertha's vocation was its thematic content: the rescue of women from selling their favors to men. Peter Swales, who was able to spend a few minutes with a summary of the journal that Marie Bonaparte had kept during her analysis with Freud in 1925 and after, remembered seeing one passage dealing with Bertha's Frankfurt years. "With glee," wrote Swales, "Freud told Marie Bonaparte what Anna O. was now doing—running a girls' home and campaigning against prostitution—all a preoccupation with sexuality!"[40]

It is in his capacity as a theorist of psychological development, however, that Freud's condescension to Pappenheim is most significant. As Breuer recognized and reported to Robert Binswanger in 1882, Bertha was not only highly intelligent and determined to reason for herself; she also felt a primary "generosity to others" and a "very lively compassion." This last trait, he wisely recommended, "is the drive which she needs to exercise at the earliest."[41]

Thus Bertha's later activities in Frankfurt expressed creative propensities whose fulfillment required only that she cease being oppressed by family members and their conventional expectations. Once she gained that freedom, she was able to become serene, not anxious; strong, not faint; decisive, not demanding; resourceful, not obstinate. But Freud couldn't envision any application of her native personality traits to a positive social role. So remote from him was a spontaneous desire to help the unfortunate—for example, a doctor's urge to heal the sick—that he could only regard it as inverted sadism.*

A few words of encouragement from Freud and Jones were all

---

* "I do not remember in my childhood any craving to help suffering humanity," Freud wrote in 1927; "my sadistic tendencies were not very strong, and so there was no need for this particular derivative to develop" (SE, 8:394).

that was needed for other Freudians to extend their intimate speculations about Anna O.'s patienthood to her life of philanthropic
deeds. Because such activity was automatically judged to be defending against unresolved intrapsychic conflict, Freudian discourse
ignored Pappenheim's acquisition and exercise of new capacities. It
is only from an "external viewpoint," as one analyst put it, that Pappenheim "could be seen as 'active and contributing.' " Regarded psychoanalytically, "she can only be seen as driven by intense compulsion."[42]
Because her father was both "idol and demon" in her mind, the
same author surmised, "Anna-Bertha never integrated her inner
self, and her reaction formation social goodness continued to operate as compensation for an enraged child within her."[43] Thus the
Oedipus complex was found to underlie Bertha's passion for right-
ing wrongs.*

For Freudians, however, the ultimate father figure is Freud himself, and Bertha's known hostility to his ideas must therefore have
been diagnostically meaningful. One analyst proposed that her incipient sexuality, "having been trampled in the transference phenomenon," was "later frightened into silence by Freud's theories."[44] And in
another formulation,

> She had escaped from nursing her father, Sigmund [sic] Pappenheim,
> by herself becoming sick. She then suffered a disappointment in trans-
> ference with her psychotherapist, Breuer. After these experiences she
> was not ready to accept the implications of another Sigmund (Freud)
> that she had a sexual conflict. . . . She did not attack Freud in her
> published work, but displaced her accusations from Freud onto the
> "traders" of girls.[45]

Even today the Anna O. case is continually revisited, and not always
so foolishly. Once various schools of psychoanalysis—Sullivanian,
Horneyan, Eriksonian, Kohutian, Winnicottian—began chafing against

---

* In a fictionalized biography that was widely regarded as authoritative, it was explained
that Pappenheim's opposition to the sex trade had been a means of "unconsciously
wishing to stem her own wild sexual impulses, or . . . wishing to prevent her mother
from having sex with her father" (Freeman 1972, p. 233).

Freud's reductive negativity and seeking a reconciliation with social psychology, each of them found lessons to be drawn from the extraordinary maturation and flowering of Bertha Pappenheim. In none of those schools, however, has the most obvious and fundamental question been addressed. If psychoanalysis first taught us that Pappenheim's life was a pathetic failure, and if psychoanalysis, employing exactly the same epistemic tools, then reached an opposite conclusion, does psychoanalysis teach us anything at all?

21

Narrative Truth

1. SHERLOCKIEREN

As we have seen, Breuer did his best to reformulate his debacle with Bertha Pappenheim in terms that would be congenial to Freud. With Freud's connivance, not only did he subtract Pappenheim's morphine addiction from the story of Anna O., allowing his readers to suppose that her strange behavior and fluctuating states were determined entirely by hysteria and by his interventions against it; he also added gratuitous "cathartic," or explosively emotional, touches to Bertha's relatively affectless reenactments of events in her recent past. But he immediately regretted having done so, and his chief desire as a coauthor was to show how different he was from the zealot Freud.

By 1895 Breuer was well aware that Freud's claims when wooing him in 1892 had been empty. Freud had proved to be a bumbling hypnotist; the symptoms he had ostensibly banished had been replaced by others; he had mistaken the agitation that he provoked for reactivated turmoil from his patients' Ur-traumas; and he had never succeeded in getting a patient to regurgitate one of those hysteria-originating experiences with the required cathartic emotion. Nor, then, necessarily, could he show that his repression-based "mechanism" for symptom production was more plausible than those put forward by other theorists, including Breuer himself.

Nevertheless, once the lightly valued *Studies* were revisited by Freudians in the twentieth century, the stories of Emmy, Elisabeth, and the others were welcomed into the canon with little objection to their anomalous features. Those souvenirs of Freud's early experience bore a fond biographical significance that overrode any doubts about their evidential standing or methodological utility. Even when Freud remarked, in a 1924 note to the Emmy narrative, that "no analyst can read this case history to-day without a smile of pity,"[1] psychoanalytic readers didn't regard the chapter as obsolete. Instead, admiring Freud's severity toward his youthful self, they cherished the story as marking a phase in his march toward mastery of the unconscious.

Here we arrive at one key to Freud's eventual success with the reading public. At some point in the early 1890s he appears to have grasped that *his own* story, told as a serial adventure of the intellect, could be made so inviting and intriguing that readers would want to participate in it vicariously. In the case histories, it is his own mind that chiefly gets "cured"—namely, of bafflement over symptoms that look at first to be mysterious and intractable. And if, in some instances, he is obliged to admit that his therapeutic efforts were foiled, he gains credibility by that show of candor.

Freud's new literary genre could work his desired effects only if its true purpose—his personal glorification—were disguised by a manifestly scientific rationale. His understanding of that requirement is apparent from a guileful autobiographical aside that interrupts the history of Elisabeth von R.:

I have not always been a psychotherapist. Like other neuropathologists, I was trained to employ local diagnoses and electro-prognosis, and it still strikes me myself as strange that the case histories I write should read like novellas [*Novellen*] and that, as one might say, they lack the serious stamp of science. I must console myself with the reflection that the nature of the subject is evidently responsible for this, rather than any preference of my own. The fact is that local diagnosis and electrical reactions lead nowhere in the study of hysteria, whereas a detailed description of mental processes such as we are accustomed to find in the works of imaginative writers enables me, with the use of a few psychological formulas, to obtain at least some kind of insight into the course of a hysteria.[2]

This passage exemplifies a Freudian specialty that we might call *the self-effacing boast*, or a demure gesture that casts the author in a better light than ever. Here he makes a show of taking the reader into his confidence and regarding his own efforts censoriously. Even to the bemused Freud, we are told, his case histories sound more like works of fiction than like scientific reports. But his seeming confession is actually a shrewd maneuver—one that heads off the reader's own perception of narrative tricks in the *Studies* and that ascribes those features not to "any preference of [Freud's] own" but to mere "description," from which "insight" is objectively drawn. In actuality, each of Freud's "novellas" puts a dramatic narrative in the place that ought to be occupied by a weighing of his explanation of the case against possible alternatives.

It might be objected that, after all, Freud's histories impute to his patients ideas that would be likely to have occurred to any person in the same situation, coping with events that did indisputably happen. But—leaving aside for now the question of whether Freud may sometimes have misreported those events—it simply isn't true that he reconstructed what anyone would have been thinking. His theory required displays of entrapment in unconscious conflict, which wasn't just unobservable; it had to be manufactured by imputing two clashing motives to the subject and designating one of them—the shameful, unacknowledgeable one—as the symptom-fomenting troublemaker.

Most of Freud's case histories are cunningly plotted works that create and then resolve suspense in a gripping manner. Readers are inclined to accept his inferences because they are conclusions in the other sense of the term: plot elements that resolve an artifactual tension. And all of the other resources of fictional narrative are put in play as well. Thus the author takes the liberty of providing crisp dialogue—not just exchanges between himself and the patient but conversations that are said to have occurred in the patient's past—as if every sentence had somehow been recorded at the time. Tension among family members and between the wise analyst and his resistant patient is a regular theme. And Freud himself, as the sleuth who meets with obstacles but ingeniously overcomes them, is the true protagonist of every tale.

In the 1890s, the model for all such detectives was Sherlock Holmes, whose literary debut in 1887 had caused an international sensation. So great was the vogue, in German-speaking countries, of Arthur Conan Doyle's master investigator that the language itself honored him with a new verb, *sherlockieren* (to track down), and a noun, *Sherlockismus* (the Holmes craze).[3] Did Freud fancy himself a Sherlock Holmes of the unconscious?

A late reminiscence by Sergei Pankeev, the Wolf Man, lends indirect support to that idea:

> Once when I happened to speak of Conan Doyle and his creation, Sherlock Holmes, I had thought that Freud would have no use for this type of light reading matter, and was surprised to find that this was not at all the case and that Freud had read this author attentively.[4]

In the same vein, Paula Fichtl, a servant in the Freud household through the last decade of his life, recalled that he would immerse himself in a detective novel almost every night and that the Holmes stories were by far his favorites.[5] But the best reason to think he had been playing Holmes in *Studies on Hysteria* is that—as we will see—he there endowed his narrative self with Holmes's uncanny knack of effortlessly deducing a subject's background, activities, and disposition.

In private life Freud enjoyed playing that same fictive role. Thus, in corresponding with Sabina Spielrein in 1909, he pretended to be uninformed about her sexual relationship with C. G. Jung, who had finally told him about it. "My reply [to Spielrein] was ever so wise and penetrating," the amused analyst reported to Jung; "I made it appear as though the most tenuous of clues had enabled me Sherlock Holmes-like to guess the situation (which of course was none too difficult after your communications)."[6]

Freud was probably influenced by Edgar Allan Poe as well as by Conan Doyle—who, anyway, had modeled Sherlock Holmes partly on Poe's preternaturally acute amateur sleuth C. Auguste Dupin. The first sentence of Freud's "Katharina" chapter—"In the summer vacation of the year 189- I made an excursion into the Hohe Tauern so that for a while I might forget medicine and more particularly the neuroses"— reads like a typical Poe opening.[7] (And, as we will see, everything in it but "summer vacation" was make-believe.)

Freud's "insight" into hysteria—the "intimate connection" he drew between causes and effects—was coextensive with his novelistic license. Authorship, for him, wasn't a means of communicating and illustrating objective psychological findings. Rather, it was his métier. And later analysts, ravished by close acquaintance with such vivid figures as Dora, Little Hans, and the Rat Man, would confuse his artistry with science. They would emulate it as best they could in their own writing, and in their training institutes they would make it the didactic core of initiation into the psychoanalytic style of thought, which was itself a reduction of human experience to a few standard plot elements.

Freud's narrative segments in *Studies on Hysteria* can be regarded as snapshots of the stages in his progression from a naïve reciting of awkward facts to a total shaping of the reader's experience. The earliest, and therefore the crudest, of his tales was that of "Emmy von N.," in which he supplied ample evidence not only that the case had turned out badly but also that the patient had made a fool of him. One indiscretion in particular wouldn't be repeated: the inclusion of case notes from the first three weeks of treatment.

Never again, after writing his Emmy chapter, would Freud allow his readers to know that he had applied a hodgepodge of conventional therapies, including twice-a-day massage of the patient's "whole body" while he was softening her resistance to his ideas. Nor (except in the Dora case, reported in 1905) would he allow us to learn that he had needlessly alarmed his patient with counterproductive remarks, or that he had been ordered to shut up and allow her to ramble on as she pleased. And this was the first and last time he would be so gauche as to reveal that the net effect of his efforts had been to foster an "aversion" to his own person.[8]

Freud would surely have preferred to apply a touch-up brush to the Emmy case, but he was prevented from doing so by Breuer's close familiarity with the course of therapy. The same limitation applied, at least in part, to the next-treated but last-presented of his four major cases, that of "Elisabeth von R." But Freud as author had now hit upon the suspense-inducing device, which would serve him well thereafter, of depicting himself as having faced, and then brilliantly solved, the puzzle that had obstructed a full understanding and cure of the case.[9]

Never mind that his solution—Elisabeth/Ilona's leg pains stemmed from a repressed desire to marry her brother-in-law—was outlandish on several counts. Never mind, too, that his great moment of Holmes-like ratiocination—proving Elisabeth's love for her brother-in-law by noting her pained expression when she once rose to greet him—constituted a hermeneutic pratfall. The whole chain of inferences made for a fetching story, especially when capped by the report that Freud (but no one else?) had caught sight of a wondrously healed Elisabeth dancing with athletic grace.

It was Freud's recourse to novelistic interior monologue that enabled him to overrule Ilona Weiss's self-understanding and replace it with his own version of what she must have felt. On the day that her brother-in-law became a widower, according to Freud, she told herself, "Now he is free and you can be his wife."[10] This sounds like something said to Freud by the patient, but she denied ever having entertained such an idea. Or again: "As we worked through these recollections, it became clear to Elisabeth that her tender feeling for her brother-in-law had been dormant in her for a long time."[11] Freud would provide such pseudo-corroboration in a number of his most famous case studies, implying that his patients, somewhere within their minds, had capitulated to his foolproof interpretations. While never claiming in so many words that the avowals had been made, he would leave that impression with unsuspecting readers.

Freud's narrative task was simpler, however, when he judged that none of his assertions could be checked. Hence the difference of texture and tone, in the *Studies*, between the strained and occasionally murky tales of Emmy and Elisabeth and the seamless one about "Miss Lucy R." Lucy, never identified to posterity, was a lowly English governess domiciled on the outskirts of Vienna; she wouldn't be reading psychological tracts there or anywhere else. Not coincidentally, then, the narrator-hero Freud asks just the right questions of the compliant textual Lucy, who is smitten by her therapist's astuteness; without difficulty he elicits the very secrets that were needed to validate his guesses; and, in the bargain, he cures her of her olfactory hallucination.

2. GO TELL IT ON THE MOUNTAIN

As for "Katharina," she too was a subordinate woman who wouldn't be available to contradict Freud's story about her. Although her encounter with him occupies the fewest pages of the major cases in *Studies on Hysteria*, that segment is the one in which Freud grants himself the most license to vaunt his deductive powers. In this instance, however, he was wrong to think that his departures from the truth would never be found out. Here, then, we can judge how far he would go, when feeling accountable to no one, in order to align a case history with his theory of the hour.

In a letter to Wilhelm Fliess of May 30, 1893, Freud reported that he was just then arriving at a fresh diagnosis, *virginal anxiety*, which he defined as "a *presentient dread* of sexuality, and behind it things [that virgins] had seen or heard and half-understood."* A few lines below in the same letter, he announced, "My family is going to Reichenau tomorrow."[12] That was their favorite vacation spot, in a resort at the foot of a mountain called the Raxalpe (or simply the Rax) in the Semmering range, fifty miles southwest of Vienna. And it was from there, on August 20, that he laconically disclosed to Fliess, "Recently I was consulted by the daughter of the innkeeper on the Rax; it was a nice case for me."[13] Needless to say, it proved to be a case of "virginal anxiety."

One day around the middle of August, the inveterate hiker Freud, stopping at the slopeside lodge on the Rax, had apparently been drawn aside for an impromptu consultation by a waitress, roughly eighteen years old, who was indeed the daughter of the innkeeper. Having learned from the guestbook that he was a physician, she is said to have

---

* FF, p. 49; emphasis as found. "Virginal anxiety," in Freud's view at the time, was not a neurosis in its own right but one possible source of hysteria. As we will see, however, he was already beginning to reconsider the array of psychological disorders, which would soon have to make way for a new entity, "anxiety neurosis."

asked for advice about asthma attacks that had begun tormenting her two years before. That was presumably her whole complaint—not hysteria, not anxiety, but asthma, an affliction that would have been especially worrisome in thin mountain air.

According to the case history, however, Freud's questioning elicited an account of numerous symptoms that had been accompanying "Katharina's" attacks, including giddiness, choking and crushing sensations, a fear of imminent death, fear of assault from the rear, and hallucinations of an unidentified man's horrible face. All but the last two of these, we may observe, were plausible concomitants of asthma; but to Freud's way of thinking all of them pointed to the same explanation, the hysterical reenactment of anxiety previously experienced when Katharina had been flooded with a sexual excitement that she couldn't handle. It was quite a windfall for Freud that Katharina freely reported (if she did) the very symptoms he already believed to indicate "dread of sexuality, and behind it things [that virgins] had seen or heard and half-understood."

Katharina had no idea why she had contracted asthma, but Freud, with Holmes-like quickness of mind, had already figured it out:

> I had found often enough that in girls anxiety was a consequence of the horror by which a virginal mind is overcome when it is faced for the first time with the world of sexuality.
>
> So I said: "If you don't know, I'll tell you how *I* think you got your attacks. At that time, two years ago, you must have seen or heard something that very much embarrassed you, and that you'd much rather not have seen."
>
> "Heavens, yes!" she replied, "that was when I caught my uncle with the girl, with Franziska, my cousin."

Whereupon, with a singular absence of virginal embarrassment, Katharina told how, two years earlier on a neighboring mountain where her aunt and uncle had been managing another inn, she had peered in a window and seen that same uncle on his bed, fully clothed but lying on top of young Franziska, also clothed. Katharina's terrified reaction had been to experience her first asthma attack—proof, we are meant to gather, that asthma, or one variety of it, is a psycho-somatic disorder and that its gasps and wheezes reproduce the over-heard sounds of intercourse.* (But Freud, ever careless with details, forgot to have Katharina overhear any sounds at all.)

The next exchange tells us more about Freud's innocence than Katharina's. He asks her whether she understood the meaning of the scene that so alarmed her. "Oh no," she replies. "I didn't understand anything at that time. *I was only sixteen.* I don't know what I was frightened about."[14] After all, what could a sixteen-year-old worker at a seasonal lodge—a love nest for both licit and adulterous couples, a home for cats, dogs, goats, and pack animals in heat, a rooming house for experienced waitresses and chambermaids, and a place where unaccompanied men of means approached working-class girls on a daily basis—have possibly known about sex?

At any rate, when Katharina's aunt heard the story, she is said to have interpreted its meaning without difficulty. Her husband and Franziska had long been lovers, but the reader supposes either that she hadn't known about it or that she had wanted to keep her niece in the dark. Now the aunt had had enough. After some stormy months, she gathered up her children and niece, moved to the adjacent mountain, and was allowed to take over management of its lodge, abandoning her hus-band to the embraces of the now pregnant Franziska.

It will be important to bear in mind that Freud's theory of hysteria formation, as of 1895, envisioned a two-step process, First, the victim would undergo a *traumatic* experience but, being too frightened by it or too inexperienced to take in its meaning, she would isolate it in a repressed "psychical group" while bottling up its affect. Later, a related *auxiliary* experience would reactivate the earlier feelings and render them horrifying, with the result that the previously stored excitation would now be converted into somatic symptoms.†

---

* "In many cases, as in Dora's," Freud later wrote, "I have been able to trace back the symptom of dyspnoea or nervous asthma to the same exciting cause—to the patient's having overheard sexual intercourse taking place between adults" (SE, 7:80). This was his automatic and unvarying interpretation of every asthmatic attack.

† This two-stage theory, as we will see, was announced in Freud's 1894 paper "The Neuro-Psychoses of Defence" (SE, 3:42–61). It is exemplified in *Studies on Hysteria* not

Thus, if Katharina had fallen ill soon after witnessing the near coupling of her uncle and cousin, this must have been the auxiliary second step of her hysterogenesis. But what, then, was the traumatic step one, and why had she still been somewhat in the dark about sexual intercourse after the culminating shock? Even at age eighteen, two years later, she purportedly exclaimed to Freud, "Oh, if only I knew what it was I felt disgusted at!"[15]

That outburst sounds inauthentic not just per se but also in view of the sordid discoveries and fierce recriminations to which Katharina had been a party as her aunt and uncle were splitting up. Her continued semi-ignorance, belied by the unblushing candor of her narration, was straining Freud's virginal-anxiety theme to the breaking point. At the same time, however, it wouldn't do for the mystery of step one—what had been the initial trauma?—to be spontaneously solved by Katharina instead of being teased forth by Freud. "*I* had no idea either," he assures us, as if he hadn't known exactly what kind of information he had been seeking from Katharina's memories. "But I told her to go on and tell me whatever occurred to her."[16] And so Katharina, after recounting the quarrels that led to the family breakup, revealed, "to [Freud's] astonishment," that her drunken uncle had tried to have sex with *her* when she was just fourteen, and not once but on various later occasions.[17]

A literal reading of Freud's text would require us to accept that there on the mountainside, confiding in a new acquaintance, Katharina reproduced the exact dialogue that had unfolded between her uncle and herself during the first such attempt, when, down in the valley's lodge, she was awakened one night by feeling his body pressing against hers:

> "What are you up to, Uncle? Why don't you stay in your own bed?" He tried to pacify her: "Go on, you silly girl, keep still. You don't know how nice it is."—"I don't like your 'nice' things; you don't even let one sleep in peace."[18]

---

only by "Katharina" but also by the story of "Miss Lucy R.," in which the "traumatic" moment is said to have occurred only months before the "auxiliary" one (SE, 2:123). In "Katharina" the two events are separated by years.

Freud soon resumes in the same imaginative vein when describing
another hotel scene. In a suite with her uncle, Katharina wakes up to
find him about to enter the adjacent chamber, where Franziska, for
some reason, happened to be staying:

> "Goodness, is that you, Uncle? What are you doing at the door?"—
> "Keep quiet. I was only looking for something."—"But the way out's
> by the *other* door."—"I'd just made a mistake" . . . and so on.[19]

Try, if you can, to picture Katharina "doing" these alternating voices
for the edification of a prying stranger. A reader would need the faith
of Bernadette in order to believe that Freud is quoting his informant
here.

Even less credible is the idea that Katharina's uncle tried to copulate with her again and again without her ever comprehending that his
actions were sexually motivated. But this marvel, too, is a bagatelle in
comparison with the central impossibility of Freud's tale: that when
Katharina, two years later, saw her own would-be multiple seducer
atop her cousin in his bed, she still didn't have a clear idea of what she
was observing.

It would seem that if one half of the Katharina story is true, something must be awry with the other half. The victim of serial fondling
and propositioning couldn't have been surprised, much less rendered
asthmatic and hysterical, simply by seeing her molester behaving in
character once again—and with the same woman who had already
aroused her suspicions of an affair. And contrariwise, if Katharina at
age sixteen wasn't sure she was observing a sex scene, she probably
hadn't been repeatedly menaced by the same predator at fourteen and
after. A reasonable surmise would be that the deviations from truth in
Freud's case history occurred at the points where they were needed by
his two-step theory of hysteria and by his predetermined emphasis on
the sexual innocence of adolescents—an emphasis, we may note, that
would soon undergo such a reversal that he would be representing
three-year-olds as scheming to kill their same-sex parent and have sex
with the other one.

For Freud when writing this case history, age fourteen was still a "pre-sexual period";[20] and therefore, when Katharina's uncle rubbed his erect penis against her in bed, the action ought to have "produced no effect on the child"[21]—no consciously recognized effect, that is. Yet even Freud hesitated to assert that a sixteen-year-old, watching an act of naked penetration, wouldn't register what she was seeing. This must be why Katharina's uncle and cousin are depicted as having been fully clothed atop the blankets. But a few pages later, the forgetful Freud refers to the moment when Katharina had "caught sight of the couple in intercourse."[22] If that was how they customarily did it, through layers of male and female Victorian garments, Franziska's pregnancy was no less miraculous than the Virgin Mary's.*

Now, however, for an unsettling surprise. In an English translation of 1924, after four German editions and two English editions of *Studies on Hysteria*, Freud appended the following note at the end of his Katharina chapter: "I venture after the lapse of so many years to lift the veil of discretion and reveal the fact that Katharina was not the niece but the daughter of the landlady. The girl fell ill, therefore, as a result of sexual attempts on the part of her own father."[23]

This is vintage Freud in its intellectual and ethical laziness with regard to his already published work. Almost thirty years after the fact, in the seventh iteration of his case history (not counting translations into languages other than English), he tells us that he has been fibbing all along on a point of cardinal importance. Yet even this time, instead of simply telling the truth, he spins the same misleading yarn before announcing in a footnote that it contains a fictitious element at its core.

Freud's changing a father into an uncle is understandable on prudential grounds. But his revelation that the child molester and adulterer was Katharina's own father demolishes whatever is left of the case history's intended lesson. If her father was trying to force incest upon her, Katharina was a victim not of disturbing fantasies about what grownups do in the dark but of the profoundest betrayal and abandonment. And if, later, she caught him in flagrante with her cousin, she

---

* Freud never did learn how to describe a sex act from the perspective of a "primal scene" observer. The most comical instance is the contortionist feat supposedly witnessed by the tiny Wolf Man—an event that Sergei Pankeev himself, much later, revealed to have been impossible on other grounds as well. See Obholzer 1982; Mahony 1984.

must have realized that her parents' marriage and the stability of her own life stood in peril. So, perhaps, did her physical safety, given her father's fury at her as the cause of his wife's desertion. All this could have made for a stunning psychological analysis, worthy of Dostoevsky. Instead, Freud twisted what he was told—*if* that was what he was told—into a trivial and unconvincing case of adolescent confusion over sex.

3. FACTS ARE STUBBORN THINGS

This is where matters stood until 1988, when Peter Swales, having performed one of his daring feats of independent scholarship, established Katharina's identity with a high degree of probability, reconstructed her history, and pondered some further liberties Freud may have taken for the sake of his thesis.[24] Katharina's actual name was Aurelia Kronich, and her parents were Julius and Gertrude Kronich. The lodge they had managed, the Baumgartnerhaus, owned by the Austrian Tourist Club, was situated at 4,880 feet on the Schneeberg, directly facing the Raxalpe. Freud conversed with Aurelia (if he ever did) at the Raxalpe's recently opened rival lodge, the Erzherzog Otto-Schutzhaus ("Ottohaus"), in the third week of August 1893.

One of Aurelia and her siblings' duties on the Schneeberg and elsewhere, Swales revealed, had been to dress in folk costumes for festive occasions and even to yodel on demand, as if to personify the rustic Alpine life. Freud fell in with this theme by having Aurelia speak in a peasant dialect. Aurelia, however, was no Heidi. She had spent more than half of her life in a Viennese tenement, just across the Danube from Freud's own childhood district of Leopoldstadt.

No doubt Aurelia had seen a good deal of hard reality by the age of ten. That was when her family, in the hope that the move would cure the father, Julius, of early-stage tuberculosis, heavy drinking, and womanizing, asked for and received permission to take over management of the Baumgartnerhaus. But the tall and handsome Julius, before getting serious with Gertrude's niece Barbara Göschl (aka Franziska), is reputed to have seduced one after another of his female lodge employees.

When interviewed in the 1980s, descendants of the Kronich line were able to corroborate the main outlines of Freud's story about Aurelia's having told her mother of the affair with Barbara, about the acrimonious dissolution of Gertrude and Julius's marriage, and about Gertrude's relocation to the Ottohaus on the Rax. Other elements of the case history, though, drew only puzzlement. For example, Aurelia's aged daughter and her granddaughter were sure that, physically and by temperament, "Katharina" resembled not Aurelia but her sister Olga—who, however, was too young to have plausibly served as Freud's informant. But here Freud may simply have been trying to make it harder for Aurelia to be recognized.

Further discrepancies were more troubling. In Swales's words:

> [The relatives] feel that had Aurelia been sexually molested by her father as an adolescent, then certainly in later life she would have confided this at least to her daughter Vilma, with whom she was particularly close. . . . [But] no one in the family ever heard anything of the kind. Furthermore, Aurelia did not display any symptoms of asthma—neither, for that matter, did Olga—nor did she suffer from a nervous condition.*

Not even Freud had the effrontery to claim that, in an hour or so, he had freed Katharina from asthma and panic attacks. He merely wrote that he hoped she had "derived some benefit from our conversation."[25] We must wonder, then: did Freud, or perhaps the distraught Aurelia in dialogue with Freud, exaggerate the menace and the persistence of Julius's drunken advances to her? Had there been any such episodes at all? (Remember, they were needed for Freud's main purpose of illustrating his two-step theory of delayed hysterical conversion.) Again, did Freud overdramatize or even concoct some of Aurelia's symptoms—for instance, the hallucination of an unidentified male face that proved, under Freud's sharp questioning, to be that of her uncle/ father? And had Aurelia, whose frank and easy manner of responding

---

* Swales 1988, pp. 111–112. Had Aurelia, then, really told Freud that she was asthmatic, or did he insert asthma into the case because he already held a sexual theory of its origin?

betrayed no sign of pathology, really been hysterical, or were her anxieties justified by her objective situation, not two or four years previously but just when Freud was interviewing her?

Very striking, with respect to this last issue, is Swales's proof of a significant misrepresentation in Freud's chronology of the events that brought Gertrude and Aurelia to the Rax. According to Freud, two years had elapsed since Katharina had precipitated her family's disintegration by tattling about her "uncle" and Franziska, and she and her "aunt" had already been at the Ottohaus for eighteen months. In fact, however, Gertrude Kronich had been granted permission to manage the not yet opened Ottohaus only in April 1893, less than five months before the Freud-Aurelia meeting. Thus the tempestuous events at the Baumgartnerhaus must have been fresh in Aurelia's memory when she spoke with Freud. Perhaps she really did live in fear of a sudden assault from her aggrieved father. Swales proposes that her state of mind in August 1893 was a compound of fear, worry over an uncertain future, and self-castigation for having wrecked her family through her indiscreet report to Gertrude about what she had seen.

By Swales's calculation, Aurelia Kronich may have just turned eighteen at the time of the key event, the window scene, in January 1893. Freud, however, made "Katharina" sixteen at that moment, in the evident hope that she would thus look more susceptible to a crackup over unmanageable "excitation." As for her uncle/father's incestuous advances, we cannot know whether Freud fabricated all of them, but they ought to remain under suspicion, for several reasons.

The supposed incidents at age fourteen were scarcely germane to Aurelia's current predicament, as she felt oppressed by the enmity of her now absent yet lurking father. Nor was the sordid family dishonor a matter to be blurted out, much less play-acted in dialogue, to a strange (in both senses) male visitor. By representing "Katharina" as a naïve bumpkin, Freud tried to make her impolitic confession sound more plausible; but the working-class Aurelia at eighteen surely knew that sexual innuendo from an unknown middle-aged man merited a good deal of reserve.

In addition, if Freud's version of events were true, Aurelia ought to have shunned and hated Julius Kronich from age fourteen onward; but she assuredly didn't. No descendants mentioned any long-standing animus between the two, who had worked and traveled together in Aurelia's adolescent years. Freud himself wrote that Katharina bore her uncle/father no ill will and that she placed the blame for her family's misfortune entirely on herself. Moreover, Swales demonstrates that as recently as November 1892, when Aurelia was seventeen, she and Julius were still on cordial terms. In that month she began compiling a book of recipes, one inscription for which consisted of verses signed by Julius. Aurelia evidently cherished that book, which was handed down to a daughter and granddaughter.

Once we have grasped what Aurelia must have been enduring in the summer of 1893, Freud's sexualization of her predicament appears to be not just off base but creepy. "Tell me just one thing," he asks. "What part of his body was it that you felt that night?"[26] There is erotic stimulation here, but it belongs to Freud, giving himself and his readers the soft-pornographic thrill of vicariously groping a teenage virgin. And when the literary Katharina assents to Freud's broad hint only by her facial expression, he remarks to us, "I cannot penetrate farther into her" *(ich kann nicht weiter in sie dringen).** Even if the question and mute response never occurred, the titillation is there on the printed page, where much of Freud's future eroticism would be invested.

When it is read in the context of its retrieved historical background, the Katharina narrative leaves two strong impressions. First, there is Freud's unwillingness or inability to weigh factors other than the ones he was looking for. As a psychologist whose nominal vocation was helping people to cope with whatever was bothering them, he appears to have failed in his hour with Aurelia Kronich, displacing her actual plight with his recent hobbyhorse of virginal anxiety. As he told Fliess, "it was a nice case for me"—a case that he could perceive only in terms of his preconceptions. And second, the Katharina story shows

---

* In the *Standard Edition*, this clause was translated as "I could not penetrate further" (SE, 2:132). The omission of "into her" reveals editorial discomfort with Freud's prurience. As for the difference in verb form, Freud chose to narrate much of his chapter in racy "you are there" style, but Strachey, doubtless judging that the past tense would make a more respectable impression, silently altered the text throughout.

us, more clearly than any of his other early case histories, that he felt no compunction about adjusting facts in order to simulate the outcomes he desired.

Even when Freud's facts were right, he tended to falsify his means of having learned them. Consider some of the things he "deduces," from his first glimpse of Katharina. Her "dress and bearing" tell him that she "must no doubt be a daughter or relative of the landlady's."[27] He decides to "try a lucky guess" that she has been disturbed by a first-time confrontation "with the world of sexuality,"[28] and he is immediately vindicated by a recounting of the window scene, about which he previously knew nothing. He acquires the complete Franziska story and its aftermath just by asking Katharina to say whatever occurs to her, "in the confident expectation that she would think of precisely what I needed to explain the case."[29] But all of this is a sham, because everything veridical in it was already familiar knowledge to everyone, residents and summer visitors alike, in the environs of Reichenau.

If Freud had really sought refuge from his demanding practice by making a special "excursion into the Hohe Tauern," 200 miles farther away from Vienna than the Raxalpe, we could accept his claim to have known nothing about the family that maintained a "refuge hut" on one of its highest peaks. Instead, he was partway up a mountain he had been climbing each August, sometimes as often as three times a week, in every year but one since his marriage in 1886—in other words, again and again for six summers. Down in Reichenau village, where his family was typically installed for the entire season, the scandal of adultery and divorce at the Baumgartnerhaus and the resultant transfer of Gertrude Kronich and her children to the new Ottohaus on the Rax must have been the chief piece of gossip, as well as the most important commercial news, in the summer of 1893.

On August 18–20 of that year Freud was an overnight guest at the Ottohaus, whose other guests surely knew why its manager lacked a husband on the premises to help her run the establishment.* Thus Freud had plenty of opportunity, before meeting Katharina face to face,

---

* Note that Freud, when arriving at the "refuge hut," already knew that it had only a "landlady" (*Wirtin*) and not an accompanying landlord, as would have been the norm.

to observe her working with her mother and be brought up to date about her from his fellow hikers. But his worst hypocrisy, so far as the genuine elements of the story were concerned, was to feign ignorance of Julius's locally notorious relations with Barbara Göschl, of their discovery and disclosure by Aurelia, and of the events that followed—all of which he recast as a theory-confirming surprise.

By 1895, we have seen, Freud had already awarded himself a license to invent, suppress, alter, and rearrange facts in the interest of enhanced self-portraiture and theoretical vindication. In the present instance, thanks to Swales's research, the imposture has been exposed for anyone to perceive. Only rarely, after 1895, would Freud allow his manipulations to be so nakedly exposed. But the Katharina chapter puts us on notice that its author—who, unlike Conan Doyle, was really quite careless about maintaining consistency in his tales—would stop at nothing in manufacturing "evidence" of his imaginary prowess.

22

Arraying the Neuroses

1. IMPOSING ORDER

When we last saw Freud holding forth at some length about the neuroses, it was in the final chapter of *Studies on Hysteria*, written and published in 1895. There, after a polite bow to his "honoured friend Josef Breuer," he let it be known that "fresh points of view" had recently taken him in a new direction:[1]

> I was fortunate enough to arrive at some serviceable findings in a relatively short time. In the first place I was obliged to recognize that, in so far as one can speak of determining causes which lead to the *acquisition* of neuroses, their aetiology is to be looked for in *sexual* factors. There followed the discovery that different sexual factors, in the most general sense, produce different pictures of neurotic disorders. And it then became possible, in the degree to which this relation was confirmed, to venture on using aetiology for the purpose of characterizing the neuroses and of making a sharp distinction between the clinical pictures of the various neuroses.[2]

This account of step-by-step induction has been naïvely credited by readers who wish to believe that Freud, in his young therapeutic practice, had been conducting a program of research. It is supposed that at some point after January 1893, when the Breuer/Freud "Preliminary Communication" was published, Freud's work with patients had alerted him to the momentous finding that the neuroses have a sexual basis. In fact, however, two draft papers that were sent to his friend Wilhelm Fliess in the weeks just before and after the debut of the "Preliminary Communication" show that he already held that opinion and was seeking to build on it through sheer cogitation.[3] It is clear from those texts and others that he and Fliess had been speculating together about sexual causes for some time. And a letter of September 29, 1893, indicates that Freud regarded all neuroses as sexual before he had begun, deductively, to work out how hysteria might figure in the etiological scheme.[4]

In the months surrounding Freud's assertion of independence from Breuer in the last chapter of *Studies on Hysteria*, he published two ambitious papers that deserve to be considered together:

- "The Neuro-Psychoses of Defence" (May and June 1894).[5]
- "On the Grounds for Detaching a Particular Syndrome from Neurasthenia under the Description 'Anxiety Neurosis'" (January 1895).[6]

And then there were two follow-up papers reflecting further thoughts and responding to objections:

- "Obsessions and Phobias: Their Psychical Mechanism and Their Aetiology" (January 1895).[7]
- "A Reply to Criticisms of My Paper on Anxiety Neurosis" (July 1895).[8]

Unlike Freud's previous psychological writings, each of which sought to align him with an established authority such as Charcot, Bernheim, Forel, Janet, or Breuer himself, these papers expound a proprietary conception of the neuroses. At a time when his exact contemporary Emil Kraepelin was about to revolutionize psychiatry with his 1896 classification of the psychoses, Freud here attempted to arrange and explain the neuroses in an even more sweeping fashion.[9] No one had attempted such a synthesis, which clustered already recognized neuroses by general type, redefined one syndrome (neurasthenia), added a new one (anxiety neurosis), and announced a precise etiology for each disorder, all within an overarching structure of sexual causation.

Freud believed he had unearthed a fundamental difference between two categories of neurosis, the *psychoneuroses* and what he would soon call the *current neuroses* (commonly misnamed "actual neuroses").* The crucial pathogen in every psychoneurosis was supposedly a repressed traumatic memory; hence all psychoneuroses were ideogenic and rooted in the past. But a current neurosis, though it too had a history, bypassed the mind. Its cause was a habitual sexual practice or deprivation, directly affecting the soma by disrupting the regulation of blood chemistry.

Freud's starting point, not just for the current neuroses but for his whole program of subsuming all of the neuroses to one perspective, was *neurasthenia*, the congeries of nervous upsets that ranked as the most frequently diagnosed malady of the late nineteenth century. Indeed, Freud called it "the commonest of all the diseases in our society,"[10] and he reported that he often encountered it in his practice.[11] Because all of the listed symptoms of neurasthenia could also be found in other disorders, and because some of those symptoms were often missing from a given case, there was no scientific rationale for regarding them as constituting a syndrome.

If Freud had thought clearly about the matter, he might have initiated a significant conceptual reform. Instead, his proposed innovation only extended the error. From neurasthenia he carved out a second, equally arbitrary, disorder: *anxiety neurosis*. Now sufferers from chronic anxiety, along with such concomitant effects as melancholy, irritability, vertigo, phobias, and intolerance of loud noises, supposedly possessed an affliction of their own. Meanwhile, neurasthenia would

---

* Freud's adjective *aktuell* had nothing to do with "actuality." Since the correct translation of *aktuelle Neurose* is "current neurosis," I will depart from tradition and employ it.

   As I have mentioned, in this early period Freud used *neuro-psychoses* and *psychoneuroses* interchangeably.

still include "intracranial pressure, spinal irritation, and dyspepsia with flatulence and constipation"—but just why, readers weren't told.*

Freud assigned each of the two current neuroses its own type of causation. Both were notably androcentric, not to say autobiographical. When neurasthenia isn't simply produced by a "hereditary taint," Freud wrote, it is brought on by an improper expenditure of sexual substance, almost always by means of masturbation. That vice, by repeatedly discharging chemicals that ought to have been stored for their role in heterosexual intercourse, not only disrupts other somatic functions; it also distracts the subject from proper object choice, lowers his ability to manage sexual tension in the future, and thus results in reduced potency.

Anxiety neurosis that isn't simply inherited, in contrast, stems from *frustration* of the sex act through prolonged abstinence or impotence or through such practices as coitus interruptus and premature ejaculation, all of which "dam up the libido."[12] No wonder, then, that attacks of anxiety exhibit such markers as heavy breathing, sweating, and palpitations. In Freud's view, these aren't mentally generated symbols of coitus but coital reflexes themselves, finding an outlet in an unintended context.

In both of the current neuroses, Freud proposed, the nervous system, which ideally regulates itself and thus stands ready to absorb the impact of external stimuli, is obliged to cope with endogenous (internal) disruptions. It does so unthinkingly, as it were. In the psychoneuroses, by contrast, a sexual *idea* is presented to the mind, which disapproves of that idea for one reason or another and thus obliges it, through repression, to find another outlet.

Freud maintained that in hysteria, repression usually *converts* unacceptable thoughts into bodily symptoms such as those featured in Charcot's *grande hystérie*. But in obsessions and compulsive acts, the sexual idea is *displaced* onto another idea—one that may lack manifest sexual content but is nevertheless either dwelled upon (an obsession)

---

* SE, 3:90. "Intracranial pressure" and "spinal irritation" have long since vanished from the medical textbooks, and historians have had difficulty reconstructing what discomforts were intended.

or ritually enacted (a compulsion), as if this substitute were the dangerous original thought. In the case of hallucinations, the subject rejects that thought so energetically that, so long as the delusive experience is in progress, reality itself is denied. And finally, a paranoiac acknowledges the existence of the shameful thought but *projects* it onto someone else.

It would be hard to overstate Freud's hubris in advancing these claims, which stand in marked contrast to those of the painstaking and methodical Kraepelin. Having learned scientific method under the experimentalists Erb, Flechsig, and Wilhelm Wundt and having compiled extensive clinical records from his hospitalized psychotics, Kraepelin eschewed etiological stabs in the dark. Instead, he built a solid evidential basis for his descriptions of psychiatric phenomena, which he offered in a spirit of collaboration with present and future researchers. His identification of two distinct psychoses, dementia praecox (schizophrenia) and manic-depressive insanity (bipolar disorder), would prove to be a lasting contribution to medical knowledge.

Freud saw many fewer patients than Kraepelin and was scarcely interested in psychological research. He had shown no ability to reach correct diagnoses or to avoid tautology in his reasoning. Such evidence as he could cite derived from four unreliable sources: snap judgments gleaned from briefly interviewed patients, inconclusive longer treatments, worry about himself, and the Anna O. case, which contradicted his theory. He was claiming to understand the inner workings of two major neuroses, hysteria and neurasthenia, that his colleagues would soon come to regard as artifactual. Yet his claims were more comprehensive and more dogmatically stated than Kraepelin's. He offered them as settled facts that were to be believed on his authority.

Freud wished to show that all neurotics, including the sufferers from psychoneuroses, lack the only way to keep a mature nervous system in healthy equilibrium: frequent heterosexual intercourse ending in orgasm. A number of other thinkers, including Josef Breuer, could concede some plausibility to that idea. The question, though, was whether theory on this level of abstraction was helpful for understanding actual cases, which might or might not be ruled by sexual factors. The whole psychogenic movement, from Delboeuf, Möbius, Strümpell, Forel, and

Janet to Paul Dubois and Breuer himself, upheld the principle that psychological phenomena are best understood in psychological terms. Freud, however, wishing to establish a sexual common denominator for all neuroses, was drawn toward a physiological framework as a means of convincing himself and others that materialist knowledge was on his side.

This tendency was heralded in the closing sentences of the 1894 "Neuro-Psychoses of Defence":

> I should like, finally, to dwell for a moment on the working hypothesis which I have made use of in this exposition of the neuroses of defence. I refer to the concept that in mental functions something is to be distinguished—a quota of affect or sum of excitation—which possesses all the characteristics of a quantity (though we have no means of measuring it), which is capable of increase, diminution, displacement and discharge, and which is spread over the memory-traces of ideas somewhat as an electric charge is spread over the surface of a body.
>
> This hypothesis . . . can be applied in the same sense as physicists apply the hypothesis of a flow of electric fluid. It is provisionally justified by its utility in co-ordinating and explaining a great variety of psychical states.[13]

Commentators who praise the psychoanalytic Freud for having cut his ties to physical science in favor of a pure psychology haven't understood how much this circuit of nerve impulses meant to him. As he would underscore in his Postscript to the "Dora" paper, published in 1905, "It is the therapeutic technique alone that is purely psychological; the theory does not by any means fail to point out that neuroses have an organic basis."[14]

Freud's quantifying idiom gave him a pass to cross the mind-body border any number of times without having to trouble himself over an exchange of currencies. The trick lay in applying make-believe mathematics to "amounts" or "sums" (*Beträge*) of both affect (*Affekt*) and excitation (*Erregung*), as if the two qualities—one psychical, the other physiological—were interchangeable. This blurring of domains wasn't

needed for the purely somatic "current neuroses," nor for those psychoneuroses, such as obsessive-compulsive disorder, that supposedly
change sexual ideas into nonsexual ones. It was invaluable, however,
for lending plausibility to the mechanics of hysterical conversion from
ideas to behaviors. Instead of having to explain how an act of defense
by a shadowy ego can persuade a body part to symbolize the event it
is repressing, Freud could just assert that "the sum of excitation, being
cut off from psychical association, finds its way all the more easily
along the wrong path to a somatic innervation."[15]

Thus, for example, "Elisabeth von R." (Ilona Weiss), informed by
Freud that she was enamored of her brother-in-law, was said to have
"repressed her erotic idea from consciousness and transformed the
amount of its affect into physical sensations of pain."[16] Such a claim,
requiring us to envision the repressing mind and the malfunctioning
limb as two stations in telegraphic communication along "the wrong
path," was granted an air of scientificity by being couched in quasi-
numerical terms. An exact amount of affect—but how much was
that?—had followed the neuronal route from mind to body, and Elisabeth had felt a pain (albeit two years later).

Despite Elisabeth's supposed repression and conversion, Freud also
wanted to claim that she had become fleetingly conscious of her shameful love for her brother-in-law. Hence he apportioned her feelings "in
a kind of algebraical picture, [whereby] we may attribute a certain
quota of affect to the ideational complex of these erotic feelings which
remained unconscious, and say that this quantity (the quota of affect) is
what was converted."[17] Just enough units of affect were left in Elisabeth's
head, supposedly, for her to recognize the correctness of Freud's understanding of her case. In actuality, Elisabeth found his interpretation preposterous. Yet his numerical jargon has lulled readers into supposing
that he must have traced his patient's problems to their source.

2. BACILLI OF THE MIND

According to the origin myth of psychoanalysis, Freud alone had the
courage to acknowledge the importance of sexuality in the formation
of neuroses. As we have seen, however, hysteria had been regarded as

a sexual disorder since antiquity, and any number of nineteenth-century physicians had anticipated Freud's emphasis on too little, too much, or too irregular sexual activity as a provocation to illness. He was by no means alone, for example, in connecting nervous symptoms to premature ejaculation and coitus interruptus.

As for habitual masturbation, in Freud's day it was regarded as a broad-spectrum noxa, generating harms that ranged from impotence to insanity. The popularizer (not the original proponent) of neurasthenia, the American George M. Beard, counted masturbation as one behavior among others—drinking and smoking, overwork, being caught up in the frenzied pace of modern life, even retiring from business—that could deplete the individual's "nerve force."* Beard also proposed a subtype, "sexual neurasthenia," for which masturbation was, again, named as a possible but not invariable source.[18]

Because the alleged pathogens of Beardian neurasthenia were nearly as various as its effects, no refutation of his account was feasible. Freud, however, regarded masturbation as the "specific cause" of neurasthenia, in the sense that Robert Koch had identified a certain microbe as the specific cause of tuberculosis.[19] Just as an animal that is inoculated with *Bacillus kochii* will always contract tuberculosis and no other disease, and just as nobody who lacks that infection can possibly be tubercular, so, according to Freud, a chronic self-abuser will contract neurasthenia and only neurasthenia; and so, too, chronic frustration of the sex act will result in no other syndrome than anxiety neurosis.

Shortly after the publication of Freud's article on the current neuroses in January 1895, the noted Munich psychiatrist Leopold Löwenfeld pointed out one conspicuous weakness in his argument.[20] Anxiety, Löwenfeld remarked, often results from simple fright, without a sexual component. The cause-and-effect relationship in such

---

* Beard 1881. Since first calling attention to neurasthenia in 1869, Beard had continued to expand its scope until, in a best-selling book of 1881, a vast number of nervous symptoms were included. For many years thereafter, Freud subscribed to Beard's omnibus disease with as much incuriosity as the Western lay public. Nor, though he attempted to modify Beard's conception in 1895, did he ever recant his faith in the genuineness of neurasthenia. By the 1920s most physicians were ready to concede that there had never been any such disorder; but Freud, as was his practice when medical opinion took an inconvenient turn, merely avoided the topic.

cases could hardly be tighter; the anxiety begins at once with the experience of terror. How, then, could Freud maintain that the real cause of anxiety was sexual?

Freud had much to say about this in his "Reply to Criticisms" article, but not before indulging in a question-begging slight that was to become routine in his later polemics. Physicians have already glimpsed the sexual basis of the neuroses, he wrote, but they dare not acknowledge it:

> Such behaviour must have a deep-seated cause, originating perhaps in a kind of reluctance to look squarely at sexual matters. . . . At all events, one had to be prepared to meet with resistance in venturing upon an attempt to make something credible to other people which they could without any trouble have discovered for themselves.[21]

Löwenfeld, Freud was hinting, suffered from sexual anxieties of his own, and that is why he had failed to admit the obvious validity of Freud's own reasoning.

Throughout his "Reply," Freud intimated that the burden of proof fell on Löwenfeld and anyone else who questioned his etiologies. But it was Freud's responsibility to establish, first, that sexual causes possess a unique determining status; second, that each specific cause is found in all instances of "its own" neurosis and in no others; and third, that psychologically healthy people rarely engage in the noxious practices in question. Instead of tackling those hard tasks, Freud cavalierly granted—as if it really didn't matter—that his theory in its present state displayed "gaps and weaknesses" and that he had "scarcely brought forward any examples" to bolster his case.[22]

That shortage, which Freud never remedied, was a grave defect, because his claims were epidemiological in nature. Only by correlating sexual habits with the presence or absence of neuroses in a large sampling of patients could he begin to make good on his claims. Nevertheless, he cheekily contended that "the presence of the specific sexual factor can, in the majority of cases, be demonstrated with certainty."[23] As usual, he was blustering his way past objections that couldn't be satisfactorily answered.

Interestingly, the early letters and drafts of papers that were sent to Fliess show a clear understanding of the requirement that would be ducked in the papers of 1895. In his "Draft A" Freud acknowledged the logical necessity of studying "men and women who have remained healthy."[24] And in the February 1893 "Draft B" he announced,

> By way of preparation I have begun a collection: one hundred cases of anxiety neurosis; likewise, I would like to collect a corresponding number of male and female cases of neurasthenia and the much rarer periodic mild depressions. A necessary counterpart would be a second series of one hundred cases of nonneurotics.[25]

A subsequent lecture by Fliess contained a passage, probably written by Freud, that confidently predicted the good outcome of this study, in which Fliess himself would presumably supply the nonneurotic control cases.[26]

It seems, however, that this sensible plan was quickly forsaken. In subsequent letters, pleading ill health, depression, worry, and fatigue as reasons for slow progress on his *sexualia* (the current neuroses), Freud made no mention of even trying to gather statistics. Though he knew that a smattering of anecdotes couldn't bear the weight of his still-evolving theory, a combination of impatience and ambition apparently drove him to publish his current-neuroses synthesis anyway, hoping that its tone of authority would compensate for the absence of pertinent evidence.

Freud kept changing his mind about etiologies with dizzying frequency. In "The Neuro-Psychoses of Defence" of May and June 1894, both obsessions and phobias were said to operate by the same mechanism, transposing repressed affect to a nonsexual idea that either dominates thought (an obsession) or is shunned in fear (a phobia). But by January 1895, in "Obsessions and Phobias," he had reversed himself: "The mechanism of phobias is entirely different from that of obsessions."[27] Now phobias were just a subtype of anxiety neurosis, lacking any psychical mechanism. In the same month, however, Freud's paper on the current neuroses announced that there were actually two types of phobias, one of which was a psychoneurosis after all.[28]

More troubling than this jumble of unsupported claims is Freud's refusal at every turn to reveal that he had altered his theory. In each instance he played the lawgiver who has simply discovered the truth. He had already cultivated that manner in his ill-fated cocaine pronouncements a decade earlier. Now he was following the same playbook: stay on the offensive, demean your critics, and cover your tracks as completely as possible.

3. SECOND OPINIONS

As I have indicated, the topic of sexuality was the casus belli between Freud and Breuer. In utilizing the fourth and final chapter of *Studies on Hysteria* to announce the exclusively sexual origin of all neuroses, Freud was turning the book into a self-consuming artifact. Readers could perceive that the seeming consensus of Chapter 1, the former "Preliminary Communication," was null and void. As for the specimen case of Anna O. in Chapter 2, it obviously held divergent meanings for the two authors. Freud made the point explicitly and with palpable spite: the Anna O. matter "was not considered at all by its observer from the point of view of a sexual neurosis, and is now quite useless for this purpose."[29]

But that wasn't all. Freud also deconstructed *his own* case studies from Chapter 2. Emmy, Lucy, Katharina, and Elisabeth had all been featured as typical hysterics, but now Freud maintained that he had misdiagnosed all four women. Emmy's hysteria was deemed secondary to a "severe anxiety neurosis" stemming from her alleged "sexual abstinence." Unfortunately, Elisabeth's problem, like Anna O.'s, hadn't been "investigated as a sexual neurosis." So, too, Lucy's anxiety "did not become visible, or it escaped me." But since both Elisabeth and Lucy were suffering from unrequited love, they too must have contracted anxiety neuroses. And Katharina could now be understood as having fallen victim to yet another combination of anxiety neurosis and hysteria. "The former created the symptoms," according to Freud, "while the latter repeated them and operated with them."[30]

These suspiciously monotonous adjustments raised more questions than they answered. If Lucy, for example, had harbored an anxiety neurosis—supposedly caused by sexual deprivation, without any psychological component—how could she have shed her symptoms as soon as she reconciled herself to continued sexual unfulfillment? The same objection applies to Elisabeth's alleged release from leg pain. As for Emmy and her "abstinence," we saw that her multiple affairs were known to just about everyone but Freud. And, most outlandishly, how could a one-hour chat with the previously unseen Katharina have shown Freud that, in her case, an anxiety neurosis had passed its symptoms along to a hysteria? In reclassifying "virginal anxiety" as a subspecies of anxiety neurosis instead of retaining it as a contributor to hysteria, Freud was ignoring his own etiological criteria. Whereas an anxiety neurosis was said to come into play automatically through a toxic buildup, Katharina's alleged disorder supposedly involved her *fear* of sexuality.

By adding a nonpsychological current neurosis to each of the major cases that he included, Freud provided himself with alibis for poor or questionable-looking outcomes. But he also ensured that in a book titled *Studies on Hysteria*, none of his examples could be regarded as isolating either the traits or the effective treatment of the disorder in question. Why, then, hadn't he gone back and replaced the four ambiguous cases with more illustrative ones?

The answer couldn't be disclosed: Freud had nothing better to offer than Emmy and company. Hence an improvisation was called for:

> And if, instead of these four, I did not report *twelve* cases whose analysis provides a confirmation of the psychical mechanism of hysterical phenomena put forward by us, this reticence was necessitated by the very circumstance that the analysis revealed these cases as being simultaneously sexual neuroses, although certainly no diagnostician would have refused them the name of hysteria. But an elucidation of these sexual neuroses would overstep the bounds of the present joint publication.[31]

Freud told his readers that he was now holding twelve sets of corroborative case notes—twelve!—in his drawer. Out of regard for Breuer, though, they couldn't be deployed. We might think that Freud would have wanted to say *something* more specific about them. But he dared not do so, because, it appears, they were fictitious.

A close reading of Freud's "Psychotherapy" chapter in *Studies on Hysteria* reveals further confusion and evasion. According to one sentence, unmixed cases of hysteria are "rare"; two paragraphs later they are nonexistent; but two pages farther on, they are back again.[32] Likewise, the cathartic method is "very well able to get rid of any hysterical symptom," yet Freud's inability to apply that method to hysteria was what supposedly drove him to reconsider his whole view of the neuroses.[33] He couldn't hypnotize deftly enough to remove his hysterics' symptoms, but the same technique had allegedly worked to perfection on his obsessives.[34] Was he capable, then, of hypnotizing obsessional neurotics but not hysterics? Or, more probably, did he boast of success with the obsessives because readers of the *Studies* would find no pertinent case histories from which they could form a judgment of their own?

In none of his case histories had Freud been able to offer a straightforward exemplification of the cathartic method. Now he had compounded the problem. If psychogenic neuroses were typically interwoven with "current" ones that resulted from unhealthy practices, where did that leave Freud as the co-promoter of a memory-based psychotherapy? Bedeviled by his own equivocations, he sank into verbal quicksand:

> It remains for me to mention the apparent contradiction between the admission that not all hysterical symptoms are psychogenic and the assertion that they can all be got rid of by a psychotherapeutic procedure. The solution lies in the fact that some of these non-psychogenic symptoms (stigmata, for instance) are, it is true, indications of illness (*Krankheitszeichen*), but cannot be described as ailments (*Leiden*); and consequently it is not of practical importance if they persist after the successful treatment of the illness. As regards other such symptoms, it seems to be the case that in some roundabout way they are carried off along with the psychogenic symptoms, just as, perhaps, in some roundabout way they are after all dependent on a psychical causation.[35]

Such incoherence was put to shame by the focused rationality of Breuer's prose as, in his theoretical Chapter 3, he punctured the fallacies in Freud's representation of the unconscious. Breuer's clarity was facilitated by the detachment he felt from the contemporary battle over psychological theory and method. Freud, however, needed to proclaim therapeutic success, even as his intellectual trajectory was taking him toward an extreme physiological determinism that discouraged both empathy and medical solicitude.

PART SIX

. . . .

OFF THE DEEP END

. . . .

Was it, as I suppose, another example of Freud's simpleminded gullibility?

—James Strachey to Ernest Jones*

---

* Quoted by Borch-Jacobsen and Shamdasani 2012, p. 284.

23

The Secret Sharer

1. A REVENANT

Wilhelm Fliess was a Berlin internist (not a rhinologist, as is commonly assumed) whose ethnicity, education, and training were very similar to Freud's.[1] He had come to Vienna in the fall of 1887 for further medical instruction. There, at Josef Breuer's urging—for Breuer and the intellectually adventuresome Fliess were already on friendly terms, and they would remain so—Fliess attended *Privatdozent* Freud's university lectures on brain anatomy and was impressed by what he heard. Freud's letters to Fliess, beginning after the latter's return to Berlin in November, reveal that each doctor had found an eager audience in the other. Each hoped to explain the source of the neuroses, and each nurtured a vision of achieving immortality by forging a new scientific paradigm; both regarded themselves as Darwinian materialists but also felt attracted to Romantic vitalism; and one of Fliess's emergent doctrines was the innate bisexual constitution of all human beings, an idea that would bear a special fascination for Freud.

The two physicians were friends from 1887 until the turn of the century, and for most of that span, beginning in 1892, Fliess was the most important presence in Freud's life, both intellectually and emotionally. The later Freud, however, would strive to relegate his long-term comrade to oblivion. Fliess received no mention in the 1914 *History of the Psycho-Analytic Movement*, whose second sentence declared that "psycho-analysis is my creation; for ten years I was the only person who concerned himself with it."[2] Nor, unless we count one nameless allusion to "the only friend of mine who was at that time interested in my work," did Fliess appear in the 1925 *Autobiographical Study*.[3]

Freud's apostles were only too willing to join him in a conspiracy of silence. A dramatic series of events, however, threatened to spring Fliess from anonymity, and finally did so. After Fliess's death in 1928, his widow gathered Freud's letters and sold them to a Berlin book dealer with the wise stipulation that under no circumstances could they be purchased by their writer. When Hitler came to power in 1933, the letters were smuggled past the Nazis and safely held in Paris. There they were bought by Marie Bonaparte, who, because her faith in Freud and psychoanalysis was absolute, believed that their availability to scholars would contribute innocuously to the history of modern psychology. And since she was a princess who was accustomed to having her way, she resisted when Freud begged her to sell him the letters—no doubt for consignment to his fireplace.

In the later 1940s, when international psychoanalysis was recomposing itself under the guidance of Anna Freud, its directorate began to grasp the full dimensions of the Fliess problem. For one thing, the letters revealed Freud to have been in most respects the subordinate and more credulous party. Another embarrassment was the abundant evidence that he had by no means ended his involvement with cocaine. Then, too, there was a psychosexual dimension to the Freud/Fliess relationship that would be certain to raise questions about Freud's disposition and to cast doubt on the myth of his happy marriage. Above all, the letters to Fliess refuted the contention that the master, working in isolation, had transcended the neurology and physiology of his day by fashioning a "pure psychology" from his patients' revelations and his self-study.

Anna Freud, to whom Marie Bonaparte consigned the letters, deserves credit for having countermanded her father's instruction that all of his manuscripts be posthumously destroyed.* But the decision to

---

* Because nearly all of Fliess's end of the correspondence is missing, Freud surely destroyed the letters himself, along with hundreds or thousands of less compromising documents.

publish a selection of the letters, including drafts of theoretical papers for which Freud had solicited Fliess's advice, wasn't taken without Machiavellian calculation by the chief editors, Anna herself and Ernst Kris. Initially, the Freudian renegade Jeffrey Masson recounts, Ernst Freud and his father's last physician, Max Schur, planned to publish a complete edition of the Fliess letters.[4] At that point, we may assume, Anna Freud exercised her veto. Although Marie Bonaparte was listed as an editor, she was displeased by Anna's adulteration of the record. She later leaked some omitted portions of the Freud/Fliess correspondence to Schur, whose subsequent revelations undermined Anna and Kris's legend building.[5]

The eventual book—*Aus den Anfängen der Psychoanalyse* (1950) and its translation, *The Origins of Psycho-Analysis* (1954)—would provide just enough information about the Freud/Fliess relationship to keep scholars busy and forestall a demand for access to the full archive, which was to remain off limits. And the bowdlerized text and its tendentious editorial apparatus would minimize inconsistencies with official lore and point the way for later Freudian apologists to incorporate Freud's temporary need for Fliess into a story of heroic self-mastery. In this manner some, but by no means all, of the truth about Freud and Fliess could be fitted into a new and more dramatic discovery narrative for the birth of psychoanalysis. With the full publication of the Fliess letters by Masson in 1985, however, all of those coordinated efforts would begin to unravel.

2. REDISTRIBUTED LIBIDO

One urgent task for the editors of *The Origins of Psycho-Analysis* would be to turn down the emotional temperature of Freud's affection for Fliess. The surviving letters, we will see, contained many expressions of homoerotic infatuation that ill suited the Freud legend. The sheer fact of love for another male, from the perspective of seventy years ago, could have made Freud look too abnormal to have gathered his psychological knowledge with the objectivity of a neutral observer. Some of his conclusions could start to look like products not of psychoanalytic research but of a personal aversion to womankind.

We cannot understand the role of Fliess in Freud's emotional economy without first remarking on his condition as a husband. When marrying in 1886, he had hoped that Martha Bernays would save him from depression, nervous exhaustion, fear of abandonment, and paranoid rage. Instead, he found himself beset with further resentments and anxieties. Even Jones, who went out of his way to sentimentalize the marriage as "the haven of happiness [Freud] had yearned for," had to admit that his nervous symptoms—chiefly indigestion, constipation, and "moodiness in a pronounced degree"—"reached [their] acme some years after his marriage."[6]

Superficially, the Freud household bore an aspect of efficient harmony. Martha humored Sigmund in every way she could, while he in turn, by acceding to her domestic decisions and routines, found himself relieved of care about matters that bored and annoyed him. He was free to arrange his time as he pleased, indulging his taste for café reunions, urban and mountain walking, nocturnal letter writing, weekly card games with friends, B'nai B'rith activities, and Baedeker-guided travel that rarely included his wife.

But the Freuds—unlike, say, Mathilde and Josef Breuer—were very unequal housemates who were long accustomed to an absence of intimacy. Having "lost her figure" and jeopardized her health in bearing six children, Martha would thenceforth strike Sigmund, who was five years older, as a used-up woman who belonged in the nursery or parlor, tending to the next generation. (Her "bad teeth," he would inform the world, had figured in his most important dream.)[7] For her part, Martha was heard to describe psychoanalysis, especially insofar as it pertained to the minds of children, as "a form of pornography."[8]

What was most drastically missing from Freud's domestic existence, causing him to tell Carl Jung's wife in 1911 that his entire marriage had been "amortized," was sexual pleasure.[9] In 1894, not yet thirty-eight years old, he confided to Fliess that his libido had "long since been subdued."[10] It hadn't been—not permanently—but Freud, probably still a faithful husband, believed otherwise, partly because he was then terrified by symptoms that we will consider later, but also because the thought of lovemaking with Martha had become unappealing to him. And after an exhausted Martha's pregnancy with the unanticipated Anna came to light in 1895, the couple's sexual estrangement became extreme. But the loss of that libidinal outlet only magnified the weight Sigmund would ascribe to thwarted sexuality in neurosogenesis.

Freud left us a remarkable if oblique record of the frustration that tormented him in his marriage and apparently drove him, at length, to seek satisfaction elsewhere. His complaints would be set forth with minimal disguise in two papers, "'Civilized' Sexual Morality and Modern Nervous Illness" (1908) and "The Taboo of Virginity" (1918).[11] Ostensibly, the generalizations that he expounded there had been gleaned from clinical experience. But Freud never presented the case material from which his inferences about marital tribulations had supposedly been drawn. If there is a confessional element in virtually all of his psychological writings, here there seems to be nothing but autobiography writ large.

Intercourse within marriage, Freud would write, is gratifying for a few years at most, and then "the marriage becomes a failure in so far as it has promised the satisfaction of sexual needs." Contraceptives cannot be employed, because they "hurt the fine susceptibilities of both partners and even actually cause illness." The loss of physical affection then "puts a stop as well to the mental sympathy between them."[12] Freud didn't lay all of the responsibility for that outcome on the female party. Young men who try to save themselves for marriage through a long wait, he wrote, are usually driven to the immoral and enervating practice of masturbation. And "every man whose libido, as a result of masturbatory or perverse sexual practices, has become habituated to situations and conditions of satisfaction which are not normal, develops diminished potency in marriage."[13]

Such a weakling, Freud believed, is ill equipped to negate the deleterious effects of his bride's prudish upbringing. Hence,

A marriage begun with a reduced capacity to love on both sides succumbs to the process of dissolution even more quickly than others. As a result of the man's weak potency, the woman is not satisfied, and she remains anaesthetic even in cases where her disposition to frigidity, derived from her education, could have been overcome by a powerful sexual experience. A couple like this finds more difficulties, too, in the prevention of children than a healthy one, since the husband's diminished potency tolerates the use of contraceptives badly. In this perplexity, sexual intercourse, as being the source of all their embarrassments, is soon given up, and with this the basis of married life is abandoned.[14]

But this generalizing of marital discord was as close as Freud could come to an equitable view of his misery. Even twenty-two years after the wedding, bitterness toward his sexually and intellectually scorned wife hadn't abated. A virgin bride, he wrote, "has nothing but disappointments to offer the man who has saved up all his desire for her."[15] As a result of having tried not to think about the erotic challenge lying ahead, such women "are scared away from *any* form of thinking, and knowledge loses its value for them."[16] And after thirty-two years of living with Martha, the still grumbling Freud reported that a bride's disposition is permanently soured by defloration. It binds her to the perpetrator, he declared in "The Taboo of Virginity," but it also "unleashes an archaic reaction of hostility towards him."[17] "The second half of a woman's life," he deduced from his experience at Berggasse 19, "may be filled by the struggle against her husband."[18]

Innumerable men have proved themselves unequipped for married love. Freud, however, superadded an element of weirdness that was all his own. Women—*all* women—impressed him as sinister creatures whose genital concavity bears a menace of "castration" to any male who ventures across its threshold. And he believed that every man dreads being "weakened by the woman, infected with her femininity and of then showing himself incapable."[19] Even successful coupling struck him as a depressing ordeal. "The effect which coitus has of discharging tensions and causing flaccidity," he remarked, "may be the prototype of what the man fears; and realization of the influence which the woman gains over him through sexual intercourse, the consideration she thereby forces from him, may justify the extension of this fear."[20]

Even worse, Freud divined that the secret ambition of every female was to *acquire* the envied penis by absorbing and severing it. Thus all women were monsters at heart. No wonder this particular victim-to-be couldn't approach any such creature as a suitor until age twenty-six. And when he finally did so and actually acquired a fiancée, he had informed her right off that she brought to his mind the folkloric "Melusina," who happened to be a serpent below the waist.[21] The very tenderness of women, he would remark in his little book on Leonardo da Vinci, conceals a "ruthlessly demanding" sensuality, "consuming men as if they were alien beings."[22]

Here, then, were the broodings that would lend classical psychoanalysis its tone of grim fatalism. That doctrine's bogeyman, castration, instead of deriving from close clinical observation of either women or men, came straight from Freud's interior house of horrors. It was daring on his part to publish such evidence of his morbidity for all to see. He did so, however, under the misapprehension that all men were similarly warped.

As if on cue, Freud encountered Wilhelm Fliess scarcely a year after graduating from fretful bachelorhood to the role of self-doubting and underperforming husband. A "slightly drab" Martha, according to Peter Gay, "virtually made Fliess necessary" for the ever-curious Freud.[23] Yet the *Brautbriefe* show Martha Bernays to have been lively and playful, well read, poetical, and eager to share in Sigmund's endeavors. Freud's need for Fliess was determined not by Martha's dullness but by the structure of his personality. As Freud recalled in one of his last letters to Fliess, Breuer had told Ida Fliess "how lucky she was that I did not live in Berlin and could not interfere with her marriage."[24]

The supplanting of Martha by Fliess didn't become apparent overnight. After Fliess's marriage to Ida Bondy in 1892, however, Freud was emboldened to be more candid about his feelings, since his friendship with a married man could hardly be suspect. Switching from *Sie* to *Du* in the wake of Fliess's honeymoon, Freud wrote that "the comforting thought welled up in me: he is now well taken care of and in good hands. This certainty also set the tone for my correspondence with you. You will not misunderstand it."[25]

The tightening of the Freud/Fliess bond can be charted through the salutations of Freud's letters, which began in 1887 with the circumspect "Esteemed friend and colleague" and advanced to "Dear friend and colleague" (1888), "Dear friend" and "Dearest friend" (1890), "My beloved friend" (1893), and "Dearest Wilhelm," "My dear," and "Dearest" (1895), with forays into "Dear Magician," "Hail, cherished Wilhelm!," "Daimonie," and "*Carissimo Guglielmo*," before subsiding to "Dear Wilhelm" again as the relationship began to cool.* But this gradualism was merely tactical, dictated by a need to keep from alarming the steadfastly heterosexual Fliess. Freud had set out immediately to win Fliess's affection, just as he had done with the handsome and gifted Ernst Fleischl a few years earlier. As he confessed in 1898, "Eleven years ago I already realized that it was necessary for me to love you in order to enrich my life."[26] "No one," he told Fliess in 1900, when their tie was fraying, "can replace for me the relationship with the friend which a special—possibly feminine—side demands."[27]

Freud's messages to Fliess are love letters in the full sense of the term. They flatter the *inamorato* while attempting to steer him away from potential rivals, notably Breuer. They callously discuss the inadequate state of sexual relations at home. As in the *Brautbriefe*, moreover, the letters voice a continual anxiety about the dear one's health. Likewise, they indulge in frequent hypochondriacal complaints for which a tender sympathy is expected. And they abound in expressions of elation and anguish, depending on whether or not Fliess has been recently seen or has responded promptly enough to the latest epistle.[28] "Here I live in ill humor and in darkness until you come," Freud writes from Vienna to Berlin, just as he had once written from Vienna to Wandsbek; "I get things off my chest; rekindle my flickering flame at your steadfast one and feel well again; and after your departure, I again have been given eyes to see, and what I see is beautiful and good."[29]

---

* On the assumption that Fliess saved all of Freud's letters, we can infer that their frequency reflected the waxing and waning of Freud's ardor. Only eleven letters survive from the period 1887–92. Each year thereafter saw more correspondence, peaking at forty-four letters by Freud in 1899 alone. After 1900 the two men were scarcely in contact, and the exchanges ended rancorously.

Ought we to conclude, then, that Freud's primary sexual orientation was to his own gender? That question was frequently on his mind, and he found it deeply worrisome. He told himself, however, that a fulfilled demand for intense male friendship was precisely what enabled him to remain heterosexual. But this was a heterosexuality that, for now at least, was largely divorced from feeling. In turning his back on Martha, Freud was devaluing someone who had joined him in the hygienically restorative but degrading act of sex. Love of Fliess was conceived from the outset as a loftier matter.

3. THE BELIEVER

In the eyes of Freud's modern editors, the most troubling aspect of his relationship with Fliess was his acquiescence to ideas that appeared to have only one merit: they were proposed and cherished by the beloved. It might be hoped that a mind as keen as Freud's would be capable of holding Fliess's propositions at arm's length and coolly assessing their rationality. In the whole archive, however, there isn't one instance of Freud's subjecting a Fliessian notion to impersonal scientific critique. Fliess, we can tell, did habitually perform that service for Freud; but Freud's desire to gratify Fliess, like his earlier prostration before Charcot, appeared to switch off the analytic portion of his brain.

Among the Fliessian propositions embraced by Freud, the ones concerning a syndrome called the "nasal reflex neurosis" (hereafter NRN) have become most notorious. Fliess wasn't the inventor of the NRN, but he was its most avid and expansive proponent, and his best-known surgeries were designed to cure it.[30] In this instance Freud's credulity would have serious consequences for himself and others.

The broadest premise behind the NRN diagnosis was the reflex model of disease, assumed by Charcot and others but already in retreat as the germ theory kept gaining adherents.[31] According to reflex theory, an illness occurs when one part of the body disrupts a quite distant part that shares with it a nervous pathway and perhaps also a homology of tissue. Just such a homology really exists between the mucous membranes of the nose and those of the male and female genitals;

and, as others had observed before Fliess, sexual arousal in either gender causes "erections" within the nose.

An affinity for reflex theory therefore prompted Fliess to look for deterministic links between nasal anomalies and "female troubles." According to Fliess, specific "genital spots" within the nose were in two-way communication with the reproductive system. The noxious practice of masturbation, he believed, was likely to impair those spots, which in their turn could trigger excessive menstrual bleeding, irregular periods, and even difficult childbirth. Indeed, so far as Fliess was concerned, nosebleeds themselves were manifestations of "nasal dysmenorrhea."[32]

Whichever kind of site was thought to be involved in a given case, Fliess's initial recourse was to treat it by topically applying cocaine to the supposed source of reflex action in the nose. When the anesthetic effect inevitably wore off, his next option was to cauterize the malfunctioning nasal tissue with electricity. And if the patient's trouble below still persisted, Fliess's last recourse was to remove the responsible portion of the nose—a piece of "turbinate bone" or concha. From 1895 onward, that was his surgical pièce de résistance, for which any number of patients were apparently referred to him by Freud among others.

Fliess regarded the nose as a control center for other organs and their maladies as well. Thus, in the style of nineteenth-century fad diagnoses, the NRN got blamed for a host of miscellaneous woes, from migraines and gastritis to muscle pains, cardiac irregularities, and troubled breathing. And once Freud had become smitten with Fliess, it was a foregone conclusion that he would begin seeing the NRN wherever he looked. "I am now making this diagnosis very often," he told his friend in May 1893, "and agree with you that the nasal reflex is one of the most frequent disturbances."[33] He expected that it would soon become known as "Fliess's disease."[34]

It is often assumed that the NRN was entirely Fliess's obsession and that Freud went along with it rather thoughtlessly. The truth is that Fliess depended on his Viennese partner not only for encouragement but also for help in forging the etiological links that appeared to warrant surgical intervention. That Freud's assistance was quite definite can be inferred from his "Draft C," probably sent to Fliess in April 1893.

There he commented on the text of a lecture on the NRN that Fliess would soon be delivering. The presentation needed to be strengthened, Freud wrote, by greater stress on "*our* etiological formula," a sexual one.[35] Freud had convinced his friend that the NRN was a variant of neurasthenia, and he wanted Fliess to insist that all neurasthenia is brought about by the vice of masturbation. Fliess not only complied; he inserted into his lecture some language probably written for the occasion by Freud.[36]

But Freud's involvement with the NRN wasn't limited to its classification or even to the notion of its ultimate source. He was also concerned with the physiological mechanism itself. On that point he took Fliess's side against a more drastic reflex-neurosis theorist, the Swiss urologist Alexander Peyer. In 1890 Peyer had claimed that certain stomach pains can be eradicated by gynecological or urethral surgery, depending on the patient's gender.[37] Freud disagreed with Peyer, but only on a technicality. The urethra, he reassured Fliess, might itself be a "reflex organ," in which case it wouldn't qualify as the proper site for surgery.[38] As we will see in Chapter 26, however, quite enough havoc could be wreaked by targeting the nose as the proper site for rectifying malfunctions elsewhere in the organism.*

Beginning in 1895, Freud felt obliged to check his own hypotheses against rules laid down by another of Fliess's pet theories. I refer to the recently announced Fliessian laws of periodicity, or what came to be known as *biorhythms*. Periodicity was now the common denominator of all of Fliess's constructs, including the NRN. If Freud hoped to retain his friendship, he had no choice but to lend his assent to everything Fliess had to say on the topic.

Fliess's starting point was the twenty-eight-day menstrual cycle, which, he claimed, could be detected in the intervals between attacks of nasal bleeding, migraine, and various other afflictions. He kept noting, however, that the attacks in question often *weren't* separated by twenty-eight days. For that matter, menstruation itself didn't always

---

* Freud's faith in the NRN diagnosis long outlasted the friendship with Fliess. As late as 1937, speaking to Marie Bonaparte, he was still privately expressing a measure of confidence in Fliess's theory (Freud 1986, p. 15).

occur when expected. But here Fliess's theory of universal bisexuality spared him from misgivings. Through abstruse calculations, having chiefly to do with the time between the end of one period and the start of the next one, he inferred that males, too, had a "menstrual cycle" of biorhythms, namely, twenty-three days. And since all females were partly male and vice versa, any variations from a twenty-eight- or twenty-three-day pattern could be explained by interference from the opposite-gender period.[39]

Already by 1897, in his book on female sexual organs and the nose, Fliess had brought this mathematizing to the brink of mysticism. There he claimed that "the whole organic world" is governed by the two interacting sex periods and that, within a human family, a single rhythm is maternally transmitted through the generations, determining "the day of our death just as much . . . as that of our life."[40] The spectrum of diseases was said to obey the same laws.[41] And in his magnum opus of 1906, *The Course of Life*, which purported to cover not just man but every organism, Fliess took further liberties with numbers, now purporting to find significance in manipulations of 23^2, 28^2, 28×23, $3 \times 28 \pm 2 \times 23$, and so forth.[42]

As some of Fliess's contemporaries protested, Fliess's means of reaching predictions were the sheerest quackery. Any positive integer whatsoever could be generated by his favorite formula of $x \times 23 \pm y \times 28$. One doesn't need mathematics, however, to see where he first went astray. If one means of predicting an outcome has proved wrong, the sensible response isn't to keep combining it with other means until the desired result is obtained, but simply to drop it.

Freud, however—besotted with Fliess, indifferent to logic, and destined to lard his own theory with stopgap provisos that could forestall refutation—saw nothing amiss with Fliess's calculations. "I read through your manuscript at one sitting," he enthused in 1896, with reference to *The Relationship between the Nose and the Female Sexual Organs*. "I was exceptionally pleased with its plain assurance, the lucid, self-evident connections between the individual themes, the unpretentious unfolding of its riches, and . . . its wealth of glimpses of new riddles and new explanations."[43]

Freud believed he could now fortify his own theory of anxiety neurosis by using "the menstrual period as its physiological model."[44] Doubts that he was feeling about his theory of repression, he added two months later, might be resolved by an appeal to the interplay between "male and female menstruation in the same individual."[45] Five months after that, appealing to "special multiples of the 28-day female period," he arrayed the psychoneuroses according to Fliessian periodicity.[46] And he also convinced himself that "the intellectual nature of males," vis-à-vis the irrationality of women, could be explained by reference to Fliessian numerology.[47]

4. "MY STRUCTURE ON YOUR BASE"

Freud's deference to his friend was partly rooted in intellectual and practical disadvantages of which he was painfully conscious. Like many other Viennese, he looked up to cosmopolitan Berlin. Meanwhile, at home, he still felt cowed by the stern materialism of Brücke, who had expected all hypotheses to be operationalized and tested. But Freud had struggled with his science courses, and he knew that he would always be an outsider to mathematics. In addition, he lacked a record of successful treatments; and even if his cases had turned out well, they would still have been too few in number to underwrite any psychological laws. Fliess, in contrast, possessed abundant clinical records deriving from physical examinations of the kind that Freud, the mental "neurologist," rarely conducted. And Fliess appeared to have effortlessly mastered every discipline relating to the functioning of the human organism.

It wasn't merely Fliess's apparent rigor that appealed to Freud; it was his supreme self-confidence and the breathtaking scope of his program. His goal was nothing less than to uncover the *Entwicklungsmechanik*, or developmental mechanism, of all life forms and to explain how it regulates human functions. One might expect that such reductionist hubris would set off an alarm for crank theory, but Freud was transfixed. And he yearned to forge a comparably majestic synthesis of his own. As he wrote to Fliess on January 1, 1896,

I see how, via the detour of medical practice, you are reaching your first ideal of understanding human beings as a physiologist, just as I most secretly nourish the hope of arriving, via these same paths, at my initial goal of philosophy. For that is what I wanted originally, when it was not yet at all clear to me to what end I was in the world.[48]

Surely, it may be thought, Freud's "philosophy"—his total vision of the nature of mind—never intersected Fliess's pseudoscientific *Entwicklungsmechanik*. But Freud himself took a different view. "Perhaps with your help," he humbly wrote to his idol, "I shall find the solid ground on which I can cease to give psychological explanations and begin to find a physiological foundation!"[49] As he avowed, his highest aspiration was to build "my structure on your base."[50] Presumably, the anchoring of his notions in physiology would lend them the authority of materialist science.

Ever since the appearance of Frank J. Sulloway's monumental *Freud, Biologist of the Mind* in 1979, it has been clear to serious inquirers that Fliess influenced the full blossoming of psychoanalytic theory more profoundly than any other person. The 1985 publication of the complete and uncensored file of letters from Freud's side of the relationship rendered that inference even more certain. To be sure, Freud was guided along his path by Fleischl, Charcot, Bernheim, Breuer, Anna von Lieben, and Janet. But if his ultimate system were to be stripped of elements inspired or inflected by Fliess, it would lack the grand intellectual sweep that has so often been praised as a sign of genius-level originality.

This isn't to say that Freud simply adopted Fliess's preexisting notions, as he had Charcot's in 1885. Rather, the two men worked together, sharing a taste for radical theory on questions of mutual concern. Much of what Freud would ascribe to "clinical experience" and even to "psychoanalytic research" derived in part from hunches that had been developed in two-man "congresses" held in Berlin, Nuremberg, Breslau, Berchtesgaden, Salzburg, Innsbruck, and elsewhere.*

---

* Lacking Fliess's letters, we can only surmise how Freud affected his thinking. Clearly, though, Freud left a mark on Fliess's system of thought. The latter's 1897 book *The*

Freud hadn't needed Fliess in order to place sexuality at the center of his theory. The influence, indeed, may have flowed in the other direction. "And if he gave me bisexuality," Freud reminisced in 1937, "I'm the one who previously gave him sexuality."[51] In Freud's therapeutic experience, however, sexuality had been largely the stuff of traumatic memories. It came back to him from Fliess as biochemistry; and psychoanalysis as Freud then developed it became a theory of the whole organism, coping in various ways with the need to discharge its "excitation."

What Freud and Fliess had most in common, apart from reaching for the stars, was their commitment to a Darwinian framework of understanding. *Homo sapiens* was to be regarded as existing on a continuum with all organisms, and thus any human trait must be shared with, or have evolved from, a function that can be observed in other animals. At some crossroads in the *Homo* line, adaptation must have favored the partial redirecting of instincts, or of one particular instinct, that had found a more immediate outlet in "lower" species.

For both men, that instinct had to be the sexual one. Among the basic human needs, only the urge to mate could be indefinitely postponed and subjected to severe deformation by custom; and the intrepid sexologist Krafft-Ebing had already brought scientific order to the range of "perversions" that take hold when either the aim or the object of sexual feeling differs from heterosexual intercourse.[52] Such pliability convinced both Fliess and Freud that all culture must be fashioned from the raw stuff of sexuality.

Freud would attach the already familiar term *sublimation* to this process, which operates, he would maintain, through *reaction formation* against sexual feelings that are blocked by revulsion, anxiety, or fear. Sublimation would come to be regarded as his noblest idea, entailing a tragic awareness that "civilization" (*Kultur*) exacts a steep price in neurosis and lost libido. But the supposed inevitability of that sacrifice, raising it beyond the level of individual psychological histories,

---

Relationship between the Nose and the Female Sexual Organs contained at least a dozen references to Freud's ideas about masturbation, hysteria, anxiety neurosis, neurasthenia, and other matters. For a detailed study of each man's effect on the other, see Schröter 1989.

was Fliess's contribution, deriving from his developmental outlook. And on occasion, before the friendship ended, Freud said so in print. "It is true," he wrote in 1898,

> that the organization and evolution of the human species strives to avoid any great degree of sexual activity during childhood. It seems that in man the sexual instinctual forces are meant to be stored up so that, on their release at puberty, they may serve great cultural ends. (W. Fliess.)*

Here Freud was characterizing sexual *latency*—another "discovery" that had actually come from Fliess. When Freud later asserted, in his 1905 *Three Essays on the Theory of Sexuality*, that the latency period "is organically determined and fixed by heredity," he explicitly credited the notion to Fliess.[53] But the subsequent erasure of Fliess from psychoanalytic history would make both latency and sublimation appear to have been inferences from Freud's clinical experience. Psychoanalysts would never inquire how the evidence for such high-level concepts, standing at several removes from observation, could possibly have been gathered and corroborated "on the couch." And, of course, it hadn't been.

Fliess possessed a theory of *repression* as well. Indeed, he may have worked it out in dialogue with Freud. If so, their congresses must have featured some tortuous discussion, for they construed repression divergently. In order to account for hysteria, Freud had posited the repression of traumatic memories and their accompanying affects. For Fliess, however, repression begins in the womb as the inevitable and most basic step of individuation: the partial suppressing of innate bisexuality in favor of one strand of sexual growth. In his view, a bisexual tendency remains in force, peripherally, throughout every life—and so, then, does repression, with or without the prompting of traumatic experience.

The use of a single word, *repression* (*Verdrängung*), to cover Freud's

---

* SE, 3:280–281. This passage, with its smuggling of "great cultural ends" into a nominal materialism, might cause us to ask whether Freud, a passionate Darwinian, had really understood *The Origin of Species*.

and Fliess's initial senses of the term—one psychological, the other biochemical—would seem to invite confusion. Freud, however, welcomed just such a blurring of boundaries. Fliess's idea of built-in repression seemed to lend his own concept a welcome dimension of physicality, and thus he was glad to make room for a variant of it in psychoanalytic doctrine.

Because Freud, in Jones's words, exhibited "a pronounced mental bisexuality" in feeling attracted to both men and women, we can readily understand why he was drawn to Fliess's ideas on that topic.[54] But Fliess, who was chiefly concerned with "male" and "female" chemistry in the phased emergence of traits and events, didn't regard such dual object choice as normal. He did, however, posit that all *neurotics*, however heterosexual in outward behavior, are unconsciously fixated on a member of their own sex. Freud could hardly count himself as an exception. He would endorse the idea in his *Three Essays* and, again, credit its origin to Fliess.[55]

Both Freud and Fliess were taken with Ernst Haeckel's *biogenetic law*, which had been extrapolated—mistakenly, as it happens—from a conjoining of Darwinism with some striking facts of embryology. Haeckel had excited the scientific world in 1866 by appearing to demonstrate that "ontogeny recapitulates phylogeny," whereby a given animal, from embryo to adult, goes through stages mirroring its predecessor species. Fliess's developmental system was a meditation on that erroneous premise. A child, he believed, is born in possession of traits and behaviors that were adaptive for prehuman ancestors but are maladaptive now; hence, early development must accomplish the shedding of those traits.

Freud agreed. In Sulloway's précis of his reasoning,

> if lower animals indeed possess a widened sphere of sexual interests paralleling their heightened sense of smell; and if mankind has lost such "polymorphously perverse" sexual interests in the course of human evolution; then, according to Haeckel's law, the child must necessarily recapitulate both the process by which the zones were gradually extinguished in man and the concomitant acquisition of olfactory "disgust" toward those zones.[56]

Much that looks arbitrary and peculiar in classical Freudian theory becomes comprehensible—though hardly justifiable—in the light of this recapitulatory perspective. According to Fliessian biology, growth within the womb is already a sexual phenomenon, the first of several "thrusts" (*Schübe*) of sex chemicals toward rendering the post-pubescent individual suited for intercourse and reproduction. When Haeckel's biogenetic law is then taken into account, the human baby must be seen as more abundantly and diversely sexual than either the socially disciplined older child or the "normal" monosexual adult, now deprived of all conscious erotic aims except the one that will bring more babies into existence. From this viewpoint, the infant's waking activities—chiefly sucking milk from a nipple and excreting—are regarded as sexually pleasurable activities from which libido must be gradually withdrawn if "civilization" and adaptive object choice are to prevail.

Here, then, was the foundation of Freud's stages of childhood development: the oral, anal, and finally genital "organizations of the libido," into the last of which he would insert his trademark Oedipus complex. But though Freud and Fliess would each attempt to spy on an infant son, hoping to catch sight of spontaneous erections that might give a palpable lift to the idea of childhood sexuality, their whole worldview had been deduced from unsound premises. And, once elaborated, the psychoanalytic theory of maturation would become a pyramid of neo-Fliessian dogmas, divorced from the observation of actual children.

Now we can appreciate the dilemma registered by the editors of *The Origins of Psycho-Analysis*. Freud had embraced all of Fliess's ideas without showing even a flicker of critical judgment. Some of those ideas struck Anna Freud and her colleagues as ridiculous. Other ideas, the developmental ones, sounded better; but that was because they had long been standard psychoanalytic lore, having been appropriated by Freud in his usual sequence of first supplying acknowledgment and then withdrawing it. Moreover, some of the prose in his letters to Fliess suggested a mind in turmoil, lurching among half-articulated brainstorms without engagement in consecutive reasoning.

One task for Freud's editors, then, was simply to put the most damning evidence under the rug. As Borch-Jacobsen and Shamdasani have shown, in 1946–47 an operation of relentless "shortening work" (*Kürzungsarbeit*) was conducted, with the mutually acknowledged goal of circumventing awkward themes and utterances.[57] Out of 284 letters from Freud to Fliess, only 168 were represented, and all but 29 of them underwent diplomatic and often silent alteration.

The Fliessian influence on Freud's psychoanalytic concepts was suppressed. So was the whole topic of his continued or resumed use of cocaine. Again, Fliess's biorhythms and his NRN were treated as follies to which Freud had been passively attracted, but never to the detriment of his objective clinical work. And flirtatiously suggestive language addressed to Fliess was carefully neutered. Where, for instance, Freud had written that he would bring to the next reunion a "temporal lobe lubricated for reception," in the *Origins* he was merely "all agape."[58] Such repairs show, in their very triviality, how worried the postwar Freudians were about their late leader's "feminine" side.

Once they had resolved to treat Freud's intimacy with Fliess as a mere detour on the road to psychoanalysis, his editors were free to demean both Fliess's intellect and his stability. It was Fliess alone, according to Kris's introduction to the *Origins*, who suffered from a "tendency to cling dogmatically to a once-formed opinion."[59] Freud had "tried to elevate him to his own level," but in vain; Fliess's "obstinacy and lack of objectivity" were irremediable.[60]

Fliess was certainly obstinate, but it may be doubted whether he was more irrational than Freud. His neo-Darwinian interests, including biorhythms, primal hermaphroditism, and evolutionary recapitulation, were widely shared in his day. Sexologists, including Krafft-Ebing himself, respected him.[61] And Breuer, though he was made uneasy by Fliess's imaginative flights, didn't dismiss his reasoning out of hand. Breuer even believed in the NRN—so completely, indeed, that he sent a number of female patients, including his thirteen-year-old daughter, Dora, to Berlin for nasal surgery by Fliess.*

---

* See Hirschmüller 1989a, pp. 144, 314, 316, 318–319. No one has been able to say why the sober physiologist Breuer became an advocate of Fliess's nasal interventions. Because those treatments involved liberal applications of cocaine, however, they probably yielded placebo effects that were then mistaken for cures. In addition, Breuer

All of those facts were known by the principal editors of *The Origins of Psycho-Analysis*. If they had placed Fliess within his scientific context, however, they would have been sketching Freud's context, too, and then the virgin birth of psychoanalysis would have been exposed as unhistorical. Moreover, if Freud's engagement with the Fliessian system had been considered representative of his unimpeded intellectual powers, his failure to display any skepticism toward the quirky elements of that system would have called into question his acumen as a scientific thinker. As we will later see, it was deemed better to pathologize both Fliess and Freud and then to assert that Freud had almost miraculously managed to get well on his own.

himself, perhaps influenced by Fliess, was said to have reversed his opposition to cocaine and to have begun prescribing it for his patients (Ebner-Eschenbach/Breuer 1969, p. 24).

Breuer's fullest assessment of Fliess appears in a 1904 letter to the philosopher Friedrich Jodl. While reserving judgment about claims for which the evidence wasn't yet convincing, Breuer called Fliess "one of the most powerful intellects I have ever come across" (Hirschmüller 1989a, p. 156).

24

The Freudian Neuron

1. A HOBBYHORSE

The strangest episode in Freud's intellectual life unfolded between April and October 1895. Off and on during that period, in feverish late-night sessions, he produced, for the eyes of Fliess alone, a manuscript unlike any that preceded or followed it. As we will see, his effort didn't stop there; but the October document is the one that survived. It stands as the most obscure work in the Freud canon. Indeed, most Freudians believe that it doesn't belong there; and that was Freud's subsequent opinion, too. Almost immediately, he apologized to Fliess for having burdened him with such a confused and eccentric text, and he wanted it to be destroyed.

Freud had been working on his "Psychology for Neurologists," as he provisionally called it, for over a month when he told Fliess about his plan. Subsequent reports on June 12, August 6, and August 16, 1895, expressed elation and despair by turns. But after visiting with Fliess in Berlin in early September, Freud was so enthusiastic that, on the train trip home, he immediately began a lengthy, ordered summary of his ideas—hoping, as he confided on September 23, that Fliess would correct and supplement the forthcoming drafts.[1]

On October 8, 1895, Freud mailed Fliess two notebooks—100

manuscript sheets—containing the 40,000 words of what we now know as either the *Entwurf einer Psychologie* ("Outline of a Psychology") or the *Project for a Scientific Psychology*.[2] Both titles originated with the editors of the truncated Freud/Fliess letters of 1950 and 1954; and because James Strachey acceded to the latter name when retranslating the text for the *Standard Edition*, the *Project* title has prevailed in English. But Freud hadn't placed any title on his text, because he regarded it as incomplete.

What Fliess received in October was the first three parts of a four-part exposition. Part II, called "Psychopathology," was at best half completed; it had a section "A" but no "B." And Part IV would never arrive. Yet that last segment, in which Freud had planned to link "the psychopathology of repression" to the workings of the nervous system, was meant to set out the raison d'être of the whole undertaking.

Freud's letters continued to swing between euphoria and gloom until, seven weeks after having sent his document, he expressed regret that he had ever "inflicted" it on Fliess. The whole enterprise, he announced despondently, had amounted to "a kind of madness."* But because he didn't ask for Parts I–III to be returned, they stayed with Fliess and eventually found their way to Marie Bonaparte and thence to Anna Freud. We owe our knowledge of the manuscript partly to the fact that Freud never wished to hear of it again.

Why, then, should we ourselves dwell on the *Project*? Wouldn't we do better to skip a failed experiment and keep focusing on the principal thread of Freud's development toward psychoanalysis? But that development, we have seen, proceeded less through reflections drawn from cases than through top-down speculation with Fliess. Regarded in the light of the correspondence that accompanied and followed it, the *Project* lies directly in the Freudian mainstream. Indeed, it says more about Freud's most tenacious beliefs than do the circumspect works of his "maturity."

Ernest Jones counted twenty-three themes in the *Project*, twenty of

---

* 11/29/95; FF, p. 152. But "madness" sounded unnecessarily self-deprecating to the editors of the 1954 *Origins of Psycho-Analysis*; they translated *Wahnwitz* as the milder "aberration."

which, he perceived, had later figured in psychoanalytic theory.[3] As Sulloway observed,

> there, in the neuroanatomical language of the *Project*, . . . are the concepts of primary and secondary processes; the principles of pleasure-unpleasure, constancy, and reality testing; the concept of cathexis; the theories of psychical regression and hallucination; the systems of perception, memory, unconscious and preconscious psychical activity; and even Freud's wish-fulfillment theory of dreams.[4]

Most of those fundamental notions had been expounded only fleetingly before surfacing in the *Project*.[5] And several of them—Sulloway names them as reality testing, the distinction between primary and secondary processes, and the wish-fulfillment theory of dreams—made their first appearance there.[6]

Especially striking in this regard is the *Project*'s discussion of sleep and dreaming. It substantially anticipated the groundbreaking Chapter 7 of *The Interpretation of Dreams*, which wouldn't see publication until November 1899. That chapter came late in the dream book because Freud wished to imply that he had inferred the mechanism of dream production from a myriad of carefully analyzed instances. In actuality, his theory was virtually complete in October 1895—by which time, so far as we know from the *Project*, only one dream, his own "Irma's Injection," had been submitted to his method of analysis.

We can understand, then, why most knowledgeable Freudians wish that the *Project* had never been resuscitated. Not only is the work scarcely intelligible to most readers; it shows Freud puzzling out important premises without any reference to clinical findings. The whole unwelcome Fliess connection, moreover, is epitomized in the *Project* and the letters pertaining to it. The wish to impress Fliess had been uppermost in Freud's thoughts; and when Fliess raised objections to certain aspects of the text, Freud could muster neither evidence nor reasons in his cause. All he could do was apologize and abase himself, as if selective disapproval from "the Kepler of biology," as Freud called him, had robbed him of all conviction.[7]

Even so, some Freudians, following the example of the renowned neurologist Karl Pribram and the psychoanalyst Merton Gill, take a more sanguine view of the *Project*. In 1976 Pribram and Gill published *Freud's "Project" Re-assessed: Preface to Contemporary Cognitive Theory and Neuropsychology*, a work claiming that the *Project*, far from constituting a perverse jeu d'esprit, had offered a well-conceived "biological cognitive control theory, based on an explicit neuropsychology."[8] And they declared Freud's effort to have been prescient in anticipating such features of modern neuronal theory as "local graded potential changes" in the electrical resistance of neurons.[9]

Was the *Project*, then, a work of genius after all? Or ought Pribram and Gill to have heeded a sage warning from Strachey: "There is a risk that enthusiasm may lead to a distortion of Freud's use of terms and may read into his sometimes obscure remarks modern interpretations that they will not bear"?[10]

2. NEUROLOGY FOR ONE

The central object of Freud's attention in the *Project* was the neuron, which had been given its name, but not discovered, by Heinrich von Waldeyer-Hartz four years earlier.[11] Ever since the theory of organic cells was launched in the 1830s, investigators had suspected that the nervous system contains a base unit in enormous quantities. Reasonably accurate, but not very detailed, drawings of the neuron's main parts—the *cell body* with its nucleus, the *axon* that transmits a charge, and the *dendrites* that receive it—already existed in the 1860s, but their relations and mode of functioning had to await improvements in microscopy and tissue staining. Waldeyer's unified theory was facilitated by Camillo Golgi's silver nitrate stain and by exquisite drawings (also indebted to Golgi) by Santiago Ramón y Cajal, who had already described a de facto neuron in 1889. Ramón y Cajal then continued, after 1891, to reveal crucial properties of the neuron—above all, the one-way transmission of its charge across the synapses between one neuron's axon branches and another's dendrites.

Adherents of psychoanalysis have supplied a predictable footnote to this story. We know that Freud and his successors belatedly credited him, rather than Carl Koller, with the discovery of cocaine anesthesia.

He nursed no such illusion about the neuron, but the Freudian community's hopes were ignited by two erroneous claims in the 1930s to the effect that Freud's early cell studies in the 1880s had resulted in a near miss. Jones needed no further encouragement to assert that the young Freud had been "trembling on the very brink of the important neurone theory" but had once again "narrowly missed world fame."[12] And more recently, Mark Solms has claimed that in 1884 Freud had "paved the way, in part, for the neurone theory" and set forth its "basic elements," though not distinctly enough to be called its discoverer.[13]

Even non-Freudians have taken seriously the idea that the younger Freud may have been a neuron pioneer. If so, however, it is odd that none of the familiar innovators—neither Ramón y Cajal nor Waldeyer, nor Golgi, nor Wilhelm His, nor August Forel, nor Albert von Kölliker—saw fit to acknowledge their debt to him. Kölliker did mention Freud, but only as one of twelve inquirers, starting with Helmholtz in 1842, who held that nerve fibers are attached to the cell body.[14] And, in fact, Freud's contribution lay precisely there. His 1884 paper had dealt with fibrils that make up nerve fibers and with the attachment of those fibers to the axon.[15] That anatomical demonstration was only peripherally germane to the neuron theory, which had to do mainly with the means and directionality of conduction between neurons.

By the time Ramón y Cajal and Waldeyer made their historic announcements, the busy physician Freud had set aside his microscope for good. Nerve composition held so little interest for him in the years just preceding the *Project* that when, in 1893, he referred to "the modern histology of the nervous system," he alluded to the neuron only vaguely and failed to include Waldeyer among its named exponents.[16] Simo Køppe may be justified, then, in surmising that the neuron-centered *Project* of 1895 exemplified that lightbulb experience "when an author suddenly gets the notion to structure his current problems" by invoking "a very radical and reductionistic theory without any previous sign in his official production."[17]

"I am tormented by two aims," Freud wrote to Fliess in May 1895: "to examine what shape the theory of mental functioning takes if one introduces quantitative considerations, a sort of economics of nerve forces; and, second, to peel off from psychopathology a gain for normal psychology."[18] The latter of those goals will sound familiar to any experimental psychologist; normal functioning can be illuminated by the study of deficits and pathologies. But Freud's other aim was more remote and more ambitious.

In the *Project* he would be attempting to sketch a nervous system that registers stimulation from within and without; that partly disposes of that stimulation through reflex action; that inhibits or "binds" the rest of it, making it available for various uses; that operates largely outside the subject's consciousness; that refashions sense data and drive-generated desires into images that play on a mental screen; that reserves small quantities of its energy for testing those images against reality, so that appropriate self-interested action can be carried out; and that, when it malfunctions, does so in a way that yields the familiar symptoms of the neuroses and psychoses.

Such an undertaking was not unique in kind. A number of mid-nineteenth-century physicians, seeking some organic basis for the freedom and compassion that appeared to be excluded by their own materialism, had speculated boldly about the relation between mind and brain. The authors of such tracts included the University of Vienna's own Carl von Rokitansky and Josef Hyrtl; and Theodor Meynert's "brain mythology" was in part an expression of the same quest. Meynert perceived in the brain the fossil record of human evolution, whereby a "secondary ego," capable of empathy and altruism as well as intellectual discipline, had been superimposed on a "primary ego" that demanded the gratification of animal needs.[19]

In venturing into such vast terrain, Freud also had a recent example to follow: a tract by Sigmund Exner, his former teacher and senior colleague in Ernst Brücke's Physiological Institute, and Brücke's successor in the university chair of physiology. In the year before Freud undertook his speculations in April 1895, Exner published his much-discussed *Outline of a Physiological Explanation of Psychical Phenomena*, a work that resembles the *Project* in several key respects.*

---

* Exner 1894. See J, 1:380–381. Jones reminds us that Freud may also have been inspired, with respect to cerebral physiology, by the appearance in 1893 of Ernst Fleischl von Marxow's posthumous collected papers.

It is hard to believe that Freud could have dared to write a neuropsychological manifesto without having the example of Exner's *Outline* before his eyes.

But there were two cardinal differences between Exner's undertaking and Freud's. Exner, a distinguished physiologist who had made important discoveries about perception, vision, and the brain, had wished to construct a model of the nervous system that would rest on well-established experimental findings. Freud, however, would be devising his theory entirely from abstract considerations. And second, some of those considerations would be idiosyncratic. Freud meant to model, and thus to legitimize, psychological operations in whose existence he alone believed.

Indeed, the immediate impetus for Freud's speculations was almost certainly his dissatisfaction with Breuer's "Theoretical" chapter in *Studies on Hysteria*. Although he still shared some important tenets with his former collaborator, he wanted, as he told Fliess, to "wholly dissociate [him]self" from that chapter.[20] He didn't say why, but the reason is apparent. Breuer had attempted to show that someone could fall victim to hysteria without involving "defense" against sexual trauma—and defense, alias repression, was now the centerpiece of Freud's conception of the way the mind works in neurosis, psychosis, and everyday life.

The real point of the *Project*, in fact, would be to show that a normal "primary defense," the blockage and diversion of excitation, forms the neurological underpinning for "secondary defense," or repression. If Freud could secure that linkage, he believed, the array of concepts he had mobilized to explain the psychoneuroses—not just repression but also regression, abreaction, and even symbolic symptom formation—could be represented as possessing a solid organic basis. And if so, no setbacks in his therapeutic work would ever compel him to forgo the ongoing codification and elaboration of those ideas.

"The intention," begins the *Project*, "is to furnish a psychology that shall be a natural science: that is, to represent psychical processes as quantitatively determinate states of specifiable material particles, thus making those processes perspicuous and free from contradiction."[21] Freud could not have known that there are some 86 billion of those "material particles" in the brain alone, or that the nucleus of each neuron contains a genome consisting of some 20,000 genes. Indeed, he didn't know the most important facts of all: that neurons are situated apart from one another; that each of them generates the electrical force that it needs; that they are always switched either "on" or "off," with no intermediate state; and that their function is to transmit information, not energy. Those handicaps would cause him to think hydraulically about transactions that, in fact, require only minuscule amounts of electricity as one neuron simultaneously activates many of its neighbors.

Like most other inquirers in his era, Freud conceived of the nervous system as a continuously linked network of "pipes" conveying a charge. Such a conception left nothing for neurons to do but to cope, as best they could, with excitation that was forever bombarding them from the external world and the body's own animal demands. Ideas and actions, then, could result only from an accumulation of nervous energy beyond a threshold level. But why, then, weren't the neurons and the nervous system as a whole being continually flooded with over-stimulation? That was the question Freud had to address but couldn't answer satisfactorily in the current state of his knowledge.

"What distinguishes activity from rest," he wrote, "is to be regarded as Q, subject to the general laws of motion."[22] He didn't venture to characterize the nature of Q, the excitation impinging on the nervous system. He simply referred to it as "quantity." Inside the system, Q was transmuted to $Q\eta$—"Q-eta"—a force of more manageable intensity that *cathected* (occupied) individual neurons or clusters of them.* Freud was inconsistent in labeling those two kinds of energy, but the difference between them was clear enough. A given sum of Q, the activating force, would impart a proportional electric current (Q-eta) to the nerves, which would then absorb, divert, or discharge that current, depending on the mental function to be served.

For the enactment of those transactions, Freud posited the existence

---

* *Cathexis* was the *Standard Edition*'s translation, in 1922, of Freud's *Besetzung*, "occupation" or "possession." (See SE, 3:63n.) At first Freud disapproved of that Greekifying neologism, but then he warmed to it.

of three kinds of neurons, which he named φ (phi), ψ (psi), and ω (omega).[23] Phi neurons, he divined, were thoroughly permeable, so as to be always ready to receive new sensations. Psi neurons, in contrast, did retain at least some "quantity," so as to record and hold memories. And omega neurons possessed not only a peculiar exemption from "quantity" but also an ability to turn other neurons' quantities into qualities, thus endowing the mind with consciousness.

Mysterious as the $\varphi\psi\omega$ system may appear to us, Freud envisioned it as operating in a straightforward mechanical way. Although the neurons in his model were attached to one another, "contact barriers" could nevertheless block some or all of one neuron's Q-eta from continuing along a path of conduction. In such events, the contact barrier would shunt Q-eta, by means of a "side-cathexis," onto a lateral neuron, where it could now serve a desired function. Here was "defense" on the most elemental level; but Freud regarded even complex repression, as in the isolation of a painful memory from awareness, as working by means of the same mechanism.

Freud didn't claim that he had encountered any evidence for his neuronal scheme. At present, he wrote, "nothing is known in support of the distinction" between phi and psi neurons; and ideally, "we should not have *invented* them [but] *found* them already in existence."[24] With an indolent wave toward empiricism, he added that "testing our theory upon factual material" would be a worthwhile endeavor. But the founder of psychoanalysis was never disposed to take such pains, and he wouldn't have known how to begin doing so.

Was the *Project* even minimally coherent? Couched, for pages at a time, in a maddening shorthand—"If $Q\eta$ in φ gives rise to a cathexis in ψ, then $3(Q\eta)$ is expressed by a cathexis in $\psi_1 + \psi_2 + \psi_3$"—it has struck some readers as sheer gibberish.[25] Others have grappled with Freud's argument but judged it to be circular. An explanation cannot succeed if it merely supplies a new name for the phenomenon to be explained. Freud appeared to be flouting that rule when he accounted for consciousness by referring to a hypothetical "consciousness neuron," omega, which had no other attributes than consciousness itself and a baffling absence of quantity.

We can accede to Pribram and Gill's judgment that many apparent obscurities in the *Project* would be intelligible to a trained neurologist. At the same time, however, those coauthors largely overlooked the hydraulic nature of Freud's model, with its sums of energy coursing through a system that can protect itself from overload only by erecting diversionary barriers. That drastic scenario caused Freud to decree, erroneously, that neurons tend to divest themselves of quantity and to seek a state of total rest.[26] Thanks to his terminological confusion—he repeatedly wrote that the nervous system tends toward *constancy* when he really meant *inertia*—Pribram and Gill mistook his neuronal nihilism for the more defensible and demonstrable law of homeostasis, or the equalizing of positive and negative forces.[27]

As soon as Freud, in the *Project*, contemplated internally generated needs for food, sex, and respiration, he had to face a major challenge to neuronal inertia. In order to receive nourishment, for instance, the organism must remain in a state of tension until food has been located and ingested; a repeated early return to stasis would soon prove fatal.[28] The inertia principle, then, was untenable. But Freud conceded only that in certain circumstances—including the need to breathe!—"the nervous system is obliged to abandon its original trend to inertia."[29] Belief in that trend had already become a permanent article of his faith. It would eventuate in the quasi-mystical "Nirvana principle" and "death instinct" that would occupy him in *Beyond the Pleasure Principle* (1920).

Although the *Project* was meant to cover a formidable number of mental functions, the undertaking wouldn't be worthwhile, by Freud's reckoning, unless it could successfully negotiate the gap between normal and abnormal psychology. But when he turned to that task in Part II, "Psychopathology," he found himself at sea. Promising a neuronal account of psychopathology in general, he settled for dealing only with hysteria; and even at that, he neglected his main novelty, the hysterical conversion of repressed affect into symbol-bearing somatic impairments. It was more prudent to stay within the psychical domain and speculate about the neuronal economy of substituting one *idea* for another. But even then, Freud had to retreat from $\varphi\psi\omega$ calculations and revert to the commonsense language of his recent papers on the psycho- and "current" neuroses.

3. THE *PROJECT*'S GHOST

It is easy to understand the relief with which Freudians have greeted Freud's November 29, 1895, repudiation of the *Project* as a folly that he was now putting behind him forever. But one need only continue reading the uncensored Fliess letters to see that this was a false ending. It was in June 1896, for example, seven months after calling the *Project* crazy, that Freud pleaded for Fliess's help in exchanging psychological propositions for physiological ones.[30] His project had by no means concluded with the *Project*.

Indeed, scarcely a week after his November 1895 disavowal, Freud's hopes had been revived by a remark from Fliess that the work was still salvageable and might lead to a publication.[31] After three further weeks, again inspired by Fliess, he sketched some lineaments of a "completely revised" theory.[32] The work then continued, off and on, for many more months, until, on December 6, 1896, more than a year after the famous admission of failure, victory was proclaimed. Freud announced that he had now discerned the relations among the elements of the nervous system that must be yielding perception, consciousness, preconsciousness, and unconsciousness.[33] He had arrived at nothing less than the "topographic" model of the mind—one of the triple pillars of Freudian metapsychology.[34]

He had done so, moreover, not by generalizing from clinical data but by pressing ahead with his neuronal modeling. The letter of December 6, 1896, contained such formulations as these:

> Our psychic mechanism has come into being by a process of stratification. . . . The different registrations are also separated . . . according to the neurones which are their vehicles. . . . W [*Wahrnehmungen*] are neurones in which *perceptions* originate. . . . The neurones of consciousness would once again be perceptual neurones and in themselves without memory.[35]

The same letter showed that at the end of 1896 Freud was still moving toward Fliess's variety of reductionism, not away from it as friendly historians would have us believe. His letters throughout that year display a continuing effort to blend his neuronal ideas with Fliess's system. All of his "$\varphi\psi\omega$ theories," he wrote on January 1, would need to be completely revised in the light of Fliess's nose-related explanation of migraine headaches.[36] And now it was clear to him that a "surplus of Q" in "nasal regions" "forces its way into ψ and . . . the free ψ energy flows to the seat of the eruption."[37]

In its extended epistolary context, then, the *Project* offered copious signs that the Freud of the mid-1890s was not an empirical psychologist. Rather, he was a manic speculator, "fantasizing, interpreting, and guessing," as he himself confided to Fliess, toward "bold but beautiful" revelations.[38] The whole *Project* affair pointed toward a conclusion that he would embrace, with injured but truculent pride, several years later, at a time when Fliess no longer respected him: "I am actually not at all a man of science, not an observer, not an experimenter, not a thinker. I am by temperament nothing but a conquistador—an adventurer, if you want it translated—with all the curiosity, daring, and tenacity characteristic of a man of this sort."[39]

It was a foregone conclusion that Ernst Kris and Anna Freud would omit that definitive self-assessment—the most revealing confession Freud ever made—from *The Origins of Psycho-Analysis*. Neutralizing the effect of the *Project* per se, however, was a trickier affair. As usual, the correct line was laid down by Ernest Jones. Yes, he granted, the *Project* was ingenious—even, in its way, "a magnificent *tour de force*"[40]— but it was still beholden to the old-fashioned scientism of Freud's teachers, whereby brain physiology was deemed more authentic than psychology. The *Project*, then, was just "a last desperate effort to cling to the safety of cerebral anatomy."[41]

At the same time, wrote Jones, the *Project* stood apart as an airy philosophical exercise, divorced from the inferences of the consulting room. "Never again until the last period of his life," wrote the house biographer, "and never before so far as we know, did Freud indulge in deductive reasoning as he did here."[42] Although Freud's "scientific imagination" had found a cathartic release, Jones added, he soon happily "returned to the empirical experience of his clinical observations"[43]— and *that* was what bestowed the gift of psychoanalysis on the world. Jones's readers were thus being asked to forget what they had just been told: that fundamental elements of Freud's theory were already crystallized in an exercise of neurological fantasy.

Though crude and easily refuted, Jones's attempt at damage control was good enough for the 1950s, when psychoanalysis was flourishing. A more sophisticated approach would be needed later. It was supplied, in a closely reasoned argument, by Mark Solms and Michael Saling in 1986. The real lineage of psychoanalysis, those authors claimed, runs not through the *Project* but through *On Aphasia* four years earlier.[44] Here, then, was an attempted "side-cathexis" in the realm of genealogy, not just circumventing the *Project* but putting a more respectable pre-analytic work in its place.

In *On Aphasia* Freud had explicitly rejected the idea that a mental function can be housed within specific nervous units.[45] Although he had seemingly gone on to support that very idea in the *Project*, Solms and Saling held that the *Project* wasn't really a neurological tract but only a misguided attempt at "translation" of Freud's solid clinical knowledge.[46] That knowledge, they said, outlasted the *Project* and, once rejoined with the sound epistemic principles that had governed *On Aphasia*, it allowed psychoanalysis to evolve along cogent scientific lines. Freud "abandoned the *Project* and continued to explain his clinical findings in terms of a psychological theory"; and "any aspects of the *Project* that were retained in later psychoanalytic theory . . . were not neurological constructs at all."[47] But Solms and Saling, no less than Jones, were trying to exorcise facts that wouldn't go away. Nothing about *On Aphasia* had been uniquely "Freudian." It was in the *Project*, rather, that Freud announced his theory of sleep, dreaming, and dream interpretation, and also where he developed his principles of neuronal inertia and of primary and secondary processes. There, too, he significantly amplified "defense," which now encompassed normal as well as abnormal operations. And a year later his ongoing meditation on the neuron issued directly in his topographic model of the mind. To exclude the *Project* from the parentage of psychoanalysis would be as willful as denying the relevance of *The Origin of Species* to *The Descent of Man*.

An essential aspect of the psychoanalytic legend is the assertion of a clean break between Freud's "physiological" early phase and his "psychological" mature one. Presumably, then, such common psycho-analytic terms as *excitation* and *cathexis* had been stripped of the neuro-logical meaning they possessed in the *Project*. When Solms and Saling declared that the remnants of the *Project*, in their later embodiment, "were not neurological constructs at all," they were adhering to the establishment's line. Yet neither Jones nor Solms and Saling could offer evidence in favor of their view; they were simply echoing a claim insis-tently made by Freud himself.

Freud adopted a strangely urgent tone when distancing his theory from its organic premises. "Psycho-analysis," he wrote in 1915, "must keep itself free from any hypothesis that is alien to it, whether of an anatomical, chemical or physiological kind."[48] In the same year he wrote, as if referring to anyone but himself, "Every attempt . . . to think of ideas as stored up in nerve-cells and of excitations as travelling along nerve-fibres, has miscarried completely."[49] And again, in 1916: "I know nothing that could be of less interest to me for the psychological under-standing of anxiety than a knowledge of the path of the nerves along which its excitations pass."[50]

Indeed, with characteristic slyness, Freud managed to reverse the linkage he had forged between neurology and psychoanalysis. On sev-eral occasions he predicted that scientists would someday discover a neurochemical basis for phenomena that he had been obliged to explain in macroscopic observational terms:

> We have found it necessary to hold aloof from biological consider-ations during our psycho-analytic work and to refrain from using them for heuristic purposes, so that we may not be misled in our impartial judgement of the psycho-analytic facts before us. But after we have completed our psycho-analytic work we shall have to find a point of contact with biology; and we may rightly feel glad if that contact is already assured at one important point or another.[51]

Or again: "We must recollect that all our provisional ideas in psychol-ogy will presumably some day be based on an organic substructure."[52]

Such admissions, which are almost always greeted as tokens of

Freud's modesty and deference to hard science, were actually his way of projecting a false assurance that he had taken his ideas entirely from therapeutic experience; that, accordingly, he couldn't be charged with reliance on outdated physiology; that sheer attention to patients' behavior had enabled him to correctly interpret effects whose ultimate cause is body chemistry; and that, consequently, he was destined to be vindicated by the men in laboratory coats. If readers were to suspect that the causal reasoning behind his zero-sum allocations of "libido" among various "objects" and "aims" had been worked out long in advance, and by reference to a defunct understanding of the nervous system, the game would have been up.

Was Freud's master concept of psychical energy, alias "psychical intensity," anything other than Q-eta, or the *Project*'s quantity of imagined nerve force? Strachey—who, to his credit, faced the significance of the *Project* for later theory—noted that equivalence in several of Freud's works ranging in date from 1895 to 1915.[53] Pribram and Gill, likewise feeling no reason to deny the persistence of Freud's neurological framework, went a good deal farther:

> Our analysis shows that Freud initially formulated the mechanisms of mental function on the basis of his biological and neurological knowledge. He then chose, for a variety of reasons, to leave these neurological foundations implicit—indeed on occasion to deny their existence. Nevertheless he kept the mechanisms basically intact.[54]

The brain researchers Robert McCarley and J. Allan Hobson, no friends to psychoanalysis, reached the same conclusion:

> Freud's psychic model was quite simply derived from the physiological constructs of the "Project." The psychic and neural agencies are virtually the same, their organizational sequence and function are the same, the direction of flow of energy is the same, and the reflex model is retained. The psychic "elements" share the properties of the "Project's" "neurons" in that "excitation" is "transmitted" according to "conductive resistance." "Association" results from "facilitating paths."

Freud even talked about "currents of excitation." In short, virtually the entire neural model of the "Project" was retained despite Freud's assertion of creating a psychological model.[55]

Independently, moreover, the information scientist Don R. Swanson examined all of Freud's metapsychological remarks over a forty-year period, deploying such crucial terms as *excitation, energy, cathexis, quantity of affect, sensory current,* and *impulse,* and found that those concepts retained the operational meaning they had held in the *Project.*[56] That fact ought to have been worrisome news for Freudians. As Swanson knew, nothing resembling Freud's nerve force Q-eta has been found to exist. To recapitulate, the human organism doesn't send sums of energy through its neurons in proportion to stimulation received; nor, a fortiori, is that energy subject to division and diversion; nor, therefore, is the nervous system involved in redirecting the traffic of "quantity."

Just such redirection, however, was the essence of Freud's "defense," and everything he would assert about the maintenance of order in the psyche depended on it. Dreams were compromise formations because the strength of scandalous wishes had to be "defended against"; errors were provoked by the same mechanism, as were neurotic symptoms; even our laughter at jokes resulted from defense against aggressive thoughts; and sublimation, the very engine of civilization, worked by a defensive siphoning off of quantity from the sex drive. Behind each of those supposed effects lay the *Project*'s mistaken conservation-of-energy model and its "side-cathexes."

As E. M. Thornton noted in the 1980s, the "conversion" of thoughts into symptoms that symbolize them was an ancient and medieval, not a modern, idea—namely, the idea of possession by movements of the spirit.[57] For that very reason, Freud would need to place it within an objective-looking frame of reference, with imagined quantities of stimuli flowing between one "innervation" and another. But his simu-lacrum of rigor couldn't withstand examination. Hence his need to characterize the "psychical apparatus" as only a fictive construct after all—a mere metaphor that would have to suffice until something better came along.

"In developing a new science," Freud would tell his American pupil Smiley Blanton, "one has to make its theories vague. You cannot make things clear-cut."[58] Mixing quanta with qualia and energetics with exegetics, he had forged in psychoanalysis the clever absurdity of an *ambiguous science*.[59] Its oxymoronic character was—and remains, for science-envying humanists—the principal source of its appeal. Where else could we turn for an interpretive free-for-all that is sanctioned by a tale of exploratory and therapeutic heroism yet also by a sober idiom of mechanical cause and effect? The real significance of the *Project* is that it equipped the psychoanalytic Freud with that idiom, safely detached from testable propositions.

25

Diminished Capacity

1. A SECOND "COCAINE EPISODE"

As Ernest Jones delicately acknowledged, a "change in his personality . . . seems to have come over [Freud] in the early nineties," whereby "moods and intuition" were permitted greater sway than immersion in clinical data.[1] One such mood was a proud but disorienting sense that he had come into possession of knowledge beyond the ability of his colleagues to fathom or even face. Sexuality, he declared to Fliess in April 1893, is "the key that unlocks everything."[2] But "I am pretty much alone here in the elucidation of the neuroses," he added in May 1894; "They look upon me as pretty much of a monomaniac, while I have the distinct feeling that I have touched upon one of the great secrets of nature."[3]

That feeling was most dramatically embodied in the *Project for a Scientific Psychology*. As we have seen, the main reason why the *Project* has caused so much uneasiness among Freudians is that, in writing it, Freud didn't bother to pretend that he was resting his conclusions on clinical evidence. That text, though never published in his lifetime, inaugurated a radical tendency in his manner of reasoning: a thrust toward ultimate reduction. Now he believed he could X-ray the mind whenever he wished, discounting surface contours of circumstance and behavior while appealing to explanatory factors at the deepest cellular level, to which he alone could penetrate through sheer intellection.

The *Project*'s manner of composition also appears to have been new. After a busy workday in the summer and fall of 1895, Freud would typically be exhausted by 10 p.m. Somehow, though, he then revived and gave himself over to intense and excited speculation. "During the past weeks," he told Fliess in May 1895, "I have . . . spent the hours of the night from eleven to two with . . . fantasizing, interpreting, and guessing."[4]

A typical report of such a nocturnal feat was that of October 20, 1895, written during what was already a "three-day migraine." "Now listen to this," Freud wrote:

> During an industrious night last week, when I was suffering from that degree of pain which brings about the optimal condition for my mental activities, the barriers suddenly lifted, the veils dropped, and everything became transparent—from the details of the neuroses to the determinants of consciousness. Everything seemed to fall into place, the cogs meshed, I had the impression that the thing now really was a machine that shortly would function on its own. . . . Naturally, I can scarcely manage to contain my delight.[5]

As we recall, however, this exhilaration was bordered by plunges into disillusionment and depression. Just a few days before "everything became transparent," everything had gone dark. "For two weeks," Freud wrote, "I was in the throes of writing fever, believed that I had found the secret, now I know that I still haven't, and have again dropped the whole business."[6]

At one earlier period in his life, in 1884–85, Freud had repeatedly experienced late-night "intellectual elation," one of whose effects had been to "alienate [him] from [his] surroundings" as he glimpsed a more audacious order of knowledge. A cocaine user at the time, he had sat up with the combined morphine and cocaine addict Ernst Fleischl, who, when jolted into alertness by injected cocaine, would race from topic to topic with Mephistophelean ease, dazzling Freud/Faust with visions of previously unsuspected marvels. Now, after midnight in 1895,

Freud was the only person left awake in Berggasse 19; but his stimulant hadn't changed. As even the psychoanalytic loyalist George Makari concedes, the *Project* was "fueled by cocaine."[7] And it may have been a brief abstention from cocaine that left Freud puzzled and mortified by "the state of mind in which [he] hatched the psychology."

No one has taken the 1890s cocaine factor more seriously than did Anna Freud and the other postwar shapers of the Freud legend. They displayed their concern by almost completely withholding relevant information both from *The Origins of Psycho-Analysis* and from Jones's cagily supervised biography. The censorship couldn't be total, for in *The Interpretation of Dreams* (1900) Freud had repeatedly alluded to his preoccupation with the drug. Among his seventeen long dreams analyzed in the book, no fewer than eight explicitly involved cocaine. And in discussing the centerpiece dream, "Irma's Injection," he had remarked that he "was making frequent use of cocaine at that time to reduce some troublesome nasal swellings."[8] The raw fact of cocaine consumption, then, was undeniable. But the psychoanalytic establishment pretended that cocaine had left Freud's mental state unaffected, and the letters that pointed to a different conclusion were suppressed.

Jones played his part through a deft misdirection gambit. In a chapter titled "The Cocaine Episode," as we recall, he candidly reviewed and deplored Freud's excesses of 1884–87, implying that the termination of that youthful folly had laid to rest the matter of drug craving. As for the nineties, he allowed that Fliess had counseled Freud to take cocaine as a medicine; but Jones said nothing about either self-directed use or cognitive and emotional consequences. For all we could discern from reading Jones, Fliess's prescription might as well have been for eye drops or antacid.

Jones knew exactly what he was doing. In a 1952 letter to Siegfried Bernfeld, he estimated that Freud had used cocaine "off and on for fifteen years."[9] Thus he privately believed, but wanted the public to remain unaware, that the drug had influenced Freud until 1899.* And

---

* Kurt Eissler, who surpassed even Jones in his access to privileged information, remarked that "Freud stopped using [cocaine] after 1900" (Eissler 2001, p. 25n).

in another 1952 letter, this one to Bernfeld's wife, Jones confessed that he was "afraid that Freud took more cocaine than he should though I am not mentioning that [in the biography]."[10] It was precisely because Jones belatedly perceived, and was appalled by, a connection between cocaine and the airier claims of psychoanalysis that he channeled his readers' curiosity to the less significant "cocaine episode" of the 1880s.

Jones's confidential reference to cocaine use "off and on for fifteen years" supplies us with a precious datum. Because the bachelor Freud is known to have cherished the drug for its imagination-inflaming aphrodisiac capacity, most students of his life have assumed that he stopped consuming it around the date of his marriage.[11] Perhaps he did, temporarily, but we have no evidence pointing to that result. Besides, it was the married state, not chaste bachelorhood, that entailed a chronic performance anxiety for which cocaine might have appealed as a remedy. And it was ten months *after* the wedding that Freud wrote his anti-Erlenmeyer polemic, in which he boasted of his personal habit without saying whether or not it was ongoing at the time.

In 1887, we perceive, Freud retained both his affection for the drug and his belief in its safety for nonaddictive personalities such as his own. (In fact, however, he was already addicted to nicotine.) His first surviving reference to cocaine in the Fliess correspondence, in May 1893, tells of self-initiated recourse to the drug: "A short time ago I interrupted (for one hour) a severe migraine of my own with cocaine; the effect set in only after I had cocainized the opposite side as well; but then it did so promptly."[12] As Jones reminds us, Freud was "a martyr to migraine throughout his life."[13] Overlooking cocaine's vasodilating rebound effect of producing further headaches, he had apparently treated his migraines with cocaine at least until 1887; and here he was doing so again in 1893.

Whether or not there was an "off and on" hiatus between two cocaine phases in Freud's life, we know that his relation to the drug took a novel turn in the 1890s. Earlier, he had hoped to achieve renown by tying his name to the propagation of a medical wonder. Now, however, he would become Fliess's cocaine patient, taking the drug on his friend's counsel as well as on his own initiative and reporting only to Fliess about its effects.

It may seem ironic that Freud appointed Fliess to be his drug physician. After all, Fliess's awareness of cocaine, like that of other European healers, was ultimately traceable to Freud's own 1884 essay "On Coca"; and Fliess isn't known to have exhibited an interest in cocaine before making Freud's acquaintance. But in the nineties, Freud's continued or resumed use of cocaine was reinforced by Fliess's theory about its curative power; and, as we will now see, the side effects of the cure prompted Freud to reach for even more cocaine.

2. NASAL MANEUVERS

Let us try to sort out this complex matter with a reconstructed history. When Freud, despite all that had recently emerged about the dangers of cocaine, told his new friend about his successes with the magical medicine, Fliess evidently tried cocaine therapy on his German patients' miscellaneous ills. He favored brushing the undiluted powder directly into the sufferer's nostrils. Thanks to the absorptive property of mucous membranes, that method of delivery provided exceptionally quick access to the reward centers of the brain, yielding analgesic and euphoric relief from whatever symptoms the patient had been experiencing. Follow-up was apparently judged to be unnecessary.

In this manner Fliess rashly inferred that cocaine must be efficacious against a host of problems, including menstrual pain, gastrointestinal distress, neuralgia, migraine, and irregularities of heartbeat and breathing; and on that basis he assembled his version of the nasal reflex neurosis. It allegedly operated in both directions. A digestive pang could trigger inflammation in the "stomachache spot" (*Magenschmerzstelle*) within the nose, but another inflammation in that spot could be the cause of a gastric upset. And how had Fliess located the stomachache spot in the first place? Simple: a few minutes after a cocaine application to a certain part of the nose, the gastric pain would vanish, proving, to Fliess's satisfaction, the existence of a reflex circuit.[14]

As we know, Freud had already been prescribing cocaine for his patients' and his own neuralgias, migraines, and chronic indigestion, among other miseries; and he rarely neglected to describe his current medical state to Fliess. Suddenly all was clear to Fliess: Freud himself

must be a victim of the nasal reflex neurosis! Without noticing the spu-
riousness of Fliess's diagnostic and therapeutic reasoning—which, after
all, only duplicated his own logic when he had first declared cocaine
to be a panacea—Freud humbly accepted that conclusion and began
the indicated regimen of powdering his nose with laboratory-grade
cocaine.

The inevitable result was swelling, infection, and necrosis of the
affected tissue.* Unsurprisingly, Fliess, too, began undergoing the same
damage. But because neither Freud nor Fliess wished to blame cocaine for
any untoward effects, they interpreted their nasal problems as further
proof that the NRN had them in its grip. And thus they took quixotic
remedial action, applying still more cocaine to their injured nostrils.

A new development now rendered Freud more dependent than
ever on his friend. Since 1889 he had been suffering from an occasional
irregular heartbeat, but in the spring of 1894 the condition became
more alarming. During a period of attempted abstinence from cigars—
for Fliess had continually urged him to quit smoking—he had suddenly
experienced "a severe cardiac misery":

> The most violent arrhythmia, constant tension, pressure, burning in
> the heart region; shooting pains down my left arm; some dyspnea
> [shortness of breath], all of it essentially in attacks extending contin-
> uously over two-thirds of the day; . . . and with it a feeling of depres-
> sion, which took the form of visions of death and departure.[15]

Once his symptoms had spontaneously abated over a two-day
period, Freud swallowed his pride and consulted Breuer, wishing to
learn whether the correct diagnosis was mere hypochondria, nicotine
withdrawal, or, as he suspected, chronic myocarditis; Breuer sensibly
advised him to get examined by a cardiologist. Before doing so, however,
Freud brought his worries to Fliess. "You people," as he put it—
referring to actual physicians as opposed to mere psychotherapists—
"know what to make of it all."[16] Over the next several years, while

---

* For the physiology of those effects, including the temporary relief as well as the
rebound, see Thornton 1984, pp. 137–138.

obsessing about Fliess's own health as if he feared losing a protective parent, Freud repeatedly described his latest symptoms (now mostly nasal) and begged to be told any withheld truth about his weakened heart. "I would like you to continue to be right," he told Fliess in April 1895, "—that the nose may have a large share in it and the heart a small one."[17]

Neither Freud nor Fliess nor Jones nor Max Schur wished to consider that Freud's heart condition may itself have been a cocaine effect, brought on by years of oral ingestion followed by the more drastic regimen prescribed by Fliess. But even if we suppose, as Freud himself did, that a flu virus initially caused his heart to skip, his greatly intensified symptoms in 1894 were almost surely cocaine related. And he had good professional reasons to draw that inference if he had been disposed to do so.

Physicians had already remarked on many cases of cocaine-induced tachycardia—a phenomenon that had been self-experimentally corroborated and reported by W. A. Hammond in the same 1886 lecture that Freud had summoned to his defense against Erlenmeyer.* In his talk to the New York Neurological Society on November 2, 1886, Hammond referred to his own "palpitation" and "exaggerated action of the heart" after a cocaine injection. His patients, too, had experienced "extraordinary action of the heart, increased temperature and blood-pressure, and indisposition to sleep."[18] Since 1885, moreover, the medical journals had been telling of fatal cardiac arrest during surgeries in which cocaine had been placed in direct contact with mucous membranes, especially nasal ones.[19] The ability of cocaine to produce cardiac symptoms is now so well known that in 2008 the American Heart Association warned physicians to ask apparent victims of a heart attack if they had recently used the drug.[20]

Having chosen to regard himself as a victim of the nasal reflex neurosis, Freud could not expect cocaine to suffice as the means of cure.

---

* Incidentally, Hammond also told of "an inordinate desire to write" while he was in the grip of cocaine insomnia. "He wrote eight or ten pages of foolscap," according to the summary of his talk, "and thought that it was the best that he had ever written, but the next morning he found that it was the most extreme nonsense" (Hammond 1886, p. 638).

As we know, Fliess envisaged three progressive therapies for the NRN: nasally applied cocaine, cauterization of the offending "spot" within the nose, and surgical removal of the usual locus of infection, a swollen turbinate bone. Each action rendered the next one more likely, causing injury and inflammation that told Fliess he was combating a stubbornly recalcitrant disorder. And thus it was that Freud, having already had his "stopped up" nose cauterized twice by November 1893, underwent at least two more operations at Fliess's hands: one in January 1895 and the other in the following August.[21]

The nature of those treatments is uncertain. It is possible that by mid-1895 Freud, having reached stage three of Fliessian debilitation, submitted to a bone removal. That was what Schur apparently believed.[22] Jones, however, surmised that both procedures were cauterizations, supplemented by "constantly prescribed" cocaine treatment, "in which Fliess [but not Freud?] was a great believer."[23] By the summer of 1895, we find Freud pleading with his scalpel-wielding friend to "let me off as far as anatomical health is concerned and endeavor only to reinstate functional health," presumably through further cauterization.[24] Nevertheless, when he did come to Berlin for more treatment, he was still sufficiently trusting to bring along his brother Alexander—allegedly another sufferer from neurasthenia—for a nasal procedure of his own.

In order to make sense of Freud's health reports in 1895, we need to bear in mind that he rejoiced in persistent nasal trouble because it told him that Fliess had been right: he was suffering from a mere neurosis, not a failing heart. Hence his exhilaration on January 24, March 4, April 20, and April 27 of that year:

In the last few days I have felt quite unbelievably well. . . . Last time I wrote you . . . that a few viciously bad days had followed during which a cocainization of the left nostril had helped me to an amazing extent. . . . The next day I kept the nose under cocaine, which one should not really do; that is, I repeatedly painted it to prevent the renewed occurrence of swelling; during this time I discharged what in my experience is a copious amount of thick pus; and since then I have felt wonderful, as though there had never been anything wrong at all.

On the last day you were here, I suddenly discharged several scabs from the right side, the one not operated on. As early as the next day there appeared thick, old pus in large clots. . . . Since then the nose has again been flooded, only today has the purulent secretion become somewhat less dense. . . . Though not designed to make one feel at ease, this information affords some pleasure because it emphasizes once again that the condition of the heart depends upon the condition of the nose.

If empyema [pus accumulation] is the main problem, then the aspect of danger is eliminated, and the continuation of the symptoms for a few months will not kill me. . . . Today I can write because I have more hope; I pulled myself out of a miserable attack with a cocaine application.

Since the last cocainization three circumstances have continued to coincide: (1) I feel well; (2) I am discharging ample amounts of pus; (3) I am feeling *very* well. Thus I want nothing further to do with a heart condition.[25]

We see, then, that Freud's intellectual support of Fliess's disputed syndrome—a support that otherwise appears incomprehensibly obtuse— was at least partly determined by concern about his own health. Scientific doubts, though they must have occurred to him, counted for little when weighed against the fear of imminent death. And that fear in turn ensured that Freud would be immoderate with the drug that always restored his peace of mind. As he put it succinctly on June 12, 1895, "I need a lot of cocaine."[26]

3. THE COCAINE SELF

In the 1890s, cocaine appears to have figured in some of Freud's traits that, though observable in his earlier years, now stood out as a significant cluster. His wild and frequent mood swings, ranging from joy to the blackest depression, were more pronounced in this period than in any other; they suggest the rush and backlash from cocaine. So, too, cocaine may account for the extraordinary vividness of his midnineties

10. *The psychiatrist Theodor Meynert, Freud's mentor, later his foe*

11. The master hypnotherapist Hippolyte Bernheim

12. Pierre Janet, Freud's chief rival as a psychological theorist

13. Josef and Mathilde Breuer

14. Bertha Pappenheim, alias "Anna O."

15. Anna von Lieben, the patient who most influenced Freud

16. Freud and his dear friend Wilhelm Fliess, about 1895

17. Emma Eckstein, patient to both Freud and Fliess

18. Otto Bauer and his sister Ida, alias "Dora"

dreams, whose interpretation would soon form a cornerstone of psycho-analytic theory. Again, as Louis Lewin would put it in 1924, long-term cocaine use brings "weakness of the sexual functions accompanied by augmented erotic desires."[27] Freud lived the same paradox, experiencing both a heightened obsession with sexuality—notably emphasizing its "perversions"—and more frequent bouts of impotence.

Then, too, there is the familiar tendency of cocaine to incite irratio-nal hostility to the user's well-wishers, especially if the latter express reservations about the drug. To be sure, Freud had displayed a para-noid streak before ever trying cocaine. Nevertheless, it is suggestive that just when Fliess became (after Fleischl) Freud's second "cocaine brother," Freud developed a searing if intermittent contempt for Breuer.* Except on the days when Breuer made a special effort to praise Freud's ideas and thus appeared to be a splendid fellow after all, he now personified for Freud the intellectual cowardice and obstruc-tionism of establishment science and medicine.

This was no small matter as a sign of personality change. Freud's longtime mentor, the dedicatee of *On Aphasia*, had been the man he most admired in the world and the one to whom he was most indebted for the launching of his career. To talk with Breuer, Freud had told his fiancée, had been "like sitting in the sun"; "he radiates light and warmth."[28] But when Breuer now tried to decline Freud's repayment of an early loan, Freud seized upon the gesture as an insult. "Hatred was directed against Breuer," observed an uneasy Jones, "and love towards Fliess."[29]

That love constituted a revival, with greatly increased intensity, of Freud's drug experience from the mideighties. In that period his affec-tionate bond with Fleischl had been sealed with jointly consumed cocaine. Now he experienced a second flowering of his homoerotic tendency, and the same elixir as before was loosening his inhibition, allowing him to voice his adoration without shame. Once again, too, cocaine must have compensated him for a painful awareness of being more emotionally vulnerable than the man who obsessed him. Other

---

* We saw, much earlier, that cocaine imparted loquacity and courage to the constitu-tionally shy Freud. Was it cocaine, then, that emboldened him to defy four of his seniors—Meynert, Charcot, Bernheim, and Breuer—who had treated him with cordial solicitude?

differences of temperament and opinion during the new couple's periodic "congresses" may also have been smoothed over by cocaine.

Some of the notions that Freud proposed in letters to Fliess, moreover, give off a "druggy" air of strangeness:

> The use of a condom is evidence of weak potency; being something
> analogous to masturbation, it is a continuous causation of [the
> patient's] melancholia.[30]

> What would you say if masturbation were to reduce itself to homo-
> sexuality, and the latter, that is, male homosexuality (in both sexes)
> were the primitive form of sexual longing? (The first sexual aim, anal-
> ogous to the infantile one—a wish that does not extend beyond the
> inner world.) If, moreover, libido and anxiety both were male?[31]

The same qualities can be found in passages expressing Freud's
struggle to purge his mind of every reservation about Fliess's own
"science":

> My capacity to participate fully in your results increases as they reach
> perfection, the more the law and the idea [behind them] shine through.
> In the as-yet-uninterpreted numbers I as a layman could not find
> what appears so promising to you; in your present communication I
> even found some links to fantasies of my own with which at one time
> I had wanted to illuminate your discoveries (that 12 as a factor of
> 23 represents the factor 10 of 28, the former having the male character;
> the latter, the female one). As you will remember, I also started with
> the approximate identity of the product
> $$12 \times 23 = 10 \times 28 \text{ (period of gestation)},$$
> but did not, I admit, know what to do with the difference, which for
> you became the starting point for further solutions. . . .
>   . . . Care has been taken to make sure that the communication of
> results will teach nothing to one in whom no indication of the pre-
> ceding mental work has remained.*

---

* 11/15/97; FF, p. 282. Note that the sentence beginning "Care has been taken" makes
no sense at all. The connoisseur of all such confusion is Robert Wilcocks (1994, 2000).

Freud's prostration before Fliess fits strangely with his belief in his own power to divine psychological laws. Both dispositions, however, express the same loss of empirical perspective. As Fliess was fondly informed in 1897, "Only someone who knows he is in possession of the truth writes as you do."[32] In the mouth of a working scientist, engaged in trying to draw warranted inferences from an opaque array of data, those words would have constituted an accusation of anti-empirical hubris. For Freud at that hour, however, "the truth" could be directly apprehended by a prepared mind; and the work of preparation, in his case, had been done not by careful research but by cocaine.

When Breuer, lecturing in November 1895, tried to convince his peers in the Vienna College of Physicians that the junior author of *Studies on Hysteria* was not a fanatic, he felt obliged to acknowledge a problem that others had apparently noticed as well:

> The objection might also perhaps have been raised that a lack of coherence makes itself felt in Freud's disquisitions; now, there is something to that, but one should not forget that we have provisional conclusions before us, that every theory is a temporary structure.[33]

Breuer knew, of course, that there was nothing provisional about Freud's reduction of all psychoneurotic etiology to "defense" against repressed sexuality. Freud's theory was indeed a temporary structure, not because he entertained it in a tentative spirit but because it answered only to his shifting guesswork. And Breuer's private opinion was that Freud was nearing a state of outright psychosis. "According to him," Freud told Fliess on March 1, 1896, "I should have to ask myself every day whether I am suffering from moral insanity or paranoia scientifica." *

---

* FF, p. 175. Freud rendered the term "moral insanity" in English.

In 1911 Freud would publish a psychoanalytic study of the paranoid-schizophrenic Daniel Paul Schreber (SE, 12:3–82). Interestingly, he would feel a strong identification with Schreber, based chiefly on a shared wish to fend off homosexuality. "I am Schreber, nothing but Schreber," he would write to Sándor Ferenczi in 1910 (12/3/10; Freud/Ferenczi 1993, p. 239).

In theory, "paranoia scientifica" could be averted by the straight-forward means of standing back from one's hypotheses and executing tests of their adequacy. As a psychologist, however, Freud had never been able to take that step. Now, as his claims expanded in scope, their arbitrariness stood out more starkly. His criterion of proof—namely, the feeling that everything is hanging together nicely—was satisfied in every instance.

It is revealing that such extreme laxity doesn't characterize Freud's writings on topics other than psychology and cocaine. Those writings included, in the 1890s, *On Aphasia* (1891); a collaborative book (with Oskar Rie) on children's cerebral paralyses (1891); two books of his own on the same theme (1893, 1897); and several briefer contributions to neurology. Except for *On Aphasia*, Freud disprized such works and privately scoffed at their favorable reception. He told Fliess that he had turned them out perfunctorily and that he bitterly resented his col-leagues' resistance to the texts that really mattered to him, his cherished pronouncements about the neuroses.[34]

It was as if there were two Freuds now: a sober, respectable, but insincere one who still observed scientific protocols, and a cocaine-driven hothead who could tolerate that timid world no longer. His ability to write the conventional works proves that at this time he didn't need to stay high in order to fend off withdrawal symptoms. Instead, he appears to have deliberately employed cocaine for inspira-tion when writing about the psyche, exactly as he had done with the theme of cocaine itself in the preceding decade.

As Freud was drafting such nonpsychological works as the 1897 *Infantile Cerebral Paralysis*, his awareness of knowledgeable readers and their scientific etiquette ensured an orderly presentation of data, a gearing of claims to that evidence, and respectful references to per-tinent literature in the field. But he couldn't write about psychology without inhabiting the persona of a Promethean rebel. In such texts, therefore, predecessors were to be obliterated, not cited; a foolproof clinical method would be announced but not spelled out sufficiently for others' use and evaluation; and that method would be underwritten not by examinable records but by deceptive assurances of success.

As the nineteenth century drew to a close and Freud's orthodox credentials for a professorship grew sufficiently ample, he would drop neurology altogether and cast his lot with psychoanalysis. When fortified by cocaine, he would already be at least occasionally convinced of his own greatness; and as a small group of followers, and then a larger one, accepted him as a genius, the drug itself would no longer be needed. Now, apparently, the cocaine self could do without cocaine.

Back in the midnineties, however, Freud's emotions and his theory were still in turmoil. He could make his way only with the aid of two crutches, Fliess and cocaine. Meanwhile, he was dealing with actual patients who trusted him, at least initially, to understand their nervous agitation and to provide efficacious remedies for it. How would his two dependencies affect his care of such patients?

26

Dire Therapy

1. A FRIEND OF THE FAMILY

According to two of Freud's best-informed (and also friendliest) biographers, Lisa Appignanesi and John Forrester, one patient in the last decade of the nineteenth century was exceptionally influential in pointing him toward what they regard as the core doctrine of psychoanalysis: that both dreams and neurotic manifestations are disguised expressions of wishes.[1] This was Emma Eckstein, who, Appignanesi and Forrester held, participated in every stage of that doctrine's development.

One might suppose, then, that Eckstein figures prominently in Freud's memoirs and in the postwar biographical literature that helped to shape the golden age of psychoanalysis. But no; with one trivial exception, Freud never mentioned her name in a publication.[2] And that name appears only once in Ernest Jones's three-volume, 1,357-page *Life and Works*, in a list of women of a "perhaps masculine cast" (that is, with minds of their own) who were "important" to Freud.[3] Jones offered no clue as to the nature of Eckstein's importance.

Anna Freud once remarked to Ernst Kris that she had experienced "the greatest pleasure in omitting the Eckstein case history" from *The Origins of Psycho-Analysis*.[4] Not until 1966 did any Freudian—it was the relatively candid Max Schur—dare to say anything in print about

Eckstein's treatment. Even then, although Schur knew her identity, she was presented to his readers as an anonymous "Emma"; and she remained "Emma" in his 1972 memoir, *Freud: Living and Dying*.* Psychoanalysis, in short, had honored an Eckstein taboo—and, as we will see, with good reason.

Emma Eckstein was the fourth among eight surviving children of a Viennese inventor and industrialist, Albert Eckstein, who amassed a fortune by manufacturing parchment; he died of locomotor ataxia, the last stage of neurosyphilis, in 1881. One of Emma's brothers, Friedrich (Fritz), a learned dilettante who inherited the management of Albert's business and almost drove it into bankruptcy, was a companion of Freud's in conversation and weekly card games. And Emma herself was close to Freud's sister-in-law Minna Bernays. In fact, the two families often vacationed together. As was customary among friends, these social ties obliged Freud, treating the allegedly neurotic Emma in her own house, to waive her fees during the first years of her therapy. But he was probably glad to do so in that period, because Emma—perhaps encouraged by Freud's only unreserved intellectual admirer at the time, Minna—trusted his judgment and was unusually compliant about serving as a guinea pig for untested procedures.

This is not to say, however, that Emma came to Freud without ideas and opinions. Despite his wealth, Albert Eckstein had been a committed socialist, and so were several of his children. They concurred, politically, with their family friend Victor Adler, the most famous Austrian Social Democrat (and Freud's resented rival in college days and after). One of the older daughters, Therese Schlesinger, would become a leading socialist-feminist and, in 1918, would be among the first women elected to the post-imperial parliament.[5] A younger brother, Gustav, also participated in socialist causes; he was an associate of the Marxist theoretician Karl Kautsky. Not surprisingly, Emma herself was both a socialist and a feminist.

In 1899 and 1900 Emma, writing for the same left-wing and feminist

* The first published mention of Emma Eckstein as Freud's patient of 1894–97 occurred in Swales 1983b, p. 361 and note. Jeffrey Masson, who had enjoyed full access to the Freud papers, had privately confirmed Swales's supposition to that effect (personal communication from Swales to me, 5/5/15).

magazines to which her sister Therese had already contributed, published essays denouncing abuses stemming from class and gender
inequality. One of her articles deplored the sexual exploitation of maid-
servants by entitled men.[6] In a book review she railed at women who
teach their daughters to shun unmarried mothers.[7] And her one
extended publication, a thirty-eight-page booklet, dealt in part with the
pathetic sexual ignorance and consequent timorousness of well-bred
nubile women.[8]

These writings call to mind Bertha Pappenheim, another sheltered
child of privilege who acquired a critical perspective on her upbringing and who took up the cause of reform. For Eckstein, however, there
would be no escape to a life of bold leadership. After her two older
sisters found husbands and moved away, she became the de facto head
of her mother's household of six persons. When she began treatment
with Freud, probably in 1894 at age twenty-nine, her life was consumed by worries, chores, and a grave physical disability. She never
married and, indeed, never moved out of the family home.

2. HYSTERO-NEURASTHENIA

There is no Eckstein case history that could help us understand what
problems this patient brought to Freud, how he regarded the progress
of her psychotherapy, or what prompted him to put her briefly in the
hands of another doctor. Nevertheless, the key events of 1895–96
were vividly narrated in Freud's letters to Fliess. Those documents and
others supply a likely sense of the two physicians' motives and assumptions as they proceeded to collaborate on her case. But what, exactly,
was ailing her?

We know that Freud initially treated Eckstein for hysteria. That is
hardly a surprise. Though Freud took intellectual comfort from hybrid
diagnoses, he was apt to find hysteria wherever he looked—even in
patients who, like Ilona Weiss ("Elisabeth von R."), were suffering
from patently organic deficits and were otherwise normal. Eckstein
resembled Weiss in experiencing, over many decades, sharp leg pains
that made walking almost impossible for her. In 1894 she was also
manifesting other symptoms that Freud folded into her hysteria: gas-

trointestinal distress and dysmenorrhea, or extreme pain during menstruation.

Those two troubles could have had the same cause, for dysmenorrhea is often accompanied by nausea, diarrhea, or constipation. The most frequent cause of dysmenorrhea itself, we now know, is a hormonal imbalance. But a number of other conditions can bring it on, some of which were known in Freud's time, including ovarian cysts or abscesses that develop from them. And, not incidentally, an ovarian cyst in turn can produce intense radiating leg pain. Freud may not have remembered these facts from his medical schooling, but in any case, he had no grounds for assuming that menstrual and digestive woes, any more than a difficulty in walking, are definitive signs of hysteria. And we will see that his stubbornness on that point held fateful consequences for Eckstein.

As for hysteria's own etiology, Freud's view of it in 1894–95 was less than clear. Although he had already started to distinguish himself from mainstream neurologists by publicly criticizing the theory of hereditary degeneration, in private he remained a believer. When analyzing Emma Eckstein's nephew Albert Hirst in 1903 and again in 1909–10, for example, he told Hirst that his grandfather's syphilis had predisposed the whole Eckstein line, into the second generation and presumably beyond, to contracting neurotic illnesses. And Freud had said so, Hirst related to Kurt Eissler, with considerable emphasis on the point.[9]

Degeneration and psychological trauma, however, could be regarded as complementary rather than mutually exclusive causes of hysteria. We have seen that in the midnineties, as with "Katharina," Freud was pursuing a two-stage account of hysteria formation based on "defense" against the recollection of sexual shocks; and he was still hopeful that probing for hysterogenic traumas might prove therapeutic. According to the theory, a misconstrued erotic incident, having befallen a virgin prior to the onset of sexual awareness, would get repressed, and thereby become hysterogenic, but only when a second such incident reawakened that memory—now more or less understood—and rendered it horrifying.

One such case is discussed in the 1895 *Project for a Scientific*

Psychology, and without doubt it is Eckstein's. (Writing for Fliess's eyes only, Freud called the patient in question "Emma.") It seems that she was then subject to "a compulsion of not being able to go into shops *alone*."[10] Properly speaking, this would count not as hysteria or compulsion but as a phobia—one, we may note, that could be afforded only by a member of the upper classes. But it may not have been much of a phobia, either. Freud didn't stop to think that Emma, because of her disability, had trouble going anywhere by herself.

Prodded to account for her phobia by reference to a trauma, Eckstein had been able to come up with nothing more convincing than an awkward experience at the self-conscious age of twelve. She had fled from a shop where she was discomfited by the sight of two assistants laughing together. Were they laughing at her? The memory could hardly be classified as sexual, but Freud's theory required it to be such. And so Eckstein "*was led to recall* that the two [assistants] were laughing at her clothes and that one of them had pleased her sexually."[11] In Freud's unusual, not to say impossible, view, the preteen Emma had been simultaneously humiliated and aroused, experiencing what he called a hysterogenic "sexual release" as she fled the premises in hypersensitive mortification.

Like "Katharina's" more patently sexual experience at sixteen, Emma's fright had allegedly reactivated her knowledge of an earlier incident that only became traumatic after the fact. That is to say, Freud demanded that such an incident be produced. "*Further investigation now revealed* a second memory," this one from age eight.[12] But it was even more peculiar than its predecessor. Although the young daughter of the affluent Albert Eckstein had probably enjoyed few if any opportunities to go shopping unaccompanied by a servant or family member, the adult Emma now seemed to recall that a shopkeeper "had grabbed at her genitals through her clothes"—an amazing infraction of the Viennese social order, and one that could have landed him in prison. Still more remarkably, the "recalled" molestation hadn't bothered the eight-year-old Emma. She had later returned with equanimity to the same shop, as if crotch grabbing by merchants were nothing out of the ordinary.

On several counts, Freud's "deferred action" story of Emma's surrender to phobia failed to make sense. But instead of asking himself whether he might be trying too hard to wrench her history into alignment with his theory, he considered the matter to have been satisfactorily resolved. He even drew a diagram for the *Project* indicating just how Emma's chain of unconscious associations had led to her "sexual release," thus overwhelming her ego and rendering her lastingly symptomatic.[13] But what he couldn't do in Emma's case was to claim that her reliving of traumatic scenes had dissolved her shop phobia. As he stated in the *Project*, Emma was phobic "at the present time"—that is, after the supposed derepression of her memories. Apparently, the theory of catharsis that had just been pronounced in *Studies on Hysteria* was already inoperative.

Freud never ceased to regard Eckstein as a hysteric. Already by 1895, however, he had arrived at a second diagnosis: her menstrual and digestive pains marked her as a victim of Fliess's nasal reflex neurosis. And that syndrome itself, Fliess and Freud had jointly decided, was a variant of neurasthenia, a "current neurosis" whose sole precipitating cause, we saw, was allegedly masturbation.* Emma had confessed to a history of that vice, about which she felt profoundly guilty. Evidently, then, Freud now viewed Eckstein as a self-abuser who suffered simultaneously from two neuroses, or a hybrid "hystero-neurasthenia."

Freud used that term for the first time in a book review that he wrote around the end of February 1895.[14] Ostensibly discussing Paul J. Möbius's sensible little book *Die Migräne*, Freud went on to propose the existence of two bizarre new entities, the "back migraine" and the "heart migraine." The latter syndrome was exemplified by "a colleague of about fifty"—obviously Freud himself—who suffered from attacks of arrhythmia and severe anxiety. As for back migraine, the female patient whom he cited as its exemplar may or may not have been Eckstein, who resembled her in progressing from common headaches in youth to more severe pain; but Eckstein was surely on his mind when he attempted to add hystero-neurasthenia to the medical lexicon.

---

* As Fliess wrote in the final, italicized, sentence of his 1893 book on the NRN, "*A majority of so-called neurasthenics are nothing other than sufferers from the reflex neurosis*" (Fliess 1893, p. 79).

We recall how Freud, writing the concluding chapter of *Studies on Hysteria* in early 1895, went back over the cases he had described as hysterical and casually added a current-neurosis label to each one, thus evading blame for his failure to have "abreacted" the several hysterias. Now, in the same period, he was inventing a new double syndrome, which, insofar as it applied to Eckstein, neatly divided her illness between Fliess's terrain and his own. Both before and after Fliess's involvement, Emma would be Freud's responsibility as a hysteric; but meanwhile she was to be Fliess's special kind of neurasthenic. It was Freud's deference to Fliess, rather than the objective lineaments of Eckstein's malady, that brought about this compromise. There would be nothing halfway, however, about her experience as the recipient of Fliess's ultimate remedy for the nasal reflex neurosis.

3. COMPLICATIONS

Fliess, it will be remembered, was prepared to apply three serial treatments for the NRN: cocaine brushed into the nose, cauterization, and surgical removal of a "spot" of twisted nasal bone that supposedly governed a misfiring sexual or digestive function. The third option, however, hadn't been tried before February 1895, and Fliess was chafing to add it to his repertoire. Most scholars have inferred that Emma Eckstein, though her care hadn't progressed beyond stage one, was chosen by Freud and Fliess to be the pioneering subject for the stage three surgery.

There is evidence to suggest, however, that Freud himself, not Eckstein, may have been the first patient to undergo Fliess's bone excision. On January 24, 1895, just ahead of Fliess's February 1–24 stay in Vienna, Freud confided:

> Now only one more week separates us from the operation, or at least from the preparations for it. The time has passed quickly, and I gladly avoid putting myself through a self-examination to ascertain what right I have to expect so much from it. My lack of medical knowledge once again weighs heavily on me. But I keep repeating to myself: so far as I have some insight into the matter, the cure must be achiev-

able by this route. I would not have dared to invent this plan of treatment on my own, but I confidently join you in it.[15]

We know that Fliess worked *some* nasal procedure on Freud before dealing with Eckstein. In the passage above, Freud couldn't have been thinking of cauterization, for he had already endured that treatment on two occasions. His reference to "one more week," meaning the very start of February; his use of the term "operation" (*Operation*); and his mention of a novel plan that worried him all seem to imply an innovative surgery on himself. So, too, in a letter of March 4, written after Fliess's return to Berlin, Freud said of a recent photograph showing himself and Fliess together, "my pleasure in having you close by my side *after the operation* clearly shows."[16] If all of these clues don't point to surgery on Fliess's own nose—for such an operation did indeed occur—then they must refer to a risky procedure applied to Freud.[17] If so, however, no "cure" occurred. Freud reported no lasting abatement of his physical and psychological complaints, and the condition of his nose appears to have worsened.

It cannot be said, then, that Freud self-tested the safety and worth of Fliess's new surgery before allowing it to be practiced on Eckstein. Rather, he appears to have offered both himself and the defenseless Emma to Fliess as experimental subjects. Neither physician took adequate trouble to ascertain whether Eckstein's symptoms might point to some diagnosis other than the fantastic NRN, and independent medical opinions were not solicited.

Instead, as Max Schur noted, Freud "asked Fliess (as he had also done in the case of many other patients) to examine [Eckstein] for any pathology of the turbinate bones and the sinuses which might be a factor contributing to her hysterical abdominal symptoms."[18] The answer to such a question was predictable, especially since Emma's nose had probably been degraded already by therapeutic applications of cocaine. And about a week *after* her surgery, Freud informed Fliess that he had told Breuer "about the analysis of Eckstein, with which you are not really familiar either."[19] Thus Freud and Fliess hadn't even discussed the psychological aspects of Emma's case; she had simply been surrendered into Fliess's care.

On or shortly before February 23, 1895, Fliess extracted from Eckstein's nose a portion of turbinate bone—probably, in modern parlance, part of the left middle concha. That segment constituted the Fliessian "stomachache spot," which, its discoverer would later write, was often inflamed "in the case of women who masturbate."* Fliess returned to Berlin immediately after the surgery, leaving the patient to be visited by Freud as she convalesced.

Freud's first letter after the event made no mention of Eckstein. Instead, it dealt briefly with a neutral-sounding newspaper report about Fliess's latest medical proposal: to ease labor pains by applying cocaine to the mother's nose.[20] In a letter of March 4, however, an account of Eckstein's state was the fourth among seven numbered items, following an expression of delight over the dual portrait photograph, an assurance to Fliess that he was "blameless" for what was now being talked about as the bad outcome of the cocaine-for-childbirth experiment, and the conveying of a hope that Fliess and his wife had by then recovered from influenza. "Fourth," wrote Freud,

> Eckstein's condition is still unsatisfactory: persistent swelling . . . ; pain, so that morphine cannot be dispensed with; bad nights. The purulent secretion has been decreasing since yesterday; the day before yesterday . . . she had a massive hemorrhage, probably as a result of expelling a bone chip the size of a heller [a small coin]; there were two bowls full of pus. Today we encountered resistance on irrigation; and since the pain and the visible edema had increased, I let myself be persuaded to call in [the surgeon Robert] Gersuny. (By the way, he greatly admired an etching of *The Isle of the Dead* [by Arnold Böcklin].) He explained that the access was considerably narrowed and insufficient for drainage, inserted a drainage tube, and threatened to break [the bone?] open if that did not stay in. To judge by the smell,

---

* Freud marked this passage, presumably with approval, in his copy of Fliess's 1902 book *On the Causal Connection between Nose and Sex Organ* (Masson 1984, p. 77). His belief in the rationality of the Eckstein surgery appears to have survived later developments of her case.

all this is most likely correct. Please send me your authoritative advice. I am not looking forward to new surgery on this girl.*

A surprising development prompted Freud, four days afterward, to write in a more urgent mode, yet so reluctantly that "for a day I shied away from letting you know about it."[21] Eckstein's condition had worsened after the insertion of Gersuny's drainage tube:

Two days later I was awakened in the morning—profuse bleeding had started again, pain, and so on. Gersuny replied on the phone that he was unavailable till evening, so I asked [Dr. Ignaz] Rosanes to meet me. He did so at noon. There still was moderate bleeding from the nose and mouth; the fetid odor was very bad. Rosanes cleaned the area surrounding the opening, removed some sticky blood clots, and suddenly pulled at something like a thread, kept on pulling. Before either of us had time to think, at least half a meter of gauze had been removed from the cavity. The next moment came a flood of blood. The patient turned white, her eyes bulged, and she had no pulse. Immediately thereafter, however, he again packed the cavity with fresh iodoform gauze and the hemorrhage stopped. It lasted about half a minute, but this was enough to make the poor creature, whom by then we had lying flat, unrecognizable. . . . At the moment the foreign body came out and everything became clear to me—and I immediately afterward was confronted by the sight of the patient—I felt sick. After she had been packed, I fled to the next room, drank a bottle of water, and felt miserable. The brave Frau Doctor [unidentified] then brought me a small glass of cognac and I became myself again. . . . [Eckstein] had not lost consciousness during the massive hemorrhage; when I returned to the room somewhat shaky, she greeted me with the condescending remark, "So this is the strong sex."[22]

---

* FF, pp. 113–114. Enclosed with this letter was a concise "Case History" (pp. 115–116), not of Eckstein but of Freud himself, detailing "a private Etna" of scabs and pus—aftereffects of treatment by Fliess. Here is further evidence favoring the hypothesis that Freud himself had undergone turbinate-bone surgery in early February.

After this near fatality, Freud had understood that Eckstein needed twenty-four-hour care, and on the following day he transferred her to a private sanatorium, where her nasal bone would be broken again to allow for curettage of the wound. Meanwhile, he feared that the case was turning into a major embarrassment for Fliess. The pus-soaked gauze was a stinking token of Fliess's carelessness. "So we had done her an injustice," wrote Freud; "she was not at all abnormal [after the surgery]."[23] This can only mean that until then, Freud and Fliess had interpreted Eckstein's bleedings, after the first one, as psychogenic "conversions"—but this excuse had now been refuted.

Freud, however, hastened to absolve Fliess of responsibility:

> That this mishap should have happened to you; how you will react to it when you hear about it; what others could make of it; how wrong I was to urge you to operate in a foreign city where you could not follow through on the case; how my intention to do my best for this poor girl was insidiously thwarted and resulted in endangering her life—all this came over me simultaneously. I have worked it through by now. . . .
>
> I really should not have tormented you here, but I had every reason to entrust you with such a matter and more. You did it as well as one can do it. . . . Of course, no one is blaming you, nor would I know why they should. And I only hope that you will . . . rest assured that it was not necessary for me to reaffirm my trust in you once again.[24]

Every commentator has noticed how frantic and feeble these denials were.

Over the ensuing month, Freud's sparse references to the case implied that Eckstein, though suffering "hysterical attacks at night,"[25] was regaining her health. But on April 11 he reported the worst crisis yet—one that was more upsetting by virtue of its unexplained nature. Now Emma, still in her sanatorium, was bleeding abundantly with new nasal packing in place, and "we do not know what to do."[26] Writing from the deepest gloom, Freud predicted that "this Eckstein affair" was "rapidly moving toward a bad ending"—the patient's death.[27] And this time, Freud couldn't summon the will to exculpate Fliess. "I am really very shaken," he confessed, "to think that such a mishap could have arisen from an operation that was purported to be harmless."[28]

Tended by Gersuny, Rosanes, and two other physicians, Karl Gussenbauer and Moriz Weil, Emma was out of danger by April 20. Fliess, however, was beside himself with resentment at the thought that his colleagues, including Freud, must be gossiping about his incompetence. He apparently wrote to Freud declaring that nothing much had been wrong with Eckstein after the surgery, that her bleeding was merely a periodic phenomenon in accordance with his mathematical laws, and that her overhasty doctors ought to have simply waited for it to stop. And he demanded that Gersuny, now the chief physician in the case, formally absolve him of responsibility for Eckstein's troubles.

Freud replied emphatically that "there could be no question of biding one's time. There was bleeding as though from the carotid artery; within half a minute she again would have bled to death."[29] And now he had to reassure Fliess, but with a hint of impatience, that his own faith was as strong as ever:

> The writer of this is still very miserable, but also offended that you deem it necessary to have a testimonial certificate from Gersuny for your rehabilitation. For me you remain the physician, the type of man into whose hands one confidently puts one's life and that of one's family—even if Gersuny should have the same opinion of your skills as *Weil*. I wanted to pour forth my tale of woe and perhaps obtain your advice concerning E., not reproach you with anything. That would have been stupid, unjustified, and in clear contradiction to all my feelings.[30]

The Eckstein case was placing a strain on the Freud/Fliess relationship, and Freud was growing exasperated with this female interloper who had been requiring so much attention. "Eckstein once *again* is in pain," he wrote on April 27; "will she be bleeding next?"[31] A month later, however, Eckstein was "finally doing very well,"[32] and almost a full year would pass before her name resurfaced in a letter.

Through that whole interval, however, Eckstein—who, curiously, seemed to bear no ill will toward either Freud or Fliess—had been

Freud's psychological patient; and Freud had been seeking to extract from her an "unconscious" rationale for her episodes of prolonged bleeding. At last his prodding was rewarded. On April 16, 1896, in a sprightly mood, he heralded "a completely surprising explanation of Eckstein's hemorrhages—which will give you much pleasure. I have already figured out the story, but I shall wait to communicate it until the patient herself has caught up."[33] No confession, we understand, had been extracted from Eckstein; like Fliess, she was to be told in due course the result of Freud's reconstruction.

On April 26, 1896, the new science of psychoanalysis—named as such just a few weeks earlier in Freud's French-language paper on "Heredity and the Aetiology of the Neuroses"—yielded the following triumphant finding, proudly imparted to Fliess:

First of all, Eckstein. I shall be able to prove to you that you were right, that her episodes of bleeding were hysterical, were occasioned by *longing*, and probably occurred at the sexually relevant times (the dame [*Frauenzimmer*], out of resistance, has not yet supplied me with the dates).[34]

And Freud elaborated on May 4:

As for Eckstein—I am taking notes on her history so that I can send it to you—so far I know only that she bled out of *longing*. She has always been a bleeder, when cutting herself and in similar circumstances; as a child she suffered from severe nosebleeds; during the years when she was not yet menstruating, she had headaches which were interpreted to her as malingering and which in truth had been generated by [auto]suggestion; for this reason she joyously welcomed her severe menstrual bleeding as proof that her illness was genuine. . . . She described a scene from the age of fifteen, in which she suddenly began to bleed from the nose when she had the wish to be treated by a certain young doctor who was present.[35]

What Freud had unearthed looks like a pertinent history of hemophilia—overlaid, however, by "scenes" and motivational suppositions that were probably artifacts of his demand for theoretically congenial information. Whether that demand was conveyed through his pressure technique—which he was still using in late 1895—or through free association is immaterial, since both methods were well adapted to imparting the therapist's suggestions. Freud had now assembled his case for a witchlike power on Emma's part to express her desires through spurts of blood.[36]

This, then, was the Freudian version of the bleeding undergone by Emma after the initial postoperative crisis:

When she saw how affected I was by her first hemorrhage when she was in the hands of Rosanes, she experienced this as the realization of an old wish to be loved in her illness, and in spite of the danger during the succeeding hours she felt happy as never before. Then, in the sanatorium, she became restless during the night because of an unconscious intent of longing [*Sehnsuchtsabsicht*] to entice me to go there; since I did not come during the night, she renewed the bleedings, as an unfailing means of rearousing my affection. She bled spontaneously three times and each bleeding lasted for four days, which must have some significance. She still owes me details and specific dates.[37]

Here, confided only to Fliess, was the most appalling example of Freud's thenceforth habitual tendency to invoke hysterical conversion whenever he found it expedient to do so. In this instance his spitefulness toward the annoying Eckstein and his wish to curry favor with Fliess are unmistakable. And his reasoning was strained, to say the least.

Upon observing Freud's pallor after her gauze had been removed, Emma had reacted with scorn: "So this is the strong sex." Why, clinging to life a few hours later, would she have been mooning over him, "happy as never before"? Again, in the sanatorium Emma had nearly bled to death (an odd way to get attention) when Freud was already present. An artery had probably been weakened by Fliess and/or Rosanes, but now Freud didn't care. He was accusing a mutilated patient, led into danger by himself and nearly killed by his bosom friend, of having emitted quantities of blood in the service of typical female wiles. Note, too, that Freud was ready to ascribe Fliessian numerological "significance" to "specific dates" that hadn't yet been revealed. Here again, the meaning of Eckstein's case was being politically apportioned between Fliess's explanatory framework and his own.

This letter of May 1896 has posed the ultimate test of faith for latter-day believers in Freud's greatness. If they can accept what he was saying here, they can swallow anything. Appignanesi and Forrester, for instance, contemplating the alleged love call issued by Eckstein's vascular system, passed the test with agility:

> So Freud shows how this terrible accident had been employed by Emma's unconscious wishes to her advantage. What is remarkable is the sureness of touch he displays in wending his way towards using the traumatic bleeding scene for the purposes of advancing Emma's *analysis*.[38]

For less acculturated readers, though, the Eckstein case may serve as the crowning example of Freud's tendency to explain all medical phenomena to his personal advantage.

4. THE LONG GOODBYE

Three further aspects of Emma Eckstein's life story bear on our effort to understand Freud's intellect and character: his anointment of her as a psychoanalyst, her publications as they were affected by Freud, and her eventual parting of the ways with him, provoked by yet another contest between psychosomatic and organic diagnoses. These are disparate topics, but when considered together they prepare us for traits that Freud was to exhibit in abundance when trying to manage the larger psychoanalytic movement.

Only one tantalizing scrap of information tells us that Emma Eckstein became the first psychoanalyst after Freud himself. His letter to Fliess of December 12, 1897, related that a *patient* of Eckstein's had corroborated an important point of analytic theory.[39] Eckstein had "deliberately treated her patient in such a manner as not to give her the slightest hint of what would emerge from the unconscious."[40] We don't know who that patient was, but it is clear from Freud's reference that he trusted Eckstein's clinical judgment as completely as he trusted his own.

What training, one wonders, qualified Eckstein to practice psycho-analysis? We know only that she was in continual therapy with Freud from 1894 through at least January 1897. Evidently, the therapy itself constituted her professional initiation. But since nothing further was said about her therapeutic work by either Freud or Emma or her heirs, we may assume that this budding career ended soon after it began. The fact that Freud credentialed one of his patients—one who would return for two more bouts of his treatment—suggests how eager he was to propagate his influence at a time when his theory was still in flux.

In any case, around 1900 Eckstein published articles and a booklet manifesting her socialist and feminist principles. Her leading topic, however, was one that crystallized from her years of association with Freud. It was his most enduring and preoccupying theme, albeit one that would be overlooked by later Freudian cohorts: masturbation. In her 1904 booklet *The Sexual Question in Childrearing*, drawing largely on works she had borrowed from Freud, Eckstein seconded his grim assessment of the nervous havoc caused by early practice of that vice.[41]

Masturbation, Eckstein wrote, "is an insidious enemy for the child. Unnoticed and unsuspected, it slinks into the nursery and works away there, assiduously and with no hindrance, at its goal of destroying the youth and strength, both physical and mental, of its victims."[42] Agree-ing with a well-known authority in his complaint that "universities do not offer courses on how to treat masturbation effectively," she endorsed the use of preventive bandages and nightclothes, and she especially recommended enlisting children's self-regard so that they would experience "disdain for [their] own feelings" of premature excitement.[43]

It is tempting to scoff at Eckstein's alarmism, but in doing so we would miss the most important clue to her continuing respect for Freud. In her youth it had been customary not just to oppose childhood mastur-bation but to punish it with threats, grisly devices, clitoral surgery, and condemnation of the child as a devilish sinner. In describing the psychological consequences, Eckstein was surely drawing on personal experience. "The mere fact," she wrote, "that an older, more experienced person provides him with enlightenment as to the character as well as the frequency of this practice is often sufficient to help him and free him from his misery."[44]

That "older, more experienced person" in Eckstein's life was Freud, and she never ceased being grateful to him for having treated her as redeemable and worthy instead of monstrous. His reassurance about the normality of *impulses* to masturbate, which ought to be resisted but not demonized, would be repeated in his analysis of her nephew, Alfred Hirst.[45] But it was the socially conscious Eckstein, not the secretive, guilt-ridden Freud, who judged the scare tactics against early masturbation to be a detriment to public health and who risked self-exposure by pleading for a more compassionate approach to the problem.

In 1904 Freud tried, unsuccessfully, to do Eckstein a favor by publishing a flattering review of her booklet on sex education.* By 1905, however, their relationship appeared to be unraveling. Emma had gone back into analysis with Freud, but on November 30, 1905, he wrote her a peevish letter giving several reasons why he no longer considered her a suitable client. She had been dragging him down, Freud complained, with her emotional demands, with her request for a waiver of his fees, and with her resentment of his perfectly objective statement—a contribution to her therapy, so it appears—that she was unattractive to men.[46]

This last point was characteristically tactless but probably correct. Not only was Emma unable to walk; according to her niece, the eminent pediatrician Ada Elias, "her face was disfigured—the bone was chiseled away, and on one side caved in."[47] But Freud assumed no responsibility for her asymmetrical visage. The trouble Emma had been causing him, he told her, reminded him of "the elemental bitchiness [*elementar-frauenzimmerlichen*] with which I constantly have to struggle."[48]

---

* Freud's review was turned down by the editor of Vienna's *Neue Freie Presse*. In 1907, however, he did praise Eckstein's booklet in an open letter to the editor of a hygiene journal. See Masson 1984, pp. 241–244.

In 1909–10, Eckstein was Freud's patient once again for at least six months. This time, however, something may have gone more seriously awry, for around this time Emma tried to kill herself.[49] And, in an incident that may or may not have been related to her suicide attempt, she and Freud lived through their terminal quarrel about her condition.

Complaining of severe stomach pains, Emma had consulted a surgeon who found and removed several uterine abscesses. Although her symptoms persisted, she felt that the discovery of an organic problem vindicated her long-held suspicion that Freud's hysteria diagnosis was wrong. And if that was so, her years in psychoanalysis, to say nothing of her misadventure with Fliess, had prevented her from receiving appropriate care.

In order to settle the dispute, Freud had Emma examined by Dr. Dora Teleky, a Viennese surgeon whom he knew well. Indeed, he had reason to believe that Teleky would second his view of the case, because, almost uniquely among physicians, she had attended his lectures on psychoanalysis. But Freud's hope was misplaced. In a subsequent letter to the journalist Emil Ludwig, Teleky recorded what had then occurred:

> I saw that the abscesses still persisted, or that a fresh abscess had formed on the site of the incision. I made a new incision and at one stroke freed the patient of her pains. When I later told this to the master at his home, he blew up. With biting scorn he asked me whether I actually believed that hysterical pain could be cured by the knife. Quaking, I objected that an obvious abscess must be treated. Despite the fact that the patient was cured of all complaints, Dr. Freud became so unfriendly to me that I was obliged to break off the discussion and leave him.*

This account tallies with what Albert Hirst recounted in his unpublished autobiography:

---

* Ludwig 1947, p. 115. Teleky was also interviewed by Kurt Eissler in 1956. Her statements at that time, which Freud scholars haven't been allowed to see, must have been of considerable interest; Eissler ordered them locked away for sixty-four years, until 2020.

Dora claimed that she had found the source of Emma's illness and had cured it. She thus confirmed Emma in her rejection of Freud's diagnosis of a recurrence of her old neurosis. When I told that to Freud the next day he was furious. He took Dora's "diagnosis" as a fake. That to him was a matter of course. He called it a highly unprofessional interference with a patient under another doctor's care. He immediately withdrew from the case, saying: "That is Emma's end. Now she will never get well."[50]

For whatever reason, Freud's heartless prophecy or curse came true. As Hirst continued:

Emma was up and about for a short time, but soon returned to her couch on which she had lived so long. She survived, as a hopeless invalid, for another ten [actually fourteen] years. It may be unjust to him, but I had the impression, or let me say, the suspicion, . . . that Freud was not unhappy to be rid of a burdensome charity case.[51]

As I have mentioned, ovarian cysts and abscesses can bring about the cluster of grave symptoms Eckstein had contracted in her adolescence. She had retained those symptoms except for one period of remission, which Freud chalked up to the healing virtue of psychoanalysis. Now, in 1910, the immediate effect of an abscess removal was the restoration of her ability to walk. The linkage of cause and effect appears to be straightforward. If Emma soon became immobile again and stayed that way for her remaining fourteen years, what are the odds that her final problem was hysteria rather than, say, new growths on her reproductive organs? And wouldn't a doctor and friend have urged her to be physically examined once again?

Freud wasn't quite through with the Eckstein case. Emma had been dead for thirteen years when, in 1937, he decided that her story might be of use to him in his essay on handling recalcitrant cases, "Analysis Terminable and Interminable." It wasn't necessary, he calculated, to mention the harrowing events of 1895, or to point out that the patient had been reanalyzed twice without experiencing a tangible benefit, much less that she had tried to kill herself. Nor, of course, did Freud reveal that he had granted this sick woman the title of psychoanalyst. His account would be at once more condensed and more psychologically colorful than the actual course of events.

The anonymous patient, assuredly Eckstein, had hoped for a cure of her inability to walk, a condition "obviously of a hysterical nature":

> An analysis lasting three-quarters of a year removed the trouble and restored to the patient . . . her right to a share in life. . . . I cannot remember whether it was twelve or fourteen years after the end of her analysis that, owing to profuse haemorrhages, she was obliged to undergo a gynecological examination. A myoma was found, which made a complete hysterectomy advisable. From the time of this operation, the woman became ill once more. She fell in love with her surgeon, wallowed in masochistic phantasies about the fearful changes in her inside—phantasies with which she concealed her romance—and proved inaccessible to a further attempt at analysis. She remained abnormal to the end of her life.[52]

27

Self-Seduced

1. SEEK AND YE SHALL FIND

Our story of Freud's development has now reached a point of intersection with educated public opinion. Almost everyone who is aware of psychoanalysis has heard of the "seduction theory": Freud's 1895–97 etiology of hysteria, obsessional neurosis, and paranoia, whereby the indispensable causative factor in those disorders was asserted to be repressed memories of childhood sexual abuse. For at least two years, "seduction" stood between the vaguer doctrine of *Studies on Hysteria*, which allowed for hysteria-inducing traumas as late as adulthood, and the *echt*-psychoanalytic idea that the patients' repressed sexual *fantasies*, not their experiences, are the key pathogenic factor.

As we will see in this chapter and the next, there are heated differences of judgment about the theory and the reasons for its demise. First, however, we must address a problem of nomenclature. The general understanding of Freud's "seduction theory" has been shaped by orthodox psychoanalysts, who chose that term in order to imply a symmetry with the Oedipus complex: patients who thought, mistakenly, that they had been abused had themselves, according to the oedipal doctrine, been bent on seduction of a parent. But *seduction*, a process of winning consent to active sexual relations, is an inappropriate term to characterize the acts to which Freud initially believed his patients to have been subjected as children—acts of genital fondling, digital penetration, and rape, forced upon helpless victims. Granted, Freud himself sometimes called such deeds seductions; but that doesn't mean that we should do so. Henceforth, I will be referring to Freud's ill-fated *molestation theory*.*

By October 15, 1895, Freud had convinced himself that "hysteria is the consequence of a presexual *sexual shock*"—one, that is, occurring before puberty.[1] And on November 2 he told Fliess that "one of the cases gave me what I expected"—exactly the evidence of "infantile abuse" that he was requiring.[2] Further "confirmations" were not slow to arrive. That was what would usually happen when Freud got a new idea, right or wrong, and tried it out on his patients.

Freud, it is clear, "discovered" early sexual traumas in the memories of his hysterics only after demanding that they materialize. The demand itself was made necessary by three things: a stubborn insistence, a therapeutic frustration, and a tenet that he would soon be discarding.

His insistence, first, was on sexual causation and repression. In *Studies on Hysteria* he had staked his reputation on the central importance of those factors, and there could be no turning back. The therapeutic frustration, second, lay in his failure either to elicit the recall of adequately traumatic *post-childhood* experiences or to effect cures after hearing of such mundane events as Emma Eckstein's having seen two clerks laughing. And the soon-to-be-forsaken tenet, third, was the asexuality of childhood. So long as Freud clung to that idea, he could assert that prepubescent sexual encounters were uniquely suited to wounding the nervous system in an inconspicuous way that would become pathogenic only later.

This idea of "deferred action" or "belatedness" (*Nachträglichkeit*) smoothed Freud's hermeneutic path all too conveniently. No longer was he vexed by the bland quality of his patients' initial mnemonic offerings. The burden of pathogenicity had been shifted to earlier "memories" that the patients *didn't recall at all*. Now Freud would tell a given patient

---

* See Triplett 2005. Triplett's preferred term is "infant genital trauma theory." We will see, however, that Freud's theory encompassed other ages as well.

what kind of sexual trauma she was withholding from consciousness; he would indicate the youthful age range from which the "memory" must be drawn; and then, if the requisite event still wasn't proffered, he would "reconstruct" it himself by drawing inferences from the patient's behavioral signals and from her responses to his own broad hints. With this protocol it was impossible for him to come up empty-handed. It was also a near certainty, however, that the resultant "early traumatic memories" would be artifacts of his method.

In *Studies on Hysteria* Freud had already revealed his procedure for arriving at precise dates of early events in a patient's life: "we can repeat to him the dates of the possibly relevant years, the names of the twelve months and the thirty-one numbers of the days of the month, assuring him that when we come to the right number or the right name his eyes will open of their own accord or that he will feel which is the right one."[3] This was roughly the same protocol, and just as scientific, as the means by which the horse Clever Hans, not long afterward in Germany, was speciously demonstrated to be a mathematician.[4]

How early must the uncovered trauma have been? According to Freud, a passive sexual experience, in order to qualify as hysterogenic, had to occur no later than ages eight to ten—a span that he designated, bizarrely, as the threshold of "sexual maturity."[5] As for the lower limit, it extended "as far back as memory itself—that is, therefore, to the tender age of one and a half or two years!"[6] The existence of such memories, Freud granted, could be detected only through "the symptoms of the illness," which, psychoanalytically interpreted, admitted of no other explanation.[7]

As we know, toddlers do form memories, but rarely if ever long-term ones, the only kind that might be reactivated in much later childhood or adolescence. No one should have known that fact better than Freud. His former mentor Theodor Meynert had discovered that long-term memory must await the gradual development of brain myelination (nerve sheathing). Densely tangled myelin fibers were what Freud himself had aspired to render more visible through his gold chloride staining method. And, building on research by Meynert's archrival Paul Flechsig, he had done valuable studies of incipient myelination in embryonic and infant brains. Thus his molestation theory depended on a curious "repression" of his own scientific knowledge.

Can we declare flatly that none of Freud's clients in this period volunteered a genuine recollection of having been sexually abused in childhood? Certainly not. But any such freely volunteered information, we must understand, didn't concern him. "The scenes [of molestation]," he wrote, "must be present as *unconscious memories*; only so long as, and in so far as, they are unconscious are they able to create and maintain hysterical symptoms."[8]

Thus, when one patient recalled, unbidden, that her father had molested her from ages eight to twelve, Freud wasn't interested. "I told her," he wrote to Fliess, "that similar and worse things must have happened in her earliest childhood."[9] Such remarks show that Freud was by no means aiming, as Masson and others have alleged, at exposing and curbing an epidemic of abuse.[10] He was entirely absorbed in winning assent to his etiological scheme.

So, too, Freud turned his back on the whole cohort of lower-class patients to whom he had been introduced at the Salpêtrière. Now the proletariat, which he regarded as routinely tolerating childhood sexual abuse, was judged too brutish to produce hysterics—a point that would have flabbergasted Charcot.[11] As Freud stated in a draft paper,

> Where there is no shame (as in a male person), or where no morality comes about (as in the lower classes of society), or where disgust is blunted by the conditions of life (as in the country), there too no repression and therefore no neurosis will result from sexual stimulation in infancy.[12]

Even within the narrow socioeconomic range of his patients, Freud was focused on causal speculation rather than on ministering to actual victims of abuse. Only rarely and perfunctorily did he refer to the psychological effects—fear, disorientation, guilt, self-devaluation, a sense of powerlessness—typically registered by a child entrapped in what he oddly called "love-relations" (*Liebesverhältnis*) with an adult.[13] More often, he assumed that even under "brutal assault," producing "grave sexual injuries,"[14] the child wouldn't be much bothered, because the purpose of those acts was obscure to her. She would respond to them merely "with indifference or with a small degree of annoyance or fright."[15]

But the older the child, the more likely it was, in Freud's privately expressed opinion, that she would actually enjoy the abuser's genital stimulation. Such was his psychological crudity at a time when his theorizing answered less to the anguish of suffering patients than to brain/genital reflex lore; to Fliessian periodicity, bisexuality, and "male and female menstruation"; to his own mechanical conception of the current neuroses; and to his grand aim of reducing mental events to waves of neuronal excitation. Those preoccupations incapacitated him for grasping what the rest of humanity intuitively knows: that positive sexual experience is a function not just of secretions, agitated tissues, and discharges but of whole persons whose need to feel respected is fulfilled in the encounter.

As Freud prepared to go public with his molestation theory in early 1896, he was still unsure why *any* sexual experience ought to be disagreeable. "For repression in the sexual neuroses," he wrote to Fliess on New Year's Day, he needed "an explanation of the release of unpleasure"—a release that he tried at first to cast in terms of energy transfers between neurons of "quantity" and "quality."[16] But he wasn't ready to expose his phi-psi-omega "gibberish" [*Kauderwelsch*], as he false-modestly demeaned it, to the skepticism of the medical world.[17] Instead, still thinking along Fliess's developmental lines, he would appeal to the interpolation of puberty "between the experience and its repetition in memory."[18]

In hereditarily susceptible individuals, Freud supposed, the chemical changes that constitute puberty impart disgust to the renewed memory of early sexual impressions. But why disgust instead of further pleasure? Perhaps, Freud hazarded to Fliess, "the neighborhood in which the sexual organs are naturally placed must inevitably arouse disgust during sexual experiences."[19]

Thus, instead of considering the unique horror, for a child, of being made someone else's sexual plaything, Freud folded the problem of molestation into his general attitude toward copulation. Unlike the piecemeal gratification of "zones" and "spots," the full heterosexual act struck him as degrading and anxiety provoking. In his judgment circa 1896, then, it wasn't abuse per se that produced neuroses, but rather the repressed memory of abuse as perceived through a revulsion that overtakes all post-pubertal humans. He would soon lose faith in his theory, but the joyless negativity that lay behind it would accompany him always.

2. GOING PUBLIC

We now know, from Freud's letters to Fliess throughout 1896 and much of 1897, that his linking of sexual abuse to the psychoneuroses was fraught with doubts and difficulties. He could never be sure, for example, of the differential age ranges within which a molestation would yield either hysteria, obsessional neurosis, or paranoia, nor of the ages beyond which a second trauma would *not* prove pathogenic.* And some of his hypothesizing was no sooner offered than retracted.

This was hardly the right time, then, for Freud to be trumpeting his molestation theory of neurosogenesis to the world. But that is exactly what he did. On February 5, 1896, he sent off two papers for publication: the French-language "Heredity and the Aetiology of the Neuroses" and the German "Further Remarks on the Neuro-Psychoses of Defence." Then on April 21 he delivered a lecture, "The Aetiology of Hysteria," to Vienna's prestigious Circle for Psychiatry and Neurology. An extended version of that lecture, under the same title, was published in installments that began on May 31. And those initiatives were meant to be historic. Both of the papers that were mailed on February 5 contained, for the first time, the signature term *psychoanalysis*,† designating an undescribed method that, according to Freud, had already proved dazzlingly successful.

---

* In January 1897 Freud told Fliess of a "red-hot" idea that had just occurred to him: "The determination of a psychosis . . . as opposed to a neurosis seems to be that sexual abuse occurs before the end of the first intellectual stage, that is, . . . before the age of 1¼ to 1½ years. . . . Epilepsy, I believe, belongs to the same period" (1/14/97; FF, pp. 221–222).

† Since "Heredity" was published before "Further Remarks," at the end of March, it is traditionally regarded as having officially launched Freud's science.

The decision to announce and defend his molestation theory in a collegial lecture was especially daring on Freud's part. Some members of his audience would have recalled his irresponsible pronouncements about cocaine and his role in the torment and death of their beloved colleague Fleischl. Many of them also knew about his pugnacious advocacy of Charcotian "male hysteria," a syndrome that he now relegated to the background. (As he insouciantly told his auditors, "This view of course leaves hysteria in men out of account.")[20] And virtually all listeners would know that in the recently published *Studies on Hysteria*, only one case (Katharina's) had even approximated the new criteria for hysterogenesis.

Whenever tentativeness and tact were called for, however, it was Freud's policy to redouble the adamancy of his claims. And so he now mobilized his full arsenal of braggadocio. The molestation etiology of the psychoneuroses, he told his April auditors, amounted to nothing less than a "*caput Nili*"—the long-sought source of the Nile, from which any further insight must necessarily flow.[21] After "the most laborious and detailed investigations" over many years, he had verified that a molestation was involved "in every case of neurosis."[22] "In the end," he wrote, "*we infallibly come to the field of sexual experience*."[23] As for the thesis that post-pubertal traumas can cause illness only in conjunction with earlier ones, "analysis demonstrates [that fact] in an irrefutable fashion."[24] Thus there could be no room for doubt that the keen new method known as psychoanalysis was "completely reliable."[25]

Likewise, Freud announced that a full analysis, because it exposes the molestation traumas that have made patients sick, always yields therapeutic success. "We cure them of their hysteria," he announced, "by transforming their unconscious memories of the infantile scenes into conscious ones."[26] If a given patient was only partially or temporarily healed, that just showed that further anamnestic work remained to be done, for it was axiomatic that "a complete psycho-analysis implies a radical cure of the hysteria."[27]

As for his means of gathering clinical evidence, Freud credited himself with the same uncanny discernment of which he had boasted in the final chapter of *Studies on Hysteria*. In his lecture, he told the assembled physicians that he could track any number of a patient's ramifying associations:

> The associative chains belonging to the different symptoms begin to enter into relation with one another; the genealogical trees become intertwined. Thus a particular symptom . . . calls up not only the earlier links in its own chain but also a memory from another chain, relating to another symptom. . . . This experience accordingly belongs to both series, and in this way it constitutes a nodal point. Several such nodal points are to be found in every analysis. . . . Going still further back, we come upon nodal points of a different kind. Here the separate associative chains converge.[28]

Speaking to a restive audience, Freud even lingered over a grandiose, self-flattering analogy. He likened himself to a combined explorer and archaeologist who enlists the natives to excavate local ruins, whereupon

> the fragments of columns can be filled out into a temple; the numerous inscriptions, which, by good luck, may be bilingual, reveal an alphabet and a language, and, when they have been deciphered and translated, yield undreamed-of information about the events of the remote past, to commemorate which the monuments were built. *Saxa loquuntur* [the stones speak]![29]

Modern academic humanists, overlooking the fact that Freud was here embellishing an endeavor that would come to nothing, have been ravished by such eloquence. The medical professors in his audience, however, couldn't be distracted from their wish to know the evidential basis of his claims.

Freud knew that he had to say *something* about his data, even if they were nonexistent. In his "Further Remarks" paper, dealing sequentially with hysteria, obsessional neurosis, and paranoia, he implied that he had become familiar with just one case of paranoia.[30] Nevertheless, he claimed to have unearthed the syndrome's etiology. But he gave his major attention to hysteria, specifying that he had treated thirteen cases of the disorder. That, too, was a pitiably small sample from which to generalize. Moreover, in that essay Freud neglected to say that he had removed or even mitigated anyone's neurosis.

He did state, however, that seven of the thirteen abusers were themselves children who had taken advantage of younger playmates. Then he categorized the "foremost" *adult* abusers as nursemaids, governesses, servants, and especially teachers, the last of which groups figured in molestations "with regrettable frequency."[31] Here Freud's inability to do arithmetic betrayed him. Four *main* classes of adult perpetrators, along with smaller classes, were now being held responsible for a grand total of six victims.

On April 21, delivering "The Aetiology of Hysteria," Freud laid claim not to thirteen cases but to eighteen, each of which, he said, had cost him more than 100 consultation hours. It appeared, then, that during the previous ten weeks over 500 hours (5×100) had been occupied with new cases alone. And now Freud announced "therapeutic success"—though only, and ambiguously, "where the circumstances allowed"—with all eighteen patients.[32]

Not one word of this was true. Compare Freud's public assertion with his reports to Fliess:

- May 4, 1896: "My consulting room is empty.... [I] cannot begin any new treatments, and ... none of the old ones are completed."[33]
- December 17, 1896: "So far not a single case is finished."[34]
- January 3, 1897: "Perhaps by [Easter] I shall have carried one case to completion."[35]
- March 29, 1897: "I am still having the same difficulties and have not finished a single case."[36]

Freud did, however, offer his audience two vivid stories of hysterical vomiting, illustrating that his demand for a second, earlier, memory "leads in every instance to the reproduction of new scenes of the character we expect."[37] But then he added,

I shall not return any further to these examples, for I have to confess that they are not derived from any case in my experience but are inventions of mine. Most probably, too, they are bad inventions. I even regard such solutions of hysterical symptoms as impossible.[38]

Members of the Circle for Psychiatry and Neurology could have been forgiven for wondering whether their speaker was in his right mind. Yet this self-defeating passage also appeared in the essay version that began to be published forty days later.

All of Freud's rhetorical cunning was needed—but it didn't suffice—to compensate for his failure to produce objective data. "Shall I put before you," he asked his colleagues, "the actual material I have obtained from my analyses? Or shall I rather try first to meet the mass of objections and doubts which, as I am surely correct in supposing, have taken possession of your attention? I shall choose the latter course."[39] Although the objections and doubts were addressed "first," nothing came second. Freud occupied the bulk of his lecture with shadow boxing against criticisms that he haughtily declared to be of slight or zero merit.

The questions that a skeptical hearer would have wanted him to answer surely included these:

- How could Freud be certain, on the basis of his slender practice, that all psychoneurotics have been abused in childhood? And since he granted that some victims of childhood abuse don't become neurotic, what factor (apart from the all-purpose alibi "heredity") immunizes them from falling ill?
- By what criterion could Freud establish that a given memory—especially an "astonishingly trivial" one—is pathogenic?[40]
- What allowance had he made for suggestion, placebo effects, and experimenter bias? Can false "retrieved memories" prove just as therapeutic as true ones?
- If the premature sexual events aren't experienced as distressing at the time, how can they be counted as traumatic? Why aren't they just permanently forgotten? And is it plausible to hold that the memory of an experience conveys more emotional power than the experience itself?
- If initially solicited, relatively recent "traumatic sexual memories"

don't suffice to account for a neurosis, why should they be *added*, causally, to early-childhood memories that may or may not exist? Shouldn't the inquirer pause to ask whether the whole sexual-memory etiology has failed to be supported?

- Where was the evidence to show that a cure is accomplished whenever an analysis is completed? And hadn't Freud recently made the same therapeutic claim, in *Studies on Hysteria*, before he had even thought of retrieving "infantile scenes"?

- If it was Freud, and not his patient, who transformed her unconscious memories into conscious ones, in whose mind did they now reside? Had an actual recollection been achieved, or was the "restored memory" a product of Freud's manipulations?

All of these points had doubtless occurred to Freud. Some of them, however, he simply chose to ignore. He mentioned some others but said, without explanation, that he was postponing consideration of them.[41] (The postponement never ended.) And he had recourse to a third tactic, which would soon become his favorite: he declared that without familiarity with the psychoanalytic method, critics weren't entitled to pass judgment on its findings.[42] As for explaining what that method was, he begged off on the grounds that he was running out of lecture time. Significantly, he offered the same alibi in the published "Aetiology"—a five-installment essay that could have been indefinitely extended.

Freud gave a full and believable answer to only one of the questions I have listed, the last one: did psychoanalysis actually *restore* early memories of trauma? "Before they come for analysis," he wrote,

the patients know nothing about these scenes. They are indignant as a rule if we warn them that such scenes are going to emerge. . . . [A]nd, even after they have gone through them once more in such a convincing manner, they still attempt to withhold belief from them, by emphasizing the fact that, unlike what happens in the case of other forgotten material, they have no feeling of remembering the scenes.[43]

Thus what Freud elsewhere called a newly conscious memory—the prize retrieved by psychoanalytic probing—was nothing of the kind.

Instead, it was an inference drawn by himself from "scenes" that were themselves generated, he confessed, only "under the most energetic pressure of the analytic procedure, and against an enormous resistance."[44] Because the "conscious memories" never did return (and how could they have done so, dating from ages as young as one and a half?), Freud lacked any evidential support for his "reconstructions." The most essential feature of the molestation theory was therefore insubstantial.

That conclusion ought to have been patent to Freud himself. But it wasn't, because he had already bidden farewell to the stage of his career in which independent evidence mattered to him. His new criterion was *internal consistency*. The strongest proof of his theory, he declared in "The Aetiology of Hysteria," was "the relationship of the infantile scenes to the content of the whole of the rest of the case history":

> It is exactly like putting together a child's picture-puzzle: after many attempts, we become absolutely certain in the end which piece belongs in the empty gap; for only that one piece fills out the picture. . . . In the same way, the contents of the infantile scenes turn out to be indispensable supplements to the associative and logical framework of the neurosis, whose insertion makes its course of development for the first time evident, or even, as we might often say, self-evident.*

Self-evident indeed. The flaw here was that "the associative and logical framework of the neurosis" and "the whole of the rest of the case history," rather than being free-standing realities, were themselves produced by Freud's theory. But so naïvely solipsistic had Freud become that he could now actually declare, in his "Heredity" paper, "The ideas put forward here are not in harmony with the psychological theory [of anyone else]; but they agree perfectly with my own speculations [on the neuroses of defense]."[45]

Agreeing with his own self: from now until the end of his career,

---

* SE, 3:205. Shortly after writing those words, Freud lost faith in the thesis they were meant to place beyond doubt. One might suppose, then, that he had thought better of his puzzle-completing approach to validation. But if we look ahead to his 1923 "Remarks on the Theory and Practice of Dream-Interpretation," we see the formula reiterated (SE, 19:116).

that would be the only proof of correctness Freud would require. Or, as he would put it in 1933, "Applications of analysis are always confirmations of it as well."[46]

3. THE FIRST RECOVERED MEMORY MOVEMENT

Freud's oral presentation of "The Aetiology of Hysteria" was the most consequential public event of his career. Although his molestation theory was implausible and unsupported, he had fancied that its truth would melt all doubts among the eminent psychiatrists and neurologists in his audience. Instead, they were dumbfounded by the whimsicality of what they heard. Rather than pose questions to the speaker, they waited in silence for him to sit down. The only comment, we gather from Freud's report to Fliess, came from the session's chairman, Richard von Krafft-Ebing: "It sounds like a scientific fairy tale" (Es klingt wie ein wissenschaftliches Märchen).[47]

To hear those condescending words spoken by the world's foremost authority on pedophilia must have been a nightmarish experience for Freud. Though he still hoped to be made an honorary professor someday, the dismissal of his molestation argument told him that there could be no hope of an entente between his new science and mainstream medicine. Was it time, then, for him to ponder where he might have gone wrong? The thought was unacceptable to him. His lecture, he told Fliess,

> was given an icy reception by the asses [Eseln] and a strange evaluation by Krafft-Ebing. . . . And this, after one has demonstrated to them the solution of a more-than-thousand-year-old problem, a caput Nili. They can go to hell, euphemistically expressed.[48]

Freud had just made his final attempt to play well with others. Thenceforward he would be an all-or-nothing proponent of revealed truths.

What Krafft-Ebing and his colleagues rejected was, in their opinion, a set of fantastical claims that deserved to be immediately forgotten. Freud himself, however, was a therapist as well as a theorist, and he was already applying his theory to treatment of his patients until, one by one, they gave up on him. At some undetermined point, furthermore, he decided that the chief abusers weren't nursemaids and governesses but *fathers*. Whether Freud had held that opinion all along and diplomatically avoided voicing it isn't known. But we do know, from the Fliess correspondence, that he vigorously pursued the "paternal etiology" with one patient after another while saying nothing about it in print.

In our own recovered memory movement of the 1980s and '90s, we saw a model of what Freud's efforts, had they been successful, could have wrought a century earlier. Patients who came to modern memory therapists complaining of depression, anxiety, or nervous exhaustion were led to believe that their condition must have stemmed from a willed forgetting of horrible abuse, most often committed by a father or stepfather. As a result, families were shredded and "perpetrators"— deemed guilty on no evidence besides the induced "memory" itself— were exposed to shame, loss of employment, and even imprisonment.* And the accusing daughters (as most of them were), instead of acquiring "the courage to heal," typically severed ties with their parents and fell into deeper anger, depression, and confused identity. Under further hypnotic prodding, often enhanced by "truth serum" drugs, some patients were led to conclude that "Satanic ritual abuse" had driven them to develop multiple personalities.[49]

No such tsunami followed Freud's efforts in 1896–97, but not because of prudent restraint on his part. We know, from the example of deputy psychoanalyst Emma Eckstein, that he wished to propagate his new memory therapy and that he especially looked forward to smoking out guilty fathers. "My confidence in paternal etiology has risen greatly," he told Fliess on December 12, 1897; Eckstein "obtained from [her female patient], among other things, the identical scenes with the father."[50]

What spared Freud from becoming known as the instigator of a

---

* The other major aspect of this craze was the indictment and conviction of "molesting" caregivers on the basis of uncorroborated testimony by children. The two halves of the movement had in common *suggestive interrogation*, which corrupted the accusers' memory before any study of the facts could be undertaken.

conceivably worse scourge than the cocaine epidemic was the short-tempered brusqueness of his manner with patients. Our modern memory doctors, some of whom persist even today, have been subtler, leading their charges stepwise, through gently solicitous quizzing, to reach their own "realization" that they had been abused in childhood. Freud, in contrast, was apt to announce his suspicion almost at once and then to demand that it be ratified without delay. As he put it in *Studies on Hysteria*, "the principal point is that I should guess the secret and tell it to the patient straight out."[51]

Freud was still recommending that blunt procedure years later, *after* coming to doubt his molestation theory. Once having classified a patient's symptoms and posited their etiology, he wrote in 1898,

> we may then boldly demand confirmation of our suspicions from the patient. We must not be led astray by initial denials. If we keep firmly to what we have inferred, we shall in the end conquer every resistance by emphasizing the unshakeable nature of our convictions.[52]

In practice, however, "every resistance" was *not* conquered. As Freud wrote to Fliess about one recalcitrant client,

> When I thrust the explanation at her, she was at first won over; then she committed the folly of questioning the old man himself, who at the very first intimation exclaimed indignantly, "Are you implying that I was the one?" and swore a holy oath to his innocence.
>
> She is now in the throes of the most vehement resistance, claims to believe him, but attests to her identification with him by having become dishonest and swearing false oaths. I have threatened to send her away and in the process convinced myself that she has already gained a good deal of certainty which she is reluctant to acknowledge.[53]

Confronted with a negation of everything they knew about their history, Freud's patients concluded that his problems must be worse than theirs. They mocked his self-vaunted ability to glean memories from the cradle. In *The Interpretation of Dreams* he would report that his explanations had met with "disbelief and laughter" (*Unglauben und Gelächter*).[54] Patients, he said, "used to parody this newly gained knowledge by declaring that they were ready to look for recollections dating from a time at which they were not yet alive."[55]

Although no repression-based accusations passed from Freud's consulting room into the public arena, what remains interesting is his initial success in cajoling his patients, in a dimly lit chamber, to visualize "scenes" of forgotten molestation. It was Freud, not the patients, who couldn't tell the difference between such psychodrama and traumatic recall. Consider some representative accounts, presented to Fliess with no indication that the narrated events might suffer from implausibility:

- "When she was two years old, [her father] brutally deflowered her and infected her with his gonorrhea. . . . [A year later her mother] tears the clothes from her [own] body. . . . Then [the mother] stares at a certain spot in the room, her face contorted by rage, covers her genitals with one hand and pushes something away with the other. . . . Shouting and cursing, she bends over far backward, again covers her genitals with her hand, whereupon she falls over forward, so that her head almost touches the floor; finally, she quietly falls over backward onto the floor."[56]

- At age six or seven months, according to Freud, the same patient saw her mother "bleeding nearly to death from an injury inflicted by the father." "Can one doubt," Freud asked, "that the father forces the mother to submit to anal intercourse?"[57] His proof was that at age seventeen the patient became hysterical *when she heard about an operation for hemorrhoids.*

- "Would you please try to search for a case of childhood convulsions that you can trace back . . . to sexual abuse, specifically to *lictus* [licking] (or finger) in the anus. . . . For my newest finding is that I am able to trace back with certainty a patient's attack that merely resembled epilepsy to such treatment by the tongue on the part of his nurse. Age 2 years."[58]

- "The early period before the age of 1½ years is becoming ever more significant. I am inclined to distinguish several periods even within it. Thus I was able to trace back, with certainty, a hysteria . . . which occurred for the first time at 11 months and [I could] hear again the words that were exchanged between two adults at that time! It is as though it comes from a phonograph."[59]

- "Will you believe that the reluctance to drink beer and to shave was elucidated by a scene in which a nurse sits down *podice nudo* [with bare buttocks] in a shallow shaving bowl filled with beer in order to let herself be licked, and so on?"[60]

For madcap self-deception on the part of a psychotherapist, such passages remained unmatched until, nearly a century later, a new generation of memory spelunkers—some of them psychoanalysts—revived both Freud's molestation theory and his facile means of drawing inferences.

To be sure, the five examples above are all taken from private letters. Freud wasn't reluctant, however, to tell everyone how such scenes could explain neurotic symptoms. "Thus, in one of my cases," he related to his audience of physicians, "the circumstance that the child was required to stimulate the genitals of a grown-up woman with his foot was enough to fixate his neurotic attention for years on to his legs and to their function, and finally to produce a hysterical paraplegia."[61]

What Freud had done in this instance was to "read back" from a foot problem to an indefinite foot-themed sexual drama; to require his patient to fashion a story that met that specification; and then to insert the story into his theory machine for generating "conversion." The metamorphosis of repressed memory into paraplegia, though it had occurred entirely within Freud's head, bore potential import for his patient, who was being steered away from appropriate orthopedic care and toward crank therapy.

The "memories" that Freud solicited in the midnineties were too outlandish to be credited; but why, then, did he advance them so uncritically? Some of his descriptions for Fliess retained the euphoric and "phonographic" immediacy of direct experience, as if he were still sharing in the conjured vision as it emerged. We may recall, in this connection, that he was then treating both his patients' and his own "nasal reflex neuroses" with substantial amounts of cocaine. Both parties, then, may have been suggestible—in short, effectively hypnotized—when one of them tried to attune his mental frequency to the other party's unconscious.

Such enchantment with bizarre images is especially notable in Freud's reports about the "memories" of Emma Eckstein, who was still his patient while also serving as his apprentice. Unquestionably, it was she about whom Freud wrote on January 24, 1897, "Imagine, I obtained a scene about the circumcision of a girl. The cutting off of a piece of the labium minor (which is even shorter today), sucking up the blood, after which the child was given a piece of the skin to eat."[62]

No one has been able to say how Freud could have compared two measurements, decades apart, of Eckstein's apparently twice-truncated vaginal lip. But if he thought that the labium had been *further shortened*, he must have believed in the reality of the whole grisly tale. He was investing his faith, then, in a childhood episode that sounded exactly like Satanic ritual abuse.

Freud's comment when introducing this passage renders that comparison unavoidable. "I am beginning to grasp an idea," he wrote:

> it is as though in the perversions, of which hysteria is the negative, we have before us a remnant of a primeval sexual cult, which once was—perhaps still is—a religion in the Semitic East (Moloch, Astarte). . . . I dream, therefore, of a primeval devil religion with rites that are carried on secretly, and understand the harsh therapy of the witches' judges.[63]

Here was a milestone in Freud's devolution from the scientific attitude. Thanks to a patient's fantasy that had been teased forth by his own obsession with sadistic erotica, Freud believed himself to be in contact with phylogenetic memory traces. Moreover, those traces told him that even then, in 1897, there might exist a pre-Mosaic cult that was committing sexual atrocities in service to an idol. Freud had retired his microscope for good and had replaced it with a crystal ball.*

---

* The fullest discussion of this incident and its relation both to male and female circumcision and to Freud's Jewish identity is Bonomi 2015. Bonomi, however, is himself a

As for "the harsh therapy of the witches' judges," Freud's new-found belief that he could hear emanations from the remote past in his patients' utterances had aroused his curiosity about "hysteria" in Counter-Reformation sorcery trials.[64] Like his fellow psychologizing historian Charcot, he was more interested in the victims' irrationality than in that of their persecutors. Indeed, he discounted torture and terror as inducements to witchcraft confessions, which he now regarded as having resulted not from the rack but from the aftereffects of infantile sexual abuse on the already impaired female mind.

In Freud's opinion, then, the unfortunate women who would say anything to avoid being burned alive had been "guilty"—not of having consorted with Satan, but of having acquired a devilish imagination. Their judges had been "therapists" in the sense of having had to confront preexistent psychical material of a disgusting nature. Freud felt a strong kinship with those inquisitors—who, he hinted, may themselves have been abused in childhood.[65] Indeed, his vision of a modern sex cult shows how close his worldview was to their own.

According to Freud's theory in 1897, the hysteria of Emma Eckstein had resulted from early molestation. Her psyche, then, ought to have rhymed with those of her "witch" predecessors. So, naturally, witchlike manifestations emerged from her analysis. "Eckstein has a scene," Freud wrote to Fliess, "where the diabolus sticks needles into her fingers and then places a candy on each drop of blood."[66] Here there could be no question of an actual memory on Emma's part. Instead, she was giving Freud what he demanded at that moment: seeming evidence that infantile sexual abuse supplies the fantasy material of demonology.

Psychoanalysis would remain a theory about possession, not by the Devil but by bad thoughts that take up residence in the unconscious and compel perverse behavior. Soon Freud would drop the idea that neurotics had been molested and would assert, rather, that their own incestuous thoughts had made them sick; in so doing, he would be rendering his theory more medieval in spirit. He realized that fact and

---

"recovered memory psychoanalyst" who, largely overlooking the problem of suggestion, endows Eckstein with a likely history of mutilations.

embraced it. As he would write in 1923, "The demonological theory of those dark times has won in the end against all the somatic views of the period of 'exact science.' The states of possession correspond to our neuroses, for the explanation of which we once more have recourse to psychical powers."[67]

28

The Breakthrough That Wasn't

1. THE SETBACK

The most widely discussed letter that Freud ever wrote was sent to Fliess on September 21, 1897. In dramatic terms, ranging in tone from mournful to stoical to manically relieved, it announced the demise of the molestation theory. "I no longer believe in my *neurotica*," Freud confessed.[1] And into the wastebasket with his theory went all of his worldly hopes. "The expectation of eternal fame was so beautiful," he wrote, "as was that of certain wealth, complete independence, travels, and lifting the children above the severe worries that robbed me of my youth. Everything depended upon whether or not hysteria would come out right."[2] But it hadn't.

Freud spelled out no fewer than eight frustrations—six, if we discount redundancies—tending to doom his theory:

- "the continual disappointment in my efforts to bring one analysis to a real conclusion"; "the running away of people who . . . had been most gripped [by analysis]"; and "the absence of . . . complete successes";
- "the possibility of explaining to myself the partial successes in other ways, in the usual fashion";

- "the surprise that in all cases, the *father*, not excluding my own, had to be accused of being perverted [*pervers*]";
- "the realization of the unexpected frequency of hysteria, . . . whereas surely such widespread perversions against children are not very probable";*
- "the certain insight that there are no indications of reality in the unconscious, so that one cannot distinguish between truth and fiction that has been cathected with affect";
- resignation to the likelihood that, if even "in the most deep-reaching psychosis the unconscious memory does not break through," it wouldn't do so in the treatment of a neurosis, either.[3]

Overlooking, for now, the big anomaly in this list—why had fathers been implicated "in all cases"?—we must acknowledge that here, for once, Freud had engaged in severe and largely cogent self-criticism. Two considerations must have been especially troubling for him. First, the absence of good clinical results was a grave matter, and not just because Freud knew that cures were regarded as the gold standard of validation. In claiming to have successfully treated eighteen cases of molestation-induced hysteria, he had committed a scientific fraud—indeed, a third fraud after pretending to cocaine expertise and then lying about therapeutic outcomes in *Studies on Hysteria*. If his retraction were now to become known, the already accomplished loss of his clientele would be topped by public exposure as a cheat.

Even more shaming, however, was a thought so terrible that Freud could refer to it only through circumlocution: "the possibility of explaining to myself the partial successes in other ways, in the usual fashion." He had realized, if only temporarily, that his patients' "scenes" had probably been tailored to his demands, in which case he had been foolishly blind to the problem of suggestion. And the charge of suggestive contamination, so patently warranted, threatened to

---

* This epidemiological consideration was an unwelcome fruit of a research effort conducted by a German-American pupil of Freud's, Felix Gattel. See Sulloway 1992, pp. 513–515.

delegitimate his entire clinical method and any future conclusions it might yield.

This was a moment, then, that called for a basic reappraisal on Freud's part—a critique that could draw him back toward accountability to empirical norms. There was no sign, however, either then or later, that he was capable of conducting such an orderly retreat. He could either give up or press straight ahead, but he couldn't learn from his mistakes. Thus, while in one sentence he struck the note of surrender that we have heard before—"Now I can once again remain quiet and modest, go on worrying and saving"[4]—a ray of hope was already breaking through his gloom. "Can it be," he dared to ask, "that this doubt merely represents an episode in the advance toward further insight?"[5]

For believers in the legend, the answer to that question was, and remains, an emphatic *yes*. Many of them, in fact, have regarded this very letter as heralding the true birth of psychoanalysis. In their view, the demise of "seduction" enabled Freud to perceive, almost at once, that the real cause of his patients' hysteria was their unresolved oedipal feelings—urgings toward patricide and incest. It is even suspected that such swelling insight was what pushed the molestation theory aside. As Ernst Kris phrased it in a note to the redacted edition of the Fliess letters, Freud

> had drawn near to the Oedipus complex, in which he recognized the aggressive impulses of children directed against their parents, but had still remained faithful to his belief in the reality of the seduction scenes. It seems reasonable to assume that it was only the self-analysis of this summer that made possible rejection of the seduction hypothesis.[6]

According to Kris, then, Freud may have sounded chastened on September 21, but he was just clearing away the last obstacle to a revelation that already lay within his reach.

Unsurprisingly, James Strachey espoused a similar view. When Freud renounced "seduction" in 1897, according to the editor of the *Standard Edition*, his discovery of the Oedipus complex was "almost simultaneous."[7] Ernest Jones, always more florid than Strachey, went farther, transforming what Freud had called "this collapse of everything valuable" into a triumph.[8] "Well might he be elated," wrote Jones, "for with the insight he had now gained he was on the verge of exploring the whole range of infantile sexuality and of completing his theory of dream psychology—his two mightiest achievements. Eighteen ninety-seven was the acme of Freud's life."[9] And three decades later Peter Gay added: "If the ground of reality had been lost, that of fantasy had been won. It had been a strenuous and upsetting time, but the rewards were dazzling."[10]

For the first editors of the Fliess correspondence, however, pondering what to include and exclude, the September 21 letter posed some delicate problems. Although Kris, Anna Freud, and Marie Bonaparte welcomed the letter's multipronged assault on "seduction," in certain respects Freud had said too much. He had admitted, for example, that he hadn't finished a single analysis (*eine Analyse*) to support his molestation theory. Of course, the editors remembered his very different assurance in "The Aetiology of Hysteria," where he claimed to have successfully treated eighteen cases. The enemies of psychoanalysis couldn't be given the satisfaction of catching the founder in an untruth. And so, in 1950, *eine* silently became *meine*, and all was well; Freud hadn't finished *his own* analysis![11]

No less worrisome was the letter's unsuitability to the purpose that Anna Freud and her associates wanted it to serve in psychoanalytic historiography: as the definitive turn toward a fantasy-based (not molestation-based) account of the psychoneuroses. With the complete file of correspondence lying before them, the editors couldn't fail to be drawn up short by letters from December 1897 that reaffirmed a "paternal etiology."[12] Those passages showed that the molestation theory was still being applied, by both Freud and Emma Eckstein, several months after he had disavowed it. Out came the scissors, then; the vexatious letters were excluded, and readers of *The Origins of Psycho-Analysis* would never learn that Freud's decisiveness on September 21 had been only provisional.

The assistance of censorship was needed, we see, for Freud to be portrayed as a man who held himself consistently accountable to scientific logic. In actuality, even so frivolous a datum as the untrained Eck-stein's eliciting an incestuous "scene" from her patient—perhaps her only patient—could momentarily reinflate his hope that his molesta-tion theory might win approval after all. The famous letter had implied a need for sweeping methodological reform, but if the outlook for acceptance was brightening, Freud wasn't inclined to interfere.

There was no clean break, then, in September 1897. Nor is it the case, however, as Masson alleges, that Freud secretly adhered to his molestation theory until 1901 and then, in 1905, renounced it merely in order to make peace with scandalized authorities.[13] Ingratiation might have done Freud some good in the years leading up to his delayed academic promotion in 1902, but he was in no frame of mind to placate "the asses" who had doubted him.[14]

Throughout the rest of 1897 and 1898, Freud remained in a state of anxious uncertainty about the cause and proper treatment of hyste-ria. He hadn't thought of anything to replace "seduction" when, in February 1898, he once again told Fliess, "The cases of hysteria are proceeding especially poorly. I shall not finish a single one this year either; and as for the next one, I shall be completely without patient material."[15] "My work," he confided in August of the same year, "now appears to me to have far less value, and my disorientation to be com-plete; . . . another entire year has gone by without any tangible pro-gress in the theory."[16] And "this year," he wrote in October 1898, "I even gave up lecturing so as not to have to talk about anything that I still hope to learn myself."[17] This was Freud at a time when, according to his hagiographers, his mind had been liberated by possession of the oedipal key to repression, guilt, neurosis, and psychosexual development.

It may have been on January 3, 1899, that Freud really, but still privately, abandoned hope for his molestation theory. That was when he informed Fliess that "to the question 'What happened in earliest childhood?' the answer is 'Nothing, but the germ of a sexual impulse existed.'"[18] There, finally, he had made a turn (by no means unprob-lematic) toward the *sexual constitution* of children as accounting for the disturbances that could eventuate in hysteria. But even then, he was loath to retract his claims of 1896. For years thereafter, his published writings simply avoided the topic of "seduction."

As for the Oedipus complex, it is true that the basic idea was disclosed to Fliess on October 15, 1897.[19] But the new concept didn't yet strike Freud as posing an alternative to the authenticity of molestations recovered from the earliest years of life, much less to the proposition that hysteria is caused by repressed memories of that abuse. Nor did he attempt to propagate the new concept. The several papers he published between 1898 and 1900 are devoid of references to it.

The world wouldn't be briefed about the sexual and homicidal designs of toddlers on their parents until Chapter 5 of *The Interpretation of Dreams*, published at the turn of the century.[20] Even then, nothing would be said about therapeutic applications. And when, in 1906, Freud finally admitted, in a chapter inconspicuously contributed to someone else's book, that he had changed his mind about "seduction," he neglected to ascribe any importance to the Oedipus factor.[21] The notion that repressed oedipal wishes constitute "the *nuclear complex* of every neurosis" was launched only in a lecture that he delivered in 1909 and published in the following year.[22] In sum, then, the story of how "the discovery of the Oedipus complex" liberated Freud from his molestation theory is a hoary fable and nothing more.

2. FREUD'S *RASHOMON*

The psychoanalytic establishment's effort to date "the discovery of the Oedipus complex" from 1897 was a desperate project whose goal was to turn his moment of greatest confusion into that of greatest insight. The urgency of the project stemmed from the Freudians' perception of an enormous risk—one that was potentially deadly for psychoanalytic theory altogether. In 1896 Freud had overruled his patients' denial that they had been sexually abused in childhood, and now he saw that they had probably been right to contradict him. On what basis, then, could he later assert that they had "only fantasized" molestations that had been nobody's idea but his own?[23]

In his *Autobiographical Study* of 1925, Freud dared to mention the possibility that he "had perhaps forced" daydream scenes of molestation upon his patients.[24] Three sentences later, however, he banished that disturbing thought: "I do not believe even now that I forced the seduction-phantasies on my patients, that I 'suggested' them."[25] This was the full extent of his public soul searching. On numerous other occasions he strove to obscure what had really happened. His intellectual heirs in the 1950s were merely completing a job of disinformation that had occupied Freud himself, intermittently, for a quarter century.

From 1905 onward, Freud attempted to jettison a necessary minimum of the molestation theory without having to admit that he had been utterly deluded about it. His first solution was to maintain that he had merely "overrated the importance of [early] seduction in comparison with the factors of sexual constitution and development."[26] Allegedly, then, the "seductions" had been real, and thus Freud's method of detecting them had been impeccable.

In an essay published in 1906, "My Views on the Part Played by Sexuality in the Aetiology of the Neuroses," Freud substantially reiterated this position. Quite by accident, he reported, his clinical data from hysterics in 1896 had included a disproportionate number of actual "seductions." Hence he had "over-estimated the frequency of such events (though in other respects they were not open to doubt)."[27] Once again, then, he was blameless; he had correctly interpreted the evidence, but "by chance" the evidence itself had been skewed.[28]

Freud's 1906 apologia contained further exercises of fast shuffling. Ten years earlier, he wrote, he hadn't been able to distinguish between true and false childhood recollections, but now he could do so; he knew which of his patients had been molested and which had only fantasized the assault. How had he gained that knowledge? The claim was a bluff, put forward with no explanatory details. Freud couldn't describe a single case in which he had determined that a former "memory" was false. Nor, apparently, had he notified any of his ex-patients that they could now stop worrying about having been abused. That would have been humiliating, as the patients would surely have reminded him that they had scoffingly rejected the "memories" with which he had tried to saddle them.

In his 1914 *History of the Psycho-Analytic Movement*, Freud ventured a new line of argument. Molestations that had been "not open to doubt" in the 1906 account were now said to have never occurred at all. The contrary belief, he wrote, "broke down under the weight of its own improbability in definitely ascertainable circumstances."[29] Though he offered no details, Freud here assayed the first in a series of mutually clashing versions of the "seduction" evidence that had once impressed him.

Initially, Freud recounted in his *History*, he had noticed merely that "something in the past" appeared to be implicated as a pathogen in cases of neurosis.[30] Lacking awareness of infantile sexuality, he had assumed that any sexual factors must date from puberty or later. But to his amazement, "the tracks led still further back into childhood and into its earliest years."[31] Readers could never guess that the tracks in question were not clinical evidence but Fliess's biogenetic speculations about sexual development, supplemented by Freud himself as an armchair physiologist.

The story continued:

> On the way, a mistaken idea had to be overcome which might have
> been almost fatal to the young science. Influenced by Charcot's view
> of the traumatic origin of hysteria, one was readily inclined to accept
> as true and aetiologically significant the statements made by patients
> in which they ascribed their symptoms to passive sexual experiences
> in the first years of childhood—to put it bluntly, to seduction.[32]

The statements made by patients. Here, in a phrase that drew no attention to itself, was the great untruth that would become canonical in psychoanalytic accounts of the molestation theory. The 1896 papers had plainly stated that it was Freud, not his patients, who had "reconstructed" their childhood traumas. Likewise, he had disclosed that even after extorting "scenes" through "the strongest compulsion of the treatment," he couldn't get any patient to regard such a coerced image as a memory; all of them "assure me . . . emphatically of their unbelief."*

---

* SE, 3:204. Even today, however, the myth of "statements" persists. Freud's female patients, according to Élisabeth Roudinesco, "often recounted these episodes [of childhood sexual abuse] during treatment with an abundance of details" (Roudinesco 2016, p. 57). Some opponents of psychoanalysis, too, still accept Freud's word about what he was "told." Thus Rebecca Solnit: "Freud's patients, amazingly, found their way to telling

From 1914 onward, Freud could profess that he had been fooled not by his own reckless method but by stories to which he had lent too sympathetic an ear. And it was his awakening from this understandable mistake, readers would be told in the *History*, that gave us psychoanalysis:

> If hysterical subjects trace back their symptoms to traumas that are fictitious, then the new fact which emerges is precisely that they create such scenes in *phantasy*, and this psychical reality requires to be taken into account alongside practical reality. This reflection was soon followed by the discovery that these phantasies were intended to cover up the auto-erotic activity of the first years of childhood, to embellish it and raise it to a higher plane. And now, from behind the phantasies, the whole range of a child's sexual life came to light.[33]

Here Freud asserts not only that infantile sexuality is the key developmental reality uncovered by psychoanalysis, but also that the means of its discovery was the reinterpretation of scenes that his patients had invented in order to disguise their early masturbation. But even if they had freely narrated tales of molestation (and they hadn't), the motive Freud here imputes to them for having done so would be incredible. According to him, it was less shameful to fantasize that one had been raped for years by a family member than to admit that one had fondled one's genitals at, say, age two. (And how was a patient supposed to have remembered that?) Still more fundamentally, the only patient to whom Freud's explanation might even vaguely apply was Freud himself, the producer-director of all those fantasies.

If the Oedipus complex, an intrafamilial scenario, was going to serve as the centerpiece of Freudian doctrine, the "seducers" Freud had named in 1896—nursemaids, governesses, servants, teachers, and older playmates—would have to be replaced by parents, who would then be exonerated by the new theory. In his 1916–17 *Introductory Lectures on Psycho-Analysis*, accordingly, he claimed that girls who report

---

what they had suffered, and at first he heard them. . . . Then he repudiated his findings" (Solnit 2014, p. 4).

molestation in childhood "fairly regularly" accuse their fathers of the crime.[34] And in 1925 he reiterated, "with female patients the part of seducer was almost always assigned to their father."[35]

This revised history would bear profound implications for the practical conduct of psychoanalysis. When the father is named, Freud declared, "there can be no doubt either of the imaginary nature of the accusation or of the motive that has led to it"—namely, the motive of repressed *yearning for* paternal incest.[36] This was a forensic judgment: because every girl wishes to copulate with her father, all who complain of having endured such incest are only fantasizing. So, notoriously, Freudian analysts dismissed some women patients' veridical confessions along with their pleas for help. The feminist backlash against such callousness was a major source of the anger that fueled "recovered memory" therapy in recent decades.

Freud had one more card to play, after 1925, in the game of turning "seduction" to new ends. By the time he wrote his 1931 essay "Female Sexuality," he had conceived a new idea about little girls. Before they form their Oedipus complexes, he now decided, they are fixated on their *mothers*. Naturally, then, "what his female patients had told him" mutated once again. They "regularly accuse their mother of seducing them," he wrote. "This is because they necessarily received their first, or at any rate their strongest, genital sensations when they were being cleaned and having their toilet attended to by their mother (or by someone such as a nurse who took her place)."[37] It would seem, then, that the molestation theory had come full circle, ending with a revelation that, for females anyway, the sexual abuse is authentic and half-innocently performed by mothers or their surrogates.

In his 1933 *New Introductory Lectures on Psycho-Analysis*, however, Freud reverted to his father etiology one last time:

In the period when [my] main interest was directed to discovering infantile sexual traumas, almost all my women patients told me that they had been seduced by their father. I was driven to recognize in the end that these reports were untrue and so came to understand that hysterical symptoms are derived from phantasies and not from real occurrences.[38]

If Freud's modern readers were disposed to think logically in response to his claims, they would perceive that the alibi of his having been told about molestation always made a poor fit with psychoanalysis. Both the molestation theory and its orthodox Freudian successor relied indispensably on the proposition that memories or fantasies must be unconscious in order to count as pathogenic. Indeed, the very act of repressing them was assumed to have initiated the process of neurosis formation.

Thus, when Freud wrote, fictitiously, of his patients' communications (*Mitteilungen*), reports (*Berichte*), and stories (*Geschichten*) about their imagined childhood abuse, he was undermining his own theory. He did so anyway in order to forestall the most destructive outcome of all: the public's awakening to a realization that *both* his patients' "repressed memories" *and* their "unconscious fantasies," which psychoanalytic therapy supposedly brought to consciousness and gradually reconciled with "the ego," were spurious artifacts of his method.

3. THE SECOND DISCOVERY NARRATIVE

Why didn't Freud simply tell the truth about how he had "discovered the Oedipus complex"? The real story was confided to Fliess in the letter of October 15, 1897, already mentioned. There he announced,

> I have found, in my own case too, [the phenomenon of] being in love with my mother and jealous of my father, and I now consider it a universal event in early childhood. . . . Everyone in the audience was once a budding Oedipus in fantasy and each recoils in horror from the dream fulfillment here transplanted into reality.[39]

Freud went on to apply his hypothesis to another budding Oedipus, Hamlet, who cannot kill his murderous and incestuous uncle Claudius because, Freud reasoned, Shakespeare unconsciously sensed that Claudius has carried out Hamlet's own desires.

Unquestionably, Freud had "discovered an Oedipus complex" in his own mind. But the later Freud, we remember, cultivated an image of himself as a methodical inductivist who had arrived at his sexual theses reluctantly, in obligation to unignorable clinical evidence. He couldn't very well admit that the Oedipus complex had turned up through sheer introspection. And it would have been still harder to explain how he had known, instantly, that the oedipal phenomenon was "a universal event in early childhood." Only a mystic, not a psychologist, could have made such a claim without appearing to have forsaken the ethos of his calling.

These problems became acute once Marie Bonaparte had shared the Fliess correspondence with the postwar inner circle. As I have indicated, an editorial solution was agreed upon. If Freud's letters to Fliess had to be sampled in a book, the one letter that heralded the birth of the Oedipus complex could hardly be omitted; but in other respects the record would be skewed to minimize his intellectual confusion and his deference to Fliess's judgment.

It would be granted that a temporarily neurotic Freud, at a crisis point in his career, had felt a need for support from somebody; and that somebody just happened to have been Fliess. The new story said that Freud had summoned his peerless courage and had performed upon his own self the world's first psychoanalysis—and in the process he had unearthed the Oedipus complex. That discovery had rendered him normal again, had liberated him from Fliess, and had allowed him to give the rest of us our acquaintance with the deepest mystery of the unconscious.

This was the theme of Kris's introduction to the selective Fliess correspondence, a deft feat of evasion implying that the only symptom of Freud's "neurosis" had been his admiration for Fliess. In that case, it was more or less believable that Freud could have mustered great inner resources to retrieve key memories from his childhood and to cure himself of his dependency. Jones then imparted a mythic dimension to the imagined feat. "It is as if [Freud] divined all along," he declaimed, "that the path he was treading would sooner or later lead to terrible secrets, the revealing of which he dreaded but on which he was nevertheless as determined as Oedipus himself."[40] And again: "What a daemonic intuition must have been at work! Perhaps we are nearing a clue to the mysterious problem of how it was that just this man was destined to discover psychoanalysis and reveal the unconscious mind of man."[41]

We are nearing a clue, all right, but not to Freud's channeling of the seer Teiresias, attuned to a hidden dimension and fated to be made the oracle of a truth from which all others shrank. The Oedipus complex, as we will now see, was called into existence by a private need of its inventor. And far from constituting an actual discovery, it signaled a retreat from obsessive ideas about his own history that he found too painful to endure.

29

The Labyrinth of Reproaches

1. "YE HOVERING FORMS"

"The most exceptional event in the life of Sigmund Freud," the Canadian psychoanalyst Patrick Mahony has written, "was undoubtedly his self-analysis."[1] But what was it, exactly, and when did it begin and end? As Mahony showed, there has been no agreement on either point. Jones, Kris, Max Schur, Erik Erikson, Didier Anzieu, and Freud himself, among others, supplied conflicting and sometimes self-contradictory accounts.[2] The venture that is alleged to have given rise to psychoanalysis is so elusive that some skeptical historians doubt whether it occurred at all.[3]

If by *self-analysis* we mean introspection that uses dreams and memories to generate reflections about one's personality, we could say that Freud's self-analysis began on the morning of July 24, 1895, when he awoke from the dream now known as "Irma's Injection" and began to assess its significance.[4] A few years later it would serve as the "specimen dream" of *The Interpretation of Dreams* and thus, subsequently, as the most minutely inspected occurrence in the corpus of psychoanalytic writings. Freud, however, didn't start referring, even privately, to a "self-analysis" until 1897. And not until the second edition of *The Interpretation of Dreams* in 1909 did he publicly mention that he had undertaken to analyze himself. The composition of that book, he had allegedly realized after the fact, had been "a portion of my own self-analysis, my reaction to my father's death—that is to say, to the most important event, the most poignant loss, of a man's life."[5]

If, however, the self-analysis is typified by the passages referring to it in the Fliess letters, mourning had nothing to do with it. Indeed, it is hard to detect any signs that Freud was upset by his father's long-expected death; he seems to have taken it quite in stride. Jacob figures in *The Interpretation of Dreams* as having failed to live up to the heroic role that the boy Sigismund had expected of him; but even that narrative was drawn not from the intense soul searching of 1897–98 but from simple reminiscence, long remembered.

In certain fevered moods, the Freud of 1897 was thinking of his father in an entirely different way. On February 8 of that year, Fliess was informed about Jacob's responsibility for long-past monstrous acts. Freud, the theorist of "conversion," had just finished telling his friend that certain adult headache symptoms betray a childhood scene of forced oral sex, "where the head is held still for the purpose of actions in the mouth."[6] "Unfortunately," he added, "my own father was one of these perverts and is responsible for the hysteria of my brother . . . and those of several younger sisters."[7]

Here Freud was obeying the logic of his molestation theory, which decreed that all psychoneuroses are traceable to early sexual abuse. He believed that he detected psychopathology not only in himself but also in his siblings. That is what made Jacob not only a suspect but, to Sigmund's way of thinking, an exposed reprobate. For, if several members of the same generation were hysterics who had been raised by a common father, his guilt was a foregone conclusion.

It is remarkable that Freud, in a phase when he surely wished to bury his old differences with Jacob over religious observances and the choice of a career, would be leveling this outrageous accusation against him. There is no way we can bridge the chasm between such slander and other passages that manifest affection and a rational assessment of his father's ingratiating qualities. Days after Jacob's burial, for example, Fliess was told, "I valued him highly, understood him very well, and with his peculiar mixture of deep wisdom and fantastic light-heartedness he had a significant effect on my life."[8] We can only surmise that

Freud's "cocaine self" was responsible for the lurid charges that weren't being tested against conscious memories.

Here we may note that Jones, following the script of the postwar legend, ascribed to Freud "a very considerable psychoneurosis" that had held sway through the 1890s.[9] It was, Jones ventured, an "anxiety hysteria" consisting chiefly of "extreme changes of mood":

> The alternations of mood were between periods of elation, excitement, and self-confidence on the one hand and periods of severe depression, doubt, and inhibition on the other. In the depressed moods he could neither write nor concentrate his thoughts (except during his professional work). He would spend leisure hours of extreme boredom, turning from one thing to another, cutting open books, looking at maps of ancient Pompeii, playing patience or chess, but being unable to continue at anything for long—a state of restless paralysis.[10]

This description calls to mind Freud's letters from Paris in 1885–86, when, oppressed by feelings of inadequacy and neglect, he absented himself from the Salpêtrière and moped in his hotel room day after day, consoled only by Victor Hugo and cocaine. But his condition in 1897 was worse. As he wrote to Fliess on June 22, 1897,

> I have never before even imagined anything like this period of intellectual paralysis. Every line is torture. . . . I have been through some kind of neurotic experience, curious states incomprehensible to [consciousness], twilight thoughts, veiled doubts, with barely a ray of light here or there.[11]

Not surprisingly, then, the famous self-analysis was itself a twilight phenomenon, discontinuous and murky. The first inkling of the Oedipus complex, far from triumphantly concluding the process, was just one passing incident within it. Three weeks later Freud reported that his "self-analysis is once more at a standstill; or rather, it slowly trickles on without my understanding anything of the course it takes." Nine days after that, "my self-analysis remains interrupted." When three further weeks had elapsed, "I often dream whole days away." And after another month the self-analysis was "still groping about, entirely in the dark."[12] Nor did Freud ever report that the process had reached a satisfactory conclusion, or indeed any conclusion at all. Nor, as we will later see, is it true that his self-analysis freed him from reliance on Fliess.

At his low points in 1897, Freud's frame of mind was as different as it could be from the cool detachment of a researcher. This was the period in which he thought he could hear the voices of a patient's mother and father when the patient herself had been eleven months old. During this time, as the psychoanalyst Carlo Bonomi observes, "his production of theory was permeated by visceral sensations and oneiric visions."[13] Fundamental tenets of psychoanalysis were being acquired in a dazed, dreamlike state. But that wasn't all. Freud's dreams themselves struck him as providing evidence about his past—evidence that he then accepted with scarcely more reserve than that of a dreamer in the deepest sleep.

Here it will be important to distinguish between two approaches to dream-based knowledge, both of which were assayed by Freud but with different results. The more rational method is the one exemplified in *The Interpretation of Dreams*, where Freud, musing on his file of recorded associations to many dreams, attempted to specify the traits, desires, concerns, and feelings that must have determined each dream's incidents and images. That procedure was far from foolproof, but it was spared from complete wildness by the fact that Freud already knew the facts about himself that he found relevant to each of his narrated dreams. His theory of dream formation could be completely wrong—indeed it was, as we will see—without impugning his characterological insights, which could have been proffered without any reference to dreams at all.

The self-analysis at its most intense pitch, however, purported to draw *new* information from dreams. Freud's tacit theory, exemplified only in the Fliess letters, held that dreams give us access to early-childhood events, the memories of which were repressed and hence kept unrecoverable by any other means. If we have a question about a deed that we may have committed or endured, no matter how remote in time, sooner or later a dream will supply the answer.

The self-analytic Freud, then, regarded dreaming itself, and not just after-the-fact analysis of "dream thoughts," as a tool of investigation. Supposedly, it could be applied night after night as one dream-encased "recollection" stirred a question that another dream could soon be expected to answer. As Freud confided to Fliess,

> my self-analysis, which I consider indispensable for the clarification of the whole problem [of hysterical etiology], has continued in my dreams and has presented me with the most valuable elucidations and clues. At certain points I have the feeling of being at the end, and so far I have always known where the next dream-night would continue.[14]

As Freud was well aware, his belief that dreams can reveal arcane knowledge aligned him with popular superstition and against the scientific mainstream, especially in positivist Vienna. If he nevertheless made that leap, it was because, like Faust, he had reached a point of intellectual and emotional frustration that rendered him willing to risk his reputation for a stab at visionary truth. At times he did remind himself that memories extracted from dreams would need to be corroborated; but he made only desultory attempts in that vein. As he later told Fliess about his means of reaching conclusions, "there is no question of deliberation." Rather, "wild things" seemed to be "at work on the lowest floor"; and the powers that were stirring, he believed, would tell him what he needed to know.[15] He concluded that letter by quoting the dedication to Goethe's verse drama: "Again ye come, ye hovering forms."[16]

This irrationalist frame of mind was epitomized in Freud's reaction to a scene from one dream about childhood experience that he recounted to Fliess. "I find nothing like this in the chain of my memories," he reasoned; "so I regard it as a genuine ancient discovery."[17] Here Freud was declaring that *because* he couldn't remember the incident, he could confidently assign it an early date in his babyhood. He was automatically

excluding a possibility that would have occurred to any other psychologist, presumably including the author of *The Interpretation of
Dreams*: that this was no memory at all but an oblique reflection of
his dreaming thoughts at the time.

2. HAUNTED—BUT BY WHAT?

The leisure to engage in a protracted examination of his own mind was
granted to Freud by his inability to retain patients in the period when
he was haranguing them to admit that they had been sexually abused.
In the whole 1895–1900 span, he had kept only two long-term clients,
Emma Eckstein and a certain "Herr E.," now known to have been the
wealthy idler Oskar Fellner.[18] Both treatments were flops. We have seen
how preposterous Freud's judgments about Eckstein were in 1897, the
year when she realized that his diagnosis of her "hysterical" lameness
must have been wrong from the start. As for Fellner, he remained symptomatic and poorly understood in 1900, after five squandered years in
Freud's care.[19]

These frustrations, amplified by Freud's sinking feeling about his
molestation theory, nagged at his self-esteem, which was further challenged by a *positive* development in the same period. In 1897 Richard
von Krafft-Ebing and Hermann Nothnagel nominated him for an honorary professorship in the University of Vienna—a cherished prize, but
one that could have been rendered unreachable by anti-Semitism or by
his colleagues' acquaintance with the less savory aspects of his record.
Never before had he so keenly felt that he was standing under pitiless
judgment.

It is instructive to see how many shames are alluded to in *The
Interpretation of Dreams*. They range from the trivial—Freud's expen-
ditures of family money on indulgences (*Liebhabereien*) such as cigars
and antiquities—to the grave: his imprudent glorification of cocaine in
the 1880s, his addicting of Fleischl, his part in the mutilation of Eckstein, the fatal overdosing of Mathilde Schleicher, and the complaint
by other uncured patients that they had been given the wrong treatment. And some dreams conjured figures, such as Breuer, Fliess, Leopold Königstein, and the pediatrician Oscar Rie, who knew of Freud's

missteps and appeared to be holding them against him.[20] To be sure, Freud put the matter differently, maintaining that some of his reported dreams were, in effect, self-justifying rejoinders to his critics. The rejoinders, however, are to be found not in the dream reports but only in his post-dreaming analyses, whose emphasis on vindication signaled that he was feeling inadequate and harried.

Although Freud had drawn comfort, as a preadolescent, from the daydream of becoming a great warrior and leader, his real adult dreams appeared to tell him that he had never attained the status of a man. The theme of castration is repeatedly implied in his associations to those dreams, from "The Botanical Monograph" and "Goethe's Attack on Herr M." through "The Bird-Beaked Figures" and "Dissecting His Own Pelvis." His self-analysis—the intended cure for a self-identified mental disorder—only made him more keenly aware that all of his failures were intertwined.[21] "Neurotic impotence always comes about in this way," he told Fliess when he had "remembered," in a dream, that his nursemaid, a molester, had complained of his sexual clumsiness in babyhood. And the same dream, he added, "was full of the most mortifying allusions to my present impotence [*Unvermögen*] as a therapist."[22]

The psychosexual aspect was clearly dominant in the dreams Freud privately narrated to Fliess. That shouldn't surprise us. Freud's marital sex life, such as it had been, was in abeyance, and his relations with Fliess were beginning to show an ominous strain. Of particular note is the anxiety he felt vis-à-vis Fliess's theory of universal bisexuality. That theory per se, as I have said, wasn't meant to imply that all men are somewhat inclined to homosexual object choice. One of its corollaries, however, was that left-handed men (like Freud) are more "feminine" than others.[23] As Fliess grew distant from him, Freud was confronted with the realization that he was the needy party in the relationship. But why? What had "feminized" him, causing him to fear women and to lavish affection on another male?

It is surely significant that Freud's letters to Fliess at this time dwelled on the fraught topic of masturbation—the very practice for which little boys were typically threatened with "castration" (severing of the penis, not the testicles). We recall that he assigned masturbation the sole responsibility for neurasthenia, the "current neurosis" that had supposedly afflicted him throughout his long engagement to Martha Bernays. Now—as will be illustrated in the "Dora" treatment of 1901—he was coming to believe that hysteria, too, was masturbation related. Hysteria would surely be contracted if a child who had fallen into onanism then tried to forgo the habit. This was the view of a man who told Fliess in August 1897 that he was coping with his own "little hysteria."[24]

Hysterical symptoms, Freud wrote two months later, are nothing other than "a substitute for the discontinued movements of masturbation."[25] And after another two months he declared, "The insight has dawned on me that masturbation is the one major habit, the 'primary addiction,' and it is only as a substitute and replacement for it that the other addictions—to alcohol, morphine, tobacco, and the like—come into existence."* "Doubt arises," he added, "whether analysis and therapy must come to a halt at this point and content themselves with transforming hysteria into neurasthenia."[26] Masturbation might be curbed for a while, then, but the urge to masturbate was incurable.

In Freud's world, it appears, all roads led to masturbation. Virtually every upsetting experience caused a child to start masturbating, and later her options were to keep masturbating and become neurasthenic or to stop and become hysterical. As Freud's theory backed off from traumatizing shocks, such as a nursemaid's sexual abuse, the causal significance of *self*-abuse only magnified. To have been an early masturbator, as we have seen, was such a disgrace that the recollection of it had to be repressed, giving way to fantasies of having been raped by a parent.

Readers may hesitate to believe that the Freud of the late nineties was still personally obsessed with masturbation. A remarkable piece of indirect evidence, however, not only settles the matter but offers an important clue as to why masturbatory fantasy was such a fraught issue for Freud. I refer to a convoluted paper, "Screen Memories," whose composition in 1899 interrupted his writing of *The Interpretation of Dreams*.[27]

---

* 12/22/97; FF, p. 287. Cocaine, the drug that had served Freud as a love potion, didn't need to be mentioned. Indeed, it couldn't be mentioned to Fliess in this context without implying that both he and Fliess, his fellow user, were masturbators.

This essay introduces us to a former patient of Freud's known as "Mr. Y.," "a man of university education, aged thirty-eight," who is now plagued by persistent mental scenes, some of which may be either fantasies or memories. By means of adroit interrogation, the wise psychoanalyst Freud will sort it out for him. But as Siegfried Bernfeld demonstrated in 1946—much to the consternation of Anna Freud, we may be sure—the "former patient" was none other than Freud himself.[28] "Screen Memories" is a quasi-autobiographical, obliquely confessional work. And Freud's patient surrogate in "Screen Memories" doesn't hesitate to imply, as the proper Viennese neurologist Sigmund Freud never would, that his violent fantasies were entertained during acts of masturbation.[29]

"Mr. Y." finds that his thoughts keep reverting to the idea of "gross sexual aggression" against members of the opposite sex.[30] Specifically, he has reveled in the prospect of brutally deflowering a bride. So, we recall, did his author, that "big wild man with cocaine in his body" who once half-jocularly notified Martha Bernays that she was going to be made his rough toy. On that occasion, as we saw, Freud wasn't venting his caveman testosterone but using cocaine to subdue doubt about his sexual adequacy. And later we inferred that a fear and loathing of the female genital apparatus was never far from his thoughts. He and his double, Mr. Y., apparently fantasized that the conquest of that monster, which he would one day liken to Medusa, could be accomplished only through rape.*

Freud's alter ego in "Screen Memories" confesses that he derives a kinky thrill from one particular image of bride ravaging. The scenario, evidently too off-color to be described in the essay, initially resisted bubbling up to his consciousness because of its "incompatibility with the dominant sexual disposition."[31] This would seem to mean that

---

* The terror symbolized by Medusa's snaky severed head, Freud would write in 1922, "occurs when a boy, who has hitherto been unwilling to believe the threat of castration, catches sight of the female genitals, probably those of an adult, surrounded by hair, and essentially those of his mother" (SE, 18:273). "Since the Greeks were in the main strongly homosexual," he added, "it was inevitable that we should find among them a representation of woman as a being who frightens and repels because she is castrated" (ibid., p. 274). But it was Freud himself who hated women for thus discomposing him and who longed to punish them for that offense.

despite the manifest heterosexuality of the envisioned act, whatever it is, the satisfaction that it promises is homosexual.

Freud approaches this delicate theme through the device of a story-within-the-story. Mr. Y. seems to remember an episode from his earliest years in which he and a slightly older boy snatched away a little girl's bunch of flowers, causing her to cry. The doubtful authenticity of that "memory" is a pivotal issue in the essay. More significant for our purpose here, though, is the interpretation that the unflappable "Freud" stencils on the scene, thus winning immediate assent from his admiring double. To steal flowers, they implausibly agree, is to *deflower*. But in this instance two males, not one, are said to have committed the deed. And so "Freud" asks his former patient, "Can you make any sense of the idea of being helped in deflowering someone?"[32]

Although "Screen Memories" as a whole is a work of disguised fiction, Freud believed that the "deflowering" scene corresponded, however metaphorically, to something that had really happened. As he told Fliess, "I have also long known the companion of my misdeeds between the ages of one and two years; it is my nephew, a year older than myself. . . . The two of us seem occasionally to have behaved cruelly to my niece, who was a year younger."[33]

This nephew was John (Johann) Freud, and his sister was Pauline. The children of his very senior half-brother Emanuel, the elder son of Jacob and Sally Kanner Freud, they were slightly older than the future psychoanalyst. "This nephew and this younger brother [Julius]," Freud informed Fliess, "have determined . . . what is neurotic, but also what is intense, in all my friendships."[34] If so, it is meaningful that Freud thought of John as having been his co-conspirator against a girl; for Freud, whose mental life was conducted in the shadow of prototype figures and revenants, mentioned in *The Interpretation of Dreams* that he regarded both Fleischl and Fliess as "new editions" of John.[35]

Ernest Jones astutely deciphered what Freud was implying in the tale of two little boys snatching flowers from a girl. "To 'hunt in couples,'" he wrote, "means sharing one's gratification with someone of one's own sex."[36] Here we may recall that Freud, in a sickly letter to his fiancée, once characterized Fleischl as a more suitable consort for her than himself.[37] That text wasn't just a homoerotic tribute to Fleischl's charms; it reads like a fantasy in which the untamed Martha is being paired with a man who meets every requirement for both satisfying and ruling her. As for Fliess, he and Freud had wreaked accidental but callously unrepented havoc on the supposed bleeder-from-longing Emma Eckstein; and Freud had shared with Fliess his excitement over wild images of torture allegedly extracted from her witchlike unconscious.

Freud believed that his homoerotic tendency wasn't a matter of genetic inclination. Rather, it had to do with an acquired resentment and fear of women, whom he could dominate, in fantasy, only with the assistance of a stronger male. It seemed to him that he had felt that way for nearly all of his life. In fact, however, there had been a time when defenseless females had been at his sole disposal. And he remembered that time all too vividly, with no merciful repression to blot out his guilt.

3. IT'S SOMETHING YOU DID

Looking back from middle age, Freud seemed to recall having been threatened by his father for peering, aghast, at the "castrated" genitals of his baby sisters. Here is what he wrote in *The Interpretation of Dreams* about the dream of "a man" who was surely himself:

> The dream combined two opportunities he had had as a little boy of seeing little girls' genitals: when they were *thrown down* and when they were *micturating*. And . . . it emerged that he had a recollection of being *chastised* or threatened by his father for the sexual curiosity he had evinced on these occasions.[38]

As in "Screen Memories," Freud calculated that he could risk this degree of candor by pretending that the memory belonged to someone else. At the same time, both texts manifested a "compulsion to confess," even if the misdeed in each instance appears to have been a minor one. Surely, however, it stands as a token for acts that could never be specified to readers, but that continued to prey on Freud's mind.

"It is only reproaches which have something in them that 'sticks,'"

Freud declared in *The Interpretation of Dreams*; "it is only they that upset us."[39] If he was maximally upset in his self-analytical period, it was probably because he felt assailed both by the reproaches of others and by guilt for something he had done long before to one or more girls. That burden, it seems likely, had already been weighing on him when he devised his molestation etiology and spelled it out in his three papers of 1896. Indeed, if we follow the signs that Freud's theorizing had everything to do with his own case, those papers become plausible if indirect guides both to his early activities and to his strategy of guilt management.

It is widely assumed that the "seduction" papers, which are more often cited than read, concentrated exclusively on the traumatizing effects of sexual violence on children who would later turn out to be hysterics. But unexpectedly, the papers lay considerable emphasis on the molester's remorse, a sentiment that could lead, Freud declared in "Further Remarks on the Neuro-Psychoses of Defence," to shame, hypochondria, social anxiety, and other handicaps. And that heavy burden would be incurred not for having been "seduced" or for having masturbated but *"for having carried out the sexual act in childhood."*[40]

Freud's molestation theory, it should be emphasized, was not just an etiology of female hysteria. It was also meant to explain two largely male syndromes, obsessional neurosis and paranoia, which he regarded as issuing from different means of coping with mortification for premature sexual activity. Some of the abusers who cause hysteria in females, he wrote in "The Aetiology of Hysteria," are not adults but boys who have themselves been lured into a behavior-altering sexual experience by an adult. Their own initiation renders them obsessive, and their obsession then turns them into compulsive predators.[41]

But some girls, too, according to "Heredity in the Aetiology of the Neuroses," can be rendered obsessional. When molested by a boy (why only by a boy?), they experience "enjoyment"; and their self-castigation for having felt such outlawed pleasure can get transformed into obsessional symptoms.[42] That is too bad, of course; but a man who, in his boyhood, has imposed sexual abuse on a girl can feel better about it after realizing, with Freud, that she must have found his manipulations agreeable at the time.

With or without a "companion of misdeeds," I infer, the child Sigismund had crossed a sexual line with at least one girl, not when he was one or two years old but at an age when an indelible memory would have been formed. Here we may recall the configuration and circumstances of his family. Bearing children with little respite until Sigismund reached the age of ten, the often feverish Amalie had been regarded as continually at risk for tuberculosis. As a consequence, and in spite of the Freuds' poverty, she had passed three months of nearly every year in a spa, accompanied by just one of her children—probably the youngest in each instance. As the eldest, Sigismund would be left at home, increasingly saddled with responsibility to manage his sisters. And one of his tasks, in the absence of hired assistance, would have been to clean and diaper the girls who were not yet toilet trained.

Attend, now, to what Freud wrote in his "Further Remarks" paper of 1896. In the majority of cases that he purported to summarize,

> it turned out that blameless children were the assailants; these were mostly *brothers who for years on end had carried on sexual relations with sisters a little younger than themselves*. No doubt the course of events was in every instance similar to what it was possible to trace with certainty in a few individual cases: the boy, that is to say, had been abused by someone of the female sex, so that his libido was prematurely aroused, and then, a few years later, *he had committed an act of sexual aggression against his sister*, in which he repeated precisely the same procedures to which he himself had been subjected.[43]

Again, in "The Aetiology of Hysteria" Freud remarked that "a brief relationship with a strange boy, who afterwards becomes indifferent, will leave a less powerful effect on a girl than *intimate sexual relations of several years' standing with her own brother*."[44] Freud claimed to have confirmed his theory through the confession of one patient who, admittedly, couldn't recall "*his earliest sexual experiences with his sister*" but remembered "scenes of that kind from later childhood, and the fact that there had been sexual relations dating further back."[45] And yet again: "Far-reaching consequences" ensue for both brother and sister when their relations are *prolonged beyond puberty*."[46]

None of the children, whether abusers or victims, who are referenced in these passages were ever mentioned again or even discovered to have existed. The incest cases that were "unearthed" through an appeal to the molestation theory dried up when the theory itself was dropped. Those cases, I infer, never needed explaining; they were artifices, invented to lend an appearance of substance to a scheme whose real impetus was personal.

It is easy to discern that Freud's own childhood situation was on his mind as he wrote his "seduction" papers. Note, for example, that the sisters in most such cases are only slightly younger than the molesting brother. Why should that be a rule for the general population? Again, why, "in every instance," should there be a lapse of "a few years" before the victim turns victimizer? Why, unless Freud was trying to forgive himself, should a brother who molests his sister "for years on end" be judged "blameless" (*schuldlos*)? And why is the originating perpetrator always "someone of the female sex"?

A striking instance of Freud's entanglement with such material is found in his letter to Fliess of June 20, 1898, in which he discusses Conrad Ferdinand Meyer's novella *The Female Judge* (*Die Richterin*). Among other sensational themes, the book deals with a love affair between step-siblings. For Freud, that plot element is proof positive— but why?—that the author was defending against a memory of childhood incest with his own sister, a deed for which Freud imagines the boy's having been "surprised in the act and scolded" by his mother.[47] Meyer, he further implies, had been seduced in childhood by a female servant. "In all analyses," Freud informed his correspondent, "one therefore hears the same story twice: once as a fantasy about the mother; the second time as a real memory of the maid."[48]

Another literary analysis, this one of Wilhelm Jensen's novel *Gradiva*, revealed Freud's sister-incest preoccupation once again. Because the protagonist encounters a woman who proves to have been one of his childhood companions, Freud leapt to the conclusion that the author had incestuously coveted his younger sister. Freud even wrote to Jensen, hoping for confirmation of his surmise. No, Jensen testily replied; he had never had a sister.[49]

We can only speculate about what the youthful Freud did, and with whom, and how frequently. But for whatever it is worth, Didier Anzieu cited the possible significance of Freud's "Botanical Monograph" dream, which represented him as opening a folded plate containing a flower. The dream, Anzieu proposed, suggests "a past, carnal action—opening the folded 'flower' of a girl, in other words her sexual organs, . . . where the little boy imagines he can see the results of castration."[50]

One of Freud's associations to the same dream is consistent with that reading. He was reminded of his clearest—practically his only— memory from age five, when he and his nearly three-year-old sister Anna, the next-born child after Julius, had been given a picture book to destroy, and they absorbed themselves in "blissfully pulling the book to pieces (leaf by leaf, like an artichoke . . .)."[51] Anna, incidentally, was the only sister for whom the adult Freud seems to have felt no affection, and hers was the wedding that he didn't attend.

It might be argued that Freud mistook remembered desires for actual events. But if so, why did he need to review those desires so intensively at age forty-one? In any event, what matters for the origin of his etiologies—both the molestation theory and its eventual successor, the Oedipus complex—isn't his long-past actions but his state of mind in 1896–99. And we can say with some assurance that he was gloomily self-preoccupied, fearful that he had damaged at least one sister through sexual improprieties, and bent not on atonement but on uncovering prior malefactors onto whom his own guilt might be shunted.

4. WHO WAS TO BLAME?

This way of regarding Freud's self-analysis makes sense of its several bizarre elements. Scholars have been puzzled, for example, by the fact that the miscellaneous abusers whom he categorized in 1896 had condensed into "the father" in 1897. But the original list was merely Freud's way of simulating broad and effective clinical experience; and then he brought "the father" under indictment because he wished to believe that his sisters had already been sexually initiated before he had taken any liberties with them. If they had then grown up to be hysterics, the fault lay entirely with Jacob.

A dream that Freud mentioned to Fliess on May 31, 1897, but omitted from *The Interpretation of Dreams* was pressed into service to that end:

> Recently I dreamed of [having] over-affectionate feelings for Mathilde [his firstborn child], only she was called Hella. . . . The dream of course shows the fulfillment of my wish to catch a *Pater* as the originator of neurosis and thus puts an end to my ever-recurring doubts.[52]

Here is a fine example of discordance between a dream and the wishful gloss that Freud laid on it. His dream had depicted him, not his late father, as incestuously aroused toward his daughter. But because Freud was himself a father, he chose to believe that he had merely been a "Jacob figure" in his dream. The alleged purpose of the dream, then, had been to confirm the thesis that Jacob, not Freud himself, had been "the originator of neurosis" within his family.

The same naïveté can be found in another dream report to Fliess, this one in October 1897. Freud's "seduction" papers, we have seen, arbitrarily maintained that boys who sexually abuse younger girls have themselves been abused, not by a "Pater" but by an adult woman. Now a dream told Freud that he himself had been a victim of one such harpy.

His Freiberg nursemaid, Freud wrote to Fliess on October 3, 1897, had been his sexual initiator; but he didn't reveal what she had done to him.[53] A day later, having dreamed again, he could be somewhat more specific. "Today's dream," he wrote,

> has, under the strangest disguises, produced the following: she was my teacher in sexual matters and complained because I was clumsy

and unable to do anything. . . . Moreover, she washed me in reddish water in which she had previously washed herself.*

Freud told Fliess that the "reddish water" dream had employed "disguises"—which is to say that he had to dismiss some of its manifest content in order to reach the meaning he was disposed to favor. Nevertheless, this is the dream that he judged to have been veridical *because* he couldn't recall the scene that it depicted. That is, he regarded the incident as having been repressed in the period before he was capable of forming long-term memories. The flimsiness of that reasoning reflects his desperation in seeking to pin responsibility for his sexual awakening on a villainess.

Freud described his dream-conjured nursemaid to Fliess as "an ugly, elderly, but clever woman"—in effect, a witch.[54] The dream told him that she had been his *Urheberin,* or "female originator," when he was about two years old.[55] But a *Heber* is also a "lifter" or "raiser." Freud was apparently accusing the nurse of having been the first person to give him an erection—one that supposedly wilted, since in the dream she scolds him for ineptitude. This is the sense in which his sexual insecurity could be traced, however dubiously, to one lustful and perverted woman.

Freud sensed, however, that there was a more plausible candidate for the role of overstimulator: his mother. When Sigismund was born in 1859, Amalie Nathanson Freud was twenty-one years old and wedded to a struggling merchant, twice married before, who was twenty years her senior.† In such conditions, it would have been understandable if the passionate and impulsive Amalie, who never hid her partiality to her firstborn son, had eroticized her early care of him. If so, Sigismund was soon placed in a double bind. Accustomed to his mother's

---

* 10/4/97; FF, p. 269. This nursemaid is widely presumed by Freud scholars to have been Monika Zajíc, the fortyish unmarried daughter of the Freuds' Czech Catholic landlords, who lived across the hall from their one-room Freiberg apartment. Whether or not the identification is correct, the nursemaid was well remembered in family circles as having served a jail term after she was denounced by Freud's half-brother Emanuel for having stolen money and toys.

† Indeed, Amalie was only a year older than her stepson-neighbor Philipp—a fact that has led some commentators (e.g., Krüll 1986; Vitz 1988) to speculate about a possible affair.

caresses, he was suddenly displaced by his baby brother Julius when he was seventeen months old and then further neglected when, in short order, Julius died of dysentery, Amalie drew back in mourning for him, the nurse was sent to jail, and Sigismund's sister Anna was born.

Although Freud appears to have believed that Amalie had ignited his sexuality and then deserted him, he couldn't bear to accuse her of having done so on purpose. Hence his investment of faith in another October dream, which told him that between the ages of two and two and a half, his "libido toward *matrem* was awakened . . . on the occasion of a journey with her from Leipzig to Vienna, during which we must have spent the night together and there must have been an opportunity of seeing her *nudam.*" *

This was another questionable memory: Amalie wasn't likely to have stripped naked in a cramped train cabin. Freud himself hedged on that detail. But his dream evidently convinced him that *some* glimpse of his mother's crotch, far from inducing the terror that he elsewhere ascribed to such proof of female castration, had stirred his infantile lust. In this manner, though stopping short of putting the blame directly on Amalie's double-bind conduct toward him, he made her into his passive and innocent "originator."

Elsewhere in Freud's writings, we can find hints that he did privately hold Amalie accountable not only for his premature eroticism but also for the homosexual aspect of his makeup. Here, for instance, is what he wrote about the cause of "inversion" in his 1905 *Three Essays on the Theory of Sexuality*:

> In all the cases we have examined we have established the fact that the future inverts, in the earliest years of their childhood, pass through a phase of very intense but short-lived fixation to a woman (usually their mother), and that, after leaving this behind, they identify themselves with a woman and take *themselves* as their sexual object. . . . Their compulsive longing for men has turned out to be determined by their ceaseless flight from women.[56]

* 10/3/97; FF, p. 268. Freud had been nearly four, not two, when his family transferred from Leipzig to Vienna.

These lines were composed by a man who had long been in "cease-less flight from women" and who obsessed about the attraction he felt toward certain men, most recently Fliess. His account of how a boy is rendered homosexual was a mistake that would cause untold harm both to gay men, whom he would stigmatize as neurotic, and to their maligned mothers. Yet his intent had been only to generalize from a sincerely felt view of what had been done to him by Amalie.

In 1897, however, Freud found that indictment too depressing to be openly entertained. Nor could he ever face it squarely. If he had indulged the full measure of resentment he had built up against his mother, he would have felt himself to be completely unloved and adrift in a hostile world. For the remainder of his life he sanctified his early oneness with her. As late as 1933 he would write, in a most unpsycho-analytic vein, that the tie between a mother and a son is "the most perfect, the most free from ambivalence of all human relationships."[57] In his view, he had dwelled within that maternal utopia only for the eleven months (actually seventeen) before he was joined by Julius.

Here is Freud in 1931, writing about a child's typical reaction to the arrival of a sibling:

> It is a remarkable fact that a child, even with an age difference of only eleven months, is not too young to take notice of what is happening. But what the child begrudges the unwanted intruder and rival is not only the suckling but all the other signs of maternal care. It feels that it has been dethroned, despoiled, prejudiced in its rights; it casts a jealous hatred upon the new baby and develops a grievance against the faithless mother.[58]

As if to remove any doubt about the autobiographical reference of the discussion, Freud added two reflections whose private significance is now obvious. He characterized the child as feeling aggrieved because its nurse "was sent away by the mother too early."[59] How could that be a regular event for children everywhere? And, Amalie's *goldener Sigi* added, "Nor does it make much difference if the child happens to remain the mother's preferred favourite. A child's demands for love are immoderate, they make exclusive claims and tolerate no sharing."[60]

One more October dream from Freud's self-analysis seemed to tell him that this jealousy was the source of his precocious guilt formation. "I greeted my one-year-younger brother (who died after a few months) with adverse wishes and genuine childhood jealousy; and . . . his death left the germ of [self-]reproaches in me."[61] At a later age, registering his mother's sadness and emotional distance and feeling somehow to blame for it, Sigismund must have fantasized that he had murdered his baby brother through "the omnipotence of wishes." Indeed, he would never be entirely liberated from that self-castigation.[62] But surely it didn't date from an age when he could scarcely talk; nor, on the other hand, had he waited to experience the feeling consciously until analyzing a dream at forty-one.

If, as Freud claimed, Julius as well as John had determined the character of his later friendships, we have one explanation of why those relations were always undermined by jealousy. In truth, however, Freud's whole attempt to derive his adult personality from traumatic events could never be more than inconclusive guesswork. He may simply have been "born that way"—insecure, somewhat bisexual, and susceptible to morbid anxiety. His mother, with her long absences from home and her understandable preoccupation with his siblings, became the focus of his melancholy; but none of his dream-informed reconstructions of his early past, each with its outlandish infractions of verisimilitude, can tell us what her conduct was actually like.

As many modern Freudians have granted, the notion of the Oedipus complex itself was a "reaction formation" against Freud's sense of abandonment by Amalie. In conceiving of fathers and sons as rivals for the embraces of a mother whose own motives were left out of consideration, Freud would fill a chasm in his psyche with a myth of masculine striving that turned every boy, beginning with himself, into a little hero at the mercy of a paternal ogre. It suited his mother-excusing myth to represent castration threats as emanating from the sexually possessive father, as if the latter would be seriously concerned about sexual rivalry from a five-year-old. The real menace to Sigismund's organ was more likely to have been voiced by the coarse Amalie. Hostility to a mother, Freud would write in 1931, reaches an apex "if the mother forbids pleasurable activity with the genitals—often with severe threats and every sign of displeasure—activity to which, after all, she herself had introduced the child."[*]

Most horrible of all for Sigismund had been the image of "castrating" parental intercourse, which he and all other little boys were allegedly doomed to witness at least once. The adult Freud recalled having believed that women, just like men, originally bear penises, in which case his childish logic had told him that Amalie's member must have been severed in the brutal sex act. Hence his peculiar fantasy of the not-yet-castrated "mother with a nurturing penis/breast"—an obsession he would foist onto Leonardo da Vinci in the most "projective" of his later cultural studies.[63] And Leonardo, he would assert, had been rendered homosexual in disposition, yet also inhibited, by his removal from the company of his mother after she had awakened his sensuality. His mother's "excessive tenderness," wrote Freud, caused Leonardo in later years to repress and sublimate his sensuality, resulting in "his sexual inactivity for the whole of his later life."[†]

Freud's need to preserve the image of an inviolate mother, in contrast to the witchlike Freiberg nursemaid, was the obverse side of his misogyny. He couldn't imagine that a properly maternal woman would willingly subject herself to the indignity of intercourse; and though he recognized that men are compelled to spill their seed, he was sure that they would prefer to do so with "debased" women, leaving the sacred maternal image unsullied.[64]

"Anyone who is to be really free and happy in love," wrote Freud in one of his more oracular pronouncements, "must have surmounted his respect for women and have come to terms with the idea of incest with his mother or sister."[65] This saying, though elusive, has been regarded as very wise. In fact, however, like much else in classical psychoanalytic theory, it had more to do with Freud's idiosyncrasies than with the psychology of others. Just because *he* had chosen his mother

---

[*] SE, 22:123. Note Freud's unwarranted guess that the novelist Conrad Ferdinand Meyer must have been "surprised in the act [of incest] and scolded" *by his mother* (p. 532 above). True, Meyer's father died when he was young; but there is no scolding at all to be found in *Die Richterin*.

[†] SE, 11:135. The Florentine authorities who once put Leonardo on trial for pederasty held a different view of his capacity for sexual expression.

and a sister as his first objects of libidinal desire, he assumed that all boys do the same. If they are then unnerved by fear or guilt, as he was, they can never be "free and happy in love." A more candid dictum might have been, "If you molest your little sister and continue to do so as she grows older, you may find it hard to forgive yourself and to overcome your self-disgust. Good luck to you, then, when you climb into bed with your wife."

PART SEVEN

LITTLE BIG MAN

It was no small thing to have the whole human race as one's patient.

—Freud, "The Resistances to Psycho-Analysis" *

---

* SE, 19:221.

30

Wishing Makes It So

1. A SHORTCUT TO SUCCESS

In 1897–99 Freud lost faith in his molestation theory, wearied of his self-analysis, continued being defied by most of his patients, and—as we can tell from expressions of worry and propitiation in his letters—was subjected to Fliess's increasing disbelief in his whole mode of thinking. He longed to supplant his "feminine" reliance on intuition with a "masculine" physiology of psychosexual development, but the only such physiology that lay at hand was Fliess's; and his subservience to Fliess was already a humiliation that he needed to put behind him.

Freud's health, moreover, was as worrisome as ever. In 1898, a lingering infection after the flu left him with chronic difficulty in breathing. A similar condition had sparked his fear of heart failure some years earlier, and now the same anxiety returned. The infection also caused an outbreak of boils, one of which, on his scrotum, left him tormented and exhausted; it was lanced in November 1898. As for the bouts of depression that had periodically incapacitated him for creative effort, they continued to plague him in that year. Nor would the postdate publication of *The Interpretation of Dreams* in November 1899 (with an official date of 1900) lift the gloom. "I have been going through a deep inner crisis," Freud told Fliess in March 1900;

you would see how it has aged me. . . . I have had to demolish all my castles in the air. . . . No one can help me in the least with what oppresses me; it is my cross, I must bear it; and God knows that in adapting to it, my back has become noticeably bent.[1]

Meanwhile, the cumulative effects of drug use, after so much habituation, must have been taking a heavy toll. Jones, we recall, privately estimated that Freud took "more cocaine than he should" over a period spanning fifteen years. That calculation would place the withdrawal in 1899, and there is some intriguing evidence to suggest that Jones was right. But if so, the withdrawal process itself may have resulted in some mental clouding.

It was in 1899 that Freud began systematically, and uncharacteristically, to rely on the ingestion of wine, with the likely intention of trying to suppress a need for cocaine. The first hint of such a program can be found in a letter of February 19, 1899.[2] Later, on June 16, Sigmund reported that Martha had "counted the bottles and took charge of them lest in my loneliness I succumb to the consolation of drink."[3] On June 27 he wrote, "I am gradually becoming accustomed to the wine; it seems like an old friend. I plan to drink a lot of it in July."[4] And he confided on July 8, "I cannot manage more than two hours a day without calling on Friend Marsala for help. 'He' deludes me into thinking that things are not really so bleak as they appear to me when sober."[5]

The turn-of-the-century segment of Freud's career was one of especially discouraging experiences with patients. In a letter to Fliess of May 16, 1897, for example, he lamented, "A proud ship was wrecked for me just a few days after my return [from the latest meeting with Fliess]":

> My banker, who was farthest along in his analysis, took off at a critical point, just before he was to bring me the last scenes. This certainly also damaged me materially, and convinced me that I do not yet know everything after all about the mainspring of the matter. But refreshed as I was, I easily took it in stride and told myself, "So I shall wait still longer for a treatment to be completed."[6]

In his next paragraph Freud reported that yet another patient was preparing to bolt. The lack of one successful case after eleven years of trying was not, of course, something to be "taken in stride."

Considering all of these troubles, we wouldn't expect the period 1897–1900 to have been a productive one for Freud. Yet these were precisely the years that psychoanalytic historians have celebrated as the blossoming of his genius. And, indeed, there can be no doubt that a logjam was broken.

In spite of setbacks and self-doubts, during this span Freud wrote the entirety of his huge *Interpretation of Dreams*; he interrupted the task to write three complicated essays, "Sexuality in the Aetiology of the Neuroses" (1898), "The Psychical Mechanism of Forgetfulness" (1898), and "Screen Memories" (1899); he composed most of the book that would make him world famous, *The Psychopathology of Everyday Life* (1901); he would interrupt that task in early 1901 to write (but not publish) his complex and extensive "Dora" case history; he envisioned *On Dreams* (1901), a little book that would render his dream theory more accessible to general readers; he collected material for another popular work, *Jokes and Their Relation to the Unconscious* (1905); and he looked ahead to the ambitious treatise that would become, in 1905, *Three Essays on the Theory of Sexuality*.

Here, then, is a mystery. Nothing in the record suggests that Freud had begun at last to relieve patients of their mental suffering, much less to reach a definitive understanding of how the neuroses are formed. It seems, on the contrary, that he largely suspended trying to fathom individual cases, including his own. Yet that retreat, instead of causing him to despair of ever besting his rivals among psychological authorities, allowed him to intuit how the same end might be reached more directly. He would devise and publish a theory about dreams that would also double as a model of the mind; and by leading the public to believe that his theory derived from, and was validated by, a successful clinical practice, he would award himself the status of a proven healer.

Freud disclosed his intention to write a dream book in a letter to Fliess of May 16, 1897. Fliess, who had not enjoyed their most recent "congress" and had begun to recoil, had gotten back in touch and had encouraged Freud to proceed with a grand study of psychosexual development. Freud didn't feel ready to do so, but a different scheme was ripening. "I have felt impelled," he wrote, "to start working on the dream, where I feel so very certain—and in your judgment am entitled to."[7] Thus he chose to believe that the flagging collaboration was being revived on a new basis. "I hope that now you will remain your old self again for a long time," he pleaded, "and will let me go on taking advantage of you as a kindly disposed audience. Without such an audience I really cannot work."[8]

Several further letters show a linkage between Freud's commitment to the planned book about dreams and his frustration in other enterprises. On February 9, 1898, for example, he confided, "My self-analysis is at rest in favor of the dream book."[9] And on June 9, 1899, he wryly observed that "the 'silence of the forest' is the clamor of a metropolis compared to the silence in my consulting room. This is a good place to 'dream.'"[10]

Self-analysis and the analysis of others would now make way for an armchair theoretical exercise, yet one that also offered a prospect of popular appeal. Freud turned to dreams partly because he had collected several years' worth of his own dream reports and analyses, constituting a narrow but fascinating resource; partly because those materials could enable him to forge a bond with nonspecialist readers; and partly because dream interpretation, especially if it was going to be largely personal, could be conducted without a need to check his inferences against the condition and progress of patients.

Freud, then, was planning to circumvent his failure either to effect cures or to explain the neuroses. And if the plan worked, he could use dream theory as a bridge for returning to unsolved problems and declaring them solved. The progress that he made, or thought he made, in understanding dreams would endow him with a sense that vast further insight was now within his reach. As he told Fliess on January 4, 1899,

> I want to reveal to you only that the dream schema is capable of the most general application, that the key to hysteria as well really lies in dreams. . . . If I wait a little longer, I shall be able to present the psy-

chical process in dreams in such a way that it also includes the process in the formation of hysterical symptoms.[11]

That was just a small fraction of what Freud would attempt in the last two chapters of *The Interpretation of Dreams*, where he would assemble a deductive foundation not only for hysteria but for virtually every expression of a divided psyche. "The Psychology of the Dream-Processes" (the title of his concluding chapter) would later prove applicable not only to every psychoneurosis but to the formation of jokes and errors as well.

Still farther ahead lay all history, custom, myth, and literature. It would be obvious to Freud that the human mind, in all times and places, had contained the same warring agencies that he identified in his dream book. The same conflicts, too, had been faced by everyone—and, remarkably, they would prove to be Freud's own conflicts over incestuous desire, envy, aggression, and sexual identity. But would this be authentic knowledge, gleaned from observation? Or, rather, would it culminate the process, at work since Freud's introduction to cocaine, of reducing the world to the size and shape of his obsessions?

2. AUTHORSHIP THERAPY

In order to get started on *The Interpretation of Dreams*, Freud had to convince himself that Fliess approved of the undertaking. That, however, was untrue. Fliess, growing impatient with Freud's succession of brainstorms that were never followed up by testing, had come to suspect that his friend was incapable of objective observation. As he would put it in August 1901, in the most cutting insult Freud would ever receive, "the reader of thoughts merely reads his own thoughts into other people."[12] But the Freud/Fliess relationship had already reached a point of no return in their congress of 1898, when Freud had unaccountably taken credit for Fliess's conception of universal bisexuality, and when he had remained unconvinced by his astonished colleague's attempt to correct his memory. Later, Freud had admitted his error; but Fliess continued to suspect that Freud was bent on intellectual thievery.

Nevertheless, Fliess behaved generously during every stage of Freud's composition and proofreading of *The Interpretation of Dreams*. He painstakingly criticized the draft chapters, suggesting changes whose general effect was to bring the discourse into closer proximity to the mainstream idiom of science. And at first Freud took his advice, even when it cost him the sacrifice of examples that were dear to him. Most notably, he dropped a too-revealing dream on which he had counted heavily as a demonstration, and he bowed to Fliess's insistence on the inclusion of a chapter surveying the extant literature on dreams—a requirement that Freud, convinced that he was now the sole authority in the field, regarded as a mere sop to fussy colleagues.

But Fliess's objections to *The Interpretation of Dreams* were comprehensive and fundamental. He was in principle a conventional empiricist. Ideas about people had to be tested on people; and without a weight of positive results there could be no excuse for retaining a hypothesis. Yet now Freud was proposing to base a universal psychological theory on nothing more substantial than his own acknowledged and unattributed dreams plus a few others, interpreted in the light of concepts that had found no corroboration in either research or psychotherapy.

In September 1899, when the complete manuscript had already been sent off for publication. Fliess complained that Freud, as the main represented dreamer, seemed to be "too witty"—a remark that Freud brushed off as posing no threat to his argument. "It is certainly true that the dreamer is too witty," he countered, "but neither is it my fault nor does it involve a reproach. All dreamers are equally insufferably witty, and they need to be because they are under pressure and the direct route is barred to them."[13]

Freud was either missing or pretending to miss Fliess's point, which was that his linguistic facility had led him to equip the dreaming mind with his own waking capacity for multilingual punning. How could Freud, having conducted no research, assure himself that images flashing through everyone's dreams are caused by clever wordplay such as he could always supply after the fact? Fliess must have been irritated by Freud's reply, which simply reaffirmed the challenged model of how each dreamer must circumvent "the censorship." That censorship itself was Freud's invention, no less arbitrary than every other construct in his hermeneutic.

Fliess was also repelled by the idea that Freud might besmirch a scientific exposition with indecorous references to his private deeds and thoughts. He was doubly alarmed because he knew the central role that Freud ascribed to sexual factors in every mental economy. Was Freud, then, going to make the public his confidant for tidbits about his relations with Martha or even with Fliess himself?

For several months, Freud tried to mollify Fliess by removing draft material that the latter regarded as unseemly. As the writing progressed, however, he became convinced that self-display, within certain limits of caution, was unavoidable if *The Interpretation of Dreams* were to do justice to the selfish and indecorous unconscious. In May 1899 he declared, "I have decided that I cannot use any of the disguises, nor can I afford to give up anything."[14]

As if it possessed a will of its own, *The Interpretation of Dreams* was turning into a one-of-a kind tome—audaciously presumptuous, disarmingly confessional, and punctuated with droll social and political commentary that amounted to satire on the self-approbation of the bourgeoisie.[15] The book would prove to be an embodiment not just of Freud's ideas but of "Freud," a shrewdly skeptical personage, alert to all folly and urbanely amused by it, with whom readers could empathize so keenly that the truth or falsity of his theory would feel irrelevant. Or rather, the vividness of that personage would serve as a warrant for the accuracy of his theory. Fliess, Freud saw, was never going to approve or even understand such a production. And Freud no longer cared; he was breaking free.

A major feature of the metamorphosis signaled by *The Interpretation of Dreams* was a shift of perspective that we can call *the opening to culture*. Hitherto, Freud had ignored but not conspicuously flouted the axiom that an explanation can be deemed adequate only if it accounts for the phenomena at hand more fully and economically than rival propositions. Now, however, he just presumed that his ideas were correct and sought to amplify their scope through analogies to myths, literary and artistic works, and practices known to linguistics, folklore, anthropology, and history. Here again, Freud's authorial persona was going to take center stage, but now it would be showing another aspect. This Freud would be a uniquely sagacious authority, commanding vast swaths of knowledge and teaching us that all human behavior, past as well as contemporary, has been "Freudian" in the deep structure of its motivation. And if we wanted to experience such insight ourselves, we would need him as our guide.

Freud would truly be breaking new ground in the *Interpretation*, not as a scientist but as a literary artist. Coolly attaching his cultural allusiveness to the triviality and occasional sordidness of dream imagery, he would defy existing genres with a boldness that bears comparison to James Joyce's in his astounding *Ulysses* of 1922. Like that work, the *Interpretation* would constitute a studied insult to the graybeards, prudes, and hypocrites who had tried in vain to keep the author down. In its blend of lawgiving, whimsy, digressiveness, self-disclosure, and mockery of the high and mighty, the shaggy treatise would be Freud's testament of all-around emancipation.

He knew how radically he was departing from academic etiquette. His title, *Die Traumdeutung*, deliberately echoed the name of the masses' favorite pseudoscience, astrology (*die Sterndeutung*). His Latin epigraph from *The Aeneid*, meaning "If I cannot bend the higher powers, I will stir up the underworld," struck a note of Luciferian rebellion. And he repeatedly sided with the folk against the professors' alleged belief that dreams are meaningless discharges of energy. Indeed, the resultant atmosphere of *social* subversion, though it was detached from any overt program and, indeed, was antithetical to Freud's centrist politics, imparted an extra resonance to the book's emphasis on suppressed powers that could foil "the censorship."[16] The *Interpretation* would feel like an all-purpose exposé of what the authorities have wanted to keep us from knowing.

The great achievement of Freud's book, considered solely as a rhetorical product, would be its enlistment of the reader in supposed teamwork against the guardians of conventional opinion. If the author was risking everything by his opposition to them, it had to be flattering to be welcomed into his confidence. Instead of being presented with a dry exposition of analyzed data, the reader would become Freud's companion on an entertaining journey whose destination, it was promised, would be unorthodox wisdom. As Fliess was told on August 6, 1899,

> The whole thing is planned on the model of an imaginary walk. At the beginning, the dark forest of authors (who do not see the trees), hopelessly lost on wrong tracks. Then a concealed pass through which I lead the reader—my specimen dream with its peculiarities, details, indiscretions, bad jokes—and then suddenly the high ground and the view and the question: which way do you wish to go now?[17]

Note Freud's assured tone, quite merited for once, and note that he intended to offer his reader a sense of freedom while never loosening his grip. A skeptic would surely balk at the use of just one analyzed "specimen dream" ("Irma's Injection") to establish trust in Freud's thesis, but doubts would be kept at bay by what Stanley Edgar Hyman once called the book's "voices, struggles, soliloquies, and stage movement."[18]

Sensing the affective impact of his text and the emergence of a literary vocation, Freud composed much of the dream book in excited bursts. "No other work of mine," he told Fliess in May 1899, "has been so completely my own, my own dung heap, my seedling and a *nova species mihi* on top of it."[19] Near the end, four months later, he remarked, "I am afraid it is *stuss*"—Yiddish for "bunk"—but instead of reconsidering vulnerable claims, he kept on writing at a pace of eight to ten pages a day.[20]

Still more revealing is an aside in a letter of August 27, 1899, when Freud was inspecting a partial set of proofs: "Every attempt to make [the book] better than it turns out by itself," he wrote, "gives it a forced quality. So it will contain 2,467 mistakes—which I shall leave in it."[21] When has any other author intentionally allowed errors to mar his book? But Freud believed that his slips would be *characteristic of him* and therefore of interest to his biographically inquisitive readers. And he was already looking ahead to *The Psychopathology of Everyday Life*, where he would analyze the supposed reasons for the most instructive blunders in the earlier work.

Freud's revelations about his sometimes grotesque dreams and about the low motives behind them still tempt unprepared readers to believe that they are seeing the hand of an admirably forthright and unassuming author.* According to Freud, it is his dreams alone that exhibit ambition, jealousy, or hostility; the man himself, a paragon of objectivity, stands aside in wonderment at the primitive impulses of his unconscious. And the very fact that he is willing to disclose those impulses marks him as a courageous and self-sacrificial inquirer. But this is all a calculated pose, and one that doesn't prevent Freud from surreptitiously inflating his achievements and his reputation whenever he can.

Let us consider one such instance of self-advertisement through dream analysis: Freud's discussion, in the *Interpretation*, of his "Open-Air Closet" dream. In it, Freud sees an outdoor toilet smeared with excrement that he then washes off with a stream of urine. Why had the dreamer, unlike the reader, felt no disgust? Freud's answer is that "the most agreeable and satisfying thoughts," relating to his own supposed greatness, had governed the dream. His subsequent analysis turns shit into both cultural and promotional gold:

> What at once occurred to me in the analysis were the Augean stables which were cleansed by Hercules. This Hercules was I. The hill and bushes came from Aussee, where my children were stopping at the time. I had discovered the infantile aetiology of the neuroses and had thus saved my own children from falling ill. The seat (except, of course, for the hole) was an exact copy of a piece of furniture which had been given to me as a present by a grateful woman patient. It thus reminded me of how much my patients honoured me. . . . The stream of urine which washed everything clean was an unmistakable sign of greatness. It was in that way that Gulliver extinguished the

---

* Freud claimed to have collected "over a thousand" dream reports from his practice—a rich trove of data. But because the dreamers were "neuropaths," he thought it best to disqualify most of them and instead to focus on dreams "derived from an approximately normal person," himself (SE, 4:104, 105). Of the 160 dreams discussed in his monograph, 50—including all of the important ones—were acknowledged as his own. It is clear, however, that many of the others were his as well.

great fire in Lilliput—though incidentally this brought him into dis-
favour with its tiny queen. But Gargantua, too, Rabelais' superman,
revenged himself in the same way on the Parisians by sitting astride
Notre Dame and turning his stream of urine upon the city. . . . And,
strangely enough, here was another piece of evidence that I was the
Superman. The platform of Notre Dame was my favourite resort in
Paris; every free afternoon I used to clamber about there on the towers of the church between the monsters and the devils. The fact that
all the faeces disappeared so quickly under the stream recalled the
motto: "*Afflavit et dissipati sunt*,"* which I intended one day to put
at the head of a chapter upon the therapy of hysteria.[22]

An author who could deploy such a range of resources, even while
falsely boasting of his discovery of "the infantile etiology of the neuroses" and his possession of an effective treatment for hysteria, would
prove irresistible to modern intellectuals. They wouldn't bother to ask
whether urination indeed signifies greatness; whether Freud's rebellious
patients, who "invariably contradict my assertion that all dreams are
fulfillments of wishes,"[23] had really "honoured" him; and whether the
idea of such honor was an actual "dream thought" or rather a calculated afterthought. But as soon as such doubts are entertained, the cultural trappings of Freud's interpretation appear in a harsher light, as
marks not of sophistication but of sophistry.

The same guile characterizes a later paragraph in the "Closet"
analysis. Freud's theory requires him to supply a "day residue" for the
references that supposedly constituted his dream thoughts. On the day
in question, he says, he had delivered a lecture that had fallen far short
of his usual standard. But an audience member disagreed,

> telling me how much he had learnt from me, how he looked at every-
> thing now with fresh eyes, how I had cleansed the *Augean stables* of
> errors and prejudices in my theory of the neuroses. He told me, in
> short, that I was a very great man. My mood fitted ill with this paean

---

* "He blew, and they were scattered"—from an inscription of medals commemorating
the English defeat of the Spanish Armada in 1588. "He" is presumably God.

of praise; I fought against my feeling of disgust, went home early to
escape from him, and before going to sleep turned over the pages of
Rabelais and read one of Conrad Ferdinand Meyer's short stories.[24]

And so, with a few deft strokes, Freud has supplied an uplifting but
surely counterfeit impetus for his ugly dream; he has depicted himself
once again as an adulated benefactor of humanity; and, with surpass-
ing gall, he has judged himself to be innocent of pride.

3. IN YOUR DREAMS

From the mid-twentieth century until today, physiological and neuro-
cognitive research has yielded a number of well-corroborated findings
about dreams and the dreaming state. Although the brain scientists
and the analysts of dream reports operate on different sets of assumptions, they are almost unanimous in putting aside the Freudian model,
which turns out to have been erroneous on every point. Freud held, for
example, that dreaming takes place in order to preserve sleep; that it
occurs only shortly before waking; that emotions felt in dreams tend
to be inappropriate to the dream's represented action; that the segments of a dream never possess an inherent narrative continuity; that a
"residue" of reference to the day's events can invariably be noted; that
repression accounts for the quick forgetting of dreams; and that the
dreams of small children typically convey simple wishes. No, says the
modern research: these were just Freud's guesses, and he guessed wrong
every time.[25]

It is often said, nevertheless, that although Freud's theory was premature, he deserves credit for having brought dreams within the purview of science. But this is only a half-truth at best. Dreaming was
already an object of psychological study in the latter half of the
nineteenth century, and for a long while such specialists as Karl Albert
Scherner, Johannes Volkelt, W. Robert, Alfred Maury, and Hervey de
Saint-Denis remained better known than Freud. Agreed, the hegemony
of psychoanalysis brought dream *meaning* into sharper focus. One
consequence, however, was a retardation of physiological inquiry for a
full half-century. Moreover, it was only after discarding the psychoan-

alytic model that cognitivists were able to assign due importance to manifest (literal) dream content, which, as we will see, held no significance in Freud's theory.[26]

When Freud began writing *The Interpretation of Dreams*, he hadn't forsaken the quasi-mystical conception of dreaming that had allowed him, in his self-analysis, to "reconstruct" events of his early childhood through dreaming about them. Dreams, he wrote there, "have at their disposal the earliest impressions of our childhood."[27] Now, however, he would be trying to glean only childhood sexual *wishes*, not memories, from those dreams. The wishes had supposedly lodged themselves in the dreamer's unconscious and remained obliquely active through the intervening decades. According to Freud, they were the motivating engine of every adult dream, joining forces with up-to-date desires and "day residue" concerns to fashion a sleeping hallucination that escapes censorship through disguise of its true meaning.

The idea that childhood sexual wishes are first repressed and then transmuted in dreams excluded any possibility that their existence might be subject to disconfirmation. The further claim that they are now, in adulthood, casting about for a means of camouflaged expression further encumbered Freud's already homuncular notion of the psyche. (Do wishes make plans, adopt disguises, and hitch rides?) And to say that the infantile wish thesis remained uncorroborated in the *Interpretation* would be an understatement. It is as if Freud had assigned himself two tasks, to propound a fundamentalist dogma and to make relatively plausible sense of remembered dreams, without ever recognizing that he had neglected to conjoin them.

In the judgment of contemporary dream investigators, only a minority of dreams appear to express wishes of any kind, let alone infantile sexual ones. Sigmund and Martha's engagement letters show that their dreams were no exception. Freud had sometimes consoled his fiancée for her disconcerting dreams, and he experienced plenty of his own. "Last night," he wrote to her on January 13, 1886,

> I dreamed I was fighting for your sake. It's such an unpleasant feeling
> to want to start fighting and yet feel paralyzed. I often dream that,

and it comes at the place in the dream where I have to pass my doctor's examination, a task that had tormented me for years.

What wish could be conveyed by the repetition of such a frightening dream? Yet Freud's treatise abounded in attempts to name the contemporary wish beneath a dream's felt anxiety. When stumped, he even posited a masochistic wish for punishment. And then in his second edition he outdid himself in self-absorption, asserting that when his patients underwent bad dreams, their motive must have been a wish to prove him wrong.[28] The more Freud strained to patch his theory with such alibis, the farther he strayed from his tenet about *infantile sexual* wishes.

We need only recall a few of our own recent dreams to see that the wish notion is contrary to experience. But why, then, did Freud insist on it? As a number of scholars have proposed, the only plausible source for this notion is his own *Project for a Scientific Psychology*.[29] Indeed, that is just where we find the first rudimentary statement of the theory. Freud began writing his *Interpretation* shortly after becoming reconciled at last to the impossibility of his ever completing the *Project*. But he didn't give up on its central idea; what couldn't be accomplished with neurons, he reasoned, might be transposed to the psychology of dreaming. Like the *Project*, the dream theory conceived of the human organism as a passive reflex machine requiring an initial input to make it go. The unconscious wish was the stimulus needed for putting the machine into reverse, yielding a hallucinatory vision instead of an action at the motor end.

Much that is obscure in the Freudian dream system can be understood, though not justified, in these terms. Ludwig Wittgenstein and others, for example, have wondered who was being deceived by "the censorship" and how a wish could be gratified in a dream if the dreamer herself wasn't aware of it. Such problems didn't occur to Freud, because he was still thinking of a mechanical model whose tendency was to discharge excitation and thus to restore a state of rest. He had confused himself by holding fast to what Malcolm Macmillan calls "a theory of a mental apparatus without a bodily or organic core."[30] And further confusion ensued, because thoughts do not carry "sums of excitation" and thus aren't subject to the mechanical reinforcements that could push them through the Freudian gates leading to consciousness.

"Every attempt that has hitherto been made to solve the problem of dreams," Freud wrote,

> has dealt directly with their *manifest* content as it is presented in our memory. . . . We are alone in taking something else into account. We have introduced a new class of psychical material between the manifest content of dreams and the conclusions of our enquiry: namely, their *latent* content, or . . . the "dream-thoughts," arrived at by means of our procedure. It is from these dream-thoughts and not from a dream's manifest content that we disentangle its meaning.[31]

Patently, Freud's "new class of psychical material" had been created in order to discount what dreams actually display and to wrench each analyzed dream into a congenial pattern. Thus the putative dream thoughts were a pure artifact of the theory. "Our procedure" was no more rational than the use of ciphers to turn Biblical verses into prophecies of modern events.

In Freud's theory, dream thoughts were rendered suitable for disguised representation by "the dream work," consisting chiefly of two supposed mechanisms, *condensation* and *displacement*. The former allowed one dream image to represent any number of dream thoughts, thus awarding Freud a license to keep on interpreting ad libitum. And displacement was even more generous. On the premise that the dreamer must hide her unacceptable ideas from herself, the theory warranted Freud to propose, as a given dream thought, either an opposite idea to the one shown in the dream or simply a different one. The range of possible transformations would thus be limited only by Freud's bounteous ingenuity.

His other two mechanisms of dream work have received less attention, but they shouldn't be overlooked as tools of his apriorism. *Representability* permitted dream thoughts to be embodied in images, thus granting Freud the right to call a dream image a symbol, a pun, a rebus, or even a palindrome. Representability had its own unique rules, whereby, for example, a sequence of images pointed to a causal connection in the thoughts; or two images together could signify an either/or relationship between the thoughts behind them; or an absurdity in the dream meant criticism or derision within the thoughts. (As if absurdities weren't a common feature of dreams!)

No less arbitrary was *secondary revision*. It performed the dream work's final job, reshaping the embryonic dream so as to endow it with storytelling coherence. Freud needed to invoke secondary revision because, as we all know, dreams often do display a strong thematic connection between one narrative element and its abrupt successor. Freud, however, insisted that every part of a dream answers only to its own independent thoughts. Here, then, in secondary revision, was a "mechanism" whose sole purpose was to minimize, as a mere afterthought, the plotlike character of many dreams.

Freud's theory depended ultimately on an impression he had gleaned from his upper-class female patients and perhaps also from his own anxieties: that the mind is a delicate contraption, easily thrown into disrepair by sexual urges and fantasies. No one in the world, according to Freud, can stay asleep without the aid of two internal censors, one guarding the portal between "the unconscious" and "the preconscious"—that is, between the inexpressible and the not-yet-expressed—and the other located between the preconscious and consciousness, where offensive material can finally be allowed covert display. But the cultural provincialism of that idea is apparent. Sheltered women who have been taught to abhor their bodily functions aren't typical of humankind; and even they surely experience dreams in which the censorship, if such a thing exists, is distinguished by its absence.

Dreaming is a brain function, and the peculiar traits of dreams correlate with the recorded activation and deactivation of brain modules, largely but not entirely in the REM state.* Probably, then, dreaming is an accidental by-product of physiological operations occurring during sleep. There is no doubt, however, that human dreams draw upon specifically human feelings and intelligence and that they have access

---

* The last neuroscientist to hold out for the Freudian wish theory claims that dreams originate in the dopaminergic system, the source of appetitive interests (Solms 1997). Nightmares, however, are hardly appetitive, and blockage of dopamine production doesn't inhibit dreaming. For references and discussion, see Domhoff 2003, p. 141.

to such well-known tools as metaphor and metonymy.[32] In his tortuous and undemonstrable theory of dream formation as self-deceit, Freud erred by granting too little sway to the direct carryover of ordinary waking fears, worries, desires, and capacities to the motor-inhibited and staccato experience of dreaming.

4. MANIFESTLY ABSURD

The fundamental assumption of clinical dream interpretation, as set forth in Freud's alleged masterpiece, was that the dreamer's verbal associations to her dream report could lead a methodologically prepared analyst back to the thoughts that had been worked over by the two agencies of censorship and then metamorphosed into dream scenes. However pleasant, neutral, horrifying, or self-critical the dream might have appeared to the dreamer, its ruling thoughts would almost always prove to have been selfish and aggressive (a judgment that may tell us more about Freud than about dreams). And then, at the base of it all, there was that infantile sexual wish, a postulate so remote from the actual experience of dreaming that even Freud couldn't provide examples of it in actual dreams.

In practice, Freud was at once the dreamer, the provider of associations, and the interpreter of many reported dreams. Several problematic aspects of the theory resulted from that circumstance. Freud's own dream thoughts, for instance, were supposedly repressed—that is why they had had to undergo disguise—yet he was able to identify any number of them with alacrity. In what sense, then, had they been unavailable to consciousness or even unfamiliar to the waking Freud?

The specimen dream of "Irma's Injection" affords a typical instance of the problem.* The dream thoughts that Freud detected behind its

---

* "A large hall—numerous guests, whom we were receiving.—Among them was Irma. I at once took her on one side, as though to answer her letter and to reproach her for not having accepted my 'solution' yet. I said to her: 'If you still get pains, it's really only your fault.' She replied: 'If you only knew what pains I've got now in my throat and stomach and abdomen—it's choking me'—I was alarmed and looked at her. She looked pale and puffy. I thought to myself that after all I must be missing some organic trouble. I took her to the window and looked down her throat, and she showed signs of recalcitrance, like women with artificial dentures. I thought to myself that there was really no need for

sequence of images were quite diverse. They included reflections about his wife's birthday celebration and her sixth pregnancy; a botched surgery and a dissatisfied psychotherapeutic patient; professional rivalry and accusations of negligence; the sulfonal-induced death of Mathilde Schleicher and the frightening illness of another Mathilde, Freud's daughter; his rheumatic shoulder; Ernst Fleischl's poisoning with cocaine; and Fliess's theory of sexual chemistry, all bundled together by an overriding wish for self-exculpation. But not a single one of those ideas had been "repressed." They were all either immediate daily concerns of Freud's or holdovers from past crises that must have bothered his conscious mind.

Freud gave fair warning that he knew more about the meaning of "Irma's Injection" than he was willing to tell the public. As he would explain in a 1908 letter to his follower Karl Abraham, he considered the dream's actual core theme to have been "sexual megalomania."[33] "Irma's Injection" had bodied forth the congruence, in his imagination, between clinically "overcoming resistance" in female patients and seducing them. And because his wife might have died in childbirth, Freud had been thinking about her possible successor as a mate. His dream had included representations of three other women, each of whom might have more than satisfactorily replaced Martha in his bed. The fact that two of them were widows at the time had especially excited him. As he told Abraham, "There would be one simple therapy for widowhood, of course."[34] This added dimension, so out of har-

---

her to do that.—She then opened her mouth properly and on the right I found a big white patch; at another place I saw extensive whitish grey scabs upon some remarkable curly structures which were evidently modelled on the turbinal bones of the nose.—I at once called in Dr. M., and he repeated the examination and confirmed it. . . . Dr. M. looked quite different from usual; he was very pale, he walked with a limp and his chin was clean-shaven. . . . My friend Otto was now standing beside her as well, and my friend Leopold was percussing her through her bodice and saying: 'She has a dull area low down on the left.' He also indicated that a portion of the skin on the left shoulder was infiltrated. (I noticed this, just as he did, in spite of her dress.) . . . M. said: 'There's no doubt it's an infection, but no matter; dysentery will supervene and the toxin will be eliminated.' . . . We were directly aware, too, of the origin of the infection. Not long before, when she was feeling unwell, my friend Otto had given her an injection of a preparation of propyl, propyls . . . propionic acid . . . trimethylamin (and I saw before me the formula for this printed in heavy type). . . . Injections of that sort ought not to be made so thoughtlessly. . . . And probably the syringe had not been clean" (SE, 4:107).

mony with the ascetic Freud known to his admirers, is enlightening; but again, the newly revealed dream thoughts are said to have been on his *conscious* mind on the day of dreaming.

The fact that Freud could give a dream one astoundingly detailed analysis and then, much later, a very different one points to an excess of license in his method. Where does interpretation stop? The afterlife of "Irma's Injection" isn't reassuring. By 1984 the psychoanalytic literature already contained ten different readings of that dream, each of which laid claim to being authoritative.[35] Since then the analysts have kept adding layers of complication to "Irma," never realizing that in doing so they are exposing a fatal absence of discipline in their procedure.

That flaw wasn't yet apparent to those few early observers, such as C. G. Jung and Eugen Bleuler, who welcomed *The Interpretation of Dreams* as a scientific breakthrough. Jung urged Freud to recast the treatise as a textbook so that others could learn just how a given dream was to be translated into its meaning. And Bleuler earnestly set out to apply the *Interpretation*, just as it was, to the understanding of his own dreams. He soon discovered, however, that the book provided no method at all. So many avenues of possible analysis were available to every dream, without any guidelines for choosing some and rejecting others, that the whole apparatus was useless. That realization transformed the empirically conscientious Bleuler from an advocate into an opponent of psychoanalysis.[36]

If there is no end to the associations that a given dream report can inspire, the question must be raised whether associations tell us anything about the actual cause of the dream. Freud assumed that a dreamer's first remarks after reporting her dream belonged to a chain of ideas leading inexorably back to the dream's formation. But that supposition is challengeable on several grounds, including the suggestive context of every therapeutic session. Of course the dreamer may recall a genuine link between her concerns and the dream; but all such links show the straightforward meaningfulness of the *manifest* dream, which was only an obstacle to interpretation à la Freud.

Chapter 2 of *The Interpretation* was meant to dazzle its readers with a barrage of plausible connections to "Irma's Injection," dissolving any resistance to the emphatic conclusion that "*a dream is the fulfilment of a wish.*"[37] But not only was it illogical to hold that one dream alone could satisfactorily establish the wish fulfillment thesis; each of Freud's publicly recounted themes in "Irma" engaged a worry, not a wish. Unless one was already a believer in the Freud legend, moreover, the "condensation" of so many thoughts into one dream could look like a synthetic construct. It is suspect, for example, that his immediate associations to the dream purportedly included a reference to his daughter Mathilde's near-fatal diphtheria, which she actually endured two years later.[38]

"At the turn of the twentieth century," wrote the philosopher of science Clark Glymour with distaste in 1983, "Freud once and for all made his decision as to whether or not to think critically, honestly, and publicly about the reliability of his methods. *The Interpretation of Dreams* was his answer to the public, and perhaps to himself." Glymour was not strictly correct. Well before launching the dream book, Freud had already made a definitive break with the ethics of scientific reporting. Now, however, he was posing as the absolute master both of his presented dreamworld and of psychological explanation in general. Accordingly, the scope of his assertions was about to become much broader.[39]

31

Sexual Healing

1. SIBLING RIVALRY

In the nineteenth century, Freud couldn't write psychological discourse at all unless he was mentally addressing a supportive friend—a role first filled by Breuer and then by Fliess. As we have seen, however, while Fliess was still available for practical assistance in 1897–99, his trust in Freud's judgment had vanished. In the same period, he was being gradually supplanted by another ideal reader, and an important one: Minna Bernays.

Ernest Jones, who understood that he was required to circumvent the question of Freud's intimacy with his sister-in-law, still felt obliged to concede that "to some extent" Freud's isolation in the 1890s had been alleviated by Minna as well as by Fliess.[1] "She certainly knew more about Freud's work than did her sister," wrote Jones in a later passage, "and he [privately] remarked once that in the lonely nineties Fliess and she were the only people in the world who sympathized with it."[2] As Didier Anzieu recognized in 1975, Minna "gradually came to provide Sigmund with greater creative stimulation than Fliess—a fact which must certainly have helped Freud to withdraw from Fliess."[3]

Martha Freud's sister was no scientist, and the objections that Fliess and other fact-minded critics held against *The Interpretation of Dreams* would have meant little to her. What she admired was imaginative freedom, a quality that Freud, too, had longed to indulge even while he felt somewhat constrained by the ethos of incremental "contributions to knowledge." Fliess was the one who insisted that Freud survey the literature on dreams, but it was probably Minna who, overruling her sole remaining rival for Freud's affection, backed his desire to include shocking examples and to speculate without hindrance. And Minna may well have inspired him to begin detaching himself from the Fliessian numerology that he had previously accepted with uncritical docility.

We can locate approximately when that shift of attitude occurred. As late as May 1899 Freud was still reflexively employing Fliess's system of mechanical explanation and prediction.[4] But just five weeks later, on July 3, reminiscing about a walking tour that he and his friend had taken near the outset of the decade, he wrote these startling lines to Fliess:

> Between Salzburg and Reichenhall you were, as usual, blind to the beauties of nature. . . . At the time I felt somewhat overwhelmed by your superiority. . . . Furthermore, I vaguely sensed something I can express only today: the faint notion that this man had not yet discovered his calling, which later turned out to be the shackling of life with numbers and formulas.[5]

Nothing in Freud's previous remarks about Fliess's science prepares us for that blast of humanistic disdain.

Minna Bernays's importance for psychoanalysis has been largely overshadowed by controversy over her putative sexual liaison with Freud—a controversy that members of the profession have until recently put down to Freudicidal malice. Today, as that affair has come to seem more plausible, they are more inclined to withhold judgment, taking refuge in the truism that the merits of Freud's theory are unaffected by biographical facts. It is probably no coincidence, however, that when Minna replaced Fliess as Freud's primary audience, he became even more cavalier about disregarding scientific norms.

On the day that Freud first encountered Martha Bernays, he also met Minna, who, just shy of seventeen, was already engaged to a friend of Freud's, the student of Sanskrit literature Ignaz Schönberg. That fact alone, to say nothing of her status as a four-years-junior sister, ensured that Sigmund's overt romantic attentions would be directed to Martha. But there can be no doubt that he also had his eye on Minna. "Almost from the moment Freud took a passionate interest in Martha Bernays in April 1882," wrote Peter Gay, "he was drawn to her younger sister Minna, intelligent, lively, and caustic."[6] And the point wasn't lost on Minna, who is said to have mischievously teased Martha, "It is very kind of Herr Doctor to take so much interest in *us*."[7]

The temperaments of the Bernays sisters could hardly have been more contrasting. Whereas Martha was known for her sweetness and equanimity, Minna was energetic, outspoken, cocky, and sardonic. She resented her mother's autocratic sway, to which Martha always reflexively bowed, and Sigmund relied on her to take his part against both Emmeline and his future brother-in-law, Eli. Martha read books deemed suitable for young ladies, but Minna devoured, recalled in detail, and passed sharp judgment on every work, in several languages, that she could manage to acquire. She was as irreligious as Martha was pious—a matter of no small importance to Freud. Her engagement to Ignaz Schönberg at sixteen, leapfrogging her older sibling as a fiancée, attested both to the fascination she could exert and to her lack of respect for convention.

It was Minna to whom Freud, writing from Paris in 1885, described the "nudities," the absence of "shame or fear," and the lawless sexual mores of the locals.[8] Minna, not Martha, was urged to read Victor Hugo's *Notre-Dame de Paris*—a book that featured not only blasphemy, Faustian taboo-breaking, sadistic torture and hangings, and excretion on a civic statue but also prostitution, penile erection, a sex-crazed priest who hides his secret cell "as carefully as his pudendum," and many groping and smooching assaults on the virtue of an abandoned maiden—strong literary fare for a protected twenty-year-old virgin.[9]

"But why do I turn to you and what do I want from you, little sister?" Freud asked in an 1882 letter to Minna. "I have to turn to you, because in every respect you are the closest to me."[10] Once he was engaged, Freud regarded himself as belonging to a virtual household—he called it "the circle"—that comprised Minna and Schönberg as well as Martha and himself. "They looked forward to being a happy quartet together," wrote Jones:

> Freud once remarked [to Martha] that two of them were thoroughly good people, Martha and Schönberg, and two were wild passionate people, not so good, Minna and himself: two who were adaptable and two who wanted their own way. "That is why we get on better in a criss-cross arrangement; why two similar people like Minna and myself don't suit each other especially; why the two good-natured ones don't attract each other."[11]

Freud's lines were meant to be reassuring, but he was telling his bourgeois fiancée, while she was being schooled for the role of obedient housewife, that he and her sister were the "wild passionate" ones who were inclined to do just as they pleased.

In one of those too-perfect reports in *The Interpretation of Dreams* that appear to have been invented to showcase Freud's deductive skill, he describes a dreamed architectural scene that translates neatly into a picture of rear-entry (but not anal) intercourse—a lifelong preoccupation of his. The last two sentences of his analysis tell us what was on his mind:

> The assistance attributed by the dreamer to his wife forces us to conclude that in reality it was only consideration for her that restrained the dreamer from making attempts of this kind. It turned out that on the dream-day a girl had come to live in the dreamer's household who had attracted him and had given him the impression that she would raise no great objections to an approach of that kind.[12]

The "girl [who] had come to live in the dreamer's household" can only be Minna.

As it happens, events were indeed entwining her fate with Sigmund's. Schönberg, whose academic aspirations soon called him to England, was already suffering from the tuberculosis that would kill him in 1886. Freud expressed solicitude for him; but his later consolation letter to Minna tactlessly referred to his dead friend's "moral weakness" and "rigidity," and it urged her to banish regret, burn the love letters, move in with the Freuds for a while, and look forward to unspecified "curious things, worthy of being experienced."[13]

The scandal-shy psychoanalytic establishment has manifested its unease over Minna in several ways, one of which has been to emphasize her stolid, sexless aspect in later years: "She grew heavier, more jowly, becoming exceedingly plain."[14] A photograph of her at eighteen, however, shows the slender figure and the alert, amused, and impudent visage that appealed to Freud in the 1880s and '90s. And right from the start, his letters to "Dear Minning," "Dear Minnich," and "My beloved Minna" were affectionate, confiding, and at times insinuating. He informed her in 1886 that he was proud to be associated with such a beautiful woman. And in the same letter, written several months before his wedding, he invited her to visit him in his sumptuous new apartment, adding, "If you weren't my sister-in-law, you could even stay [wohnen] with me."[15]

Minna, for her part, would put her hypercritical faculty in abeyance and lend encouragement to whatever ideas Freud was willing to share. And share them he did. He asked her to read the proofs of his Bernheim translation. He informed her about his book on aphasia and his treatment of Anna von Lieben. And the first indication that we have of his interest in writing a volume about dreams is a letter to Minna in April 1893.[16]

Until recently, Minna Bernays has figured in psychoanalytic histories as a perpetually grieving spinster, somewhat in the Miss Havisham line, whom the generous Freuds spared from a lifetime of poverty and lowly domestic jobs by inviting her, in 1896, to live permanently with them and to assist Martha in raising their six children. By no means, however, did Minna regard herself as a poor relation or a charity case. As the children in her care grew up, they found their aunt to be not only a harsh disciplinarian but also aloof and arrogant; and they began to notice that her relationship with their father was the only one she cared about. The jealous Anna in particular found her to be insufferably possessive, as if Minna and not Martha were the real *Frau Professor Freud*. And, in fact, those would be Minna's exact habitual words, in the twentieth century, when picking up the telephone at Berggasse 19.[17]

2. THE CURE FOR NERVOUS ILLNESS

When Minna joined the Freud household for good in 1896, Sigmund and Martha had long since ceased communicating about his ideas, which she found revolting; and their conjugal relations, for a number of reasons, appeared to have subsided three years before. (An unplanned exception had yielded Anna Freud, born in December 1895.) Never suspecting that her future husband would resist taking adequate contraceptive precautions, Martha had looked forward to having just three children. Now, after the difficult and dangerous birth of Anna, her sixth baby in nine years, she suffered a nervous collapse whose chief symptom was an inability to put a single word on paper. Sigmund mentioned it in a casual postscript to Fliess.[18] Of greater interest to him, however, was her heightened adamancy in refusing further intercourse.

In the resultant atmosphere of tension and resentment, Sigmund, no doubt using the pretext that Martha needed more help, took revenge by inviting Minna into the home and openly preferring her company.* She, not Martha, would be Sigmund's companion in games of tarock or mah-jongg after dinner. She would read his texts and flatter his amour propre. She would become his trusted private secretary. And in later years, when psychoanalysis had swelled into an international movement, she would serve as its hostess, making arrangements and coping with the pilgrims whose adulation threatened to distract her Sigi from his all-important contemplation and writing.

Most conspicuously, Minna would become his elegantly attired travel companion. The frugal and dowdy Martha, who suffered from constipation and diarrhea, among other complaints, had neither the interest nor the capacity to accompany her husband on his fast-paced summer hiking trips in the Alps and his visits, Baedeker in hand, to historic towns and cities in Italy, Germany, and Switzerland. But Minna, at least until a mysterious illness debilitated her after one such adventure in 1900, could and did keep up with him; and even before she had fully recovered from that affliction, the trips resumed.

---

* The cost of maintaining another relative, especially one with Minna's tastes, far exceeded an added governess's pay; and Martha might well have expected her sister to move in with their widowed mother in Hamburg.

The couple's first day-long walk alone occurred in 1897, and their first overnight trip in the following summer. In 1900 they were alone together from August 26 until September 9. Munich, Nuremberg, and Meran (now Merano) were the way-stations of a 1903 trip that lasted for two weeks. A three-week voyage ensued in 1905; it included an eight-day stay, for just the two of them, at one hotel in Genoa. And the summer custom prevailed again in 1907, 1908, 1913, 1919, 1921, and 1923, the last four trips involving month-long "cures" at spas.[19] In 1919, with the family drastically short of funds, Sigmund and Minna spent their month together in the posh spa of Bad Gastein while Martha, in a sanatorium, was convalescing from a near-fatal bout of the Spanish flu.[20]

A person would have to be awfully slow-witted not to detect a pattern here. Because the only warrant for psychoanalytic propositions has been trust in the veracity and sterling character of Freud, however, just such imperceptiveness has been mandated by allegiance to his movement. Jones, for example, who surely knew better, lulled his readers into believing not only that Sigmund had been "puritanical" and "quite peculiarly monogamous" but also that between the chaste in-laws "there was no sexual attraction on either side."[21] That was the most risible statement in Jones's three volumes—but it was also, in its very absurdity, the one that most plainly revealed Anna Freud's puppet strings. The gullible Peter Gay was taken in. While noting worriedly that some of Freud's writings "whisper of luxuriant erotic fantasies persisting through the years," Gay wished to believe that his ascetic idol had felt, and acted upon, "an aversion to extramarital adventures."[22] And most recently, the loyalist Élisabeth Roudinesco, repeatedly urging that Freud put sexuality behind him and even established a personal "cult of abstinence," has asserted that the Minna affair "doubtless never happened" and is a pure figment of Freud bashers.[23]

The truth is that Freud had arrived at an ethical position exactly opposite to the one Jones, Gay, and Roudinesco ascribed to him. Already in the midnineties, with his papers on neurasthenia and anxiety neurosis, he had declared as a medical principle that sexual satisfaction is essential to both physical and mental health. Like his moralizing successor D. H. Lawrence, he believed that no vows or conventions must be allowed to take precedence over such fulfillment. And he felt so strongly on the point that he became something of an activist against bourgeois sexual morality—a role that would endear him to the flappers and philosophers of the Jazz Age, with whom he had nothing else in common.

Freud's most famous declaration of non-obligation to loveless marriage would be made in his strikingly gauche essay of 1908, "'Civilized' Sexual Morality and Modern Nervous Illness."[24] There he offered the world a scarcely disguised picture of his wife as frigid, incurious, neurotic, and spiteful, all because she had entered marriage in a state of sexual ignorance. Only "a very few procreative acts" (just one, really) would be allowed by such a prude—a frustration, Freud opined, that would drive any virile man to consort with prostitutes.[25] He didn't say *any virile man but me.* "All who wish to be more noble-minded than their constitution allows," he proclaimed, "fall victim to neurosis; they would have been more healthy if it could have been possible for them to be less good."[26] And the doctor wrote out his Rx for all to see: "The cure for nervous illness arising from marriage would be marital unfaithfulness."*

Already in 1905, responding to a questionnaire about Austria's restrictive divorce law, Freud had advocated what he called "successive polygamy," or the replacement of an unsatisfactory spouse with a more congenial one. After all, he reflected, most married men already get their good sex outside the home.[27] Behind his endorsement of serial marriage lay the tacit opinion that an unhappy spouse was entitled to take matters into his or her own hands.

Later, in answering a 1915 query from the American neurologist James J. Putnam, Freud would declare, "I stand for an infinitely freer sexual life."[28] He added that he had personally made use of such free-

---

* SE, 9:195. Did Freud visit prostitutes? His ethical position sanctioned the practice, and his domestic situation encouraged it. When Marie Bonaparte asked him whether he had frequented brothels, he refused to answer (Roudinesco 2016, p. 25). Of an anonymous dreamer in *The Interpretation of Dreams* he wrote, "He had only seldom visited a brothel—only two or three times in his life." The same dreamer "in his boyish curiosity . . . had occasionally, though only seldom, inspected the genitals of a sister who was a few years his junior" (SE, 4:333). The two "seldoms," in two adjacent sentences, are evocative of a wish to mitigate guilt.

dom "only so far as I considered myself entitled to define the limits of what is permissible in this area"—a subtle admission that he hadn't allowed society's nominal rules to inhibit him.[29] And in 1921, having urged one of his analytic protégés to divorce his wife and marry his mistress, he would defend his action thus: "I thought it the good right of every human being to strive for sexual gratification and tender love if he saw a way to attain them, both of which he had not found with his wife."[30]

Transparent though Freud's behavior with Minna would appear to an outsider, psychoanalysts held fast to the party line until 2006, when the German sociologist Franz Maciejewski published a sensational-looking datum.[31] On August 13, 1898, Freud had signed the register of the Hotel Schweizerhaus in Maloja, Switzerland, for two nights in a double room, as "*Dr. Sigm. Freud u Frau/Wien.*" The "wife" was Minna. In Maciejewski's view and that of many others, the Minna thesis had been proved. Whereupon most Freudians ceased to protest; Jones's supposed "Puritan" must, after all, have adopted his wife's sister as his paramour.

But those loyalists who have held out for an innocent interpretation of the hotel register were justified in being unmoved by Maciejewski's news.[32] There were a number of benign explanations for the "doctor and wife" registration, such as the fact that Swiss hotels at the time would have refused to accommodate an openly unmarried couple. Both in 1898 and again in 1900, Freud *told Martha* that he and Minna were passing as spouses; he reported to her from one hotel, no doubt with forced jocularity, that he was avoiding the company of recognized colleagues who could have noted that he was being accompanied by "the incorrect wife" (*der nicht richtigen Frau*).[33] Those words alone suffice to weaken the forensic value of Maciejewski's titillating discovery.

But Freud's conduct in that summer of 1898 certainly did manifest his preference for Minna's company over Martha's. After spending only a week or so with his family in the Austrian resort town of Aussee and having a congress with Fliess near there, he left for Munich, where he and Minna embarked alone on a trip of some seventeen days, traveling through the Austrian, Swiss, and Italian Alps by train, carriage, and foot. In their joint letters to Martha, they dissembled the fact that they were staying in luxury hotels instead of modest inns. Nevertheless, they openly expressed the pleasure they took not only in sightseeing but also in one another. "Naturally," wrote Minna in one letter, referring to her recently purchased travel attire, "Sigi finds me extremely elegant."[34]

Martha, stranded with six children, was evidently outraged, and when Sigmund returned she demanded comparable treatment to Minna's. The sullen spouses then set out for Dalmatia, but Martha developed colitis-like symptoms and couldn't proceed. Sigmund left her behind at Ragusa (now Dubrovnik) and continued alone. These details are redolent of Minna-related strife between the Freuds. Yet the fact that Martha still expected some consideration and wanted to travel with Sigmund may suggest that she wasn't yet convinced of an accomplished sexual betrayal.

It is important, in fact, to recognize that Sigmund and Minna were almost certainly not practiced lovers in that summer of 1898. The investigator who has looked most closely into all of the pertinent data, Peter Swales, has shown, in both published and unpublished work, that Freud's sojourn with Minna aroused his erotic hopes but also put them on hold.[35] Swales argues persuasively that Freud did approach Minna sexually in the summer of 1898; that he was rebuffed in a less than definitive way, leaving him with hope for later success; and that he returned to Vienna in a carpe diem mood. The lesson that he then drew from a dream ("The Three Fates") was clear: "One should never neglect an opportunity, but always take what one can even when it involves doing a small wrong. One should never neglect an opportunity, since life is short and death inevitable."[36] So much for Jones's "Puritan."

There is powerful evidence to show that two years later, another overture by Freud was favorably received. If Sigmund and Minna weren't already lovers before the summer of 1900, they certainly were before that summer was over. Some of the proof lies right before us in the Fliess correspondence—not, of course, in the correspondence as sanitized by Kris and Anna Freud, but in the full archive published in 1985.

On August 26, 1900, Sigmund and Minna undertook a solitary

jaunt through the South Tyrol that ended on September 9 with a dubiously rationalized event, Freud's leaving Minna in the spa town of Meran. First, however, came an idyll that can only be characterized as a honeymoon. It included a several-day stopover in Trent (Trento), a day trip from there to a picturesque castle, an expensive carriage ride at Minna's request over a precipitous pass to the Austrian-border hamlet of Lavarone, and then a no less expensive descent to Riva, on Lake Garda, where, after one night in an unpleasant hotel, the couple relocated to the annex of the majestic Hotel-Pension du Lac.

Back in Vienna, Martha was now sending telegrams asking her husband to return at once. But Sigmund, normally a restless traveler who preferred to spend no more than one night anywhere, was in no hurry to leave, and he and Minna passed another four nights in their lakeside retreat. Nor was that the end of their escapade. In spite of Martha's entreaties, the couple then proceeded to Lake Maggiore for further time alone, sailing from one town to another so as to spend a second night by the water. Even after Sigmund deposited Minna in Meran, 150 miles to the northeast, he didn't return to Vienna but, for unknown reasons, headed all the way back to Milan and Genoa. Something conclusive, implacable, appears to have taken hold of his will.

The real smoking gun is a letter written to Fliess from Vienna on September 14, 1900. The former companions had held their last, extremely acrimonious, congress in that same summer; and Fliess had found Freud's aggressiveness toward him so alarming that he actually feared an intention of murder.[37] But now Freud had news that he simply couldn't keep to himself. Although, or perhaps because, the two men were now estranged, Freud wanted Fliess to know how ecstatic he had been with someone else at his side. And it is clear from the letter that Fliess already knew Freud's feelings and intentions toward Minna.

Freud began by narrating a vexatious journey with his wife that had been followed by several obligatory rendezvous with other relatives. But then there had been a dramatic change. "Finally," wrote Freud, "—we have now reached August 26—came the relief. I mean Minna."[38] Relating their travels, he gushed over the "extraordinarily beautiful" Castel Toblino and the spectacular road to Lavarone, where "we found the most magnificent forest of conifers and undreamed-of solitude."[39]

And then the descent to Lake Garda: "We finally stopped for five days at Riva, divinely accommodated and fed, luxuriating without regrets, and untroubled."[40]

The German for that last is striking: *eine Schwelgerei ohne Reue und Trübung*. A *Schwelgerei* is a debauch. And surely, if Sigmund and Minna weren't a sexual pair in Riva, there would have been no cause for him to say that their untroubled time was passed *ohne Reue*: lacking remorse, repentance, or contrition.

3. REMORSE AFTER ALL

Why had Freud dropped Minna off in Meran before he zigzagged alone to Milan, Genoa, and finally home? According to Jones, Minna was to be treated in Meran for her "tuberculosis."[41] But what tuberculosis was that? Jones made no further reference to it in his biography. Though Minna had once, as an adolescent, been sent to Sicily to recover from a lung ailment, no TB had ever been detected; and just recently she had been traversing mountain passes and otherwise having a grand time with Freud.

Sigmund informed Martha on September 1, before the halcyon days and nights on Lakes Garda and Maggiore, that Minna would be in Meran for one or two weeks, recovering from her "coughing."[42] Sometime between September 5 and 12, she settled into the pricey Hotel Erzherzog Johann—a typical choice for the strong-willed Minna, who, though the family bank account was then perilously low, could get Sigmund to pay for whatever she desired. Around September 26, however, she transferred to the modest Pension Mon Repos outside of town. Shortly thereafter, Freud wrote to Fliess that Minna would be away for "a few weeks or months" owing to her "pulmonary apicitis," or inflammation of the lungs.[43]

Minna's change of residence could lead us to think that she had hoped for the short visit first mentioned by Freud, but that she had learned something about her condition that required a longer and more economical stay in Meran. Then, since Mon Repos was a recuperative facility, it would seem that she was coping with the aftermath of a medical procedure. On October 14 Freud wrote cryptically to

Fliess, "the news from Meran [is] favorable."[44] But it would be six weeks altogether before Minna reappeared in Vienna. As for the daily correspondence that must have circulated between Minna and the anxious Freuds, it has disappeared, along with every letter between Sigmund and Minna for the seven years following September 1898.*

What we know is that within a month of her return, Minna became gravely ill, suffering from intermittent fever, a racing heartbeat, sharp stomach pains, and bloody stools appearing to contain mucus and shreds of tissue. Those symptoms weren't pulmonary. The medical researcher E. M. Thornton judged them to be consistent with a diagnosis of septic abortion, resulting from a crude attempt to end a pregnancy.†

Thornton's opinion was expressed orally to Peter Swales, who had tracked down Minna's whereabouts in Meran and reconstructed the whole August-to-October episode. In a groundbreaking 1982 article, he drew only one clearly erroneous conclusion, later amended when the whole Fliess correspondence came to light. Swales had inferred that Minna remained in Meran through February 1901, when in fact she was back in Vienna by the third week in October. In other respects, his detective work appears to have been uncanny—for the telltale "debauch" letter was still unpublished, and the guardians of the Freud Archives had refused to let him examine it.

Swales's key evidence for the pregnancy and abortion, however, was supplied by published sources. Freud, with a recklessness that must leave us dumbfounded, sometimes illustrated psychological phenomena with items from his covert life, placing himself under further suspicion by declaring that he couldn't say more "without doing serious mischief in important directions."[45] Or again, if he didn't break off analysis of a certain dream, "I should be obliged to betray many things which had better remain my secret."[46] Both of those cautions were

---

* Bizarrely, Gay counted the missing correspondence as weighing *against* any impropriety on Freud's part (Gay 1990, pp. 164–179). In a 2006 letter to Swales, however, he admitted that the evidence for an affair had become stronger, and he pledged to revise his biography accordingly if the opportunity arose (private correspondence; copy in my possession).

† Minna's elevated temperature and heart rate and her abdominal pain were suggestive of septicemia; her bloody and clotted stools may have been caused by subsequent peritonitis.

issued regarding his discussion of the "Table d'hôte" dream, to which he kept referring in his 1901 booklet *On Dreams*. The dream itself tells us little of interest, but one of Freud's attempts to explain its origin bears directly on the reason for Minna's presence in Meran.

Freud had probably experienced the dream in late September 1900, several weeks before Minna's return. Interpreting it in *On Dreams*, he recounted that he had recently "paid out a considerable amount of money on behalf of a member of my family of whom I am fond"— someone, moreover, with whom he had taken several "*cab-drives*" (including an "expensive" one) not long before.[47] Although Freud had "not hesitate[d] for a moment" when deciding to spend the money, he now declared, "*I regret having made the expenditure.*"[48] And while he designated the "relative" with masculine pronouns, he recalled having thought, anomalously, that "love of that sort would not be 'free of cost.'"[49] Later in the text he returned to the point, lamenting, "I wish I might for once experience love that cost me nothing."[50]

Likewise, in the nearly simultaneous *Psychopathology of Everyday Life*, Freud reverted to the same dream and its meaning for him. He related that he had withdrawn a sum of money that was sent to a relative absent "for purposes of cure."* And he added that he "regretted this expenditure," even though he hadn't had "a feeling of regret" when he promised to pay.[51]

It makes no sense for Freud to have "regretted" paying a medical bill for a sick relative, whether male or female, especially after having *not* regretted it at first. Such a miserly sentiment would not have been confessed to the public. It would seem, then, that he felt bad not about having *spent* the money—a simple loss of funds—but about having *provided* it for a regrettable purpose, one that had somehow been necessitated by "love." Only in the Minna context can that feeling be understood. Freud was remorseful over the killing of his paramour's fetus. In retrospect—so he thought, anyway, in his guilty brooding— he would have preferred to risk the consequences of allowing the baby to be born.

---

* SE, 6:120. The *Standard Edition* says "for purposes of medical treatment," thus obscuring the fact that Freud's term *Kurgebrauch* implied a spa—Meran, of course.

Freud's writings generally avoided the topic of abortion, but an important exception was noted by Swales. Delayed traumatic symptoms, Freud wrote in 1920, can result from "the killing of an unborn child, which had been decided upon without remorse and without hesitation" (*ohne Reue und Bedenken*).[52] What Swales couldn't have known in 1982, but understandably emphasizes today, is that Sigmund and Minna's lovefest on the banks of Lake Garda had also been conducted *ohne Reue*. In the later passage we perceive, to Freud's credit, that his conscience still tormented him twenty years after a decision that had spared his career, his sister-in-law's honor, and his illicit affair with her.

· 32 ·

The Unborn Avenger

1. TOO MANY COINCIDENCES

As can be seen, the question of whether Freud had a sexual relationship with his sister-in-law at the turn of the century remains open only for readers who prefer legend to fact. Yet I haven't mentioned the main evidence that was brought to light by Swales in 1982. That evidence must now be reviewed, not only because of its forensic value but also because it amounts to an object lesson in how to apprehend Freud's texts with due awareness of their guile.

When Freud returned to Vienna from his adventures with Minna in September 1900, feeling "outrageously merry and well," he was supercharged with energy and enthusiasm.[1] It was at this juncture that he experienced the burst of creativity that would yield, within a few months, *On Dreams* and *The Psychopathology of Everyday Life*. The first task that Freud set himself was to write the essay that would serve as Chapter 2 of the *Psychopathology*, "The Forgetting of Foreign Words." (Chapter 1 would be "The Forgetting of Proper Names," revised from the 1898 paper "The Psychical Mechanism of Forgetfulness.") Once regarded as the most stunning exhibit of repression, free association, and Freud's deductive genius, the chapter is now—ever since Swales's explosive article of 1982—the most controversial of all his writings.

In order to illustrate the unconsciously determined failure to recall a foreign word, Freud recounted an instructive recent experience:

> Last summer—it was once again on a holiday trip—I renewed my acquaintance with a certain young man of academic background. I soon found that he was familiar with some of my psychological publications. We had fallen into conversation—how I have now forgotten—about the social status of the race to which we both belonged; and ambitious feelings prompted him to give vent to a regret that his generation was doomed (as he expressed it) to atrophy, and could not develop its talents or satisfy its needs. He ended a speech of impassioned fervour with the well-known line of Virgil's in which the unhappy Dido commits to posterity her vengeance on Aeneas: "Exoriare. . . ." Or rather, he *wanted* to end it in this way, for he could not get hold of the quotation and tried to conceal an obvious gap in what he remembered by changing the order of the words: "Exoriar(e) ex nostris ossibus ultor." At last he said irritably: "Please don't look so scornful: you seem as if you were gloating over my embarrassment. Why not help me? There's something missing in the line; how does the whole thing really go?"
>
> "I'll help you with pleasure," I replied, and gave the quotation in its correct form: "Exoriar(e) ALIQUIS nostris ex ossibus ultor." ["May SOMEONE rise up from our bones as an avenger."]
>
> "How stupid to forget a word like that! By the way, you claim that one never forgets a thing without some reason. I should be very curious to learn how I came to forget the indefinite pronoun 'aliquis' in this case."
>
> I took up this challenge most readily, for I was hoping for a contribution to my collection. So I said: "That should not take us long. I must only ask you to tell me, *candidly* and *uncritically*, whatever comes into your mind if you direct your attention to the forgotten word without any definite aim."[2]

With the fictitious dialogue of "Screen Memories" in mind, the reader of this opening passage ought to be having a déjà vu experience. Once more we meet an anonymous man "of academic background," which is to say, someone possessing credentials for a grasp of psychoanalytic reasoning. More remarkably, this fellow, who hasn't been analyzed by Freud, is one of the few people in the world who, by the summer of 1900, has read his psychological writings with open-minded sympathy. And more remarkably still, he knows of Freud's doctrine about motivated forgetting, a theory that had been illustrated only once, in a specialist journal of psychiatric neurology.*

The young acquaintance again elicits no sense of the unusual from Freud when he finishes off a peroration with the abandoned Dido's cry from *The Aeneid*. He assumes that the vacationing doctor will have the corrected wording on the tip of his tongue—and his assumption is instantly confirmed. Indeed, Freud is confident that it will be child's play for him to solve the much chancier mystery of why the word *aliquis* couldn't be recalled.

Freud's certainty of success here recalls his equally unbelievable assurance when he supposedly invited Katharina, the girl at the mountain lodge, to free associate "in the confident expectation that she would think of precisely what I needed to explain the case." Needless to say, he is right again. Each of the interlocutor's reported thoughts will point to the same cause of the slip, obviating any need on Freud's part to reassess false leads and failed hypotheses. Other psychologists, I believe, haven't found reality bending to their will in this ideal manner.

Herr Aliquis, as he has come to be known in the secondary literature, begins his share of the task by dividing *aliquis* into *a* and *liquis*, to which he ties *Reliquien* (relics), *liquefying*, *fluidity*, and *fluid*. The term *relics* then reminds him of St. Simon of Trent, who was thought by Christians to have been murdered by Jews in childhood so as to obtain his blood for a ritual purpose; and thus the traveler proceeds to think about the recent revival of the same pernicious falsehood. In a book by a certain *Kleinpaul*, he adds, those murdered babies are characterized as "new editions" of the crucified Saviour. Next, Herr Aliquis

---

* This was the original version of Freud's "Signorelli" analysis, published in 1898 in the *Monatsschrift für Psychiatrie und Neurologie* (SE, 3:287–297). Before August 1898, not even Fliess was aware that Freud had developed the concept of the "parapraxis" (*Fehlleistung*).

dwells briefly on St. Augustine's remarks about women. And then he mentions that he recently met an old gentleman, *a real original*, named Benedikt, who looked like "a huge bird of prey." Clearly, this champion associator bears no resemblance to those patients who, when commanded by Freud to say whatever occurred to them, protested that "nothing comes to mind."

Freud now interrupts to point out that Herr Aliquis has been arraying, alongside the church father Origen (="original"), a string of saints: Simon, Augustine, Benedict, and Paul; whereupon the man volunteers that he has also been thinking of St. Januarius, a "calendar saint" whose relics in Naples are expected to liquefy on certain holy days. If they fail to bleed, major trouble could ensue. And finally, with embarrassed hesitancy, Herr Aliquis confesses that he "suddenly" recalls something else: that he has been anxiously awaiting news from "a lady" that could prove "very awkward for both of us."[3]

At this point Freud turns himself into an avatar of Poe's C. Auguste Dupin, who, in "The Murders in the Rue Morgue," traces the strolling narrator's exact sequence of thoughts over the previous fifteen minutes. In this instance the straight man voices his own chain of associations; but Freud, like Dupin, nonchalantly demonstrates his command of their meaning, as if the task were no more challenging than brushing his teeth. He has already deciphered the news feared by Herr Aliquis:

"That her periods have stopped?"

"How could you guess that?"

"That's not difficult any longer; you've prepared the way sufficiently. Think of *the calendar saints, the blood that starts to flow on a particular day, the disturbance when the event fails to take place, the open threats that the miracle must be vouchsafed, or else....* In fact, you've made use of the miracle of St. Januarius to manufacture a brilliant allusion to women's periods."

"Without being aware of it. And you really mean to say that it was this anxious expectation that made me unable to produce an unimportant word like *aliquis*?"

"It seems to me undeniable."[4]

By now Herr Aliquis is so unnerved by Freud's godlike omniscience that he calls a halt to the exchange. Freud must turn to the reader in order to complete his analysis:

> The speaker had been deploring the fact that the present generation of his people was deprived of its full rights; a new generation, he prophesied like Dido, would inflict vengeance on the oppressors. He had in this way expressed his wish for descendants. At this moment a contrary thought intruded. "Have you really so keen a wish for descendants? That is not so. How embarrassed you would be if you were to get news just now that you were to expect descendants from the quarter you know of. No: no descendants—however much we need them for vengeance."[5]

Supposing for the moment that there really was a Herr Aliquis, we may ask whether Freud has plausibly explained his failure to recall one word from the 9,896-line *Aeneid*. Back in 1974, in an acute book-length critique of the *Psychopathology*, the linguist Sebastiano Timpanaro showed that the forgetting of a word in a quotation can result from a variety of factors, any of which would require less suspension of disbelief than the unproven concept of repression.[6] The "roundabout associative path" of Herr Aliquis's supposed thoughts, with its "every appearance of artificiality," adds further degrees of implausibility. If Freud had been the canny skeptic that he represents himself as being, he would hardly have been satisfied with the least parsimonious explanation of what looks like a very ordinary failure of recall.

Moreover, Freud's attempt to illustrate the intricate workings of repression is doomed, logically if not rhetorically, by an irreparable flaw: Herr Aliquis *has not repressed* his concern about a possible pregnancy. It would seem that for some time he has been brooding about nothing else. By having him "suddenly" bring that concern to mind, Freud is hinting that the worry usually resides below the level of consciousness; but a person doesn't anxiously anticipate "a piece of news" without awareness of doing so.

"You've made use of the miracle of St. Januarius to manufacture a brilliant allusion to women's periods," Freud tells Herr Aliquis. Well, *someone* has done exactly that, and a simple test can be applied to determine who it was. If we could show that Herr Aliquis's mental images were inspired by Freud's own experience, the already high likelihood that Freud himself was the "manufacturer" would rise to a certainty.

In this connection, we must be struck by Herr Aliquis's report of having recently met a unique-looking old man named *Benedikt*. (Strachey spelled the name *Benedict*, but that was a mistranscription, and possibly not an innocent one.) Freud was very familiar with the aging Viennese maverick Moriz Benedikt, "a real original" indeed, whose bald pate and long beaklike nose also matched Herr Aliquis's "bird of prey." Benedikt, we recall, had supplied Freud's letter of introduction to Charcot. If Freud, in the story, refrains from commenting on the coincidence of his interlocutor's having met his own eccentric Viennese colleague, it must be because Freud the author is drawing on his store of references to supply make-believe associative material.

Here are some further parallels that Swales establishes between Herr Aliquis and Freud:

- The career of the ambitious Herr Aliquis has been hamstrung by the denial of full rights to Jews, and he is angry about it. In September 1900 Freud, having recently learned that his candidacy for a professorship had been rejected once again, felt the same resentment with especial keenness. That is when he sat down to write the *aliquis* chapter. Two years later, inscribing a copy of *The Interpretation of Dreams* to Theodor Herzl, the founder of Zionism, he praised that "fighter for the human rights of our people."[7]
- *The Aeneid* was a beloved text of Freud's. He quoted it in "Screen Memories," and it supplied his defiant epigraph to *The Interpretation of Dreams*. He didn't take those passages directly from Virgil's poem, however, but from a work by a writer he greatly admired, the German socialist Ferdinand Lasalle. In a collection of Lasalle's writings that Freud was reading in the summer of 1899, the Jewish author, yearning for vengeance against gentile wrongs, ended the text of a speech with these words: *Exoriare aliquis nostris ex ossibus ultor.*
- Dido's call for an avenger against the Romans was meant by Virgil to prophesy the Carthaginian Hannibal's near conquest of Rome.

As we know, the semitic Hannibal was the historical figure with whom the youthful Freud most closely associated himself. Indeed, his Hannibal identification was being strongly revived at the turn of the century.

- Herr Aliquis reports that he has been to Trent and seen the relics of the murdered child St. Simon. In the very summer when the conversation allegedly took place, Freud himself visited the same town in the company of Minna Bernays. It is impossible that the Baedeker-wielding Freud would have missed seeing Trent's main touristical asset, the Church of St. Peter, where the relics were housed. Tellingly, however, he fails to mention any such visit either to Herr Aliquis or to the reader.

- Freud's interest in the persecution and vilification of Jews, which St. Simon's alleged martyrdom in the fifteenth century had continued to incite, was intensified by at least one contemporary "blood libel" trial in Europe. (Another one, not mentioned by Swales in 1982, was a journalistic sensation during Freud's writing of his chapter.) The modern expert on blood libel was Rudolf Kleinpaul, an author Freud greatly admired. Herr Aliquis mentions him, but the personage Freud doesn't let on that he has ever heard of him.

- Herr Aliquis's phrase "new editions," characterizing examples of reincarnation, appears in metaphorical contexts about a dozen times in Freud's published writings. It would appear prominently in his postscript to the "Dora" case, drafted in the year following the *aliquis* essay.[8]

- Herr Aliquis reflects on St. Augustine's negative view of women. In the "Dora" case history, written four months after the *aliquis* chapter, Freud quotes St. Augustine on our common disgrace, as human beings, in having to enter the world from the vagina, "between urine and feces."

Swales traced all but one of Herr Aliquis's associations to Freud's own reading, experience, and passionate concerns. The exception was the putative liquefaction of St. Januarius's blood in Naples, a city that Freud hadn't ever visited. In the narrative, Freud has to be informed about the Neapolitan tradition by the more widely traveled young man. "We must wonder, then," Swales wrote in 1982, "if Freud happened to read about the famous Roman Catholic blood-miracle around this time, perhaps in a newspaper, causing him spontaneously to associate it with the symbolically congruent matter of menstruation."[9]

Swales's question was answered in 2001 when Richard Skues, in most respects a resolute defender of Freud, published an article disarmingly titled "On the Dating of Freud's *Aliquis* Slip." Among other evidence supporting Swales's thesis, Skues reported the following precious discovery. On September 23, 1900, the newspaper that Freud never failed to read, Vienna's *Neue Freie Presse*, contained a review by the Jewish-Danish author Georg Brandes of two travel books, one of which included a visit to the famed chapel in Naples—"this very chapel," in words quoted by Brandes, "in which the blood of St. Januarius several times a year is so kind as to transform itself from a solid to a liquid state."[10] And, as it happens, Brandes was Freud's very favorite contemporary author. Freud had attended a lecture of his in Vienna six months earlier, had "reveled in listening to it," and had sent an inscribed copy of *The Interpretation of Dreams* around to Brandes's hotel as a tribute.[11]

Freud had been home from his summer travels for almost two weeks when Brandes's review materialized before his gaze. Hence we can be sure that the *aliquis* event, with its central emphasis on the miracle of St. Januarius, didn't occur on a summer "holiday trip." But there is no reason to think that it occurred at all, and every reason to think otherwise. On the day following the appearance of Brandes's reference to the Neapolitan saint, Freud wrote to Fliess that he was now at work on *The Psychopathology of Everyday Life*.[12] "I was hoping for a contribution to my collection," Freud tells us in the chapter itself. The invented tale of Herr Aliquis was his response to a dearth of authentic illustrative material for "the forgetting of foreign words."*

---

* Could there have been a real Herr Aliquis after all? The leading candidate, very weakly supported, has been Freud's brother Alexander. One proponent of that identity, Albrecht Hirschmüller, feels obliged to admit that it would have been imprudent for Freud to have implicated his brother in causing an illicit pregnancy. But—no problem!

But of course it was more than that. Herr Aliquis was Freud, and Freud was awaiting news from Meran about whether a certain lady had "liquefied" on schedule or had missed her period. He was not so adept at covering his tracks, however, as he fancied himself to be. Thinking, perhaps, of Minna's whereabouts, he had Herr Aliquis call the lady an Italian; but in doing so he forgot that such a person, descended from the sackers of Carthage and Jerusalem, could hardly give birth to an avenger of the Jews. Minna Bernays, with a genetic boost from the would-be Maccabee Freud, could have done so. The hero, however, would be stabbed to death in his mother's womb.

As Timpanaro noted in 1974, abortion is the real theme behind Freud's emphasis on the infanticide of St. Simon of Trent.[13] Freud, in a footnote to his chapter, had his imaginary companion say that *exori-are* reminded him of *exorcism*; then, amending his note for the 1924 edition, he accepted another psychoanalyst's proposal that "exorcism would be the best symbolic substitution for repressed thoughts about getting rid of the unwanted child by abortion."[14] Freud's guilty brooding hadn't stopped.

2. THE AFTERMATH

Minna Bernays's illness persisted and evolved, for reasons unknown, not for weeks or months but for five years, after which time she was mobile again but still not fully well. Her invalidism ought to have given Freud plenty of time to reconsider the prudence of conducting an affair with his sister-in-law. It would have been understandable if the two parties had agreed to take a big step back. And we can suppose that Minna—who had remained a virgin nanny in the Freuds' household for four years, had probably fended off advances by Sigmund in 1898, and had now suffered in body and spirit—would have welcomed that resolution.

After Minna's recovery, however, this wouldn't have been Freud's view of the matter. A man who makes love to his mistress on summer

---

"The concealment was obviously good enough that, up until now, hardly anyone has publicly expressed this supposition" (Hirschmüller 2002b, p. 398).

holidays and, for the rest of the year, pays for her upkeep at home isn't likely to leave her untouched there. And what about the whole years, later ones, when Minna and Sigmund were unable to travel alone? Freud had been a tyrant in all of his dealings with Martha. He was still a tyrant, and now at last he had a sexual relationship that actually pleased him. As for Minna herself, she was surely in love with him, and she depended on his goodwill and largesse for shelter from a society that had little use for penniless spinsters.

It was long believed that Aunt Minna's bedroom at Berggasse 19 was adjacent to Sigmund and Martha's, a circumstance that would have discouraged adultery. That arrangement, however, dated only from 1920, when Freud was sixty-four. Previously, Minna's room, in a huge complex, had been as far from the conjugal one as it could possibly be, and the nocturnal Sigmund could have visited it with impunity in predawn hours.[15]

In 1969 there was published an interview, actually recorded in 1957, between Jung and one of his American admirers, John M. Billinsky. Jung had told Billinsky and at least two other people about his first visit to the Freud apartment in 1907, when he was startled by the contrast between the roles of the Bernays sisters. "I am sorry that I can give you no real hospitality," Freud had apologized; "I have nothing at home but an elderly wife."[16] (Martha was not yet forty-six.) Hours later, Jung tried to engage Martha in conversation about Sigmund's work, "but I soon discovered that Mrs. Freud knew absolutely nothing about what Freud was doing. It was very obvious that there was a very superficial relationship between Freud and his wife."[17] A "very good-looking" Minna, however, "not only knew enough about psychoanalysis but also about everything that Freud was doing."[18]

A few days later during Jung's weeklong stay in Vienna, Minna, no doubt perceiving that a psychoanalytic heir apparent was being anointed, allegedly drew him aside:

> She was very much bothered by her relationship with Freud and felt guilty about it. From her I learned that Freud was in love with her and

that their relationship was indeed very intimate. It was a shocking discovery to me, and even now I can recall the agony I felt at the time.[19]

That language, though unambiguous, was euphemistic. As we now know from Billinsky's handwritten notes, Jung had actually told him in so many words that Minna and Sigmund were engaged in "sexual relations."[20]

Of course the psychoanalysts fought back, demeaning Jung's motive and denying that Minna would have unburdened herself to a stranger. Some other observers, however, had long since inferred the state of affairs that was reportedly confessed to Jung. One of them was Oscar Rie, who was not only Fliess's brother-in-law, a close friend of Freud's for forty-five years, and the co-author of his book on infantile paralyses, but also the personal physician of all three principals—Sigmund, Martha, and Minna. Rie is said to have remarked, "For children, Freud went with Martha; for pleasure, he took Minna."[21]

As might be expected, Freud's lawless behavior with Minna, which he never explicitly disavowed or tried to explain away, resulted in long-lasting anxiety within his extended family and much gossip among the psychoanalytic elite. Sándor Ferenczi, who knew Freud very well and tried to draw him out on the topic, teased him about it with a punning rhyme. Hadn't Sigmund and Minna voyaged "*de lit-à-lit* [from bed to bed] *en Italie*"?[22]

But this was no joking matter. Freud never contemplated practicing the "successive polygamy" that he would advocate in his 1905 questionnaire response. Instead, he demanded different services from two simultaneous wives, according no concessions to wife number one in compensation for his intimacy with the other. Martha would continue as his domestic attendant while being shown, every day, that in her husband's opinion she deserved nothing better. The effect on her was noted by Jung in 1907. In a 1953 interview with Kurt Eissler that Eissler embargoed for fifty years, Jung dodged the Minna issue but recounted that Martha had struck him as "totally washed out, ego-disturbed, ego-disturbed."[23]

Even Jones, obliged to perjure himself by swearing that Sigmund loved only Martha, adoringly, for fifty-seven years, couldn't resist flashing us a few semaphores behind Anna's back. "Everything points to a remarkable concealment in Freud's love life," he observed; and elsewhere, "One sensed an invisible reserve behind which it would be impertinent to intrude, and no one ever did," and "there were features about his attitude that would seem . . . to justify the word privacy being replaced by secrecy."[24]

What Jung was told by Minna in person made a profound if confused impression on him. Could the inventer of psychoanalysis, with its ethic of arduous probing for the truth, have been concealing a double life for the sake of advancement? When Freud and Jung were visiting the United States in 1909 and exchanging comments on each other's dreams, the clandestinely well-informed Jung pressed Freud to explain a dream, involving Martha, Minna, and himself, that Freud reported but then refused to discuss. When pressed, according to Jung, Freud had recoiled and exclaimed, "But I cannot risk my authority!"[25]

This incident, which Jung confided to others at the time, was a watershed moment for him. Now he knew for sure what he had scarcely been willing to believe two years earlier. He wasn't offended by adultery, with which he was more at ease than Freud, but he ceased looking up to his surrogate father; and from then on the most serious fracturing of the psychoanalytic movement would be unavoidable.

33

Girl Trouble

1. DOMESTIC AFFAIRS

Although Freud had planned a concluding chapter of *The Interpretation of Dreams* on "Dreams and Neuroses," he had lacked any successful cases to draw upon, and thus the chapter had remained unwritten.[1] In mid-October 1900, however, just before Minna Bernays's delayed return from Meran, he acquired a patient whose reported dreams, in a projected year-long analysis, *might* offer a key to understanding or even removing her "hysteria." The hope of a cure disappeared with the patient herself when she deserted him less than three months later, after some sixty-five sessions. Nevertheless, Freud believed she had given him the required demonstration of correspondence between dream imagery and hysterical symptoms.

That is why he interrupted the composing of his *Psychopathology of Everyday Life* for three weeks, in the first month of 1901, to write up this patient's case, initially named "Dreams and Hysteria: A Fragment of an Analysis." The new paper, Freud told a no longer sympathetic Fliess, was "the subtlest thing I have written so far."[2] Indeed, it would be hailed not only as the first of Freud's major case studies—the others are considered to be the narratives of Little Hans, the Rat Man, the psychotic Schreber, and the Wolf Man—but as the most fascinating and instructive of them all. And perhaps it is, though not for the reasons customarily given.

Freud's famous patient, "Dora," was actually Ida Bauer, who turned eighteen shortly after entering treatment with him. (He variously called her eighteen and "almost nineteen.") Only in 1978 did her identity become widely known,[3] and even now she is still Dora to students of her case, many of whom continue to saddle her with the disagreeable traits and motives that were first specified by Freud. As part of a fresh look at the case, I will employ the real names not only of Ida but also of the four adults who principally figured in her dramatic story:

- *Filipp Bauer*, Ida's father, a wealthy textile entrepreneur with two factories in what is now the Czech Republic, but was then part of Austria-Hungary.
- *Katharina Gerber Bauer*, Ida's mother. She and Filipp married in 1881. She will be *Käthe* below.
- *Hans Zellenka* (Freud's "Herr K."), a shopkeeper in Meran (Freud's "B.").
- *Giuseppina Zellenka*, Hans's wife (Freud's "Frau K."). She will be *Peppina* below.

When Ida was born to Käthe and Filipp Bauer on November 1, 1882, her address in Vienna was Berggasse 32, just a block away from Freud's later residence and consulting room. Her only sibling, Otto, was fourteen months older.* The most important events of her childhood concerned her father's health. When Ida was six, Filipp contracted tuberculosis, and the family relocated to Meran, 250 miles to the southwest, for its pure mountain air. Already blind in one eye, Filipp suffered a detached retina in the other eye when Ida was ten or eleven. Becoming involved in his care, she evidently learned that he had contracted

---

* Having earned a law degree and written a well-regarded book, Otto Bauer would become a leading socialist. In 1914 Freud advised him to give up politics, a futile realm, and turn to teaching. "Don't try to make people happy," Freud told him. "People don't want to be happy" (Decker 1991, pp. 159–160). Otto disregarded Freud's opinion, and after the empire's collapse he became the first foreign minister of the Austrian Republic.

syphilis before his marriage. That disease probably explained his most alarming crisis, which occurred in 1894, when Ida was twelve. Filipp then underwent an attack of temporary paralysis and mental confusion.

As Freud relates, Käthe Bauer and her husband barely got along. Partly because of his diseases, we can suppose, she became a compulsive cleanliness fanatic, devoting virtually all of her waking time to washing, tidying, and disinfecting. Unwilling or unable to keep dealing with Filipp's need for care, she enlisted Peppina Zellenka to nurse him. Peppina appears to have done so all too well, for the nurse and patient became sexually involved.

Peppina's husband, Hans, was aware of that fact, and understandably, he wanted the relationship to cease. But he was in no position to complain about extramarital adventures. Peppina's frequent absences facilitated his own avocation of skirt chasing. Moreover, he didn't shrink from pedophilia, with a special target in mind: the twelve-year-old daughter of his wife's lover, Filipp. Brashly, he plied Ida with flowers, gifts, and flattering attentions.

Käthe seems to have been too focused on decontaminating her house to notice the danger into which Ida was falling. And Filipp, though he is said to have loved his daughter, was no less distracted than his wife. One day when Ida was thirteen—Freud claimed she had been a year older—Hans contrived to get her alone in his Meran shop, where he grabbed and kissed her.* The terrified Ida managed to twist away and flee, but she confided in no one at the time. Perhaps she couldn't explain to herself what had happened, but she also must have been reluctant to tell her parents, for by then the adult Bauers and Zellenkas, in spite of their disparity of wealth and class, were on perversely cordial terms, and Ida must have sensed the disbelief and annoyance with which her accusation would have been greeted.

A further complication was that Ida herself had become a virtual member of the Zellenka family, enjoying Peppina's apparently sincere friendship, admiring her beauty, sharing her confidences about her

---

* Freud's consistent inflation of Ida's age obscured some of the horror of her treatment by himself and others. It isn't known whether his misstatements were deliberate or merely careless. See Mahony 1996, pp. 18–19.

loveless marriage, and caring affectionately for her two young children. According to Freud, Ida also colluded in the Filipp-Peppina affair by making space for the adulterers when they were together. We can't be sure, however, that she comprehended the nature of their relationship, much less that she actively fostered it.

There matters stood until June 1898, when Ida, by Freud's reckoning, was sixteen (she was really fifteen and a half). The Zellenkas invited her for an extended stay at an Alpine lake where they had rented a summer house. Filipp transported her, expecting to return to Meran alone a few days later. Early in the visit, however, Hans, confronting Ida after a boat ride across the lake and declaring that he "got nothing out of his wife," openly propositioned her. She slapped him and hurried away.

When Ida took a nap later on the day of the confrontation, she awoke to find Hans standing by her bed, menacingly declaring that he could enter "his own room" whenever he pleased. And when, on the following day, she tried to lock the door so she could change her clothes without fear of intrusion, she found that the key was missing. She needed no further evidence in order to realize that it would be hazardous for her to remain alone with the Zellenkas. Three days later, she insisted on leaving with her father, though without telling him why. She waited two more weeks before reluctantly telling her mother what had happened, whereupon Käthe relayed the story to her husband.

Here, then, was a crucial test for both families. The adult Bauers might have been expected to support their daughter and face up to the destructive consequences of Filipp's affair with Peppina. And surely Peppina could be counted upon to take Ida's part against the predatory Hans. But the test was failed on both sides. Hans, replying to a letter of inquiry from Filipp, expressed high regard for Ida and declared himself to be entirely innocent; yet when quizzed in person after his return to Meran, he went on the offensive, calling Ida's story a delusion brought on by delving into forbidden literature about sexual intercourse. Peppina, acting on her own selfish motives, had evidently supplied him with that tactically useful information about Ida's reading.*

---

* Peppina reportedly said that Ida had been studying *The Physiology of Love* (1896), by the same Paolo Mantegazza whose transports over the coca leaf had so impressed

The Bauers believed Hans's story, or pretended to. Thus Filipp got to keep his mistress, and he and Käthe together could retain their friendship with the "exonerated" Zellenkas. The only loser was Ida, traduced by all four adults and belittled as a sexually twisted hallucinator. Her now furious demands that the Filipp-Peppina relationship be ended and that all ties with the Zellenkas be broken were treated as further manifestations of an unbalanced mind.

In 1899 the Bauers moved briefly to Reichenberg, near Filipp's factories, before deciding that Vienna ought to be their permanent home. To Ida's consternation, they were soon joined there by the Zellenkas, and Ida perceived that the liaison between her father and Peppina was still intact. The recent death of her favorite aunt—possibly the only person in her milieu who had merited her trust—was a further inducement to depression. When she then left a questionably sincere "suicide letter" where her parents would be likely to find it, Filipp decided that she ought to enter treatment with Freud.

Filipp and Freud were already on excellent terms when Ida's therapy began. Filipp had previously consulted the Viennese neurologist about his own symptoms in 1898; and Freud, diagnosing late-stage syphilis, had prescribed accordingly, somehow producing either the reality or the appearance of a remission.* Freud had also met Ida, immediately labeling her a hysteric because she exhibited a persistent cough. Once the Bauers had settled in Vienna, Filipp revisited Freud on several further occasions. Now he wanted Freud to talk Ida out of her supposedly delusional ideas, which included not only her "false memory" of the lakeside incident but also her belief that there was something improper about his impeccably virtuous relations with Peppina.

Freud in 1884. But it was another book of Mantegazza's, *The Sexual Relations of Mankind* (1885), that dealt graphically with the sex act.

* Freud's conventional remedy for syphilis was mercury, a horrific neurotoxin; and the reader may recall that he advocated prescribing higher doses of it if the patient were simultaneously administered the wonder drug cocaine. In the Dora write-up, he boasted of having removed Filipp's symptoms with just one application of medicine—a feat beyond the most sanguine claims of syphilis specialists, who typically offered their patients widely spaced infusions of mercury in a regimen lasting for years.

2. TAKING SIDES

What chiefly distinguished Ida Bauer from Freud's usual patients was her youth and the involuntary nature of her presence in his office. She didn't know it, but she was there in order to be turned back into the obedient daughter she had been before the onset of teenage rebelliousness. In her own opinion, however, her "aggression" was entirely merited by adult misconduct. Vexingly for Freud, her relations with him would follow the same course traced by most of her predecessors. She would listen to his questions and assertions, take note of what she judged to be his insensitive monomania, and decide that it would be pointless to continue. As she remarked of the treatment on its final day, December 31, 1900, she had decided to "put up with it till the New Year" but not beyond.[4]

Apart from conceding that Ida was "a girl of intelligent and engaging looks," Freud had nothing good to say about her.[5] Her personality, he believed, was inherently contrary, a fact that was demonstrated by her immediate disputing of practically everything he ventured regarding her motives in the two-family imbroglio. Yet if we discount Freud's editorializing and simply attend to Ida's words and actions, we can make out a more sympathetic person.

Though she was starved for forthright affection within her family, Ida was nevertheless capable of expressing love for Peppina's two children. We can also discern in her an admirable independence of mind—a trait, we remember, that Freud (making an exception for Minna) then regarded as unbecoming a lady. Ida understood her parents' weakness and cowardice; she saw that both pairs of adults had been willing to sacrifice her to their self-interest; and, noting that her brother Otto had been given every advantage and opportunity, she linked her plight to her inferior status as a female. Rather ominously from Freud's point of view, her ordeal at the lake had provoked her, at the precocious age of seventeen, into "attending lectures for women and . . . carrying on more or less serious studies."[6]

It is no exaggeration to say that Freud grew to despise Ida Bauer. At times her very presence seems to have disgusted him. "For several days on end," he reported at one point, "she identified herself with her mother by means of slight symptoms and peculiarities of manner, which gave her an opportunity for some really remarkable achievements in the direction of intolerable behaviour."[7] (Freud never met Käthe, either then or later.)

Freud regarded his patient as an antagonist, to be tripped up and scolded wherever he could find an opening to do so. "I let her go on talking," he reported, "and she suddenly recollected that it was [Hans's] birthday . . . —a fact which I did not fail to use against her."[8] Or again, when Ida appeared one day suffering sharp abdominal pains, Freud's immediate response was, "Whom are you copying now?"[9] And when she reported that she had recently endured an attack of appendicitis and a chronically dragging foot, Freud brushed aside the diagnoses made by the specialists who had examined her.[10] The "appendicitis," he declared, had been a phantom pregnancy, issuing in a hysterical childbirth—the memory of which she must have repressed—and the lameness stood for her "false step" in having failed to protect against the imaginary conception.*

But Freud was never granted the catharsis of winning Ida's agreement to such interpretations. She "had grown accustomed to laugh at the efforts of doctors, and in the end to renounce their help entirely."[11] Before being handed over to Freud, the depressed and sullen Ida had been subjected to hydrotherapy and electrical stimulation, useless therapies that Freud himself had trusted in the early years of his practice. Only as a favor to her father had she consented to sign on with Freud. And when she saw his unsubtle way of assimilating her every utterance to his sexual theory, she was less offended than amused.

After Freud pronounced his "satisfaction at the result" of a two-hour dream analysis, for example, Ida saucily retorted, "Why, has anything so very remarkable come out?"[12] And when he told her that a jewel case, mentioned in one of her dream reports, signified the female genitals, she snapped, "I knew you would say that"—a line that was

---

* In the common circumstance of "pelvic appendicitis," the psoas muscle can be impinged, affecting locomotion. This may not have been Ida's problem, but Freud, as a physician, ought to have considered it. See Stadlen 1989.

rendered still funnier by Freud's huffy footnote: "A very common way of putting aside a piece of knowledge that emerges from the repressed."[13]

Less amusing today, however, is Freud's response to the story of adultery, child abuse, prevarication, and betrayal that Ida recounted to him. Although he wanted to dismiss parts of that story as exaggerated, he was finally obliged to believe every word of it. But his belief was unaccompanied by even the slightest concern over Ida's trial. Not once, in a case history that occupies 115 pages of the *Standard Edition*, did he acknowledge his patient's traumatization at the hands of unscrupulous elders. Nor, apparently, had he done so in person.

Freud's hectoring of the slandered and pathologized Ida stands in marked contrast to his reluctance to criticize the other principals, especially the two philandering husbands. Here we may observe that he began analyzing Ida just a month after returning from his own sequence of trysts with his sister-in-law. Like Filipp as described by his daughter, Sigmund had spent lavishly on the woman he loved and had written deceptively chatty letters home when he was away with her. Other parallels must have been even more striking to the superstitious Freud. Ida's tale was largely set in Meran, where Minna remained at the time of telling. And the big lake on whose far side Hans had invited Ida to become his lover was probably Garda, the very site of Sigmund and Minna's recent "debauch without remorse." Dissatisfied husbands who sought relief outside their marriage were not about to be judged harshly by Freud.

The worst miscreant in Ida's story was Hans. Freud, however, found him altogether appealing. "I happen to know [Hans]," he told his readers, "for he was the same person who had visited me with the patient's father, and he was still quite young and of prepossessing appearance."[14] So smitten by Hans was Freud that he couldn't fathom why Ida hadn't immediately assented to his proposition, which "was not in the least tactless or offensive."[15] And why, asked Freud, "did her refusal take such a brutal form, as though she were embittered against him?"[16] The fifteen-year-old Ida's brutality, we recall, consisted of one slap that sufficed to forestall the embrace of a practiced roué.

It was Hans's first sexual advance, however—the coerced kiss in his empty shop—that most dramatically elicited Freud's indulgence toward the predator and his contempt for the victim. Freud's commentary on this point deserves to be studied by everyone who has regarded him as a moral authority:

> This was surely just the situation to call up a distinct feeling of sexual excitement in a girl of fourteen [really thirteen] who had never before been approached. But [Ida] had at that moment a violent feeling of disgust, tore herself free from the man, and hurried past him to the staircase and from there to the street door. . . .
>
> In this scene . . . the behavior of this child of fourteen was already entirely and completely hysterical. I should without question consider a person hysterical in whom an occasion for sexual excitement elicited feelings that were preponderantly or exclusively unpleasurable; and I should do so whether or not the person were capable of producing somatic symptoms.[17]

A number of influences were doubtless at work behind these pronouncements, including Freud's ill-feeling toward Ida, his attraction to Hans, his mechanical model of the hydraulic flow and blockage of libido, his ethic of imperative libidinal satisfaction for frustrated husbands, and his own history with childhood sexual abuse. Most significant of all, however, is simply his want of psychological understanding. For years he had been theorizing about sexual trauma as a prompt for the outbreak of neuroses; but when presented with an actual sexual assault on a terrified child, he declared the victim's *unpleasure* to be an infallible sign of hysteria.

We have previously remarked that Freud was fond of telling female patients that they were in love with certain unattainable men. It didn't matter if the woman denied having nurtured such a feeling; in that case she must have been unconsciously in love. Much of Freud's time with Ida was devoted to insisting, against her firm denial, that she had loved Hans Zellenka and, in spite of everything, that she still did. "How [Ida] managed to fall in love with the man about whom her beloved friend [Peppina] had so many bad things to say," Freud granted, "is an interesting psychological problem." But it was easily solved: "contraries get on together" within the unconscious.[18] And drawing another cliché from his romance novelist's hoard, he declared that, after all, Hans's intentions were honorable.

According to Freud, the middle-aged paterfamilias Hans had wanted to divorce his wife and marry his teen heartthrob. What a pity, then, that he had misinterpreted her slap as a definitive rejection of his plan. "If he had disregarded that first 'No,' and had continued to press his suit with a passion which left room for no doubts," Freud opined, "the result might very well have been a triumph of the girl's affection for him over all her internal difficulties."[19] Even as Ida bade Freud a civil farewell on the day she walked out, he persisted in believing that she was "waiting till [Hans] could marry her."[20]

In this portion of his argument, Freud combined moral crudeness with what can only be characterized as willful blindness. Ida had given him sufficient information to prove beyond doubt that Hans wasn't contemplating divorce and remarriage to her. Yet Freud couldn't recognize the meaning of the very facts that he was passing along from Ida to his readers.

For one thing, Hans had denounced his "future wife" to her parents as a sex-obsessed confabulator. Second, he doesn't appear to have ever mentioned marriage, either at the lake or during the presentation of a gift on the following Christmas. Third, she had recently spotted him prowling furtively behind her through the streets of Vienna—hardly the conventional behavior of a suitor. Fourth, a governess in the Zellenka household had revealed to Ida, just prior to the lakeside proposition, that Hans had persistently wooed her, won her submission, and then spurned her, a series of events that would soon cause the deceived woman to be unemployed. Fifth, and most insultingly, Hans had recycled with Ida the very same seduction line he had worked on the governess. And sixth, immediately thereafter his conduct had resembled that of a potential rapist, not a would-be fiancé.

The prospective marriage of Ida and Hans was Freud's impractical idea of how to comply with Filipp Bauer's main charge to him—to get Ida to stop complaining about his relationship with Peppina. Among other flaws in the scheme, it would have left the deserted Peppina alone to raise two small children by herself—unless, of course, Filipp were to marry Peppina, thus stranding Käthe. Peppina and Käthe, however, weren't paying Freud's bills; Filipp was. And Freud showed, in his pattern of behavior throughout the psychoanalysis, that he was serving as Filipp's agent.

Even before the treatment began, Freud had resolved to yield nothing to Ida:

> I felt quite convinced that she would recover at once if only her father were to tell her that he had sacrificed [Peppina] for the sake of her [Ida's] health. But, I added, I hoped he would not let himself be persuaded to do this, for then she would have learned what a powerful weapon she had in her hands, and she would certainly not fail on every future occasion to make use once more of her liability to ill-health.[21]

Thus we see that Freud, in encouraging the adulterous Filipp to retain his mistress, recommended a course of action opposite to the one that, in his professional judgment, could immediately clear up Ida's "hysteria." Under no circumstances could an obstreperous young female be allowed to wield "a powerful weapon" against a male. This explains why Freud never revealed to Ida that he agreed with her contentions that her father and Peppina were lovers and that the lakeside incident had actually occurred. On the contrary, he tried to convince her that her insistence on those points was a sign of illness. And her reproaches against others, he kept telling her, were merely projections of criticisms whose real target was her jealous, insubordinate, smutty-minded, and secretly guilty self.

The only ethical party in the whole affair, including Freud, was Ida herself. She alone upheld the nominal morality of her class by resisting indecent overtures and by attempting to persuade others to honor their vows. She had even insisted that her own governess be fired when she perceived that the woman was making a play for Filipp. Freud, however—now himself the lover of his children's governess—mentally assimilated Ida to the licentious servant order, assigning her the fictive name ("Dora") that his sister Rosa had bestowed on a nursemaid,[22] and sneering, as Ida was abandoning him, that she had given two weeks' notice, "the time characteristic for a person in service."[23]

3. THE EXISTING PICKLOCKS

As we will see, Freud was infuriated when Ida suddenly pinched off both his income stream and his investigation of her mind. It had already become clear to him, however, that she wasn't going to join that handful of patients, notably Anna von Lieben, Emma Eckstein, and Oskar Fellner, who had been willing to wait almost indefinitely to reap some benefit from his method. Nevertheless, he was far from believing that his eleven weeks of prodding and provoking had gone for naught. He felt that, by having *prevented* Ida from receiving the trust and validation that she expected, and then by relating two of her dreams to her symptomatology, he had exposed her repressions to the light. Freud told his readers that Ida might have continued in therapy if he had shown "a warm personal interest" in her. But that "would have been tantamount to providing her with a substitute for the affection she longed for"[24]—an error of technique that he would admonish all analysts to avoid.

In contemplating Ida's "hysteria," Freud faced a precious opportunity to clarify his approach to the psychoneuroses—reconsidering the genuineness of hysteria as an illness, weighing the relative merits of several etiologies, and disembarrassing himself of burdensome contradictions. There were just two obstacles to such pruning. First, Freud had never shown a capacity for testing psychological hypotheses; and second, he didn't want to do so. Heaping explanations atop one another was his idea of showing mastery of a case. As he told Fliess in just the second week of treatment, Ida's hysteria had "smoothly opened to the existing collection of picklocks."[25] And, as I have mentioned, so reluctant was the first psychoanalyst to be caught revising his premises that he would begin his narrative with a raw falsehood: Ida's case was going to "substantiate" his already abandoned etiological views of 1895 and 1896.[26]

Like anyone else in her era and part of the world, Ida Bauer had experienced a number of illnesses that bore lingering aftereffects. No doubt she had also "somaticized" tension and anger resulting both from Filipp's affair and from Hans's stalking and slandering her; and it is plausible to think that she had employed some symptoms, such as headaches and "fainting fits," as bargaining chips in trying to influence her parents. Freud acknowledged the element of hypochondria when he surmised that an end to Filipp's affair would have caused Ida to "recover at once." But real hysteria, he believed, was more deeply seated, and he still expected that its key determinants would be found in early childhood.

Ida's episodes of coughing, sometimes lasting for weeks, were of especial interest to Freud.* Unfortunately, he supplied us with two times of origin for this trait. On one page he asserted that Ida began coughing at age twelve; on another it was at age eight.[27] But he concentrated his explanatory hypotheses on the later period, when Ida was already being approached by Hans Zellenka. Her cough, Freud observed, was sometimes accompanied by aphonia, or loss of voice. Without asking whether the two effects may have belonged to a single physical condition, he forged a symbolic bridge between the aphonia and Ida's alleged love for her pursuer.

When Hans was in town, Freud hypothesized, Ida wanted to speak only to him, and when he was away she couldn't speak at all. All it took for Freud to secure this thesis was an alleged symmetry of events: Ida's "attacks" had lasted some three to six weeks, and so, it was claimed, had Hans's travels. But even this dubious correlation had failed to hold in more recent years. Did Freud, then, reassess or modify his claim? "Later on," he wrote, "it no doubt became necessary to obscure the coincidence between her attacks of illness and the absence of the man she secretly loved, lest its regularity betray her secret."[28] Hysteria, it seems, had played a clever trick by getting Ida to lose her voice at misleading times.

But the cough per se, as opposed to the aphonia, required a separate attribution of cause. Ida, Freud believed, complained too much about her father's bad behavior. This could mean, by Freud's logic, that she was actually in love with him, and not in a conventional daughterly way. The possibility hardened into a certainty: Ida had incestuous designs

---

* It may be of organic significance that Ida was the daughter of *two* tubercular parents (Deutsch 1990, p. 38). Filipp, by the way, still showed symptoms of tuberculosis at his death in 1913 (Decker 1991, p. 159).

on her father. Moreover, Freud's clinical experience had supposedly "confirmed over and over" that each hysterical symptom depicts a sexual fantasy.[29] Now, where does a cough occur? Why, in "the throat and the oral cavity," of course.[30] Therefore, Ida must have been coughing because she wished to suck her father's penis. That is what a triumphant Freud told his virginal patient.

Though he didn't like to brag, Freud couldn't resist informing his readers that one of Ida's coughing spells (among many more to come) had ceased "a very short time after she had tacitly accepted this explanation."[31] In fact, she had flatly rejected it. Her later "acceptance" was "tacit," we can gather, because she didn't care to dwell on her therapist's sick idea.

Freud had still another reason for favoring his interpretation of Ida's cough. He thought he had teased from her an admission that her father was impotent, thus entailing the inference that the Filipp/Peppina relationship must have involved unorthodox sex acts. But was Filipp really impotent? Freud's first inference to that effect rested on a frivolous game with words. Ida had characterized her father as *ein vermögender Mann*, a man of means—a phrase that Freud, for no good reason, reversed to *ein unvermögender Mann*, an impotent man.[32] Whether Ida had really "confirmed this interpretation" must remain conjectural.[33]

According to Freud, Filipp couldn't penetrate Peppina, and so the lovers must have resorted to oral sex performed by her upon him. Just how that scenario relates to Filipp's alleged impotence is unclear, as is Peppina's motive for always giving but—so far as we are told—never receiving satisfaction. Nonetheless, it was Freud's opinion that Ida longed to take Peppina's role with Filipp—and, further, that her coughing also signified a wish to perform the same service for Hans.

But if Ida, in Freud's opinion, wanted to fellate both her father and Hans, which desire was the stronger of the two? Freud was never at a loss to resolve such questions by rendering the matter more complicated than it already was. Ida, he determined, had redoubled her incestuous fantasy merely as a defensive maneuver, thus sparing herself from surrender to her true inamorato, Hans. Later in Freud's career, this priority would be reversed: the Oedipus complex would be held to serve as the driving force behind all subsequent object choice. But in 1901, and again in 1905 when "Dora" was finally published, he still regarded incest wishes that persisted after puberty as requiring a special motive.

Freud had some further notions to propose. Having deemed Filipp unfit for any kind of sex but fellatio, he would nevertheless tell Ida that she desired to offer her entire "jewel case" to him; and before long, even her cough was said to "represent sexual intercourse with her father."[34] Nor was that all; Freud regarded Ida as a lesbian, too. One of his regrets about the truncation of the case was that he had "failed to discover in time," and thus inform the patient, that the strongest current of her eroticism was her "deep-rooted homosexual love" of Peppina.[35]

In 1901, Freud was no longer clinging to his molestation theory; but neither had he arrived at the dogma that hysterics have oedipally fantasized experiences of parental rape. What he wanted now was an explanation of hysteria that would still be trauma based but would allow for more varied shocks than sexual abuse alone. One such shock, he now believed, was *the primal scene*, a child's witnessing or overhearing parental intercourse and being terrified by the experience. It was likely that he himself had undergone such an initiation in his family's one-room flat in Freiberg—so why shouldn't just about every hysteric have been subjected to the same fright? The primal scene would become a routine feature of Freud's theory, highlighted in such cases as those of the Rat Man and the Wolf Man. And here in 1901, it was making its psychoanalytic debut as the *fons et origo* of Ida's hysteria.

Since the age of eight, Ida had suffered from dyspnea, or shortness of breath. She would remain asthmatic for the rest of her life, a fact that could weigh against a psychosomatic etiology.[36] For Freud, however, the case was transparent. Ida's wheezing, like Katharina's (if it really occurred), reminded *him* of coital heavy breathing, and therefore she must have heard her father, never fully recovered from tuberculosis but not yet impotent, huffing and puffing in the conjugal bed.

With the "fact" of Ida's primal scene established, Freud had no trouble intuiting the rest of the story:

> The sympathetic excitement which may be supposed to have occurred
> in [Ida] on such an occasion may very easily have made the child's

sexuality veer round and have replaced her inclination to masturbation by an inclination to anxiety. A little while later, when her father was away and the child, devotedly in love with him, was wishing him back, she must have reproduced in the form of an attack of asthma the impression she had received. She had preserved in her memory the event which had occasioned the first onset of the symptom, and we can conjecture from it the nature of the train of thought, charged with anxiety, which had accompanied the attack. The first attack had come on after she had over-exerted herself on an expedition in the mountains, so that she had probably been really a little out of breath. To this was added the thought that her father was forbidden to climb mountains and was not allowed to over-exert himself, because he suffered from shortness of breath; then came the recollection of how much he had exerted himself with her mother that night, and the question whether it might not have done him harm; next came concern whether *she* might not have over-exerted herself in masturbating—an act which, like the other, led to a sexual orgasm accompanied by slight dyspnoea—and finally came a return of the dyspnoea in an intensified form as a symptom.[37]

Note how Freud's reconstructions presumed to capture the exact sequence of Ida's unconscious thoughts at age eight, yet without the benefit of any data besides her asthma.

Among the gratuitous assumptions in Freud's account, one ranked as the causal linchpin not just of Ida's case but of every other hysteric's, too: childhood masturbation. Ida had been a thumb sucker and a bed wetter—both signs of masturbation in Freud's judgment—and additionally, she suffered from abnormal vaginal discharges, or leukorrhea, which he regarded as not just a result but an actual "admission" (*Eingeständnis*) of having masturbated.[38] And now he could assert that all of Ida's accusations against her four seniors were merely deflected self-reproaches for having played with herself—an idea that one modern Freudian, joining many predecessors, has hailed as "a powerful interpretive paradigm."[39]

In order for hysteria to be contracted, Freud's theory now held, masturbation must give way to repression. But he also wanted to convict Ida of *ongoing* involvement in the disgraceful practice. That was the alleged meaning, during one analytic session, of her nervously inserting a finger into her miniature purse, which "was nothing but a representation of the genitals."[40] And masturbation, again, explained her stomach pains—the very same pains that he elsewhere ascribed to her emulation of a malingering cousin.[41] As Freud, commenting on Ida's upset stomach, memorably informed his readers,

> It is well known that gastric pains occur especially often in those who masturbate. According to a personal communication made to me by Wilhelm Fliess, it is precisely gastralgias of this character which can be interrupted by the application of cocaine to the "gastric spot" discovered by him in the nose, and which can be cured by the cauterization of the same spot.[42]

Thus Ida was both an ex-masturbator and a current one—a conundrum, but one whose very incoherence attested to the strength both of Freud's masturbation hobbyhorse and of his antagonism to his patient.

4. THE CLINCHING PROOF

Freud's dream theory, as we saw, asserted that every dream is animated by a repressed sexual wish that has persisted since childhood. In neither of his two dream books, however—*The Interpretation of Dreams* and its compact sequel, *On Dreams*—had he been able to exemplify that point. In fact, he would never succeed in doing so. But what most excited him about his "Dora" case was the testing ground it provided for another bold hypothesis: the dreams of a hysteric can lead their interpreter back to the infantile factors that had brought the illness into existence. This was the very tenet that had underwritten Freud's own abortive self-analysis.

Ida presented Freud with two dream reports, each of which poignantly expressed a dilemma she had felt at a time of betrayal.[43] In the first instance, she was said (however implausibly) to have had the following dream many times, beginning with each of the three nights preceding her escape from Hans Zellenka:

A house was on fire. My father was standing beside my bed and woke
me up. I dressed quickly. Mother wanted to stop and save her jewel-
case; but Father said: "I refuse to let myself and my two children be
burnt for the sake of your jewel-case." We hurried downstairs, and as
soon as I was outside I woke up.[44]

Whatever else this dream may have meant, it clearly shows Ida's
sense of emergency, her concern for threatened family harmony, and
her wish for rescue by her father. Under Freud's questioning, she recalled some relevant associations to the jewel case, to her having
dressed quickly, and to the danger of fire in both the Zellenka house
and her own home. Anomalously, however, Freud showed more interest in very recently expressed thoughts of Ida's, which he then asserted,
nonsensically, to have "appeared in the dream" when it originally
occurred.*

The associations that mattered the most to Freud, however, were
not Ida's but his own. The room, a *Zimmer*, reminded him of *Frauenzimmer*, a demeaning term for *woman* that we have encountered before.
"The question whether a woman is 'open' or 'shut,'" he observed
apropos of nothing, "cannot be a matter of indifference. It is well known,
too, what sort of 'key' effects the opening."[45] And to Freud, as we have
seen, the jewel case meant Ida's genitals.

Without explaining why, moreover, Freud reversed the dream's
manifest emphasis, ruling that it concerned Ida's wish to grant sexual
access to both Hans and her father. Through still more obscure maneuvers, he purported to show that the dream concerned, at its deepest
level, childhood bed-wetting, the Freudian opposite of fire. And because
Freud held masturbation to be the cause of bed-wetting, he regarded
Ida as once again obliquely confessing that she had been a masturbator.

Here, then, Freud was performing an operation to which he now
attached revolutionary significance: deducing psychopathology from a

---

* In a 1924 edition, nineteen years after the first publication of his paper, Freud rectified
his blunder; but he did so not by admitting the error but by silently altering the text of
his original dialogue with the patient (see SE, 7:66 and n).

dream. But the flaw in his procedure is apparent. In order to arrive at a phenomenon such as bed-wetting, he had to apply several of his unsupported transformational rules to the manifest dream content; and the choice of which rules to invoke was governed by predetermined conclusions. As always, then, Freud "learned" only what he already believed.

In a subsequent association, Ida mentioned that she had smelled smoke on each awakening at the lake. Since she had quite recently experienced the dream again—though apparently without smelling smoke afterward—Freud associated the smoke with his own cigar-consuming self, and reasoned, "she would like to have a kiss from me."[46] That deduction tells us nothing about Ida but a good deal about her fantasizing therapist.

Ida's second dream occurred just before she broke off the treatment, and Freud employed it to sum up the case. It depicted her father as having died, leaving the affectless dreamer to search for the funeral in an unknown town. Refusing the assistance offered by a stranger in a dense wood, Ida's dream self was unable to reach a railroad station that she saw before her. But then she found herself back at home, only to be told that her mother and others were already at the cemetery.[47]

Ida experienced this dream after she had resolved to stop seeing Freud and thus to cease cooperating with her father's wishes. The dream appeared to represent her inability to square accounts with Filipp, her anxiety about proceeding on her own, and, nevertheless, her determination to do so without further guidance. For Freud, however, seething with annoyance over his patient's imminent departure, the "cruel and sadistic" dream was dominated by her "*craving for revenge*," a theme he had also foisted upon her at various earlier junctures in his analysis.[48] And by soliciting her associations and then freely digressing from them, he once again arrived at conclusions that lacked pertinence to the manifest dream—namely, the "facts" of her simulated appendicitis, her phantom pregnancy, and her "false step."

This time, moreover, Freud surpassed even himself in prurient symbol mongering. He had relentlessly quizzed the eighteen-year-old Ida not only about Hans Zellenka's "erect member" (which, she vainly objected, she *hadn't* felt pressed against her during the kiss) but also about the source of her knowledge regarding sexual matters, as if such curiosity were a damning trait.[49] Now he perceived several dream images, including the "thick wood," as pubic references. His interpretation was "confirmed" by the following reflections:

> She had seen precisely the same thick wood the day before, in a picture at the Secessionist exhibition. In the background of the picture there were *nymphs*.
>
> ... The use of *Bahnhof* ["station"; literally, "railway court"] and *Friedhof* ["cemetery"; literally, "peace-court"] to represent the female genitals was striking enough in itself, but it also served to direct my awakened curiosity to the similarly formed "*Vorhof*" ["vestibulum": literally, "fore-court"]—an anatomical term for a particular region of the female genitals. ... Now, with the addition of "nymphs" visible in the background of a "thick wood," no further doubts could be entertained. Here was a symbolic geography of sex! "Nymphae," as is known to physicians though not to laymen ..., is the name given to the labia minora, which lie in the background of the "thick wood" of the pubic hair. But anyone who employed such technical names as "vestibulum" and "nymphae" must have derived her knowledge from ... anatomical textbooks or from an encyclopaedia.[50]

Here Freud was displaying his lifelong obsession with the "castrated" female crotch, and he was showing that his method of dream interpretation, far from constituting a means of deep access to his patients' minds, was suited to erasing the boundary between those minds and his own. It was Freud alone who could look at nymphs in a painting and see genital lips. And he had failed to notice the obvious fact that *Vorhof* and *Nymphae* were his own terms, not Ida's. Here was a level of confusion that disqualified its subject as an observer, much less an interpreter, of his patients' traits.

So far as Freud was concerned, however, all of the puzzle pieces in his "Dora" case were now ready for assembly:

- Ida Bauer had been predisposed to hysteria by her father's syphilis.
- Having sucked her thumb until the age of four or five, she had developed permanent oral yearnings.
- Although she was primarily a hysteric, a paranoid tendency manifested itself in nasty accusations against others (accusations that just happened to be true).
- But she also masturbated to fantasies deriving from the primal scene—thus causing her to become asthmatic—and now her oral fixation made her crave to fellate her father.
- At age eight, she suddenly stopped masturbating, acquired a conscious sexual disgust, and began coughing, a stand-in for sucking a penis.
- Another symptom, a vaginal discharge, expressed a confession: "I used to be a masturbator."
- At twelve, Ida made the acquaintance of the handsome Hans Zellenka and transferred much of her erotic fantasy life to him; but she protected herself from committing actual sex acts through the novel expedient of intensifying her unconscious fantasies of oral incest.
- Still, she manifested her love of Hans by falling mute whenever he was out of town. To cover its tracks, however, her hysteria arranged to render her mute when he was at home, too.
- When, before she had reached puberty and again two years later, the amiable Hans offered himself to her, she was abnormally inhibited by the disgust that had arisen when she first forswore masturbation.
- Her only recourse, then, was to turn homosexual, and she did so—but without noticing the fact.

If Ida had been induced to believe these propositions, or indeed any one of them, she might truly have lost her mind. Freud, in contrast, considered himself to have exercised the strictest empiricism. "I take no pride in having avoided speculation," he wrote of the concepts underlying his analysis; "the material for my hypotheses was collected by the most extensive and laborious series of observations."[51]

5. NO HARD FEELINGS

Freud would see Ida one more time, fifteen months after the abrupt termination. She paid a call on him, partly to update him on her story but also to consult him about a painful facial neuralgia. (He was, after all, technically a neurologist.) Now she was feeling better on the whole, and in Freud's postscript to the case history he didn't fail to take credit for the improvement. "I am not inclined to put too low a value," he wrote, "on the therapeutic results even of such a fragmentary treatment as [Ida's]."[52]

Over those fifteen months and in the four years before his paper saw publication, Freud had had time to ponder Ida's recalcitrance as a patient. In a discussion that has been universally admired by psychoanalysts, he faulted himself for not having taken sufficient account of the *transference*—that is, of the fact that Ida had seen him as a "new edition" of her father and had therefore punished him, Freud, for grievances whose real object had been Filipp. Thus Freud, instead of reviewing his many debatable interpretations, continued to rate his understanding of the case as impeccable. Surely Ida's protests against those interpretations would have ceased—wouldn't they?—if he had explained to her that she was emotionally incapable of passing objective judgment on his claims.

Ida's most interesting news concerned the Zellenkas. She had heard that one of their two children—we now know that the girl's name was Clara—had succumbed to a lingering illness. Ida had loved her, and she felt compassion for the parents:

> She took the opportunity of their loss to pay them a visit of condolence, and they received her as though nothing had happened in the last three years. She made it up with them, she took her revenge on them, and she brought her own business to a satisfactory conclusion. To the wife she said: "I know you have an affair with my father"; and the other did not deny it. From the husband she drew an admission of the scene by the lake which he had disputed, and brought the news of her vindication home to her father. Since then she had not resumed her relations with the family.[53]

She took her revenge on them. That was Freud's construal of the nineteen-year-old Ida's achievement in clearing the air with those who had wronged her, and presumably in forgiving them as well. Ida had recognized, as the ever spiteful Freud could not, that the death of a child reduces every other concern to triviality. If she had really been hysterical, this brave and magnanimous conduct could have served as the proof of her recovery.

Freud's behavior during his own reunion with Ida attests that there had been no comparable mellowing on his side. He had received her termination of the analysis as an act of sheer malice against himself, and now "one glance at her face . . . was enough to tell me that she was not in earnest" about getting relief from her neuralgia.[54] Noting that she had made her request on April Fool's Day, he refused to treat her. Instead, he reverted to his habit of playing calendar games with symptoms.

Ida, Freud ascertained, had been in pain for exactly a fortnight. "I could not help smiling," he told his readers, for just a fortnight earlier the news of his finally approved academic promotion had been announced. "Her alleged facial neuralgia was thus a self-punishment— remorse at having once given [Hans Zellenka] a box on the ear, and at having transferred her feelings of revenge on to me."[55] Freud evidently believed that Ida, perceiving that the doctor whom she had treated so rudely now bore the exalted title of professor, realized how badly she had behaved and, as penance, inflicted neuralgia on herself. But then Freud made his own try at turning the other cheek. "I do not know what kind of help she wanted from me," he declared, "but I promised to forgive her for having deprived me of the satisfaction of affording her a far more radical cure for her troubles."[56] If Freud had effected that radical cure, it would have been the only one in his career.

With Freud's posthumous blessing, Ernest Jones called Ida "a disagreeable creature who consistently put revenge before love."[57] But it was Freud, not Ida, who had payback in mind. It chiefly took the form of his trying to rush her case history into print just weeks after the treatment ended, while she was still an eighteen-year-old resident of Vienna who bore both the history and the overt symptoms described in his report. Over the objections of both Fliess and Oscar Rie, he had submitted the document twice for publication in 1901, receiving a complaint from one scandalized editor and an outright rejection from the other.[58] When his study finally saw print in 1905, Ida, now married with a son, was still in the city. (She would remain there until fleeing from the Nazis to France and America in 1939.) Freud, it appears, would not have been altogether displeased if she had become publicly identified as the orally fixated masturbating hysterical homosexual "Dora."

In 1923 (not 1922, as he recalled), Freud's disciple Felix Deutsch realized that he had "Dora" herself briefly in his care for Ménière's disease; and in 1957, after her death in 1945, he published a paper characterizing her anonymously to his colleagues. Ida had been very unhappy in 1923. She was laboring under more physical problems than ever; her husband was unfaithful; and, incomprehensibly to Deutsch, "she denounced men in general as selfish, demanding, and ungiving."[59] Almost as if to illustrate Ida's point, Deutsch joined the psychoanalytic chorus of condescension. He quoted an anonymous informant as having told him later that she was "one of the most repulsive hysterics" he had ever encountered.[60] At least, according to Deutsch, she had felt honored to have been Freud's famous patient. But in a letter to his wife, Deutsch was honest: Ida had "nothing good to say about analysis."[61]

The case study of "Dora," we have seen, wasn't just the story of a therapeutic fiasco. It was also the product of a mind that conjoined illogic and bizarre ideas with misogyny, prurience, and cruelty. By including his account of the follow-up visit, with its stark contrast between Ida's generosity and his own petty vindictiveness, Freud completed what must surely be the most damning self-portrait in any case study.

Yet that same text would serve as the Freudian movement's most cherished document—a compelling tale, a model explication of hysteria, a testament to the master's methodological self-criticism, and a valuable lesson that transference must never be neglected. Along with the major histories to come, "Dora" would adorn the curriculum of every psychoanalytic institute. And for decades, everyone would assume

that the poor outcome of the case was entirely owing to the uncooperative patient and her deflection of a father conflict onto Freud.

It may appear as though the psychoanalytic community and its
well-wishers simply clothed the naked emperor because he was their
ruler. No, the metamorphosis was wrought by Freud with an ingenuity
and persistence unchecked by any regard for truth. He had braced the
Dora tale with self-serving fibs, placing the narrative in a fictitious
context of deductive triumph and healing with all patients except the
one at hand.

Freud assured the readers of "Dora" that he was building on the
solid foundation of his teamwork with Breuer. "In not a single [case],"
he asserted, "have I failed to discover the psychological determinants
which were postulated in the *Studies*."[62] But his departure from
Breuer, exclusively emphasizing the sexual factor, now explained
"the whole effectiveness of the [newer] treatment," which was "far
superior" to Breuer's mode; "there can be no doubt that it is the
only possible one."[63] And he even hinted at concurrence from other
psychoanalysts (who, except for the already retired Emma Eckstein,
didn't yet exist), for he generalized about "our patients" and "our
case histories."[64]

Lest anyone disbelieve that every symptom represents an unconscious theme, the imaginary Freudian team had verified the point "in
every other case and in every other instance."[65] With neurotics less
stubborn than Dora, Freud added, "improvement will be admitted by
the patient and his relatives and will approximate more or less closely
to a complete recovery."[66] And he emphasized that his innumerable
successes in "clearing up the symptoms" were owing to the truth of his
theory.[67]

Such tactics cushioned the impact of the Dora case's failure. But
the positive appeal of Freud's essay lay elsewhere, in its invitation to
the reader to share in forensic work that was both intellectually and
sexually thrilling. As we have seen, nothing at all was detected; but it
was the *role* of triumphant puzzle solver that would prove irresistible
to psychoanalytic readers. "He that has eyes to see and ears to hear,"
wrote Freud, once again channeling Sherlock Holmes, "may convince

himself that no mortal can keep a secret. If his lips are silent, he chatters with his finger-tips; betrayal oozes out of him at every pore."[68] The novelty of Freud's erotic "findings" about Dora added spice to his readers' fantasy of accompanying him as he sifted the lascivious contents of a teenage girl's mind—but really just his own—all the while offering assurance that a cold surgical decorum was being observed.

Unanimity about the brilliance of the Dora history—"this beautiful little monograph," Jones called it[69]—remained unbroken until the 1960s. Then Erik Erikson stirred some unrest by discreetly suggesting that Freud might have done better to notice that his patient had been an adolescent at the time of her ordeal.[70] Not until 1983, however, did a psychoanalyst, Rosemarie Sand, dare to point out that Freud had failed to support his hypotheses or even to distinguish between the patient's fantasies and his own.[71]

With the full emergence of modern feminism, however, the repulsive qualities of Freud's text became impossible even for some male analysts to ignore. As one of them wrote in 1996, the Dora case

> is one of the great psychotherapeutic disasters; one of the most remarkable exhibitions of a clinician's published rejection of his patient; spectacular, though tragic, evidence of sexual abuse of a young girl, and her own analyst's published exoneration of that abuse; an eminent case of forced associations, forced remembering, and perhaps several forced dreams. . . . The case, the published history, and the subsequent reception can be called an example of continued sexual abuse. Dora had been traumatized, and Freud retraumatized her. And for roughly half a century the psychoanalytic community remained either collusively silent about that abuse or, because of blind adoration, simply ignorant of it.*

---

* Mahony 1996, pp. 148–149. I question only the claim that Freud exacerbated Ida's suffering. Like many of his early patients, she seems to have enjoyed taunting him, and his zealotry and hostility may have helped her to realize that she could depend on no one but herself.

In a later and no less scathing discussion of the same case history, however, the same psychoanalyst paused long enough to call the perpetrator of this disgrace "one of the world's greatest geniuses."[72] Blind adoration, indeed. If the grotesqueries of "Dora," once fully exposed, can't dislodge that faith from the initiated, we must wonder whether anything can.

34

A Law unto Himself

1. UNTRANSFORMED

"In 1901 Freud, at the age of forty-five, had attained complete maturity, a consummation of development that few people really achieve."[1] So began the middle volume of Ernest Jones's authorized biography. To be sure, Jones conceded, "a few personal idiosyncrasies" remained in place, along with "some vexatious disturbances" of a probably psychosomatic kind. That wasn't surprising, according to Jones; we could hardly expect the discoverer of psychoanalysis to have shed all traces of his "Herculean struggles" against the surly trolls of the unconscious. But having "obtained the insight and knowledge that made possible the life's work for which his name has become famous," the Freud of 1901 was prepared to meet his future "storms, stresses and tribulations" with clear-headed equanimity and courage.[2]

Jones granted that until the twentieth century, Freud had shown a predilection for reliance on other thinkers:

A profound self-confidence had been masked by strange feelings of inferiority, even in the intellectual sphere, and he had tried to cope with these by projecting his innate sense of capacity and superiority on to a series of mentors on some of whom he then became curiously dependent for reassurance.[3]

Jones was engaging in double-talk here. What manner of "profound self-confidence" is compatible with "strange feelings of inferiority"? But the biographer was willing to recognize this much weakness because, in his hero's progress, all debts to others were now declared to be a thing of the past. From 1901 onward, Jones proclaimed, Freud would be refining knowledge that had emerged entirely from the workings of his solitary genius.

In actuality, the psychoanalytic Freud would compile an extraordinary record of borrowing ideas, with only the most glancing gestures of acknowledgment. "The theme of plagiarism," observed Paul Roazen, "can be found almost everywhere one turns in Freud's career."[4] The sociologist Robert K. Merton counted over 150 occasions of disputed priority in his psychological writings.[5] And more often than not, Freud was the one who falsely accused others of stealing from him.

In some cases he really forgot whose idea had come first—a quirk of memory that doesn't inspire confidence in his general ability to think straight about the mind.[6] One such episode, as we have seen, occurred in 1898, when Freud, having previously expressed gratitude to Fliess for the notion of universal innate bisexuality, alarmed the latter by claiming the idea as his own. This was confusion, not plagiarism, but Fliess now distrusted a man who was given to appropriating ideas, whether deliberately or not. And when Fliess then read, in the manuscript of *The Interpretation of Dreams*, that the author's "unconscious" harbored death wishes against him, he wanted nothing further to do with Freud.*

Once abandoned, Freud passed from conflicted forgetfulness to focused revenge. He did reluctantly admit, in the first (1905) edition of his *Three Essays on the Theory of Sexuality*, that he had "become acquainted through Wilhelm Fliess with the notion of bisexuality."[7] Such was his bitterness over having been jilted, however, that he buried Fliess among eight other authors whose contributions were supposedly of comparable value.[8] And by tactically omitting any reference to

---

* Fliess took Freud's murderous intent so seriously that at the ex-friends' final, August 1900, congress at the Tyrolean resort of Achensee, according to well-remembered family lore, he actually dreaded that Freud meant to shove him off a precipice (Swales 1989b).

Fliess's 1897 book on the same topic, he misleadingly implied that all of the eight competitors had preceded him. In his second edition (1910), moreover, he made so bold as to delete the words "through Wilhelm Fliess" from the sentence I have just quoted. Freud was inching his way toward the total erasure of Fliess that he would consummate in his *History of the Psycho-Analytic Movement* (1914) and his *Autobiographical Study* (1925).

Especially telling against the "maturity" claimed by Jones was another stab at Fliess in the second edition of the *Three Essays*. Pursuing a vendetta that had been ongoing for seven years, Freud added Otto Weininger's 1903 *Sex and Character* to the books that had supposedly preempted Fliess. Here was Freud's spitefulness in its most craven embodiment. Weininger's theory of bisexuality was simply Fliess's, leaked to him at Freud's instigation by Freud's pupil Hermann Swoboda, who *also* pirated Fliess in a 1904 book of his own. Not satisfied with using both Weininger and Swoboda as his proxies in a campaign to undermine Fliess, Freud maliciously implied in 1910 that it was Weininger who had influenced Fliess and not the other way around.[9]

When Fliess confronted Freud with the justified suspicion that Freud had used Swoboda to rob him of credit for his theory of bisexuality, Freud at first professed a perfect innocence. Then, however, he was trapped into confessing the truth. The affair was sordid, but it did inspire Jones to produce his unintentionally funniest sentence: "It was perhaps the only occasion in Freud's life when he was for a moment not completely straightforward."[10]

In the twentieth century, we can see, Freud extended his early record of intellectual parasitism but took greater pains than before to hide his sources; and he revived his old habit of launching sneak attacks on the figures who had meant the most to him. Only by adding hostile footnotes to the books he had volunteered to translate, we recall, had he dared to break from Bernheim and Charcot. Now he was ignobly plotting against Fliess while cannibalizing the portions of Fliess's theory that could lend psychoanalysis an appearance of grounding in biological science. Still later, as we have seen, he would smear both Breuer and Carl Koller, circulating a demeaning lie about the former and promoting the myth that Koller had robbed him of credit for being the real discoverer of cocaine anesthesia.

Such conduct is hardly suggestive of the serenity that is said to have resulted from Freud's self-analysis in the late 1890s. The principal trait he had then sought to understand was his unwelcome bisexual tendency, which had caused him to feel both love and ill will toward Fliess. Although the self-analysis had yielded no reliable knowledge, it had been an anguished effort at fathoming his neurosis. After 1900, however, Freud was largely through with introspection. "I no *longer* have any need for that full opening of my personality," he told Ferenczi in 1910, spurning an overture to a more confiding friendship.[11]

Indeed, Freud allowed that defensiveness to be translated directly into psychoanalytic theory. As Fliess withdrew from him, he sought to put all of the blame on his ex-friend's psychosexual makeup. Fliess, he told himself, had turned paranoid, and he had done so because of an inability to tolerate his own homosexual impulses. Paranoia, then, was a projection of repressed homosexuality. ("I don't love him; he hates me.") As Freud would write to Jung in 1908, Fliess "developed a lovely [*schöne*] paranoia after throwing off his affection for me. . . . I owe this idea [of repressed homosexuality as the cause of paranoia] to him, i.e., to his behaviour."[12]

It was Freud himself, we know, who wrestled with homosexual impulses and who, coincidentally, had displayed a marked paranoid tendency ever since the early 1880s.[13] Now, however, he convinced himself that he had been rendered normal by overcoming his attachment to Fliess. The "piece of homosexual investment" in his personality, he told Ferenczi, had been "withdrawn and utilized for the enlargement of my own ego. I have succeeded where the paranoiac fails."[14] But there are numerous indications that Freud had by no means overcome his old feelings for Fliess; he just remained out of touch with them until some reminder of the old intimacy sent him into a panic, or indeed into a faint.[15]

Freud's own paranoid strain was manifested not only in his obsession with enemies but also in his feeling of exemption from the psychoanalytic law that everyone is selfish and aggressive at heart. As he told James J. Putnam in 1915,

I believe that when it comes to a sense of justice and consideration for others, to the dislike of making others suffer or taking advantage of them, I can measure myself with the best people I have known. I have never done anything mean or malicious, nor have I felt any temptation to do so. . . . Why I—and incidentally my six adult children as well—have to be thoroughly decent human beings is quite incomprehensible to me.[16]

Freud had always regarded himself as an ethically superior man, but he had struggled against self-condemnation for tragic blunders and misdeeds. By 1915, as we see here, introspection had largely given way to delusion. Although he would remain suspicious and embittered, a perfect stonewalling would shield him from reproaches for the rest of his life.

2. GIANT AMONG PYGMIES

If Jones was determined to show us an altered personage, he would have done better to choose 1902, not 1901, as a boundary line. Freud learned nothing new in that year, but his long-delayed academic promotion marked a permanent change in his situation and attitude. Renominated for the professorship in 1901, he enlisted two socialite ex-patients, Elise Gomperz and the Baroness Marie von Ferstel, to intercede with the education minister and bribe him with the gift of a coveted painting.[17] Or, as Gay put it fastidiously, Freud "now found ways of forcing [his conscience] to moderate its strenuous claims on his rectitude."[18]

Historians disagree about the efficacy of that step; perhaps Freud was going to be promoted anyway in 1902.[19] What we know for sure is that his contempt for the system of privilege was reinforced by his apparent success in gaming it. Now he would make maximal use of his new title while feeling less allegiance than ever to the university that had bestowed it. So, too, any remaining scientific scruples that had been imparted by that university would be trumped forever by "the Professor's" sovereign word. And now he would be free to go all-out in the quest for more glorious prizes than a mere prefix to his name.

As "the Professor," Freud could recruit followers and, in their presence, trade the role of frustrated outsider for that of wise leader. The respect that he then commanded was gratifying, though never sufficient to banish his insecurity and render him more open-minded. Instead, the acquisition of a small but fanatical army would redouble his dogmatism, provide a field of exercise for his authoritarian leanings, and introduce a new anxiety that would be managed badly: a fear of betrayal and usurpation.

The Freud of 1902 wanted to found a movement not for free psychological inquiry but for promulgating his own theory and practice of psychoanalysis. To that end it was essential to enlist men who would feel inferior to him. Most of them were doctors, but none was a psychologist by training. An early follower, Max Graf (a musicologist and the father of "Little Hans"), remembered that Freud had asked him to gather writers and artists to attend the Wednesday evening meetings that would finally yield the Vienna Psychoanalytic Society.[20] As Fritz Wittels, an early member of Freud's circle who did have medical training, reminisced,

> It did not matter if the intelligences were mediocre. Indeed, [Freud] had little desire that these associates should be . . . critical and ambitious collaborators. The realm of psychoanalysis was his idea and his will. . . . What he wanted was to look into a kaleidoscope lined with mirrors that would multiply the images he introduced into it.[21]

Freud acquired a circle of obstreperous admirers—nearly all of them Viennese Jews, and all drawn to radical ideas—who met in his smoke-filled study for freewheeling discussion.* The original participants were Freudians only in a loose sense; at first Freud had to tolerate their deviations and their often savage tirades against one another. Privately, he regarded them as a sorry lot of crackpots—"the gang," he called them—who, so long as they made up his only constituency, offered little hope of spreading the psychosexual gospel.[22]

---

* No local gentile would join the Vienna Psychoanalytic Society until 1908 (Klein 1981, p. 93). The original members, though they quarreled about everything else, regarded themselves as a Jewish avant-garde.

What a contrast those mediocrities formed to the company Freud had once kept with the likes of Breuer, Exner, Fleischl, Paneth, Königstein, and Koller! Being treated as an equal by such talented scientists had been incomparably more flattering than playing the Professor to Paul Federn, Isidor Sadger, Max Kahane, Wilhelm Stekel, and Rudolf Reitler. The promising young anatomist who had studied under the great Brücke and Meynert had come a long way down.

The first Freudians regarded their leader as a quasi-divine figure. Coming across *The Interpretation of Dreams*, Hanns Sachs had "found the one thing worth while for me to live for; many years later I discovered that it was the only thing I could live by."[23] Graf wrote of the Wednesday society's early meetings, "There was an atmosphere of the foundation of a religion in that room. Freud himself was its new prophet. . . . Freud's pupils—all inspired and convinced—were his apostles."[24] Another member of the original band characterized it as "a sort of catacomb of romanticism, a small and daring group, persecuted now but bound to conquer the world."[25] And Stekel, who hailed the other early converts as "brothers of an order,"[26] recalled feeling himself to be "the apostle of Freud who was my Christ!"[27]

The actual deliberations of Freud's Wednesday Psychological Society were considerably more mundane than such raptures would suggest. Their intellectual level is well represented by the minutes of the March 6, 1907, meeting—a historic event, for the Swiss psychiatrists Carl Jung and Ludwig Binswanger were in attendance for the only time, and psychoanalysis was about to break out of Vienna.* It is remarkable, however, that the visitors weren't disheartened by what they heard.

In that session, the physician Alfred Adler presented the case of a Russian Jewish stutterer whose compulsive symptoms included submerging himself in the bathtub until he had counted to a certain number, either 3, 7, or 49. The patient himself associated those figures with his religion: "3 is the sacred number . . . ; 7 is the Jewish holy number; $7 \times 7 = 49$; this is the Jewish Jubilee year." But Adler, pursuing his pet

---

* Binswanger, the son of Robert Binswanger (p. 349 above), would become the founder of existential psychoanalysis.

theory of "organ inferiority," had obliged the patient to recall feeling that his penis compared unfavorably in size to those of his brother and father. In discussion, Otto Rank (who, like Adler, would later break with Freud) helpfully remarked that "the numbers 7 and 49—the small and the big Jubilee year—represent the small and the big penis." Freud, not to be outdone, chimed in with the observation that "3 may perhaps represent the Christian penis; 7 the small, and 49 the large Jewish penis. The smaller Jewish penis is represented in the compulsion by the larger number."[28]

Jung and Binswanger, having no knowledge of Freud's long flirtation with numerology, couldn't believe that such a display typified the man they were getting to know. During their stay in Vienna (one week for Jung, two for Binswanger), the twenty-six-year-old Binswanger had been especially smitten by a manner that was cordial and kindly yet also suggestive of deep, even mysterious, sagacity. "Freud impressed me most strongly," Binswanger recalled,

during the evenings when I saw him in his study or consulting room. . . . What enchanted me was not merely the time Freud devoted to me . . . after a day of hard work, in his quiet, dimly lit study which even then contained important works of ancient and Oriental art, but even more the indefatigable, detailed, and most instructive and stimulating manner in which he answered my eager questions. Freud sat behind his desk, smoking a cigar, his hand resting on the arm of his chair or on the desk; occasionally he would pick up an art object and gaze at it, then keenly yet benevolently scrutinize his visitor, never asserting his superiority and always citing case histories rather than going into theoretical explanations.[29]

Could this be the same short-tempered, contentious, and resentful Freud whom we encountered in the Dora case? Here, instead, was a personage self-fashioned to incarnate the penetration of his science. Ingratiating and seductive, he was making full use of stage props in his den of wisdom while projecting an air of infallibility. And his case examples must have sounded to Binswanger as if they emanated from a vast store of corroborative material. The bedazzled young man would hardly have been inclined to dispute points of theory with such an august presence.

Jung, too, found Freud "extremely intelligent, shrewd, and altogether remarkable." "And yet," he added, "my first impressions of him remained somewhat tangled; I could not make him out." What troubled Jung, apart from Minna Bernays's revelation of her concubinage, was Freud's bitter, morbid insistence on decomposing all cultural manifestations into their supposed roots in twisted sexuality. When Freud reiterated that demand, Jung related, "his tone became urgent, almost anxious, and all signs of his normally critical and skeptical manner vanished."[30]

Freud's character hadn't changed during the early years of the twentieth century. The novelty was his studied self-assurance—a pose that the observant Jung, unlike Binswanger, understood to be a form of advertisement. The product to be sold was psychoanalysis, and the prospective buyer was Jung himself, who, by importing the doctrine back to the Zurich of August Forel and Eugen Bleuler, might do Freud the vital service of effacing its ethnic and geographic provincialism. To the outrage of Freud's neurotic-and-proud-of-it Viennese circle, he intended to transfer his headquarters to a Protestant stronghold and to maneuver Jung into position as his successor.*

Jung had already been attracted to *The Interpretation of Dreams*, and now he decided, not without misgivings, to risk tying his fortunes to Freudian psychology. But he couldn't be won over by Freud's attempts to school him in doctrinaire materialism. "I had a strong intuition that for him sexuality was a sort of *numinosum*," or spiritual entity, Jung reminisced in his old age. And he was reminded of a later conversation in Vienna:

> I can still vividly recall how Freud said to me, "My dear Jung, promise me never to abandon the sexual theory. That is the most essential thing of all. You see, we must make a dogma of it, an unshakable bulwark."

---

* In the April 6, 1910, meeting of the society, Wittels spoke against the proposed move: "Each of us has a neurosis, which is necessary for entry into Freud's teachings; whether the Swiss have, is questionable" (Nunberg and Federn 1962–75, 2:468).

He said that to me with great emotion, in the tone of a father saying, "And promise me this one thing, my dear son: that you will go to church every Sunday." In some astonishment I asked him, "A bulwark—against what?" To which he replied, "Against the black tide of mud"—and here he hesitated for a moment, and then added—"of occultism."[31]

Occultism? Freud had posed his admonition to the man who would become the twentieth century's foremost occultist. And what about Freud himself? In spite of his self-positioning as an Enlightenment thinker, his deepest affinity was with Romantic vitalism—the *Naturphilosophie* that his professors had scorned as prescientific.

Even so, he didn't dare tell Jung what the coming psychoanalytic revolution actually meant to him. We can only surmise that meaning ourselves. But clues are not lacking, and scholars who understand that psychoanalysis was always a dream of glory, never a science, have been able to piece them together plausibly.

3. A JOB FOR SUPERMAN

The Freud of the early twentieth century was seeking vindication for what he regarded as a decade of suffering (1892–1902), with negligible solace or support, while he had developed psychological insights of fundamental importance. Thus, when Jung and Binswanger first visited him in 1907, he dwelled repeatedly on his "scientific Calvary" (*wissenschaftlichen Leidensweg*), when the world was ungratefully spurning his message.[32] But there had been no consistent message to be spurned. The decade of "splendid isolation," as Freud later glamorized it, had for the most part been one of sporadic, premature stabs at theorizing followed by misgivings, backtracking, and renewed despair. And though he claimed to be able to cure psychoneuroses, he knew that he had never done so.

By 1902, however, Freud had come to regard himself as a fated personage; and it was this conviction of chosenness that rendered him charismatic in the eyes of his disciples. We can catch the flavor of his new self-conception in a passing remark that occurs in the Dora case history: "No one who, like me, conjures up the most evil of those half-tamed demons that inhabit the human breast, and seeks to wrestle with them, can expect to come through the struggle unscathed."[33] The demons were only paper cutouts of Freud's devising, but in his view he had seized insights that human beings hadn't been meant to acquire. With Freud as its Prometheus, the species might yet find equanimity by ceasing to fear its own forbidden impulses.

The twentieth-century Freud radiated a sense of world-historical mission. This was the man who, without having made a single corroborated discovery, would compare himself favorably to Copernicus and Darwin.[34] He really seems to have felt that he had visited the mental underworld, retrieved memories from an impossibly early age, perceived in a flash how those memories illuminated everyone else's mind as well as his own, and undergone a gnostic vision of how our species had formed its familial and social bonds.

It didn't matter, for his recruitment of followers in his lifetime or even posthumously, whether they regarded him as saintly or Satanic, an upholder of Western rationality or its most subversive foe. In 1930, for example, the German author Arnold Zweig told him, admiringly, that psychoanalysis had "reversed all values, . . . conquered Christianity, disclosed the true Antichrist, and liberated the spirit of resurgent life from the ascetic ideal."[35] The philosopher Richard Wollheim, without saying what benefits he had in mind, wrote in the 1980s that Freud did "as much for [humanity] as any other human being who has lived."[36] And more recently, Christopher Bollas—who has been called "perhaps the most prolific and widely read psychoanalytic author at work today"[37]—declared that the human race nurtured, for thousands of years, a "phylogenetic" yearning for a theory of the unconscious, a need supplied at last by "the Freudian Moment," which "changed man forever." Psychoanalysis, according to Bollas, "arrived at the moment when its implementation might rescue humanity from self-destruction."[38]

It wasn't Prometheus, however, but Oedipus who had become the key mythological figure for Freud. Since high school, where he translated a familiar passage from *Oedipus Rex* in his final examination, he had yearned to win Oedipus's instant fame and authority through some feat that would be comparable to the canny Theban's solving of the Sphinx's riddle. But his self-analysis in the later nineties, plunging him into turbulent thoughts about the damage he had undergone from sexualized care by his mother, followed by the damage he himself had inflicted on a sister, had brought forward the other half of the Oedipus myth: incest and its punishment.

Freud's anxiety and dread of failure, he had come to believe, stemmed from castration threats to which he had been subjected as a masturbating boy. The masturbation itself, with Amalie Freud as its evident object, had expressed an incest wish that persisted into adulthood, keeping alive his irrational fear of retribution and rendering him wary of intimacy with fully grown exemplars of the precastrated, emasculating female sex. And now, in the twentieth century, he was ready to extrapolate from his case to everyone else's: all of humanity was being deterred from incest only by a taboo that was redirecting the blocked libido into either sublimation or neurosis. As for his illicit acts with a sister, they too could be explained in part, and therefore excused, by the infantile sexuality that was already programmed into every child.

Freud's oedipal obsession never abated. When explaining his dream of "Irma's Injection" to Karl Abraham in 1908, for example, he recounted that he had named his three daughters after *three mothers*, Mathilde Breuer, Sophie Paneth, and Anna Hammerschlag Lichtheim, whom he then appointed the *godmothers* of those girls. His Irma dream, he disclosed, had expressed a fantasy of seducing all three mothers. And the very act of endowing his daughters with their names had evidently been a symbolic sexual appropriation. To Freud's mythy way of thinking, any mother was *the* mother—his own—and to "possess" the mother's name was to have sneaked past the incest barrier. As he told Abraham with unhealthy glee, the original Mathilde, Sophie, and Anna were "the three godmothers of my daughters, and I have them all!"[39]

In the fantasy of world conquest that now preoccupied Freud, only a uniquely courageous man, prepared to withstand abuse from every quarter, would be equipped to realize and state the momentous truth that everyone is incestuous at heart and that morality, which has kept us in chains through the millennia, is really just an internalization of the paternal castration threats that dissuade little boys from trying to copulate with their mothers. We can see this project taking shape as early as "Draft N," sent to Fliess on May 31, 1897:

Definition of "Holy"

"Holy" is something based on the fact that human beings, for the benefit of the larger community, have sacrificed a portion of their sexual liberty and their liberty to indulge in perversions. The horror of incest (something impious) is based on the fact that, as a result of communal sexual life (even in childhood), the members of a family remain together permanently and become incapable of joining with strangers. Thus incest is antisocial—civilization consists in this progressive renunciation. *Contrariwise, the Superman.*[40]

Here, generalizing anthropologically from his zero-sum conception of libidinal investment, Freud was saying that the mass of humanity is induced to exchange a portion of erotic freedom for maintenance of social cohesion. It all starts with blocked gratification of the primary desire for incest. Widespread incest would confine sex within the family and thus thwart civilization's most basic desideratum, healthy propagation of the species. Hence the ruling clerics' sermonizing for holiness, or virtue in renunciation of instinct. But not quite everyone, Freud told Fliess, is humbled by that propaganda. *Dagegen der Übermensch.* The Superman understands how and why the others are cowed; and, armed with that empowering knowledge, he lives by his own rules, or possibly by no rules at all. Incest, then, is his prerogative.

"I was the Superman," wrote Freud in *The Interpretation of Dreams* when analyzing what he believed to be the feeling of omnipotence behind his "Open-Air Closet" dream.[41] But the Superman was also, of course, Friedrich Nietzsche's superior individual, uninhibited in both intellect and sensuality by virtue of having spurned the fear-mongering priesthood that keeps the rest of humanity in line. On February 1, 1900, Freud would tell Fliess, "I have just acquired [the collected works of] Nietzsche, and I hope to find words for much that remains mute in me."[42]

Freud wouldn't need to open those volumes, however, in order to feel Nietzsche's sway.[43] One of his early friends, Joseph Paneth, was personally acquainted with the philosopher, who had been adulated among Freud's university classmates in the *Leseverein*. The revered text was then Nietzsche's first book, *The Birth of Tragedy* (1872), an exuberant tribute to the Dionysian Richard Wagner. Remarkably, Nietzsche had called Wagner *the modern Oedipus*. And for Nietzsche there was nothing coincidental about the conjunction of two roles, riddle solver and incestuous taboo breaker, within a single mythic figure. "Oedipus," Nietzsche had written, "murderer of his father, husband of his mother, Oedipus the solver of the Sphinx's riddle! . . . How else could nature be forced to reveal its secrets, other than by victorious resistance to her, i.e. by some unnatural event?"[44]

Christianity, for Nietzsche, was the institutionalized revenge of the weak upon the strong, who were now encouraged to cast it aside. That counsel was emboldening for Freud. It is hardly news, by now, that psychoanalytic theory constituted a thoroughgoing inversion of Christian principles, with sexual gratification triumphant over virtuous sacrifice for heaven, and with the clinical interview serving as a mock confessional in which absolution could be granted without any need for repentance. Only gradually has it been realized, however, that this remissive order, instead of having been deduced from efficacious treatments of neurotics, answered to Freud's craving to pull down the temple of Pauline law.

One of Freud's favorite lines from Virgil, we recall, was Dido's prophecy of the Semitic warrior Hannibal, "May someone rise up from our bones as an avenger!" Hannibal was the real-life figure whom Freud, both in boyhood and in the aftermath of his father's death, embraced as his primary role model. Freud, too, wanted to conquer Rome, a synecdoche for Christianity. As the new Hannibal, he meant to overthrow the whole Christian order, earning payback for all of the bigoted popes, the sadists of the Inquisition, the modern promulgators of "blood libel" slander, and the Catholic bureaucrats who had held his professorship hostage.

Oddly, however, between 1897 and 1901 he found himself reluctant to approach "the mother of cities" even as a visitor. This was his "Rome phobia," a mental block that he was willing to acknowledge but not to elucidate. "My longing for Rome," he confessed to Fliess in 1897, "is . . . deeply neurotic."[45] Ten weeks later, "the yearning for [Rome] becomes ever more tormenting."[46] And "Rome is still distant," he relayed in March 1899; "you do know my Roman dreams."[47] Yet on September 2, 1901, in the company of his brother Alexander, he did enter Rome without feeling anxious. That "fulfillment of a long-cherished wish," he told Fliess, was at once "overwhelming" and "slightly diminished," "as such fulfillments are if one has waited too long for them."[48]

The most that Freud would say on the matter in *The Interpretation of Dreams*, when discussing a whole series of his dreams about Rome, was that "the wish to go to Rome had become in my dream-life a cloak and symbol for a number of other passionate wishes."[49] Buried in a footnote to the second (1911) edition of the dream book, however, would be a reference that hinted at the foremost of those wishes. An oracle of the ancient Tarquin kings, Freud wrote, had "prophesied that the conquest of Rome would fall to that one of them who should first kiss his mother."* Had Freud "kissed his mother" and thus liberated himself from his phobia?

He had assuredly "kissed" Minna Bernays in August 1900—an experience whose aftermath included euphoria and a rush of creativity. The fulfillment of his long-imagined seduction appears to have served as a signal that it was time to put indecisiveness aside and become an activist in reaching his destiny. His immediate and rapid composition of the *aliquis* story, with its theme of vengeance against persecutors and its disregard for truth, bespeaks just such motivation.

As the sister of Freud's wife, Minna Bernays was regarded in Judaic law as an incestuous sex object. For the atheist Freud, that would have constituted one of her attractions. He also seems to have fantasized her as one of his own sisters. From the outset of their dealings in 1882, he

---

* SE, 5:398. Freud credited Otto Rank with that observation; but Rank, at the time, was being fed ideas by Freud, who gained an appearance of corroboration for his own notions by having his disciples state and illustrate them "independently." See Swales 1982a, p. 19.

always called her *sister* or *little sister* (*Schwesterchen*), never *sister-in-law*.

But that wasn't all. As various scholars have observed, Minna was also a maternal figure for Freud.[50] Before moving in with his family, she had served as a nursemaid in his natal Moravia, and now, as a resident of his apartment, she occupied a comparable role for his own children. Thus, for Freud, she had become a double of his Freiberg nurse, whom he repeatedly characterized as his "second mother"—a cardinal theme of his self-analysis. Freud was now living with two mothers, one of whom had become his mistress.[51]

It has also been pointed out that Minna wasn't just a mother but a virgin mother—in short, potentially a figure of the Catholics' Mary. And insofar as she represented Freud's nurse, Catholicism may have been entailed once again, for Sigmund's parents had told him that the fanatically devout woman had taken him to mass and filled his head with superstition about "God Almighty and hell."[52] To possess Minna, then, could have meant, first, to commit symbolic incest with the mother of God; second, to "kill" the father God by means of this ultimate sacrilege; and third, to nullify the authority both of Austria's established church and of its Vatican parent—thereby, in Freud's internal drama, freeing his people from two millennia of religious persecution.

4. INFINITE MIND

The most pronounced indication of Freud's retreat from empiricism would be his gradually emergent affinity for the paranormal.[53] To be sure, as Henri Ellenberger exhaustively proved, the whole psychodynamic tradition had arisen from claims of unnatural cognitive power; and parapsychology, or the study of such claims, had become a recognized, if marginal, field of inquiry with the founding of the Society for Psychical Research in 1882. We have seen that both the late Charcot and the early Janet were naïvely hospitable to paranormal assumptions. But psychology, as Janet soon realized, would be self-hobbled if it welcomed "realities" that appear to be physically impossible. Freud, however, became progressively more enamored of the occult.

Already in 1896, writing to Fliess, he had professed himself willing to believe in "the symbolic presentiment of unknown realities."[54] By 1910, led on by Ferenczi, who jestingly called himself "the Court Astrologist of Psychoanalysis," he had gone considerably farther in that direction.[55] In 1911 he became a corresponding member of the Society for Psychical Research, and he remained such until his death. By the 1920s he had consulted a soothsayer, attended at least one séance with his daughter Anna, frequently exchanged "thought reading" with her, and confessed to Jones that he believed in "clairvoyant visions of episodes at a distance" and even in "visitations from departed spirits."[56] In 1921 he wrote to the Anglo-American student of medium-ship Hereward Carrington, "If I had my life to live over again I should devote myself to psychical research rather than to psychoanalysis."* It was all that Jones and the equally worried Max Eitingon could do to dissuade him from announcing a public merger between his "science" and the paranormal.

Telepathy, or the communication of thoughts between two parties at a substantial distance, was the unlikely power that most attracted Freud. He wrote two revealing papers on the topic, "Psycho-Analysis and Telepathy" (1921) and "Dreams and Telepathy" (1922), and he drew upon those works for a lecture, "Dreams and Occultism," included in his *New Introductory Lectures on Psycho-Analysis* (1933).[57] Although colleagues managed to keep one of the essays from being published during Freud's lifetime, and although all three pieces contain token signs of skepticism, together they leave no doubt that the first psychoanalyst had become an outright mystic, subscribing to the capacity of ideas and images to fly across hundreds of miles and reconstitute themselves within a second mind.

After much weaseling in "Dreams and Telepathy," Freud blurted out his conviction that "sleep creates favourable conditions for telepathy"— a point that he repeated in "Dreams and Occultism."[58] For Freud, not even the inaccuracy of a dream prophecy disqualified it from being

---

* Quoted by J, 3:392. The society's founder, Frederic W. H. Myers, who decisively influenced Janet's youthful experiments in telepathy, was an early admirer of *Studies on Hysteria*, which he understood to be a treatise about coaxing hidden knowledge from the bottom of the mind (J, 1:250n).

deemed telepathic. His inclination was to believe that a given dream, bearing only an approximate resemblance to an event elsewhere, must have been *obliquely* prophetic. "We must admit," he wrote in one instance, "that it is only the *interpretation* of the dream that has shown us that it was a telepathic one: psycho-analysis has revealed a telepathic event which we should not otherwise have discovered."[59] A scientist wielding Occam's razor would have proceeded in the opposite spirit, judging, à la Hume, that a rough correspondence between dream and reality is far too weak to warrant belief in the miracle of telepathic transmission.

The miraculous, however, had become everyday reality for Freud, and not always to the benefit of his equanimity. He felt himself to be almost literally pursued by bad fortune, and he engaged in propitiatory acts to ward it off. Seized by existential fear, he was convinced that the fates had determined just when he was going to die. When the appointed year, at age fifty-one, left him still breathing, he didn't decide that he could now think about himself more objectively; he rejuggled the magic formula and arrived at a new terminus: sixty-one. Meanwhile, telephone numbers and the numbers of hotel rooms held frightening messages for him.[60]

In the most candid and pained of his biographical chapters, Jones came to grips with Freud's occultism and deplored it. Freud, Jones admitted, was prone to credulity. But then, didn't his genius consist precisely in an "exquisite oscillation" between that trait and skepticism?[61] It was a good thing, Jones ventured, that Freud had been initially susceptible to dubious, even ridiculous, ideas, for by that means he could break with conventional thinking and open himself to some vital notions that would prove their merit after all.

Unfortunately for that argument, Freud's minor hedging about the paranormal manifested no skepticism whatsoever, but only a hesitancy to reveal how stubbornly naïve he remained after having heard rational objections from Jones himself and others. Moreover—and this is more important—his occultism was no hobbyistic sideline. What he didn't say, but clearly believed, was that the psychoanalytic interview itself was a process of paranormal thought transference and had been such from the start.

The free-floating attention that he recommended for clinical practice was meant to attune the therapist's unconscious to that of the
patient, picking up signals that would have been jammed by either
party's exercise of conscious will. That sense of special rapport, which
survives within modern psychoanalysis,* explains why Freud was
unmoved whenever a patient denied that a posited childhood event
could have occurred. Freud *saw* the primal scene that the Wolf Man
declared to have been implausible, and he *heard* the parents' conversation over a patient's crib from thirty years before. Likewise, he knew
for a certainty what thoughts his patients were repressing. If those
thoughts had invaded his own mind, where else could they have originated but in the patient's unconscious?

The power that Freud granted himself wasn't limited to telepathy.
He fancied that through sheer intellection he could take recovered
memories and assign them determinative significance for a patient's
present neurosis. All he required for that feat was to perceive a thematic likeness between the supposed childhood event and an adult
symptom. No scientist, without even bothering to test one causal
hypothesis against others, could be so easily satisfied. Yet Freud, as we
have witnessed, thought he could trace an unbroken chain of causes,
through layer upon layer of the psychical cavern, without losing his
way or even encountering a difficult choice of paths to follow.

He also allowed himself to take verbal associations, whether the
patients' or his own, and transmute them directly into engines of symptomatology. Anna von Lieben, Ilona Weiss, Emma Eckstein, and Ida
Bauer, we saw, had all supposedly been rendered lame by the thought
of "missteps" or "a wrong footing." So, too, because *Jungfrau* means
"virgin," Freud believed that a view of the great mountain must have
aroused "Herr E." to masturbate over it at age fourteen.[62] And the same
patient's later womanizing was explained with similar logic. "He failed
to pass in botany," Freud told Fliess; "now he carries on with it as a
'deflorator.'"[63]

What we observe in such examples is a style of "investigation"

---

* The psychoanalyst Carlo Bonomi, e.g., writes of "the feelings of clairvoyance that we,
as psychoanalysts, value and praise so highly in our practice" (2015, p. 91).

whereby findings can be reached without a need to gather any facts. Freud's world, as Michel Onfray puts it, was "a theater in which hats are penises, locks are vaginas, boxes are uteruses, money is fecal matter, a loose tooth is a wish to masturbate, the loss of hair is castration."[64] The materializing of any such item, even in a dream, made it impossible for Freud not to see confirmation of his hunches wherever he looked. Pre-interpreted words and gestures provided his evidence for those same interpretations. As he stated without apology in "Dora," "I handle unconscious ideas, unconscious trains of thought, and unconscious impulses as though they were no less valid and unimpeachable psychological data than conscious ones."[65]

Most of the tendencies I have reviewed were in play by the early 1890s. What changed in the twentieth century, when Freud was emboldened by the acquisition of disciples, was both the adamancy and the range of his irrationalism. Thus he could no longer be swayed by reminders that he was out of step with basic scientific knowledge. When Joseph Wortis, for example, reminded him in 1934 that biologists then rejected the Lamarckism whereby memories can be passed down the generations through the germ plasm, Freud replied, "But we can't bother with the biologists. We have our own science."[66]

This was not just a matter of adherence to a minority position in a scientific controversy. (If it were, Freudians could point out that modern knowledge of gene expression has given a limited second life to the inheritance of acquired characteristics.) Freud wasn't saying that he favored some technical argument for Lamarck over Mendel; he was saying that psychoanalytic belief takes precedence over *any* contrary judgments. Indeed, the telepathic Freud was now indifferent even to the laws of physics. In short, he had become an outright antiscientist.

All knowledge now stood within Freud's reach. He knew, for example, that the Ur-father, at the dawn of humanity, had been murdered by his sons; that the control of fire had awaited renunciation of a "homosexual" urge to pee on it; and that weaving had been invented by the first woman to thread her pubic hairs in order to hide her "castration." Perhaps, Freud hazarded in his *New Introductory Lectures*, "the great insect communities" practice telepathy within their ranks.[67] He told Karl Abraham in 1917 that he and Ferenczi planned "to put Lamarck entirely on our ground and to show that his 'need,' which creates and transforms organs, is nothing but the power of *Ucs.* [unconscious] ideas over one's own body."* And no inquiry would be required before he asserted that instincts of "life" and "death" are coursing through all creatures, and that their fluctuating ratio explains the major patterns of human history. The truth had announced itself to his mind.†

5. CASE MANAGEMENT

Already by the turn of the century, Freud's expanding grandiosity was grossly out of scale with his therapeutic record. Yet he had to present himself not only as a healer but as a uniquely successful one, for it was the alleged superiority—not just the efficacy—of psychoanalytic therapy that underwrote his claim of having flushed the unconscious from its lair. Hence, when he told the broad public about his therapeutic regimen, he withheld no superlatives regarding its benefits. Psychoanalysis, he pronounced, was "the only possible method of treatment for certain illnesses," which he didn't bother to name.[68] His routine was producing "successes second to none of the finest in the field of internal medicine."[69] Its "undeniable therapeutic success . . . far exceeded any that had previously been achieved."[70]

Without good-looking cases, however, there could be no convincing histories to back up those general assertions. Freud lacked a single ex-patient who could attest to the capacity of the psychoanalytic method to yield the specific effects that he claimed for it. That is why he reverted so often to Breuer's "Anna O.," a case that, while no more efficacious than his own morphine-sodden treatment of Anna von Lieben, had been repackaged in *Studies on Hysteria* as a cure. As for his own extended cases, Freud had no choice but to write up some of them, disguising or excusing their poor results, endowing them with literary appeal, and portraying himself as having mastered every intellectual

---

* Freud/Abraham 2002, p. 361. Freud and Ferenczi partially carried out this wild project; see Freud 1987b.

† In 1953 Jung recalled that when he and Freud once disagreed, "He said to me: 'But it must be so!' I asked: 'Why then?' 'Because I have thought it!' " (quoted by Borch-Jacobsen and Shamdasani 2012, p. 162).

challenge they posed. In those tasks of marketing he was spectacularly effective. That is where his "genius" will be found—not in having understood anyone's mind but in having created an impression of success from stories that, regarded objectively, constitute evidence of his own obsession, coercion, and want of empathy.

In two instances, however, the stories themselves were entirely flattering to Freud. We have seen that for "Screen Memories" (1899) he manufactured the analysand, "Mr. Y.," who could then be represented as a fawning admirer of both the analyst and his theory. And in the following year the *aliquis* chapter of *The Psychopathology of Everyday Life* was constructed on the same duplicitous model.* In thus concocting fictions that showcased both his latest ideas and his fantasized infallibility as a sleuth, Freud could be sure that there would be no dissatisfied ex-patients or family members to challenge his representations. The only danger was that the whole sham might someday come to light.

But what if it did? Even then, attachment to Freud might prove emotionally stronger than disillusionment. This is just what happened when, in 1946, Siegfried Bernfeld circumspectly exposed "Screen Memories" as an "unknown autobiographical fragment"—that is, an imposture. Neither Bernfeld nor Jones professed to see an ethical issue in Freud's having foisted the essay's fantasmal Mr. Y. on physicians, potential patients, and recruits to his movement. As for James Strachey, he only regretted that "the intrinsic interest of this paper has been rather undeservedly overshadowed by an extraneous fact."[71] Yet Freud's claim that he had been able to "relieve [Mr. Y.] of a slight phobia by means of psycho-analysis" already constituted medical fraud, for he was publishing false evidence of the effectiveness of his regimen.[72]

Freud himself was well aware that he had cheated. When the hour arrived in 1906 for a first collection of his psychoanalytic papers, he chose to withhold "Screen Memories." Too many facts identifying him as Mr. Y. had become known since the date of composition. But with

---

* Albrecht Hirschmüller, who believes that scientific probity is important, has written that his whole intellectual world would crumble if he had to admit that Herr Aliquis was a fictitious character (Hirschmüller 2002b). What, then, does he think about the proven case of Mr. Y.?

Herr Aliquis, Freud was more brazen. Because the *aliquis* chapter constituted the most admired portion of his most popular book, he left it scarcely unaltered through all eleven editions, expressing gratitude in each to his "former travelling-companion" for having facilitated an excellent demonstration of memory blockage. "My purpose," he averred, "is . . . particularly well served when a person other than myself, not suffering from nervous illness, offers himself as the object of such an investigation."[73]

A man who has been found to practice such deceit in two instances will surely stretch the truth in other narratives.* It is not surprising, then, that Freud, unlike genuine researchers, went out of his way to destroy the notes for his case histories, along with other materials he had utilized in his published writings. But he failed to do so on one occasion. After his death, his notes for three and a half months of treating the "Rat Man" (Ernst Lanzer) in 1907 were found among his effects. They can now be read by anyone in the *Standard Edition*, and they convey a clear message regarding what Jones was pleased to call Freud's "flawless integrity."[74]

The psychoanalyst Patrick Mahony, preparing to devote a book to the Rat Man case, found to his regret that Freud had switched the chronological order of some events; lengthened the timeline, extending three and a half months into a full year of thoughtful effort; pretended to have deduced facts that had simply been told to him; and falsely claimed that, within the period corresponding to the notes, he had cured Lanzer of his rat obsession and restored him to psychological health.[75] In a word, Freud's published case history was largely feigned. Its difference from "Screen Memories" and *aliquis* was only a matter of degree.

From Freud's way of proceeding we can derive the most general principle of his reportage, whether or not a given patient had ever existed: *theory precedes and dictates evidence*. Or, as Albert Moll incisively put it in 1909, "The impression produced in my mind is that the theory of

---

* For further deception in the *Psychopathology of Everyday Life*, see Swales 2003, where it is shown that Freud's forgetting of the name *Signorelli* was explained on demonstrably specious grounds. I would go a step farther and propose that Freud, for whom the Italian artist was a powerfully meaningful figure, hadn't forgotten the name at all.

Freud . . . suffices to account for the clinical histories, not that the clinical histories suffice to prove the truth of the theory."[76] No more shaming condemnation of one scientist by another can be imagined.

Freud's stories of solved cases belong not to the genre of the clinical report but to that of detective fiction. As we have seen, their portrait of Freud himself as a master of ratiocination is no more legitimate than if Arthur Conan Doyle had claimed to possess the mental powers of Holmes. As Poe, the genre's founder, asked after an admirer had credited him with the acuity of his protagonist, Dupin, "Where is the ingenuity of unraveling a web which you yourself (the author) have woven for the express purpose of unraveling?"[77]

35

Imposing His Will

1. NEVER AN ENTHUSIAST

Freud was not the all-daring, all-risking hero or villain that he has sometimes been taken to be. Because his trademark therapy became a lucrative quasi-medical business, his fantasy of subversion would need to be obscured even from most of his fellow analysts. He was, after all, only a closet Antichrist, one whose grandiosity was veiled by a stance combining tragic resignation with solicitous "advice for living." In most people's eyes he wasn't Doctor Faust but only the solicitous Doctor Freud, who would help us all to become more normal. And meanwhile, his devilish rupture of the incest taboo was just a peculiarly callous adultery that he was afraid to confess to anyone.

Unlike, say, Havelock Ellis, Margaret Sanger, or the gay activist Magnus Hirschfeld, Freud doesn't match up well with the liberation he has been taken to represent. Fluid gender identity, for example, is just what he was desperate to overcome in his own case. Thanks to his troubled history, moreover, he couldn't imagine male psychosexual development without assigning a key role to gruesome castration threats. Additionally, the model whereby he reduced psychological effects to a play of libidinal flows and blockages expressed a determinism that was inherently fatalistic.

Even as a critic of mores, furthermore, Freud was reluctant to press

very hard. His liberal counsel was spurred not by concern for the mis-
education and torment of millions but by frustration within his marriage.
He gave only brief attention to the plight of girls and women, those
potential shrews to their long-suffering husbands. One ex-patient, Irma-
rita Putnam, told Paul Roazen that Freud "used to think that women
should have the same sexual freedom as men, but . . . he had changed
his mind subsequently."[1] As for homosexuals, we have noted that
Freud ascribed their "perversion" to eroticized maternal care; and he
concurred with his society's judgment that their sexual practices were
abominable.

At the end of the nineteenth century and the beginning of the
twentieth, one topic—masturbation—provided a litmus test of authenticity for claimants to sexual enlightenment. Albert Moll, Havelock
Ellis, and others, dissatisfied with old-wives' lore about the evils of
self-abuse, took the trouble to collect data showing that avid masturbators were no more likely than anyone else to fall mentally or physically ill.[2] As that awareness spread, the medical taboo on masturbation
gradually dissipated. Freud, however, never wavered in his allegiance
to backward dogma. Clearly, he felt that he himself had been permanently injured by overindulgence in "the primary addiction." And when
his son Oliver, as a troubled adolescent, approached him with the hope
of being reassured that his self-manipulation was developmentally
normal, he was brusquely rebuked. Oliver could never again feel close
to his father.[3]

Psychoanalysts were expected to march in step behind Freud's anti-
masturbatory banner. Between 1910 and 1912 the Vienna Psychoanalytic Society devoted no fewer than eleven sessions to discussing the
ravages of the vice, and though dissenting voices were raised, Freud
remained adamant. Not only was masturbation toxic to the body,
producing neurasthenia; it also violated propriety by virtue of its
fantasy-based hedonism, its undermining of potency in marriage, and
its sheer abnormality as a deviation from heterosexual coupling.[4] The
pope himself would have found nothing objectionable in that stand.

As we have seen, Freud regarded masturbation—either its continuing practice or its abrupt and traumatic abandonment—as the precipi-

tating agent of most neuroses. Through the first decade of the twentieth century, his relentless grilling of patients was chiefly focused on uncovering their histories in that regard. Albert Hirst recalled that when he entered treatment with Freud at age sixteen, the therapist immediately required him to sit "in the position in which I masturbated."[5] Other patients were enjoined not to masturbate for the duration of their care, lest a "current neurosis" be triggered.[6]

But in most cases willpower alone, Freud believed, was insufficient to keep the hand from straying downward. In two 1910 letters, one to Ludwig Binswanger and the other to the Swiss psychiatrist Alphonse Maeder, he recommended that a masturbation-addicted male patient be subjected to treatment with a "psychrophore"—a catheterlike device for inserting ice water into the urethra.[7] If Freud's name were to evoke the image of a psychrophore instead of a couch or a cigar, we would be spared much needless discourse about his sponsorship of erotic freedom.

Freud knew that his claims of healing power for psychoanalysis lacked any basis in fact. From time to time he even intimated, amid many claims to the contrary, that patients ought not to expect good results. Therapeutic success, he wrote in his "Little Hans" case history of 1909, "is not our primary aim. We endeavour rather to enable the patient to obtain a conscious grasp of his unconscious wishes."[8] In a 1912 letter to a fellow analyst he observed, "The therapeutic point of view . . . is certainly not the only one for which psychoanalysis claims interest, nor is it the most important."[9] Freud's pupil Abram Kardiner recalled his declaring, "I have no great interest in therapeutic problems. . . . I am much too occupied with theoretical problems all the time."[10] Finally in 1932, when he felt himself to be generally revered, he admitted to the world that he had "never been a therapeutic enthusiast."[11]

By then, little harm could be done to Freud's movement by a belated show of candor; if anything, he was garnering further points for modesty. Suggesting that psychoanalysis hadn't yet reached its full potential was one of his standard ploys. But it had been essential for him to conceal his therapeutic doubts from the laity until his greatness as a thinker was widely taken for granted. The alleged "successes second to none" didn't just drum up business for Freud and his fellow practitioners; they were proffered as validation of the postulates in his theory of mind.

Some of Freud's later patients did aver, vaguely, that they had benefited from their analyses.[12] Already by 1910, such was his shamanic aura that a stroll around the city of Leyden with Gustav Mahler was said to have permanently cured the composer of impotence.[13] But this was faith healing, not psychoanalysis. The gain in confidence that Mahler and some others experienced appears to have been related to their awe of Freud—a very great man, they believed in advance. He had blessed them, they felt, by forgiving the flaws they disclosed to him. A priest in a confessional could have brought comparable relief to burdened seekers.

More typical was the experience of "the female homosexual," Margarethe Csonka, the subject of one of the longer case histories (1920).[14] Csonka had been sent to Freud by her father for alteration of her sexual preference. Even Freud admitted that the treatment had failed. He boasted in his case study, however, that he had traced "the origin and development" of his patient's homosexuality "with complete certainty and almost without a gap."[15] Actually, Csonka had kept him busy analyzing fabricated dreams that were designed to satirize his preconceptions. Freud was just wary enough to suspect that *her dreams* were trying to deceive him, but not wary enough to perceive that Csonka herself was the trickster. After each session, having retired to a café, she would amuse her girlfriend with uproarious accounts of her therapist's fatuity.[16]

What Csonka had perceived in Freud was the same obtuseness and dogmatism that we have noted in his clinical efforts from the early 1890s onward. But something had changed—for the worse. The Oedipus complex, which had been an incidental and not-yet-named feature of the mental model Freud sketched in *The Interpretation of Dreams*, had loomed ever larger until it impressed him as the key to all psychological conflict—indeed, to the whole psychosexual development of *Homo sapiens*, beginning from the epoch of the primal horde. The effect of that conviction on Freud's therapeutic endeavors was to render them more peremptory and question begging than ever.

We can perceive this quality most starkly in a case whose "patient," the five-year-old "Little Hans" (Herbert Graf), wasn't seen by Freud even once before his problem was determined to be an oedipal one. The whole matter was settled through Freud's chats with Hans's father, Max, an early believer in psychoanalysis. Hans had developed a horse phobia after seeing a horse collapse, terrifyingly, in the street. That was too superficial a connection for Freud. He just knew, without needing to question Hans about his feelings, that the boy had transferred onto horses his fear of castration for wanting to stuff his "widdler" into his unsuspecting mother.[17]

The same instant wizardry was apparently at work in Mahler's miracle cure. At least Freud asked Mahler some questions, but the diagnosis was foreordained. What Mahler was told, we gather, was that his conjugal impotence derived from a fixation on his mother. Go ahead, Freud advised, have sex with your mother/wife and enjoy it; I know that the taboo can be safely broken. That was a morale booster for Mahler, though hardly a sign that the universal Oedipus complex actually exists.

Having detected it in Mahler, we are told, Freud asked him why he hadn't chosen a wife with the same name as his mother, Marie. But behold, the middle name of Mahler's wife proved to be Maria, and he called her Marie! Can this story be believed? Does an oedipal fixation make every woman undesirable except those bearing one's mother's name? In that case, why hadn't Freud himself proposed to an Amalie? Here, surely, was further crude *Sherlockismus* by Freud, whose favorite mind-reading stunt, as we have seen, was "conjecturing" details that he already knew.

One of Freud's psychoanalytic trainees in the 1920s, Clarence Oberndorf, learned just how adamant he could be in defense of his instant interpretations. On the first day of consultation, Oberndorf brought Freud a dream report: he was riding to an unknown place in a carriage drawn by two horses, one white and one black. According to the memoir of Oberndorf's friend Abram Kardiner, Freud declared at once that Oberndorf "could never marry because he didn't know whether to choose a white woman or a black woman."[18] Oberndorf, who had been raised in Jim Crow Atlanta with an abhorrence of "race mixing," realized that the interpretation was wild. The two men tangled over the dream for months, "until Freud got tired of it and discontinued the analysis. Freud was unequivocal in his condemnation of Oberndorf's character and of his ability."[19]

If the Oberndorf analysis hadn't been aborted, we can be fairly sure what course it would have taken. Freud had decided that his own nervousness was explained by permutations of the Oedipus complex that had been triggered by eroticized maternal care in his infancy, leaving him saddled with doubts about his sexual orientation. That was all the evidence he needed to declare, as he did in the Csonka history, that "a very considerable measure of latent or unconscious homosexuality can be detected in all normal people."[20] Even clients who came to him with no psychological complaints at all, such as apprentice analysts seeking to be trained, received the boilerplate diagnosis. Those who weren't already overt homosexuals were unconscious ones, and their Oedipus complexes were to blame.

Thus Kardiner himself was told by Freud that he had been sexually overstimulated by his mother and, fearing punishment for his resultant incest wish, had become an unconscious homosexual.[21] Kardiner was taken aback, but fortunately he was able to compare notes with other students and learn that, "as with the Oedipus complex, unconscious homosexuality was a routine part of everyone's analysis."[22] Indeed, "Once [Freud] located the Oedipus complex and worked through the unconscious homosexuality, there wasn't anything much left to do."[23]

In the nineties Freud had clung to a hope that memory retrieval might actually produce cures. Once he stopped trying and instead applied the oedipal diagnosis to every case, he saw no further need to involve himself in his patients' emotional storms. Indeed, he no longer cared whether they benefited from treatment. "We do analysis for two reasons," Theodor Reik heard him say: "to understand the unconscious and to make a living."[24] Ferenczi recalled the same judgment: "Patients only serve to provide us with a livelihood and material to learn from. We certainly cannot help them."[25]

Now Freud felt entitled to violate all of his own precepts about technique. As Janet Malcolm observed in 1982, he

> conducted therapy as no classical Freudian analyst would conduct it today—as if it were an ordinary human interaction in which the analyst could shout at the patient, praise him, argue with him, accept flowers from him on his birthday, lend him money, and even gossip with him about other patients.[26]

Be an impassive, attentive listener, Freud advised his colleagues; but with some patients he held forth incessantly, scarcely allowing them to put in a word while he told jokes and grumbled about his pet peeves. On the other hand, some clients were allowed to talk randomly; but Freud, instead of "listening with the third ear," sometimes slept through their monologues.* Never analyze friends or family, Freud wrote; but he did so all the time, typically winning the complicity of one relative by divulging what had been confidentially said about her by another.

So, too, indiscretion about the content of analyses served Freud as a means of keeping members of his circle dependent on him. Thus he demanded reports from Ferenczi about Ferenczi's analysis of Jones; kept Jones himself up to date on his analysis of Jones's mistress; and tattled to both Ferenczi and Jung about secrets he was prying from women who were sexually involved with them.[27] The common denominator of all this indulgence was a simple principle: Freud, standing beyond the reach of anyone's criticism, was entitled to his whims.

Having abandoned hope of therapeutic gains, Freud also lost whatever sympathy he had once felt for patients experiencing mental anguish. Though he held all of humanity in low regard, he especially despised his complaining neurotics, who had trapped him into putting up with their deplorable weaknesses. "Patients," he told Ferenczi, "are a rabble" (*ein Gesindel*).[28] "I prefer a student ten times more than a neurotic," he

---

* Already by 1898 Freud told Fliess, "I sleep during my afternoon analyses" (3/15/98; FF, p. 303). The implication wasn't that he dozed off occasionally but that this was an efficient means of budgeting his time. With age and illness, however, the practice may have become involuntary.

said to Joseph Wortis (himself a student) with "a disparaging gesture and a laugh."[29] And a shocked Ludwig Binswanger reported that he would never forget the exact words of Freud's reply when asked how he felt about his patients: "I could throttle every one of them." (*Den Hals umdrehen könnte ich ihnen allen.*)[30]

2. STEADY WORK

It may be asked why Freud continued to accept patients at all. The answer can be stated in one word, but it is the word that, in most Freud studies, dare not speak its name: *money*.[31] A critic who so much as mentions the topic is regarded as having displayed anti-Semitism or "Jewish self-hatred." Freud himself, however, was privately candid about what he called his "money complex." As he told Jung, "I don't like to count on the gratitude of my respected fellow men, but prefer to make lots of money myself."[32]

The theme of money has been with us from the outset of our study. The strongest motive behind Freud's early ventures with his gold chloride stain and with cocaine had been a desire to lift himself out of poverty. We recall, too, that when his molestation theory looked unviable in 1897, he mourned the loss of "certain wealth" and its concomitant benefits. Especially given his struggles in a society that was increasingly hostile to the aspirations of Jews, we can hardly begrudge him his determination to join the middle class and prosper.

The question, though, is whether a desire for wealth, as opposed to medical solicitude or scientific curiosity, had become a paramount motive in Freud's life. As we saw, he had begun angling for "goldfish" as soon as he could, and he had adopted a lifestyle out of proportion to his means. His colleagues, notably Breuer, had been shocked by his willingness to keep affluent patients in treatment for as long as five years without signs of consistent improvement. And he had made no secret, among his friends, that he wanted his professorship chiefly in order to attract high-paying clients and to raise his fees.

Freud's acquisitiveness wasn't lost on his patients. Albert Hirst observed to Paul Roazen that the analyst had been extremely "money-minded," and the American visitor Joseph Wortis was taken aback by "an over-emphasis on money matters."[33] Even Martha Freud, as her husband wrote to Jung in 1911, objected to his "losing [himself] in the business of money-making."[34] He had set out, early in the twentieth century, to become very rich, and between 1906 and 1914 he did so. His fortune then vanished in the war; but from 1919 onward, accepting only clients who could pay him in inflation-resistant currencies (the dollar was especially strong), and hiding his earnings from the tax authorities, he became wealthier than ever.*

In 1974 the Wolf Man, Sergei Pankeev, told the journalist Karin Obholzer that before he lost his estate to the Bolsheviks, he was charged forty crowns per hour by Freud, or the equivalent of a day and a half's stay in a first-class sanatorium, including medicine and care.[35] There were six such hours each week except on holidays and during summer vacations. Pankeev's four-year analysis, it has been estimated, cost him the rough equivalent of 500,000 euros at their 2010 value.[36] And Freud was then allotting as many as seven more daily hours for consultations with other patients.

The little gifts that Freud bestowed on certain patients expressed his favoritism toward them but were also, in some instances, donated in anticipation of greater gifts in return. When the Wolf Man's treatment paused in July 1914, Freud proposed that Pankeev, in order to "keep his feeling of gratitude from becoming too strong," would do well to offer his analyst a substantial present. It proved to be a museum-quality antique Egyptian statuette of a princess, evidently chosen by Freud himself.[37]

Other offerings may have been more consequential. We recall that it was two ex-patients who intervened on behalf of Freud's academic promotion; they did so at his explicit urging.[38] In the family lore of one of them, the Baroness Marie von Ferstel (the original goldfish), it was

---

* Freud's hatred of the United States was sharpened, not alleviated, by his acceptance of well-off American clients. Having shed his lowly origins, he found Americans grievously lacking in respect for class distinctions. Above all, as Ernst Falzeder points out, Freud "strove for money, wealth, fame, and independence, but he did not want to be beholden to those who could make this possible" (Falzeder 2012, p. 108).

said that Freud had also sweet-talked her into giving him the deed to a
villa, which he had promptly sold. The story is uncorroborated, but its
existence attests to the perception by many patients' families that Freud
was more of a confidence man than a therapist. The baroness herself
came around to that opinion, which she then imparted, emphatically,
to anyone who would listen.[39]

Surely, the reader will protest, this is going too far. But is it? Sándor
Ferenczi, who knew Freud very well and had followed his development with fascination, reluctantly decided that his teacher had dis-
carded any ethical scruples as a therapist. In 1932 Ferenczi confided to
his diary that Freud had long since despaired of his ability to be of
any use to people in mental pain; "yet by the concealment of these
doubts and the raising of patients' hopes," Ferenczi observed, "patients
do become caught."[40]

We have already observed that Freud actively promoted a regimen
that he considered to be ineffective. He offered it to some patients
whom he regarded as hypochondriacs and to others whom he knew to
be too psychotic for assistance by any form of talk therapy. When the
condition of troubled patients deteriorated under his care, he didn't
abandon or even alter the treatment but kept right on collecting their
fees with no terminus in view.[41]

Consider some representative examples, all of which are discussed
in Borch-Jacobsen's useful compilation *Les Patients de Freud*:

- Anna von Vest, whose "paralyzed" legs were supposedly ready for
  waltzing after one week of treatment by Freud in 1903, kept retreat-
  ing to her bed as a means of summoning him again. Her family
  gathered that she was a malingerer, and even Freud resisted some
  of her entreaties, reassuring her that she had been cured once and
  for all. Nevertheless, Anna became his patient again in 1904, 1907,
  1908, 1910, and 1925, never showing more than transitory gains.
  In a letter to her of November 14, 1926, Freud expressed regret that
  he hadn't been able to bring her analysis to a successful conclusion.
- Viktor von Dirsztay, probably psychotic from the outset and
  assuredly so in later years, consulted Freud without benefit for some

1,400 hours in 1909–11, 1913–15, and 1917–20. In 1935 he killed himself.

- Elfriede Hirschfeld was a prisoner of obsessional rituals. In 1921 Freud told colleagues that her prior history made her an unlikely candidate for analysis, but that "I was sufficiently curious, ignorant, and interested in earning money to start an analysis" without placing her in a clinic, where he apparently thought she belonged. Hirschfeld consulted Freud off and on for seven years, sometimes as often as twelve times a week, for a total of about 1,600 hours. Two years into the regimen, Freud told Jung that her symptoms had considerably worsened. In the fourth year, he wrote to Oskar Pfister that she had no chance of being cured; but the treatment continued. And in the fifth year, 1912, Freud observed to Jung with typical sangfroid, "she is beyond any possibility of therapy, but it is still her duty to sacrifice herself to science."[42]

- After four years and five months in analysis with Freud, Sergei Pankeev was pronounced cured of various phobias and obsessions and, for good measure, of constipation. Or rather, that is what Freud, who knew better, chose to claim in his dramatic case history of the Wolf Man. In reality, during the next sixty years Pankeev ricocheted among psychoanalysts, none of whom could benefit him. Near the end of his life he told Karin Obholzer, "the whole thing looks like a catastrophe. I am in the same state as when I first came to Freud, and Freud is no more."[43]

- Carl Liebmann, the Rheingold Beer heir, nurtured a jockstrap fetish that prompted Freud to regard him as an obsessional neurotic and therefore as treatable by psychoanalysis. Others deemed him psychotic. Charging the equivalent of nearly $300 an hour, Freud accepted him as a patient in 1925. Soon the doctor learned that he was dealing with a paranoiac, and later he added the designation of schizophrenia as well. Nevertheless, he kept Liebmann in treatment for five years. The doomed man spent his final period in McLean Hospital, entertaining one and all with reminiscences of Freud and reciting what he believed he had learned about himself from the master: "I am my father's penis!"[44]

What stands out in the histories of those long-term patients who weren't simply deranged is the extent of their willing subservience to Freud, as if they had granted him a power of attorney over their most important decisions. Freud's aura of wisdom, the initiation into the elite company of the analyzed, the coaxing forth of intimate confessions, the tantalizing, ever renewed promise of good results to come, and the threat of the ultimate horror, "regression" to outright homosexuality, were as effective in producing dependency as they were ineffective for recovery. Freud made full use of that dependency, not by treating it as a "transference" to be resolved on the couch but as a means of aggregating all power and initiative to himself.

3. LEADING FROM WEAKNESS

Freud was bent upon founding a scientific movement, and to outward appearances he did just that. But isn't a *scientific movement* a contradiction in terms? There is no "natural selection movement" nor any "string theory movement" or "asteroid extinction theory movement." Biologists, physicists, and geologists simply go about their work; and when they disagree with one another, their first impulse isn't to round up supporters and denounce their adversaries; they try to make the best case for their position by appealing to the burden of evidence. It is the accessibility of that evidence to all parties that guarantees a measure of civility and order in debate. "Scientific movements" are needed only by pseudosciences, whose hallmark is precisely a refusal to be bound by common standards of validation.

Freud's behavior as a leader expressed his predicament as a defender of the indefensible. Thanks to his rhetorical adeptness, he would prove to be a superbly effective ambassador to the laity. At no point, however, could he engage in substantive, research-informed debate with the many critics of his system. He had to dodge such interchanges because, as we have seen, the case for psychoanalysis was entirely a matter of faith in his word. Hence he insisted that only bona fide members of his own school were qualified to pass judgment on his conclusions. He answered his detractors not by addressing their reasoning but by accusing them of cowardice, mental illness, and thralldom to the defense mechanisms that were featured in his theory.

Even psychoanalysts, if they made so bold as to question one of Freud's dictates, were subjected to withering sarcasm. "One hears of analysts," he wrote,

> who boast that, though they have worked for dozens of years, they have never found a sign of the existence of a castration complex. We must bow our heads in recognition of the greatness of this achievement, even though it is only a negative one, a piece of virtuosity in the art of overlooking and mistaking.[45]

Such language cowed some followers into conformity while driving others to give up on Freud and establish rival schools.

In theory, Freud and his first-generation cohort of analysts were fellow investigators who shared clinical findings and adjusted their concepts accordingly. But that isn't what happened in actuality. Freud was willing to incorporate ideas from any source, including his followers, but it was all for the greater glory of *his* creation, over which he intended to have the final say. He could never grant what his subordinates wanted from him: comradely respect and allowance for some independence of judgment beneath his rule. As a young man at the Salpêtrière, he hadn't grasped how Charcot, by quashing legitimate scientific differences with his staff, was courting fallacies and ensuring his later downfall. Now Freud would become the new Charcot and seal his long-term posthumous fate.

Psychoanalysis was supposed to bring insight and liberation to the repressed, but its own practitioners, so long as they remained loyal to Freud, trembled in fear of his wrath and collapsed into Orwellian groupthink. One negative remark from him could tell the other insiders, annihilatingly, that a formerly respected analyst had been "insufficiently analyzed." And Freud didn't hesitate to employ that weapon with ruthless cunning. As Jung bitterly complained to him in 1912, "You go around sniffing out all the symptomatic actions in your vicinity, thus reducing everyone to the level of sons and daughters who blushingly admit the existence of their faults. Meanwhile you remain on top as the father, sitting pretty."[46] In the words of the psychoanalyst Robert Holt, "Freud was often deceptive, manipulative, and Machiavellian. He schemed with his favorites to get rid of others for whom he expressed contempt, riding roughshod over them when they got in the way of his grand design."*

The sharpest instrument of Freud's plotting was his "Secret Committee," proposed in 1912 to combat backsliding—or, as Louis Breger bluntly puts it, "to stifle debate and impose censorship."[47] Its original members, in addition to Freud, were Jones, Ferenczi, Rank, Abraham, and Sachs. Max Eitingon was added in 1919. The final member, after deaths and desertions left an opening, was Anna Freud, who would discreetly advance the defunct Committee's agenda after World War II.

The little team, with its special gold rings for members and its oath of unswerving loyalty to Freud's dogma, operated, with interruptions, from 1913 until 1936, but its existence remained hidden until 1944. The Committee worked behind the scenes to attack, ridicule, and blacklist defectors, thus enforcing an orthodoxy that couldn't be sustained by less conspiratorial means.[48] Interestingly, the idea of establishing such a cabal had been proposed by none other than Ernest Jones. But as Freud's slander of both Breuer and Koller illustrates, he himself set the Committee's vicious tone.

Although the Committee assassinated only reputations, not people, its atmosphere was distinctly Stalinist, each member acting with awareness that at any time he might incur Freud's displeasure and be transferred to the hit list. That, indeed, is just what happened to Ferenczi. His offense was to differ with Freud on a point of clinical technique. In 1929, and continuing until his death in 1933, he was shunned and vilified. And Jones, Ferenczi's former analysand and pupil, perpetuated Freud's fatwa, repeating in his biography the lie that Ferenczi had been demented in his final years.[49]

On the whole, it was easy for Freud to tell which of his associates

---

* Holt 1992, pp. 21–22. Holt went on to charge that psychoanalytic training institutes still duplicate Freud's authoritarianism, systematically "infantilizing" not only their candidates but also their nonteaching members (pp. 23–24).

deserved to be reclassified as unpersons: it was those who had challenged one or more of his teachings. His paranoid tendency, however, broadened the range of threatening figures. The obverse side of his belief in telepathy was a sense that his mind might be subject to invasion by malefactors. Hence his preoccupation with doubles, revenants, and experiences of déjà vu.* Was someone eavesdropping on his brain?

Consider the enmity that Freud contracted against his promising but depressive student Viktor Tausk, who died in 1919. The approval of the first psychoanalyst was all that mattered to Tausk.[50] But he was doing too well, intellectually, for Freud's comfort. He appeared to be articulating points of theory that were still gestating in his mentor, who suspected that Tausk was employing thought transference to steal his ideas before he could articulate them.

Freud's first prophylactic against that threat was to render Tausk abject by refusing to analyze him and by assigning him an analyst, Helene Deutsch, who was junior to himself in the profession. But then Freud began obsessing that Tausk's influence on Deutsch might be contaminating her for her role as his own analysand. (Psychoanalysts other than Freud were often in analysis themselves.) He told Deutsch that she must choose forthwith between Tausk and himself. Robotically, Deutsch dismissed Tausk, who, unable to imagine a meaningful existence that was unsanctioned by Freud, promptly committed suicide. In an icy letter to Tausk's former lover, Lou Andreas-Salomé, Freud expressed grim satisfaction over Tausk's disappearance from the analytic scene. "I confess," he wrote, "that I do not really miss him; I had long realized that he could be of no further service, indeed that he constituted a threat to the future."†

---

* As Freud would write in his paper on "The Uncanny," the feeling that someone else is one's double "is accentuated by mental processes leaping from one of these characters to another—by what we should call telepathy—, so that the one possesses knowledge, feelings and experience in common with the other. Or it is marked by the fact that the subject identifies himself with someone else, so that he is in doubt as to which his self is, or substitutes the extraneous self for his own" (SE, 17:234).

† Freud/Andreas-Salomé 1966, p. 98. For a long while, suicide was an occupational hazard of the psychoanalytic profession, whose practitioners tended to be no less unbalanced than their patients. Between 1902 and 1938, at least 9 of the 149 members of the Viennese Psychoanalytic Association killed themselves (Falzeder 1994, p. 182). "Monroe Meyer and I once discussed with Freud the suicides of two analysts in Vienna,"

5. UNRESTRAINED

Only in one enterprise was Freud able to mold another human being entirely to his own ends. Psychoanalysis stops at the nursery door, his disgusted wife had admonished when he wanted to peer at the spontaneous erections of a son. But when his anorexic and depressed daughter Anna reached fourteen, he invited her to attend sessions of the Vienna Psychoanalytic Society, where she learned about penis envy, female masochism, the equation of femininity with the extinction of "masculine" clitoral sensation, and every daughter's normal desire to fornicate with her father—concepts to which she would remain strictly faithful thereafter.

In person and in correspondence, the teenage Anna kept Sigmund apprised of her unsuccessful efforts to stop masturbating and fantasizing about being beaten by him. When she was eighteen, he began telling would-be suitors, such as Jones himself, to keep their distance from his Anna/Antigone. And at twenty-two, she began the first of two secret analyses on her father's couch, six days a week, lasting a total of four years. Now she would be Papa's girl for the rest of a long life.

Just weeks after undertaking his daughter's analysis, Freud began writing one of his most intricate clinical papers, "'A Child Is Being Beaten': A Contribution to the Study of the Origin of Sexual Perversions."[51] Out of "a large number of cases," all of which featured beating fantasies and masturbation, he had allegedly selected six for close study.[52] Curiously, however, Anna was the only patient of Freud's whose beating fantasies have ever come to light. As the world would begin to understand later, it was Freud's own daughter, and only his daughter, whose onanistic activity and fantasies inspired him to chart regression to "the pregenital, sadistic-anal" organization of the libido.[53]

Anna's induction into the psychoanalytic profession was no less an inside job. In May 1922, hoping to be accepted as a full colleague at age twenty-six, she read her own paper, "Beating Fantasies and Day-

---

Abram Kardiner would write. "His eyes twinkling, he commented, 'Well, the day will come when psychoanalysis will be considered a legitimate cause of death'" (Kardiner 1977, p. 70).

dreams," to the assembled Vienna Psychoanalytic Society. Just this once, a candidate for admission to the company of practicing analysts wrote up the content of her own analysis, which was the only one with which she was directly acquainted. The society's members, all but one, were not to know that she had been the patient, not the analyst.

Anna's presentation was a swindle. Her acceptance, however, was never in doubt. Although one clueless listener protested that the patient whom Anna described sounded like "a totally abnormal person whose incompetence and inferiority would absolutely emerge in real life,"[54] the chairman of the session—her father, of course—judged her paper to be excellent. He didn't let on that he had been the masochistic masturbator's psychoanalyst. Six months later, Anna began treating patients of her own.

Readers can decide whether they consider Freud's cloning of himself in his daughter to have been a happy stroke for psychoanalysis or a crime, the abduction of a soul. (But why not both?) There can be no question, however, about the destructive effects of other interventions when Freud saw no barrier to the exercise of absolute power. The locus classicus, though it came fully to light only in 1988, is the Horace Frink affair, which starkly illustrates what had become of the earnest young medical student of the 1870s.[55]

Frink was a brilliant, witty, but very disturbed American practitioner of psychoanalysis who underwent a training analysis with Freud in 1921 at age thirty-eight. Failing to perceive that Frink was manic depressive (bipolar), Freud found him altogether delightful, and he began to conceive of Frink as his American Jung—the gentile who could be entrusted with the stewardship of psychoanalysis in the New World.

The married Frink, like many psychoanalysts of his era, was carrying on a protracted affair with one of his patients. This was Angelika Bijur, heiress to a New York bank fortune. Though she, too, was married, Freud began to envision a financial windfall for his movement. He used the first weeks of Frink's training analysis in Vienna to impress upon him the therapeutic benefit of deserting his wife and children, suing for divorce, and marrying the heiress—who, summoned to Vienna by a dangerously depressed Frink in the fifth month of his analysis, was told by Freud that, unless she divorced her husband and married Frink, disaster was sure to ensue. As Angelika later recalled, Freud said that otherwise Frink "would never again try to come back to normality and probably develop into a homosexual though in a highly disguised way."[56]

Angelika, who truly loved Frink, was persuaded to demand a divorce from her shocked and infuriated husband. Freud, she explained to him in the company of a "dazed" Frink, had laid his blessing on the proposed remarriage. Shortly thereafter, Frink's wife, Doris, reluctantly consented to a divorce. But then Horace and Angelika began having second thoughts. In September 1921 Freud wrote to Frink assuring him that the remarriage would form the capstone to his now "complete" analysis.[57]

Freud's letter had the desired effect; the twin divorces were set in motion. An emotionally exhausted and wretched Doris Frink boarded a train to Albuquerque with her two young children to try to begin a new life. But Abraham Bijur wasn't so cooperative. He drafted an open letter to Freud, meant for publication in the New York newspapers, denouncing his meddling in the lives of people he hadn't even met and asking, "Great Doctor, are you savant or charlatan?"[58] Luckily for Freud, however, Bijur died of cancer in May 1922, before his letter could be published. Shown a copy later, Freud scoffed that it was a silly appeal to hypocritical Yankee public opinion.

Horace Frink's psychological condition deteriorated once again, and Freud, still insistent on the remarriage, took him back into analysis for two more periods, April to July and November to December 1922. Now not even Freud, one might think, could miss the signs of psychosis as Frink, alternating between hyperactivity and stupor, mistook his bathtub for a grave and pictured Angelika as looking "queer, like a man, like a pig."[59] But Freud, seeing only "excellent grim humor" in Frink's dissociated behavior, was undeterred.[60] He didn't tell "Angie Frink," as he now called her, how strangely Frink was acting. And in November he wrote the following unforgettable lines to Frink:

> May I still suggest to you that your idea that Mrs. B had lost part of her beauty may be turned into her having lost part of her money. . . .

Your complaint that you cannot grasp your homosexuality implies that you are not yet aware of your phantasy of making me a rich man. If matters turn out all right let us change this imaginary gift into a real contribution to the Psychoanalytic Funds.[61]

One week after Frink went into a brief remission, he and Angelika married in Paris. In January 1923, at Freud's insistence, an unpopular Frink was unanimously elected acting president of the New York Psychoanalytic Society. In April, however, he heard that Doris was dying of pneumonia. He rushed to see her, but, excluded from her room, he couldn't apologize for all that had occurred in the past two years.

After that, Frink redirected his self-loathing at his new wife, whom he physically attacked. In March 1924 he took a leave from his executive office and checked himself into the Henry Phipps Psychiatric Clinic at Johns Hopkins, in the care of the notable anti-Freudian Adolf Meyer. Both Frink and Angelika now began to blame psychoanalysis for having ruined their lives. "I have so far not met any analist [sic]," wrote Angelika to Meyer, "who does not appear to me an obvious neurotic, lost in their theory and unable to deal with life."[62]

Freud was never able to collect his windfall of dollars. Eventually, Angelika divorced Frink, but not before he twice attempted suicide. In later years, despite a few more bad episodes, he remarried again and found a measure of peace. A year before he died of a heart attack at age fifty-three, a daughter asked him what message he would send to Freud if he could. "Tell him," replied Frink, "he was a great man, even if he did invent psychoanalysis."[63]

Are We Being Freudian Yet?

By 1895, in writing the concluding chapter of *Studies on Hysteria*, Freud was ready to tell the world that he had devised an efficacious new therapy, based on Josef Breuer's "cathartic method" but improving on it—for Breuer hadn't grasped that every psychoneurosis is traceable to the repressed memory of a sexual trauma. A year later, in two articles, he gave a name to the new procedure: psychoanalysis.

No good Freudian, however, would agree that Freud was then practicing psychoanalysis. In 1896 he was immersed in his molestation theory (commonly misnamed "seduction theory"), whereby all sufferers from hysteria were presumed to have repressed a memory of sexual molestation in childhood; and his therapeutic technique was aimed at uncovering those experiences. But soon Freud decided that he had been mistaken; and psychoanalysis, as commonly understood, was initiated when he began searching for the opposite of molestation—namely, guilty sexual thoughts on the part of little boys, who feared punitive "castration" because their "Oedipus complexes" had made them aspire to murder their fathers and to copulate with their mothers. (The "female Oedipus complex" would have to be patched together as an afterthought.)

There is something odd here, beyond the oddity of the Oedipus complex itself. Freud *thought* he was practicing psychoanalysis in 1896. Little seems to have changed in his clinical procedure between his emphases on molestation and on the Oedipus complex, which is said to have been revealed to him in the very next year, 1897. Why, then, isn't psychoanalysis dated from 1896, as announced by Freud? The answer is that Freudians regard the molestation theory as an embarrassment. In postdating psychoanalysis, they are avoiding the unpleasant thought that the same method, applied by the same intellect to the same cohort of patients, yielded opposite findings within a matter of months. Isn't that a black mark against the method?

Of course, much did change in Freud's conception of psychoanalysis—both the clinical technique and the theory—in the decade following 1896. Indeed, it is worthwhile to review some of the features that are now regarded as classically psychoanalytic and to see how spread out they are in time and how they changed their meaning. Just a handful of them were present at the outset—a fact that must prompt us to ask whether "psychoanalysis" originally constituted a breakthrough in understanding and cure or merely a hopeful career move.

a. **Repression and the unconscious.** Yes, those ideas were important from the start. But the way in which they were construed would be significantly modified.

b. **Resistance.** Already in 1896, a patient's resistance to interpretations posed by Freud was counted as a sure indication that certain thoughts were being held under repression. The nature of those interpretations, however, changed as his theory evolved. Thus the early patients had been resisting ideas that Freud himself later considered to have been wrong.

c. **Trauma-based etiology.** By 1896 Freud had in hand his two-step etiology of hysteria, featuring primary and then auxiliary traumas, both of which were allegedly needed to launch the disorder.[1] But the kind of trauma that counted, and the age range within which it was supposed to have occurred, would soon be revised.

d. **Conversion, symbolization, compromise formation.** The hysterical conversion of repressed thoughts into bodily symptoms was one of Freud's earliest psychological ideas. So was his belief that the symptom would act out, or symbolize, the initiating trauma. (An insult that feels like "a slap in the face" causes facial neuralgia, etc.) But not until *The Interpretation of Dreams* in 1900 would Freud argue that a symptom, like a dream, expresses a *compromise* between repressed and repressing thoughts. If that new tenet was true, all of his previous interpretations of symptoms had been wrong.

e. **Sublimation.** It was Freud's belief that the energy needed for cultural achievements, broadly construed, must be siphoned off from sexual instinct. Sublimation was the envisioned means by which a sexual aim could be replaced by a nonsexual one. Here, then, was an important if vague item of Freudian "economics." But we hear nothing about it before 1908.[2]

Along with repression, *regression, projection, denial, reaction formation,* and a few other concepts as well, sublimation came to be counted, rather mysteriously, as a *mechanism of defense.* Freud never listed those mechanisms, but his daughter Anna did so in 1937, thus finally imparting a formal order to the topic.[3]

f. **Free association.** It was probably around 1896 that Freud began trying to replace his "pressure technique" with free association, whereby the therapist, noting gaps and hesitancy in the patient's oral narrative, encourages her to speak whatever thoughts come to mind. Further dialogue, when certain new expressions have been singled out as cues for more associating, presumably leads to the uncovering of repressed memories or other censored thoughts.

Free association proved to be the most universal and enduring tool of psychoanalysis in all of its many schools. Freud himself placed a high value on it as an avenue into the unconscious. Yet he didn't mention it in print until 1904, when at last he contributed a chapter to Leopold Löwenfeld's book on clinical technique.[4]

Once again, the nature of the privileged psychical material shifted over time; and needless to say, inferences from the patients' associations always kept pace with the latest dogma.* So, too, in the many schools of psychoanalysis that have succeeded Freud's, free association leads infallibly to each school's favored kind of truth. The obvious reason is that each hub of training and propagation has its own idea of what constitutes a significant utterance.[5] Free association, then, is and has always been a farce; yet Freudians dare not call it into question as a reliable epistemic instrument.

g. **Dreams and blunders.** Freud was privately absorbed in dream interpretation in 1896, but it formed no part of psychoanalysis as he publicly introduced it. And *The Interpretation of Dreams* (1900) became self-contradictory in later editions. Originally, Freud held that only the dreamer's verbal associations to her dream report can explain the symbols in the dream. But when Wilhelm Stekel and Otto Rank, in 1909 and 1914, urged him to include *universal* sexual symbols, he could think of no objection to doing so.

As for "Freudian slips," their exposition in *The Psychopathology of Everyday Life* (1901) helped to make the author a celebrity, but they would never play a serious therapeutic role.

h. **Transference and countertransference.** Not until 1905, in the postscript to his "Dora" case history, would Freud begin placing theoretical weight on transference: the patient's emotional entanglement with the therapist, supposedly resulting from her putting him in the place of a parent who was loved and/or hated in early childhood.[6] Even in 1905, Freud regarded transference only as a nuisance to be dealt with before substantial progress could be made. As for countertransference, or the therapist's reciprocal involvement, it wasn't mentioned until 1910, and Freud attached little importance to it except as a risk to objectivity.[7]

---

* Freud's recalcitrant American client Joseph Wortis recalled that Freud "would wait until he found an association which would fit into his scheme of interpretation and pick it up like a detective at a line-up who waits until he sees his man" (Wortis 1940, p. 844). Wortis meant a witness, not a detective, but his point about Freud's pouncing was vividly conveyed.

i. **The Oedipus complex, the castration complex, infantile sexuality.** For the first generations of Freudians, the Oedipus complex was Freud's greatest discovery and the very heart of psychoanalysis. They were agreeing with the master; repressed oedipal wishes, he declared, constitute "the *nuclear complex* of every neurosis."[8] He didn't say so, however, until 1909, in a lecture that was published in the following year. If he was right in 1909, he had lacked this indispensable knowledge for the first thirteen years of his analytic career.

The castration complex, deriving from a child's alarmed perception of anatomical differences between the sexes, and then from fear of punishment for incest wishes, was considered to be integral to the overcoming of the Oedipus complex. Both complexes depended on the assumption that children are fully sexual creatures—a belief at which Freud privately arrived in 1899. Yet it was only in 1905, in *Three Essays on the Theory of Sexuality*, that he characterized the "polymorphous perversity" of infantile sexuality; and it was much later, between 1913 and 1923, that he laid out every child's *pregenital stages* of oral, anal, and phallic eroticism, with *fixation points* to which adult neurotics may have regressed.

j. **Metapsychology.** Freud's highest aim was to model the whole mind in its normal and abnormal functions, showing mutually opposed agencies and energies. *Metapsychology*, a word he privately coined in 1896, was his term for that enterprise.[9] Eventually, he would devise three overlapping mental models, known as the *topographical*, the *dynamic*, and the *economic*.

The first public indication of this interest is found in Chapter 7 of *The Interpretation of Dreams*, with the topographical distinction between the conscious, preconscious, and unconscious realms. Although the dynamic triad of *ego*, *id*, and *superego* is widely considered to encapsulate the psychoanalytic vision, it went unmentioned until 1923.[10] As for the "economics" of energy transfers, enabling a given mental force to pass a threshold of inhibition and thus to get expressed, Freud was wedded to the idea as early as 1895.

The idea itself, however, lacked any operational meaning. "Psychical energy" was an undetectable phenomenon that amounted merely to a redundant manner of representation: if something happened, a sufficiency of energy must have been exerted. Thus the "economic model" was adaptable to any and all assertions Freud wished to pose regarding the mind. And those assertions, once again, kept changing without his ever setting forth data to justify the moves.

When we note how incrementally the elements of classical psychoanalysis were assembled, it becomes apparent that what Freud established in 1896, when his theory was entering its period of maximum turbulence, was little more than a brand name for a product in beta development. His subsequent aim would be to protect and promote his brand, irrespective of its run-ins with evidence and logic. Thus, for example, when he gave up on futile memory retrieval and made "analysis of the transference" into the focus of treatment, he didn't admit that no one had been healed under the former dispensation, much less that his regimen was now devoted to coping with a problem caused by the regimen itself. Psychoanalysis, whatever it was, had to be depicted as marching ever forward.

This commercial mentality is what set Freud apart from the ethical scientists and physicians of his era. Members of those groups, loyal not to a business but to the idea of objective inquiry, felt constrained to abandon measures and beliefs that had failed to garner empirical support. But Freud, who cared only about the cause to which his name was attached, found it imperative to inflate his results, to make promissory claims, to meet objections through sophistry, scorn, and ad hoc tinkering, and to pile further theory atop postulates that had never been validated.

Each of the many later schools of psychoanalysis has adopted certain Freudian concepts and jettisoned others, but never on the basis of empirical trials. There has never been a moment when we could say, "*This* is psychoanalysis." The name, then, is just a placemarker for whatever any given psychoanalyst happens to be practicing and declaring at any given time.

NOTES

Citations by name and date refer to the Works Cited beginning on page 709. For abbreviated titles see p. xvii. When dates of letters through 1886 are given without further information, they always refer to engagement letters that were still unpublished when this book was completed.

PREFACE

1   See especially Ellenberger 1970; Levin 1978; McGrath 1986; Sulloway 1992; Macmillan 1997; Davidson 2001; Tauber 2010.

2   See, e.g., Van Rillaer 1980; Thornton 1984; Grünbaum 1984, 1993; Zwang 1985; Szasz 1990; Puner 1992; Torrey 1992; Esterson 1993; Israëls 1993, 2006; Scharnberg 1993; Wilcocks 1994, 2000; Webster 1995; Gellner 1996; Erwin 1996; Farrell 1996; Macmillan 1997; Cioffi 1998; Dufresne 2000, 2003; Bénesteau 2002; Eysenck 2004; Meyer et al. 2005; Buekens 2006; Pommier 2008; Borch-Jacobsen 2009; Onfray 2010.

3   Williams et al. 1997.

4   Robins et al. 1999, p. 117.

5   Tauber 2010, p. 1. Independent scholars, reviewing the Freudian experiments purporting to validate Freud's master concept of repression, have found fatal design flaws in every one of them. See Eysenck and Wilson 1973; Holmes 1990; Pope and Hudson 1995; Erwin 1996; Pope et al. 2007; McNally 2003; Rofé 2008.

6   See Borch-Jacobsen and Shamdasani 2012.

7   See Makari 2008. But precisely because Makari is a Freudian believer, he fails to grasp the meaning of the history he narrates so well.

8   See, e.g., Louis Breger's generally shrewd *Freud: Darkness in the Midst of Vision* (2000). The Freud whom Breger accurately depicts would have had no means of ascertaining which, if any, of his "visions" were true.

9   Cioffi 1998, p. 32.

1: BETWEEN IDENTITIES

1   J, 1:19. See generally Gresser 1994.
2   See Feiner 2002, 2004.
3   SE, 4:197.
4   M. Freud 1957, p. 11. See also Margolis 1996.
5   SE, 4:196.
6   Klein 1981, p. 48.
7   Ibid., p. 46.
8   Heer 1972, p. 6.
9   Knoepfmacher 1979a, pp. 294–296.
10   McGrath 1974, p. 249.
11   SE, 20:8–9; translation modified.
12   12/6/74; FS, p. 73.
13   9/18/74; ibid., pp. 60–61.
14   4/11/75; ibid., p. 109.
15   See especially McGrath 1974, pp. 33–52.
16   Quoted by Klein 1981, p. 48.
17   Scheuer 1927; McGrath 1974.
18   9/18/72; Freud 1969, p. 420; translation modified. Meseritsch was a Czech town that had contained an independent Jewish community since the seventeenth century.
19   6/28/75; FS, p. 121.
20   8/14/78; FS, p. 169.
21   9/16/83; FMB, 2:252.
22   3/21/86. (Dates without a further citation indicate as yet unpublished *Brautbriefe*, or engagement letters.)
23   8/5/85.
24   Quoted by Klein 1981, p. 51.
25   Bernfeld 1951, pp. 216–217.
26   See Gilman 1985, 1986, 1993a.
27   See Knoepfmacher 1979b.
28   For Freud's curious leaning toward Christianity in various respects, see Vitz 1988.
29   SE, 23:1–138; see Yerushalmi 1991.
30   It is by no means certain that anti-Semitism caused the delay of Freud's promotion to honorary professor. See Gicklhorn and Gicklhorn 1960.

2: GETTING BY

1   Solms 2002, p. 32.
2   Shepherd 1991.
3   Robinson 2001.
4   Solms 2002, p. 19.
5   Ibid., p. 21.
6   J, 1:40.
7   9/19/01; FF, p. 450.
8   A. B. Freud 1940, p. 336.

9   Trosman and Wolf 1973, p. 231.
10   SE, 20:8.
11   7/17/73; FS, p. 24.
12   12/11/74; FS, p. 78.
13   3/7/75; FS, p. 95.
14   3/7/75; FS, p. 96.
15   Brentano 1973, pp. 101–110; Tauber 2010, pp. 48–53.
16   Schur 1972, p. 68.
17   SE, 20:9.
18   J, 1:58.
19   SE, 20:8.
20   Ibid., p. 253.
21   A. B. Freud 1940, p. 337.
22   SE, 20:253.
23   Freud 1877; Bernfeld 1949, p. 166.
24   Ibid., p. 169.
25   For a detailed analysis of Freud's work under Meynert, see Hirschmüller 1991, 1992.
26   Hirschmüller 1991.
27   Ibid., pp. 201–202, 208.
28   5/29/84; L, p. 111; FMB, 3:373.
29   Freud 1884h.
30   Bernfeld 1949, p. 187.
31   J, 1:54.
32   Bernfeld 1949, p. 186.
33   Ibid., pp. 186–187.
34   Freud 1927, p. 394.

3: FORSAKING ALL OTHERS

1   2/7/73; Freud 1969, p. 422.
2   2/27/75; FS, pp. 92, 93.
3   Ibid., p. 93.
4   FS, pp. 133–138, 187–188.
5   9/4/72; FS, p. 17.
6   3/19/08; L, p. 272.
7   J, 1:99.
8   L, p. viii.
9   Quoted by Trosman and Wolf 1973, p. 231.
10   1/13/86.
11   12/14/85; emphasis as found. The term "*break down*" is in English.
12   6/30/84; L, p. 118; FMB, 3:430.
13   10/23/83; L, p. 70; FMB, 2:362.
14   1/16/84; L, p. 89; FMB, 3:71.
15   10/17/84; L, p. 123.
16   2/10/86; L, p. 210.
17   Quoted by Swales 1983, pp. 5, 17.
18   See, e.g., SE, 9:201.

19   SE, 22:133–134.
20   Quoted by J, 1:140.
21   6/28/82; FMB, 1:126.
22   8/14/82; L, p. 23; FMB, 1:283; translation modified.
23   8/2/82; FMB, 1:242.
24   2/23/86.
25   FMB, 2:413.
26   1/16/84; L, p. 89; FMB, 3:71; 7/23/82; L, p. 18; FMB, 1:214; 8/29/83; L, p. 52; FMB, 2:191.
27   7/8/82; FMB, 1:173; emphasis as found.
28   10/23/83; L, p. 71; FMB, 2:363.
29   Mill 1880.
30   11/15/83; L, p. 76; FMB, 2:425.
31   Ibid.; translation modified.
32   J, 1:122.
33   Ibid., p. 110.
34   7/26/84; FMB, 3:486–487.
35   Quoted by J, 1:114–115.
36   Quoted by J, 1:117.
37   8/3/82; FMB, 1:248.
38   See 10/25/82; FMB, 1:546–549.
39   6/22/86.
40   6/23/86.
41   7/6/86.
42   Quoted by J, 1:148; emphasis as found.
43   6/22/86; emphasis as found.
44   6/25/86.
45   Ibid.
46   6/27/86.
47   Ibid.
48   6/23/86.
49   6/22/86.
50   6/27/86.
51   Ibid.
52   6/18/86.
53   7/7/86.
54   7/2/82; FMB, 1:144.

4: WHITE MAGIC

1   2/2/86; L, p. 202.
2   3/29/84; L, pp. 101–102; FMB, 3:223.
3   2/14/84; L, p. 99; FMB, 3:147.
4   Freud 1879, p. 468.
5   Bernfeld 1949, p. 181.
6   Freud 1884e, f, g.
7   10/25/83; L. pp. 72–74; FMB, 2:370.

8   See, e.g., 10/9/83; FMB, 2:321; 10/15/83; FMB, 2:339; 1/7/84; FMB, 3:48.

9   Upson 1888.

10   SE, 3:231.

11   These passages are quoted by Quinn 1994, the source of the present discussion. See also Quinn 1992, 1993. I am grateful to Dr. Quinn for sending me a copy of his 1994 manuscript.

12   L, pp. 107–108; translation modified; FMB, 3:278.

13   CP, pp. 15–19.

14   Ibid., p. 70; SK, pp. 77–78. Cohen 2011 (p. 60) cites one further *Gazette* article on morphine cures from 1881.

15   For cocaine's worldwide history, see Gootenberg 2001 and Karch 2006.

16   5/12/84; FMB, 3:326.

17   J, 1:81.

18   59/84; FMB, 3:320.

19   6/19/84; FMB, 3:411.

20   Freud 1884c.

21   Haas 1983, p. 176; SK, p. 14; CP, p. xvii.

22   CP, p. 66; SK, p. 71.

23   CP, p. 58; SK, p. 60.

24   CP, p. 58; SK, p. 59.

25   CP, p. 65n; SK, p. 71n.

26   Mantegazza 1975, p. 41; emphasis as found.

27   CP, p. 71; SK, p. 79.

28   CP, p. 64; SK, pp. 68, 69.

29   CP, p. 71; SK, p. 79.

30   CP, p. 71; SK, p. 79.

31   CP, pp. 55, 63; SK, pp. 55, 67.

32   CP, p. 63; SK, p. 67.

33   CP, p. 59; SK, p. 61.

34   CP, pp. 64, 62; SK, pp. 68, 66; translation modified.

35   CP, p. 62; SK, p. 66.

36   CP, p. 60; SK, p. 62.

37   Bernfeld 1953, p. 601.

38   J, 1:84.

39   Ibid., p. 91.

40   FMB, 3:381.

41   10/26/84.

42   6/2/85.

43   6/15/85.

44   6/29/84; L, p. 115; FMB, 3:427.

45   5/4/85.

46   CP, p. 51; SK, pp. 45–46.

47   CP, p. 73; SK, pp. 81–82; translation modified.

48   5/4/85.

49   6/2/84; FMB, 3:381.

50   J, 1:84–85.

51   For the effect of cocaine on Freud's psychoanalytic conception of libido, see Swales 1989a.

5: A FRIEND IN NEED

1   SE, 20:9.
2   See Schorske 1980.
3   6/27/82; L, pp. 11–12; FMB, 1:120; translation modified.
4   SE, 5:421–422.
5   10/28/83; FMB, 2:376.
6   J, 1:11.
7   L, p. 12; FMB, 1:120, 122.
8   6/27/82; L, p. 11; FMB, 1:120.
9   4/21/84; L, pp. 107–108; FMB, 3:278; translation modified.
10   Hirschmüller 2002a, p. 71.
11   FMB, 3:319.
12   CP, p. 64; SK, p. 68.
13   5/7/84; FMB, 3:316.
14   FMB, 3:319–320.
15   Ibid., p. 319.
16   CP, p. 71; SK, p. 79; translation modified.
17   FMB, 3:326.
18   Ibid., pp. 325–326.
19   Ibid., p. 329.
20   Ibid., p. 326.
21   Ibid., pp. 351–352.
22   Ibid., p. 359.
23   Ibid., p. 447.
24   Freud 1885b.
25   CP, p. 109; SK, p. 85.
26   6/12/84; FMB, 3:401.
27   CP, p. 117; SK, p. 106; translation modified.
28   J, 1:96.

6: THE WRONG DISCOVERER

1   Newton 1995, pp. 86–87.
2   See Von Oettingen 1933; Marret et al. 2004.
3   Cited by Martin-Duce 2002, p. 188.
4   Grinspoon and Bakalar 1985, pp. 22–23; Altman et al. 1985.
5   Quoted by Becker 1974, p. 283.
6   Ibid., p. 284.
7   See Stepansky 1999, pp. 44–45; Imber 2010; Markel 2011.
8   CP, p. 97; SK, p. 89; emphasis added; translation modified.
9   10/10/84; cf. J, 1:88.
10   Quoted by Becker 1974, p. 294.
11   10/11/85.
12   10/29/84; Freud/Minna Bernays 2005, p. 96.

13   10/18/84.
14   12/12/84.
15   Ibid.
16   3/4/85, 3/7/85.
17   10/1/84.
18   1/12/85.
19   Ibid.
20   1/1/86; quoted by Becker 1974, pp. 306–307.
21   4/6/85.
22   1/6/85; quoted by Becker 1974, p. 301.
23   8/1/85.
24   4/6/85.
25   1/1/86; quoted by Becker 1974, p. 307.
26   Quoted by Becker 1974, p. 308.
27   8/29/85.
28   Quoted by Becker 1974, p. 313.
29   SE, 4:170. (The official publication date was 1900.)
30   The discussion that follows is much indebted to Israëls 1999 and Bénes-
      teau 2002.
31   SE, 20:14–15
32   Becker 1974, p. 293.
33   J, 1:79–80.
34   2/27/85.
35   3/27/85.
36   4/6/85.
37   Bernfeld 1953, pp. 595–596.
38   Wittels 1924, p. 25.
39   Bénesteau 2002, pp. 146–147.
40   Sachs 1946, p. 71.
41   See, e.g., 5/12/84.
42   Roazen 1995, pp. 5–6.
43   Ibid., p. 6.
44   Meller 1934.
45   Quoted by Israëls 1999, p. 31.
46   Ibid., pp. 31–32.
47   J, 1:87.
48   Ibid., pp. 87–88.
49   Eissler 1971, p. 159.
50   Ibid.

7: EXPERT JUDGMENTS

1   Hirschmüller 1995, p. 123.
2   10/5/84.
3   Merck 1884.
4   Merck 1884, 1885a.
5   CP, pp. 78–79; translation modified.
6   Ibid., p. 80; translation modified.

7   Anon. 1884.
8   Grinstein 1971, pp. 254–258.
9   Anon. 1884, p. 502.
10   Israëls 1999, p. 82.
11   Freud 1884d, p. 505; emphasis as found.
12   10/11/84.
13   10/21/84.
14   10/28/84.
15   Freud 1885a.
16   Bernfeld 1953, pp. 596–597.
17   J, 1:92.
18   CP, p. 98; SK, p. 90; translation modified.
19   11/12/84.
20   CP, pp. 98–99; SK, p. 91; translation modified.
21   Quoted by Aeschlimann 1980, p. 67.
22   CP, p. 101; SK, p. 94; translation modified.
23   3/7/85.
24   Hirschmüller 1995, pp. 129–131.
25   Ibid., p. 129.
26   Merck 1885b.

8: THE SURVIVOR

1   10/29/84, 6/26/85.
2   See 3/10/85, 7/18/85.
3   4/3/85.
4   L, p. 138.
5   J, 1:161.
6   See 6/24/85, 6/26/85, 7/18/85.
7   6/24/85.
8   7/18/85.
9   5/21/85.
10   6/26/85.
11   5/26/85; L, p. 147; translation modified.
12   Letters characterizing Freud's late-night vigils with Fleischl include those
      of 4/16/85, 5/21/85, 6/15/85, 7/14/85, 5/1/86, 5/8/86, and 5/30/86.
13   FMB, 3:447.
14   See 2/5/85.
15   See, e.g., Borch-Jacobsen and Shamdasani 2012, p. 265; Cohen 2011,
      p. 107.
16   L, p. 69.
17   5/21/85.
18   8/1/85.
19   4/5/86.
20   4/7/86.
21   5/30/86.
22   Cited by Israëls 1999, p. 117.
23   Breuer 1974.

24   Ibid.
25   Breger 2000, p. 73.

9: EXIT, PURSUED

1   Erlenmeyer 1885.
2   Erlenmeyer 1887, 2006.
3   Erlenmeyer 1885, p. 290.
4   Ibid., pp. 290–291.
5   Ibid., pp. 297–298.
6   Ibid., p. 298; emphasis as found.
7   J, 1:93.
8   Karch 1998, p. 59.
9   See Imber 2010; Markel 2011; Crews 2011.
10   Quoted by Streatfeild 2001, p. 132.
11   Ibid.
12   Quoted in CP, p. xxxii.
13   Erlenmeyer 1886, p. 483.
14   Ibid., p. 483.
15   Ibid.
16   SK, p. 121.
17   Freud 1887.
18   CP, p. 171; SK, p. 123; emphasis as found.
19   CP, p. 172; SK, pp. 124–125.
20   Bernfeld 1953, pp. 607–609.
21   Smidt and Rank 1885.
22   Compare Obersteiner 1884, 1885, to Obersteiner 1886a, b.
23   CP, p. 176; SK, p. 131.
24   See, e.g., Haas 1983, p. 194n; Springer 2002, p. 22.
25   CP, p. 173; SK, p. 126.
26   Hammond 1886; see the discussion that followed his talk.

10: A FRENCH CONNECTION

1   J, 1:75.
2   See, e.g., SE, 20:13.
3   L, p. 154; translation modified.
4   Makari 2008, p. 26.
5   See 2/23, 3/6, 3/9, 3/21, and 3/23/86.
6   See 11/28/85, 2/10/86, and 3/5/86.
7   J, 1:71–72.
8   See Ellenberger 1970; Evans 1991; Crabtree 1993.
9   Gicklhorn and Gicklhorn 1960, p. 77.
10   Shorter 1992, p. 152.
11   7/1/85.
12   In all of these connections, see Fichtner and Hirschmüller 1988, pp. 107–110, and Hirschmüller 1989a, pp. 91–95.
13   Charcot 1886–93.

14   López Piñero 1983, pp. 29, 44–45; Goetz 2007, p. 104.
15   Goetz et al. 1995, p. 76.
16   As Jan Goldstein observes, some of Charcot's contemporaries did already use the term *névrose* in its modern sense of a nonpsychotic ("neurotic") mental ailment (Goldstein 1987, p. 334).
17   Quoted by Didi-Hubermann 2003, p. 15. See also Micale 1985.
18   Quoted by Goetz et al. 1995, p. 20.
19   For a sample of Charcot's authoritative style, see Furst 2008, pp. 122–152.
20   For contemporary reactions to Charcot's gaze, see Ellenberger 1970, pp. 92–93.
21   Quoted by Cesbron 1909, p. 198.
22   Showalter 1985, 1993.
23   See, however, pp. 187–188 below.
24   Goldstein 1987, p. 334.
25   Hustvedt 2011, p. 37.
26   Goetz et al. 1995, p. 170.
27   Charcot 1886–93, 3:4.
28   For the full set of distinctions that Charcot drew between epilepsy and hysteria, see Charcot 1877–81, 1:306–315, and Charcot and Marie 1892, p. 639.
29   See, e.g., Charcot 1887/88, p. 229.
30   Charcot 1886–93, 3:335.
31   Janet 1895, p. 601; Owen 1971, p. 209.
32   Ibid., p. 336.
33   Quoted by Goetz et al. 1995, p. 206.
34   Charcot 1887/88, p. 207.

11: THE TRAVESTY

1   Janet 1907, p. 21.
2   Quoted by Shorter 1992, p. 186.
3   Charcot 1984, p. 67.
4   Bourneville and Regnard 1876–80, 2:125.
5   Goldstein 1987, p. 331.
6   Ellenberger 1970, p. 99.
7   Marie 1925, p. 580.
8   Hacking 1998, p. 33.
9   See Gastaut 1954; Thornton 1984, pp. 43–49; Gauld 1992, p. 308; Goetz et al. 1995, p. 192; Webster 1995, pp. 55–85. For the gradual shrinkage of the hysteria diagnosis as such organic defects became better understood, see Micale 1993.
10   See Eames 1992.
11   Charcot 1875–87, 3:253.
12   Ibid., 1:230.
13   Ibid.
14   Charcot 1877–81, 1:387.

15 Charcot and Marie 1892, p. 632. For the nineteenth-century shift of emphasis, in defining the essence of the feminine, from the uterus to the ovaries, see Laqueur 1987.
16 Micale 2008, p. 154.
17 Richer 1885, p. 34.
18 Charcot 1984, p. 67.
19 Shorter 1992, p. 181.
20 Harrington 1988, pp. 23–28. See also Harrington 1987.
21 Nicolas 2004, p. 13.
22 Quoted by Harrington 1988, p. 25.
23 See Goetz et al. 1995, pp. 197–200; Hustvedt 2011, p. 121.
24 Binet and Féré 1905.
25 Harrington 1988, pp. 31–33.
26 Hacking 1995, pp. 172–173; Nicolas 2004, pp. 19–20.
27 Hustvedt 2011, p. 127.
28 Ibid., pp. 55–58.
29 See, e.g., Munthe 1936, p. 219.
30 See Duyckaerts 1992.
31 Delboeuf 1886, p. 258.
32 Ibid., p. 124.
33 Ibid., p. 127.
34 Ibid., p. 140.
35 Ibid., p. 269; emphasis as found.
36 The fullest, and also the most provocative, study of the *Iconographie* is Didi-Huberman 2003.
37 Quoted by Hustvedt 2011, p. 96.
38 Quoted by Shorter 1992, p. 185. For a subtle analysis of the patients' rebellion, see Porter 1993, pp. 256–257.
39 Bourneville and Regnard 1876–80. There was also a later publication, the *Nouvelle Iconographie* . . . , which ran from 1888 to 1918.
40 Charcot 1886–93, 3:15.
41 Goetz et al. 1995, p. 241.
42 Marshall 2007.
43 Raymond 1896, p. 15.
44 Delboeuf 1889, p. 65.
45 Charcot 1886–93, 3:476.
46 Charcot 1984, p. 68.
47 Ibid., p. 69.
48 Hustvedt 2011, pp. 195–202.
49 Charcot 1877–81, 1:235.
50 Binet and Féré 1905, pp. 310–311; Shorter 1992, pp. 182–183.
51 For a vivid account of Charcot's poking and pressing the naked belly of a female patient amid a circle of male onlookers, see Charcot 1888/89, p. 276.
52 Bourneville and Regnard 1876–80, 2:128.
53 Charcot 1887/88, p. 176.
54 Hustvedt 2011, pp. 46, 175, 203.
55 Evans 1991, p. 38.

12: ATTACHMENT THERAPY

1   12/3/85; Freud/Minna Bernays 2005, p. 129.
2   Ibid., p. 128.
3   10/23/85.
4   SE, 6:261.
5   10/21/85.
6   11/24/85.
7   11/12/85.
8   See also 11/17/85.
9   11/19/85.
10   11/24/85; L, p. 185.
11   11/24/85.
12   12/1/85, 12/3/85.
13   12/1/85.
14   Ibid.
15   Ibid.
16   12/7/85.
17   Charcot 1875–87; Freud 1886.
18   12/11/85. Jones mistakenly asserted that the whole letter had been drafted
     by Louise Ricchetti.
19   I translate from the French, which appears in Jones's English edition
     (1953, p. 229) but not in his American one.
20   SE, 20:12.
21   12/14/85.
22   1/10/86.
23   1/13/86.
24   Charcot 1892–94.
25   1/27/86.
26   1/28/86.
27   1/10/86.
28   SE, 9:235–241.
29   Ibid., p. 241.
30   1/20/86.
31   SE, 3:16.
32   1/19/86.
33   4/19/86.
34   L, pp. 201–202; translation modified.
35   Ibid., p. 202; translation modified.
36   Ibid.
37   For Freud's idea and its long-delayed implementation, see pp. 324–325
     below.
38   1/13/86.
39   3/19/86.
40   Quoted by Goetz et al. 1995, p. 200.
41   Furse 1997, p. xv. The critic is Elaine Showalter.
42   2/10/86.

13: IN DUBIOUS BATTLE

1   Bernheim 1884, 1886.
2   3/18/86.
3   See, e.g., 3/5, 3/6, 3/8, and 3/18/86.
4   SE, 1:3–15.
5   Ibid., p. 6.
6   Ibid., p. 8; emphasis in the original German.
7   Ibid., p. 11.
8   Ibid., p. 12.
9   Ibid., p. 11.
10   Ibid., p. 13.
11   The papers were delivered on 5/11 and 5/27/86; see J, 1:229.
12   See Bernfeld 1952, pp. 39–46, and Ellenberger 1993, pp. 437–442. The
        most useful brief summary of the occasion and its importance is Sullo-
        way 1992, pp. 35–42.
13   See p. 173–174 above.
14   See Charcot 1984, pp. 18, 23.
15   Carter 1980, p. 265n.
16   See Ellenberger 1970, p. 301.
17   Quoted by Sulloway 1992, p. 39.
18   Ibid., p. 38.
19   SE, 1:23–31.
20   Ibid., p. 25.
21   Ibid., p. 26.
22   Ibid.
23   Ibid., p. 27.
24   Ibid., p. 31.
25   Ibid.
26   SE, 20:15–16; translation modified. "Opposition" bears an initial capital
        letter in the *Standard Edition*'s translation, but since all German nouns
        are capitalized, this orthography makes more of Freud's *in die Opposi-
        tion gedrängt* than he probably intended.
27   Bernfeld 1952, p. 44.
28   See Gicklhorn and Gicklhorn 1960.
29   Bénesteau 2002, p. 186.
30   Sulloway 1992, p. 42.
31   See Bénesteau 2002, p. 186.
32   7/12/92; FF, p. 32.
33   SE, 4:438.
34   12/28/87; FF, p. 17.
35   Bernheim 1889.
36   SE, 1:56–57.
37   Ibid., p. 57.
38   Ibid., p. 43.
39   See FF, p. 20.
40   8/29/88; FF, p. 24.
41   SE, 1:77.

42   Ibid., pp. 77–78.
43   Ibid., p. 78.
44   Ibid.
45   Ibid., p. 79.
46   Gauld 1992, p. 352.
47   Ibid., pp. 342–343.
48   Charcot 1887/88; see Gelfand 1988, p. 583.
49   Bernheim 1892. See also Bernheim 1896.
50   Charcot 1892–94.
51   SE, 1:133, 135–136.
52   Ibid., p. 136.
53   Ibid., p. 139.
54   Ibid., pp. 142–143.
55   Charcot 1894, p. 8n.
56   Gelfand 1988, p. 587.
57   Ibid., p. 582.
58   Meige 1993, p. 343.
59   See Gicklhorn 1969, p. 38.
60   SE, 3:22.
61   Ibid., p. 19.
62   Ibid., pp. 21, 23.
63   Ibid., p. 22.
64   Ibid., pp. 22–23.

14: MEDICINE MAN

1   J, 1:143.
2   6/16/86.
3   Ibid.
4   4/18/86.
5   See 2/21/86, 2/25/86.
6   See 4/14/86.
7   See 6/28/86.
8   8/25/86; Freud/Minna Bernays 2005, p. 169.
9   Quoted by J, 1:148.
10   See 5/10/86.
11   See 7/7/86 and the letter to Minna Bernays of 8/25/86, in Freud/Minna
     Bernays 2005, p. 168.
12   See 5/17/86.
13   5/17/86.
14   5/29/86.
15   See 10/3, 10/18, and 10/24/84.
16   See 11/28/84.
17   Erb 1883, pp. 349, 352.
18   See 5/29/86.
19   3/31/85.
20   SE, 20:16.
21   Gay 1989, p. 62.

22	Freud 1987a, p. 177.
23	See, e.g., 5/26/86, 6/13/86.
24	SE, 20:16.
25	J, 1:235.
26	10/24/87; L, p. 226.
27	See Showalter 1993, p. 297.
28	SE, 1:36.
29	Ibid., p. 55; emphasis as found.
30	SE, 2:267.
31	See Bonomi 1997, 2015.
32	See SE, 1:50.
33	Ibid.
34	SE, 14:13.
35	Bonomi 1997, p. 39.
36	L, p. 217.
37	Ibid., p. 166.
38	See Kern 1973, p. 314n.
39	J, 1:95.
40	Ibid., p. 96.
41	See 2/23/86.
42	Ibid.
43	See 3/21/86.
44	4/25/86.
45	5/15/86.
46	SE, 6:166.
47	Ibid., p. 146.
48	See also Webster 1995, pp. 142–143.
49	Hirschmüller 1989b; Borch-Jacobsen 2011, pp. 28–31.
50	Jolles 1891, p. 1914.
51	Hirschmüller 2005, p. 1032. See also Jolles 1891.
52	See Voswinckel 1988; Hirschmüller 1989b.
53	Freud 1891, p. 1914.
54	Hamilton 2002, p. 889.
55	FS, pp. xiv–xv.
56	Ibid., p. 186.
57	For Eissler's attempt to sanitize the record, see Borch-Jacobsen 2011, p. 45.
58	FS, p. 192.
59	I thank Peter Swales for supplying me with copies of three newspaper articles and two official death records.
60	SE, 3:301–322; 5:486. See also p. 528 below.
61	SE, 5:486.

15: TENDING TO GOLDFISH

1	FF, p. 18.
2	For *névroses*, see p. 162 above. "Neurosis," coined by William Cullen in 1769, has changed its meaning several times. See López Piñero 1983.

3   Shorter 1992, pp. 219–220.
4   Porter 1993, p. 245.
5   Swales 1997, p. 119.
6   See Hacking 1998.
7   Decker 1977, p. 57.
8   Freud/Pfister 1963, pp. 61–62.
9   SE, 2:123.
10   Ibid., p. 265.
11   Quoted by Hartman 1983, p. 567.
12   SE, 12:133.
13   Ibid., p. 132.
14   Quoted by Hartman 1983, p. 567.
15   Ansbacher 1959. Key research about Freud's patients by Henri Ellen-
           berger, Albrecht Hirschmüller, Peter Swales, Ulrike May, Karin Obhol-
           zer, Paul Roazen, and Ines Rieder and Diana Voigt, among others, is
           usefully assembled in Borch-Jacobsen 2011, a book containing much
           further information gleaned from Kurt Eissler's interviews with relatives
           of Freud's patients.
16   J, 1:154; 2:415.
17   J, 2:391.
18   Ibid., p. 390.
19   Drucker 1978.
20   12/2/1909; Freud/Jung 1974, p. 270. My quotations in this paragraph
           can all be found in an essential essay, Swales 1997, to which this whole
           section of the chapter is indebted.
21   9/21/99; FF, p. 374.
22   M. Freud 1957, pp. 24, 33.
23   Schur 1972, p. 247; Freud/Ferenczi 1993, 1:169. See generally Burke
           2006.
24   Freud/Ferenczi 1993, 1:169.
25   FF, p. 368.
26   J, 1:151; Swales 1997, pp. 115–116.
27   9/21/99; FF, p. 374.
28   9/27/99; FF, p. 375.
29   Borch-Jacobsen 2011, p. 82.
30   FF, p. 27.
31   Quoted by Hirschmüller 1978, pp. 157, 160.
32   Swales 1986a, p. 49.
33   2/4/88; FF, pp. 18–19.
34   SE, 7:298.
35   SE, 7:295.
36   Freud 1987a, p. 167.
37   SE, 20:17.
38   SE, 2:108; emphasis as found.
39   SE, 1:108.
40   Quoted by Ellenberger 1993, p. 286.
41   SE, 1:113.
42   Forel 1889, pp. 58, 61.

43   SE, 2:100n.
44   FF, pp. 21–22.
45   Swales 1986a.
46   Ibid., p. 73. These are Swales's words.
47   Ibid.
48   Forel 1889, p. 69.
49   Binet and Féré 1905, pp. 48–151, 221.
50   SE, 7:298.
51   SE, 2:302.
52   See Freud 1987a, p. 111.
53   SE, 1:108.
54   Ibid., p. 109.
55   Ibid., p. 111.
56   Ibid., p. 107.
57   Ibid., p. 111.
58   Ibid.
59   Ferenczi 1988; diary entry of 5/1/1932, p. 93.
60   Binet and Féré 1905, pp. 9–14.
61   See Duyckaerts 1992, pp. 89–90.

16: LESSONS TAKEN AND APPLIED

1   SE, 20:17. See also 23:285.
2   Perry and Laurence 1984, p. 19.
3   See Schiller 1982.
4   Cited by Shorter 1992, p. 242.
5   Ellenberger 1993, pp. 104–118, 301.
6   Frank J. Sulloway's forty-two dense pages on this topic (1992, pp. 277–319) ought to be required reading for anyone who wishes to comment about Freud's originality.
7   Ellenberger 1970, p. 762.
8   See J, 1:181. For the conferences themselves, see Société 1890; Berillon 1890; Ellenberger 1970, pp. 758–761; Alvarado 2010.
9   Société 1890, pp. 146–151.
10   Ibid., p. 150.
11   Janet 1889, pp. 436–440.
12   Delboeuf 1889, p. 71.
13   2/8/97; FF, p. 229.
14   Cited by Borch-Jacobsen in Freud 2015, p. 97.
15   7/28/89; Freud/Minna Bernays 2005, p. 209.
16   SE, 2:177.
17   Ibid., p. 176.
18   Ibid., p. 179.
19   Ibid., p. 178.
20   Swales 1986a, p. 51. The words are Swales's own.
21   Delboeuf 1889, p. 10; Duyckaerts 1992, pp. 89–90.
22   See Swales 1986a, pp. 35–36.
23   See 10/19/82; FMB, pp. 377–379.

24   SE, 1:56.
25   Bernays 1970.
26   See Macmillan 1997, pp. 14–18.
27   SE, 2:177.
28   Ibid., p. 70.
29   Ibid., p. 178.
30   SE, 1:48.
31   Borch-Jacobsen 2011, p. 43.
32   FF, p. 61.
33   Freud/Minna Bernays 2005, p. 233.
34   In Freud 2015 (pp. 98–102, 168–173), Borch-Jacobsen gives a revealing account of the case, resting on previously unpublished correspondence.
35   See ibid., pp. 108–109, 363.
36   Quoted by Swales 1986a, p. 55.
37   Ibid.
38   Quoted by Borch-Jacobsen in Freud 2015, p. 383n.
39   Scammell 2009, p. 8.

17: TRAUMAS ON DEMAND

1   SE, 2:48–49.
2   Ibid., p. 49.
3   For a fine summary of Fanny's life and therapy, see Ellenberger 1993, pp. 273–290.
4   Ibid., pp. 286–289.
5   SE, 2:65.
6   Ibid., p. 73.
7   Ibid., pp. 103–104.
8   Ibid., p. 65n. For anxiety neurosis, see pp. 399–401 below.
9   Andersson 1979, p. 11; see also Ellenberger 1993, p. 282.
10   SE, 2:50, 51n, 54, 64, 86.
11   Ibid., p. 102.
12   Ibid., p. 104.
13   Ibid., p. 51.
14   Ibid., pp. 61–62.
15   Ibid., p. 62n.
16   Ibid., pp. 52–53.
17   Ibid., p. 56.
18   Ibid., p. 56n.
19   Ibid., p. 103.
20   Ibid., p. 77.
21   Ibid., p. 84.
22   Ibid., p. 105n.
23   Borch-Jacobsen 2011, p. 37. I am translating Freud's German via Borch-Jacobsen's French.
24   SE, 20:27.
25   Ibid.

26   Ibid.
27   See Fichtner and Hirschmüller 1988, p. 116 and n.
28   SE, 16:451–452.
29   Ibid., p. 451.
30   SE, 19:195.
31   SE, 20:41.
32   SE, 16:449.
33   SE, 2:109.
34   Ibid., p. 110.
35   Macmillan 1997, p. 85.
36   SE, 2:111.
37   Ibid., p. 154.
38   Ibid., p. 139.
39   Ibid., p. 106.
40   Ibid., p. 118.
41   Thornton 1984, p. 160; Webster 1995, pp. 158–159.
42   SE, 2:121.
43   Ibid., pp. 137–138.
44   Ibid., pp. 135, 137.
45   Ibid., p. 135.
46   Ibid., pp. 135, 137.
47   Ibid., p. 137.
48   Ibid., p. 140.
49   Ibid.
50   Ibid., p. 161.
51   Ibid., p. 150.
52   Ibid., p. 152; emphasis as found.
53   Ibid., p. 150; emphasis as found.
54   Ibid., p. 149.
55   Ibid., p. 154.
56   Ibid., p. 153.
57   Ibid., pp. 140–141, 146.
58   Ibid., pp. 146–147.
59   Ibid., p. 164.
60   Ibid., p. 168; emphasis as found.
61   Ibid., pp. 168–169.
62   Ibid., p. 174; translation modified.
63   Ibid., p. 164.
64   Ibid., p. 155.
65   Ibid., p. 166.
66   Ibid., p. 159.
67   Ibid.
68   Ibid., pp. 159–160.
69   Ibid., p. 160.
70   Borch-Jacobsen 2011, p. 59.
71   Quoted by Gay 1989, p. 72.
72   Peter Swales, personal communication.

73   Gay 1989, p. 72.
74   Ibid., p. 71.
75   Ibid., p. 72.

18: NOW OR NEVER

1   Janet 1892, p. 352. See also Macmillan 1997, pp. 66, 94.
2   SE, 1:169.
3   Ibid., p. 170; emphasis as found.
4   Ibid., p. 169.
5   SE, 20:13–14.
6   J, 1:233.
7   SE, 1:157–158.
8   Ibid., p. 159.
9   SE, 3:75.
10   Ibid., pp. 141–156.
11   Ibid., pp. 157–185.
12   See, e.g., Janet 1925, pp. 601–602.
13   But see Swales 1986a, p. 63n., suggesting that Freud may have known
        Breuer as early as 1874.
14   Elisabeth Ullmann, quoted in Hirschmüller 1989a, p. 56.
15   Hirschmüller 1989a, pp. 229–255.
16   SE, 2:3.
17   Ibid., p. 6; emphasis as found.
18   Ibid., p. 3.
19   Ibid., p. 7n.
20   Janet 1901, p. 495.
21   SE, 2:12–16.
22   Ibid., p. 14.
23   Ibid., p. 7.
24   Janet 1925, 1:188–190.
25   6/28/92; FF, p. 31; translation modified.
26   Freud/Fliess 1954, p. 62.
27   SE, 1:147n. Even Masson's correction, "witticisms," was somewhat euphe-
        mistic.
28   FF, p. 32.
29   Ibid.
30   12/18/92; FF, p. 36.
31   SE, 2:12.
32   Ibid., p. 244.
33   Ibid., p. 123.
34   Ibid., p. 214.
35   Ibid., p. 223.
36   Ibid., pp. 235–236.
37   Ibid., p. 287.
38   Ibid., p. 228.
39   Ibid., p. 245.
40   Ibid., p. 244.

41   Ibid., p. 250.
42   Ibid., pp. 270, 276, 281, 295; emphasis added in each instance.
43   3/1/96; FF, p. 175; emphasis as found.

19: THE FOUNDING DECEPTION

1   SE, 16:280.
2   Ibid., p. 257.
3   Ibid., p. 279; translation modified.
4   Grubrich-Simitis 1997, p. 26.
5   Hirschmüller 1989a, p. 100.
6   SE, 2:23.
7   Ibid., p. 24.
8   Ibid., p. 25.
9   Ibid., p. 29.
10   Ibid., p. 28.
11   Ibid; translation modified.
12   Ibid., p. 30.
13   Ibid.
14   Ibid., p. 32.
15   Ibid., p. 33.
16   Ibid., pp. 35–36.
17   Ibid., p. 36.
18   Ibid., p. 40.
19   Ibid., pp. 40–41.
20   Ibid., p. 43.
21   Ibid.
22   See, e.g., Swales 1986b; Schweighofer 1987; Borch-Jacobsen 1996; Shorter 1997.
23   Borch-Jacobsen 1996, p. 84.
24   SE, 2:46.
25   See, e.g., Bernheim 1965, p. 190.
26   SE, 2:46.
27   Ellenberger 1972.
28   SE, 2:46.
29   Hirschmüller 1989a, pp. 293–296.
30   Ibid., p. 358; 1989a, p. 286.
31   Macmillan 1997, pp. 20–24.
32   Hirschmüller 1989a, p. 115.
33   J, 1:225.
34   Ellenberger 1972, p. 279; Hirschmüller 1989a, p. 116.
35   Forrester 1990, p. 26.
36   Borch-Jacobsen 1996, p. 21.
37   Quoted by Hirschmüller 1989a, p. 295.
38   Quoted by Cranefield 1958, p. 319; translation modified.
39   Skues 2006, p. 7.
40   Hirschmüller 1989a, p. 295; emphasis added.
41   Ibid., p. 291.

42   Skues 2006, p. 37.

43   This is the estimation proposed by Schweighofer 1987.

44   Quoted by Cranefield 1958, p. 319; emphasis as found.

45   Hirschmüller 1989a, p. 295.

46   Ibid., p. 293.

47   See, e.g., Goshen 1952; Orr-Andrawes 1987; Merskey 1992; Thornton 1984; Webster 1995; Rosenbaum and Muroff 1984. Most of the twentieth-century reinterpretations are discussed in Micale 1989.

48   A number of commentators have remarked on the pharmacological aspect of the case. See, e.g., Thornton 1984; Orr-Andrawes 1987; Gilhooley 2002; Ramos 2003.

49   Hirschmüller 1989a, pp. 305–306.

50   Swales 1986b.

51   SE, 2:28, 30.

52   Ibid., p. 30.

53   Hirschmüller 1989a, p. 290.

54   Ibid., p. 306.

55   J, 1:225.

56   In this paragraph and the next I follow Ramos 2003, which in turn draws on standard medical texts.

57   Ramos 2003, p. 242.

58   Hirschmüller 1989a, p. 296.

59   Ibid., p. 293.

60   Ibid., p. 294.

61   Ibid.

62   SE, 20:21.

20: ADJUSTING THE RECORD

1   SE, 2:21.

2   Cranefield 1958, p. 320.

3   See, e.g., SE, 6:257; 8:235; 20:20.

4   SE, 2:246–247.

5   Ibid., p. 200.

6   J, 1:255.

7   SE, 2: xxvi.

8   SE, 14:12. "Untoward event" appeared in English.

9   SE, 20:26.

10   See Skues 2006, pp. 57–62.

11   6/2/32; L, p. 413; translation modified.

12   Ibid.

13   Israëls 1999, pp. 158–164.

14   FMB, 2:385.

15   Ibid., p. 391.

16   Borch-Jacobsen and Shamdasani 2012, pp. 271–273.

17   SE, 2:41n.

18   J, 1:224–225.

19   Hirschmüller 1989a, p. 293.

20 Skues 2006, pp. 93–110.
21 Borch-Jacobsen 1996, p. 32n.
22 J, 1:226.
23 Ellenberger 1970, p. 483; Ellenberger 1972.
24 Tolpin 1993, pp. 158–159.
25 Castelnuovo-Tedesco 1994, p. 59.
26 Britton 1999, p. 2. Britton's history is sternly corrected by Esterson 1999.
27 Schweighofer 1987, pp. 60–61, 132.
28 Gay 1989, p. 67.
29 Eissler 2001, p. 177.
30 Ibid.
31 J, 1:225.
32 Ibid.
33 Information about Pappenheim's Frankfurt years can be found in Edinger 1968; Jensen 1984; Guttmann 2001; Brentzel 2002; Konz 2005.
34 Quoted by Edinger 1968, p. 83.
35 Quoted by Jensen 1970, p. 288.
36 SE, 16:274.
37 Quoted by Forrester and Cameron 1999, p. 934.
38 Ibid.
39 Ibid.
40 Quoted by Borch-Jacobsen 1996, p. 98.
41 Hirschmüller 1989, p. 277.
42 Kavaler-Adler 1991, p. 168.
43 Ibid., pp. 160–161.
44 Steinmann 1984, p. 130.
45 Karpe 1961, p. 23.

21: NARRATIVE TRUTH

1   SE, 2:105.
2   Ibid., pp. 160–161; translation modified.
3   Sherwood 1985, p. 17. See also Hyman 1962, Reve 1994, pp. 16–24; Rohrwasser 2005.
4   Gardiner 1972, p. 135.
5   Berthelsen 1987, p. 38.
6   6/18/09; Freud/Jung 1974, pp. 234–235.
7   SE, 2:125.
8   Ibid., p. 78.
9   The classic exposition of this strategy on Freud's part is Fish 1986.
10 SE, 2:167.
11 Ibid., p. 158.
12 5/30/93; FF, p. 49.
13 FF, p. 54.
14 SE, 2:128; emphasis added.
15 Ibid., p. 129.
16 Ibid.; emphasis as found.

17   Ibid.
18   Ibid., p. 130.
19   Ibid., pp. 130–131.
20   Ibid., p. 133.
21   Ibid.
22   Ibid., p. 131.
23   Ibid., p. 134n.
24   Swales 1988.
25   SE, 2:133.
26   Ibid., p. 131.
27   Ibid., p. 125.
28   Ibid., p. 127.
29   Ibid., p. 129.

22: ARRAYING THE NEUROSES

1   SE, 2:255, 256.
2   Ibid., p. 257; emphasis as found.
3   FF, pp. 37–44.
4   Ibid., p. 56.
5   SE, 3:41–61.
6   Ibid., pp. 85–115.
7   Ibid., pp. 69–82.
8   Ibid., pp. 119–139.
9   This was the fifth edition of Kraepelin's already influential *Psychiatrie*
        (Kraepelin 1896).
10   SE, 1:35.
11   Ibid., p. 118.
12   The early Freud placed heavy emphasis on the noxious effects of those
        practices. See SE, 1:177n, 181, 184, 190–194; 3:81, 100–102, 109–110,
        268.
13   SE, 3:60.
14   SE, 7:113.
15   SE, 2:116.
16   Ibid., p. 164.
17   Ibid., p. 166.
18   Beard 1884.
19   See, e.g., SE, 3:136. See also Carter 1980.
20   Löwenfeld 1895.
21   SE, 3:124–125.
22   Ibid., pp. 124, 134.
23   Ibid., p. 137.
24   FF, p. 38.
25   2/8/93; FF, p. 44.
26   FF, pp. 46–47n.
27   SE, 3:80.
28   Ibid., pp. 96–97.

29	SE, 2:259.
30	Ibid., p. 260.
31	Ibid., pp. 260–261; emphasis as found.
32	Ibid., pp. 259, 261.
33	Ibid., pp. 256, 261.
34	Ibid., p. 256.
35	Ibid., p. 265.

23: THE SECRET SHARER

1	I thank Peter Swales for the information regarding Fliess's speciality.
2	SE, 14:7.
3	SE, 20:65.
4	Masson 1984, p. 206.
5	Schur 1966, 1972.
6	J, 1:151, 170.
7	SE, 4:110 and n.
8	Martha Freud, quoted by René Laforgue in Ruitenbeek 1973, p. 342.
9	See Freud/Jung 1974, p. 456.
10	4/25/94; FF, p. 69.
11	SE, 9:177–204; 11:191–208.
12	SE, 9:194.
13	Ibid., p. 201.
14	Ibid., pp. 198–199.
15	Ibid., p. 198.
16	Ibid., p. 199; emphasis as found.
17	SE, 11:208.
18	SE, 22:133.
19	SE, 11:198–199.
20	Ibid., p. 199.
21	6/19/82; L, pp. 8–9; FMB, p. 93.
22	SE, 11:108.
23	Gay 1989, pp. 60, 61.
24	8/7/01; FF, p. 447.
25	6/28/92; FF, p. 31.
26	8/26/98; FF, p. 323.
27	5/7/00; FF, p. 412.
28	For commentary, see Abraham 1982–83; Krüll 1986; Garner 1989.
29	1/3/99; FF, p. 339.
30	See Sulloway 1992, pp. 147–150; Bonomi 2015, pp. 63–64.
31	See Shorter 1992, pp. 64–68.
32	Fliess 1897, p. iii.
33	5/30/93; FF, p. 49.
34	"Draft C" [1893]; FF, p. 45.
35	FF, p. 45; emphasis added.
36	FF, p. 47n.
37	Shorter 1992, p. 51.

38 See Draft C/2, which appears only in the German edition of the Fliess letters (Freud 1986, pp. 36–39).

39 See Fliess 1897, pp. 133–145.

40 Ibid., p. iv.

41 Ibid., pp. 156–190.

42 Fliess 1906; see Sulloway 1992, p. 141.

43 3/1/96; FF, p. 173.

44 Ibid., p. 174.

45 6/30/96; FF, p. 193.

46 Ibid., p. 210.

47 Ibid., p. 212.

48 FF, p. 159.

49 6/30/96; FF, p. 193.

50 12/4/96; FF, p. 204.

51 Freud 1986, p. xv.

52 Krafft-Ebing 1886.

53 SE, 7:177 and n.

54 J, 2:422.

55 SE, 7:166n.

56 Sulloway 1992, p. 199.

57 Borch-Jacobsen and Shamdasani 2012, pp. 237–239.

58 6/30/96; FF, p. 193; Freud 1954, p. 169.

59 Freud 1954, p. 4.

60 Ibid., pp. 8, 14.

61 Sulloway 1992, p. 149.

24: THE FREUDIAN NEURON

1 FF, p. 139.

2 Ibid., p. 141.

3 J, 1:392.

4 Sulloway 1992, p. 119.

5 See, e.g., FF, pp. 172, 180, 216, 266, 301–302.

6 Sulloway 1992, p. 130.

7 7/30/98; FF, p. 320.

8 Pribram and Gill 1976, p. 14.

9 Ibid., p. 61.

10 SE, 1:293.

11 The following discussion is indebted to Amacher 1965; Pribram and Gill 1976; McCarley and Hobson 1977; Swanson 1977; Levin 1978; Køppe 1983; Mancia 1983; Shepherd 1991; Sulloway 1992; Macmillan 1997.

12 J, 1:50.

13 Solms 2002, pp. 20–21.

14 See Køppe 1983.

15 See Freud 1884b.

16 SE, 1:160.

17 Køppe 1983, p. 24.

18	5/25/95; FF, p. 129.
19	See Amacher 1965.
20	6/22/94; FF, p. 83.
21	SE, 1:295.
22	Ibid.
23	Ibid., pp. 299–302, 309–310.
24	Ibid., pp. 302, 303; emphasis as found.
25	Ibid., p. 315.
26	Ibid., p. 296.
27	See McCarley and Hobson 1977; Swanson 1977; Køppe 1983.
28	SE, 1:297.
29	Ibid.
30	See p. 428 above.
31	12/8/95; FF, pp. 154–155.
32	1/1/96; FF, pp. 159–160.
33	FF, pp. 207–208.
34	See p. 663 below.
35	FF, pp. 207–208; emphasis as found.
36	Ibid., p. 159.
37	Ibid., p. 161.
38	5/25/95; 8/6/95; FF, pp. 129, 135.
39	2/1/00; FF, p. 398.
40	J, 1:383.
41	Ibid., p. 384.
42	Ibid.
43	Ibid.
44	Solms and Saling 1986. See also Forrester 1980; Greenberg 1997.
45	Freud 1953, p. 55.
46	Solms and Saling 1986, p. 400.
47	Ibid., pp. 400, 401.
48	SE, 15:21.
49	SE, 14:174.
50	SE, 16:393.
51	SE, 13:181–182.
52	SE, 14:78. See also SE, 7:278–279; 16:388–389, 436; 20:152–153, 231; 21:240, 242–243.
53	SE, 21:242n.
54	Pribram and Gill 1976, p. 10.
55	McCarley and Hobson 1977, p. 1219.
56	Swanson 1977, pp. 608–611.
57	Thornton 1984, Chapter 16.
58	Blanton 1971, pp. 47–48. See also SE, 20:57–58.
59	See Lothane 1998, p. 60.

25: DIMINISHED CAPACITY

1	J, 1:241–242.
2	"Draft C," c. 4/93; FF, pp. 45–46.

3   5/21/94; FF, p. 74.
4   5/25/95; FF, p. 129.
5   FF, p. 146.
6   10/15/95; FF, p. 144.
7   Makari 2008, p. 71.
8   SE, 4: 111.
9   Quoted by Swales 1983, p. 12n.
10   Quoted by Trosman and Wolf 1973, p. 231.
11   See, e.g., Scheidt 1973, pp. 406–407; Bonomi 2015, p. 125.
12   5/30/93; FF, p. 49.
13   J, 1:308.
14   See Fliess 1897, p. 109.
15   4/19/94; FF, p. 67.
16   Ibid., p, 68.
17   4/20/95; FF, p. 125.
18   Hammond 1886, p. 638.
19   Thornton 1984, pp. 131–133.
20   See Stengle 2008; Vongpatanasin et al. 1999; Tuncel et al. 2002.
21   See 11/27/93; FF, p. 61; J, 1:309; Schur 1972, p. 82.
22   Schur 1972, p. 82.
23   J, 1:309.
24   6/12/95; FF, pp. 131–132.
25   FF, pp. 106, 115–116, 126, 127.
26   Ibid., p. 132.
27   Quoted in CP, p. 248.
28   Quoted by J, 1:167.
29   J, 1:308.
30   8/23/94; FF, p. 94.
31   10/19/99; FF, p. 380.
32   12/12/97; FF, p. 285.
33   Quoted in FF, p. 151n.
34   See 5/21/94; FF, p. 74.

26: DIRE THERAPY

1   Appignanesi and Forrester 2005, p. 133.
2   See p. 482n. below.
3   J, 2:421.
4   Quoted by Borch-Jacobsen and Shamdasani 2012, p. 244.
5   See Magaziner 1975, pp. 216–219.
6   Eckstein 1899–1900.
7   See Masson 1984, pp. 236–237.
8   Eckstein 1904.
9   See Lynn 1997, p. 82.
10   SE, 1:353; emphasis as found.
11   Ibid.; emphasis added.
12   Ibid., p. 353; emphasis added.
13   Ibid., p. 356.

14   Freud 1895, p. 140. In 1896 and 1898 Freud continued to speculate about connections between neurasthenia and "defense" neuroses; see, e.g., SE, 3:168; 265–266.
15   FF, p. 107.
16   Ibid., p. 113; emphasis added.
17   For the hypothesis that Fliess, not Freud, underwent a serious nasal operation in February 1895, see the editorial note to Freud 1986, pp. 105–106n.
18   Schur 1972, p. 80.
19   3/4/95; FF, p. 114.
20   2/25/95; FF. p. 112.
21   3/8/95; FF, p. 118.
22   Ibid., pp. 116–117.
23   Ibid., p. 117.
24   Ibid., pp. 117–118.
25   3/13/95; FF, p. 120.
26   FF, p. 124.
27   Ibid., p. 123.
28   Ibid., p. 124.
29   Ibid., p. 125.
30   Ibid.; emphasis as found.
31   Ibid., p. 128; emphasis as found.
32   5/25/95; FF, p. 130.
33   Ibid., p. 181.
34   FF, p. 183; emphasis as found; translation modified.
35   Ibid., p. 186.
36   For the persistence of "pressure," see "Draft J"; FF, p. 156.
37   FF, p. 186; translation modified.
38   Appignanesi and Forrester 2005, p. 137; emphasis as found.
39   FF, p. 286. For discussion, see p. 499 below.
40   Ibid.
41   Masson 1984, p. 237.
42   Eckstein 1904, p. 9.
43   Ibid., pp. 13, 15, 18–19.
44   Ibid., p. 19.
45   Lynn 1997, pp. 79–80.
46   Masson 1984, pp. 248–249.
47   Ibid., p. 70.
48   Ibid., p. 248; translation modified.
49   Lynn 1997, p. 81.
50   Quoted by Masson 1984, pp. 249–250.
51   Ibid., p. 250.
52   SE, 23:222.

27: SELF-SEDUCED

1   10/15/95; FF, p. 144; emphasis as found.
2   11/2/95; FF, p. 149.

3   SE, 2:112.
4   See Sebeok and Rosenthal 1981.
5   SE, 3:165, 166.
6   Ibid., p. 165.
7   Ibid., pp. 165–166.
8   Ibid., p. 211; emphasis as found.
9   4/28/97; FF, p. 238.
10   Masson 1984.
11   SE, 3:207, 210.
12   "Draft K"; FF, p. 163.
13   SE, 3:215.
14   Ibid., pp. 152, 164.
15   Ibid., p. 155.
16   FF, pp. 159–160.
17   Ibid., p. 160.
18   "Draft K," included with the letter of 1/1/96; FF, p. 163.
19   Ibid.
20   SE, 3:201.
21   Ibid., p. 203.
22   Ibid., pp. 149, 199, 220.
23   Ibid., p. 199; emphasis as found.
24   Ibid., p. 155.
25   Ibid., p. 162.
26   Ibid., p. 211.
27   Ibid., p. 206.
28   Ibid., pp. 198–199.
29   Ibid., p. 192. For discussion of Freud's rhetoric in this full passage, see
        Orrells 2011. For his use of the archaeological metaphor in general,
        see Armstrong 2005.
30   SE, 3:174.
31   Ibid., p. 164.
32   Ibid., p. 199.
33   FF, p. 185.
34   Ibid., p. 218.
35   Ibid., p. 220.
36   Ibid., p. 233.
37   SE, 3:196.
38   Ibid.
39   Ibid., p. 203.
40   Ibid., p. 200.
41   See ibid., pp. 210, 213–214.
42   See ibid., pp. 199, 204.
43   Ibid., p. 204.
44   Ibid., p. 153.
45   SE, 3:154.
46   SE, 22:146.
47   4/26/86; FF, p. 184.
48   Ibid.

49   See Loftus and Ketcham 1996; Ofshe and Watters 1996; Pendergrast
        1996; Pope 1997; McNally 2003; McHugh 2008.
50   FF, p. 286.
51   SE, 2:281.
52   SE, 3:269.
53   1/3/97; FF, pp. 220–221.
54   SE, 5:451–452; translation modified.
55   Ibid., p. 452.
56   12/22/97; FF, pp. 288–289.
57   Ibid., p. 289.
58   1/12/97; FF, pp. 223–224.
59   1/24/97; FF, p. 226.
60   1/17/96; FF, p. 218.
61   SE, 3:215.
62   FF, p. 227.
63   Ibid.
64   For Freud's reading in the literature of demonology, see Swales 1989c.
65   See 1/17/97; FF, p. 225.
66   1/17/97; FF, pp. 224–225.
67   SE, 19:72.

28: THE BREAKTHROUGH THAT WASN'T

1   FF, p. 264.
2   FF, p. 266.
3   9/21/97; FF, pp. 264–265.
4   Ibid., p. 266.
5   Ibid., p. 265.
6   Freud 1954, p. 216.
7   SE, 7:128.
8   FF, p. 266.
9   J, 1:267.
10   Gay 1989, p. 96.
11   Freud 1950, p. 187; FF, p. 266n.
12   See 12/12/97; FF, p. 286; 12/22/97; FF, pp. 288–289.
13   Masson 1984.
14   For a definitive critique of Masson's position, see Esterson 1998.
15   2/9/98; FF, p. 299.
16   8/31/98; FF, p. 325.
17   10/23/98; FF, p. 332.
18   FF, p. 338.
19   See "Draft N," FF, p. 250; pp. 272–273; and p. 601 below.
20   SE, 4:260–266.
21   SE, 7:275–277.
22   SE, 11:47; emphasis as found.
23   See Cioffi 1998 [1974], pp. 199–204; Schimek 1987; Israëls and Schatzman
        1993; Scharnberg 1993; Webster 1995; Macmillan 1997; Israëls 1999;
        Esterson 2001; Borch-Jacobsen 2009. The one psychoanalyst in this

grouping, Jean Schimek, subsequently protested the appropriation of his article for "Freud bashing" (Crews et al. 1995, p. 77).

24   SE, 20:34.
25   Ibid.
26   SE, 7:190.
27   SE, 7:274.
28   Ibid.
29   SE, 14:17.
30   Ibid.
31   Ibid.
32   Ibid.
33   SE, 14:17–18; emphasis as found.
34   SE, 16:370.
35   SE, 20:34.
36   SE, 16:370.
37   SE, 21:238.
38   SE, 22:120.
39   FF, p. 272.
40   J, 1:307.
41   J, 1:54.

29: THE LABYRINTH OF REPROACHES

1   Mahony 1979, p. 67.
2   Ibid., pp. 67–68.
3   See, e.g., Borch–Jacobsen 2009, p. 161.
4   See SE, 4:107–120.
5   Ibid., p. xxvi.
6   FF, p. 230.
7   Ibid., pp. 230–231.
8   11/2/96; FF, p. 202.
9   J, 1:304.
10   Ibid., pp. 305–306.
11   FF, pp. 253–254.
12   11/5/97, 11/14/97, 12/3/97, 1/4/98; FF, pp. 277, 281, 284, 291.
13   Bonomi 2015, p. 88.
14   10/3/97; FF, p. 268.
15   10/11/99; FF, p. 379.
16   Ibid. For discussion of the self-analytic Freud's references to Faust and to Goethe's own quest for knowledge of his origins, see Anzieu 1986, p. 238.
17   10/4/97; FF, p. 269.
18   See Rudnytsky 1987; Davis 1990; Micale 2008. Peter Swales disclosed Fellner's identity in a lecture (1996) that was delivered from notes and never written up (personal communication).
19   3/11/00; FF, p. 403.
20   For Königstein's dissatisfaction with his old friend, see Swales 1983, pp. 27–35.

21   8/14/97; FF, p. 261.
22   10/4/97; FF, p. 269.
23   See, especially, 1/4/98; FF, pp. 292–293.
24   8/14/97; FF, p. 261.
25   10/27/97; FF, p. 275.
26   12/22/97; FF, p. 287.
27   SE, 3:299–322.
28   Bernfeld 1946.
29   SE, 3:318–320.
30   Ibid., p. 317.
31   Ibid.
32   Ibid., pp. 318–319.
33   10/3/97; FF, p. 268.
34   10/3/97; FF, p. 268.
35   See SE, 5:421–425.
36   J, 1:11.
37   See pp. 78–79 above.
38   SE, 4:201; emphasis as found.
39   SE, 5:481–482; translation modified.
40   SE, 3:171; emphasis added.
41   Ibid., p. 208.
42   Ibid., p. 155.
43   Ibid., pp. 164–165; emphasis added.
44   Ibid., p. 210; emphasis added.
45   Ibid., p. 206; emphasis added.
46   Ibid., p. 208; emphasis added.
47   FF, p. 318.
48   Ibid., p. 317.
49   J, 2:343.
50   Anzieu 1986, pp. 287–288.
51   SE, 4:172.
52   FF, p. 249.
53   10/3/97; FF, p. 268.
54   FF, p. 268. Élisabeth Roudinesco mistakenly relies on Freud's dream as a source of information about his real nursemaid (Roudinesco 2016, p. 15).
55   10/3/97; FF, p. 268.
56   SE, 7:145n.
57   SE, 22:133.
58   Ibid., p. 123; translation modified.
59   Ibid., p. 122.
60   Ibid., p. 123.
61   10/3/97; FF, p. 268.
62   See, e.g., SE, 22:123.
63   SE, 11:57–137.
64   See SE, 11:177–190.
65   Ibid., p. 186.

30: WISHING MAKES IT SO

1   3/23/00; FF. pp. 405–406.
2   Ibid., p. 345.
3   Ibid., p. 355.
4   Ibid., p. 357.
5   Ibid., p. 359.
6   Ibid., pp. 243–244; translation modified.
7   Ibid., p. 243.
8   Ibid.
9   Ibid., p. 299.
10   Ibid., p. 354. "The Silence of the Forest" was the title of a contemporary painting.
11   Ibid., p. 338; translation modified.
12   8/7/01; FF, p. 447.
13   9/11/99; FF, p. 371; translation modified.
14   5/128/99; FF, p. 353.
15   See, e.g., Welsh 1994.
16   See Schorske 1980; McGrath 1986.
17   FF, p. 365.
18   Hyman 1962, p. 312.
19   5/28/99; FF, p. 353.
20   9/6/99; FF, p. 369; translation modified.
21   FF, p. 368.
22   SE, 5:469; translation modified.
23   SE, 4:146.
24   Ibid., p. 470; emphasis as found.
25   See Hobson 2002; Domhoff 2003.
26   See Vande Kemp 1981; Schwartz 2000.
27   SE, 4:163.
28   SE, 4:151–152.
29   See, especially, Sulloway 1992; Macmillan 1997; Appignanesi and Forrester 2005.
30   Macmillan 1997, p. 281.
31   SE, 4:277.
32   See States 1988; Lakoff 1993, 1997.
33   Freud/Abraham 2002, p. 21.
34   Ibid. For discussion, see Appignanesi and Forrester 2005, pp. 117–133.
35   See Langs 1984.
36   See Mayer 2001–2.
37   SE, 4:121; emphasis as found.
38   Wilcocks 1994, pp. 246–253.
39   Glymour 1983, pp. 70–71.

31: SEXUAL HEALING

1   J, 2:6.
2   Ibid., p. 387. Jones's informant was Freud's daughter-in-law Lucie Freud.

3   Anzieu 1986, p. 527.
4   5/25/99; FF, p. 351.
5   FF, pp. 358–359.
6   Gay 1990, p. 165.
7   J, 1:104; emphasis as found.
8   12/23/85; L, pp. 187–188.
9   Hugo 2002, p. 243. For the unexpurgated *Notre-Dame*, see p. 565
         above.
10   8/22/82; Freud/Minna Bernays 2005, p. 37.
11   J, 1:164–165. The letter is from 12/27/83; FMB, 2:541.
12   SE, 5:397.
13   2/7/86; L, pp. 204–205; translation modified.
14   Gay 1989, p. 76.
15   5/7/86; Freud/Minna Bernays 2005, p. 151.
16   4/27/93; ibid., p. 237.
17   Behling 2005, p. 77.
18   3/7/96; FF, p. 177.
19   Freud 2002, passim.
20   Gay 1989, p. 382.
21   J, 2:5, 421; 1:153.
22   Gay 1989, p. 163.
23   Roudinesco 2016, pp. 128, 149, 237, 475.
24   SE, 9:177–204.
25   Ibid., pp. 194, 195.
26   Ibid., p. 191; translation modified.
27   See Boyer 1978.
28   7/8/15; L, p. 308.
29   Ibid.; translation modified.
30   Quoted by Edmunds 1999, p. 264.
31   Maciejewski 2006a, 2006b, 2008.
32   See, e.g., Hirschmüller 2007; Lothane 2007.
33   Freud 2002, p. 131.
34   Quoted by Tögel 2002, p. 107.
35   Swales 1982a; 1982b; 1986b; 2003. Swales 2003 is focused on the events
         of 1898.
36   SE, 4:207.
37   Swales 1989b.
38   FF, p. 423.
39   Ibid.
40   Ibid.
41   J, 1:336.
42   Tögel 2002, p. 126.
43   9/14/00; FF, p. 423.
44   FF, p. 427.
45   SE, 5:671.
46   Ibid., p. 640.
47   Ibid., pp. 656–657, 672; emphasis as found.

48   Ibid., p. 672; emphasis as found.
49   Ibid., p. 656.
50   Ibid., p. 672.
51   SE, 6:120.
52   SE, 18:167.

32: THE UNBORN AVENGER

1   9/14/00; FF, p. 424.
2   SE, 6: 8–9; emphasis as found.
3   Ibid., p. 11.
4   Ibid.
5   Ibid., p. 14.
6   Timpanaro 1976.
7   Quoted by Falk 1977, p. 7.
8   SE, 7:116–118.
9   Swales 1982, p. 12.
10   Skues 2001, p. 1197.
11   3/23/1900; FF, pp. 406–407.
12   9/24/1900; FF, p. 425. Masson's translation is inaccurate; see Skues
        2001, pp. 1195–1196, n. 12.
13   Timpanaro 1976, p. 42.
14   SE, 6:12n.
15   See Gay 1990, p. 165.
16   Quoted by Kerr 1993, p. 136.
17   Ibid.
18   Ibid.
19   Ibid.
20   See Rudnytsky 2011, p. 16.
21   Kerr 1993, p. 137.
22   12/26/12; Freud/Ferenczi 1993, p. 453.
23   Quoted by Gale 2015, p. 62.
24   J, 1:124; 2:408.
25   Jung 1973, p. 158.

33: GIRL TROUBLE

1   3/15/98; FF, p. 303.
2   1/25/01; FF, p. 433.
3   See Rogow 1978. Further context can be found in Decker 1991.
4   SE, 7:105.
5   Ibid., p. 23.
6   Ibid.
7   Ibid., p. 75.
8   Ibid., p. 59.
9   Ibid., p. 38.
10   Ibid., pp. 101–103.
11   Ibid., p. 22.

12   Ibid., p. 105.
13   Ibid., p. 69 and n.
14   Ibid., p. 29n.
15   Ibid., p. 38n; translation modified.
16   Ibid.
17   Ibid.; translation modified.
18   Ibid., p. 61.
19   Ibid., p. 109.
20   Ibid., p. 119.
21   Ibid., p. 42.
22   See SE, 6:241.
23   SE, 7:107.
24   Ibid., p. 109.
25   10/14/00; FF, p. 427.
26   SE, 7:7.
27   Ibid., pp. 22, 27. Freud wrote "in her eighth year," but another reference (p. 21) shows that he meant age eight, not seven.
28   Ibid., p. 39.
29   Ibid., pp. 46–47.
30   Ibid., p. 47.
31   Ibid., p. 48.
32   SE, 7:47.
33   Ibid.
34   Ibid., pp. 70, 83.
35   Ibid., pp. 104n, 120n.
36   Deutsch 1990, p. 38.
37   SE, 7:80.
38   Ibid., p. 75.
39   Makari 1997, p. 1074.
40   SE, 7:77.
41   Ibid., p. 38.
42   Ibid., p. 78.
43   The two dreams are sensitively discussed in McCaffrey 1984.
44   SE, 7:64.
45   Ibid., p. 67n.
46   Ibid., p. 74.
47   Ibid., p. 94.
48   Ibid., pp. 98, 110; emphasis as found.
49   Ibid., p. 99; translation modified.
50   Ibid., pp. 99–100; emphasis as found.
51   Ibid., p. 113.
52   Ibid., p. 120.
53   Ibid., p. 121.
54   Ibid., pp. 120–121.
55   Ibid., p. 122.
56   Ibid.
57   J, 2:256.
58   Mahony 1996, pp. 139–142. See also SE, 7:4–5.

59   Deutsch 1990, p. 37.
60   Ibid., p. 43.
61   Quoted by Mahony 1996, p. 16.
62   SE, 7:24.
63   Ibid., pp. 12, 49.
64   Ibid., p. 18.
65   Ibid., p. 41.
66   Ibid., p. 115.
67   Ibid., p. 85.
68   Ibid., pp. 77–78.
69   J, 1:364.
70   Erikson 1962.
71   Sand 1983.
72   Mahony 2005, pp. 37–38.

34: A LAW UNTO HIMSELF

1   J, 2:3.
2   Ibid., p. 4.
3   Ibid., p. 3.
4   Roazen 1969, p. 88.
5   Merton 1976.
6   See Trosman 1969.
7   SE, 7:220 and n; translation modified.
8   Ibid., p. 143n.
9   For discussion of these complex doings, see Sulloway 1992, pp. 223–229.
10   J, 1:315.
11   10/6/10; Freud/Ferenczi 1993, p. 221; emphasis as found.
12   2/17/08; Freud/Jung 1974, p. 121; translation modified.
13   See Farrell 1996.
14   10/6/10; Freud/Ferenczi 1993, p. 221.
15   See, e.g., Breger 2000, pp. 240–244; Geller 2007, pp. 157–158.
16   7/8/15; L, pp. 308–309.
17   See J, 1:339–341; Gay 1989, pp. 136–139.
18   Gay 1989, p. 139.
19   See Gicklhorn and Gicklhorn 1960.
20   Graf 1942, p. 470.
21   Wittels 1924, p. 134.
22   Binswanger 1956, p. 4.
23   Sachs 1944, pp. 3–4.
24   Graf 1942, p. 471.
25   Karl Furtmüller, quoted in Handlbauer 1998, p. 24.
26   Quoted by Decker 1977, p. 185n.
27   Stekel 1950, p. 106.
28   Nunberg and Federn 1962–1975, 1:140–142.
29   Binswanger 1957, p. 3.
30   Jung 1965, pp. 149–150.

31   Ibid., p. 150.
32   Binswanger 1956, p. 12.
33   SE, 7:109.
34   SE, 17:140–141.
35   12/2/30; Freud/Zweig 1970, p. 23.
36   Wollheim 1981, p. 252.
37   Lear 2010, p. 34.
38   Bollas 2007, p. 2.
39   1/9/08; Freud/Abraham 2002, p. 21.
40   FF, p. 252; translation modified; emphasis added.
41   SE, 5:469, 470.
42   FF, p. 398.
43   For Freud's profound debt to Nietzsche and his coy attempts to deny it,
     see Rudnytsky 1987, pp. 198–223; Lehrer 1995.
44   Nietzsche 1999, pp. 47–48.
45   12/3/97; FF, p. 285.
46   10/23/98; FF, p. 332.
47   3/2/99; FF, p. 347.
48   9/19/01; FF, p. 449.
49   SE, 4:196–197.
50   See, e.g., Vitz 1988; E. M. Jones 1993.
51   See Swan 1974.
52   10/3/97; FF, p. 268.
53   See J, 3:375–407; Moreau 1976; Roustang 1983; Bénesteau 2002; Onfray
     2010.
54   10/9/96; FF, p. 200.
55   J, 3:386.
56   Ibid., p. 381.
57   SE, 18:173–194, 195–220; 22:31–56.
58   SE, 18:219; 22:37.
59   SE, 22:38; emphasis as found.
60   4/16/09; Freud/Jung 1974, pp. 218–220.
61   J, 3:375.
62   2/19/99; FF, p. 346.
63   Ibid.
64   Onfray 2010, p. 373.
65   SE, 7:113.
66   Wortis 1954, p. 84.
67   SE, 22:55.
68   SE, 18:250.
69   SE, 16:458.
70   SE, 19:202.
71   SE, 3:302.
72   Ibid., p. 309.
73   SE, 6:12.
74   SE, 10:251–318; J, 1:327.
75   Mahony 1986. Mahony's findings are concisely summarized in Esterson
     1993, pp. 62–67.

76   Moll 1913, p. 190.
77   Poe 1978, p. 521.

35: IMPOSING HIS WILL

1   Roazen 1995, p. 185.
2   Sulloway 1992, p. 185.
3   Roazen 1975, p. 15.
4   Stengers and van Neck 2001, pp. 138–141; Onfray 2010, pp. 497–504.
5   Lynn 1997, p. 74.
6   Roazen 1993, p. 181.
7   4/9/10; 4/21/10; Freud/Binswanger 2003, pp. 32, 34.
8   SE, 10:120.
9   Quoted by J, 2:125.
10   Kardiner 1977, pp. 68–69.
11   SE, 22:151.
12   See Roazen 1995; Lohser and Newton 1996; Swales 1997; Falzeder
        2007; Borch-Jacobsen 2011. Falzeder's article cites the sources for remi-
        niscences by many patients.
13   J, 2:79–80.
14   SE, 18:145–172.
15   Ibid., p. 147.
16   Borch-Jacobsen 2011, pp. 180–186.
17   See Wolpe and Rachman 1999.
18   Kardiner 1977, p. 76.
19   Ibid.
20   SE, 18:171.
21   Kardiner 1977, p. 59.
22   Ibid., p. 61.
23   Ibid., p. 84.
24   Alexander et al. 1966, p. 255.
25   Ferenczi 1988, p. 93.
26   Malcolm 1982, p. 37.
27   Roazen 1995, p. 76.
28   Ferenczi 1988, p. 93.
29   Wortis 1954, p. 18.
30   Binswanger 1956, p. 56.
31   The main exception to the rule, as might be anticipated, is Peter Swales
        (1997).
32   3/14/11; Freud/Jung 1974, p. 402.
33   Roazen 1995, p. 13; Wortis 1954, p. 22.
34   7/21/11; Freud/Jung 1974, p. 436.
35   Obholzer 1982, p. 34.
36   Onfray 2010, p. 434.
37   Obholzer 1982, p. 42.
38   See 3/11/02; FF, pp. 456–457.
39   Swales 1988, pp. 148–149.
40   Ferenczi 1988, p. 93. See also pp. 118, 186.

41	See generally Swales 1997.
42	12/17/11; Freud/Jung 1974, pp. 473–474. See also Falzeder 1994.
43	Obholzer 1982, pp. 171–172.
44	See Lynn 1993.
45	SE, 19:253.
46	12/18/12; Freud/Jung 1974, p. 535.
47	Breger 2000, p. 209.
48	See Roustang 1982; Grosskurth 1991; Bénesteau 2002.
49	J, 3:176.
50	Roazen 1969; Roustang 1983.
51	SE, 17:175–204.
52	Ibid., p. 191.
53	Ibid., p. 189.
54	Young-Bruehl 1988, p. 108.
55	Edmonds 1988; reprinted in Crews 1989, pp. 260–276.
56	Edmunds 1999, p. 264.
57	Ibid., p. 265.
58	Ibid., p. 268.
59	Ibid.
60	Ibid., p. 272.
61	Ibid., p. 270.
62	Ibid.
63	Ibid., p. 261.

APPENDIX: ARE WE BEING FREUDIAN YET?

1	See pp. 388, 487–488 above.
2	SE, 9:187.
3	A. Freud 1946.
4	SE, 7:247–254.
5	A famous admission of this fact is Marmor 1962.
6	See SE, 7:116.
7	See SE, 11:144–145.
8	SE, 11:47; emphasis as found.
9	See 4/2/96; FF, p. 180.
10	See SE, 19:12–59.

WORKS CITED

For abbreviated titles, see p. xvii.

Abraham, Ruth. 1982–83. "Freud's Mother Conflict and the Formulation of the Oedipal Father." *Psac. Rev.*, 69:441–453.

Aeschlimann, Jürg. 1980. *Rudolf Brun (1885–1969): Leben und Werk des Zürcher Neurologen, Psychoanalytikers und Entomologen*. [Medical dissertation.] Zürich: Juris.

Alexander, Franz, Samuel Eisenstein, and Martin Grotjahn. 1966. (Eds.) *Psychoanalytic Pioneers*. New York: Basic.

Altman, Adam J., Daniel M. Albert, and George A. Fournier. 1985. "Cocaine's Use in Ophthalmology: Our 100-Year Heritage." *Survey of Ophthalmology*, 29:300–306.

Alvarado, Carlos S. 2010. "Nineteenth-Century Suggestion and Magnetism: Hypnosis at the International Congress of Physiological Psychology (1889)." *Contemporary Hypnosis*, 27:48–60.

Amacher, Peter. 1965. "Freud's Neurological Education and Its Influence on Psychoanalytic Theory." *Psychological Issues*, 4:1–87.

Andersson, Ola. 1979. "A Supplement to Freud's Case History of 'Frau Emmy v. N' in *Studies on Hysteria* 1895." *Scandinavian Psac. Rev.*, 2:5–16.

[Anon.] 1884. [From Our Special Correspondent. Vienna.] "Cocaine." (Philadelphia) *Medical News*, 45:502.

Ansbacher, Heinz L. 1959. "The Significance of the Socio-economic Status of the Patients of Freud and of Adler." *Am. J. Psychotherapy*, 13:376–382.

Anzieu, Didier. 1986. *Freud's Self-Analysis*. [1975.] London: Hogarth and Institute Psa.

Appignanesi, Lisa, and John Forrester. 2005. *Freud's Women*. [1992.] London: Orion.

Armstrong, Richard H. 2005. *A Compulsion for Antiquity: Freud and the Ancient World*. Ithaca, NY, and London: Cornell U.

Beard, George Miller. 1881. *American Nervousness: Its Causes and Consequences; A Supplement to Nervous Exhaustion (Neurasthenia)*. New York: Putnam's.

_____. 1884. *Sexual Neurasthenia (Nervous Exhaustion), Its Hygiene, Causes, Symptoms and Treatment*. New York: Treat.

Becker, Hortense Koller. 1974. "'Coca Koller': Carl Koller's Discovery of Local Anesthesia." [1963.] In CP, pp. 263–290.

Behling, Katja. 2005. *Martha Freud: A Biography*. Trans. R. D. V. Glascow. [2003.] Malden, MA: Polity.

Bénesteau, Jacques. 2002. *Mensonges freudiens: Histoire d'une désinformation séculaire*. Liège: Mardaga.

Berillon, Edgar. 1890. (Ed.) *Premier Congrès International de l'Hypnotisme Expérimental et Thérapeutique: Comptes Rendus*. Paris: Doin.

Bernays, Jacob. 1970. *Grundzüge der verlorenen Abhandlung des Aristoteles über Wirkung der Tragödie*. [1857, 1880.] New York: Olms.

Bernfeld, Siegfried. 1946. "An Unknown Autobiographical Fragment by Freud." *Am. Imago*, 4:3–19.

_____. 1949. "Freud's Scientific Beginnings." *Am. Imago*, 6:163–196.

_____. 1951. "Sigmund Freud, M.D., 1882–1885." *Int. J. Psa.*, 32:204–217.

_____. 1952. "Freud's First Year in Practice, 1886–1887." *Bull. Meninger Clinic*, 16:37–48.

_____. 1953. "Freud's Studies on Cocaine, 1884–1887." *J. Am. Psac. Assn.*, 1:581–613.

Bernheim, Hippolyte. 1884. *De la suggestion dans l'état hypnotique et dans l'état de veille*. Paris: Doin.

_____. 1886. *De la suggestion et de ses applications à la thérapeutique*. Paris: Doin.

_____. 1889. *Die Suggestion und ihre Heilwirkung*. 2 vols. Trans. Sigmund Freud. Leipzig and Vienna: Deuticke.

_____. 1892. *Neue Studien über Hypnotismus, Suggestion und Psychotherapie*. Trans. Sigmund Freud. Leipzig and Vienna: Deuticke.

_____. 1896. *Die Suggestion und ihre Heilwirkung*. 2 vols. 2d. ed. Trans. Sigmund Freud and Max Kahane. Leipzig and Vienna: Deuticke.

_____. 1965. *Hypnosis and Suggestion in Psychotherapy: A Treatise on the Nature and Uses of Hypnotism*. [1888.] New York: University Books.

Berthelsen, Detlef. 1987. *Alltag bei Familie Freud: Die Erinnerungen der Paula Fichtl*. Hamburg: Hoffman und Campe.

Binet, Alfred, and Charles Féré. 1905. *Animal Magnetism*. [1887.] London: Kegan Paul, Trench, Trübner.

Binswanger, Ludwig. 1956. *Erinnerungen an Sigmund Freud*. Bern: Francke.

_____. 1957. *Sigmund Freud: Reminiscences of a Friendship*. New York: Grune and Stratton.

Blanton, Smiley. 1971. *Diary of My Analysis with Sigmund Freud*. New York: Hawthorn.

Bodde, N. M., and J. L. Brooks, G. A. Baker, P. A. Boon, J. G. Hendriksen, and A. P. Aldenkamp. 2009. "Psychogenic Non-epileptic Seizures—Diagnostic Issues: A Critical Review." *Clinical Neurology and Neurosurgery*, 111:1–9.

Bollas, Christopher. 2007. *The Freudian Moment*. London: Karnac.

Bonomi, Carlo. 1997. "Freud and the Discovery of Infantile Sexuality: A Reassessment." In Dufresne 1997, pp. 35–57.

_____. 2015. *The Cut and the Building of Psychoanalysis*. Vol. 1. London: Routledge.

Borch-Jacobsen, Mikkel. 1996. *Remembering Anna O.: A Century of Mystification*. [1995.] New York and London: Routledge.

_____. 2009. *Making Minds and Madness: From Hysteria to Depression*. Cambridge: Cambridge U.

_____. 2011. *Les patients de Freud: Destins*. Auxerre: Sciences Humaines.

_____, and Sonu Shamdasani. 2012. *The Freud Files: An Inquiry into the History of Psychoanalysis*. Cambridge and New York: Cambridge U.

Bourneville, Désiré-Magloire, and Paul Regnard. 1876–1880. *Iconographie photographique de la Salpêtrière, service de M. Charcot*. 3 vols. Paris: Progrès Médical/Delahaye.

Boyer, John W. 1978. "Freud, Marriage, and Late Viennese Liberalism: A Commentary from 1905." *J. Modern Hist.*, 50:72–102.

Breger, Louis. 2000. *Freud: Darkness in the Midst of Vision*. New York: Wiley.

Brentano, Franz. 1973. *Psychology from an Empirical Standpoint*. [1874.] Trans. Antos C. Rancurello, D. B. Terrell, and Linda L. McAlister. London: Routledge.

Brentzel, Marianne. 2002. *Anna O.-Bertha Pappenheim: Biographie*. Göttingen: Wallstein.

Breuer, Josef. 1974. [Letter to Franziska von Wertheimstein, 1893.] In *Theodor Gomperz: Ein Gelehrtenleben im Bürgertum d. Franz-Josefs-Zeit: Ausw. seiner Briefe u. Aufzeichnungen 1869–1912* (Vienna: Österr. Akad. d. Wiss.), p. 89.

Britton, Ronald. 1999. "Getting In on the Act: The Hysterical Solution." *Int. J. Psa.*, 80:1–14.

Buekens, Filip. 2006. *Freuds Vergissing: De illusies van de psychoanalyse*. Leuven: Van Halewyck; Baarn: United Media.

Burke, Janine. 2006. *The Sphinx on the Table: Sigmund Freud's Art Collection and the Development of Psychoanalysis*. New York: Walker.

Carter, K. Codell. 1980. "Germ Theory, Hysteria, and Freud's Early Work in Psychopathology." *Medical Hist.*, 24:259–274.

Castelnuovo-Tedesco, Pietro. 1994. "On Rereading the Case of Anna O.: More about Questions That Are Unanswerable." *J. Am. Acad. Psa.*, 22:57–71.

Cesbron, Henri. 1909. *Histoire critique de l'hystérie*. Paris: Asselin et Houzeau.

Charcot, Jean-Martin. 1875–87. *Leçons sur les maladies du système nerveux faites à la Salpêtrière*. 3 vols. Paris: Progrès Médical.

_____. 1886. *Neue Vorlesungen über die Krankheiten des Nervensystems insbesondere über Hysterie*. Trans. Sigmund Freud. Leipzig and Vienna: Toeplitz and Deuticke.

_____. 1886–1893. *Oeuvres completes: Leçons recueillies et publiées par Bourneville, Bernard, Féré, Guinon, Gilles de la Tourette, Brissaud, Sevestre*. 9 vols. Paris: Progrès Médical/Lecrosnier et Babé.

_____. 1887/88. *Leçons du mardi à la Salpêtrière: Policlinique 1887–1888: Notes de cours de MM. Blin, Charcot, Colin*. Paris: Progrès Médical/Delahaye et Lecrosnier.

_____. 1888/89. *Leçons du mardi à la Salpêtrière: Policlinique 1888–1889: Notes de cours de MM. Blin, Charcot, Colin.* Paris: Progrès Médical/Delahaye et Lecrosnier.

_____. 1892–94. *Poliklinische Vorträge. I Band. Schuljahr 1887–1888. Mit 99 Holzschnitten.* Trans. Dr. Sigm. Freud. Leipzig and Vienna: Deuticke.

_____. 1984. *Leçons sur l'hystérie virile.* Ed. Michèle Ouerd. Paris: Sycomore.

———, and Pierre Marie. 1892. "Hysteria[,] Mainly Hystero-Epilepsy." In *A Dictionary of Psychological Medicine Giving the Definition, Etymology and Synonyms of the Terms Used in Medical Psychology, with the Symptoms, Treatment, and Pathology of Insanity and the Law of Lunacy in Great Britain and Ireland,* ed. D. Hack Tuke, 2 vols. (London: Churchill), Vol. 1, pp. 627–641.

Cioffi, Frank. 1998. *Freud and the Question of Pseudoscience.* Chicago and La Salle, IL: Open Court.

Cohen, David. 2011. *Freud on Coke.* London: Cutting Edge.

Crabtree, Adam. 1993. *From Mesmer to Freud: Magnetic Sleep and the Roots of Psychological Healing.* New Haven, CT: Yale U.

Cranefield, Paul F. 1958. "Josef Breuer's Evaluation of His Contribution to Psycho-Analysis." *Int. J. Psa.,* 39:319–322.

Crews, Frederick. 1999. (Ed.) *Unauthorized Freud: Doubters Confront a Legend.* [1998.] New York: Penguin.

_____. 2011. "Physician, Heal Thyself." *New York Rev. Books,* Sept. 29, pp. 92–93, 97–99; Oct. 13, pp. 17–19.

———, et al. 1995. *The Memory Wars: Freud's Legacy in Dispute.* New York: New York Review.

Davidson, Arnold I. 2001. *The Emergence of Sexuality: Historical Epistemology and the Formation of Concepts.* Cambridge, MA: Harvard U.

Davis, Douglas A. 1990. "Freud's Unwritten Case." *Psac Psychology,* 7:185–209.

Decker, Hannah S. 1977. *Freud in Germany: Revolution and Reaction in Science, 1893–1907. Psychological Issues,* 11:1. New York: International Universities.

_____. 1991. *Freud, Dora, and Vienna, 1900.* New York: Free.

Delboeuf, Joseph. 1886. "Une visite à la Salpêtrière." *Revue de Belgique,* 54:142–147, 258–275.

_____. 1889. *Le magnétisme animal: À propos d'une visite à l'école de Nancy.* Paris: Alcan.

_____. 1891. "Comme quoi il n'y a pas d'hypnotisme." *Revue de l'hypnotisme,* 6:129–135.

Deutsch, Felix. 1990. "A Footnote to Freud's 'Fragment of an Analysis of a Case of Hysteria.' " [1957] In *In Dora's Case: Freud—Hysteria—Feminism,* 2d ed. [1985] (New York: Columbia U.), pp. 35–43.

Didi-Huberman, Georges. 2003. *Invention of Hysteria: Charcot and the Photographic Iconography of the Salpêtrière.* [1982.] Trans. Alisa Hartz. Cambridge, MA: MIT.

Domhoff, G. William. 2003. *The Scientific Study of Dreams: Neural Networks, Cognitive Development, and Content Analysis.* Washington, DC: Am. Psychological Assn.

Drucker, Peter F. 1978. *Adventures of a Bystander.* New York: Harper.

Dufresne, Todd. 1997. (Ed.) *Freud Under Analysis: History, Theory, Practice: Essays in Honor of Paul Roazen.* Northvale, NJ: Aronson.

_____. 2000. *Tales from the Freudian Crypt: The Death Drive in Text and Context*. Stanford, CA: Stanford U.

_____. 2003. *Killing Freud: Twentieth-Century Culture and the Death of Psychoanalysis*. London and New York: Continuum.

Duyckaerts, François. 1992. *Joseph Delboeuf, philosophe et hypnotiseur*. Paris: Empêcheurs de Penser en Rond.

Eames, Peter. 1992. "Hysteria Following Brain Injury." *J. Neurology, Neurosurgery and Psychiatry*, 55:1046–1053.

Ebner-Eschenbach, Marie von, and Josef Breuer. 1969. *Ein Briefwechsel, 1889–1916*. Ed. Robert A. Kann. Vienna: Bergland.

Eckstein, Emma. 1899–1900. "Das Dienstmädchen als Mutter." *Dokumente der Frauen*, 2:594–598.

_____. 1904. *Die Sexualfrage in der Erziehung des Kindes*. Leipzig: Modernes Verlagsbureau.

Edinger, Dora. 1968. (Ed.) *Bertha Pappenheim: Freud's Anna O*. Highland Park, IL: Congregation Solel.

Edmunds, Lavinia. 1999. "The Marriage Counselor." [1988.] In Crews 1999, pp. 260–276.

Eissler, K. R. 1971. *Talent and Genius: The Fictitious Case of Tausk contra Freud*. New York: Quadrangle.

_____. 2001. *Freud and the Seduction Theory: A Brief Love Affair*. Madison, CT: International Universities.

Ellenberger, Henri F. 1970. *The Discovery of the Unconscious: The History and Evolution of Dynamic Psychiatry*. New York: Basic.

_____. 1972. "The Story of Anna O.: A Critical Review with New Data." *J. Hist. Behavioral Sciences*, 8:267–279.

_____. 1993. *Beyond the Unconscious: Essays of Henri F. Ellenberger in the History of Psychiatry*. Ed. Mark S. Micale. Trans. Françoise Dubor and Mark S. Micale. Princeton, NJ: Princeton U.

Erb, Wilhelm. 1883. *Handbook of Electro-Therapeutics*. [1882.] Trans. L. Putzel. New York: Wood.

Erikson, Erik H. 1962. "Reality and Actuality—An Address." *J. Am. Psac. Assn.*, 10:451–474.

Erlenmeyer, Albrecht. 1885. "Ueber die Wirkung des Cocaïn bei der Morphiumentziehung." *Centralblatt für Nervenheilkunde, Psychiatrie und gerichtliche Psychopathologie*, 8:289–299.

_____. 1886. "Ueber Cocainsucht: Vorläufige Mitteilung." *Deutsche Medizinal-Zeitung*, 7:483–484.

_____. 1887. *Die Morphiumsucht und ihre Behandlung*. Berlin: Heuser.

_____. 2006. *Die Morphiumsucht und ihre Behandlung*. (Abridged reprint.) Elibron Classic Series. Boston: Adamant Media.

Erwin, Edward. 1996. *A Final Accounting: Philosophical and Empirical Issues in Freudian Psychology*. Cambridge, MA: MIT.

Esterson, Allen. 1993. *Seductive Mirage: An Exploration of the Work of Sigmund Freud*. Chicago: Open Court.

_____. 1998. "Jeffrey Masson and Freud's Seduction Theory: A New Fable Based on Old Myths." *Hist. Human Sciences*, 11:1–21.

_____. 1999. "'Getting in on the Act: The Hysterical Solution.'" [Letter.] *Int. J. Psa.*, 80:1237–1239.

_____. 2001. "The Mythologizing of Psychoanalytic History: Deception and Self-Deception in Freud's Accounts of the Seduction Theory Episode." *Hist. Psychiatry*, 12:329–352.

Evans, Martha Noel. 1991. *Fits and Starts: A Genealogy of Hysteria in Modern France*. Ithaca, NY, and London: Cornell U.

Exner, Sigmund. 1893. "Biographische Skizze." In Fleischl von Marxow 1893, pp. v–xii.

_____. 1894. *Entwurf zu einer physiologischen Erklärung der psychischen Erscheinungen*. Leipzig and Vienna: Deuticke.

Eysenck, Hans J., and Glenn D. Wilson. 1973. *The Experimental Study of Freudian Theories*. London: Methuen.

Falk, Avner. 1977. "Freud and Herzl." *Midstream*, 23:3–24.

Falzeder, Ernst. 1994. "My Grand-Patient, My Chief Tormentor: A Hitherto Unnoticed Case of Freud's and the Consequences." *Psac. Q.*, 63:297–331.

_____. 2007. "Is There Still an Unknown Freud? A Note on the Publications of Freud's Texts and on Unpublished Documents." *Psa. and Hist.*, 9:201–232.

_____. 2012. "'A Fat Wad of Dirty Pieces of Paper': Freud on America, Freud in America, Freud and America." In *After Freud Left: A Century of Psychoanalysis in America*, ed. John Burnham (Chicago and London: U. of Chicago), pp. 85–109.

Farrell, John. 1996. *Freud's Paranoid Quest: Psychoanalysis and Modern Suspicion*. New York and London: New York U.

Feiner, Shmuel. 2002. *Haskalah and History: The Emergence of a Modern Jewish Historical Consciousness*. Portland, OR: Littman.

_____. 2004. *The Jewish Enlightenment*. Philadelphia: U. Pennsylvania.

Ferenczi, Sándor. 1988. *The Clinical Diary of Sándor Ferenczi*. Ed. Judith Dupont. Trans. Michael Balint and Nicola Zarday Jackson. Cambridge, MA: Harvard U.

Fichtner, Gerhard, and Albrecht Hirschmüller. 1988. "Sigmund Freud, Heinrich Obersteiner und die Diskussionen über Hypnose und Kokain." *Jahrbuch der Psychoanalyse*, 23:105–137.

Fish, Stanley. 1986. "Withholding the Missing Portion: Power, Meaning, and Persuasion in Freud's 'The Wolf-Man.'" [London] *Times Literary Supplement*, Aug. 29:935–938.

Fleischl von Marxow, Ernst. 1893. *Gesammelte Abhandlungen*. Ed. Otto Fleischl von Marxow. Leipzig: Barth.

Fliess, Wilhelm. 1893. *Neue Beiträge zur Klinik und Therapie der nasalen Reflexneurose*. Leipzig and Vienna: Deuticke.

_____. 1897. *Die Beziehungen zwischen Nase und weiblichen Geschlechtsorganen: In ihrer biologischen Bedeutung dargestellt*. Leipzig and Vienna: Deuticke.

_____. 1906. *Der Ablauf des Lebens: Grundlegung zur exacten Biologie*. Leipzig and Vienna: Deuticke.

Forel, Auguste. 1889. *Der Hypnotismus: Seine Bedeutung und seine Handhabung: In kurzgefasster Darstellung*. Stuttgart: Enke.

Forrester, John. 1980. *Language and the Origins of Psychoanalysis*. New York: Columbia U.

———. 1990. *The Seductions of Psychoanalysis: Freud, Lacan, and Derrida*. Cambridge: Cambridge U.

———, and Laura Cameron. 1999. "'A Cure with a Defect': A Previously Unpublished Letter by Freud Concerning Anna O." *Int. J. Psa.*, 80:929–942.

Frank, Jerome D., and Julia B. Frank. 1991. *Persuasion and Healing: A Comparative Study of Psychotherapy*. Baltimore: Johns Hopkins U.

Freeman, Lucy. 1972. *The Story of Anna O*. New York: Walker.

Freud, Anna. 1946. *The Ego and the Mechanisms of Defence*. [1937.] New York: International Universities.

Freud, Martin. 1957. *Glory Reflected: Sigmund Freud—Man and Father*. London, Sydney, Melbourne, Wellington: Angus and Robertson.

Freud, Sigmund. 1877. "Beobachtungen über Gestaltung und feineren Bau der als Hoden beschriebenen Lappenorgane des Aals." *Akademie der Wissenschaften, Wien, Mathematisch-Naturwissenschaftlichen Classe*, 75:419–431.

———. 1879. "Notiz über eine Methode zur anatomischen Präparation des Nervensystems." *Centralblatt für die Medicinischen Wissenschaften*, 17:468–469.

———. 1884a. [See Anon. 1884.]

———. 1884b. "Die Struktur der Elemente des Nervensystems." *Jahrbucher für Psychiatrie*, 5:221–229.

———. 1884c. "Ueber Coca." *Centralblatt für die gesammte Therapie*, 2 (July): 289–314.

———. 1884d. "Coca." *St. Louis Medical and Surgical J.*, 47:502–505.

———. 1884e. "Eine neue Methode zum Studium des Faserverlaufs im Centralnervensystem." *Archiv für Anatomie und Physiologie, Anatomische Abteilung*, 5–6:453–460.

———. 1884f. "Eine neue Methode zum Studium des Faserverlaufs im Centralnervensystem." *Centralblatt für Deutsche Medicinischen Wissenschaften*, 22, No. 11:161–163.

———. 1884g. "A New Histological Method for the Study of Nerve-Tracts in the Brain and Spinal Chord." *Brain*, 7:86–88.

———. 1884h. "Ein Fall von Hirnblutung mit indirekten baselen Herdsymptomen bei Scorbut." *Wiener Medizinishe Wochenschrift*, 34:244–246, 276–279.

———. 1885a. "Beitrag zur Kenntnis der Cocawirkung." *Wiener Medizinische Wochenschrift*, 35:129–133.

———. 1885b. *Über Coca. Neu durchgesehener und vermehrter Separat-Abdruck aus dem 'Centralblatt für die gesammte Therapie.'* Vienna: Perles.

———. 1885c. "Ueber die Allgemeinwirkung des Cocains." *Zeitschrift für Therapie*, 3(7) (Apr.):49–51.

———. 1885d. "Ueber die Allgemeinwirkung des Cocains." *Medicinisch-Chirurgisches Central-Blatt*, 20:374–375.

———. 1887. "Bemerkungen über Cocaïnsucht und Cocaïnfurcht." *Wiener Medizinische Wochenschrift*, 37:929–932.

———. 1891. [Report on the Treatment and Death of Mathilde Schleicher.] In Jolles 1891, pp. 1913–1914.

_____. 1895. Review of *Die Migräne*, by P. J. Möbius. *Wiener Klinische Rundschau*, 9 (March 3):140–142.

_____. 1927. "Concluding Remarks on the Question of Lay Analysis." *Int. J. Psa.*, 8:392–398.

_____. 1950. *Aus den Anfängen der Psychoanalyse: Briefe an Wilhelm Fliess, Abhandlungen und Notizen aus den Jahren 1887–1902.* Ed. Marie Bonaparte, Anna Freud, and Ernst Kris. London: Imago.

_____. 1953. *On Aphasia: A Critical Study.* [1891.] Trans. E. Stengel. New York: International Universities.

_____. 1954. *The Origins of Psycho-Analysis: Letters to Wilhelm Fliess, Drafts and Notes: 1887–1902.* Ed. Marie Bonaparte, Anna Freud, and Ernst Kris. New York: Basic.

_____. 1969. "Some Early Unpublished Letters of Freud." Ed. Ernst L. Freud. Trans. Ilse Schrier. *Int. J. Psa.*, 50:419–427.

_____. 1986. *Briefe an Wilhelm Fliess: Ungekürtzte Ausgabe.* Ed. Jeffrey Moussaieff Masson. "Deutsche Fassung" by Michael Schröter. Frankfurt am Main: Fischer.

_____. 1987a. *Gesammelte Werke: Nachtragsband: Texte aus den Jahren 1885 bis 1938.* Ed. Angela Richards, in collaboration with Ilse Grübrich-Simitis. Frankfurt am Main: Fischer.

_____. 1987b. *A Phylogenetic Fantasy: Overview of the Transference Neuroses.* Ed. Ilse Grübrich-Simitis. Trans. Axel Hoffer and Peter T. Hoffer. Cambridge, MA: Harvard U.

_____. 2002. *Unser Herz zeigt nach dem Süden: Reisebriefe 1895–1923.* Ed. Christfried Tögel. Berlin: Aufbau.

_____. 2015. *L'hypnose: Textes, 1886–1893.* Ed. Mikkel Borch-Jacobsen. Paris: L'Iconoclaste.

———, and Karl Abraham. 2002. *The Complete Correspondence of Sigmund Freud and Karl Abraham, 1907–1925; Completed Edition.* Ed. Ernst Falzeder. Trans. Caroline Schwarzacher. London and New York: Karnac.

———, and Lou Andreas-Salomé. 1966. *Sigmund Freud and Lou Andreas-Salomé: Letters.* Ed. Ernst Pfeiffer. Trans. Willam and Elaine Robinson-Scott. New York: Norton.

———, and Minna Bernays. 2005. *Briefwechsel 1882–1938.* Ed. Albrecht Hirschmüller. Tübingen: Diskord.

———, and Ludwig Binswanger. 2003. *The Sigmund Freud-Ludwig Binswanger Correspondence, 1908–1938.* Ed. Gerhard Fichtner. Trans. Arnold J. Pomerans. New York and London: Other.

———, and Sándor Ferenczi. 1993. *The Correspondence of Sigmund Freud and Sándor Ferenczi.* Vol. 1. Ed. Eva Brabant, Ernst Falzeder, and Patrizia Giampieri-Deutsch. Trans. Ingeborg Meyer-Palmedo. Cambridge, MA: Harvard U.

———, and C. G. Jung. 1974. *The Freud/Jung Letters: The Correspondence between Sigmund Freud and C. G. Jung.* Ed. William McGuire. Trans. Ralph Manheim and R. F. C. Hull. Princeton, NJ: Princeton U.

———, and Oskar Pfister. 1963. *Psychoanalysis and Faith: The Letters of Sigmund Freud and Oskar Pfister.* Ed. Heinrich Meng and Ernst L. Freud. New York: Basic.

———, and Arnold Zweig. 1970. *The Letters of Sigmund Freud and Arnold Zweig*. Ed. Ernst L. Freud. Trans. Elaine and William Robson-Scott. New York: Harcourt.

Furse, Anna. 1997. *Augustine (Big Hysteria)*. Amsterdam: Harwood Academic.

Furst, Lilian R. 2008. *Before Freud: Hysteria and Hypnosis in Later Nineteenth-Century Psychiatric Cases*. Lewisburg, PA: Bucknell U.

Gale, Barry G. 2015. *Love in Vienna: The Sigmund Freud–Martha Bernays Affair*. Santa Barbara and Denver: Praeger.

Garner, Shirley Nelson. 1989. "Freud and Fliess: Homophobia and Seduction." In Hunter 1989, pp. 86–109.

Gastaut, Henri. 1954. *The Epilepsies: Electro-Clinical Correlations*. Trans. Mary A. B. Brazier. Springfield, IL: Thomas.

Gauld, Alan. 1992. *A History of Hypnotism*. Cambridge: Cambridge U.

Gay, Peter. 1989. *Freud: A Life for Our Time*. [1988.] New York: Anchor Doubleday.

———. 1990. *Reading Freud: Explorations and Entertainments*. [1989.] New Haven, CT: Yale U.

Gelfand, Toby. 1988. "'Mon Cher Docteur Freud': Charcot's Unpublished Correspondence to Freud, 1888–1893." *Bull. Hist. Medicine*, 62:563–588.

———. 1989. "Charcot's Response to Freud's Rebellion." *J. Hist. Ideas*, 50:293–307.

Geller, Jay. 2007. *On Freud's Jewish Body: Mitigating Circumcisions*. New York: Fordham U.

Gellner, Ernest. 1996. *The Psychoanalytic Movement: The Cunning of Unreason*. [1985.] Evanston, IL: Northwestern U.

Gicklhorn, Josef, and Renée Gicklhorn. 1960. *Sigmund Freuds akademische Laufbahn: Im Lichte der Dokumente*. Vienna and Innsbruck: Urban und Schwarzenberg.

Gicklhorn, Renée. 1969. "The Freiberg Period of the Freud Family." *J. Hist. Medicine*, 24:37–43.

Gilhooley, Dan. 2002. "Misrepresentation and Misreading in the Case of Anna O." *Modern Psa.*, 27:75–100.

Gilles de la Tourette, Georges. 1885. "Étude sur une affection nerveuse caracterisée par l'incoordination motrice accompagnée d'écholalie et de coprolalie." *Archives de Neurologie*, 9:19–42, 158–200.

Gilman, Sander L. 1985. *Difference and Pathology: Stereotypes of Sexuality, Race, and Madness*. Ithaca, NY: Cornell U.

———. 1986. *Jewish Self-Hatred: Anti-Semitism and the Hidden Language of the Jews*. Baltimore: Johns Hopkins U.

———. 1993a. *Freud, Race, and Gender*. Princeton: Princeton U.

———, Helen King, Roy Porter, G. S. Rousseau, and Elaine Showalter. 1993. *Hysteria Beyond Freud*. Berkeley, Los Angeles, London: U. California.

Glymour, Clark. 1983. "The Theory of Your Dreams." In *Physics, Philosophy, and Psychoanalysis: Essays in Honor of Adolf Grünbaum*. Ed. R. S. Cohen and L. Laudan (Boston: Reidel).

Goetz, Christopher G. 2007. "J.–M. Charcot and Simulated Neurological Disease: Attitudes and Diagnostic Strategies." *Historical Neurology*, 69: 103–109.

_____, Michel Bonduelle, and Toby Gelfand. 1995. (Eds.) *Charcot: Constructing Neurology*. New York: Oxford U.

Goldstein, Jan. 1987. *Console and Classify: The French Psychiatric Profession in the Nineteenth Century*. Cambridge: Cambridge U.

Gootenberg, Paul. 2001. *Between Coca and Cocaine: A Century or More of U.S.-Peruvian Drug Paradoxes, 1860–1980*. Washington, D.C.: Woodrow Wilson Center.

Goshen, Charles E. 1952. "The Original Case Material of Psychoanalysis." *Am. J. Psychiatry*, 108:829–834.

Graf, Max. 1942. "Reminiscences of Professor Sigmund Freud." *Psac. Q.*, 11: 465–476.

Greenberg, Valerie D. 1997. *Freud and His Aphasia Book*. Ithaca, NY, and London: Cornell U.

Gresser, Moshe. 1994. *Dual Allegiance: Freud as a Modern Jew*. Albany: SUNY.

Grinspoon, Lester, and James B. Bakalar. 1985. *Cocaine: A Drug and Its Social Evolution*. [1976]. New York: Basic.

Grinstein, Alexander. 1971. "Freud's First Publications in America." *J. Am. Psac. Assn.*, 19:241–264.

Grosskurth, Phyllis. 1991. *The Secret Ring: Freud's Inner Circle and the Politics of Psychoanalysis*. Reading, MA: Addison-Wesley.

Grübrich-Simitis, Ilse. 1997. *Early Freud and Late Freud: Reading Anew* Studies on Hysteria *and* Moses and Monotheism. Trans. Philip Slotkin. London and New York: Routledge.

Grünbaum, Adolf. 1984. *The Foundations of Psychoanalysis: A Philosophical Critique*. Berkeley and Los Angeles: U. California.

_____. 1993. *Validation in the Clinical Theory of Psychoanalysis: A Study in the Philosophy of Psychoanalysis*. Madison, CT: International Universities.

"Gutt." [unknown.] 1885. "Neue Artzneimittel und Heilmethoden: Über die verschiedenen Cocain-Präparate und deren Wirkung." *Wiener Medizinische Presse*, 26:1035–1038.

Guttmann, Melinda Given. 2001. *The Enigma of Anna O.: A Biography of Bertha Pappenheim*. Wickford, RI, and London: Moyer Bell.

Haas, Eberhard. 1983. "Freuds Kokainepisode und das Problem der Sucht." *Jahrbuch der Psychoanalyse*, 15:171–228.

Hacking, Ian. 1995. *Rewriting the Soul: Multiple Personality and the Sciences of Memory*. Princeton, NJ: Princeton U.

_____. 1998. *Mad Travelers: Reflections on the Reality of Transient Mental Illness*. Charlottesville and London: U. Virginia.

Hadlich, [unknown]. 1885. "Richter, Pankow: Ueber Cannabinon." *Neurologisches Centralblatt*, 4 (1885):20–23.

Hamilton, James W. 2002. "Freud and the Suicide of Pauline Silberstein." *Psac. Rev.*, 89:889–909.

Hammond, W. A. 1886. "Cocaine and the So-Called Cocaine Habit." Reported in *New York Medical Journal*, 44:637–639.

Handlbauer, Bernhard. 1998. *The Freud-Adler Controversy*. [1990.] Oxford: Rockport, MA: Oneworld.

Harrington, Anne. 1987. *Medicine, Mind, and the Double Brain: A Study in Nineteenth-Century Thought*. Princeton, NJ: Princeton U.

———. 1988. "Metals and Magnets in Medicine: Hysteria, Hypnosis and Medical Culture in Fin-de-Siècle Paris." *Psychological Medicine*, 18:21–38.

Hartman, Frank R. 1983. "A Reappraisal of the Emma Episode and the Specimen Dream." *J. Am. Psac. Assn.*, 31:555–585.

Heer, Friedrich. 1972. "Freud, the Viennese Jew." In *Freud, the Man, His World, His Influence*, ed. Jonathan Miller, trans. W. A Littlewood (Boston: Little, Brown), pp. 2–20.

Hilgard, Ernest R. 1977. *Divided Consciousness: Multiple Controls in Human Thought and Action*. New York: Wiley-Interscience.

Hirschmüller, Albrecht. 1978. "Eine bisher unbekannte Krankengeschichte Sigmund Freuds aus der Entstehungszeit der 'Studien über Hysterie.'" *Jahrbuch der Psychoanalyse*, 10:136–168.

———. 1989a. *The Life and Work of Josef Breuer: Physiology and Psychoanalysis*. [1978.] New York and London: New York U.

———. 1989b. "Freuds 'Mathilde': Ein weiterer Tagesrest zum Irma-Traum." *Jahrbuch für Psychoanalyse*, 24:128–159.

———. 1991. *Freuds Begegnung mit der Psychiatrie: Von der Hirnmythologie zur Neurosenlehre*. Tübingen: Diskord.

———. 1992. "Freud at Meynert's Clinic: The Paradoxical Influence of Psychiatry on the Development of Psychoanalysis." In *Understanding Freud: The Man and His Ideas*, ed. Emanuel E. Garcia (New York and London: New York U.), pp. 39–54.

———. 1995. "E. Merck und das Kokain: Zu Sigmund Freuds Kokainstudien und ihren Beziehungen zu der Darmstädter Firma." *Gesnerus*, 52:116–132.

———. 2002a. "Freud's Studies on Cocaine." In Van de Vijver and Geerardyn 2002, pp. 70–77.

———. 2002b. "Wer war 'Herr Aliquis'? Zu den Thesen von Peter J. Swales." *Psyche*, 56:396–402.

———. 2005. "Mathilde Schleicher." In *International Dictionary of Psychoanalysis*, Vol. 2, ed. Alain de Mijolla (Detroit: Macmillan Reference USA, 2005), p. 1033.

———. 2007. "Evidence for a Sexual Relationship between Sigmund Freud and Minna Bernays?" *Am. Imago*, 64:125–129.

Hobson, J. Allan. 2002. *Dreaming: An Introduction to the Science of Sleep*. Oxford and New York: Oxford U.

Holmes, David S. 1990. "The Evidence for Repression: An Examination of Sixty Years of Research." In *Repression and Dissociation: Implications for Personality, Theory, Psychopathology, and Health*, ed. Jerome L. Singer (Chicago: U. Chicago), pp. 85–102.

Holt, Robert R. 1992. "Freud's Parental Identifications." In *Freud and the History of Psychoanalysis*, eds. Toby Gelfand and John Kerr (Hillsdale, NJ: Analytic), pp. 1–28.

Hückel, Armand. 1888. *Die Rolle der Suggestion bei gewissen Erscheinungen der Hysterie und des Hypnotismus: Kritisches und experimentelles*. Jena: Fischer.

Hugo, Victor. 2002. *The Hunchback of Notre Dame*. [1831.] Trans. Catherine Liu. New York: Modern Library.

Hurst, Arthur F. 1920. *The Croonian Lectures on the Psychology of the Special Senses and Their Functional Disorders*. London: Frowde/Hodder & Stoughton.

Hustvedt, Asti. 2011. *Medical Muses: Hysteria in Nineteenth-Century Paris*. New York and London: Norton.

Hyman, Stanley Edgar. 1962. *The Tangled Bank: Darwin, Marx, Frazer, and Freud as Imaginative Writers*. New York: Atheneum.

Imber, Gerald. 2010. *Genius on the Edge: The Bizarre Double Life of Dr. William Stewart Halsted*. New York: Kaplan.

Israëls, Han. 1993. *Het geval Freud. 1. Scheppingsverhalen*. Amsterdam: Bakker.

_____. 1999. *Der Fall Freud: Die Geburt der Psychoanalyse aus der Lüge*. Trans. Gerd Busse. Hamburg: Europäische.

_____. 2002. *El caso Freud: Histeria y cocaína*. Trans. Julio Grande. Madrid: Turner.

———, and Morton Schatzman. 1993. "The Seduction Theory." *History of Psychiatry*, 4:23–59.

_____. 2006. *Der Wiener Quacksalber: Kritische Betrachtungen über Sigmund Freud und die Psychoanalyse*. Jena: Bussert and Stadeler.

Janet, Pierre. 1889. *L'automatisme psychologique: Essai de psychologie expérimentale*. Paris: Alcan.

_____. 1892. "L'anesthésie hystérique." *Archives de Neurologie*, 23:323–352.

_____. 1895. "J. M. Charcot, son oeuvre psychologique." *Revue Philosophique de la France et de l'Étranger*, 39:569–604.

_____. 1901. *The Mental State of Hystericals: A Study of Mental Stigmata and Mental Accidents*. [1892.] Trans. Caroline Rollin Corson. New York and London: Putnam's.

_____. 1907. *The Major Symptoms of Hysteria: Fifteen Lectures Given in the Medical School of Harvard University*. New York: Macmillan.

_____. 1925. *Psychological Healing: A Historical and Clinical Study*. 2 vols. [1919.] Trans. Eden and Cedar Paul. New York: Macmillan.

Jensen, Ellen M. 1970. "Anna O—A Study of Her Later Life." *Psac. Q.*, 39:269–293.

_____. 1984. *Streifzüge durch das Leben von Anna O./Bertha Pappenheim: Ein Fall für die Psychiatrie: Ein Leben für die Philanthropie*. Frankfurt am Main: ZTV.

Jolles, Adolf F. 1891. "Ueber das chemische Verhalten der Harne nach Sulfonal-Intoxikation." *Internationale Klinische Rundschau*, 5:1913–1916, 1953–1959.

Jones, E. Michael. 1993. *Degenerate Moderns: Modernity as Rationalized Sexual Misbehavior*. San Francisco: Ignatius.

Jones, Ernest. 1953. *Sigmund Freud: Life and Work*. Vol. 1: *The Young Freud, 1856–1900*. London: Hogarth.

Jung, C. G. 1973. *Memories, Dreams, Reflections*. [1963.] Ed. Aniela Jaffé. Trans. Richard and Clara Winston. New York: Pantheon.

Karch, Steven B. 1998. *A Brief History of Cocaine*. Boca Raton, FL: CRC.

Kardiner, Abram. 1977. *My Analysis with Freud: Reminiscences*. New York: Norton.

Karpe, Richard. 1961. "The Rescue Complex in Anna O.'s Final Identity." *Psac. Q.*, 30:1–27.

Kavaler-Adler, Susan. 1991. "Some More Speculations on Anna O." *Am. J. Psa.*, 51:161–171.

Kern, Stephen. 1973. "Freud and the Discovery of Child Sexuality." *Hist. Childhood Q.*, 1:117–141.

Kerr, John. 1993. *A Most Dangerous Method: The Story of Freud, Jung, and Sabina Spielrein*. New York: Knopf.

Kihlstrom, John F. 2001. "Dissociative Disorders." In *Comprehensive Handbook of Psychopathology*, 3d ed., ed. Henry E. Adams and Patricia B. Sutker (New York: Plenum), pp. 259–276.

Klein, Dennis B. 1981. *Jewish Origins of the Psychoanalytic Movement*. New York: Praeger.

Knoepfmacher, Hugo. 1979a. "Sigmund Freud in High School." *Am. Imago*, 36:287–300.

_____. 1979b. "Sigmund Freud and the B'nai B'rith." *J. Am. Psac. Assn.*, 27:441–449.

Konz, Britta. 2005. *Bertha Pappenheim (1859–1936): Ein Leben für jüdische Tradition und weibliche Emanzipation*. Frankfurt: Campus.

Køppe, Simo. 1983. "The Psychology of the Neuron: Freud, Cajal and Golgi." *Scandinavian J. Psychology*, 24:1–12.

Kraepelin, Emil. 1896. *Psychiatrie: Ein Lehrbuch für Studirende und Aertze*. 5th ed. Leipzig: Barth.

Krafft-Ebing, Richard von. 1886. *Psychopathia sexualis: Eine klinisch-forensiche Studie*. Stuttgart: Enke.

Krüll, Marianne. 1986. *Freud and His Father*. [1979.] Trans. Arnold J. Pomerans. New York: Norton.

Lakoff, George. 1993. "How Metaphor Structures Dreams: The Theory of Conceptual Metaphor Applied to Dream Analysis." *Dreaming*, 3:77–98.

_____. 1997. "How Unconscious Metaphorical Thought Shapes Dreams." In *Cognitive Science and the Unconscious*, ed. Dan J. Stein (Washington, DC: Am. Psychiatric Assn.), pp. 89–120.

Langs, Robert. 1984. "Freud's Irma Dream and the Origins of Psychoanalysis." *Psac. Rev.*, 71:591–617.

Laqueur, Thomas. 1987. "Orgasm, Generation, and the Politics of Reproductive Biology." In *The Making of the Modern Body*, ed. Catherine Gallagher and Thomas Laqueur (Berkeley: U. California), pp. 1–41.

LeBlanc, André Robert. 2000. *On Hypnosis, Simulation, and Faith: The Problem of Post-Hypnotic Suggestion in France, 1884–1896*. Ph.D. thesis, U. of Toronto.

Lehrer, Ronald. 1994. *Nietzsche's Presence in Freud's Life and Thought: On the Origins of a Psychology of Dynamic Unconscious Mental Functioning*. Albany: SUNY.

Levin, Kenneth. 1978. *Freud's Early Psychology of the Neuroses: A Historical Perspective*. Pittsburgh: U. Pittsburgh.

Loftus, Elizabeth, and Katherine Ketcham. 1996. *The Myth of Repressed*

Memory: False Memories and Allegations of Sexual Abuse. [1994.] New York: St. Martin's Griffin.

Lohser, Beate, and Peter M. Newton. 1996. *Unorthodox Freud: The View from the Couch*. New York: Guilford.

López Piñero, José Maria. 1983. *Historical Origins of the Concept of Neurosis*. [1963.] Trans. D. Berrios. Cambridge and New York: Cambridge U.

Lothane, Zvi. 1998. "Freud's 1895 *Project*: From Mind to Brain and Back Again." *Annals New York Acad. Sciences*, 843:43–65.

_____. 2007. "The Sigmund Freud/Minna Bernays Romance: Fact or Fiction?" *Am. Imago*, 64:129–133.

Löwenfeld, Leopold. 1895. "Ueber die Verknüpfung neurasthenischer und hysterischer Symptome in Anfallsform nebst Bemerkungen über die Freud'sche 'Angstneurose.'" *Münchener Medicinische Wochenschrift*, No. 13:282–285.

Ludwig, Emil. 1947. *Doctor Freud: An Analysis and a Warning*. New York: Hellman, Williams.

Lynn, David J. 1997. "Sigmund Freud's Psychoanalysis of Albert Hirst." *Bull. Hist. Medicine*, 71:69–93.

Macmillan, Malcolm. 1979. "Delboeuf and Janet as Influences in Freud's Treatment of Emmy von N." *J. Hist. Behavioral Sciences*, 15:299–309.

_____. 1997. *Freud Evaluated: The Completed Arc*. [1991.] Cambridge, MA: MIT.

Maciejewski, Franz. 2006a. "Späte Sensation im Freud-Jahr: Archivfund bestätigt Affäre zwischen Sigmund Freud und Minna Bernays." *Frankfurter Rundschau*, Thema Kultur, 28 Sept., p. 28.

_____. 2006b. "Freud, His Wife, and His 'Wife.'" *Am. Imago*, 63:497–506.

_____. 2008. "Minna Bernays as 'Mrs. Freud': What Sort of Relationship Did Sigmund Freud Have with His Sister-in-Law?" *Am. Imago*, 65:5–21.

Magaziner, Alfred. 1975. *Die Wegbereiter: Aus der Geschichte der Arbeiterbewegung*. Vienna: Volksbuch.

Mahony, Patrick. 1979. "Friendship and Its Discontents." *Contemporary Psa.*, 15:55–109.

_____. 1984. *Cries of the Wolf Man*. New York: International Universities.

_____. 1986. *Freud and the Rat Man*. New Haven, CT: Yale U.

_____. 1996. *Freud's Dora: A Psychoanalytic, Historical, and Textual Study*. New Haven, CT: Yale U.

Makari, George. 2008. *Revolution in Mind: The Creation of Psychoanalysis*. New York: HarperCollins.

Malcolm, Janet. 1982. *Psychoanalysis: The Impossible Profession*. New York: Vintage.

Mancia, Mauro. 1983. "Archaeology of Freudian Thought and the History of Neurophysiology." *Int. Rev. Psa.*, 10:185–192.

Mantegazza, Paolo. 1975. "Coca Experiences." In *The Coca Leaf and Cocaine Papers*, ed. George Andrews and David Solomon (New York and London: Harcourt), pp. 38–42.

Margolis, Deborah P. 1996. *Freud and His Mother: Preoedipal Aspects of Freud's Personality*. Northvale, NJ: Aronson.

Marie, Pierre. 1925. "Éloge de Charcot." *Bulletin de l'Académie de Médicine*, 93:576–593.

Markel, Howard. 2011. *An Anatomy of Addiction: Sigmund Freud, William Halsted, and the Miracle Drug Cocaine*. New York: Pantheon.

Marmor, Judd. 1962. "Psychoanalytic Therapy as an Educational Process." In *Science and Psychoanalysis*, Vol. 5: *Psychoanalytic Education*, ed. J. H. Masserman (New York: Grune and Stratton), pp. 286–299.

Marret, Emmanuel, Marc Gentili, and Francis Bonnet. 2004. "Moreno y Maíz: A Missed Rendezvous with Local Anesthesia." *Anesthesiology*, 100:1321–1322.

Marshall, Jonathan. 2007. "Dynamic Medicine and Theatrical Form at the *Fin de Siècle*: A Formal Analysis of Dr. Jean-Martin Charcot's Pedagogy, 1862–1893." *Modernism/modernity*, 15:131–153.

Martin-Duce, A. 2002. "A Developmental History of Local Anaesthesia." *Ambulatory Surgery*, 9:187–189.

Masson, Jeffrey Moussaieff. 1984. *The Assault on Truth: Freud's Suppression of the Seduction Theory*. New York: Farrar.

Mayer, Andreas. 2001–2. "Introspective Hypnotism and Freud's Self-Analysis: Procedures of Self-Observation in Clinical Practice." *Revue d'Histoire des Sciences Humaines*, 5:179–196.

McCaffrey, Phillip. 1984. *Freud and Dora: The Artful Dream*. New Brunswick, NJ: Rutgers U.

McCarley, Robert W., and J. Allan Hobson. 1977. "The Neurobiological Origins of Psychoanalytic Dream Theory." *Am. J. Psychiatry*, 134:1211–1221.

McGrath, William J. 1974. *Dionysian Art and Populist Politics in Austria*. New Haven, CT: Yale U.

_____. 1986. *Freud's Discovery of Psychoanalysis: The Politics of Hysteria*. Ithaca, NY, and London: Cornell U.

McHugh, Paul R. 2008. *Try to Remember: Psychiatry's Clash over Meaning, Memory, and Mind*. New York: Dana.

McNally, Richard J. 2003. *Remembering Trauma*. Cambridge, MA: Harvard U.

Meige, Henry. 1993. *Le Juif-Errant à la Salpêtrière*. [1893.] Paris: Nouvel Objet.

Meller, J. 1934. *Gedenkworte zum 50. Jahrestage des Vortrages von Dr. Karl Koller über das Kokain vor der Gesellschaft der Ärtze in Wien*. Vienna: Springer.

Merck, E. 1884. "Cocain und seine Salze." *Klinische Monatsblätter für Augenheilkunde*, 22:428–434.

_____. 1885a. "Cocaine and Its Salts." *Chicago Medical J. and Examiner*, 50:157–163.

_____. 1885b. "Zur Kentniß des Cocain." [Open letter.] *Wiener Medizinische Presse*, 26:1373.

Merskey, Harold. 1992. "Anna O. Had a Severe Depressive Illness." *British J. Psychiatry*, 161:185–194.

Merton, Robert K. 1976. "The Ambivalence of Scientists." In *Sociological Ambivalence and Other Essays* (New York: Free), pp. 32–55.

Meyer, Catherine, Mikkel Borch-Jacobsen, Jean Cottraux, Didier Pleux, and Jacques Van Rillaer. (Eds.) 2005. *Le livre noir de la psychanalyse: Vivre, penser et aller mieux sans Freud*. Paris: Arènes.

Micale, Mark S. 1985. "The Salpêtrière in the Age of Charcot: An Institutional Perspective on Medical History in the Late Nineteenth Century." *J. Contemporary Hist.*, 20:703–731.

———. 1989. "Hysteria and Its Historiography: A Review of Present and Past Writings." *Hist. Science*, 27: 223–261, 319–351.

———. 1993. "On the 'Disappearance' of Hysteria: A Study in the Clinical Deconstruction of a Diagnosis." *Isis*, 84:496–526.

———. 2008. *Hysterical Men: The Hidden History of Male Nervous Illness*. Cambridge, MA, and London: Harvard U.

Mill, John Stuart. 1880. *Ueber Frauenemancipation. Plato; Arbeiterfrage; Socialismus*. Trans. Siegmund [*sic*] Freud. Leipzig: Fues.

Moll, Albert. 1913. *The Sexual Life of the Child*. [1909.] Trans. Eden Paul. New York: Macmillan.

Moreau, Christian. 1976. *Freud et l'occultisme: L'approche freudienne du spiritisme, de la divination, de la magie et de la télépathie*. Toulouse: Privat.

Munthe, Axel. 1936. *The Story of San Michele*. London: Murray.

Newton, Peter M. 1995. *Freud: From Youthful Dream to Mid-Life Crisis*. New York and London: Guilford.

Nicolas, Serge. 2004. *L'hypnose: Charcot face à Bernheim*. Paris: L'Harmattan.

Nietzsche, Friedrich. 1997. *Human, All Too Human,* Vol. I. [1878.] Trans. Gary Handwerk. Stanford, CA: Stanford U.

———. 1999. *The Birth of Tragedy and Other Writings*. Ed. Raymond Geuss and Ronald Speirs. Trans. Ronald Speirs. Cambridge, England: Cambridge U.

Nunberg, Herman, and Ernst Federn. 1962–1975. (Eds.) *Minutes of the Vienna Psychoanalytic Society*. 4 vols. Trans. M. Nunberg. New York: International Universities.

Obersteiner, Heinrich. 1884. "Die Morphiumsucht und ihre Behandlung." Reported in *Congrès périodique international des sciences médicales,* 8me session (Copenhagen: C. Lange, 1886), Vol. 3, pp. 10–14.

———. 1885. "Zur interner Anwendung des Cocains bei Neurosen und Psychosen." *Wiener Medizinische Presse*, 26:1253–1257.

———. 1886a. "Über Intoxikations-Psychosen." Reported in *Wiener Medizinische Presse*, 27:116–117.

———. 1886b. "Die Intoxikationspsychosen." *Wiener Klinik*, 12:33–52.

Obholzer, Karin. 1982. *The Wolf-Man Sixty Years Later: Conversations with Freud's Controversial Patient*. [1980.] Trans. Michael Shaw. New York: Continuum.

Ofshe, Richard, and Ethan Watters. 1996. *Making Monsters: False Memories, Psychotherapy, and Sexual Hysteria*. [1994.] Berkeley: U. California.

Onfray, Michel. 2010. *Le crépuscule d'une idole: L'affabulation freudienne*. Paris: Grasset.

Orne, Martin T., and David F. Dinges. 1989. "Hypnosis." In *Comprehensive Textbook of Psychiatry*, 5th ed., ed. Harold I. Kaplan and Benjamin J. Sadock (Baltimore: Williams and Wilkins), pp. 1501–1516.

Orr-Andrawes, Alison. 1987. "The Case of Anna O.: A Neuropsychiatric Perspective." *J. Am. Psac. Assn.*, 35:387–419.

Orrells, Daniel. 2011. "Rocks, Ghosts, and Footprints: Freudian Archaeology." In *Pompeii in the Public Imagination from Its Rediscovery to Today*, ed. Shelley Hales and Joanna Paul (Oxford: Oxford U.), pp. 185–198.

Owen, A. R. G. 1971. *Hysteria, Hypnosis and Healing: The Work of J.-M. Charcot*. New York: Garrett.

Pappenheim, Else. 1980. "Freud and Gilles de la Tourette: Diagnostic Specula-tions on 'Frau Emmy von N.'" *Int. Rev. Psa.*, 7:265–277.

Paul, Gordon L. 1963. "The Production of Blisters by Hypnotic Suggestion: Another Look." *Psychosomatic Medicine*, 25:233–244.

Pendergrast, Mark. 1996. *Victims of Memory: Sex Abuse Accusations and Shat-tered Lives*. [1995.] Hinesburg, VT: Upper Access.

Perry, Campbell P., and Jean-Roche Laurence. 1984. "Mental Processing Outside of Awareness: The Contributions of Freud and Janet." In *The Unconscious Reconsidered*, ed. Kenneth S. Bowers and Donald Meichenbaum (New York: Wiley), pp. 9–48.

Phillips, Adam. 2014. *Becoming Freud: The Making of a Psychoanalyst*. New Haven, CT, and London: Yale U.

Poe, Edgar Allan. 1978. *The Collected Works of Edgar Allan Poe*. Vol. II: *Tales and Sketches*. Ed. Thomas Ollive Mabbott. Cambridge, MA: Harvard U.

Pollock, George H. 1968. "The Possible Significance of Childhood Object Loss in the Josef Breuer-Bertha Pappenheim (Anna O.)-Sigmund Freud Relationship: 1. Josef Breuer." *J. Am. Psac. Assn.*, 16:711–739.

Pommier, René. 2008. *Sigmund Freud est fou et Freud a tout faux: Essai sur la théorie freudienne du rêve*. Paris: Fallois.

Pope, Harrison G., Jr. 1997. *Psychology Astray: Fallacies in Studies of "Repressed Memory" and Childhood Trauma*. Boca Raton, FL: Upton.

———, and James I. Hudson. 1995. "Can Memories of Childhood Sexual Abuse Be Repressed?" *Psychological Medicine*, 25:121–126.

———, Michael B. Poliakoff, Michael P. Parker, Matthew Boynes, and James I. Hudson. 2007. "Is Dissociative Amnesia a Culture-Bound Syndrome? Find-ings from a Survey of Historical Literature." *Psychological Medicine*, 37: 225–233.

Porter, Roy. 1993. "The Body and the Mind, the Doctor and the Patient: Negoti-ating Hysteria." In Gilman et al. 1993, pp. 225–285.

Pribram, Karl H., and Merton M. Gill. 1976. *Freud's "Project" Re-assessed: Pref-ace to Contemporary Cognitive Theory and Neuropsychology*. New York: Basic.

Puner, Helen Walker. 1992. *Sigmund Freud: His Life and Mind*. [1947.] New Brunswick, NJ, and London: Transaction.

Quinn, Bruce. 1992. "Sigmund Freud and the History of Neurotechnique: The 'Lost' Year." *Society for Neuroscience Abstracts*, 18:181.

———. 1993. "Freud's Gold Chloride Myelin Stain: A Vignette in the History of Neurologic Science in Vienna." *Neurology*, 43(S2):A377.

———. 1994. "Myelin Stains and Myeloarchitectonics: A Neuropathology His-torical Vignette from Freud's Laboratory, and Modern Applications in Basal Ganglia Research." [Manuscript.]

Ramos, Sérgio de Paula. 2003. "Revisiting Anna O.: A Case of Chemical Depen-dence." *Hist. Psychology*, 6:239–250.

Raymond, Fulgence. 1896. *Leçons sur les maladies du système nerveux, Hospice de la Salpêtrière*. Paris: Doin.

Reve, Karel van het. 1994. *Dr. Freud und Sherlock Holmes*. Trans. Gerd Busse. Frankfurt am Main: Fischer.

Ribot, Théodule. 1881. *Les maladies de la mémoire*. Paris: Baillière.

Richer, Paul. 1885. *Études cliniques sur la grande hystérie ou hystéro-épilepsie*. Paris: Delahaye et Lecrosnier.

Roazen, Paul. 1969. *Brother Animal: The Story of Freud and Tausk*. New York: Knopf.

_____. 1975. *Freud and His Followers*. New York: Knopf.

_____. 1993. *Meeting Freud's Family*. Amherst: U. Massachusetts.

_____. 1995. *How Freud Worked: First-Hand Accounts of Patients*. Northvale, NJ, and London: Aronson.

Robins, Richard W., Samuel D. Gosling, and Kenneth H. Craik. 1999. "An Empirical Analysis of Trends in Psychology." *Am. Psychologist*, 54:117–128.

Robinson, Joseph D. 2001. *Mechanisms of Synaptic Transmission: Bridging the Gaps, 1890–1900*. Oxford and New York: Oxford U.

Robinson, Paul. 1993. *Freud and His Critics*. Berkeley: U. California.

Rofé, Yacov. 2008. "Does Repression Exist? Memory, Pathogenic, Unconscious and Clinical Evidence." *Rev. General Psychology*, 12:63–85.

Rogow, Arnold A. 1978. "A Further Footnote to Freud's 'Fragment of an Analysis of a Case of Hysteria.'" *J. Am. Psac. Assn.*, 26:331–356.

Rohrwasser, Michael. 2005. *Freuds Lektüren: Von Arthur Conan Doyle bis zu Arthur Schnitzler*. Giessen: Psychosozial.

Rosenbaum, Max, and Melvin Muroff. 1984. (Eds.) *Anna O.: Fourteen Contemporary Reinterpretations*. New York: Free.

Roudinesco, Élisabeth. 2016. *Freud: In His Time and Ours*. [2014.] Cambridge, MA, and London: Harvard U.

Roustang, François. 1982. *Dire Mastery: Discipleship from Freud to Lacan*. [1976.] Trans. Ned Lukacher. Baltimore: Johns Hopkins U.

_____. 1983. *Psychoanalysis Never Lets Go*. [1980.] Trans. Ned Lukacher. Baltimore and London: Johns Hopkins U.

Rudnytsky, Peter L. 1987. *Freud and Oedipus*. New York: Columbia U.

_____. 2011. *Rescuing Psychoanalysis from Freud: And Other Essays in Re-Vision*. London: Karnac.

Ruitenbeek, Hendrik M. 1973. *Freud as We Knew Him*. Detroit: Wayne State U.

Sachs, Hanns. 1946. *Freud, Master and Friend*. Cambridge, MA: Harvard U.

Sand, Rosemarie. 1983. "Confirmation in the Dora Case." *Int. Rev. Psa.*, 10:333–357.

_____. 2014. *The Unconscious without Freud*. Lanham, MD: Rowman and Littlefield.

Savill, Thomas Dixon. 1908. *Clinical Lectures on Neurasthenia*. 4th ed. London: Glaisher.

Scammell, Michael. 2009. *Koestler: The Literary and Political Odyssey of a Twentieth-Century Skeptic*. New York: Random.

Scharnberg, Max. 1993. *The Non-authentic Nature of Freud's Observations*. 2 vols. Uppsala: Uppsala U.

Scheidt, Jürgen vom. 1973. "Sigmund Freud und das Cocain." *Psyche*, 27: 385–430.

Scheuer, Oscar Franz. 1927. *Burschenschaft und Judenfrage: Der Rassen-anti-Semitismus in der deutschen Studentenschaft*. Berlin: Berlin-Wien.

Schiller, Francis. 1982. *A Möbius Strip: Fin-de-Siècle Neuropsychiatry and Paul Möbius.* Berkeley, Los Angeles, London: U. California.

Schimek, Jean G. 1987. "Fact and Fantasy in the Seduction Theory: A Historical Review." *J. Am. Psac. Assn.,* 35:937–965.

Schorske, Carl E. 1980. *Fin-de Siècle Vienna: Politics and Culture.* New York: Knopf.

Schröter, Michael. 1989. "Un dialogue scientifique entre Freud et Fliess: Le projet d'étude sur la neurasthénie." *Revue Internationale d'Histoire de la Psychanalyse,* 2:109–146.

Schur, Max. 1966. "Some Additional 'Day Residues' of 'The Specimen Dream of Psychoanalysis.' " In *Psychoanalysis—A General Psychology: Essays in Honor of Heinz Hartmann,* ed. Rudolph M. Loewenstein, Lottie M. Newman, Max Schur, and Albert J. Solnit (New York: International Universities), pp. 45–85.

_____. 1972. *Freud: Living and Dying.* New York: International Universities.

Schwartz, Sophie. 2000. "A Historical Loop of One Hundred Years: Similarities between 19th Century and Contemporary Dream Research." *Dreaming,* 10:55–66.

Schweighofer, Fritz. 1987. *Das Privattheater der Anna O.* Munich and Basel: Reinhardt.

Sebeok, Thomas A., and Robert Rosenthal. 1981. (Eds.) *The Clever Hans Phenomenon: Communication with Horses, Whales, Apes, and People.* New York: New York Acad. Sciences.

Shepherd, Gordon M. 1991. *Foundations of the Neuron Doctrine.* New York: Oxford U.

Shorter, Edward. 1992. *From Paralysis to Fatigue: A History of Psychosomatic Illness in the Modern Era.* New York and Toronto: Free.

_____. 1997. "What was the Matter with 'Anna O.': A Definitive Diagnosis." In Dufresna 1997, pp. 23–34.

Showalter, Elaine. 1985. *The Female Malady: Women, Madness, and English Culture, 1830–1980.* New York: Pantheon.

_____. 1993. "Hysteria, Feminism, and Gender." In Gilman et al. 1993, pp. 286–344.

Skues, Richard A. 2001. "On the Dating of Freud's *Aliquis* Slip." *Int. J. Psa.,* 86:1185–1204.

_____. 2006. *Sigmund Freud and the History of Anna O.: Reopening a Closed Case.* Basingstoke and New York: Palgrave Macmillan.

_____. 2017. "Who was the 'Heroine' of Freud's First Case History? Problems and Issues in the Identification of Freud's Patients." *Psa. and Hist.,* 19:7–54.

Smidt, H., and C. Rank. 1885. "Ueber die Bedeutung des Cocain bei der Morphiumentziehung." *Berliner Klinische Wochenschrift,* 22:592–596.

Société de Psychologie Physiologique de Paris. 1890. *Congrès International de Psychologie Physiologique, Première Session, Paris, 1890.* Paris: Bureau des Revues.

Solms, Mark. 1997. *The Neuropsychology of Dreams: A Clinico-anatomical Study.* Mahwah, NJ: Erlbaum.

_____. 2002. "An Introduction to the Neuroscientific Works of Sigmund Freud." In Van de Vijver and Geerardyn 2002, pp. 17–35.

———, and Michael Saling. 1986. "On Psychoanalysis and Neuroscience: Freud's Attitude to the Localizationist Tradition." *Int. J. Psa.,* 67:397–416.

Solnit, Rebecca. 2014. "Cassandra Among the Creeps." *Harper's,* Oct.: 4–9.

Springer, Alfred. 2002. "Kokain, Freud und die Psychoanalyse." *Suchttherapie*, 3:18–23.

Spurling, Laurence. 1989. (Ed.) *Sigmund Freud: Critical Assessments*. 4 vols. London and New York: Routledge.

Stadlen, Anthony. 1989. "Was Dora 'Ill'"? [1985.] In Spurling 1989, Vol. 2, pp. 196–203.

Starr, Karen E., and Lewis Aron. 2011. "Women on the Couch: Genital Stimulation and the Birth of Psychoanalysis." *Psac. Dialogues*, 21:373–392.

States, Bert O. 1988. *The Rhetoric of Dreams*. Ithaca, NY: Cornell U.

Steiner, Riccardo. 2000. "Die Zukunft als Nostalgie: Biographien von Mythen und Helden . . . ?: Bemerkungen über Jones' Freud-Biographie." *Psyche*, 54, Nos. 2–3:99–142, 242–282.

———. 2013. "*Die Brautbriefe*: The Freud and Martha Correspondence." *Int. J. Psa.*, 94:863–935.

Steinmann, Anne. 1984. "Anna O.: Female, 1880–1882; Bertha Pappenheim: Female, 1980–1982." In Rosenbaum and Muroff 1984, pp. 118–131.

Stekel, Wilhelm. 1950. *The Autobiography of Wilhelm Stekel: The Life Story of a Pioneer Psychoanalyst*. Ed. Emil A. Gutheil. New York: Liveright.

Stengers, Jean, and Anne van Neck. 2001. *Masturbation: The History of a Great Terror*. Trans. Kathryn A. Hoffmann. New York: Palgrave.

Stengle, Jamie. 2008. "Cocaine May Cause Heart Attack Symptoms." *AP Online*, March 17.

Stepansky, Paul E. 1986. (Ed.) *Freud: Appraisals and Reappraisals: Contributions to Freud Studies*. 3 vols. Hillsdale, NJ, and London: Analytic.

———. 1999. *Freud, Surgery, and the Surgeons*. Hillsdale, NJ, and London: Analytic.

Streatfeild, Dominic. 2001. *Cocaine: An Unauthorized Biography*. New York: Picador.

Sulloway, Frank. J. 1992. *Freud, Biologist of the Mind: Beyond the Psychoanalytic Legend*. [1979.] Cambridge, MA: Harvard U.

Swales, Peter J. 1982a. "Freud, Minna Bernays, and the Conquest of Rome." *New Am. Rev.*, 1(1):1–23.

———. 1982b. "Freud, Minna Bernays, and the Imitation of Christ." Privately printed.

———. 1983. "Freud, Martha Bernays, and the Language of Flowers." Privately printed paper.

———. 1986a. "Freud, His Teacher, and the Birth of Psychoanalysis." In Stepansky 1986, Vol. 1, pp. 3–82.

———. 1986b. "Freud, Breuer, and the Blessed Virgin." Lecture text, privately circulated.

———. 1988. "Freud, Katharina, and the First 'Wild Analysis.'" In Stepansky 1986, Vol. 3, pp. 80–164.

———. 1989a. "Freud, Cocaine, and Sexual Chemistry: The Role of Cocaine in Freud's Conception of the Libido." [1983.] In Spurling 1989, Vol 1, pp. 273–301.

———. 1989b. "Freud, Fliess, and Fratricide: The Role of Fliess in Freud's Conception of Paranoia." In Spurling 1989, Vol. 1, pp. 302–330.

_____. 1989c. "Freud, Johann Weier, and the Status of Seduction: The Role of the Witch in the Conception of Fantasy." In Spurling 1989, Vol 1, pp. 331–365.

_____. 1996. "Freud, His Ur-patient, and Their Romance of Oedipus: The Role of 'Herr E.' in the Conception of Psychoanalysis." Unpublished lecture. The Richardson History of Psychology Seminar, New York Hospital–Cornell Medical Center, New York, Dec. 4.

_____. 1997. "Freud, Filthy Lucre, and Undue Influence." *Rev. Existential Psychology and Psychiatry*, 23:115–141.

_____. 2003. "Freud, Death, and Sexual Pleasures: On the Psychical Mechanism of Dr. Sigm. Freud." *Arc de Cercle*, 1:4–74.

Swan, Jim. 1974. "*Mater* and Nannie: Freud's Two Mothers and the Discovery of the Oedipus Complex." *Am. Imago*, 31:1–64.

Swanson, Don R. 1977. "A Critique of Psychic Energy as an Explanatory Concept." *J. Am. Psac. Assn.*, 25:603–633.

Szasz, Thomas S. 1990. *Anti-Freud: Karl Kraus's Criticism of Psychoanalysis and Psychiatry*. [1976.] Syracuse, NY: Syracuse U.

Tauber, Alfred I. 2010. *Freud, the Reluctant Philosopher*. Princeton, NJ: Princeton U.

Thornton, E. M. 1984. *The Freudian Fallacy: An Alternative View of Freudian Theory*. First published as *Freud and Cocaine* (London: Blond and Briggs, 1983). Garden City, NY: Dial.

Timpanaro, Sebastiano. 1976: *The Freudian Slip: Psychoanalysis and Textual Criticism*. [1974.] Trans. Kate Soper. London: NLB.

Tögel, Christfried. 1994. "*. . . Und gedenke die Wissenschaft auszubeuten*": *Sigmund Freuds Weg zur Psychoanalyse*. Tübingen: Diskord.

Tolpin, Marian. 1993. "The Unmirrored Self, Compensatory Structure, and Cure: The Exemplary Case of Anna O." *Annual of Psa.*, 21:157–177.

Torrey, E. Fuller. 1992. *Freudian Fraud: The Malignant Effect of Freud's Theory on American Thought and Culture*. New York: HarperPerennial.

Triplett, Hall. 2005. "The Misnomer of Freud's 'Seduction Theory.'" *J. Hist. Ideas*, 65:647–665.

Trosman, Harry. 1969. "The Cryptomnesic Fragment in the Discovery of Free Association." *J. Am. Psac. Assn.*, 17:489–510.

———, and Ernest S. Wolf. 1973. "The Bernfeld Collaboration in the Jones Biography of Freud." *Int. J. Psa.*, 54:227–233.

Tuncel, Meryem, and Zhongyun Wang, Debbie Arbique, Paul J. Fadel, Ronald G. Victor, and Wanpen Vongpatanasin. 2002. "Mechanism of the Blood-Pressure Raising Effect of Cocaine in Humans." *Circulation*, 105:1054–1059.

Upson, Henry S. 1888. "On Gold as a Staining Agent for Nerve Tissues." *J. Nervous and Mental Disease*, 13:685–689.

Van de Vijver, Gertrudis, and Filip Geerardyn. 2002. (Eds.) *The Pre-Psychoanalytic Writings of Sigmund Freud*. London: Karnac.

Vande Kemp, Hendrika. 1981. "The Dream in Periodical Literature: 1860–1910." *J. Hist. Behavioral Sciences*, 17:88–113.

Van Rillaer, Jacques. 1980. *Les illusions de la psychanalyse*. Brussels: Mardaga.

Vitz, Paul C. 1988. *Sigmund Freud's Christian Unconscious*. New York and London: Guilford.

Von Oettingen, W. F. 1933. "The Earliest Suggestion of the Use of Cocaine for Local Anesthesia." *Annals Medical Hist.*, N.S. 5:275–280.

Vongpatanasin, Wanpen, Yasser Mansour, Bahman Chavoshan, Debbie Arbique, and Ronald G. Victor. 1999. "Cocaine Stimulates the Human Cardiovascular System via a Central Mechanism of Action." *Circulation*, 100:497–502.

Voswinckel, Peter. 1988. "Der Fall Mathilde S. . . . : Bisher unbekannter klinischer Bericht von Sigmund Freud." *Artzt und Krankenhaus*, 61:177–184.

Webster, Richard. 1995. *Why Freud Was Wrong: Sin, Science, and Psychoanalysis*. New York: Basic.

Welsh, Alexander. 1994. *Freud's Wishful Dream Book*. Princeton, NJ: Princeton U.

Wilcocks, Robert. 1994. *Maelzel's Chess Player: Sigmund Freud and the Rhetoric of Deceit*. Lanham, MD: Rowman and Littlefield.

_____. 2000. *Mousetraps and the Moon: The Strange Ride of Sigmund Freud and the Early Years of Psychoanalysis*. Lanham, MD: Lexington.

Williams, J. Mark G. 1997. *Cognitive Psychology and Emotional Disorders*. [1988.] Chichester, UK: Wiley.

Wittels, Fritz. 1924. *Sigmund Freud: His Personality, His Teaching, and His School*. New York: Dodd, Mead.

Wollheim, Richard. 1981. *Sigmund Freud*. [1971.] Cambridge: Cambridge U.

Wolpe, Joseph, and Stanley Rachman. 1999. "A Little Child Shall Mislead Them." [1963.] In Crews 1999, pp. 164–173.

Wortis Joseph. 1940. "Fragments of a Freudian Analysis." *Am. J. Orthopsychiatry,* 10:843–849.

_____. 1954. *Fragments of an Analysis with Freud*. New York: Simon and Schuster.

Yerushalmi, Yosef Hayim. 1991. *Freud's Moses: Judaism Terminable and Interminable*. New Haven, CT, and London: Yale U.

Young-Bruehl, Elisabeth. 1988. *Anna Freud: A Biography*. New York: Summit.

Zwang, Gérard. 1985. *La statue de Freud*. Paris: Laffont.

ACKNOWLEDGMENTS

My largest debt is to Han Israëls, both for providing me with vital documents and for posing brave and essential questions about Freud's early career. His groundbreaking 1993 book, *Het geval Freud. 1. Scheppingsverhalen*, translated into German (1999) and Spanish (2002) but not English, inspired my project.

I have also been sustained and enlightened by exchanges, across many years, with other scholars who have shown us a more human Freud than the fabled one: Jacques Bénesteau, Mikkel Borch-Jacobsen, Maarten Boudry, Louis Breger, Filip Buekens, the late Frank Cioffi, G. William Domhoff, Todd Dufresne, Allen Esterson, John Farrell, Adolf Grünbaum, J. Allan Hobson, Malcolm Macmillan, Peter Rudnytsky, Max Scharnberg, Morton Schatzman, Frank J. Sulloway, Peter J. Swales, Christfried Tögel, Hall Triplett, Alexander Welsh, and Robert Wilcocks.

To readers familiar with the literature, it will be evident that I owe more to Macmillan and Swales, in particular, than any number of citations could convey. I will be pleased if this book whets an appetite for Macmillan's great *Freud Evaluated* and for Swales's incomparable biographical studies, which I continue to urge him to gather between covers. And although Frank Sulloway has justly reconsidered the evaluation of Freud's achievement posed long ago in *Freud, Biologist of the Mind*, that work has proved to be a treasure chest of important facts and inferences. I have also relied on meticulous research by some authors—most prominently Albrecht Hirschmüller—whose judgment of Freud and psychoanalysis bears little resemblance to my own.

Special thanks are due Stewart Justman, who patiently read my draft chapters and offered shrewd advice as well as encouragement. I doubt that I could have persevered for eleven years without his expressions of faith in the outcome. Jack Shoemaker, who published my most recent book, has shown me the generosity for which he is well known. It has been a pleasure to work once again with Andrew Franklin, who will be introducing this book to British readers. As always, my most tireless line-by-line critic has also been the nearest and dearest, Elizabeth Crews.

I wrote the manuscript, but it became a book only after receiving the expert shepherding of my agent, Michael Carlisle. Without him, the project would never have come to the notice of Sara Bershtel, the publisher of Metropolitan Books, who saw possibilities where others did not. Sara is also a legendary editor—the best alive, so it is said in New York. In her case, unlike Freud's, the legend has proved to be true. And thanks to her, I was handed along to a truly brilliant copy editor, Prudence Crowther. I am also indebted to Connor Guy for his valuable editorial suggestions and many other services.

For help with (but not responsibility for) my German, I thank Katra Byram, Emily Banwell, Han Israëls, and Gerd Busse. And I am grateful for the support of friends, including Joan Acocella, William and JoAn Chace, Karel de Pauw, the late Denis Dutton, Pamela Freyd, Alan Friedman, Jacob Fuchs, E. D. Hirsch Jr., Susan Jacoby, Stephen Kennamer, Emily and William Leider, Jeffrey Meyers, Gary Saul Morson, Paul Nixon, Richard Pollak, Tom Quirk, James Samuels, the late Robert Silvers, James Wallenstein, and my daughters, Gretchen Detre and Ingrid Crews.

INDEX

ABOUT THE AUTHOR

FREDERICK CREWS is the author of many books, including the bestselling satire *The Pooh Perplex* and, most recently, *Follies of the Wise*, which was a finalist for a National Book Critics Circle Award. His works relating to psychoanalysis include *The Memory Wars* and the anthology *Unauthorized Freud*. A professor emeritus of English at the University of California, Berkeley, and a long-time contributor to *The New York Review of Books*, he is a member of the American Academy of Arts and Sciences.